한국의 토익 수험자 여러분께,

토익 시험은 세계적인 직무 영어능력 평가 시험으로, 지난 40여 년간 비즈니스 현장에서 필요한 영어능력 평가의 기준을 제시해 왔습니다. 토익 시험 및 토익스피킹, 토익라이팅 시험은 세계에서 가장 널리 통용되는 영어능력 검증 시험으로, 160여 개국 14,000여 기관이 토익 성적을 의사결정에 활용하고 있습니다.

YBM은 한국의 토익 시험을 주관하는 ETS 독점 계약사입니다.

ETS는 한국 수험자들의 효과적인 토익 학습을 돕고자 YBM을 통하여 'ETS 토익 공식 교재'를 독점 출간하고 있습니다. 또한 'ETS 토익 공식 교재' 시리즈에 기출문항을 제공해 한국의 다른 교재들에 수록된 기출을 복제하거나 변형한 문항으로 인하여 발생할 수 있는 수험자들의 혼동을 방지하고 있습니다.

복제 및 변형 문항들은 토익 시험의 출제의도를 벗어날 수 있기 때문에 기출문항을 수록한 'ETS 토익 공식 교재'만큼 시험에 잘 대비할 수 없습니다.

'ETS 토익 공식 교재'를 통하여 수험자 여러분의 영어 소통을 위한 노력에 큰 성취가 있기를 바랍니다.

감사합니다.

Dear TOEIC Test Takers in Korea,

The TOEIC program is the global leader in English-language assessment for the workplace. It has set the standard for assessing English-language skills needed in the workplace for more than 40 years. The TOEIC tests are the most widely used English language assessments around the world, with 14,000+ organizations across more than 160 countries trusting TOEIC scores to make decisions.

YBM is the ETS Country Master Distributor for the TOEIC program in Korea and so is the exclusive distributor for TOEIC Korea.

To support effective learning for TOEIC test-takers in Korea, ETS has authorized YBM to publish the only Official TOEIC prep books in Korea. These books contain actual TOEIC items to help prevent confusion among Korean test-takers that might be caused by other prep book publishers' use of reproduced or paraphrased items.

Reproduced or paraphrased items may fail to reflect the intent of actual TOEIC items and so will not prepare test-takers as well as the actual items contained in the ETS TOEIC Official prep books published by YBM.

We hope that these ETS TOEIC Official prep books enable you, as test-takers, to achieve great success in your efforts to communicate effectively in English.

Thank you.

*toeic.

토익˚
단기공략
PART

PART

7

토익
단기공략
PART 7

발행인　허문호

발행처　YBM

편집　윤경림, 이혜진, 정유상, 이진열
디자인　강상문, 박도순, 김륜형
마케팅　정연철, 박천산, 고영노, 김동진, 박찬경, 김윤하

초판발행　2022년 12월 20일
3쇄발행　2024년 9월 2일

신고일자　1964년 3월 28일
신고번호　제 1964-000003호
주소　서울시 종로구 종로 104
전화　(02) 2000-0515 [구입문의] / (02) 2000-0345 [내용문의]
팩스　(02) 2285-1523
홈페이지　www.ybmbooks.com

ISBN　978-89-17-23796-2

*toeic.

토익 단기공략

PART

PART 7

PREFACE

Dear test taker,

English-language proficiency has become a vital tool for success. It can help you excel in business, travel the world, and communicate effectively with friends and colleagues. The TOEIC® test measures your ability to function effectively in English in these types of situations. Because TOEIC scores are recognized around the world as evidence of your English-language proficiency, you will be able to confidently demonstrate your English skills to employers and begin your journey to success.

The test developers at ETS are excited to help you achieve your personal and professional goals through the TOEIC® 단기공략 Part 7. This book contains over 500 practice-test questions from Part 7 of the TOEIC® Listening and Reading Test that will help you prepare to respond to the items in that section of the test. It also includes detailed explanations of question types and language points tested, which will give you valuable insight into your abilities and how to best prepare for the test. Most of the items in this book have been taken from actual tests, so you can be confident that you will receive an authentic test-preparation experience.

Features of the TOEIC® 단기공략 Part 7 include the following.
• Actual test items from recent tests so you can be sure that they are of the same quality and difficulty as those found in actual TOEIC® tests
• Test taking tips that will help you prepare to successfully answer Part 7 test questions
• Five mock tests created from actual TOEIC Listening and Reading tests.
• Enhanced analyses and explanations of each type of test question based on the latest trends in TOEIC® tests

By studying for the TOEIC® test with the TOEIC® 단기공략 Part 7, you can be assured that you have a professionally prepared resource that will most accurately guide you through the tasks, content, and format of the test and help you maximize your TOEIC® test score. With your score report, you will be ready to show the world what you know!

We are delighted to assist you on your TOEIC® journey with the TOEIC® 단기공략 Part 7 and wish you the best of success.

출제기관이 만든
PART 7 단기 공략서

국내 유일! 출제기관이 독점 제공하는 Part 7 전략서

국내 유일 진짜 토익 문제! 출제기관 독점 제공!

최신 기출 문제 및 정기 시험과 100% 동일한 문제 품질

풍부한 최신 기출 문항뿐 아니라 토익 출제기관인 ETS가 정기 시험과 동일한
유형 및 난이도로 개발한 문제들로 구성!

ETS가 제시하는 시간 단축 공략법

Part 7에 대한 이해를 높이고 고득점 달성을 위해 체계적인 공략법과 Part 7의
관건인 시간 단축을 위한 공략법 제시!

Part 7 모의고사 5회분 제공

대부분 기출로 이루어진 Part 7 모의고사 5회분을 통해 실전에 완벽 대비!

토익 최신 경향을 반영한 명쾌한 분석과 해설

최신 출제 경향 완벽 분석 반영 및 고득점 달성을 위한 해법 제시!

토익 단기 공략

PART 7

CONTENTS

INTRODUCTION

Part 7 이렇게 나온다 ··· 014
Part 7 시간을 단축해주는 고득점 기술 ······················· 016
Part 7 패러프레이징 ··· 018

CHAPTER

1

문제 유형별 전략

UNIT 01 주제/목적 문제 ·· 024
UNIT 02 세부 사항 문제 ·· 030
UNIT 03 Not/True 문제 ··· 036
UNIT 04 추론 문제 ·· 042
UNIT 05 문장 삽입 문제 ·· 048
UNIT 06 동의어 문제 ··· 054

CHAPTER 2

지문 유형별 전략

UNIT 01 이메일/편지 ·· 062

UNIT 02 공지/회람 ·· 072

UNIT 03 광고/안내문 ·· 082

UNIT 04 기사 ·· 092

UNIT 05 웹페이지/양식 ·· 102

UNIT 06 문자 메시지/온라인 채팅 ·· 112

UNIT 07 이중 지문 ·· 122

UNIT 08 삼중 지문 ·· 134

CHAPTER 3

ETS 실전 모의고사

ETS 실전 모의고사 1회 ·· 149

ETS 실전 모의고사 2회 ·· 171

ETS 실전 모의고사 3회 ·· 193

ETS 실전 모의고사 4회 ·· 215

ETS 실전 모의고사 5회 ·· 237

출제 경향

1 — PART 7 문제 유형 및 출제 비율(평균 문항 수)

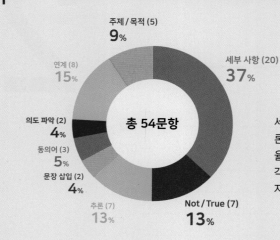

주제 / 목적 (5)
9%

연계 (8)
15%

세부 사항 (20)
37%

의도 파악 (2)
4%

동의어 (3)
5%

문장 삽입 (2)
4%

추론 (7)
13%

Not / True (7)
13%

총 54문항

세부 사항 문제가 가장 높은 비율을 차지하며 추론 문제와 Not / True 문제가 그 다음으로 출제율이 높다. 주어진 문장 넣기와 의도 파악 문제는 각각 2문항씩 고정 비율로 출제된다. 이중, 삼중 지문에서는 연계 문제가 8문항 정도 출제된다.

2 — **정답의 단서를 찾기 어려운 변형 추론 문제들이 출제되고 있다.**

대체로 (most) likely, probably와 같은 변형된 추론 문제 유형이 등장하면 지문에 정답의 근거가 명확하게 제시되지 않아서 정답을 골라내기가 쉽지 않다. 수험자가 지문을 신속하게 정독하는 실력을 가져야 풀 수 있는 문제들이 매월 꾸준히 출제되고 있다.

3 — **종합적인 독해력을 요구하는 문제가 많아지고 있다.**

일부 질문과 보기를 의도적으로 어렵게 출제해서 지문을 정확하게 해석하지 않으면 정답을 골라내기가 쉽지 않다. 수험자가 지문 전체의 종합적인 내용을 이해해야 풀 수 있는 문제들이 매월 꾸준히 출제되고 있다.

4 — **정답 보기를 유사 표현으로 바꿔 제시한다.**

지문에서 언급된 정답 단서가 보기에 나올 때는 유사어로 바꿔서 같은 의미를 지닌 다른 단어, 표현, 문장으로 대체(paraphrasing)하는 경향이 있다. 특히 후반에 등장하는 연계 지문의 보기에는 지문에 사용된 표현이 거의 등장하지 않도록 의도적으로 어렵게 출제된 문제가 점점 증가하는 추세이다.

1   자투리 시간을 잘 활용하자.

Part 7은 늘 시간이 부족하다. 시험 시작부터 시간 배분을 전략적으로 해야 한 문제도 놓치지 않고 풀 수 있다는 것을 기억하자. Listening 시험 때 Part 1과 Part 2 디렉션이 나오는 시간을 활용하면 Part 5를 몇 문항은 풀 수 있다. Part 5는 시간을 최소한으로 사용하고 Part 7에서 시간을 충분히 쓰는 것이 유리하다.

2   어려운 것부터 푸는 것이 좋다.

Part 7은 대체로 뒤로 갈수록 지문의 길이가 길고 어렵다. 그리고 아무래도 이중 지문과 삼중 지문은 문제 푸는 데 시간이 더 걸린다. 앞에서부터 풀다가 시간이 얼마 안 남은 상황에서 이중/삼중 지문 문제를 풀려면 마음이 조급해져서 지문 간의 관계를 차분히 생각하면서 풀기가 쉽지 않다. 따라서 이중/삼중 지문 문제부터 푸는 것이 도움이 될 수도 있다.

3   상대적으로 쉽고 짧은 단일 지문은 최대한 빨리 풀도록 한다.

Part 7을 앞에서부터 풀든 뒤에서부터 풀든 앞쪽에 배치된 비교적 쉽고 짧은 단일 지문 문제는 시간을 최소로 사용하도록 한다. Part 7 문제 푸는 시간은 문항당 1분 정도로 생각하면 되지만, 이런 문제들은 1분을 충분히 다 쓰지 말고 빨리 푼 다음 어려운 문제에 좀더 할애하도록 하자.

4   잘 풀리지 않는 문제는 과감히 넘어가라.

시간을 재면서 한 문항 한 문항을 푸는 것은 아니지만 잘 풀리지 않는 문제는 잡고 있지 말고 넘어가도록 한다. 그 문제 때문에 풀 수 있었던 문제를 놓치게 되는 일이 생길 수 있기 때문이다. 시간이 남으면 다시 돌아와서 천천히 읽어보도록 한다.

5   답안지 마킹도 시간 배분이 필요하다.

시험지에 문제를 다 푼 후 한꺼번에 답안지에 마킹하는 것은 좀 위험하다. 시간이 부족할 수도 있고, 마음이 급해져 실수를 할 수도 있기 때문이다. 중간중간 마킹할 시간을 배분한다든지, 답안지에 대충이라도 칠해놓고 나중에 한꺼번에 마킹을 한다든지, 답안지 마킹도 시간 관리 전략이 필요하다는 것을 기억하자.

TOEIC 소개   What is the TOEIC?

TOEIC Test Of English for International Communication (국제적 의사소통을 위한 영어 시험)의 약자로서, 영어가 모국어가 아닌 사람들이 일상생활 또는 비즈니스 현장에서 꼭 필요한 실용적 영어 구사 능력을 갖추었는가를 평가하는 시험이다.

시험 구성

구성	Part	내용		문항수	시간	배점
Listening	1	사진 묘사		6	45분	495점
	2	질의 응답		25		
	3	짧은 대화		39		
	4	짧은 담화		30		
Reading	5	단문 빈칸 채우기 (문법/어휘)		30	75분	495점
	6	장문 빈칸 채우기		16		
	7	독해	단일 지문	29		
			이중 지문	10		
			삼중 지문	15		
Total	7 Parts			200문항	120분	990점

평가 항목

LC	RC
단문을 듣고 이해하는 능력	읽은 글을 통해 추론해 생각할 수 있는 능력
짧은 대화체 문장을 듣고 이해하는 능력	장문에서 특정한 정보를 찾을 수 있는 능력
비교적 긴 대화체에서 주고받은 내용을 파악할 수 있는 능력	글의 목적, 주제, 의도 등을 파악하는 능력
장문에서 핵심이 되는 정보를 파악할 수 있는 능력	뜻이 유사한 단어들의 정확한 용례를 파악하는 능력
구나 문장에서 화자의 목적이나 함축된 의미를 이해하는 능력	문장 구조를 제대로 파악하는지, 문장에서 필요한 품사, 어구 등을 찾는 능력

* 성적표에는 전체 수험자의 평균과 해당 수험자가 받은 성적이 백분율로 표기되어 있다.

수험 정보

시험 접수 방법

한국 토익 위원회 사이트(www.toeic.co.kr)에서 시험일 약 2개월 전부터
온라인으로 접수 가능

시험장 준비물

신분증 규정 신분증만 가능
(주민등록증, 운전면허증, 기간 만료 전의 여권, 공무원증 등)
필기구 연필, 지우개 (볼펜이나 사인펜은 사용 금지)

시험 진행 시간

09:20	입실 (09:50 이후는 입실 불가)
09:30 – 09:45	답안지 작성에 관한 오리엔테이션
09:45 – 09:50	휴식
09:50 – 10:05	신분증 확인
10:05 – 10:10	문제지 배부 및 파본 확인
10:10 – 10:55	듣기 평가 (Listening Test)
10:55 – 12:10	독해 평가 (Reading Test)

TOEIC 성적 확인

시험일로부터 약 10-11일 후, 오전 6시부터 인터넷과 ARS(060-800-0515)로
성적 확인 가능. 성적표는 우편이나 온라인으로 발급 받을 수 있다. 우편으로 발급
받을 경우 성적 발표 후 대략 일주일이 소요되며, 온라인 발급을 선택하면
유효 기간 내에 홈페이지에서 본인이 직접 1회에 한해 무료 출력할 수 있다.
TOEIC 성적은 시험일로부터 2년간 유효하다.

TOEIC 점수

TOEIC 점수는 듣기 영역(LC)과 읽기 영역(RC)을 합계한 점수로 5점 단위로
구성되며 총점은 990점이다. TOEIC 성적은 각 문제 유형의 난이도에 따른 점수
환산표에 의해 결정된다.

PART

7

INTRODUCTION

PART 7 이렇게 나온다

PART 7 시간을 단축해주는 고득점 기술

PART 7 패러프레이징

PART 7 이렇게 나온다

단일 지문 29문항/복수 지문 25문항 총 54문항

Part 7은 제시된 지문을 읽고 그에 따른 문제를 풀어야 하는 유형으로, 단일 지문 10개에 29문항, 이중 지문 2세트에 10문항, 삼중 지문 3세트에 15문항으로 구성되어 있다.

PART 7 미리 보기

Questions 147-148 refer to the following memo.

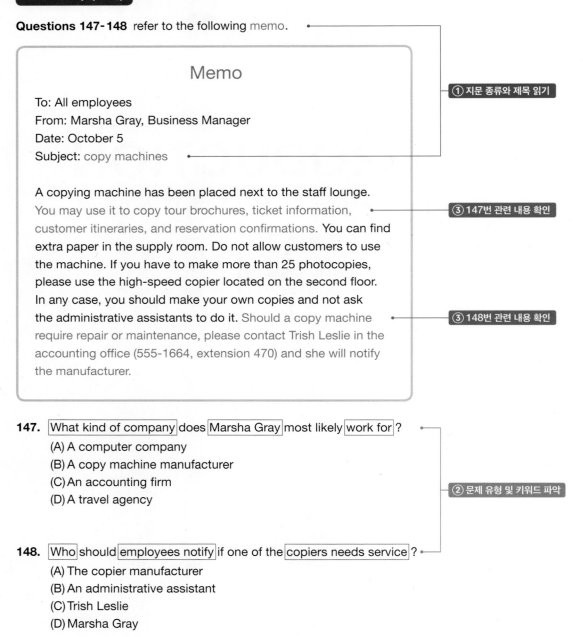

Memo

To: All employees
From: Marsha Gray, Business Manager
Date: October 5
Subject: copy machines

① 지문 종류와 제목 읽기

A copying machine has been placed next to the staff lounge.
You may use it to copy tour brochures, ticket information,
customer itineraries, and reservation confirmations. You can find
extra paper in the supply room. Do not allow customers to use
the machine. If you have to make more than 25 photocopies,
please use the high-speed copier located on the second floor.
In any case, you should make your own copies and not ask
the administrative assistants to do it. Should a copy machine
require repair or maintenance, please contact Trish Leslie in the
accounting office (555-1664, extension 470) and she will notify
the manufacturer.

③ 147번 관련 내용 확인

③ 148번 관련 내용 확인

147. What kind of company does Marsha Gray most likely work for?
(A) A computer company
(B) A copy machine manufacturer
(C) An accounting firm
(D) A travel agency

② 문제 유형 및 키워드 파악

148. Who should employees notify if one of the copiers needs service?
(A) The copier manufacturer
(B) An administrative assistant
(C) Trish Leslie
(D) Marsha Gray

PART 7 풀이 전략

① 지문의 종류와 제목을 읽고 지문의 특성을 인지하고 내용을 예상한다.

지문 유형마다 자주 다뤄지는 내용이 있으며, 전개 방식도 비슷하므로 예상하는 것이 좋다.

> **Questions 147-148** refer to the following memo.
>
> **회람** → 새로운 규정이나 시스템, 시설 정비, 행사 등을 전달하는 내용 예상
>
> copy machines
>
> **복사기 관련** → 복사기 설치, 고장 또는 사용법 등 내용 예상

② 질문을 읽고 문제 유형과 키워드를 파악한다.

정답은 대체로 순서대로 나온다는 사실을 기억하자.

> **147.** What kind of company does Marsha Gray most likely work for?
> **추론** → 앞부분에 집중
>
> **148.** Who should employees notify if one of the copiers needs service?
> **세부 사항** → 키워드 notify, service 같은 어휘가 나오는 부분에 집중

③ 지문을 읽으며 주요 내용을 파악하고, 문제와 관련된 내용이 나오면 집중해서 읽는다.

> **147.** 마샤 그레이는 어느 회사에 근무할 것 같은가?
>
> You may use it to copy tour brochures, ticket information, customer itineraries, and reservation confirmations.
>
> 여행 소책자, 티켓 정보, 고객 일정표나 예약 확인서 등을 복사하는 데 복사기를 사용하실 수 있습니다.
>
> → **정답 (D) A travel agency** 여행사
>
> **148.** 복사기를 수리해야 하는 경우 직원들은 누구에게 알려야 하는가?
>
> Should a copy machine require repair or maintenance, please contact Trish Leslie in the accounting office (555-1664, extension 470) and she will notify the manufacturer.
>
> 복사기를 수리하거나 정비해야 할 경우는 경리부 트리시 레슬리(555-1664, 내선 470번)에게 연락주시면 그녀가 제조업체에 연락을 할 것입니다.
>
> → **정답 (C) Trish Leslie** 트리시 레슬리

PART 7 시간을 단축해주는 고득점 기술

1
지문의 기초 사항을 재빨리 파악하라

- 지시문 맨 끝에 제시된 지문의 유형을 파악하도록 한다. 어떤 종류의 지문인지에 따라 내용의 전개 유형이 정해져 있으므로 준비하는 데 도움이 된다.
- 이메일/편지라면 수신자, 발신자, 제목 정도까지 확인하고 웹페이지라면 메뉴 탭, 기사와 광고는 제목도 확인하면 좋다.
- 시간을 소모하지는 말고 습관적으로 휙 한번 보는 정도면 된다.

2
질문의 키워드를 잡아라

- 질문에서 핵심이 되는 키워드만 잡고 지문을 읽으며 정답을 기다리면 된다.
- 키워드는 굳이 여러 단어를 잡으려고 노력하지 않아도 되며, 지문 내에서 문맥상 알 수 있는 주어 등은 생략하고 사건 중심으로 잡도록 한다.
- 문제 해석에 너무 시간을 뺏기지 않도록 주의하자.

3
되도록 큰 청크로 직독직해 하라

- 단어를 하나하나 해석하려고 하면 시간 낭비! 시야를 넓혀 최대한 큰 청크(의미 단위)로 보려고 노력해야 한다. 이것이 바로 읽는 속도를 높이는 축지법!

> **청크란?** '덩어리'라는 의미의 청크(chunk)는 여러 개의 단어가 모여 최소의 의미를 만드는 의미 단위를 말한다. 정확한 규칙이나 정답이 있는 것은 아니나, 대체로 문장 끊어 읽기의 기준이 되는 것이 바로 청크이다.

- 읽으면서 청크 단위로 바로 바로 의미를 파악하는 직독직해를 해야 지문 읽는 속도를 단축할 수 있다. 너무 잘게 쪼개지 않도록 유의하자. 최대한 한눈에 크게 보는 것이 시간 단축에 좋다.

4

스키밍과 스캐닝을 적절히 하라

스키밍(skimming): 대략의 내용과 주제 파악을 위해 훑어 읽기
스캐닝(scanning): 특정 정보를 찾기 위해 정독하면서 꼼꼼히 읽기

- 지문은 꼭 읽어야 할 부분이 있고, 굳이 안 읽고 건너뛰어도 되는 부분이 있다. 문제를 푸는 데 필요한 부분은 스캐닝으로 자세히 읽어야 한다.
- 키워드를 찾기 위해서는 스키밍을, 키워드를 찾은 다음에는 그 부분을 스캐닝하여 답을 찾도록 한다.
- 토익 Part 7은 정보 찾기를 위한 독해이다. 지문 전체를 하나하나 해석하는 시험이 아니라는 점을 명심하자.

5

미리 읽지 않는 것이 더 유리한 지문이 있다

- 항목으로 구분되는 형식의 지문은 미리 읽을 필요가 없다.
  문제 확인 후에 해당 항목만 찾아 읽도록 한다.

항목 형식의 지문 예
-August: Fun fitness and exercise classes
-September: Guided nature hikes on park trails (all ages)
-October: Drawing and painting lessons in the field house

- 표, 영수증, 주문서, 일정 등 양식 형태의 지문도 마찬가지로 미리 읽지 말고 문제 확인 후 관련 부분을 찾도록 한다.

6

문제 유형별 전략을 활용하라

- 문제 유형을 보면 대체로 지문의 어느 부분을 보면 좋을지 알 수 있는 경우가 많다.
- 예를 들어, 주제/목적 문제는 제목이나 앞부분, 요청 문제는 후반부, 세부 사항 문제는 핵심 키워드가 있는 곳을 찾아본다.
- 본책 Chapter 1에 제시된 문제 유형을 잘 파악하여 시간 낭비 없이 문제 풀이에 임하도록 훈련하자.

PART 7 | 패러프레이징

답은 대체로 지문의 내용과 똑같은 표현으로 제시되지 않는다. 같은 의미의 다른 표현으로 바꾸어 나오며 대체로 포괄적인 표현으로 패러프레이징 되는 경향이 있다. 패러프레이징에 강해지려면 어휘력과 논리적 사고력이 관건이다. 다양한 패러프레이징 표현이 가능하다는 것을 인지하고 실전에 임하자.

유형 1 **동의어 / 유사 표현**: 의미가 같지만 다른 표현을 사용하는 경우

질문	Q: Why should Ms. Ingersoll contact Mr. Garcia?	가르시아 씨에게 연락해야 하는 이유는?
지문	Ramon Garcia in the sales department may have some **suggestions** for you.	영업부의 라몬 가르시아가 몇 가지 **제안**을 드릴 수 있을지도 모르겠습니다.
정답	A: To ask for **recommendations** for entertainment	오락거리를 **추천**해 달라고 부탁하기 위해

● 지문의 suggestions → 정답의 recommendations

질문	Q: What is implied about the Kinsley Mirror Company?	킨슬리 거울 회사에 대해 암시하는 것은?
지문	For **several decades**, the name Kinsley has been associated with high-quality mirrors.	**수십 년 동안**, 킨슬리라는 이름은 고급 거울과 관련되어 왔습니다.
정답	A: It has been in business for **many years**.	**오랫동안** 사업을 해왔다.

● 지문의 several decades → 정답의 many years

유형 2 **포괄적 상위어 표현**: 상위 개념의 어휘를 사용하는 경우

질문	Q: What problem with her sunblock did Ms. Harrison report?	선크림에 무슨 문제가 있다고 하는가?
지문	**It feels watery and rather greasy.**	그것(선크림)이 **묽어졌고 기름기도 좀 많아진 것 같습니다.**
정답	A: **The texture changed.**	**질감이 변했다.**

● 지문의 It feels watery and rather greasy. → 정답의 The texture changed.

질문	Q: What are the articles in *Today's Space* mostly about?	<오늘의 공간> 기사는 무엇에 관한 것인가?
지문	*Today's Space* features information about houses and buildings that are known for their impressive **furnishings and décor.**	<오늘의 공간>은 인상적인 **가구와 장식**으로 유명한 집과 건물에 관한 정보를 다룹니다.
정답	A: **Interior design**	**인테리어 디자인**

● 지문의 furnishings and décor → 정답의 Interior design

유형 3 **축약 표현**: 간단히 요약하여 말하는 경우

질문	Q: What does Mr. Burnes suggest Mr. Pitts do?	무엇을 하라고 제안하는가?
지문	**For the latest package status information**, please go to **"My Account" on Worldstore.com**.	배송 상황에 관한 최신 정보를 알고 싶으면 Worldstore.com의 '내 정보'를 방문하세요.
정답	A: Visit **a Web site for more information**	더 많은 정보를 얻기 위해 웹 사이트를 방문할 것

● 지문의 For the latest package status information → 정답의 for more information
   지문의 "My Account" on Worldstore.com → 정답의 a Web site

질문	Q: What does the Kinsley Mirror Company offer that other companies do not?	다른 회사에서 제공하지 않는 무엇을 제공하는가?
지문	Unlike all of our competitors, we will **ship your products to you at no extra cost**, regardless of the size of the order.	저희 모든 경쟁자들과 달리, 저희는 주문품의 크기에 상관없이 여러분의 제품을 추가 비용 없이 배송해 드립니다.
정답	A: **Free shipping**	무료 배송

● 지문의 ship your products to you at no extra cost → 정답의 Free shipping

유형 4 **풀어 쓰는 표현**: 이해하기 더 쉬운 표현으로 풀어 쓴 경우

질문	Q: What is indicated about the Woodlawn Theater?	이 극장에 대해 명시된 것은?
지문	He began gathering the necessary funds to realize his goal by requesting **donations from several area businesses**.	그는 여러 지역 사업체에 기부를 요청함으로써 자신의 목표를 실현하기 위해 필요한 자금을 모으기 시작했습니다.
정답	A: It was purchased with **financial support from the local community**.	지역 사회의 재정 지원으로 매입되었다.

● 지문의 donations from several area businesses → 정답의 financial support from the local community

질문	Q: What is mentioned about *Mintner Photography Magazine*?	이 잡지에 대해 언급된 것은?
지문	We are looking forward to sharing your work with our **international readership**.	저희는 귀하의 작품을 세계 독자들과 공유할 수 있기를 고대하고 있겠습니다.
정답	A: It **is read around the world**.	세계적으로 읽힌다.

● 지문의 international readership → 정답의 is read around the world

✅ PRACTICE

정답 및 해설 p.002

For PREMIUM PRODUCTS Home Kitchen Refrigerator Models #770-850

You can solve many common refrigerator problems easily, saving yourself the cost of a possible service call. Try the suggestions below to see if you can solve the problem yourself before calling to have the unit serviced by a repair technician.

---

1. For whom is the guide intended?
   (A) A repair technician
   (B) An appliance owner

Please refamiliarize yourselves with the following pool safety precautions. As a recreation manager, you are responsible for discussing these regulations with your staff at your next weekly meeting.

---

2. What is the purpose of this notice?
   (A) To ensure that management staff follow regulations
   (B) To instruct guests about swimming pool use

Monika Slava [3:19 P.M.] We could hire some runners from the track team at Northern Fields University to do a foot race while wearing the shoes. Then we can transmit the statistics the shoes generate to a big screen for the audience to watch in real time.

Lin Zan [3:20 P.M.] Can Zip Strings give us a few sample pairs? We could give them away as prizes after the race.

---

3. What is suggested about Northern Fields University?
   (A) It has an organization of student runners.
   (B) Many of its students own Zip Strings shoes.

Ms. Wagner requested that an additional security guard be hired for the fourth floor. She explained that the number of visitors to this area has increased because of the recent expansion of the Greek sculpture collection.

---

4. Why does Ms. Wagner request additional security?
   (A) To protect a valuable painting
   (B) To monitor increased visitor traffic

Dear Mr. Oliver:

To follow up on our conversation of April 2, I would like to import the following items. Please confirm that these prices are correct and that the items are in stock. And let me know when I can expect the items to be shipped.

5. What is Mr. Oliver asked to do?
 (A) Mail a confirmation letter
 (B) Verify product availability

Thank you for your interest in teaching in our online business program. After reviewing your application materials, we would like to offer you an instructor's position for the upcoming semester.

6. Why was the e-mail sent?
 (A) To offer employment at a university
 (B) To provide information about a business class

Present ticket and identification with proof of age at ticket booth. Full refunds are available for reservations canceled 48 hours or more before the event date. Contact our customer service line at +64 3 555 0199 to reschedule or arrange a refund.

7. Why should a ticket holder call customer service?
 (A) To purchase additional tickets
 (B) To change a reservation date

To: All employees
From: Hamid Amari
Subject: Maintenance

The main e-mail server will be down for routine maintenance this Saturday, 22 October, from 7:00 A.M. to 11:00 A.M. Please shut down your computer when you leave on Friday night to accommodate the maintenance procedure.

8. What does Mr. Amari ask employees to do?
 (A) Turn off their computers
 (B) Make appointments with the help desk

PART

7

CHAPTER

1

문제 유형별 전략

UNIT 01 주제/목적 문제
UNIT 02 세부 사항 문제
UNIT 03 Not/True 문제
UNIT 04 추론 문제
UNIT 05 문장 삽입 문제
UNIT 06 동의어 문제

기출 전략

1. 지문의 핵심이 되는 내용을 묻는 문제 유형으로, 첫 번째 문제로 등장한다.
2. 대부분은 글의 앞부분에서 정답을 알 수 있지만, 가끔은 뒷부분이나 지문 전체를 읽어야 알 수 있는 경우도 있다.

주제/목적 질문 유형

주제	**What** is the notice **about**?	공지는 무엇에 관한 것인가?
	What is being **advertised**?	무엇이 광고되고 있는가?
목적	What is the **purpose** of the e-mail?	이메일의 목적은?
	Why was the letter **written**?	편지는 왜 쓰여졌는가?

기출 예제 풀이 전략

Q. What is the **purpose** of the e-mail?

(A) To introduce a new festival coordinator
(B) To confirm that a request has been granted
(C) To announce a music event at Sunquist Park
(D) To extend the length of time in a contract

STEP 1
질문의 키워드 잡기
글의 목적

STEP 2
지문의 앞부분 집중
음악 페스티벌에서 공식 사진사로
승인되었음을 알림

STEP 3
정답 찾기: 정답 (B)

패러프레이징
지문의 you have been approved
→ 보기의 a request has been
granted

To: saul.abramov@urkmagazine.com
From: b.perkins@yeloyamusicfestival.org
Subject: Yeloya Music Festival

We are pleased to inform you that you have been approved as an official photographer for this year's Yeloya Music Festival at Sunquist Park. Welcome to the press team!

The festival press office will contact you soon about how to pick up your media pass. If you have any questions in the meantime, please don't hesitate to contact me at 952-555-0183.

Sincerely,
Belinda Perkins, Event Coordinator

번역 p. 004

🔄 주제/목적 문제의 패러프레이징

I have decided to **accept a previous offer** from Chang & Associates.	**Q** 편지를 쓴 이유? → To **decline a job offer**
The owner of Woodcraft Designs is pleased to announce **the opening of her second store** in Falls City.	**Q** 공지의 목적? → To promote **a new retail store**
I'm writing to remind those who have not yet submitted status reports **that they are due by the end of the day**.	**Q** 이메일의 목적? → To remind employees of **an upcoming deadline**

다음 지문을 읽고 질문의 정답을 고르세요.

Letter

Dear Mr. Won,

At Nayontech, we are dedicated to responsibly recycling your computers, mobile phones, and other electronics. Our efficient collection network keeps our costs low and our services affordable. We have facilities in four countries, allowing us to minimize shipping distances and fuel consumption.

As the sustainability officer of one of the most rapidly expanding companies in Korea, your decisions about where and what to recycle have great influence. I hope you will consider the enclosed brochure about Nayontech as you choose where to send your recyclable electronic waste. For further assurance regarding the quality of our services, I encourage you to call or write any of the clients identified on the back page of the brochure. If you would like to discuss your company's specific requirements, please contact me or, if you prefer, speak with Woo-jin Park in our Seoul office.

Sincerely,
Brendan Dilks
Senior Account Manager

1. What is the purpose of the letter?

(A) To describe new environmental regulations
(B) To promote a recycling service
(C) To offer a discount to loyal clients
(D) To recommend a brand of electronic equipment

Advertisement

The Perfect Gift

Imagine sharing a new, special picture every day of the year with friends and loved ones! Gold Coast Imagination, Inc., will use images that you provide to create a personalized daily calendar using images of special people, memorable places, or important events.

Just go through your photo album and select the pictures you want to include. We will use your digital images or traditional print photographs to create a personalized gift. Birthdays, anniversaries, and the dates of special events can be indicated for no additional fee!

One of our consultants will help you choose from dozens of formats and styles. For more information, give us a call at (07) 7010 2390 or visit us online at www.gci.co.au.

2. What is being advertised?

(A) Travel postcards
(B) Photograph albums
(C) Birthday cards
(D) Personalized calendars

Questions 1-2 refer to the following letter.

난이도 ★☆☆

Kippler-Starr Bank
660 Century Avenue
Billings, MT 59102

March 27

Cecilia Feridino
90 Young Street
Billings, MT 59107

Re: Account #850981-591

Dear Ms. Feridino,

Thank you for your letter informing us about your new contact information. We have updated the information on your account, and all subsequent statements and correspondence will be sent to your current address.

Please note that we received your letter just today, and your most recent statement had already been mailed to your previous address. However, you may view your account details (including account balance, recent charges, and payments received) at any time by accessing your account online.

Thank you for being a valued customer.

Sincerely,
Carl Delgado
Customer Service Associate

주제 / 목적 문제

1. What is the letter about?

   (A) An overdue payment
   (B) A newly opened account
   (C) A change-of-address request
   (D) An incorrect account balance

2. What does Mr. Delgado suggest that Ms. Feridino do?

   (A) Visit a Web site
   (B) Call customer service
   (C) Send a payment
   (D) Fill out a form

Questions 3-4 refer to the following e-mail.

난이도 ★★☆

E-mail	
To:	Tina Scherma <tinas@writersworld.com>
From:	Christopher Lote <christopher_lote@wtj.com>
Date:	October 1
Subject:	Story submission
Attachment:	📎 Lote's essay

Dear Ms. Scherma:

I got your e-mail address from Daryl Brown, your former assistant, who also happens to be a former colleague of mine. We used to work as copy editors for *Investment Digest*.

I have been a reader of your fiction and poetry for years, and I was happy to learn that you are the new editor of *Writer's World*. I hope you will consider my short essay, which I have attached to this e-mail, for future use in the journal's nonfiction section. It is about friendship in the age of technology. I have been publishing short stories and essays for over five years, and my work has appeared in various publications, including the *Basket House Review* and *Solitude Today*.

Thank you for your time.

Christopher Lote

주제/목적 문제

3. Why did Mr. Lote send the e-mail?
   (A) To ask for a writing sample
   (B) To introduce a new employee
   (C) To inquire about a former colleague
   (D) To request consideration for publication

4. What is suggested about *Writer's World*?
   (A) It has a large editorial staff.
   (B) It focuses on issues of public policy.
   (C) It includes different types of writing.
   (D) It is circulated throughout the country.

Attention Tenants of Commerce Center Plaza

In an effort to save energy and reduce the cost of utilities, the heating in all offices will be turned down to a low temperature setting over the upcoming national holiday week, from March 15 to 22. This measure is part of a pilot program that has the potential to reduce our office complex's energy usage in the month of March by a significant amount. The savings that result will be passed on to all tenants in the form of a reduction in maintenance costs for the month. If successful, the pilot program will be extended to run heating and cooling on minimal settings during other official holidays as well as on nights and weekends.

The building management is aware that, although all offices will be officially closed during the March holiday, some employees may need to work in the building. If you are planning to occupy your office at any time during the holiday week, please contact Ralph Snyder at 627-5899 ext. 234. Arrangements will be made for your office to be ready for occupancy during the days and times you specify.

Throughout the pilot program, we welcome your input. Please send any comments and questions to the director of building management, Geraldine Teller, at 627-5899 ext. 200. On March 23, a survey to help us gather data about your experience with the program will be distributed to everyone in the building. Please take the time to complete the survey and return it to Ms. Teller at that time.

Sincerely,
The Office of Building Management
Commerce Center Plaza Office Complex

주제/목적 문제

5. What is the purpose of the notice?

(A) To explain rising utility expenses
(B) To invite tenants to a building committee meeting
(C) To announce an energy conservation program
(D) To describe an upcoming construction project

6. How does the office of building management plan to decrease costs?

(A) By making repairs only when necessary
(B) By reducing heat when offices are not in use
(C) By installing newer, more efficient equipment
(D) By following advice provided by experts

7. What is indicated in the notice as a reason to contact Mr. Snyder?

(A) To arrange to use the building during the week of March 15
(B) To offer suggestions about a proposed renovation program
(C) To report any changes in utility bills
(D) To submit requests for additional office space

8. According to the notice, what will tenants be asked to do after March 22 ?

(A) Turn off unnecessary lights
(B) Volunteer to work additional hours
(C) Elect a new director of building management
(D) Complete a questionnaire

A Victory for Melquila Customers
By Jocelyn Gilmore

As of May 15, Melquila, maker of a variety of natural dairy products, will be offering its yogurt in screw-top glass jars; to date, the product is sold only in plastic cups. The move is in part a response to complaints from customers who argue that the product loses its flavor when a cup is refrigerated after it has been opened. Many shoppers posted comments on the company's Web site, pointing to research that has shown that products packaged in glass containers retain their flavor longer than those packaged in plastic.

Asked whether the company had decided to implement the change only after Food Source, one of the nation's leading consumer groups, had backed the concerns raised by customers, Melquila's senior director of sales was surprisingly frank. "In the last five years we have been enjoying steady sales growth," Jeff Pollard said, "so maybe we did become a little too pleased with ourselves and really needed a wake-up call." He pointed out, however, that the new measure was also driven by the increased adoption of innovative production techniques and marketing strategies by dairy companies worldwide. "Obviously, Melquila has to embrace these developments if it wishes to retain and expand its market share," he said.

Melquila is well aware of the profound effect consumer sentiment can have on its financial performance. Two years ago the company was awarded the Dairy Industry Research Agency (DIRA) Gold Medal of Excellence for its cinnamon-hazelnut ice cream. DIRA had surveyed about 3,500 ice cream lovers, the majority of whom praised Melquila's product for its creamy texture, rich taste, and low-fat, low-calorie content. In the months immediately following receipt of the award, Melquila saw demand for virtually all of its products soar, resulting in a 33 percent jump in revenue. Thus, Melquila fully realizes that its fortunes are in the hands of the consumer and that ignoring customer demand may carry considerable financial risk for the company.

주제 / 목적 문제

9. Why was the article written?

(A) To announce a change in the packaging of a product

(B) To promote the various products a company offers

(C) To show that consumers research products online

(D) To describe the purchasing habits of consumers

10. Why did customers complain about Melquila's yogurt?

(A) It was sold only in major supermarkets.

(B) It featured a limited number of flavors.

(C) It did not stay fresh for very long.

(D) It was not a low-fat product.

11. Who is Mr. Pollard?

(A) The owner of one of Melquila's competitors

(B) The head of Melquila's sales department

(C) The director of Food Source

(D) The spokesperson for DIRA

12. What is indicated about Melquila?

(A) It expanded its advertising efforts two years ago.

(B) It was increasingly losing business to its competitors.

(C) It conducted a number of surveys among its customers.

(D) It saw an increase in earnings after receiving an award.

기출 전략

1. 가장 많이 출제되는 문제 유형으로 누구, 무엇, 언제, 어디서, 어떻게, 왜 등과 같은 구체적인 정보를 묻는다.
2. 질문의 키워드를 잡고 지문에서 해당 부분을 찾아 그 주변을 정독하도록 한다. 요청/제안, 앞으로 할 일 등을 묻는 문제는 주로 지문 후반부에서 답을 찾을 수 있다.

세부 사항 질문 유형

시점	**When** will the **change go into effect**?	변경 사항은 언제부터 실시될 것인가?
장소	**Where** will the free **event** be **held**?	무료 행사는 어디서 열릴 것인가?
방법	**How** will **Ms. Smith help** with the **event**?	스미스 씨는 어떻게 행사를 도울 것인가?
요청/제안	**What** is **Ms. Choi asked to do**?	최 씨는 무엇을 하라고 요청받는가?

기출 예제 풀이 전략

Q. What is the **reason for** the **closure**?

(A) A special event   (B) Weather conditions
(C) A construction project   (D) Street repairs

MEMO

From: Aideen Haran, Operations Director
To: All Bayview Avenue Employees
Date: Friday, July 26

Please be advised that beginning on Tuesday, July 30, vehicular traffic to our office building on Bayview Avenue must follow a detour along Villa Road until further notice. The closure is necessary for the site development of the city's new sports stadium. Employees who drive to the office should allow extra travel time. Commuters who normally board the city bus on Lynn Street will need to use an alternate bus stop.

STEP 1
질문의 키워드 잡기
도로 폐쇄(closure) 이유

STEP 2
키워드 주변 집중
새로운 시립 스포츠 경기장 부지 개발을 위한 도로 폐쇄

STEP 3
정답 찾기: 정답 (C)

패러프레이징
지문의 site development
→ 보기의 construction project

번역 **p. 008**

🔄 세부 사항 문제의 패러프레이징

Every story on the site will have a form at the end through which readers can post comments or **e-mail the writer directly**.	**Q** 독자들이 웹사이트를 이용하는 방법? → To **contact reporters**
Please **let us know if this is correct** by replying to this e-mail.	**Q** 요청받는 것? → **Confirm that some information is true**
On March 15, we will **set up a new customer service call center**.	**Q** 회사가 계획하는 것? → **Open a new office**
The Contractor must **obtain all required construction permits** from city authorities for the work performed.	**Q** 이 회사의 책임은? → **Getting approval** from the city to perform work

다음 지문을 읽고 질문의 정답을 고르세요.

Kang Carpet Store

2987 Claremont Boulevard Halifax, NS
902-555-0145 www.kangcarpet.ca
Special event on Saturday, May 2!

As one of our best customers, you are invited to a special event marking the introduction of Marvaclean, a new line of carpets featuring a revolutionary new carpet fiber. Factory tests show that Marvaclean carpets trap up to 25% less dirt and last longer than comparably priced carpets. And if you purchase a Marvaclean carpet at our store on May 2, you can save up to 40% off the regular price. Simply bring this notice to our store on May 2 and show it to a store employee to gain admission to the Marvaclean showroom. We look forward to seeing you!

1. How can a customer qualify for a discount on a Marvaclean carpet?
   (A) By ordering the carpet online
   (B) By recommending Kang Carpet Store to a friend
   (C) By attending a store event
   (D) By completing a customer survey

Dear Ms. Tang:

Our records show that your Organization of Industrial Designers membership is about to expire. We hope that you simply forgot, and we would like to encourage you to renew your membership before it lapses.

Last year was an exciting time for the OID as we launched our new magazine, *Light and Form*. This year we will begin making improvements to our Web site. When these changes are completed, you will be able to update your contact information, register for meetings, and pay membership dues online.

To renew your membership now, please fill out the enclosed form and mail it in the envelope provided. We have current membership status recorded as at Level A; please indicate if your membership level has changed. If you have recently renewed your membership, please disregard this notice.

Sincerely,
Olujimi Oduya
Membership Director

2. What is Ms. Tang asked to do?
   (A) Complete a form
   (B) Send an e-mail message
   (C) Visit the Web site
   (D) Call the OID offices

Questions 1-2 refer to the following e-mail.

난이도 ★☆☆

To:	Marketing Team
From:	John Mehta
Date:	Thursday, 21 January
Subject:	Business cards

Hi everyone,

Business cards will be printed next Wednesday morning and delivered to my office the following afternoon. I know some of you have changed jobs recently, and I want to make sure everyone's information is correct. If your position has changed, please reply to this e-mail no later than 5:00 P.M. tomorrow with your name and new title. If I don't hear from you, I'll assume that the information on your existing card is still correct.

Each employee will get a box of 300 cards. Please pick them up from my office by next Friday.

Thanks,

John Mehta
Administrative Assistant

세부 사항 문제

1. When will the new business cards most likely arrive in Mr. Mehta's office?

   (A) On Tuesday
   (B) On Wednesday
   (C) On Thursday
   (D) On Friday

2. Who is asked to reply to the e-mail?

   (A) Employees who have changed jobs
   (B) Employees who have recently moved to a new address
   (C) Employees who will be away when the new cards are delivered
   (D) Employees who need 300 or more business cards

Questions 3-5 refer to the following announcement.

Library Events in June

Board Game Night: Fridays, 6:00–10:00 P.M.
Play your favorite board game or learn a new one while getting to know fellow board game enthusiasts at our weekly game night in the library conference room. Bring your own game or play one from the library's collection. Games for children and adults are provided.

Basics of Drawing: June 12, 2:00–4:00 P.M.
Teens and adults can learn techniques for drawing portraits and objects using pencils and ink. Materials are provided. Space is limited. Please register at the library or on the library Web site.

Bird-Watching for Amateurs: June 16, 1:00–3:00 P.M.
Bird enthusiasts can join University of Olympia biologist and author of *Birds in Your Neighborhood* Mercedes Ortiz in the library's courtyard to observe our bird visitors. Ortiz will help participants to identify birds by their appearance.

Music Hour: June 20, 10:00–11:00 A.M.
Join our favorite children's musician Tammy Lindale for an hour of interactive music and play. Instruments and toys provided. Ideal for children ages 3–6. Registration not required, but front-and-center seating will be limited to 30 children, so get there early.

Book Lovers Gathering: June 28, 6:00–8:00 P.M.
Join other readers at the library's monthly book club meeting. This month, the group will be discussing Alfred Pedersen's new novel *Living in the City*.

세부 사항 문제

3. Which event requires participants to sign up in advance?

(A) Basics of Drawing
(B) Bird-Watching for Amateurs
(C) Music Hour
(D) Book Lovers Gathering

4. Who most likely is Ms. Ortiz?

(A) A library employee
(B) A zookeeper
(C) An artist
(D) A scientist

세부 사항 문제

5. What are participants in Music Hour encouraged to do?

(A) Pay a fee online
(B) Bring an instrument
(C) Bring a chair
(D) Arrive early

---

http://www.t-note.com/aboutus ▶

Welcome to t-note.com, the only job-search Web site dedicated exclusively to those working in or looking to join the field of translation. Submit the form below to receive an e-mail whenever a suitable job is posted. Also explore the rest of the site to find upcoming job fairs, as well as user testimonials, résumé tips, and job-search advice from translation professionals.

Click all boxes that apply. Sign up today and begin your path toward a fulfilling career in translation!

Name: _____

E-mail address: _____

Languages: ⦿ English ⦿ Spanish ⦿ French ⦿ German ⦿ Italian
⦿ Russian ⦿ Japanese ⦿ Mandarin ⦿ Cantonese ⦿ Korean ⦿ Arabic
⦿ Urdu ⦿ Hindi ⦿ Persian ⦿ Indonesian ⦿ Other _____

Types of translation experience, if any:
⦿ Administrative ⦿ Commercial ⦿ Financial ⦿ Legal ⦿ Medical
⦿ Technical ⦿ Other _____

Desired employment type:
⦿ On-site—list city or country _____
⦿ Off-site/Remote

Submit

---

6. According to the Web page, how does t-note.com differ from other job-search Web sites?

(A) Its job listings are extremely detailed.
(B) Its content is updated daily.
(C) It is specifically for people seeking jobs in translation.
(D) It can be displayed in a variety of languages.

7. What does t-note.com provide?

(A) A monthly newsletter
(B) Personalized notifications of jobs
(C) Free tickets to job fairs
(D) A professional résumé review service

8. What information is requested on the form?

(A) Number of years of experience
(B) Salary requirements
(C) Samples of recent work
(D) Preferred work location

May 16

Dr. Thomas Rennault
Department of Economics
McGruder University
543 Shoreline Road
Boston, MA 02243

Dear Dr. Rennault,

I am the vice president for operations at the Eastfield Company, a full-service investment and financial planning firm. I was in the audience last Thursday evening when you spoke about the effects of social media on measures of consumer confidence. I was impressed with your analysis of how the expansion of social media will affect economic growth in the short term.

As part of our commitment to staff professional development, Eastfield offers an in-house program of continuing education workshops for our staff members. Would you be interested in leading one of these workshops, on the same topic as your lecture? A session lasts 90 minutes, including a question-and-answer period, and typically attracts about 25 participants. Last year we had another member of your department, Dr. Carter, come to lead a group, and it was very successful.

If you are interested, please call my assistant, Daniel Wong, at 617-555-0172 to discuss compensation. We look forward to hearing from you soon.

Sincerely,
Ananya Patel
Vice President, Operations

세부 사항 문제

9. How did Ms. Patel find out about Dr. Rennault's ideas?
   (A) She heard a talk he gave on a radio program.
   (B) She was his colleague at McGruder University.
   (C) She read a newspaper article about him.
   (D) She attended a lecture that he delivered.

10. What is suggested about the employees at the Eastfield Company?
    (A) They are offered flexible work schedules.
    (B) They are encouraged to enroll in college classes.
    (C) They can attend on-site learning sessions.
    (D) They receive a bonus for improved job performance.

세부 사항 문제

11. According to the letter, who previously visited the Eastfield Company?
    (A) Researchers conducting a study
    (B) The head of a consumer organization
    (C) A professor of economics
    (D) A reporter for a finance newsletter

세부 사항 문제

12. Why should Dr. Rennault contact Mr. Wong?
    (A) To discuss the amount of a payment
    (B) To select topics for a workshop
    (C) To ask for directions to a company
    (D) To request a brochure about investment

UNIT 03 Not/True 문제

⚙ 출제 비율 10~12문제 | 54문항

기출 전략

1. 보기 중 지문의 내용과 일치하거나 일치하지 않는 것을 찾는 문제 유형이다.
2. NOT 문제는 각 보기와 지문의 단서를 일일이 대조하면서 오답을 소거해야 하므로 다른 문제에 비해 시간이 걸리는 고난도 문제에 속한다.

Not/True 질문 유형

일치하는 것
What is **true** about the **new model**?   새 모델에 대해 사실인 것은?
What is **indicated[stated]** about **J&J Airlines**?   J&J 항공사에 대해 명시[언급]된 것은?

일치하지 않는 것
What is **NOT provided** in this **invoice**?   이 주문 청구서에서 제공되지 않는 것은?
What is **NOT mentioned** as a **feature of the new Web site**?   새 웹사이트의 특징으로 언급되지 않은 것은?

기출 예제 풀이 전략

Q. What is **NOT mentioned** as being **available at Greengage Conference Center**?
(A) Free Internet access
(B) Presentation software
(C) Dining facilities
(D) On-site hotel rooms

STEP 1
질문의 키워드 잡기
콘퍼런스 센터에서 이용할 수 있는 것

STEP 2
보기와 지문 대조
- 사무 생산성 소프트웨어 일체
- 무료 인터넷 접속
- 두 군데의 식당

Greengage Conference Center

Located just 40 minutes from the Charlotte Airport, Greengage Conference Center is the perfect place to hold your next corporate event. Situated among beautiful rolling hills and woodlands, our center provides a private, serene retreat. We offer conference facilities and meeting rooms that are equipped with everything you need for multimedia presentations. We also offer a fully equipped business center with (B)a complete suite of office productivity software, (A)complimentary wireless Internet access, (D)two restaurants, and a banquet hall.

STEP 3
정답 찾기: 정답 (D)

패러프레이징
지문의 complimentary
→ 보기의 Free
지문의 restaurants
→ 보기의 Dining facilities

번역 p.013

 Not/True 문제의 패러프레이징

I've seen **some of your recent photographs on your Web site**.	**Q** 사실인 것? → She displays **her work on the Internet**.
Orders shipped to destinations overseas usually arrive in two to four weeks.	**Q** 언급된 것? → **International orders** are accepted.
At Tobbler, he was credited with **earning record-high revenues** for the company.	**Q** 토블러 사에서 강 씨가 한 일로 언급된 것? → He **increased revenues**.

다음 지문을 읽고 질문의 정답을 고르세요.

Job advertisement

20 February

Help Wanted

Full-time cashier needed for a new spice shop in Port Melbourne. Grocery or retail experience required. Must be available to start on our grand opening day next month. Employee discount available after four months on the job. Send your CV and cover letter to Walter Maughan at wmaughan@pmhs.com.au by 25 February.

1. What is indicated about the advertised job?

(A) It is a managerial position.
(B) It is part-time.
(C) It is a four-month position.
(D) It includes an employee discount.

Notice

Eckman Markets

• **Need advice on setting health goals?**
• **Want to make your favourite meals more nutritious?**
• **Looking for healthy snacks for you and your family?**

Let Eckman Markets help! We provide on-site cooking classes, personal shopping tours, and one-on-one consultations.

Come meet Jennifer Yoshimura, Accredited Practising Dietitian at Eckman Markets in Perth. You may have already read Ms. Yoshimura's blog on healthy eating or seen her being interviewed on local television. Find out more at www.eckmanmarkets.com.au/nutritionist or by stopping by Ms. Yoshimura's table by the front entrance.

2. What is NOT mentioned in the notice as something that Eckman Markets offers?

(A) Lessons in cooking
(B) Samples of products
(C) Tours of the store
(D) Help with achieving goals

Questions 1-2 refer to the following brochure.

난이도 ★☆☆

NLG Computer Repairs Ltd.

Over 25 years serving Rutland County

Computer services
- We remove viruses, malware, and other harmful programs.
- We recover data that is lost as a result of system crashes or hardware damage.
- We configure the wireless network of your home or business.
- We collect, repair, and return your computer from anywhere in Rutland County—and unlike our competition, this service is included in the charge.

IT training
If your business has recurring computer problems, ask us about our in-person training sessions. At the low cost of only £80 per hour, these sessions can be tailored specially to address the needs of your staff members and build their IT skills.

Visit our Web site at www.nlgcomputerrepairs.co.uk or call 01632 960547 for more information.

Not / True 문제

1. According to the brochure, what is unique about the business?

   (A) It offers online data storage.
   (B) It builds customized computers.
   (C) It has many locations in Rutland County.
   (D) It does not charge an additional fee for transporting customers' items.

2. What is stated about the training sessions?

   (A) They are intended for advanced learners.
   (B) They are reasonably priced.
   (C) They are available on the Internet.
   (D) They are held on a monthly basis.

Questions 3-5 refer to the following e-mail.

From:	Katya Svobodová <katya@casalopez.net>
To:	Allen Jay <anjay@santorolaw.com>
Subject:	Reservation at Casa Lopez
Date:	August 8
Attachment:	📎 Receipt for deposit

Dear Mr. Jay,

Thank you for choosing Casa Lopez for Santoro and Lamont Partners at Law's upcoming celebration. This is to confirm your reservation for the Córdoba Room on October 16 from 7:00–9:00 P.M., with seating accommodations for 108 guests. As I mentioned, for this number of guests, I would recommend round tables that each seat six people; however, other table setups can easily be arranged. As we discussed, I will have a projector set up in the Córdoba Room so that you can present a slide show about the three employees whose retirement from your company will be celebrated.

On the home page of our Web site, www.casalopez.net, you will find the link for party menus. There, you may choose from over 100 food and beverage options; click any option to find out the ingredients that the item contains and how it is prepared. Should you need assistance making menu choices, please send me an e-mail, or telephone me at 555-0174. Please make your menu selections by September 15.

This e-mail also confirms receipt of your deposit of $500; the receipt is attached. You will receive a bill for the total amount due once you have made your menu selections.

Sincerely,

Katya Svobodová
Events Manager
Casa Lopez

Not/True 문제

3. Why is an event being held on October 16?
   (A) To welcome newly hired staff members
   (B) To celebrate the opening of Santoro and Lamont's new office
   (C) To honor staff members who are retiring
   (D) To announce the appointment of a new company president

4. According to the e-mail, what can Mr. Jay find on the Casa Lopez Web site?
   (A) The invoice for his order
   (B) Descriptions of food items
   (C) A contract that he should print and sign
   (D) A seating plan for the Cordoba Room

5. What is NOT mentioned as a service that can be provided by Casa Lopez?
   (A) Offering advice in making menu selections
   (B) Setting up a projector for a slide show
   (C) Making changes to the suggested arrangement of tables
   (D) Decorating the event area

Search Update: Valvecomp West Coast Center

Following a review of the infrastructure and accessibility in fifteen cities across the United States and Canada, our site search committee has eliminated a dozen locations. Portland, Seattle, and Vancouver remain under consideration as viable locations for Valvecomp's west coast center. The committee is visiting the three cities and meeting with their respective city councils before it makes a final decision.

The committee's review of Portland, Oregon, notes that the city welcomes new and growing companies. Although Portland is distant from Valvecomp's headquarters, it is close to the Martone Motor Company, a manufacturer of engine components. Locating Valvecomp's west coast center in Portland would make getting orders to this major client efficient and cost effective.

Developing a west coast center close to the city's port area would allow Valvecomp to make shipments using all transportation modes. The Columbia River has three marine terminals, and Portland's airport is adjacent to the port. The rail network, which is undergoing some renovation, will be able to handle increased freight starting in the new year—currently only passenger trains are operating through December. Finally, trucking is a reliable option, since major highways pass through the port and Portland's downtown area.

Not / True 문제

6. How many locations is the committee now considering?
(A) One
(B) Three
(C) Twelve
(D) Fifteen

7. What is indicated about the Martone Motor Company?
(A) It is moving its facility to central Portland.
(B) It has appointed new leadership.
(C) It has just been purchased by Valvecomp.
(D) It is an important client to Valvecomp.

8. According to the report, what is true about Portland?
(A) Its airport is too small to handle freight.
(B) Its transport infrastructure is similar to Seattle's.
(C) Its rail system can begin carrying freight in the new year.
(D) Its extensive highway system is in need of repairs.

Black Creek Networking Association
15 South Walnut Avenue
Black Creek, NE 68897

Dear BCNA member,

Thank you for your patience. Enclosed is the Black Creek Networking Association Directory, the one you typically receive when renewing your annual membership. We apologize for its lateness this year. We were in the process of relocating our office and, as a result, were unable to meet the usual publishing deadline for the directory. If you would like another copy, please send your request to Patti Greenwald at membership@BCNA.net.

You can access an electronic version of the directory on our Web site using your BCNA ID and password. The text is searchable, making it easy to find the addresses and phone numbers of other BCNA members.

Please check the directory to see how you are listed. If your entry is out-of-date or incorrect, feel free to log in, click the button labeled "My account," and correct your contact information. On that same page, you can also verify the status of your membership and renew it before it expires.

We are preparing to make an interactive map of our membership for the Web site. Tech-savvy volunteers interested in helping with this task should call Ron Sanderling.

Sincerely,
Francine Cooper
Association President

Contacts:

Patti Greenwald: 308-555-0147

Ron Sanderling: 308-555-0122

Not/True 문제

9. What is the reason for the delay?
(A) The printer made an error.
(B) A shipment was lost.
(C) The BCNA office was being moved.
(D) BCNA grew more quickly than expected.

10. According to the letter, what is one of Ms. Greenwald's responsibilities?
(A) Distributing paychecks
(B) Providing additional directories
(C) Planning BCNA events
(D) Keeping official records for BCNA

11. What is NOT mentioned as something members can do online?
(A) Contact Ron Sanderling
(B) Update a directory listing
(C) Search for a telephone number
(D) Renew a membership

12. Why is BCNA seeking volunteers?
(A) To find potential members
(B) To help distribute materials
(C) To create a new feature for its Web site
(D) To survey members about new services

UNIT 04 추론 문제

⚙ 출제 비율 10~12문제 | 54문항

 기출 전략
1. 지문에 직접적으로 언급되지는 않았지만 지문 내용을 바탕으로 추론할 수 있는 정보를 찾는 문제 유형이다.
2. 지문의 내용을 충분히 파악한 후에 유추할 수 있는 경우가 많으므로 추론 문제는 마지막에 푸는 것이 유리하다.

추론 질문 유형

전체 내용
Where would this **article** most likely be **found**?　이 기사는 어디에서 볼 수 있겠는가?
To whom is the memo most likely **written**?　이 회람은 누구를 대상으로 쓰여진 것 같은가?

세부 사항
Who most likely is **Mr. Martel**?　마텔 씨는 누구일 것 같은가?
What is **suggested** about the **new model**?　새 모델에 대해 암시되는 것은?

기출 예제 풀이 전략

Q. Who most likely is **Ms. Earlham**?

(A) A lawyer　　　　　　　(B) A real estate agent
(C) A seminar leader　　　(D) An administrative assistant

STEP 1
질문의 키워드 잡기
얼햄 씨의 직업

Dear Ms. Earlham,

Congratulations on completing Savino Real Estate's seminar, "Target Marketing for Selling Condominiums." We hope you received some valuable information that will help you in your career.

STEP 2
지문 내용 읽고 보기 대조하기
부동산 세미나 수료, 경력에 도움이 되길 바란다는 말에서 직업 유추 가능

Our next seminar will be held on Saturday, August 8. It will focus on recent changes to commercial real estate law. If you sign up by July 20, you will receive 30 percent off all course materials. Register online at www.savinorealestate.com. We hope you will join us!

STEP 3
정답 찾기: 정답 (B)

Sincerely,
Anton Savino

번역 p.017

🔄 추론 문제의 패러프레이징

I very much **enjoyed your talk at the International Conference** on Public Architecture in Mumbai.	**Q** 웡 씨에 대해 추론할 수 있는 것? → He **attended a presentation** given by Ms. Cha.
Bring your résumé and **meet with human resources personnel** from school districts throughout the country.	**Q** 이 행사에 대해 암시된 것? → It helps its members **find jobs.**
Maple Leaf Literary Journal, **the most widely circulated** literary magazine in Canada, …	**Q** 잡지에 대해 암시된 것? → It **sells more copies than its competitors**.

다음 지문을 읽고 질문의 정답을 고르세요.

ATTENTION!

This freight elevator is for staff use only. It is NOT intended to be used by the general public. Customers should use the passenger elevators to the right of the fitting rooms at the back of the store.

Thank you for your cooperation and enjoy your shopping experience!

- Management

1. Where would the notice most likely be found?

(A) In a museum
(B) In a warehouse
(C) In a department store
(D) In an office building

To: Kyungbin Yi <kyi@moto.net>
From: Miguel Hernández <mhernandez@mintner_mag.com>
Date: 3 January
Subject: Your submission

We're writing with some good news. Your photograph *Coastline in Winter* has been chosen as the third-place winner in the "Views of Our World" landscape photography contest sponsored by *Mintner Photography Magazine*.

Your photograph will appear among the other winning photographs in the March issue of *Mintner Photography Magazine*. In addition, your work will be featured in a special landscape photography exhibit in Birmingham at Perivale Art Museum from 9 May to 21 May.

You will receive a prize of £400 as well as a two-year subscription to *Mintner Photography Magazine*.

Congratulations on your success. We are looking forward to sharing your work with our international readership and hope to see more of your work in the future.

2. What is implied about Ms. Yi's photograph?

(A) It is in black and white.
(B) It has previously been published.
(C) It has been purchased by a magazine.
(D) It depicts a landscape scene.

Questions 1-2 refer to the following online chat discussion.

난이도 ★☆☆

Timothy Reeder [1:09 P.M.]
Hello, Lucia. I'm back at my desk now, so I can look up the figures you asked about earlier today. Please remind me exactly what you need.

Lucia Bruhl [1:12 P.M.]
I need the updated sales figures from each of our cosmetic lines for the quarter that recently ended. The figures that I have only go up to the end of May. My computer seems to be having problems connecting to the database.

Timothy Reeder [1:14 P.M.]
All right. That shouldn't be difficult to do. I assume that e-mail is OK.

Lucia Bruhl [1:15 P.M.]
Yes, that's great. Thank you for your help.

 추론 문제

1.   What is suggested about Mr. Reeder?

    (A) He works in the IT department.
    (B) He is training Ms. Bruhl.
    (C) He works for a cosmetics company.
    (D) He wants to schedule a meeting.

2.   At 1:14 P.M., what does Mr. Reeder most likely mean when he writes, "That shouldn't be difficult to do"?

    (A) He can easily repair Ms. Bruhl's computer.
    (B) He can ship products quickly.
    (C) He can extend a deadline.
    (D) He can provide sales information.

Questions 3-5 refer to the following letter.

난이도 ★ ★ ☆

Medipro Alliance

Koningstraat 251
6511 LA, Nijmegen
The Netherlands
Telephone: 024 217 9961

Eleni Katsantonis
842 Athalassis Street
2221 Nicosia
Cyprus

Dear Ms. Katsantonis:

Because today's global business environment is profoundly interconnected and interdependent, establishing professional relationships with domestic and international colleagues is more important than ever. That is why Medipro Alliance has compiled an extensive database with information about more than 40,000 medical laboratory scientists located in 42 countries. Join Medipro Alliance today and broaden your peer-to-peer connections.

As a subscriber to our Standard Business Listing, you will have access to the name, title, and contact information of each individual included in this and any of our other databases of medical professionals, including those intended for physicians, nurses, and physical therapists. Should you subscribe to our Premium Business Listing, you will have access to the aforementioned information as well as any detailed data we have been authorized to disclose.

We are so confident you will find this service invaluable that we are happy to offer it to you free for 30 days. To sign up for this free trial, or to become a subscriber, please visit our Web site, www.mpalliance.com.nl/subscription.

Sincerely,

Marjolein Bloemenveld

Marjolein Bloemenveld
Senior Marketing Director

---

3. What is the purpose of the letter?

(A) To request updated information

(B) To attract a new customer

(C) To explain how to register for an event

(D) To recommend medical professionals

5. What service does Medipro Alliance offer?

(A) Designing Web sites

(B) Recovering lost data

(C) Providing medical training courses

(D) Facilitating professional communications

추론 문제

4. Who most likely is Ms. Katsantonis?

(A) A doctor

(B) A nurse

(C) A laboratory scientist

(D) A physical therapist

Esterwall (5 April) – Real estate investors looking to develop areas of the old city centre along Harbour Street may soon be required to follow strict new standards that have been proposed by the Esterwall Redevelopment Council (ERC).

In light of resident concerns about appropriate reuse of the area's venerable old buildings, the ERC recently drafted a set of design guidelines intended to shape future development projects in the Harbour Street neighbourhood.

Harbour Street, located at the heart of a somewhat neglected but historic area, has been eyed increasingly by investors sensing opportunity for profit. Of late, there have been half a dozen proposals to replace aging buildings with new shops and residences.

In response, the ERC is taking a strong stand for heritage preservation. "Our vision is to revitalize the area, but to do so while showcasing its original character," explains ERC spokesperson, Brad Knight. According to the proposed guidelines, structures recognized as having architectural or historical merit must be restored, whereas new structures must conform to principles of compatible design.

The ERC's draft is available online at their Web site, esterwallrc.org.uk. Hard copies are available at the Deaton Public Library.

The ERC will hold a public assembly at the Harbour Street Community Centre on 8 April at 1:30 P.M. There, ERC officials will answer questions about the proposal and citizens will be able to voice their opinions. Those unable to attend can e-mail feedback to Lorna Hu at lhu@esterwallrc.org.uk.

6. What is indicated about the Harbour Street area?
   (A) It is next to the Deaton Public Library.
   (B) It has ample parking space.
   (C) It has historic significance.
   (D) It is a popular shopping location.

7. According to the article, why should readers visit the ERC Web site?
   (A) To vote on a design
   (B) To view a document
   (C) To check library hours
   (D) To obtain a building permit

8. Why will ERC officials be at the Harbour Street Community Centre?
   (A) To plan upcoming cultural events
   (B) To welcome new residents
   (C) To launch an educational program
   (D) To discuss proposed regulations

추론 문제

9. What will Ms. Hu most likely do?
   (A) Respond to media inquiries
   (B) Inspect development projects
   (C) Gather comments from residents
   (D) Review proposals from contractors

To:	Alina Gomez <agomez@galleonair.com>
From:	Tomoko Ono <tono@szmail.net>
Re:	February stopover
Date:	March 3

Dear Ms. Gomez,

As a customer familiar with your usual high standards, I feel it is necessary to tell you about my recent unsatisfactory experience during a stopover. On February 25, my flight (GL115) from Newark to Dallas was delayed due to mechanical issues. When I finally arrived in Dallas, I had missed my connecting flight to Austin and needed a room for the night. The Galleon Airways customer service representative arranged transportation and gave me vouchers to use at the Wycliff Inn.

My brief stay at the Wycliff Inn was frustrating and unpleasant. I ordered a meal at the hotel's restaurant, but when I attempted to pay using the meal voucher given to me by the airline, I was told that the code was invalid. After paying $19.78 of my own money for my dinner, I went upstairs to visit the fitness center, only to find it closed for renovation. Finally, my room was too hot, but I was unable to turn down the heat because the thermostat was broken.

Galleon Airways had been my preferred carrier until this incident. I hope you will not renew any contract you have with the Wycliff Inn and that you will direct your passengers elsewhere in the future. I have also written to Arlen Charles, general manager of the Wycliff Inn, to describe my experience.

Since I was unable to use the voucher (#8892730), I hope that you will compensate me for my dinner. The next time I choose Galleon Airways, I will expect the exemplary service that I usually receive. Please contact me if you require additional information.

Regards,

Tomoko Ono
788 Highpoint Terrace
Kerryville, NJ 08001
856-555-0195

10. Why did Ms. Ono send the e-mail?

(A) To confirm a reservation
(B) To submit a complaint
(C) To settle a ticketing problem
(D) To inquire about a service

추론 문제

11. What does Ms. Ono imply in her e-mail?

(A) She routinely makes travel arrangements through a travel agency.
(B) She is planning to take a vacation soon.
(C) She frequently flies on Galleon Airways.
(D) She is currently employed in the hotel industry.

12. What feature of the Wycliff Inn is NOT mentioned by Ms. Ono?

(A) Its exercise facility
(B) Its heating system
(C) Its food service
(D) Its housekeeping staff

13. What does Ms. Ono request from Ms. Gomez?

(A) A receipt
(B) Flight schedules
(C) A recommendation for a hotel
(D) Reimbursement for a meal

UNIT 05 문장 삽입 문제

⚙ 출제 비율 2문제 | 54문항

기출 전략

1. 지문의 전체 흐름을 파악하여 주어진 제시문이 들어가기에 알맞은 위치를 찾는 문제 유형이다.
2. 문장 삽입 문제가 나온 경우는 반드시 그 제시문을 먼저 파악한 후에 지문을 읽어야 한다.
3. 제시문 내에 단서가 있다는 사실을 기억하라. 문맥상 힌트가 되어줄 제시문 내의 연결어, 지시대명사, 정관사를 단서로 잡고 지문을 읽어야 한다.

문장 삽입 질문 유형

In which of the positions marked [1], [2], [3], and [4] does the following sentence best belong?

"He should finish around five o'clock."

[1], [2], [3], [4]로 표시된 곳 중에서 다음 문장이 들어가기에 가장 적합한 곳은?

"그는 다섯 시쯤 끝날 겁니다."

기출 예제 풀이 전략

Q. In which of the positions marked [1], [2], [3], and [4] does the following sentence best belong?

"Save money and time by **not having to check your suitcase before boarding.**"

(A) [1]　　　(B) [2]　　　(C) [3]　　　(D) [4]

Make traveling for business easy with the Sleek-Roll carry-on bag by Careel

The compact design of this lightweight and durable case meets the requirements of all major airlines for carry-on luggage. —[1]—. Measuring just 21 x 34 x 55 centimeters and weighing a little over 2 kilograms, the Sleek-Roll carry-on bag is made with a crush-proof shell. —[2]—. Its wheels rotate 360 degrees and the collapsible handle is operated by a push button, enabling you to easily maneuver through airports and narrow airplane aisles. —[3]—.

All Careel products include a two-year warranty against breakage. —[4]—. Should your Sleek-Roll carry-on bag be damaged in flight, simply return it to us for replacement.

STEP 1

제시문 파악하기
여행 가방을 수하물로 부칠 필요 없다는 말을 기억하고 지문을 처음부터 읽는다.

STEP 2

지문 처음부터 읽으며 문맥 파악하기
기내용 가방(carry-on luggage)이라는 설명이 처음 나오는 문장 뒤에 들어가야 자연스럽다.

기내용 가방에 알맞은 콤팩트한 디자인 → 수하물로 부칠 필요 없음

STEP 3

정답 찾기: 정답 (A)

번역 p. 022

🔄 **문장 삽입 문제의 정답을 부르는 단서**

연결어	삽입문에 however / but / yet(그러나), therefore(그러므로), consequently(결과적으로), also(또한) 등의 단어가 있을 경우 앞 문장과 의미 관계를 따져 위치를 파악하도록 한다.
지시어/대명사	this, that, it, he, she 등의 대명사는 그 대명사가 가리키는 대상이 있는 문장 뒤에 삽입될 가능성이 높다.
시간 순서	before(전에), after(후에), first(처음에), since(그 이래로), and then(그러고 나서) 등의 표현은 전후 관계나 순서를 짐작할 수 있는 단서가 된다.

다음 지문을 읽고 질문의 정답을 고르세요.

Mark your calendars for History Day!

—[1]—. On September 20, the Historical Society of Shedona (HSS) will be holding its annual History Day event at Halston Field from 10 A.M. to 6 P.M. The event will feature various activities led by HSS members, including a lecture by historian Ed Topanga. The author of *Shedona: The First 100 Years*, Mr. Topanga will present an overview of the founding of our town. There will also be a furniture restoration workshop led by Ms. Linda Ogus. —[2]—. She is the owner of Rejuvenation, which specializes in restoring antique furniture. In addition, visitors to the fair are invited to tour three of the oldest homes in the town of Shedona. —[3]—. For a full schedule of events, visit the HSS Web site at www.hss.org. Admission to the event is free, but donations are encouraged.

No visitor parking is available at Halston Field. —[4]—. Therefore, attendees should plan to use the parking area on Mason Road.

1. In which of the positions marked [1], [2], [3], and [4] does the following sentence best belong?

"Whatever your age or interest, there will be something for you."

(A) [1] (B) [2] (C) [3] (D) [4]

Brigham & Jones Locksmiths

Government agencies, jewelers, and electronics retailers have all trusted Brigham & Jones with their valuable inventories and data for decades, and we hope that now you will, too. —[1]—. It is our mission to provide durable, attractive locks to secure even the smallest valuable. —[2]—. All of our locks are handmade with solid, reinforced brass and undergo extensive stress testing. During our quality control process, the locks are placed in very hot temperatures, struck with hammers, and even chopped at with a diamond-bladed knife. If any locks fail these trials, we reexamine their design and our production process to ensure we are making the most secure locks possible. —[3]—.

To celebrate our 80th anniversary, we are offering an exclusive discount to our loyal customers. —[4]—. Through the end of May, all recurring orders will receive a 5% price reduction, and shipping costs on any orders over $100 will be waived.

2. In which of the positions marked [1], [2], [3], and [4] does the following sentence best belong?

"Because of this fine craftsmanship, Brigham & Jones has led the padlock industry for 80 years."

(A) [1] (B) [2] (C) [3] (D) [4]

Questions 1-3 refer to the following e-mail.

난이도 ★★☆

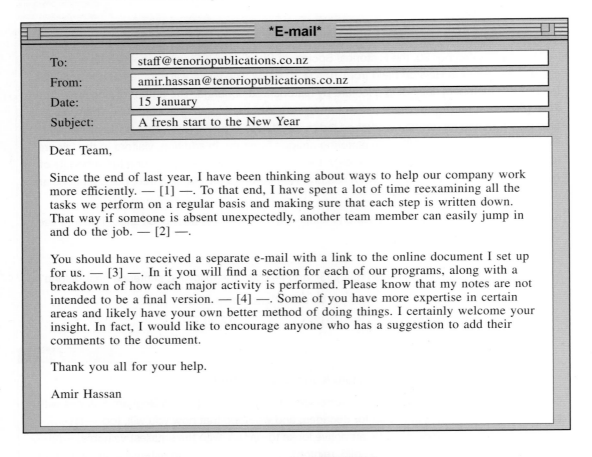

E-mail

To:	staff@tenoriopublications.co.nz
From:	amir.hassan@tenoriopublications.co.nz
Date:	15 January
Subject:	A fresh start to the New Year

Dear Team,

Since the end of last year, I have been thinking about ways to help our company work more efficiently. — [1] —. To that end, I have spent a lot of time reexamining all the tasks we perform on a regular basis and making sure that each step is written down. That way if someone is absent unexpectedly, another team member can easily jump in and do the job. — [2] —.

You should have received a separate e-mail with a link to the online document I set up for us. — [3] —. In it you will find a section for each of our programs, along with a breakdown of how each major activity is performed. Please know that my notes are not intended to be a final version. — [4] —. Some of you have more expertise in certain areas and likely have your own better method of doing things. I certainly welcome your insight. In fact, I would like to encourage anyone who has a suggestion to add their comments to the document.

Thank you all for your help.

Amir Hassan

문장 삽입 문제

1. What project has Mr. Hassan been working on?
   (A) Creating new marketing materials
   (B) Reevaluating a company's mission
   (C) Rearranging some workstations
   (D) Documenting a company's processes

2. What are the staff members encouraged to do?
   (A) Test software
   (B) Provide feedback
   (C) Work more hours
   (D) Learn new skills

3. In which of the positions marked [1], [2], [3], and [4] does the following sentence best belong?

   "They are simply a starting point."

   (A) [1]
   (B) [2]
   (C) [3]
   (D) [4]

Questions 4-7 refer to the following newspaper article.

난이도 ★★★

Delmax City Times
September 2

Personal trainer helps locals keep fit at popular gym

Three years ago, when personal trainer Carol Yoo invested her life savings to open Prism Gym, her friends were concerned. "You're taking a big risk," a colleague told her. — [1] —. However, the investment proved to be worth it.

Today, Prism Gym has 350 clients and 21 staff members. The facility offers 24-hour access and 12 personal trainers. It currently occupies a 2,200-square foot space on the second floor of the Mandel Building and will move to a larger space on the first floor of the same building next month. "I didn't think I would need more space so soon," Ms. Yoo said. — [2] —.

Yoo, a Delmax City native, previously worked as a personal trainer at the downtown Wellness Gym. She quit when Plus Fitness, Inc. bought out the facility and reduced her work hours, and soon started Prism Gym with an initial equipment purchase of $50,000. "I paid $30,000 up front, and the rest on installments. Thanks to our surprisingly rapid growth, I paid off the remaining $20,000 earlier than planned," she said. — [3] —.

Yoo has done no marketing since the gym opened. "All of our members are Delmax City residents who joined via positive word of mouth from other clients," she said. A typical member, she explained, is a beginner with little gym experience. — [4] —. Because of that, all of the Prism Gym staff are "friendly and approachable."

4. According to the article, what is true about Prism Gym?
   (A) It offers outdoor fitness classes.
   (B) It is open 24 hours a day.
   (C) It has 2,200 members.
   (D) It has multiple locations.

5. What is indicated about Ms. Yoo?
   (A) She was born in Delmax City.
   (B) She owns two fitness centers.
   (C) She used to manage Plus Fitness, Inc.
   (D) She sells her own line of exercise equipment.

6. What does Ms. Yoo say about Prism Gym's members?
   (A) They are transferred from other gyms.
   (B) They will soon appear in a marketing video.
   (C) They referred each other to the facility.
   (D) They live outside of Delmax City.

문장 삽입 문제

7. In which of the positions marked [1], [2], [3], and [4] does the following sentence best belong?

   "But the business has grown faster than I expected."

   (A) [1]　　　　(B) [2]
   (C) [3]　　　　(D) [4]

Ambo's Furniture Plus
247 Lacson Ave.

March 19

Mr. Sandalio Wi
917 Ligaya St., Apt. 3B
Manila, PH 1000

Dear Mr. Wi,

We have received news that your order was damaged upon delivery. On behalf of Ambo's Furniture Plus I'd like to apologize for the inconvenience this has surely caused. We package all of our goods in a triple layer of plastic padding, but clearly in this case it was insufficient. —[1]—. Again, we are very sorry this occurred.

Our delivery person will collect the furniture at a time that is convenient for you and of course at no charge. As soon as we have confirmation from the delivery person that the goods have been picked up, we will ship out a replacement order of the chairs. —[2]—. Unfortunately, the table you ordered was the last one in stock. —[3]—. If you would like to order a different table, please call our support line. If not, we will refund the price of the table to your credit card on file.

We hope these measures will satisfactorily resolve the matter. As a token of our gratitude for your choosing Ambo's Furniture Plus, we are including a coupon for free shipping on a future order. —[4]—. Thank you for your understanding and we look forward to doing business with you in the future.

Sincerely,

The Ambo's Furniture Plus Team

Enclosure

---

8. What is the main purpose of the letter?
   (A) To notify that an item is in stock
   (B) To resolve a problem with delivered goods
   (C) To market new products to repeat customers
   (D) To provide a customer with contact information

9. What is indicated about Ambo's Furniture Plus?
   (A) Delivery is free for large orders.
   (B) Furniture is backed by an extensive warranty.
   (C) Goods are delivered in multiple layers of padding.
   (D) Customers must bring furniture to the store to return it.

10. What is included with the letter?
    (A) An order form
    (B) An instruction manual
    (C) A product catalog
    (D) A shipping voucher

11. In which of the positions marked [1], [2], [3], and [4] does the following sentence best belong?

    "Therefore we will not be able to replace it."

    (A) [1]
    (B) [2]
    (C) [3]
    (D) [4]

Positive Change for Mechelen

Wind Dynamics, the leading producer of wind turbines and wind energy technology across Europe, has announced plans to open a production plant in Mechelen, Belgium. —[1]—. The Dutch company is spending more than €15 million to purchase, renovate, and equip the abandoned Cantek Telephone factory. The venture is expected to create about two hundred new production jobs and fifty new office jobs over the next two years. This is good news for Mechelen, an industrial area that has been hit hard by factory closures and job loss in recent years. —[2]—. Battel Builders has already been contracted to undertake the plant's transformations. —[3]—.

The plant will primarily be used for the assembly and testing of gear drives to be incorporated in the company's wind turbines. —[4]—. Wind Dynamics, in cooperation with the Mechelen Business Development Association (MBDA), will provide development grants to train its incoming workforce in green technology. Jane Arens, MBDA president, says "Mechelen is proud to be part of something that contributes to energy conservation and to the economic growth of our region."

12. What does the article mainly discuss?

(A) The appointment of a new company CEO

(B) The merger of two companies

(C) The process of producing wind turbines

(D) The opening of a facility

13. What will happen to the Cantek Telephone factory?

(A) It will be restored as a historic site.

(B) It will be used by a different industry.

(C) It will be moved to a new location.

(D) It will be demolished to create an open space.

14. Who is Ms. Arens?

(A) A Wind Dynamics employee

(B) A newspaper journalist

(C) The president of an association

(D) The mayor of a town in Belgium

문장 삽입 문제

15. In which of the positions marked [1], [2], [3], and [4] does the following sentence best belong?

"It also anticipates hiring additional workers to complete the construction project."

(A) [1]

(B) [2]

(C) [3]

(D) [4]

UNIT 06 동의어 문제

기출 전략

1. 지문 속 특정 단어가 문맥상 의미하는 바와 가장 유사한 어휘를 고르는 문제 유형이다.
2. 사전적 의미가 아니라 문맥상 대체 가능한 어휘를 골라야 하므로, 보기를 하나씩 대입하여 문맥에 어울리는지 파악해보도록 한다.

동의어 질문 유형

The word "practices" in paragraph 1, line 2, is closest in meaning to

첫 번째 단락 2행의 "practices"와 의미상 가장 가까운 것은?

기출 예제 풀이 전략

Q. The word "**yield**" in paragraph 1, line 4, is closest in meaning to

(A) allow   (B) fail
(C) follow   (D) produce

STEP 1
질문의 키워드 잡기
yield와 동의어 찾기

STEP 2
제시 단어의 앞뒤 문맥 살피기
but이라는 연결어에 주목
→ yield의 뒷문장에서 악천후에도 불구하고 밀농사가 잘됐다고 하므로 밀 생산을 의미한다는 것을 알 수 있다.

STEP 3
정답 찾기: 정답 (D)

Alma Poised for Growth

This month has seen a huge jump in sales of Condor PX brand wheat seed in Argentina. Last year, across much of this nation, there were above-average temperatures and below-average rainfall, causing fields to yield sharply less wheat overall. But despite the adverse weather conditions, Condor PX wheat did comparatively well.

Condor PX was bred by Alma Seed Company in Brazil. Although Alma has been selling Condor PX through its Argentinian distributors for several years, it was slow to catch on until now. Investors also have taken notice of Alma's rapidly improving fortunes.

번역 **p. 027**

빈출 동의어

address ① 다루다, 처리하다 deal with, handle, attend to ② 보내다 direct, refer	**issue** ① 쟁점, 문제 matter, conflict ② 발행물의 호 publication, edition
cover ① 덮다, 가리다 hide, conceal ② 다루다 address, deal with ③ 비용을 대다 pay for	**run** ① 작동하다, 운영하다 function, operate, manage ② 계속되다 continue ③ 상영하다 show
feature ① 특징 characteristic ② 기사 story, article	**serve** ① 제공하다 offer, distribute ② 일하다, 근무하다 work, function
hold ① 보유하다 keep, possess ② 개최하다 host ③ 간주하다 consider	**term** ① 기간 period, duration ② 용어 word ③ 조건 (-s) conditions

다음 지문을 읽고 질문의 정답을 고르세요.

Book review

From Coins to Credit: Banking Throughout the Ages is a concise history of banks and the banking industry from ancient times to the present. James Gallagher, who has made a career of covering financial news for several newspapers, has done a careful job of investigating his subject. Although he presents the facts carefully, Mr. Gallagher has made what could have been a dry book into one that is interesting and enjoyable. By telling amusing anecdotes about historical figures, he makes them come alive. Even people who are not particularly attracted to the subject matter will find this book engrossing.

1. The word "dry" in line 5 is closest in meaning to

(A) dull

(B) vacant

(C) arid

(D) humorous

E-mail

Dear Emery,

I am so glad that you were able to stay on as manager and that most of the store employees have stayed as well. You are a dedicated group, and it was a pleasure working with you and your team at your store. I have assisted several stores in Denver and San Francisco with their transitions, and none of them went as smoothly as yours did. Thank you for your fine work.

I am confident that everything will continue to run well. Please feel free to contact me with any questions or concerns.

2. The word "run" in paragraph 2, line 1, is closest in meaning to

(A) understand

(B) race

(C) function

(D) open

Article

TU Offers Online Classes

12 August—Last month, Tirupati University became the latest institution in the region to offer online business classes. Students can choose from a range of full-credit classes provided entirely over the Internet.

Vice Chancellor Dr. R. D. Mehta noted, "We're excited about this new direction and so are our students. They like the convenience and flexibility." Like Tirupati's traditional courses, all online classes are taught by highly qualified instructors, who are required to have an MBA or an advanced degree in a related field. According to Dr. Mehta, the university plans to expand its online class offerings in the spring.

3. The word "noted" in paragraph 2, line 1, is closest in meaning to

(A) wrote down

(B) remembered

(C) said

(D) saw

Questions 1-3 refer to the following e-mail.   난이도 ★★☆

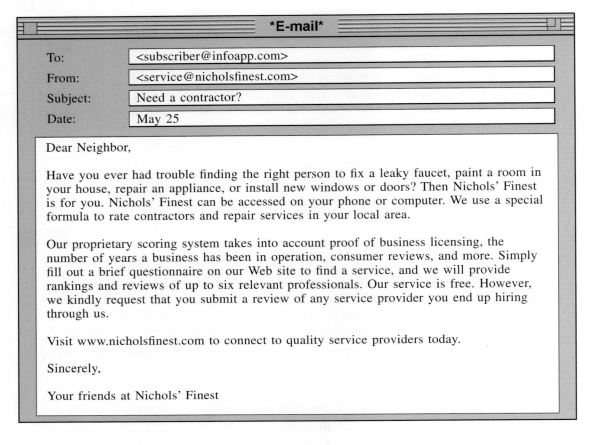

E-mail

To:	<subscriber@infoapp.com>
From:	<service@nicholsfinest.com>
Subject:	Need a contractor?
Date:	May 25

Dear Neighbor,

Have you ever had trouble finding the right person to fix a leaky faucet, paint a room in your house, repair an appliance, or install new windows or doors? Then Nichols' Finest is for you. Nichols' Finest can be accessed on your phone or computer. We use a special formula to rate contractors and repair services in your local area.

Our proprietary scoring system takes into account proof of business licensing, the number of years a business has been in operation, consumer reviews, and more. Simply fill out a brief questionnaire on our Web site to find a service, and we will provide rankings and reviews of up to six relevant professionals. Our service is free. However, we kindly request that you submit a review of any service provider you end up hiring through us.

Visit www.nicholsfinest.com to connect to quality service providers today.

Sincerely,

Your friends at Nichols' Finest

---

1. What is the purpose of the e-mail?
   (A) To advertise training programs in the home-repair industry
   (B) To promote a resource for home-repair services
   (C) To encourage business owners to register their companies
   (D) To invite new contractors to be listed in a directory

동의어 문제

2. In paragraph 1, line 4, the word "formula" is closest in meaning to
   (A) method
   (B) direction
   (C) effort
   (D) expression

3. What is requested of the consumers who use Nichols' Finest?
   (A) Payment of a registration fee
   (B) Proof of homeowners insurance
   (C) A review of a service
   (D) A referral to a friend

022 p.028 정답 및 해설 p.028

Questions 4-7 refer to the following article.

Bangalore (3 November)—Six years ago, DPQR Ltd. was founded as a tiny start-up technology firm. Today, it is estimated to be worth over £2 billion and is on the verge of offering company stock to the public for the first time. This rapid transformation can be attributed largely to the public's recent obsession with DPQR's game *Quincey*.

Quincey is one of eight games that DPQR has produced and marketed over the years, yet it is the only one to have gained such a following. According to Satya Bhavan, CEO of DPQR, *Quincey* has been downloaded onto nearly 20 million handheld devices. "To date,

people's interest shows no signs of weakening," says Ms. Bhavan.

"While the basic game is free, a tremendous amount of revenue is generated through purchases of special virtual items and upgrades that enhance game play," reports Mark Rolleau, a Finian Group market analyst. "This sales concept isn't new, but the degree of spending on this particular product is unprecedented in the industry." Investors feel that the game's popularity will continue to grow and increase company revenue to spend on development of similar games.

4. What does the article announce?
(A) The hiring of a new CEO
(B) The increase in a company's value
(C) The launch of a new device
(D) The anniversary of a successful product

5. What is indicated about DPQR?
(A) It was formerly owned by Finian Group.
(B) Its first product was *Quincey*.
(C) It has been in business for six years.
(D) Its sales of handheld devices have grown.

6. What is true about the majority of DPQR's products?
(A) They are less popular than *Quincey*.
(B) They are continually updated.
(C) They are easy to use.
(D) They are very costly to produce.

동의어 문제

7. The word "degree" in paragraph 3, line 7, is closest in meaning to
(A) achievement
(B) charge
(C) temperature
(D) extent

From:	Jeremy Chang
To:	Ann Dougal; Emily Park; Oscar Mendez
Date:	March 29
Subject:	Today's session postponed

Dear session participants,

Thank you for registering for the session on expense reporting. Unfortunately, this session will not take place today because of technical issues in our training room. We are working to reschedule the session, and you will receive an e-mail when details have been finalized.

Please note that the topics covered in this session will include departmental budgeting, business expense cards, and company reimbursement policies. This session does not include information about our new payroll system; that will be covered separately in a document to be e-mailed to all staff.

If you have any questions, please reach me by e-mail. To view a list of other learning opportunities available for employees, including next week's session on developing effective surveys, please visit our Web site at www.zurergroup.net/train.

I apologize for the inconvenience, and I look forward to seeing you soon.

Jeremy Chang

동의어 문제

8. Who mostly likely is Mr. Chang?

(A) A finance consultant
(B) A payroll specialist
(C) A repair technician
(D) A training coordinator

9. What reason is given for the postponement?

(A) Low employee interest
(B) Technical problems
(C) A change in course content
(D) A presenter's scheduling conflict

10. The word "covered" in paragraph 2, line 1, is closest in meaning to

(A) protected
(B) dealt with
(C) paid for
(D) concealed

11. What can staff expect to receive by e-mail?

(A) A registration form
(B) An employee-satisfaction survey
(C) A list of online learning opportunities
(D) A document about a company system

Gordon Financial Services

March 25

Lalita Kapoor
4200 University Place
Portland, ME 04146

Dear Ms. Kapoor,

I am writing to confirm your participation in the seminar that Gordon Financial Services is hosting in Houston, Texas, from June 2 to June 4. You have been scheduled to give your presentation on June 3.

I would also like to extend an invitation to a reception and catered dinner on the evening of the last day. This event will begin at 6:00 P.M. in the Gerald Adams Conference Center, upstairs from where our seminar proceedings have been scheduled.

The details of your stay in Houston have been arranged by my executive assistant, Pat Gorman. I am sure you will find the Grand Regent Hotel very comfortable, and it is a short walking distance from our seminar activities. Please contact the hotel directly if you have any questions about their facilities.

Let me remind you that the content of your presentation must be approved in advance by both our legal and public affairs offices. Therefore, we ask that you forward a complete copy of your presentation and any related materials to us at your earliest convenience.

Numerous colleagues have highly recommended you based on your expertise in portfolio diversification. I look forward to meeting you and learning more about your professional experience.

Best regards,

Jamal Hassan

Jamal Hassan
Vice President, Professional Development Strategies

동의어 문제

12. The word "extend" in paragraph 2, line 1, is closest in meaning to
(A) postpone
(B) lengthen
(C) reach
(D) offer

13. Where will Ms. Kapoor be giving a presentation?
(A) At a hotel
(B) At a conference center
(C) At a company's headquarters
(D) At a law firm

14. What is NOT mentioned in the letter?
(A) Seminar times
(B) A social gathering
(C) Local accommodations
(D) A presentation date

15. How did Mr. Hassan learn about Ms. Kapoor?
(A) Through her publications
(B) Through her professional reputation
(C) Through her attendance at previous seminars
(D) Through her job application

PART

7

CHAPTER

2

지문 유형별
전략

UNIT 01 이메일/편지
UNIT 02 공지/회람
UNIT 03 광고/안내문
UNIT 04 기사
UNIT 05 웹페이지/양식
UNIT 06 문자 메시지/온라인 채팅
UNIT 07 이중 지문
UNIT 08 삼중 지문

기출 전략

1. 가장 많이 출제되는 지문 유형으로, 비즈니스나 업무 관련 사항을 논하는 내용이 주로 출제된다.
2. 이메일 주소나 편지 상단의 레터헤드, 지문 마지막의 발신자 정보 등을 통해 관계를 파악하도록 한다.

기출 예제

수신자
발신자
날짜
제목

To: Diana Lopez
From: Silvio Guarda
Date: August 28
Subject: Your human resources file

Dear Ms. Lopez,

주제/목적

I have been updating GHT National employees' files, and I see that we are missing several of the documents necessary to complete your file for this year. In order to comply with company regulations, ①all employees from the editorial department must have the following items in their files:

세부 사항

• A copy of their most recent annual performance review
• A current résumé
• A completed and signed Employee Data Form

요청/제안

②Could you please assist me by submitting this documentation by Monday, September 3?

Please e-mail me or call my secretary at extension 241 if you have any questions or concerns.

발신자

Sincerely,
Silvio Guarda,
Manager Human Resources Department
GHT National

수신자 / 발신자 / 날짜 / 제목 확인

– 도메인이 있는 경우는 사내 업무 이메일인지 외부 이메일인지 확인하도록 한다.
– 제목은 이메일 내용을 압축해 놓은 것이므로 중요하다.

주제 / 목적 확인

이메일/편지를 보내는 목적이나 이유는 앞부분에 주로 나온다.

① 로페즈 씨는 누구?
편집부 직원들을 대상으로 하는 이메일임을 알 수 있음

요청 / 제안 / 연락 방법 확인

후반부에 요청 사항이나 첨부 파일, 담당자 연락처 등의 추가 정보가 나온다.

② 로페즈 씨가 해야 할 일?
위의 서류들을 월요일까지 제출해달라고 함

번역 p. 032

추론
Q1. Who most likely is **Ms. Lopez**?
A1. An editor

로페즈 씨는 누구이겠는가?
편집자

세부 사항
Q2. What must **Ms. Lopez do**?
A2. Provide additional paperwork

로페즈 씨가 해야 할 일은?
추가 서류 제출

패러프레이징 지문의 submitting this documentation → 보기의 Provide additional paperwork

정답이 보이는 단서 표현

주제 / 목적   이메일 제목 또는 글의 초반부에서 주제와 글을 쓴 목적을 알 수 있다.

Subject: Your reservation

I am writing to share a marketing idea with you.

We are pleased to let you know about a special offer.

Thank you for your interest in the Hernan Quintero Public Library.

This is a reminder that the water will be temporarily shut off tomorrow.

We would like to invite you to become a member of our Buyer Club.

제목:
~하고자 편지 드립니다
~하게 되어 기쁩니다
~에 감사드립니다
~을 알려드립니다
~하고 싶습니다

요청 / 제안   Please로 시작하는 명령문이나 Could you 등 공손한 표현을 사용하는 경우가 많다.

Please sign and return the attached document.

We ask that you call us one day in advance of your appointment.

Could you send me a biographical profile as soon as possible?

We encourage you to consult the program in advance.

~해 주세요
~해 주시길 부탁드립니다
~해 주실 수 있나요?
~하시길 권장합니다

연락 방법 / 첨부 사항   연락 방법은 웹사이트나, 이메일 주소, 전화번호 등을 알려주며, attach, enclosed, included 등의 표현이 나오면 첨부 사항이 나온다.

Please e-mail me or call my secretary at extension 241.

Attached you will find a revised sample of your business card.

I have enclosed a copy of our current catering menu.

이메일을 보내주시거나 전화주세요
~을 첨부하였습니다
~을 동봉하였습니다

이메일 / 편지   **빈출 어휘**

주문 / 구매

loyal 충실한
renew 갱신하다
subscription 구독(료)
invoice 송장, 주문서
enclose 동봉하다
undergo 겪다
account 계정, 계좌
outstanding balance 미지불 잔액
estimate 견적(=quote)

업무 / 회사 생활

regulation 규정, 규제
submit 제출하다
extension 내선번호
demonstrate 보여주다, 입증하다
qualification 자격, 자질
install 설치하다
relocate 이전하다
profitable 수익성 좋은(=lucrative)
reimburse 상환하다

감사 / 사과

encouragement 격려
devote 바치다, 쏟다
compliment 칭찬하다
appreciate 감사하다
apology 사과
compensate 보상하다
complimentary 무료의
on behalf of ~을 대표하여
courteous 공손한, 정중한

서비스

guarantee 보장하다
launch 출시하다
prompt 신속한, 즉각적인
malfunction 제대로 작동하지 않다
extend 연장하다
additional 추가의
redeem 현금이나 상품으로 바꾸다
expire 만료되다

행사

interactive 상호적인, 대화형의
expand 확장시키다, 확대하다
registration 등록
requirement 요건
organize 준비하다, 조직하다
hands-on 직접 해 보는
sign up for ~을 신청하다
attire 복장

축하 / 기념

award-winning 상을 받은
exceptional 특출한
entertain 즐겁게 하다
venue 장소
retirement 퇴직, 은퇴
authentic 진짜인
recognition 표창, 인정
plaque 명판, 상패

Questions 1-3 refer to the following e-mail.

난이도 ★★☆

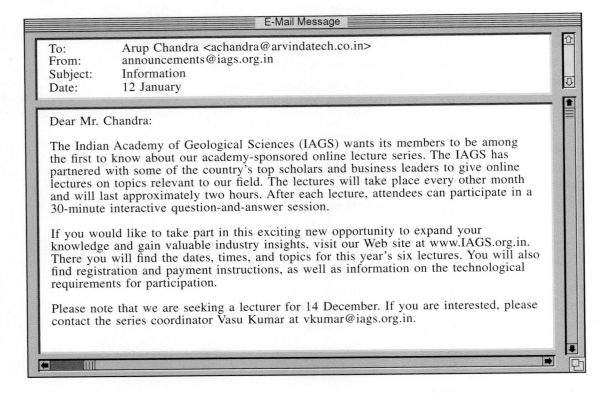

1. Why did Mr. Chandra receive the e-mail?

   (A) He is applying to study geology.
   (B) He is scheduled to give a lecture.
   (C) He is a member of IAGS.
   (D) He is organizing a lecture series.

2. What is indicated about the lectures?

   (A) They take place every month.
   (B) They are focused on a specific profession.
   (C) They are free of charge.
   (D) They will take place at IAGS headquarters.

3. What is NOT mentioned as something that can be found on the IAGS Web site?

   (A) The dates and times of the lectures
   (B) A list of lecture topics
   (C) Registration information
   (D) Profiles of the lecturers

Questions 4-6 refer to the following letter.

난이도 ★★☆

Hathley Magazine
43 Broad Street
Framingham, MA 01701

December 1

Mr. James Cho
262 South Street
Norman, OK 73070

Dear Mr. Cho,

Thank you for being a loyal reader of *Hathley Magazine*. — [1] —. As you know, each monthly issue is full of thoughtful articles by award-winning writers. — [2] —. We cover an exceptional range of topics including politics, science, culture, and world travel, to inform and entertain our readers.

To ensure that you receive uninterrupted service, please consider renewing your subscription now. A subscription to *Hathley Magazine* normally costs $39.99 per year. — [3] —. However, if you respond to this letter before January 1, we can guarantee a price of $29.99 per year. — [4] —.

We will continue to send you printed issues. You can also read the digital version on our Web site, www.hathleymagazine.com. We recently launched a mobile app, so you can even read our magazine's content on your phone or any mobile device.

We hope to hear from you soon.

Sincerely,

Rochelle Gustave

Rochelle Gustave
Subscription Services

---

4. What is suggested about Mr. Cho?
   (A) He writes articles for *Hathley Magazine*.
   (B) He is mainly interested in science topics.
   (C) He currently receives *Hathley Magazine*.
   (D) He has submitted a change-of-address form.

5. What is mentioned as a benefit of a *Hathley Magazine* subscription?
   (A) Access to an online message board
   (B) A discount at entertainment venues
   (C) A bonus atlas of world maps
   (D) Mobile access to articles

6. In which of the positions marked [1], [2], [3], and [4] does the following sentence best belong?

   "In fact, this is the best subscription price we offer."

   (A) [1]
   (B) [2]
   (C) [3]
   (D) [4]

```
*E-mail*
```

To: Anna Chen

From: Enrique Salgado

Date: 22 April

Subject: Our meeting

Dear Ms. Chen,

Thank you so much for meeting me last week. It is very exciting to receive feedback from a designer I admire so much. I'm aware that your time is valuable, and I was honored that you devoted over an hour to talking with me. It was the highlight of my visit to France.

I must say that I was surprised by what you said while reviewing my design portfolio, especially about my use of heavy fabrics. I have long been unsure about working with them, and I now feel that your encouragement will prompt me to use them more often.

You mentioned that you would be open to my working with you as a part-time intern in the future. I would like to declare that at this point in my career, having only recently graduated from the School of Fashion in Madrid, there is no place I would rather begin my professional life than at your fashion design office in Paris. Please let me know as soon as your circumstances change and you would like my assistance.

Sincerely,

Enrique Salgado

---

7. What is indicated about Mr. Salgado?

(A) He is a well-known designer.
(B) He has not completed his university degree.
(C) He is responding to Ms. Chen's e-mail.
(D) He has never held a design job.

8. Why was Mr. Salgado surprised?

(A) Ms. Chen offered to purchase his designs.
(B) Ms. Chen complimented his use of fabrics.
(C) Ms. Chen disapproved of some of the textures in his designs.
(D) Ms. Chen felt that more use of color would improve his work.

9. What is suggested about the results of the meeting?

(A) Mr. Salgado will accept only a full-time position.
(B) Mr. Salgado will return to Madrid.
(C) Ms. Chen currently has no openings for interns.
(D) Ms. Chen will refer Mr. Salgado to someone.

Loach and Greene, Solicitors at Law
121-125 Commercial Road
London E1 3LP

28 February

Sarah Ruth, Owner
Hilary's of Greenwich
198-200 Greenwich High Road
London SE10 1FN

Dear Ms. Ruth:

I am writing in reference to the retirement party that you hosted for us on 24 February. Although it was the first time I had been to your establishment, it is a favourite of our former managing partner, Padma Patel, who was honored that night by our firm. Ms. Patel has often praised the quality of your food, and indeed, for our dinner, each dish was cooked to perfection. The food was so good that I have already made plans to bring a group of friends and family for dinner soon.

I was equally impressed by the degree of professionalism demonstrated by your staff. The servers were prompt and courteous and were able to answer all our questions about the menu.

Thank you so much for this delightful experience! We look forward to making parties at Hilary's of Greenwich a new Loach and Greene tradition.

Yours sincerely,

Allan Loach
Allan Loach, Senior Partner

CHAPTER 2

UNIT 01

10. What is Hilary's of Greenwich?

(A) A cooking school
(B) A party-supply store
(C) A law firm
(D) A restaurant

11. Why was Ms. Patel honored in February?

(A) She was promoted to managing partner.
(B) She opened a new law firm.
(C) She retired from Loach and Greene.
(D) She graduated from law school.

12. The word "degree" in paragraph 2, line 1, is closest in meaning to

(A) level
(B) qualification
(C) position
(D) summary

13. What does Mr. Loach imply in the letter?

(A) He is in the process of hiring new staff members for his firm.
(B) He will do business with Hilary's of Greenwich again.
(C) He first learned about Hilary's of Greenwich from a family member.
(D) He is expecting Ms. Ruth to contact him about some questions he has.

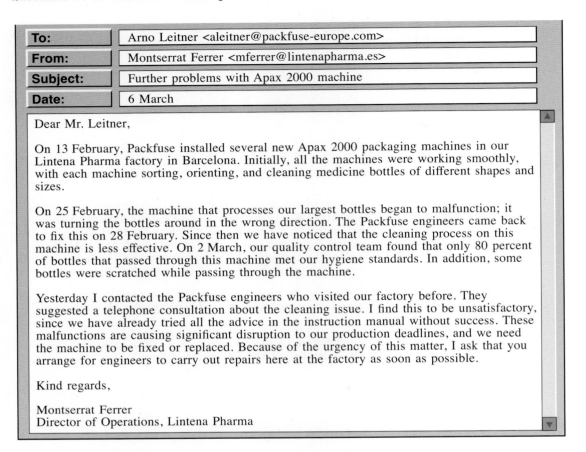

To:	Arno Leitner <aleitner@packfuse-europe.com>
From:	Montserrat Ferrer <mferrer@lintenapharma.es>
Subject:	Further problems with Apax 2000 machine
Date:	6 March

Dear Mr. Leitner,

On 13 February, Packfuse installed several new Apax 2000 packaging machines in our Lintena Pharma factory in Barcelona. Initially, all the machines were working smoothly, with each machine sorting, orienting, and cleaning medicine bottles of different shapes and sizes.

On 25 February, the machine that processes our largest bottles began to malfunction; it was turning the bottles around in the wrong direction. The Packfuse engineers came back to fix this on 28 February. Since then we have noticed that the cleaning process on this machine is less effective. On 2 March, our quality control team found that only 80 percent of bottles that passed through this machine met our hygiene standards. In addition, some bottles were scratched while passing through the machine.

Yesterday I contacted the Packfuse engineers who visited our factory before. They suggested a telephone consultation about the cleaning issue. I find this to be unsatisfactory, since we have already tried all the advice in the instruction manual without success. These malfunctions are causing significant disruption to our production deadlines, and we need the machine to be fixed or replaced. Because of the urgency of this matter, I ask that you arrange for engineers to carry out repairs here at the factory as soon as possible.

Kind regards,

Montserrat Ferrer
Director of Operations, Lintena Pharma

14. What is wrong with the malfunctioning machine?
(A) It is mislabeling the largest bottles.
(B) It is not sorting smaller bottles.
(C) It is not cleaning bottles well.
(D) It is breaking 80 percent of bottles.

15. What is suggested about Packfuse engineers?
(A) They installed most of the Apax 2000 machines incorrectly.
(B) They visited the Lintena Pharma factory twice in February.
(C) They initiated contact with Ms. Ferrer in March.
(D) They do annual quality control checks on Lintena Pharma's products.

16. The word "matter" in paragraph 3, line 5, is closest in meaning to
(A) situation
(B) importance
(C) material
(D) amount

17. What does Ms. Ferrer request?
(A) A user's manual
(B) An extended deadline
(C) A refund
(D) A service appointment

May 1

Janet Gregory
143 Tudwell St.
Eula, ID 83879

Dear Ms. Gregory,

Congratulations! We are pleased to announce your selection as one of six finalists in the fourth annual Taste of Italy cooking contest. Your recipe for spaghetti verde was selected from over 100 entries as one of the judges' favorites for creative use of authentic Italian ingredients. As one of our finalists, you have been awarded a $100 gift certificate to the fabulous Quindici restaurant, the chief sponsor of the contest.

You are also invited to prepare your recipe for a panel of judges during Jemmer City's annual Italia Festival. This year's festival will take place Friday, May 31, through Sunday, June 2. Finalists will begin cooking at 2:00 P.M. on Sunday in a tented venue just outside Quindici. Judging will take place at 3:30 P.M., with an award ceremony immediately following. The winner will receive one week of culinary instruction provided by Quindici's celebrated head chef and TV personality Armando Conti. Every day for five days, Mr. Conti will provide hands-on instruction in his cooking methods.

Once you notify us that you intend to join us for the final competition, you will be directed to complete and return a written form that will secure your place. Please call our office at (208) 555-0157 no later than Thursday, May 16 to confirm.

We look forward to hearing from you!

Sincerely,
Bartolomeo Pagnotto
Taste of Italy Coordinator
Quindici

18. Why did Mr. Pagnotto write to Ms. Gregory?
(A) To hire her as a cooking instructor
(B) To indicate receipt of her résumé
(C) To identify her as an award recipient
(D) To ask her to judge a contest

19. When must contest participants be available?
(A) On May 16
(B) On May 31
(C) On June 1
(D) On June 2

20. What is the prize for winning the Taste of Italy cooking contest?
(A) A job at a restaurant
(B) A series of cooking lessons
(C) A certificate of achievement
(D) An appearance on a TV show

21. What is Ms. Gregory asked to confirm?
(A) Her decision to participate in an event
(B) Her mailing address
(C) A reservation at a restaurant
(D) A schedule for training with a chef

Questions 22-25 refer to the following e-mail.

  난이도 ★★★

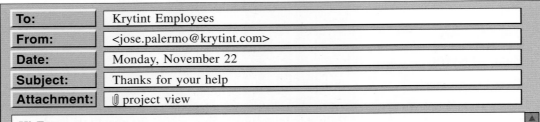

To:	Krytint Employees
From:	\<jose.palermo@krytint.com\>
Date:	Monday, November 22
Subject:	Thanks for your help
Attachment:	📎 project view

Hi Everyone,

I would like to thank those of you who continually help out around the office and to let you know that your efforts have not gone unrecognized. Many people have mentioned that they notice when things get cleaned and that a tidy office makes a big difference. Let's keep up the good work!

While the new building is looking much nicer than it did last month when we first moved in, we still have a lot of organizing to do before our clients from Grafton come next week. To this end, I have written down some projects I need your help with as soon as possible. Please view the attached document and put your name down for one of these chores. Your assistance is greatly appreciated. Please complete the job you sign up for by Friday.

Also, we have only budgeted for our cleaning company to come in three times a week, so please continue to be diligent in taking care of our office—especially on Tuesdays and Thursdays when they will not be in. The cleaning crew has been asked to clear out the refrigerator every Friday. If you have anything in there that you would like to be saved, please mark it with your name and the date so that they know not to throw it away. Colored tags are available for this purpose. They are on the top shelf of the supply closet.

Thanks for helping out during this transition!

Jose Palermo
Krytint Industries
Corporate Office Manager

---

22. What are employees being thanked for?

(A) Correcting a mistake
(B) Keeping the office clean
(C) Restocking supplies
(D) Obtaining a new client

23. What did Krytint Industries do last month?

(A) Hire a new cleaning service
(B) Purchase some office supplies
(C) Change its days of operation
(D) Relocate to a new workspace

24. What is included with the e-mail?

(A) A list of tasks
(B) A work schedule
(C) A quarterly budget
(D) A client directory

25. Why should employees use the colored tags?

(A) To label food items
(B) To mark boxes for movers
(C) To request that a space be cleaned
(D) To make changes to important documents

Woodford's Grocery
63 Guildry Street
Shrewsbury, Shropshire, SY2 1UQ
01743 499955

1 April

Dear Customer,

Exciting changes are happening at Woodford's Grocery! We hope you will visit us later this month and see the improvements we are making in order to make your shopping experience more enjoyable.

As you may know, we have been undergoing a significant renovation that is adding approximately 5,000 square metres to our store. Beginning on 10 April, our produce section will be nearly twice as big, which will allow us to offer a greater variety of fruits and vegetables and allow you to move around the store with greater ease. We are also expanding our bakery section to provide you with more of the freshly baked breads and pastries you have come to love.

We will be celebrating the renovations with a customer appreciation day on Saturday, 20 April. There will be cooking demonstrations and free tastings from our bakery and deli departments. In addition, beginning on this day we will start opening on Saturdays at 6:00 A.M. instead of 7:00 A.M. so that you can get your shopping done earlier.

To encourage you to visit the new Woodford's Grocery, we have enclosed discount coupons for a range of items, including cereals and cleaning supplies. The coupons are good until 30 April. You will also find a calendar indicating special sale days and product demonstrations. So, stop by this month, and let us help you create delicious meals for you and your family!

Sincerely,

Cecily Watkins

Cecily Watkins
Store Manager

Enclosure

---

26. What is the purpose of the letter?

(A) To announce the completion of a store expansion

(B) To advertise a custom brand of bakery goods

(C) To introduce a change in store ownership

(D) To promote a new store location

27. When will Woodford's Grocery host a special event?

(A) On April 1

(B) On April 10

(C) On April 20

(D) On April 30

28. What is included with the letter?

(A) A questionnaire

(B) A schedule of events

(C) A list of products

(D) A product sample

29. What is NOT mentioned as a change at Woodford's Grocery?

(A) A wider selection of products

(B) Increased floor space

(C) Extended hours of operation

(D) Additional cashiers

UNIT 02 공지/회람

 기출 전략

⚙ 출제 비율 2~3세트

1. 공지와 회람은 다수의 대상에게 특정 정보를 고지하기 위한 글로, 새로운 정책이나 변경 사항, 보수/점검, 행사나 강연 등을 안내하는 내용이 출제된다.
2. 지문 초반의 미래 시제(will) 문장은 발표하고자 하는 내용을 담고 있으며, 중반에는 전달 사항과 향후 일정이 안내되곤 한다.

기출 예제

제목/행사명	**ATTENTION MEMBERS**
목적/변동 안내	In observance of the national holiday next week, please note that Grissom Fitness Club's hours will be limited as follows.

전달 사항	**Monday, May 4:**	We will open as usual at 8:00 A.M. but will close early at 8:00 P.M. ①Drop-in childcare will not be affected on this day. However, ②please check with your group fitness instructor to see if your class will be held as scheduled.
	Tuesday, May 5:	The facility will be closed all day.

추가 정보	③We will resume regular opening and closing hours on Wednesday, May 6. Please contact manager
연락처	Kevin Tripper at ktripper@grissomfitness.com if you have any questions.

공지의 목적 확인
제목과 첫 단락에서 무엇을 공지하려고 하는지, 왜 공지하는지 알려준다.

전달 사항 확인
중요한 전달 사항이 나오는 부분이며 반드시 문제로 나온다.
① 이 피트니스 클럽에 대해 암시하는 것?
아이 돌봄 서비스는 영향을 받지 않음
② 그룹 수업에 대해 암시하는 것?
일정대로 하는지 강사에게 문의하라고 함

추가 공지/연락 방법 확인
후반부에는 추가 공지 사항이나 요청 사항, 연락처 등의 정보가 나온다.
③ 정상 운영으로 복귀하는 날?
5월 6일 수요일에 정상 영업 시간을 재개한다고 함

번역 p.040

추론	**Q1.** What is **suggested** about **Grissom Fitness Club**? **A1.** It offers childcare services.	그리솜 피트니스 클럽에 대해 암시하는 것은? 보육 서비스를 제공한다.
추론	**Q2.** What is **suggested** about **group classes**? **A2.** Some may be canceled.	그룹 수업에 대해 암시하는 것은? 일부는 취소될지도 모른다.
세부 사항	**Q3. Which day** will Grissom Fitness Club **return to normal hours**? **A3.** On Wednesday	그리솜 피트니스 클럽은 무슨 요일에 정상 운영 시간으로 복귀하는가? 수요일

패러프레이징 지문의 resume regular opening and closing hours → 질문의 return to normal hours

072

정답이 보이는 단서 표현

제목

공지/회람의 제목에서 주제나 목적 또는 업종 등이 드러난다.

THIS OFFICE CLOSED FOR RENOVATIONS	사무실 공사 중
Attention All Manning & Murdoch Employees	매닝 앤 머독 전 직원들께
RATE OUR SERVICES AND WIN FREE TRAVEL!	업종: 여행사

행사/공사

행사나 공사의 일정 및 내용 안내, 변경 및 유의 사항 등이 공지된다.

A new motor and handrail **can be installed**.	공사 안내
The annual Hastings Book Fair **will take place on 25 July**.	행사 일정
Escalators in the first-floor lobby will be closed **beginning on** Monday, August 1.	공사 일정
We apologize for any inconvenience this may cause.	불편에 대한 사과

업무/서비스

사내 신규 시스템이나 정책 안내, 협조 요청 사항, 규정 등이 공지된다.

I am pleased to announce that we are introducing a new program for employees.	신규 프로그램 공지
All company computers **require an update** to the operating system.	업데이트 요청 안내
Please note that the competition is only open to people aged 18 and over.	규정 안내
Canceling on the same day will result in **no refund**.	환불 규정

빈출 어휘

회의/대회

upcoming 앞으로 다가오는
summarize 요약하다
compete in 출전하다, 참가하다
feature 특별히 포함하다
proceeds 수익금
organize 준비하다, 조직하다
well attended 많은 사람이 참석한
represent 대표하다
nomination 지명, 임명
unanimous 만장일치의

공사

inconvenience 불편
maintenance 유지 보수
decrease 감소
designated 지정된
temporary 임시의, 일시적인
alternate 번갈아 생기는
extension 연장
procedure 절차, 진행
restoration 복구, 복원
renovate 보수하다

회사 생활

receptive 수용적인
constructive 건설적인
expense 경비, 비용
requirement 필요조건
potential 잠재적인
personnel 직원들, 부서 인원
performance evaluation 업무 평가
appraisal 평가
oversee 감독하다
deliberation 심사숙고

인사 이동

transfer 이동, 전근
take over 인수하다, 인계하다
administrative 관리의, 행정의
professionalism 전문성
contribution 기여
recognize 표창하다, 인정하다
notify 통보하다
tenure 재임 기간
predecessor 전임자
assume 떠맡다
accomplishment 성취, 업적

정책/규정

attention 알립니다
in observance of ~을 기념하여
resume 재개하다
revise 수정하다, 변경하다
revenue 수익, 수입
renew 갱신하다
permanent 영구적인
security 보안
violation 위반
activate 활성화시키다
mandatory 의무적인, 필수적인

지역 사회/환경

preference 선호
reside 거주하다
artificial 인공의
combination 조화
preservation 보존
prestigious 권위 있는, 명망 있는
grant 승인하다; 보조금
outreach 지원[봉사] 활동
publicize 홍보하다
municipal 시의, 지방 자치의
initiative (새로운) 계획

Questions 1-2 refer to the following memo.

난이도 ★★☆

From: Jane Musante, Director of Human Resources
To: President's Office staff, R&D staff
Subject: Notice of transfer
Date: Wednesday, March 7, 4:19 P.M.

I am pleased to announce that Hong Hanh Pham has accepted a transfer from the President's Office to the Office of Research and Development. Hong Hanh will begin training with Vernon West next week and will take over as administrative assistant in Research and Development after Vernon retires at the end of the month.

John Roussel, my colleague in the Human Resources department, is updating the job description for the administrative assistant position in the President's Office and will post the opening tomorrow. We expect to have the position filled by the end of the month.

Please congratulate Vernon on his retirement after more than 30 years with the company, and wish Hong Hanh the best as she transitions into her new role.

1. Who is leaving the company?
   (A) Jane Musante
   (B) Hong Hanh Pham
   (C) Vernon West
   (D) John Roussel

2. What is expected to happen at the end of the month?
   (A) An office will have a new administrative assistant.
   (B) The company president will retire.
   (C) A job description will be revised.
   (D) Someone in the Human Resources department will be promoted.

Questions 3-5 refer to the following notice.

난이도 ★★☆

Dunnport Light Rail

January 20

To our passengers:

Because of rising operating costs, Dunnport Light Rail will increase passenger fares beginning on March 1. The cost of tickets for adults, university students, and school-aged children will go up by 5 percent. Children five years of age and younger will continue to ride free of charge.

We apologize for any inconvenience this may cause our customers. We would like to point out that this is the first fare increase for Dunnport Light Rail service in seven years. Revenue from passenger fares is used for employee salaries and general train maintenance.

We will continue to provide you with the level of service you have come to expect. Thank you for riding Dunnport Light Rail.

3. What is indicated about Dunnport Light Rail?
   (A) It is adding new routes.
   (B) It raised its fares seven years ago.
   (C) It is responding to complaints from customers.
   (D) It is experiencing a decrease in the number of passengers served.

4. What is suggested about university students?
   (A) They can purchase monthly rail passes at a discount.
   (B) Their fare will increase by the same percentage as the fare for adults.
   (C) Their student identification cards must be renewed by March 1.
   (D) They once were able to travel on Dunnport Light Rail free of charge.

5. According to the notice, what is one way that revenue collected from fares is spent?
   (A) To pay employees
   (B) To expand rail service
   (C) To renovate stations
   (D) To improve advertising

MEMO

To: Design Team Members
From: Greta Paulson, CEO
Date: June 9
Subject: Great job!

Contreras Creative has enjoyed a tremendous year of steady work from a happy client, and you have been an integral part of that success. To show our appreciation, we will be depositing an extra $1,200 into each of your accounts this month.

I have worked with many different design teams over the years, but only on rare occasions has a team been so agreeable. You meet your deadlines, are receptive to constructive criticism, and produce your deliverables in a strategic, effective way.

It is not easy for us to forecast how many projects we will get each year, so bonuses cannot always be given on a regular basis. But please know that we very much value your hard work and professionalism, and we look forward to your future contributions!

6. What is the purpose of the memo?
    (A) To review an expense report
    (B) To announce an upcoming bonus
    (C) To summarize contract requirements
    (D) To share news about a potential new client

7. What is indicated about the members of the design team?
    (A) They often work directly with international clients.
    (B) They developed a new method for delivering products.
    (C) They were hired relatively recently.
    (D) They are open to receiving feedback.

8. The word "regular" in paragraph 3, line 2, is closest in meaning to
    (A) fixed
    (B) orderly
    (C) informal
    (D) qualified

LORENZO'S KITCHEN
PERFECT PIZZA CONTEST

Lorenzo's Kitchen announces its first ever Perfect Pizza contest. We invite local pizza enthusiasts to submit an original idea for the perfect pizza-topping combination. Our pizza makers will assemble and cook the pizzas, which will then be judged by a panel of "pizza experts," including Paulette Puccini, host of Channel 9's *Wood Fire Grill* and a regular guest on local talk shows. Prizes will be awarded for the top three entries, as follows.

- **First-Place Winner** – $50 gift card to Lorenzo's Kitchen and your pizza featured on our permanent menu.
- **Second-Place Winner** – $30 gift card to Lorenzo's Kitchen and your pizza featured on our monthly specials menu for two months.
- **Third-Place Winner** – $20 gift card to Lorenzo's Kitchen and your pizza featured on our monthly specials menu for one month.

Contest participants can pick up an entry form from the display near our main entrance. The form must contain your full name, phone number, a list of suggested toppings, and a sauce preference (red or white). Forms can be dropped in the designated box at the entrance by July 15.

Entrants must reside in Guilford City and must not work in the food industry. Limit one entry per person. Winners will be notified by July 25 by phone. Come and try the winning creations starting Saturday, August 3!

---

9. Who most likely is Ms. Puccini?

(A) A former contest winner
(B) A television celebrity
(C) A restaurant owner
(D) A cookbook author

10. What is mentioned about the Perfect Pizza contest?

(A) It is held every year.
(B) It will be judged by Lorenzo's Kitchen chefs.
(C) Only local residents may compete in it.
(D) Participants may enter it multiple times.

11. According to the notice, what will happen in August?

(A) A second contest will begin.
(B) Judges will meet to select contest winners.
(C) The restaurant will recognize winners at a ceremony.
(D) The restaurant will offer several new menu items.

난이도 ★★☆

To: All employees
From: Matthew Bennett, Chief of Operations
Date: October 4
Subject: ID badges

A new security system will be installed next Monday, October 10. When this system is fully activated, it will require that Wattley employees carry identification badges at all times. These plastic cards are embedded with digital identification codes, which will allow access electronically to all buildings on the Wattley campus.

Badges will be available on Friday, October 7, in the Human Resources Department. The supervisors of all departments have been given a schedule and will advise their staff about when their badges can be obtained. Employees will be unable to enter any Wattley facilities after October 12 without their new IDs. Please direct any questions or concerns to your manager.

---

12. What is the purpose of the memo?

(A) To inform employees of a department's new location

(B) To introduce a company policy

(C) To announce the temporary closing of a building

(D) To report a recent security violation

13. What are employees being asked to do?

(A) Attend a meeting

(B) Use an alternate entrance

(C) Sign a form

(D) Get an identification card

14. Who are employees instructed to contact with their concerns?

(A) Their department managers

(B) A security guard

(C) Human resources personnel

(D) The chief of operations

The Stewards Bay Arts Council
presents the
Spring Fling Celebration

The Stewards Bay Arts Council is excited to announce that this year's Spring Fling Celebration will be sponsored by our town's own newspaper, the *Stewards Bay Journal*. This year's celebration will feature more events than any other year. Here is just a sampling of events that will take place throughout the week of March 20.

Highlights include:
The Chefs' Best Brunch—This yearly favorite features chefs from local restaurants. This year Luisa Reyes from Oteria Restaurant will be leading the team of chefs as they prepare a scrumptious brunch buffet at the community center. Tickets are $25 per person. The proceeds go directly to support the council's art education programs at the Stewards Bay community center. Call 267-555-0122 to make reservations. Only 500 tickets are available, and this event always sells out.

The Dot Solly Jazz Band—The jazz trio will perform a free concert Saturday evening starting at 7:30 P.M. at the Terrapin Park Pavilion. Light refreshments will be available for purchase. In case of rain, the concert will be held in the Town Hall auditorium.

The Town Hall Art Show and Competition—The display is open to the public all week long during the regular Town Hall building hours. Prizes will be awarded by last year's winner, Kalib Martin, at a ceremony at the end of the week.

Look for a comprehensive Spring Fling Celebration program in next week's *Stewards Bay Journal*.

---

15. What is suggested about the Spring Fling Celebration?

(A) It will offer more events than last year.
(B) It is organized by a local business owner.
(C) It includes several nights of musical performances.
(D) It has been planned to increase area tourism.

16. What is NOT true about the Chefs' Best Brunch?

(A) It takes place annually.
(B) It raises funds for the arts council.
(C) It is usually well attended.
(D) It will feature a guest speaker.

17. According to the notice, what will be published in the local newspaper?

(A) A complete schedule of the festival
(B) Details about a culinary competition
(C) Short biographies of art show winners
(D) A map of Terrapin Park

From: Liam Perry, marketing director
To: All marketing staff
Date: August 5
Re: New line of juice products

Last week was the end of the free-sample program for our new line of fruit juices. Potential customers received complimentary bottles of the drinks and 15% discount coupons for future purchases. They were then asked to complete feedback questionnaires. The program ran from July 15 to July 31, and the discount, which applies to our full range of products, will be good until October 1.

The following briefly summarizes information gathered through the program:
- Three varieties were measured, listed here in descending order of customer popularity: Mango Mountain, Great Guava, and Yum Cocoplum
- Analysis of the feedback questionnaires showed that customers felt Yum Cocoplum contained too much sugar. (This is a surprising finding because none of the brands are artificially flavored and they all preserve the natural taste of the fruit they are based on.)
- Many customers rated the flavor combinations in Mango Mountain and Great Guava as "superb."

I would like to hold a meeting with you next week to discuss these points in more detail. Jess Bronsky is putting together the agenda for the meeting and will notify you soon of the time and place.

18. What is the purpose of the memo?
(A) To report the results of a study
(B) To request a deadline extension
(C) To recommend new product names
(D) To propose a new discount

19. What did potential customers NOT receive?
(A) A discount certificate
(B) A list of ingredients
(C) A free sample of juice
(D) A feedback form

20. What concern was reported by potential customers?
(A) Artificial ingredients were used.
(B) The discount procedure was confusing.
(C) The juice portions were too small.
(D) One of the juices was too sweet.

난이도 ★★★

Roger Wilkinson to Join
Pace and Brown Architects, Inc.

At Friday's company-wide meeting, president and CEO Cynthia Hu announced that, following a lengthy search, Pace and Brown has selected Roger H. Wilkinson as the new director of restoration projects. Beginning May 1 Mr. Wilkinson will succeed Keira Powells, who retired on January 3. Mr. Wilkinson is coming to Pace and Brown from his position as senior project designer at Bershire Blakeburns in London, where he has lived for the last ten years.

Mr. Wilkinson will be responsible for representing the firm externally and ensuring that the firm has a clear strategic direction as it expands its work in restoration and historic preservation. He brings with him many diverse talents and more than 25 years of design and project management experience. He is probably best known for his restoration work on the historic 32-story Starsham Hotel in Melbourne, for which he was awarded the Schills Medal, Australia's most prestigious design award.

21. Where would this announcement most likely appear?
(A) In a newspaper advertisement
(B) In a business textbook
(C) In a telephone directory
(D) In a company newsletter

22. Who is Keira Powells?
(A) A past president of a business
(B) A former director of a business
(C) A successful clothing designer
(D) A well-known historian

23. How long has Roger Wilkinson lived in London?
(A) For 10 years
(B) For 15 years
(C) For 25 years
(D) For 32 years

24. According to the announcement, what is Roger Wilkinson known for?
(A) Directing restoration projects at Pace and Brown
(B) Being Bershire Blakeburns' longest serving director
(C) Renovating a historic building in Melbourne
(D) Winning a major design award in London

CHAPTER 2   UNIT 02

기출 전략

1. 광고는 크게 상품/서비스 광고와 구인 광고로 나뉘며, 안내문은 제품 매뉴얼이나 시설 또는 서비스 이용법 등 다양한 내용이 출제된다.
2. 광고와 안내문은 대체로 제목과 지문 초반에 주제가 명확히 드러나는 경우가 많다. 제품 광고의 후반부에는 할인 정보, 구매 방법, 추가 혜택 등이 등장하곤 한다.

기출 예제

업체명 (주소)	**Winston's Ice Cream** 19 Market Street, Dorlinton 792-555-0197
소개	Once you try our premium ice cream and cakes, you will return again and again. Winston's is a conveniently located sweet stop for the whole family, and we are the only ice-cream shop in town with a private party room.
서비스 특장점	We offer: • 15 ice-cream varieties, ① produced right here in our shop using local ingredients • A wide selection of fruit and nut toppings • Ice-cream cakes made to order • Complimentary wireless Internet access for our patrons
영업시간 안내	Hours: Tuesday-Sunday, 11:00 A.M. to 8:00 P.M. ② Summer (May through October): Open until 10:00 P.M.
추가 정보 및 혜택	③ Wednesday is Kids Day – get a child-size serving of any flavor of ice cream at 50 percent off.

업체 확인

제목이나 앞부분에서 업체의 분야를 파악한다.

서비스 특장점 확인

항목으로 분류된 특장점은 Not/True 문제로 출제되기 쉬우므로 보기와 지문을 대조하도록 한다.

① 아이스크림에 대해 언급된 것?
지역 재료로 가게에서 만듦

추가 정보/혜택 확인

추가 정보나 예외 정보, 특별한 혜택은 문제로 출제되기 쉽다.

② 5월에 일어날 일?
여름(5월~10월)에는 영업시간이 늦어짐

③ 할인에 대해 명시된 것?
수요일은 키즈 데이로 50% 할인

번역 **p. 047**

Not/True | **Q1.** What is **mentioned** about **Winston's Ice Cream**?
A1. Its ice cream is made in the store.

윈스턴 아이스크림에 대해 언급된 것은?
아이스크림을 가게에서 만든다.

패러프레이징 지문의 produced right here in our shop → 보기의 made in the store

---

세부 사항 | **Q2.** According to the advertisement, **what** happens in **May**?
A2. The store hours change.

광고에 의하면, 5월에 무슨 일이 있는가?
가게 영업시간이 바뀐다.

Not/True | **Q3.** What is **indicated** about the **discount**?
A3. It is offered only one day a week.

할인에 대해 명시된 것은?
일주일에 하루만 제공된다.

관심 유도/소개   제목이나 첫 문장에서 소비자의 관심을 끄는 경우가 많다.

For Sale: Three 200-liter Rain Barrels	~ 팝니다
Interested in being a sponsor?	~에 관심 있으십니까?
Looking for a caterer for your special occasion?	~을 찾으십니까?
Visiting Carlin County? **Don't miss** these points of interest!	~을 방문하시나요? 놓치지 마세요.

제품/서비스 특장점 및 조건   feature, boast, 비교급/최상급 등의 표현과 if, only, offer, exclusive, limited 등의 표현을 눈여겨본다.

Home and office visits available **by appointment only**.	예약으로만 가능
This apartment **boasts** a patio with a lovely view of the harbor.	~을 자랑합니다
We offer a wide selection of plants from around the world.	~을 제공합니다
The celebration will **feature** a display of arts and crafts.	~을 특징으로 합니다
The state's **largest** outdoor food court	특장점
Stanford Employment Agency **seeks a receptionist** for a busy office.	구인 광고

안내 목적/대상   안내 목적과 대상, 그리고 어디에서 볼 수 있는 안내문인지 추론할 수 있다.

Group rates are available for parties of 12 or more.	대상: 단체 손님
Do not operate a machine without authorization.	장소: 공장
Before assembling your cabinet, please review the parts list below.	목적: 캐비닛 조립 안내

상품

ingredient 재료, 성분
made to order 주문 제작된
offer 할인 행사
electronic transfer 온라인 이체
state-of-the-art 최첨단의
rechargeable 재충전되는
sturdy 견고한
lightweight 경량의
humidity 습도

상품

patented 특허를 받은
retail price 소매가
article 물품, 물건
price estimate 가격 견적서
charge 요금; 청구하다
insert 삽입하다
compatibility 호환성, 양립성
versatile 다재다능한, 다용도의
portable 휴대용의

서비스

patron 고객, 후원자
frequent customer 단골 고객
initiation 개시, 시작
reinstatement 복구, 회복
extend 늘리다, 연장하다
terminate 끝나다, 종료하다
instruction manual 사용 설명서
consumption 소비
full refund 전액 환불

구인

requirement 요건, 필요조건
superior 우수한
paid vacation 유급 휴가
raise 임금 인상
successful candidate 합격자
certified 공인된
experienced 경험이 풍부한, 숙련된
replacement 교체, 후임자

부동산/주거

realty 부동산
venerable 고색 창연한
tenant 입주자
landlord 집주인
home improvement 주택 개조
commercial 상업적인
premises 구내, 건물
on-site 현장에서

행사/축제

donate 기부하다
fairground 축제 마당
publicity 홍보
press release 보도 자료
assignment 배정
appreciation 감사
complimentary 무료의
distribute 배포하다, 나눠주다

Questions 1-2 refer to the following information on a Web site.　　난이도 ★☆☆

Dolomino's

| Home page | **What's new at Dolomino's** | About us | Store locations |

Posted: Tuesday, October 1

Looking to save money on your next shopping trip? Take advantage of the end-of-season sale at Dolomino's, starting today. We offer an extensive inventory at competitive prices. Save up to 60% off original prices on a wide assortment of items, including shoes, jackets, shirts, clocks, microwave ovens, and fans. These discounts also apply to orders placed through our online store at www.dolominos.com. This offer cannot be combined with other offers or discount coupons. Sale ends October 10.

---

1. What is being advertised?

    (A) The availability of a new product
    (B) The opening of a new store
    (C) A contest for frequent customers
    (D) Reduced prices on products

2. What type of product is NOT mentioned as available at the store?

    (A) Household appliances
    (B) Gardening tools
    (C) Footwear
    (D) Clothing

Questions 3-4 refer to the following advertisement.

난이도 ★★☆

Job Fair
Metzger Airlines

Metzger Airlines is seeking international flight attendants and will hold a job fair on Tuesday, March 1, beginning at 9:00 A.M. at the Metzger Airlines Corporate Center in Miami.

Requirements:
- Must be able to work nights, weekends, and holidays
- Must be at least 21 years old
- Must be prepared to relocate
- Must have superior communication skills
- Must function well in stressful situations
- Must work well with others

Metzger Airlines offers all employees paid vacations, semi-annual raises, professional development courses, and much more.

Interested individuals should be prepared to submit a résumé and complete an application at the job fair. Initial Interviews will take place during the afternoon.

Successful candidates will spend six weeks at the Metzger Airlines Training Facility in Tokyo. After completion of the training program, newly certified flight attendants will be based in Barcelona or Milan.

3. What is NOT a stated requirement for becoming a Metzger Airlines flight attendant?

(A) Willingness to work on holidays
(B) Willingness to move to a new city
(C) A minimum age of 21
(D) A minimum of one year of experience

4. Where will successful candidates train to become flight attendants?

(A) In Miami
(B) In Tokyo
(C) In Barcelona
(D) In Milan

EXPLANATION OF GRADY GAS COMPANY'S FEES

Monthly Delivery Charge: This charge covers the cost of delivery of natural gas each month to residential and business customers in Grady and the surrounding area.

Service Initiation Fee: A fee of $20 will be charged to open a new residential or business account with the company and initiate service. This is a one-time fee that will appear on a customer's first bill.

Payments by Credit Card: A convenience fee of one percent will be assessed for payments made by credit card. Customers can avoid this fee by scheduling automatic monthly electronic transfers from a bank account.

Late Payment Charge: Payment is due 21 days following the conclusion of the billing period; the billing period and the payment due date are clearly indicated on the first page of all customer bills. If payment for the total amount due is received 10 or more days after the due date, a late fee of $25 will be added to the next bill.

Service Reinstatement Fee: If service is terminated due to nonpayment of a bill, a $15 fee is assessed for reinstatement of service. This fee is in addition to any late-payment charges that may be assessed. For service to be reinstated on the same day it is requested, payment must be submitted that day by 11:00 A.M., either by telephoning Grady Gas Company at 555-0141 to make a credit card payment, or by visiting the customer service center at 514 Juniper Drive.

---

5. What is the purpose of the information?

(A) To announce that delivery costs for natural gas will increase soon

(B) To provide details about how charges for gas service are determined

(C) To confirm a customer's request for an electronic transfer of funds

(D) To note that a customer service center now has extended hours

6. According to the information, a charge for what amount always appears on a customer's first bill?

(A) $10

(B) $15

(C) $20

(D) $25

7. What is indicated about Grady Gas Company?

(A) It is closing its office location on Juniper Drive.

(B) It is unable to reinstate service on the same day that a customer requests it.

(C) It provides service to business customers only.

(D) It accepts credit card payments over the phone.

Apartment available: Bright 1-bedroom apartment in Ossington

Rent: $1,700/month, including utilities

Description: Now in its fourth year of operation, Fernald Realty is one of Toronto's most innovative property management firms. — [1] —. Over the past two years, we have acquired and renovated six vintage apartment buildings in historical city neighborhoods. — [2] —.

We now have a vacant 1-bedroom, third-floor apartment in the venerable 12-story building, The Traydan. — [3] —. Newly renovated and located in the popular Ossington neighborhood, The Traydan embodies our motto of "Live Well in the City." Enjoy fresh pastries at the famous Gasparro Café, just across the street from The Traydan's lobby entrance. Then work off the extra calories at the free, 24-hour fitness center in the building's basement—or simply relax in the tenant lounge. This deluxe unit even comes with extra large closets and a view of Shaw Park. — [4] —. Please call us at 555-0127 to request a viewing.

8. What is suggested about Fernald Realty?
   (A) It plans to merge with another firm.
   (B) It also designs wooden cabinets.
   (C) Its contracts last for two years.
   (D) Its rental apartments are in older buildings.

9. What is NOT indicated about The Traydan?
   (A) It is twelve stories tall.
   (B) It has a café in the lobby.
   (C) It was recently renovated.
   (D) It has an on-site fitness center.

10. In which of the positions marked [1], [2], [3], and [4] does the following sentence best belong?

   "As we grow, we plan to keep turning such promising properties into great rental communities."

   (A) [1]
   (B) [2]
   (C) [3]
   (D) [4]

Demy NX—Getting Started   p. 4

Congratulations on purchasing a Demy NX Cordless Electric Drill! The following pages will explain the basic guidelines for operating this state-of-the-art power tool.

Batteries
Your Demy NX Cordless Electric Drill is powered by two Demy rechargeable 18-volt batteries (included in packaging). These are specifically designed for compatibility with your NX Cordless Electric Drill and with the Demy 18-Volt Battery Charger (also included). Before using the drill for the first time, charge the batteries in the charger for at least six hours. Then insert them into the drill's battery compartment (see page 7 for a detailed diagram).

Because your Demy 18-Volt Battery Charger makes use of the latest in battery charging technology, you should leave your batteries in the charger indefinitely between uses, thus ensuring that your Demy NX Cordless Electric Drill is ready to use at a moment's notice. The average life of Demy rechargeable 18-volt batteries varies depending on use. To avoid possible damage to your charger or drill, use only Demy brand batteries.

11. Where would the information most likely be found?

(A) In an advertisement for a Demy product
(B) In an instruction manual for a power tool
(C) In a book on home improvement techniques
(D) In a review of popular brands of tools

12. What is indicated about the batteries?

(A) They should be charged every two weeks.
(B) They were charged at the factory.
(C) They are covered by a limited warranty.
(D) They were designed for use with the product.

13. According to the information, where should the batteries be stored?

(A) In an air-conditioned location
(B) Inside the battery charger
(C) Inside the power tool
(D) In a protective case

14. What does the information warn against?

(A) Using a battery with a low charge
(B) Recharging a battery more than once in a two-week period
(C) Using batteries made by other manufacturers
(D) Opening the charger before the batteries are fully charged

Warm Up with Thermozest!

This winter, make your home or office a more comfortable place with the Thermozest heating system! Traditional space heaters concentrate the heat in one part of the room, leaving many cold spots. The Thermozest heating system, by contrast, warms the entire area evenly, resulting in a comfortable temperature throughout. And since only the room in use is heated, the Thermozest system reduces your energy consumption.

The Thermozest unit comes with a set of rotating wheels and a sturdy yet lightweight handle, making transferring it between locations effortless. Unlike most space heaters, which dry out the air, our patented system helps maintain normal humidity.

Orders received by mail or online by December 31 will receive a 25% discount PLUS free shipping. After that date, customers will be billed the normal retail price plus $35 shipping per unit. If you are not satisfied with our product for any reason, you may return it within 60 days for a full refund, including shipping costs.

- -

Yes! I want to start saving. Please send me _____ units.

☐ I am placing my order on or before December 31. Please apply my 25% discount, for a total price of $120 per unit.

☐ I am placing my order after December 31. Please bill me at $160 per unit, plus a shipping cost of $35 per unit.

15. What is NOT mentioned as an advantage of the heating system?

(A) It avoids making the air drier.
(B) It promotes efficient energy use.
(C) It is less expensive than similar products.
(D) It can be moved easily.

16. How can customers avoid paying a shipping fee?

(A) By ordering before a deadline
(B) By buying two or more units
(C) By signing a one-year service contract
(D) By entering a code on a Web site

17. What is the normal retail price of the heater?

(A) $25.00
(B) $35.00
(C) $120.00
(D) $160.00

Tired of dull blades? Let Skillpoint help!

Skillpoint helps restaurants, grocery stores, and commercial kitchens in the Toronto metropolitan area keep their knives in top condition. We sharpen all types of knives, no matter how dull or damaged they may be. We also work on blades for food processors, slicers, graters, and scissors.

Choose from these options:

- Bring your items to us—Every Friday between 8 A.M. and noon we are open for business at 4512 West Park Street. Have your pieces sharpened while you wait. This usually takes no more than 15 minutes.

- Visit the Downtown Farmers Market—On weekends, you can drop off your blades at our open-air booth between 9 A.M. and 1 P.M. and pick them up when you are finished with your shopping!

- Have us come to you—An experienced professional will be dispatched to your premises to sharpen all your blades on-site. We have morning, afternoon, and evening times available Monday through Thursday. Visit our Web site, www.torontosp.com, to sign up for a convenient time.

18. What service does Skillpoint offer?

(A) Purchasing used equipment
(B) Sharpening kitchen tools
(C) Rating food quality and preparation
(D) Training food service workers

19. What is NOT mentioned as a way to take advantage of Skillpoint's service?

(A) Visiting a storefront location
(B) Going to an outdoor market
(C) Receiving a visit from a representative
(D) Attending a convention for the restaurant industry

20. According to the advertisement, what can a customer do through the company's Web site?

(A) Request a price estimate
(B) Make an appointment
(C) Comment on services
(D) Read a press release

Corville Music Festival

Interested in donating some of your time while enjoying all kinds of great music? Then volunteer at the fifteenth annual Corville Music Festival! This year's festival runs from September 24 to 30 at the county fairgrounds in Corville and features music from more than 50 talented groups, including local favorites Vireos Pop Band, Jazz Marvels, and Chiang String Quartet.

Volunteers are needed to
- help with publicity—designing and posting all flyers and sending press releases—starting September 1.
- greet the musicians and help them locate their housing assignments from September 22 to 28. All out-of-town musicians will be hosted by area families.
- operate the ticket booth, direct guests to the parking areas during the festival, and provide general information.

In appreciation, each volunteer will receive a limited edition Corville Music Festival T-shirt and four complimentary tickets.

If you are interested in volunteering, please contact Marta Sedlak at msedlak@corvillemusicfest.org by August 17.

21. What is indicated about the festival?

(A) It will take place on September 1.
(B) It features a variety of music types.
(C) It is run by a professional musician.
(D) It may be rescheduled because of rain.

22. What is suggested about some of the performers?

(A) They will be donating used instruments.
(B) They will be providing posters for the festival.
(C) They will be staying at homes in Corville.
(D) They will be receiving a major award at the festival.

23. What task will NOT be done by volunteers?

(A) Selling tickets for festival performances
(B) Transporting musicians to the fairgrounds
(C) Showing visitors where to park
(D) Distributing publicity materials

24. What will volunteers receive for free?

(A) An article of clothing
(B) A pass to access backstage areas
(C) A video recording of the festival
(D) Snacks and meals on festival days

UNIT 04 기사

⚙ 출제 비율 2~3세트

1. 비즈니스, 지역, 특정 기업이나 인물, 문화 등 다양한 주제의 기사가 등장하며, 지문의 길이가 대체로 길고 수준 높은 어휘가 많이 등장하여 전반적으로 난이도가 높은 편이다.
2. 제목과 도입부에서 기사의 주제가 언급되며, 후반부에는 향후 계획이나 전망 등을 전하는 경우가 많다.

기출 예제

제목	**Welcome Bags Available**
기관 소개 행사/계획 소개	①The Fairmill Welcome Association (FWA) has decided on an exciting gift for new residents: a reusable shopping bag filled with information about the town of Fairmill. These cloth bags, which will have "Celebrate Fairmill" printed across the front, will be filled with community updates, coupons, and home-baked treats from association members.
세부 사항	②Local businesses interested in helping to fund this project can pay to have their logos printed on the back of the bags. ③Fairmill residents are encouraged to welcome their new neighbors by personally delivering these bags to each household. To sign up,
신청 방법	please go online to visit our updated community Web site at fairmillwa.org.

제목/앞부분 확인
제목이나 앞부분에서 기사의 주제를 파악한다.
① 기사가 등장할 곳?
페어밀 시 정보를 담은 백을 새 주민들에게 준다고 함

세부 사항 확인
기사의 핵심 정보 소개
② 지역 사업체들이 후원할 방법?
웰컴백 뒷면에 로고 인쇄해줌

추가 사항/신청 방법 확인
자세한 행사나 계획 소개 후 추가 사항이 나오면 문제로 출제되기 쉽다.
③ 페어밀 주민들이 요청받는 것?
웰컴백 배분에 동참 독려

번역 p.054

추론
Q1. Where would the article most likely **appear**?
A1. In a community newsletter

이 기사가 등장할 것 같은 곳은?
지역 소식지

- -

세부 사항
Q2. How can **local businesses support** the **project**?
A2. By purchasing advertising space

지역 사업체들은 어떻게 이 프로젝트를 지원할 수 있는가?
광고 공간 구매

패러프레이징 지문의 pay to have their logos printed on the back of the bags
→ 보기의 purchasing advertising space

- -

세부 사항
Q3. According to the article, **what** are Fairmill **residents asked to do**?
A3. Distribute greeting materials

기사에 따르면, 페어밀 주민들은 무엇을 하라고 요청받는가?
환영 자료 배포

패러프레이징 지문의 personally delivering these bags
→ 보기의 Distribute greeting materials

제목
제목에서 기사의 주제를 파악할 수 있다. 제목이 없는 경우는 처음 한두 문장에서 파악 가능하다.

BAC Welcomes *Timothy Kang*	티모시 강 씨를 맞이하는 BAC
NEW LOOK FOR COMPTON STREET AREA	컴프턴 가 지역에 대한 새로운 전망
Light rail keeps neighborhood industry on track	경전철이 지역 산업을 순조롭게 만들다
Rice Crop Expected to Reach Near-Record Levels	쌀 수확량 사상 최고치에 근접할 것으로 예상

육하원칙
기사는 육하원칙에 따라 주요 소식을 전한다.

Porterfield College is building its **new housing complex**.	누가/무엇을
A ground-breaking ceremony took place **last Wednesday in Leartown**.	언제/어디서
He began gathering the necessary funds **to realize his goal by requesting donations**.	왜/어떻게

인용문
기사에서는 인용문을 이용한 문제가 종종 출제된다.

"Even though a lot of visitors came into the store, many **left without making a purchase**."	상점에 대해 암시한 것은?
"I hope that they will then stop by **my establishment to enjoy a delicious meal**."	이 사람은 누구이겠는가?

경제 / 경영

sales revenue 매출 수입
negotiation 협상
ongoing 진행 중인
amass 모으다, 축적하다
treasurer 회계 담당자
tentatively 잠정적으로
multinational 다국적의
take advantage of ~을 이용하다
pay off 성공하다
base ~에 본사를 두다
innovative 혁신적인
strategy 전략

경제 / 경영

cater to ~의 구미에 맞추다
subsidiary 자회사
turn profits 이윤을 남기다
expert 전문가
investigate 조사하다, 연구하다
profitable 수익성이 있는
approval 승인
affordable (가격이) 적당한
merger 합병
enterprise 기업
entrepreneur 기업가
loyal customer base 단골 고객층

도로 / 교통

interactive 상호적인, 쌍방향의
customized 개개인의 요구에 맞춘
comprehensive 포괄적인
public transit 대중교통
congestion 혼잡
enlarge 확장하다, 확대하다
fuel-efficient 연료 효율성이 좋은
bustling 붐비는, 북적북적하는
alert 경보
take effect 시행되다
temporary 임시의, 일시적인
relocation 이전

건물 / 건설

landscaping 조경
reconstruct 재건하다
backdrop 배경, 환경
existing 기존의
establish 수립하다, 설립하다
operational 가동할 준비가 갖춰진
facilitate 용이하게 하다
accommodate 공간을 제공하다

문화 / 예술

reputation 명성, 평판
archive 기록 보관소
publicity 홍보
volume 낱권
literary 문학의
contemporary 동시대의
manuscript 원고
inspire 영감을 주다

지역 사회 / 환경

resident 주민, 거주자
fund 자금을 대다
large-scale 대규모의
initiative 계획
convert 전환하다, 개조하다
habitat 서식지
preserve 보존하다, 보호하다
extinction 멸종, 소멸

Questions 1-3 refer to the following article.

난이도 ★★☆

Tradeen County to Hold Park Project Event

Tradeen County is holding an event to recruit workers for the Park Project, a large-scale initiative that involves converting the Tradeen Canyonlands into a wildlife refuge and educational facility. More than 75 positions are available in construction, maintenance, and landscaping, as well as in marketing and education. The event will be held at the County Coliseum on Saturday, March 31.

For information about employment opportunities with the Park Project and to download an application, go to www.tradeencounty.gov. Those who register online prior to March 31 will be able to schedule an interview in advance, although walk-in candidates are also welcome on the day of the event. All interviews will be conducted between 10:00 A.M. and 4:00 P.M.

The Park Project was initiated by county officials in response to a recently passed law aimed at increasing habitat protection for wildlife.

1. Why most likely would someone attend the event?
   (A) To look for a job
   (B) To discuss a new law
   (C) To learn about protecting wildlife
   (D) To celebrate the opening of a park

2. What will people who sign up before the event be able to do?
   (A) Pay a discounted registration fee
   (B) Reserve a meeting time
   (C) Participate in a special tour
   (D) Enter the event early

3. What does the law mentioned in the article support?
   (A) Urban development
   (B) Computer education
   (C) Preserving the natural environment
   (D) Opening a university in Tradeen County

Questions 4-6 refer to the following article.

난이도 ★ ★ ☆

Discover Port Snowden
App Now Available

September 22—The Port Snowden Business Council (PSBC) announced today that a new application, called *Discover Port Snowden*, can now be downloaded at no charge on most types of tablets and mobile phones.

One of the application's most popular features is an interactive map that provides customized directions to community attractions. Also included are a directory of area restaurants, a comprehensive list of accommodations, and a monthly guide to concert, theater, and other events. Getting around is made easier with up-to-date information about public transit routes and schedules, construction zones, and traffic delays.

Jens Henningsen, the programmer who developed the application, explained, "Paper maps and brochures often become dated whenever something changes. With this application, important information can be added or changed with the click of a button."

The ability to keep information current was the primary reason the PSBC decided to take on the project. The cost of developing *Discover Port Snowden* was covered by the annual dues collected from PSBC members.

4. What is indicated about the application?

(A) It offers discounts for attractions.
(B) It has a hotel reservation feature.
(C) It can display restaurant menus.
(D) It provides information about transportation.

5. According to the article, why did the PSBC have the application developed?

(A) Because it will promote tourism
(B) Because it will be easy to update
(C) Because it will save money
(D) Because it will create jobs

6. Where did the PSBC obtain funding for the application?

(A) From sales revenue
(B) Through community donations
(C) Through additional taxes
(D) From membership fees

Yesterday the Baywood Historical Society (BHS) announced plans to have the Tower Mill reconstructed exactly as it had been designed and built over a century ago. The mill was lost to a fire a year and a half ago. Although it had not been in operation for the last 50 years, it had been a mainstay of the Baywood community since it opened. What made it such a beloved landmark was its location. Situated in an idyllic setting on the edge of town, the Tower Mill formed the backdrop for an untold number of graduations, weddings, and anniversaries. It was even featured in three television documentaries about life in rural small towns.

The project to re-create the original design of the mill was awarded to Mindseye Matters, Inc. Negotiations with a building contractor are ongoing. The Town Council has allocated $100,000 toward the project while local businesses have given donations in excess of $75,000. The BHS intends to amass an additional $50,000 through a series of fund-raising projects, to be headed by its treasurer Janeen Tsui. On June 6 BHS President Garvan Locke will discuss the project and provide historical information from the BHS archives about the original mill. Also, Ms. Tsui will outline plans for a benefit dinner tentatively scheduled for Saturday, July 27. The June 6 event will be held at 7:00 P.M. at the BHS office, 151 Waltham Road.

7. What is suggested about the Tower Mill?

(A) Its design is similar to mills in many rural towns.

(B) Its rebuilding will be financed by a variety of sources.

(C) It had been reconstructed once before, almost 50 years ago.

(D) It was located in the center of Baywood.

8. What kind of business most likely is Mindseye Matters, Inc.?

(A) Construction
(B) Photography
(C) Landscaping
(D) Architecture

9. What is NOT indicated about the Baywood Historical Society?

(A) It intends to host a fund-raising event in July.

(B) It is headed by Mr. Locke.

(C) It intends to provide regular project updates to the public.

(D) It has information about the historical development of the Tower Mill.

No More Free Parking in the City

May 21

By Alicia Granger

In an effort to limit congestion in the center of Morristown, the city council is planning changes in parking regulations. "Our streets are often at their busiest in the evening hours," said Gina Thompson, spokesperson for the Morristown City Council. "That's because residents and nonresidents alike come to our downtown area to enjoy our restaurants, theaters, and concert venues. People tend to avoid the parking garages, which charge a fee. They drive around looking for free street parking, and this increases congestion."

Currently, payment for parking on the street is required only from 6 A.M. to 5 P.M., and no parking fee is charged at night. "This needs to change," Ms. Thompson said. "We'd like to follow the example of other cities, where payment is required 24 hours a day."

If the proposed change goes into effect, it will be the second in recent months. In March, new parking meters were installed that accept both coins and credit cards, as well as special Morristown parking cards. The cards, which became available in April, can be purchased from the city.

---

10. What is suggested about Morristown?

(A) Its roads are in need of repair.
(B) It must raise funds for new road construction.
(C) It has a traffic problem.
(D) Its residents can park for free in city garages.

11. What is the city council considering?

(A) Enlarging existing parking spaces
(B) Creating new parking areas
(C) Raising the hourly rate for parking
(D) Introducing evening parking fees

12. What has recently happened in Morristown?

(A) Some downtown parking garages closed.
(B) The city council purchased additional land for parking.
(C) Parking meters were repaired.
(D) New payment options for parking were established.

Questions 13-16 refer to the following article.

Metro-Edibles Corporation Announces New Direction

May 7—Metro-Edibles Corporation has announced that it plans to develop a fast-food chain it is calling Soup and Salad Central. The new chain will be managed from Metro-Edibles' Hong Kong headquarters, and the multinational corporation hopes to eventually introduce 200 Soup and Salad Central locations throughout Asia and Europe.

"The convenience food sector has shown worldwide growth over the last decade," remarked Louis Merkey, industry analyst at Businesstrend.com. "Metro-Edibles is wisely taking advantage of this trend."

A survey conducted by Metro-Edibles over the last year revealed that consumers are choosing to purchase more wholesome foods when eating out. Neha Ramisetty,

Metro-Edibles' top executive, noted that the industry in general is placing less emphasis on fried foods and focusing more on fresh ingredients and nutritional value.

"We are offering this approach too, at an average price of US $7.50 for a lunch or dinner, with cheaper options for breakfast and snacks," said Ms. Ramisetty. "Furthermore, we will cater mostly to urban residents with faster-paced lifestyles. So we think that they will appreciate the convenience that our menu will offer."

Metro-Edibles Corp. is optimistic that Soup and Salad Central, its newest subsidiary, will start to turn profits by its second year of operations. The corporation still carries some long-term debt from money it borrowed to start current enterprises.

13. Who most likely is Mr. Merkey?
(A) A legal consultant for Metro-Edibles Corporation
(B) A Hong Kong bank officer
(C) A nutrition expert
(D) A food industry researcher

14. What is reported about Metro-Edibles Corporation?
(A) It has hired a new leader.
(B) It has been affected by slow industry growth.
(C) It investigated people's dining preferences.
(D) It is planning to relocate its headquarters.

15. What does Ms. Ramisetty NOT indicate about the meals at Soup and Salad Central?
(A) They will be less expensive than meals at similar restaurants.
(B) They will be available throughout the day.
(C) They will include healthful ingredients.
(D) They will be served quickly.

16. What is suggested about Soup and Salad Central?
(A) It replaces an unsuccessful Metro-Edibles Corporation enterprise.
(B) It will offer recipes of its menu items to customers.
(C) It is not expected to be profitable immediately.
(D) It will open locations primarily in small towns.

DA Pivots Toward South America

23 January—Deutsche Autokonzern AG (DA) announced earlier this week that it plans to build an automobile plant in Curitiba, Brazil. Pending final approval of the architectural designs, construction of the German automaker's first South American plant will begin this March.

DA's affordable, fuel-efficient cars became a popular choice with European consumers the moment they first rolled off the company's Leipzig assembly line. In a press release, the company's chief executive officer, Hans-Dietrich Kaufman, said, "We want to make our products and services available to customers throughout South America so that they, too, can enjoy our high-quality, competitively priced cars."

Market analysts point out that this news did not come as a surprise. DA had released a comprehensive strategy to broaden its presence around the world nearly three years ago. Regardless, analysts were skeptical about the construction time referred to by DA's top official. Kaufman, who worked at Bachmeier Autofabrik for 25 years before accepting the top job at DA two years ago, stated, "DA has always expected to expand its production capacity, and we are confident that our Curitiba plant will be operational in a year's time."

Market analyst Melina Nascimento notes that over the past four years the company's profits have been steadily increasing. She attributes this financial success to the fact that European consumers are impressed with DA's products and its customer service. Nascimento fully expects that South Americans will share this sentiment, resulting in a further strengthening of the company's finances.

CHAPTER 2

UNIT 04

17. According to the article, why does DA plan to build a plant in Curitiba?

(A) To facilitate a merger with Bachmeier Autofabrik
(B) To strengthen its presence internationally
(C) To produce cars based on a new design
(D) To replace the factory in Leipzig

18. What does the article suggest about DA?

(A) It has increased the price of its vehicles.
(B) It has been planning to open a new plant for some time.
(C) It owns multiple automobile plants in Europe.
(D) It faces strong competition in South America.

19. According to Mr. Kaufman, when will the new plant open?

(A) In one year
(B) In two years
(C) In three years
(D) In four years

20. Why does Ms. Nascimento believe DA will be successful in South America?

(A) It has established a good reputation outside of Europe.
(B) It will launch an extensive advertising campaign.
(C) Customers will be able to purchase cars directly from the factory.
(D) Customers will like what the company has to offer.

Dublin (30 August)—Earlier this month, two recent graduates from Dublin's Clontarf University opened the doors to their first commercial venture. Ardal McFee and Joe Healy have created Spin Cycle, a one-stop exercise and launderette destination, Ireland's first such establishment. Located on Kincora Road in a bustling neighborhood near the university, the enterprise provides a healthy diversion to the time-consuming task of doing laundry. As Mr. McFee explained, "One day as I was walking away from campus, I noticed a busy launderette with a for-sale sign in the window. I discovered that the owner was retiring to spend more time with his family and wanted to sell his shop. Joe and I thought the location was ideal for our first venture."

Mr. McFee and Mr. Healy knew from personal experience that making regular trips to a launderette was a chore. They realized that they would have to offer a creative twist to their service if they wanted to stand out. After writing a business plan and securing a commercial loan, they were able to purchase a vacant shop next to the launderette. They cut a doorway in the common wall, connecting the area to the launderette, and cleaned and painted the area. They then installed twelve stationary exercise bicycles. Spin Cycle was set for customers.

The young entrepreneurs' instincts seem to be paying off; the business is already profitable, according to McFee and Healy. Many residents in the area live in student housing or small apartments, which often cannot accommodate washing machines or dryers. At Spin Cycle, customers can leave their laundry at the front desk to be washed, dried, and folded within 90 minutes, or they can use the self-service machines. Either way, they can complete an energizing workout and leave with fresh, clean clothes.

21. What is the purpose of the article?

(A) To explain how to manage a store

(B) To announce a grand opening event

(C) To compare the ideas of two colleagues

(D) To describe an unusual business concept

22. What is suggested about Spin Cycle?

(A) It is run by a single family in Dublin.

(B) It is located on a university campus.

(C) Its customers can drop off their laundry to be washed.

(D) Its washing machines were recently replaced.

23. The word "set" in paragraph 2, line 13, is closest in meaning to

(A) certain

(B) determined

(C) distinct

(D) prepared

24. What did Mr. McFee and Mr. Healy NOT do before opening Spin Cycle?

(A) Conduct a customer survey

(B) Develop a business plan

(C) Obtain funding

(D) Renovate a space

Nairobi Daily Journal

2 April

Two supermarket chains are currently competing to be number one in Kenya. Both retailers, AT Mart and Duggan's, have announced that they are determined to place first with consumers. — [1] —.

In March, AT Mart, which is based in the United Kingdom, announced it was planning to launch its first store in Nairobi. — [2] —. It is one of the largest supermarket chains in the world. Duggan's, on the other hand, is not well-known outside of Africa, but it is South Africa's most dominant supermarket chain and has established a presence here. Now there are eight Duggan's stores in Kenya with a loyal customer base.

— [3] —. Some supermarket chains, such as Wentworth's, which is based in the United States, have not been willing to pay what they consider to be exorbitant leasing fees when their stores simply were not attracting a significant number of shoppers. As a result, Wentworth's closed all three of its stores after only two years in Kenya.

Duggan's, however, has an advantage. — [4] —. The company created its own real estate division, D Properties Ltd. This company has built four shopping complexes with Duggan's as the main tenant in each. Moreover, Duggan's has paid special attention to tailoring its product inventory to the local culture. It also has developed an effective supply-and-delivery system to service its famous on-site bakeries, butcher shops, and produce sections. AT Mart may have much wider name recognition, but it will need to be more innovative to compete against the popular Duggan's.

--Susan Kotter, Staff Reporter

25. What is the article mainly about?

(A) Business strategies that work well
(B) The competition within an industry
(C) Places to find bargains in Kenya
(D) The growth of new shopping malls

26. What is indicated about Wentworth's?

(A) It has a loyal customer base.
(B) Its branch stores were mostly in South Africa.
(C) Its business in Kenya was relatively short-lived.
(D) It is a family-owned enterprise.

27. What is NOT mentioned as an accomplishment of Duggan's?

(A) Establishing a real estate division
(B) Creating an efficient delivery system
(C) Setting up on-site bakeries
(D) Developing a global reputation

28. In which of the positions marked [1], [2], [3], and [4] does the following sentence best belong?

"Rents in desirable locations for supermarkets are often extremely high."

(A) [1]
(B) [2]
(C) [3]
(D) [4]

UNIT 05 웹페이지/양식

⚙ 출제 비율 2~3세트

기출 전략

1. 웹페이지는 기업이나 단체의 홈페이지상에서 볼 수 있는 제품/서비스 소개나 고객 후기 등이 주로 출제된다. 양식은 실생활에서 접하기 쉬운 영수증, 주문서(송장), 쿠폰, 일정표 등 단어 수가 상대적으로 많지 않은 다양한 형식의 지문이 등장한다.
2. 별표(*)나 Note(유의 사항) 등 특별 고지 항목이 자주 문제로 출제되며, 양식에서는 특히 숫자나 고유명사 같은 단편 정보를 파악해야 하는 문제가 잘 등장한다.

기출 예제

업체 정보 주요 서비스	**NORTH RIVER HOTEL** ①Same-day wash/dry/fold service

상세 서비스	• Drop off at reception before 8:30 A.M. • Ready by 6:00 P.M. • Cost: $10.00 per bag

주문 내역

ITEMS IN BAG	QUANTITY
Shirts or blouses	4
Trousers or skirts	3
Dresses	
Sweaters or vests	
Shorts	1
Socks (pair)	2

고객 정보
날짜/가격 등

②Name and room: <u>Lidia Lee, 603</u>
Received by: <u>Darnell Reed</u>
Date: <u>January 19</u>
Total cost: <u>$10.00</u>

업체 정보 및 주요 서비스

어떤 업체의 어떤 종류의 양식인지 파악한다.

① 세탁 서비스에 대해 명시된 것?
Same-day 서비스라는 점에 주목

상세 서비스 내용 및 주문 내역

항목으로 분류된 지문 형태이므로 미리 읽지 말고 문제를 먼저 보도록 한다.

고객 정보 및 날짜/가격 등

서비스를 신청한 고객의 정보, 주문 받은 사람, 날짜, 가격 등이 나와 있다.

② 리 씨는 누구?
이름과 방 호수가 나와 있음

번역 **p.063**

Not/True

Q1. What is **indicated** about the **laundry service**?
A1. It is completed in one day.

세탁 서비스에 대해 명시된 것은?
하루만에 완료된다.

패러프레이징 지문의 Same-day → 보기의 in one day

- -

추론

Q2. Who most likely is **Ms. Lee**?
A2. A hotel guest

리 씨는 누구일 것 같은가?
호텔 투숙객

정답이 보이는 단서 표현

웹페이지 탭   홈페이지에서 표시된 탭 정보를 통해 글의 주제와 목적을 가늠할 수 있다.

Home / About Us	회사 전반 소개
Our Products / Services / Menu / Features / Special Deals	상품/서비스 종류 및 특장점 소개
Customer Service / Support / Reviews / Testimonials	고객 서비스 / 고객 후기
Membership / Join Us / Register / Sign Up	회원 가입

영수증/주문서/쿠폰   물품을 통한 업종 유추, 요금 및 결제 정보, 할인 조건, 서비스 제외 품목 등과 관련된 문제가 출제된다.

Drafting pencil 6 / Steel-handle hammer / Flathead screwdriver	어떤 종류의 업체인가?
Total amount must be received by **31 October.**	언제까지 지불해야 하는가?
Order Date: August 31 Estimated Shipping Date: September 4	8월 31일에 무엇을 했는가?
Excludes clothing, bags, and shoes.	이 쿠폰에 대해 사실인 것은?
Receive the usual free shipping on **orders of $75 or more.**	어떻게 할인 받을 수 있는가?

초대장/일정표/설문지   행사 종류/대상을 유추하는 문제, 행사의 목적, 장소, 날짜, 유의 사항 등과 관련된 문제가 출제된다.

This is an open forum for **owners of small companies.**	초대장은 누구에게 보내진 것인가?
It's our **50th year** in business.	무엇을 축하하는가?
Quality of food: Poor / Fair / Good / Excellent / N/A	진술과 일치하는 것은?

빈출 어휘

청구/결제

up front 선불
remainder 나머지
balance due 미지불액
managerial 경영의, 관리의
at no extra charge 추가 요금 없이
receipt 수령, 영수증
back-order 이월 주문(하다)
deduct 빼다, 공제하다
assess 평가하다, 부과하다
deposit 보증금, 착수금(선불금)

청구/결제

estimate 견적(액); 어림잡다
in installment 할부로
incidental expense 부대 비용
measurement 치수, 측정
overdue 기한이 지난, 늦은
partial payment 부분 지불
reduction 할인
reimbursement 환급, 상환
subtotal 소계
waive a fee 요금을 면제해 주다

전자 제품/가구

trade-in 보상 판매
retrieve 되찾아 오다, 회수하다
status 상황
customized 개개인의 요구에 맞춘
fragile 취약한, 손상되기 쉬운
exclusively 독점적으로
compatible 호환이 되는
cutting-edge 최신식의
valid 유효한
instructions 설명(서), 지시

공연/행사

contemporary 동시대의
attendee 참석자
advance sale 예매
acknowledgement 접수 통지
register 등록하다
specified 명시된
intermission 중간 휴식 시간
overwhelming 압도적인
sequel 속편
usher (극장 등의) 안내인

여행

itinerary 여행 일정표
memorable 기억에 남는
off season 비수기
outskirts 변두리, 교외
restriction 제한
ruins 폐허, 유적
rural 시골풍의(= rustic)
stopover 경유, 단기간 체류
vessel 선박, 배
voyage 여행(하다)

초대

anonymously 익명으로
charity 자선 (단체)
compassionate 인정 많은
cordially 진심으로, 다정하게
credit 칭찬, 인정
decent 괜찮은, 품위 있는
devote 바치다, 헌신하다
donor 기증자
organization 단체, 기관
recipient 수상자

Questions 1-2 refer to the following invitation.

난이도 ★☆☆

San Bernardino Condominium Units
Grand Opening on Feldstone Avenue
Friday, July 7

North River Real Estate of
Springton City, BC V8B 2KO,
cordially invites you to view our
SPECTACULAR properties
available for immediate purchase!

Continuous tours from 4 P.M. to 8 P.M.
Beverages and snacks will be served.

Contact J. D. Ponge at (604) 555-0139 for
property details and mortgage information.

1. Why is an event being held?

    (A) To announce a construction plan to the community
    (B) To introduce new housing in the area
    (C) To celebrate a renovated company headquarters
    (D) To schedule employment interviews at a business

2. What most likely is J. D. Ponge's profession?

    (A) Sales agent
    (B) Interior designer
    (C) Manager of a catering service
    (D) City tour operator

Questions 3-5 refer to the following Web page.

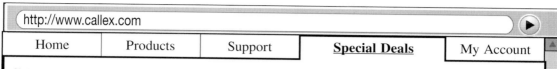

| Home | Products | Support | **Special Deals** | My Account |

Callex Electronics Trade-In Program

Do you want to get rid of your old Callex laptop or other electronic device? Is it beyond repair or past warranty? No problem! You can ship it to us and buy any new Callex device at a reduced price. The process is simple and can be done in three steps:

Step 1: Select your Callex product category from the Products page, and our online calculator will assess the value of your trade-in device.

Step 2: Ship your device within 30 days to the address provided online. Once you have shipped your device, any data that may still be contained within it cannot be retrieved. It is strongly recommended that you delete all personal information from your device prior to shipping.

Step 3: Once your device has been received, a Callex gift card will be sent to you for the final assessed amount. The card can be used at any Callex store or for online purchases in any product category.

3. What does the online calculator estimate?
   (A) How much an item is worth
   (B) How much it costs to ship an item
   (C) How long it takes to repair an item
   (D) How soon an item can be delivered

4. What are customers advised to do?
   (A) Compare prices
   (B) Erase data
   (C) Buy an additional warranty
   (D) Check a product's shipping status

5. What will customers receive?
   (A) Free repair service
   (B) Customized technical support
   (C) Notice of future sales events
   (D) Credit for future purchases

CHAPTER 2 UNIT 05

Yitsu Photo Lab
104 First Avenue
St Zacharie, QC GOM 2C0

Customer Name: _Selena Gimpl_

Special Instructions:

Please scan the enclosed photographs and print two copies of each on archival-quality paper. Be sure to save these images in digital format, and include two CDs with the order. These are old photographs, so please take great care when handling them.

Print Size: 4x6   (5x7)

Finish: (glossy)   matte

Pickup Date: _May 24th, anytime after 3:00 P.M._

Total: _$60.00_

• 10% Promotional Discount (applicable only to first-time customers)?   (Yes)   No
  Total: _-$6_
• 25% Payment Up Front (required for all orders over $30): _-$13.50_

Remainder Due at Pickup: _$40.50_

6. What is suggested about the photographs provided by Ms. Gimpl?
   (A) They are fragile.
   (B) They are brightly colored.
   (C) They show historical buildings.
   (D) They were taken with a digital camera.

7. How much money does Ms. Gimpl owe on May 24?
   (A) $6.00
   (B) $13.50
   (C) $40.50
   (D) $60.00

York Fabric and Yarn
79 Welch Road, York, UK YO31 3LP
Purveyors of fine wool, yarns, and textiles for over 70 years

Customer: Sebastian Graham
Order: 78-3L2 (placed 8 June)
Billing address: 25 Canary Road, Reading RG31 2RE
Shipping address: Glenda Graham, 13 Reed Street, Wantage OX12 2T

Quantity	Item	Unit Price	Item Price
1.5 kilograms	**Shetland Wool** *Source: Old Grove Sheep Farm, Lerwick*	£14/kilogram	£21.00
2.5 kilograms	**Leicester Wool** *Source: Arnold Farms, Arnesby*	£16/kilogram	£40.00

	Gift wrapping	Free
	Subtotal	£61.00
	Shipping	£ 7.00
	Order total	£68.00
	Amount paid with credit card	£68.00
	Balance due	£ 0.00

This is a billing receipt. The gift receipt included in the shipment does not list prices.

8. Where is the package most likely being sent?

(A) To York
(B) To Wantage
(C) To Lerwick
(D) To Reading

9. What is suggested about the merchandise?

(A) It was paid for in cash.
(B) It was bought by a sheep farm.
(C) It was purchased as a gift.
(D) It was shipped by truck.

10. What is indicated about York Fabric and Yarn?

(A) It has been in business for decades.
(B) It is an online retailer.
(C) It offers free shipping with large orders.
(D) It is planning to open a second location.

http://www.citywidesportsemporium.com.nz/about

Citywide Sports Emporium

| **ABOUT** | HOME | LOCATIONS | PRODUCTS | SERVICES |

About Citywide Sports Emporium

Business and tennis partners Grace Clay and Amelia Ross established the first Citywide Sports Emporium (CSE) at 164 Bowen Street a decade ago. They realized that most sporting goods retailers at the time were concentrating on adventure sports merchandise—for example, rock climbing and kayaking gear—and Wellington residents with less extreme interests were underserved. Two years after opening the Bowen Street shop, CSE opened a shop at 23 Lambton Quay. CSE then successfully expanded outside of Wellington. Today, CSE is the top destination exclusively for tennis, cycling, and running enthusiasts across the country.

This year CSE proudly debuted a line of clothing, Citywide Sports Attire, designed by Olympic runner Shawn Wagner. It is available at all locations and through this Web site. Click **Products** to view our comfortable and colourful clothing and footwear for men and women.

Note, too, that special services are available exclusively at our original location. These services include bicycle and treadmill reconditioning, tennis racquet restringing, and more. Click **Services** to schedule a repair or to leave an inquiry.

---

11. What is indicated about the owners of CSE?

(A) They design sportswear.

(B) They play tennis together.

(C) They are professional cyclists.

(D) They are interested in selling the CSE chain.

12. The word "established" in paragraph 1, line 1, is closest in meaning to

(A) demonstrated

(B) challenged

(C) introduced

(D) furnished

13. What is suggested about CSE?

(A) It does not sell adventure sports gear.

(B) It does not own any stores outside of Wellington.

(C) It no longer sells its products online.

(D) It no longer operates a store on Lambton Quay.

14. What is available to CSE customers only at the Bowen Street shop?

(A) Athletic shoes

(B) Exercise classes

(C) Running apparel

(D) Equipment repair

Frank's Auto Repair
112 Central Avenue

Customer Feedback Form

Your opinions are important to us. We will use the information collected in this survey to help improve our service. Please tell us how important each of the following factors is to you when you choose a business for automotive repair. Circle a number from 1-6.

	Not important				Very important	
Price	1	2	3	4	(5)	6
Convenient Location	1	(2)	3	4	5	6
Experienced Mechanics	1	2	3	4	5	(6)
Courteous Office Staff	1	2	3	(4)	5	6

Did our staff:

Clearly explain the work your vehicle needed?   No X   Yes ____

Treat you politely and with respect?   No ____ Yes X

Accurately estimate the amount of time the work would take?   No ____ Yes X

Tell you the cost before repairing your vehicle?   No ____ Yes X

Comments

I'm not sure I understand what was wrong with the car, but the mechanics were able to fix it quickly and easily. The price was reasonable, too. But it would be helpful next if I could get more information about the repair.

15. What does the customer consider unimportant when choosing a repair service?

(A) The location of the company
(B) The respect shown by the employees
(C) The experience of the company's mechanics
(D) The price of the company's services

16. With which aspect of the service was the customer NOT satisfied?

(A) The cost of the necessary parts
(B) The amount of information given about the repair work
(C) The amount of time needed to make the repairs
(D) The politeness of the employees

17. What is suggested about the customer?

(A) The customer has been to the repair service more than once.
(B) The customer will not do business with Frank's Auto Repair again.
(C) The customer was satisfied with the repair costs.
(D) The customer knew what the problem was with the car.

---

http://www.asterbooks.com/invoice_58579 ▶

Aster Books

Order Number: 58579
Order Date: February 8
Estimated Shipping Date: February 12

Ship To:
Ms. Kadija Al-Fulan
93 Carver St., Apt. 16
New York, NY 10007

Bill To:
Ms. April Drew
231 Lombard Ave.
Cherryview, NJ 08172

Title	**Author**	**Price**
Management Strategies	Leonard Forest	$32.95
Steps to Managerial Success	Eleanor Tsu	$42.49

Subtotal	$75.44
Tax	$ 5.28
Shipping and Handling	Free
Total Charged to Credit Card	$80.72

Include card (at no extra charge) if order is a gift? _X_ Yes ___ No

Message for card: Congratulations on your new job! We hope these books will be helpful in your new position. We miss you already.

Sincerely,

The staff at Drew & Ikeda Legal Services

---

18. What did Ms. Drew do on February 8?

(A) Picked up a package
(B) Canceled a shipment
(C) Purchased a gift
(D) Returned some books

19. What is suggested about Ms. Al-Fulan?

(A) She was recently hired as a manager.
(B) She has enrolled in a university course.
(C) She is Ms. Drew's supervisor.
(D) She has written a book.

20. What is indicated about Aster Books?

(A) It shipped an order at no additional charge.
(B) It publishes magazines.
(C) It sells gift certificates.
(D) It shipped an order one day after receiving it.

http://www.eypf.org.uk/

The Elise Young Poetry Festival

| Archive | **About EYPF** | Tickets | Home |

The Elise Young Poetry Festival is one of the largest poetry events in the UK, drawing renowned contemporary poets and hundreds of other attendees from all over the world. Click on the "archive" tab above to see videos of readings at past festivals, along with short biographies of the featured poets.

This year, the festival will take place on 6 and 7 July at Rosehill Gardens in Paisley. Tickets are £15 for adults and £10 for children 12 and under. Advance sale tickets will be available for purchase online beginning 20 May at http://www.eypf.org.uk/tickets (the "tickets" tab above).

Presentation Submissions

Anyone is eligible to submit his or her work for formal presentation at the festival. Submissions must include a work sample containing between 100 and 400 lines; the sample may consist of one long poem or any number of shorter pieces. Both published and unpublished work may be submitted. A video of the applicant reading the work is helpful but not required.

Submissions must be received no later than 25 March. Please refrain from inquiring about the status of your submission. All applicants will receive a letter of acknowledgement by post, and accepted applicants will be contacted by 25 April. Due to the high volume of submissions, at the conclusion of the selection process we will be able to notify only those applicants who are invited to present.

Send your work for consideration to the following address:
Elise Young Poetry Festival, c/o Carey Wood
PO Box 29001, Dundee DD1 4BG

Several open reading sessions are also held during the Festival. All those wishing to perform their poetry before an audience are welcome at these sessions, which do not require advance application.

CHAPTER 2

UNIT 05

21. What is NOT indicated as something that can be done on the festival's Web site?

(A) View recordings of past performances
(B) Read about the lives of famous poets
(C) Buy tickets to attend the festival
(D) Register to attend poetry classes

22. What is a requirement of the poetry submitted by applicants?

(A) It must be unpublished.
(B) It must be recorded on video.
(C) It must be of a specified length.
(D) It must be written in a particular formal style.

23. What will be sent to everyone submitting work to the festival?

(A) A letter confirming receipt of the work
(B) A letter indicating the reviewers' final decision
(C) A list of comments about the work
(D) A pass to an exclusive event at the festival

24. What is suggested about the open reading sessions?

(A) Members of the public may attend them at no cost.
(B) They are held before the official beginning of the festival.
(C) Poets who perform at them will receive feedback from audience members.
(D) Poets whose applications are rejected may perform at them.

기출 전략

1. 직장 동료 간에 신속한 업무 처리를 위해 즉석에서 주고받는 대화나 의견 전달 내용이 출제된다.
2. 일상 생활에서 사용되는 구어체가 등장하며, 대화 맥락상 특정 문장의 의도를 묻는 의도 파악 문제가 반드시 포함된다.

기출 예제

대화 목적 용건 언급	**Sungmi Chung (9:24 A.M.)** Tony, Mr. Bukar is asking me for everybody's sales figures for July. They were due last week. When can you send me yours?
상황 발생	**Tony Valerio (9:30 A.M.)** Sorry about that. I've been out sick. I'm working on them now.
관련 피드백	**Sungmi Chung (9:35 A.M.)** Oh-I was not aware of that. Glad you're feeling better. ① Do you think you met your goals?
	Tony Valerio (9:40 A.M.) I can't tell. I'll get it to you by noon.
추가 전달 사항	**Sungmi Chung (9:45 A.M.)** Thanks. Overall, ② we did not sell as many cars as we did in previous months, possibly because many of our sales agents were on vacation.

대화의 주제 확인

초반에 언급되는 용건에서 대화의 주제와 인물 관계도가 드러난다.

의도 파악 문제 확인

앞뒤 문장을 통해 의미를 파악한다.
① "모르겠다"의 의미?
목표를 달성했는지 묻는 질문에 대한 대답

추가 전달 사항 확인

차를 많이 못 팔았다고 덧붙이는 말에서 두 사람의 직업을 알 수 있다.
② 정 씨에 대해 암시된 것?
지난달만큼 차를 많이 팔지 못했다는 말에서 알 수 있음

번역 **p. 070**

의도 파악   **Q1.** At **9:40 A.M.**, what does Mr. Valerio most likely mean when he writes, **"I can't tell"**?
A1. He is not sure if he reached his sales objectives.

9시 40분에 발레리오 씨가 "모르겠어요"라고 쓴 의도는 무엇이겠는가?
매출 목표에 도달했는지 알 수 없다.

패러프레이징 지문의 met your goals → 보기의 reached his sales objectives

추론   **Q2. What** is **suggested** about **Ms. Chung**?
A2. She works for a car dealership.

정 씨에 대해 암시되는 것은?
자동차 대리점에서 일한다.

정답이 보이는 단서 표현

동의 / 수락   의견, 제안, 요청에 대한 동의 / 수락의 표현이 출제된다.

Can you do me a favor? – Sure. / Of course.	부탁을 들어줄 수 있다.
Let me know if you need anything else. – Will do.	필요한 것이 있으면 알리겠다.
Let me know after you decide. – Absolutely!	결정되면 알리겠다.
Would you like to join us? – Sure thing.	함께하겠다.
Do you mind if I send them tomorrow? – That's OK.	내일 보내도 된다.
It really worked out well. – Good to hear.	잘 해결되었다니 다행이다.
Can you cover my shift this afternoon? – I'd be happy to.	근무를 대신해주겠다.
We can complete that on Monday morning. – Great.	월요일 아침에 끝낼 수 있다니 잘됐다.
Could we move it to 1 P.M. instead? – Even better.	1시로 옮기는 게 더 좋다.
I have forgotten my workplace ID tag. Can you let me in? – No problem. / Shouldn't be a problem.	들여보내줄 수 있다.
What about reserving the meeting room at 2 P.M.? – That would be better for me.	회의실 2시 예약이 더 좋다.
Why don't you come to my office this afternoon? – Sounds good.	사무실에 들를 수 있다.

의구심 / 부정 / 거절   동의하지 않음, 거절, 부정 등을 나타내는 표현도 출제된다.

Do you have a minute to look at this? - Sorry about that.	볼 시간이 없다.
Do you plan to try anything? – I don't know.	시도해 볼지 모르겠다.
I'd like to organize this first. – No need.	정리할 필요 없다.
Are you at the office by any chance? – Not yet.	아직 못 갔다.
Should I order some office supplies for you? – Don't bother.	사무용품을 주문하지 않아도 된다.

빈출 어휘

업무 / 회사 생활

reminder 상기시키는 것	fill in 대신하다	approve of ~을 찬성하다
document 서류, 문서	notify 알리다	security 보안
assist 돕다, 보조하다	urgent 긴급한	figure out 이해하다
contract 계약(서)	official 공식적인	quarterly 분기의
market 시장에 내놓다	release 출시	due ~하기로 되어 있는
supply 용품	demonstrate 시연하다	proofread 교정을 보다
state 진술하다	in-house 내부의	maintenance 유지
process 처리하다	hands-on 직접 해보는	accounting 회계
payment 결제	set up 준비하다	administrator 관리자
cover 대신하다	description 설명, 소개	temporary 임시의
arrange 주선하다	confidential 기밀의	hire 신입 사원

일상 생활

accidentally 우연히	in person 직접	pull in 차를 세우다
misplace 물건을 잃어버리다	run out of ~이 바닥나다	come up with ~을 생각해 내다
break down 고장 나다	set aside 따로 떼어 두다	follow up 후속 조치하다
recognize 알아보다	take a detour 우회하다	take turns 교대로 하다
participate in ~에 참여하다	be held up 지체되다	keep track of 계속 파악하다

Questions 1-2 refer to the following text-message chain.

난이도 ★☆☆

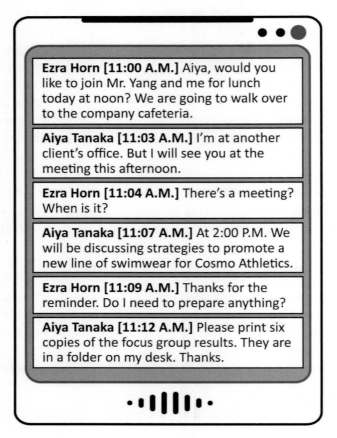

Ezra Horn [11:00 A.M.] Aiya, would you like to join Mr. Yang and me for lunch today at noon? We are going to walk over to the company cafeteria.

Aiya Tanaka [11:03 A.M.] I'm at another client's office. But I will see you at the meeting this afternoon.

Ezra Horn [11:04 A.M.] There's a meeting? When is it?

Aiya Tanaka [11:07 A.M.] At 2:00 P.M. We will be discussing strategies to promote a new line of swimwear for Cosmo Athletics.

Ezra Horn [11:09 A.M.] Thanks for the reminder. Do I need to prepare anything?

Aiya Tanaka [11:12 A.M.] Please print six copies of the focus group results. They are in a folder on my desk. Thanks.

1. At 11:03 A.M., what does Ms. Tanaka most likely mean when she writes, "I'm at another client's office"?
(A) She needs a document that she left on her desk.
(B) She cannot assist with a contract.
(C) She cannot accept an invitation.
(D) She went to the wrong building address.

2. What is indicated about an afternoon meeting?
(A) It will be moved to a larger conference room.
(B) It will focus on how to market a new product line.
(C) It will start earlier than originally scheduled.
(D) It will include a presentation by Mr. Yang.

Questions 3-4 refer to the following online chat discussion.

난이도 ★★☆

Live Chat

— □ X

Roger Varland (12:21 P.M.)
Hello. This is Kolpin Art Supply's 24-hour customer-support chat. My name is Roger. How can I help you?

Shaina Orbes (12:22 P.M.)
I have been waiting for four items I ordered online, and now I see that the order was canceled. I often order from Kolpin, and I've never had a problem before. Can you check my account?

Roger Varland (12:24 P.M.)
I'm bringing it up now. It states here that the credit card you have on file with us has expired, so we could not process the payment. If you log in to your customer account, you can update your payment information. Then you can click on your order number and the system will let you place the order again.

Shaina Orbes (12:26 P.M.)
I'll do that now. Thanks for your help!

3. Why did Ms. Orbes contact customer support?
   (A) An order did not arrive.
   (B) A product was damaged.
   (C) A package was sent by mistake.
   (D) An item is out of stock.

4. At 12:24 P.M., what does Mr. Varland most likely mean when he writes, "I'm bringing it up now"?
   (A) He is mentioning the problem to his supervisor.
   (B) He is helping Ms. Orbes create a new password.
   (C) He is applying a discount to some items.
   (D) He is looking at the details of Ms. Orbes' account.

Questions 5-6 refer to the following text-message chain.

 난이도 ★★☆

Melita Wilson [7:43 A.M.]
Unfortunately, my car broke down last night, and I won't be able to come into the office today.

Hong Zhang [7:44 A.M.]
Sorry to hear that, Melita. Is there anything important on your calendar?

Melita Wilson [7:45 A.M.]
Yes, I have an appointment today with Jing Qiwen from Adelaide Boot Manufacturers to discuss marketing strategies for next year. It's scheduled for 10:30 A.M.

Hong Zhang [7:46 A.M.]
That's an important client. We've been consulting for them for three years. Is there someone else who could cover that meeting for you, or should it be rescheduled?

Melita Wilson [7:48 A.M.]
Let's not reschedule it. It wasn't very easy to arrange. My assistant, Benjamin Kenney, has been closely involved in my work for this client, so he could fill in for me.

Hong Zhang [7:50 A.M.]
Sounds good. I'll notify Benjamin now.

5. What is suggested about Ms. Wilson?
   (A) She is unable to attend a meeting.
   (B) She is Ms. Qiwen's boss.
   (C) She is a new business owner.
   (D) She does not have any urgent projects.

6. At 7:50 A.M., what does Mr. Zhang most likely mean when he writes, "Sounds good"?
   (A) He likes Ms. Wilson's proposed marketing idea.
   (B) He thinks Mr. Kenney would be a suitable replacement.
   (C) He agrees that Mr. Kenney should be promoted.
   (D) He believes that an appointment should be rescheduled.

Questions 7-10 refer to the following online chat discussion.

난이도 ★★★

JANE KOVAR [8:48 A.M.] Hi, Stan. It's official! Our new software product, the DT-3 "Inventory Manager", is set for release next month.

STAN MILTON [8:50 A.M.] Right on schedule! I'll need to train my sales staff on how to demonstrate it—soon.

JANE KOVAR [8:52 A.M.] Ah! Larry Huang, our most experienced in-house trainer, will give your team a hands-on presentation next week.

STAN MILTON [8:53 A.M.] But he works at headquarters. Would we train there?

JANE KOVAR [8:54 A.M.] No, he'll come here via company shuttle. We'll just need to put together a program schedule. Would next Tuesday or Wednesday work for your team?

STAN MILTON [8:55 A.M.] I'll send out a group e-mail now and see what people prefer.

JANE KOVAR [8:57 A.M.] Sure. Keep me posted and we'll talk more.

MIKE BEDFORD [9:46 A.M.] Hi, sorry. I logged on late. I got an e-mail titled "Training". Do we have a workshop today? I can attend...

STAN MILTON [9:48 A.M.] Oh, no. That e-mail is about hands-on training—for the DT-3.

MIKE BEDFORD [9:49 A.M.] Ah, good. When will we train? And how long is the training?

STAN MILTON [9:50 A.M.] We're still working on it.

JANE KOVAR [9:52 A.M.] Yes, I can set up whatever you need. And, for the whole sales team, here is the password (link) to view the DT-3's full product description. Remember—it's confidential for now.

STAN MILTON [9:53 A.M.] Okay, thanks a lot.

SEND

CHAPTER 2

UNIT 06

7. Who is Larry Huang?
   (A) A warehouse manager
   (B) A software designer
   (C) A training instructor
   (D) A company president

8. Why most likely did Mr. Bedford join the conversation?
   (A) To give details about a sales meeting
   (B) To thank others for organizing an event
   (C) To confirm he can be present at an event
   (D) To discuss a problem with an e-mail program

9. At 9:50 A.M., what does Mr. Milton mean he writes, "We're still working on it"?
   (A) A team member will be absent.
   (B) A product release will be delayed.
   (C) A schedule is not complete.
   (D) A payment was not received.

10. What does Ms. Kovar provide for the sales team?
    (A) A training manual
    (B) A client list
    (C) A contract
    (D) A password

Marina Müller   15:06
A tourist from your morning tour group said she accidentally left her sunglasses on your bus. She said she was sitting toward the back on the left side. Can you check to see if they are still there?

Vincent Dumont   15:07
No problem. We're in the middle of a hike right now, but I'll check as soon as I get back to the bus.

Marina Müller   15:07
Thanks. I'll let her know.

Vincent Dumont   15:43
I'm back. Do they have red frames with square lenses?

Marina Müller   15:45
Yes. That's the pair. If it's possible, she would like to collect them at our office tonight. Your tour ends at five, but we close at six. Can you make it back within an hour? I know you're a bit far away and there might be a lot of traffic.

Vincent Dumont   15:46
It's usually not that bad. If I'm running late, I'll let you know.

[I   ] [Send]

11. What problem does Ms. Müller mention?

(A) A hiking trail is closed.
(B) A visitor misplaced an item.
(C) A bus has broken down.
(D) A tour has been canceled.

12. At 15:46, what does Mr. Dumont imply when he writes, "It's usually not that bad"?

(A) People can finish the hike in one hour.
(B) The traffic is the worst on Friday.
(C) He thinks most people enjoy the tour.
(D) He can return to the office by six o'clock.

Questions 13-16 refer to the following online chat discussion.

난이도 ★★★

Julie Perlow (10:05 A.M.)
Hello, Zoe and Otis. I offered to pick up Mr. Sato at the train station at 1:00 P.M., but I'm feeling a little sick. Could either of you do it?

Otis Hawksworth (10:06 A.M.)
I would offer to help, but I need to be in a meeting starting at 1:30 P.M.

Julie Perlow (10:09 A.M.)
Is Mr. Sato going to the same meeting? If he is, then the meeting can't start without him anyway.

Otis Hawksworth (10:10 A.M.)
I don't think so. He's coming to town to attend all the interviews.

Zoe Bergdorf (10:11 A.M.)
I can pick him up. I will be coming back to the office after lunch and can pick him up on my way.

Julie Perlow (10:12 A.M.)
Oh, that's right, Otis. I had forgotten that we're looking to fill the salesperson position this week.

Julie Perlow (10:13 A.M.)
Perfect, Zoe. That would be very helpful.

Zoe Bergdorf (10:14 A.M.)
How will I recognize him? We've never met.

Julie Perlow (10:15 A.M.)
I'll send you his employee profile. It includes a photo.

Zoe Bergdorf (10:16 A.M.)
Thanks!

CHAPTER 2

UNIT 06

13. Why is Mr. Hawksworth unable to help Ms. Perlow?
(A) He will be in a meeting.
(B) He will be at the train station.
(C) He has never met Mr. Sato.
(D) He is not feeling well.

14. Why is Mr. Sato coming to town?
(A) To attend a meeting with Mr. Hawksworth
(B) To participate in interviews with candidates for a sales position
(C) To request a job promotion
(D) To eat lunch with Ms. Perlow

15. At 10:13 A.M., what does Ms. Perlow most likely mean when she writes, "Perfect, Zoe"?
(A) She is glad that Ms. Bergdorf will bring lunch back to the office.
(B) She believes that Ms. Bergdorf is the right candidate.
(C) She is looking forward to meeting Ms. Bergdorf later in the day.
(D) She approves of Ms. Bergdorf's plan to meet Mr. Sato at the station.

16. Why will Ms. Perlow send a photo of Mr. Sato to Ms. Bergdorf?
(A) So Ms. Bergdorf can add it to Mr. Sato's application
(B) So Ms. Bergdorf can update Mr. Sato's employee file
(C) So Ms. Bergdorf can send the photo to the security desk
(D) So Ms. Bergdorf can recognize Mr. Sato

119

난이도 ★★★

Marcus Pavone (12:40 P.M.) Hi Lara, can you e-mail me your notes from the sales meeting this morning?

Lara Niu (12:41 P.M.) Do you mind if I send them tomorrow? I'd like to organize them first.

Marcus Pavone (12:42 P.M.) No need. I'm sure I can figure them out.

Lara Niu (12:43 P.M.) OK. I'm finishing up at the cafeteria now, but I'll send them as soon as I get back to my desk.

Marcus Pavone (12:44 P.M.) Great. When will that be?

Lara Niu (12:45 P.M.) In about a quarter of an hour. What's the rush?

Marcus Pavone (12:46 P.M.) I need to review some of the data for my quarterly report. It's due this afternoon.

Lara Niu (12:47 P.M.) Oh, wow! I thought that wasn't due until next Monday.

Marcus Pavone (12:48 P.M.) It was, but Tyler Kelso moved up the deadline.

Lara Niu (12:49 P.M.) OK, I'll get the notes to you soon. Let me know if you'd like me to proofread the report before you present it.

Marcus Pavone (12:50 P.M.) Thank you! Will do.

17. Why does Mr. Pavone request Ms. Niu's notes?
(A) He lost the notes that he took himself.
(B) He was not happy with some sales data.
(C) He needs them for a report he is writing.
(D) He wants to know who attended the meeting.

18. At 12:42 P.M., what does Mr. Pavone most likely mean when he writes, "No need"?
(A) He has changed his mind about needing the notes.
(B) He cannot pick up the notes in person.
(C) He will work with notes that are unorganized.
(D) He prefers to wait for the notes until next Monday.

19. What is Ms. Niu most likely doing while texting?
(A) Eating lunch
(B) Attending a meeting
(C) Collecting data
(D) Reading a book

20. What does Ms. Niu offer to do?
(A) Check a report for errors
(B) Change a report's deadline
(C) Contact Mr. Kelso
(D) Deliver a letter for Mr. Pavone

Questions 21-24 refer to the following online chat discussion.

Rolanda Tapia (4:46 P.M.) Hi Enver. I don't know if you've heard that this afternoon, a water pipe broke on the third floor in the advertising department.

Enver Atay (4:47 P.M.) I hadn't heard. Has it been fixed?

Rolanda Tapia (4:48 P.M.) Maintenance says it'll take two or three days. The floor is covered with water up here, so six of us from advertising can't be at our regular desks until Friday. We're trying to find some open space. You have a few empty desks in the accounting department, right?

Enver Atay (4:49 P.M.) We do have an extra room with three desks in it. Your staff are all welcome here. Also, let me check with my department administrator, Garcelle, about whether three of you can use the conference room on our floor. I'll add her to this discussion.

Garcelle Benoit (4:51 P.M.) Hello Rolanda and Enver, I've looked at the conference room schedule for the next three days, and there's just one meeting scheduled there tomorrow morning.

Enver Atay (4:53 P.M.) I can hold the meeting in my office instead. I'll make the change to the meeting invitation when we're done here.

Rolanda Tapia (4:54 P.M.) Perfect. Garcelle, can I leave it to you to determine where to put each person from my department? I will contact IT about getting temporary laptops set up for them.

Enver Atay (4:55 P.M.) Let me know if you need anything else.

Garcelle Benoit (4:56 P.M.) Sure thing.

Rolanda Tapia (4:57 P.M.) Thank you both so much!

21. Why did Ms. Tapia write to Mr. Atay?
(A) To get information about his staff
(B) To ask him for help with a problem
(C) To let him know some work was completed
(D) To inform him about a meeting

22. What is suggested about Ms. Benoit?
(A) She works for the accounting department.
(B) She manages the IT department.
(C) She is a member of the maintenance team.
(D) She is Mr. Atay's client.

23. At 4:49 P.M., what does Mr. Atay most likely mean when he writes, "Your staff are all welcome here"?
(A) He is pleased that new hires have joined his department.
(B) Advertising personnel can use space in his department.
(C) He wants employees to join a tour.
(D) Some colleagues can help him finish a project.

24. What will Mr. Atay most likely do next?
(A) Arrange for his office to be cleaned
(B) Request a list of names
(C) Ask the IT department for new laptops
(D) Update a meeting location

기출 전략

1. 서로 관련이 있는 두 개의 지문이 시간 순서에 따라 제시되며, 총 5문항 중 1~2문항은 연계 문제로 출제된다.
2. 첫 번째 지문은 다 읽는 것이 유리하다. 단, 항목별 분류된 부분은 나중에 답을 찾을 때 읽도록 한다.

연계 문제 풀이 전략

이메일 + 전단

Dear Team,

I have attached a flyer for a lunchtime workshop taking place next week. This is part of a corporate initiative recently launched by our CEO. The first session conflicts with our weekly team meeting, → STEP 2 but you should be able to attend one of the other two. I think it would be worth your time.

Thank you,
Amarilia Santana
Director of Quality Assurance

STEP 1
질문의 키워드 잡기
산타나 씨 팀의 다음 회의는 언제?

STEP 2
키워드 단서 찾기
지문1에서 워크숍 첫 세션이 팀 회의와 겹친다는 말이 나온다.

STEP 3
지문 간의 단서 찾기
지문2에서 첫 세션이 9월 5일임을 알 수 있다.

STEP 4
정답 도출
두 지문의 정보를 조합해보면 정답은 9월 5일이다.

September Lunch & Learn Workshop

This month's workshop will help employees understanding the nuances of budgeting, investments, and long-term financial planning. In only 60 minutes, you can increase your financial acumen while enjoying lunch with your colleagues!

Instructor: Bai Shen is an investment consultant at DBH international.

<u>Upcoming Sessions</u> (all beginning at 12:30 P.M.):
Monday, September 5 → STEP 3
Tuesday, September 6
Thursday, September 8

To register for a session, please contact Nate Steffani (ext. 8571) in Human Resources.

번역 p.077

Q. **When** will Ms. Santana's team have its **next team meeting?** → STEP 1
   (A) On September 1
   (B) On September 5 → STEP 4
   (C) On September 6
   (D) On September 8

산타나 씨의 팀은 언제 다음 팀 회의를 할 것인가?
(A) 9월 1일
(B) 9월 5일
(C) 9월 6일
(D) 9월 8일

다음 지문을 읽고 질문의 정답을 고르세요.

From: Richard Baxter
To: Jessica Shire
Sent: Tuesday, November 12, 10:12 A.M.
Subject: Sales conference

Dear Jessica,

Thanks for agreeing to take my place at the annual marketing conference in Detroit next month. Some Korean clients will be in town that week, and I need to meet with them here in the New York office. When I attended the conference last year in Chicago, I found the experience to be very rewarding and I made many useful contacts. I've contacted our travel department and asked that your flight and hotel arrangements be made. Your flight will leave Philadelphia on Sunday, December 1 at 1 P.M. and arrive in Detroit at 4:45 P.M. Your flight, hotel, and car rental will be paid in advance by EBR Industries. There is an allowance to cover the cost of your meals, but you will not be reimbursed until you return. So be sure to save all of your receipts, and submit them to the accounts payable department when you return.

The schedule for the conference seminars is as follows: On Monday from 9:00 to 11:30 A.M. is Exhibit Marketing, and from 1:30 to 4:30 P.M. is Brand Marketing. On Tuesday from 9:00 to 11:30 A.M. is Internet Marketing, and from 1:30 to 4:30 P.M. is Target Marketing.

Have a great trip!
Richard

From: Jessica Shire
To: Richard Baxter
Sent: Wednesday, December 4, 2:11 P.M.
Subject: RE: Sales conference

Dear Richard,

I got back from the marketing conference late last night. Unfortunately, the Monday morning seminar was canceled due to poor attendance, but the other seminars took place as scheduled. I took very detailed notes and will have a full written report to you by the end of the week. I hope your meetings here went well. Thank you for giving me the opportunity to represent EBR's sales department at this conference.

Sincerely,
Jessica

Q. What seminar was canceled at the conference?
(A) Brand Marketing
(B) Internet Marketing
(C) Target Marketing
(D) Exhibit Marketing

Questions 1-5 refer to the following brochure and e-mail.

난이도 ★★☆

Norburg Community Center
Space for Rent

The newly refurbished Norburg Community Center (NCC) offers space for rent for business meetings and social events. See the following details.

Rooms	Cost per Hour	Capacity (seated/standing)
Meeting Room A	$75	20/44
Meeting Room B	$100	60/126
Dining Room	$120	40/84
Event Hall	$150	80/170

- Discounted rates are available for schools and charitable organizations.
- Rooms come with tables, chairs, microphones, and projectors.
- A $25 cancellation fee will be incurred if the reservation is canceled at least 30 days in advance of the reserved date. Cancellations made less than 30 days before the reserved date will incur a $50 fee. Submit cancellation requests to reservations@norburgcommunitycenter.org.

E-mail

From:	mari.reed@joycecochranefoundation.org
To:	reservations@norburgcommunitycenter.org
Date:	June 25
Subject:	Notice of cancellation

To Whom It May Concern at the NCC,

Due to unexpected expenses, the Joyce Cochrane Foundation (JCF) is unable to host its annual volunteer appreciation dinner at the NCC as planned. As such, we are canceling the reservation made for November 14. We regret any inconvenience this may cause you.

Our charity has held this event at the NCC for the last eight years and has consistently received excellent service. Since the NCC overlooks beautiful Lake Serenity, our festive gatherings have always had an extra dimension of elegance. We look forward to holding this event at your facility next year.

Sincerely,

Mari Reed
JCF President

1. What does the brochure suggest about the NCC?
   (A) It charges an extra fee for a projector.
   (B) It was recently renovated.
   (C) It is under new management.
   (D) It provides catering services.

2. What is included in the cost of renting space at the NCC?
   (A) Pre-event setup
   (B) Cleaning services
   (C) Use of food stations
   (D) Audiovisual equipment

3. What is suggested about the JCF?
   (A) It receives funds annually from the NCC.
   (B) It was eligible for a discount from the NCC.
   (C) It has existed for less than eight years.
   (D) It is currently recruiting volunteers.

4. According to the e-mail, why must the JCF cancel its reservation?
   (A) It needs a larger space.
   (B) It has some unforeseen costs.
   (C) Its volunteers have requested an unusual menu.
   (D) Its members prefer a different location.

5. How much will the JCF have to pay as a cancellation fee?
   (A) $25
   (B) $50
   (C) $75
   (D) $100

Interstate Maritime Agency (IMA)

Home	About	Services	News	**Opportunities**

Internship Program

IMA recruits interns throughout the year. At this time, IMA's accounting, communications, and marine engineering departments are seeking interns. To qualify for an internship, applicants must:
- be in their final year of university study;
- complete an application;
- submit a résumé; and
- submit a letter of support from one of their university instructors.

Interns contribute to ongoing projects alongside IMA professionals. Interns are expected to meet scheduled deadlines, successfully collaborate with department colleagues, and work independently.

Applications can be downloaded from www.ima.ti/applications. Send all materials to Mr. Ramesh Nayak, Career Development Supervisor, IMA, 11 Sulon Road, Tankai Islands, TI442Z. Note: The selection process may take up to two months as all applications are carefully reviewed by an internal committee. Applications are retained in the IMA database for one year from the date received.

To:	Project managers
From:	Amy Perino
Date:	15 July
Subject:	For our next meeting
Attachment:	📎 Villalobos letter of interest

Hi everyone,

Starting 1 September, Alicia Villalobos will be joining us as an intern. Alicia, who has a strong command of the Spanish language, will be providing translation services in addition to performing other duties for our department. Please read the attached letter of interest she submitted with her internship application. Be ready, during our 1 August meeting, to discuss how we can best utilize Alicia's skills during the four months she will be with us. Soon after the meeting, I would like to let Alicia know which of our projects she can expect to work on.

Thanks,

Amy Perino
Director, Communications Department

6. According to the information, what must interns be able to do?
   (A) Use accounting software
   (B) Write reports in Spanish
   (C) Work as part of a team
   (D) Maintain a full-time work schedule

7. What is indicated about the internship applications?
   (A) They are saved in a database for up to two months.
   (B) They are read by a panel of IMA employees.
   (C) They must be submitted on the IMA Web site.
   (D) They must be accompanied by the applicants' work samples.

8. What is the purpose of the e-mail?
   (A) To ask managers to submit project proposals to Mr. Nayak
   (B) To announce changes in Ms. Perino's office hours
   (C) To note that a meeting for managers has been postponed
   (D) To request help in assigning work to a temporary staff member

9. In the e-mail, the word "command" in paragraph 1, line 2, is closest in meaning to
   (A) respect
   (B) mastery
   (C) instruction
   (D) appreciation

10. What is suggested about Ms. Villalobos?
    (A) She has been contracted to work at IMA for one year.
    (B) She was asked to resubmit her application materials.
    (C) She is currently a university student.
    (D) She is seeking an engineering position.

Archives of T.E. Haas on Display

DALLAS (May 2)—The archives of fiction writer T.E. Haas are now available for research at the Drayton Center, a humanities research library located at 23 Wye Street. The archives, which fill more than 140 boxes, are being housed in the Monmouth Room of the library. The bulk of the documents, which include all of his major writings and even some original handwritten copies of his earlier books, trace Haas's life and career. The archives also include character notes, story ideas, and publicity materials from the several films that were based on his works.

"T.E. Haas is one of the country's most respected writers," said Drayton Center staff member Evelyn Brownell. "His twenty-five novels and three volumes of short stories have been a treasure to literary students for many decades. In making the Haas papers available to researchers, the Drayton Center has created an exciting opportunity for students of contemporary literary studies."

The Drayton Center provides access to manuscripts, rare books, visual materials, and other documents for research purposes only. New patrons must stop at the reception desk to read and sign the Drayton Center regulations. They must also visit the second floor, where they will view a short video presentation about using the facility and handling materials. The Drayton Center is open Monday–Friday, 9:00 A.M.–5:00 P.M.

Drayton Center

Membership Regulations Agreement

Welcome to the Drayton Center. In order to provide an environment conducive to research, to preserve the collections, and to ensure ongoing access to them, patrons are expected to respect the regulations concerning use of library materials. Please read the attached document in its entirety and confirm your acceptance of the Drayton Center's regulations by signing at the bottom of the page. Submit this form at the reception desk along with a valid form of identification to obtain a one-year membership card. Please note that the Drayton Center does not allow materials to be removed from the center. All bags are subject to search when patrons exit the library.

I have read and accept the terms and conditions to use Drayton Center materials.

Date: _April 22_

Name: _Jeremy kweller_

Signature: _Jeremy kweller_

11. According to the article, what are visitors able to do at the Drayton Center?

(A) Learn how to archive materials

(B) Attend a writing workshop

(C) Listen to a lecture by a popular author

(D) View a collection of writings

12. What is NOT mentioned about T.E. Haas?

(A) He will be presenting his newest work in May.

(B) He produced handwritten copies of some of his works.

(C) He is admired by many people.

(D) He wrote several books of short stories.

13. Who is Ms. Brownell?

(A) An author

(B) A researcher

(C) A filmmaker

(D) A library employee

14. What is indicated about the Drayton Center?

(A) It is updating its policies.

(B) It is seeking new materials.

(C) It is available to researchers only.

(D) It is expanding its storage space.

15. What is Mr. Kweller required to do?

(A) Pay a membership fee

(B) Watch an informational video

(C) Provide a sample of his work

(D) Renew the materials he checked out

Water and Sewerage Authority of Antigua & Barbuda
PUBLIC NOTICE

On 4 March, the Water and Sewerage Authority of Antigua & Barbuda (WASAAB) will begin Phase 3 of the Sewerage Improvement Project (SIP) for the city of Saint John's. The aim of the project is to allow for more effective wastewater management within the city.

Over the next several months, existing sewer pipes will be replaced by new ones in the city's central business district. This work will require that a number of streets be closed to the public. Detour signs will be posted to guide motorists around the affected area. On 25 February, a timetable detailing specific street closures will be published in all local newspapers. Throughout the duration of Phase 3, this timetable will also be available on the agency's Web site at www.wasaab.gov.ag/sipp3.

While Phase 3 is scheduled to be completed by 31 May, WASAAB will make every effort to complete this phase prior to the specified deadline. Be advised, however, that the deadline may have to be pushed back should unanticipated circumstances arise.

We appreciate your patience and understanding as we complete these necessary improvements that will benefit all residents of Saint John's. If you have any questions or concerns please contact Mr. Lennox Codrington, Public Relations Officer, at 555-0139 or by e-mail at lcodrington@wasaab.gov.ag.

---

http://www.abputrans.com.ag

| About Us | Routes | **Alerts & Advisories** | Contact Us |

ABPUTRANS
Antigua & Barbuda Public Transit Service
Bus Stop Relocation

The last in the series of temporary bus stop relocations announced by ABPUTRANS in February will take effect beginning 10 June. These relocations are the result of the work being done on Phase 3 of the Saint John's Sewerage Improvement Project (SIP). The stops that will be affected are located along Bloomfield Road, between Plymouth Street and Sandalwood Lane. As of 10 June, riders who wish to board bus lines 18, 24, and 27 in the area affected should now do so along Frederick Road between Calabash Avenue and Shady Pines Lane. The temporary bus stops will be marked with bright yellow signs carrying the ABPUTRANS logo. While this measure is scheduled to be in effect through the end of June, riders are encouraged to check for the latest updates at www.abputrans.com.ag.

16. Why was the notice issued?
   (A) To address questions about a city's wastewater management
   (B) To alert the public to upcoming road closures
   (C) To inform the public about a project's approval
   (D) To invite comments on a community project

17. What is NOT indicated about Bloomfield Road?
   (A) It will be partially inaccessible to the public.
   (B) It is located in the city's business section.
   (C) It was recently introduced as a bus route.
   (D) It is used by multiple bus lines.

18. What is suggested about phase 3 of the Sewerage Improvement Project?
   (A) It involved the construction of new streets.
   (B) It was criticized by the public.
   (C) It was not widely publicized.
   (D) It was not completed as originally scheduled.

19. Where will temporary bus stops be placed?
   (A) On Calabash Avenue
   (B) On Frederick Road
   (C) On Plymouth Street
   (D) On Sandalwood Lane

20. What is supposed to happen in July?
   (A) ABPUTRANS will redesign its Web site.
   (B) ABPUTRANS will introduce a new logo.
   (C) Some buses will return to their regular route.
   (D) Some temporary bus stops will be installed.

Questions 21-25 refer to the following description and review.

난이도 ★★★

Rilker ECD-2 Cordless Drill

Rilker's ECD-2 Cordless Drill has always had plenty of power. It now boasts new and improved features that make it the most versatile drill in its price range. With the updated design of the ECD-2, you will feel confident tackling any home-improvement job, from the heaviest task to the most delicate. Take a look at these exclusive features:

Balanced Handle: The ECD-2's new ergonomic grip design features a nonslip surface and is shaped to fit your hand perfectly, minimizing fatigue.

Three Speed Settings: In addition to the previous high and low settings, there is an extra-low speed setting for precision work. All three speeds work in forward and reverse, making it easy to match the best speed and direction for each drilling task.

Fan-Cooled Motor: Rilker's patented fan-cooled system keeps the drill from overheating and decreases wear on the motor, greatly extending the drill's life.

Rechargeable Battery: Our rapid-charge 7.2-volt battery now takes only two hours to fully charge. With the ECD-2 you can return to your projects more quickly!

Customer Reviews

Online User Nathan Peltola; Detroit, MI   September 9, 10:21 A.M.
Customer Rating:  (four out of five stars)

My Rilker ECD drill finally stopped functioning after years of use. When I learned about the updated product two weeks ago, I purchased it right away. The price was very reasonable, and I can honestly say that I have never used a better drill. While completing several different carpentry projects, I was pleased to note that it works great for drilling into all kinds of wood. The handle on this new drill fits me much more comfortably, and my hand and wrist never get tired the way they did when I used the original model. I also like the slightly roomier storage case. If I have one complaint, it is that the redesigned motor with the fan is sometimes noisy and vibrates more than the motor in my previous drill. Overall though, the ECD-2 is an improvement to what was already a good product.

21. Where would the description most likely be found?

(A) In a directory of local businesses

(B) In a training manual for a carpentry class

(C) On a Web site for home-improvement Items

(D) In a brochure for a construction company

22. What is suggested about the ECD-2 drill?

(A) It has a unique cooling system.

(B) It is specially designed for professionals in the construction industry.

(C) It features a traditional style handle.

(D) Its price has never changed.

23. What is indicated about Mr. Peltola?

(A) He used to be a Rilker company associate.

(B) He owned a Rilker company product in the past.

(C) He returned a product for a refund.

(D) He recently built a house.

24. What new feature listed in the description does Mr. Peltola especially appreciate?

(A) The rapid-charge battery

(B) The improved storage case

(C) The nonslip handle

(D) The money-back guarantee

25. In the review, the word "model" in paragraph 1, line 7, is closest in meaning to

(A) pattern

(B) purpose

(C) example

(D) version

기출 전략

1. 서로 관련이 있는 세 개의 지문이 시간 순서에 따라 제시되며, 총 5문항 중 2문항이 연계 문제로 출제된다.
2. 세 개의 지문 중 두 개의 지문이 연계되며, 지문1 + 지문2, 지문2 + 지문3, 또는 지문1 + 지문3이 연계되는 문제가 출제된다.

연계 문제 풀이 전략

구인 광고 + 이메일 + 달력

Web Editor for *The Online Daily*

The Online Daily, a popular electronic publication, is seeking a Web editor. The position primarily requires that articles are checked to ensure that they adhere to grammar and style standards. A minimum of four years of editorial experience is expected.

Hello Ms. Choi,

Thank you for your interest in the Web editor position with *The Online Daily*. We would like to invite you to begin our interview process. We require that prospective hires download and complete the editing assessment on our Web site, www.theonlinedaily.com, and send it back to us by Wednesday, June 27.

Thank you.
Chelsea Trax

Name: Ana Choi		Month: June
24	Sunday	Mail three résumés
25	Monday	Start editing assessment
26	Tuesday	Submit editing assessment
27	Wednesday	Make vacation travel plans
28	Thursday	10:00: Car mechanic appointment
29	Friday	Follow-up with Ms. Trax

연계 문제 1

지문 1: 첫 번째 지문은 다 읽는 것이 좋으므로 우선 지문 1을 읽는다. 웹에디터 구인 광고이며, 최소 4년의 편집 경력이 기대된다는 내용이 나온다.

지문 2: 이메일 처음 두 문장에서 최씨가 지원했음을 알 수 있다.

→ 정답: 편집 관련 경력이 있음

연계 문제 2

지문 2: 이메일 후반부에 편집 능력 평가를 완료하여 6월 27일 수요일까지 보내라는 요청이 나온다.

지문 3: 달력을 보면 최 씨가 26일 화요일에 편집 능력 평가를 제출한다고 메모한 것을 볼 수 있다.

→ 정답: 마감일인 수요일 하루 전

번역 p. 085

---

1. **What** is **suggested** about **Ms. Choi**?

   (A) She has several years of relevant work experience.
   (B) She started her own online publication.
   (C) She has worked with Ms. Trax previously.
   (D) She prefers telecommuting to working on-site.

   최 씨에 대해 암시된 것은?
   (A) 몇 년간의 관련 업무 경력이 있다.
   (B) 온라인 출판을 직접 시작했다.
   (C) 이전에 트랙스 씨와 일한 적이 있다.
   (D) 현장 근무보다 재택근무를 선호한다.

2. **When** does **Ms. Choi** plan to **finish a required test**?

   (A) Three days before the deadline
   (B) Two days before the deadline
   (C) One day before the deadline
   (D) The same day as the deadline

   최 씨는 요구받은 테스트를 언제 끝낼 계획인가?
   (A) 마감 3일 전
   (B) 마감 2일 전
   (C) 마감 1일 전
   (D) 마감일

다음 지문을 읽고 질문의 정답을 고르세요.

Dear Ms. Herrera,

It was a pleasure meeting you and having the opportunity to show you some of our rental apartment listings. I'm sending you this e-mail just to mention a couple of important things as we move forward.

I have assigned a senior rental agent, Lisa Lepke (lisa@altafinders.com), to work with you on your search. Please feel free to contact her at 555-0143 if you have any questions at any time. I hope you've had the chance to look at the marketing flyer I gave you for the Sunmard Building. It currently has several vacant units. Thanks to an agreement with the building's property management company, my agency has exclusive authorization to lease their apartments. We can arrange viewings at any time.

I passed on your basic requirements to Ms. Lepke, noting that your maximum rental budget is $1,700 a month and that you prefer the largest unit available with a view of Sidell Park.

Once again, we look forward to working with you.

Ted Munson
Owner/manager, Alta Finders Co.

Live in the Sunmard Building

☞ Located in the city's historical theater district, just north of the downtown core, the Sunmard Building offers a variety of great living options. Residents can take in panoramic views across the city in any of the building's affordable apartments. Amenities include:

- New refrigerators and electric ovens in all units
- Private on-site gym – free for all tenants
- Spacious balconies and large hall closets

☞ The Sunmard Building is managed by Bacci Property Ltd. Visit us at www.bacciproperty.com.

This list of vacancies in the Sunmard Building has been generated for: <u>Ms. Dina Herrera</u>

#1170 1 bedroom unit facing east (downtown view), $1,675/month   Size: 677 square feet
#1432 Large studio facing south (riverside view), $1,575/month   Size: 524 square feet
#1214 1-bedroom unit facing west (view of Sidell Park), $1,775/month   Size: 636 square feet
#1502 1-bedroom unit facing west (view of Sidell Park), $1,690/month   Size: 611 square feet

---

1. What most likely is true about Bacci Property Ltd.?

(A) It rents spaces through Mr. Munson's company.
(B) It manages both commercial and residential properties.
(C) It was founded by Lisa Lepke.
(D) It plans to merge with another company.

2. What unit most likely would fit Ms. Herrera's requirements?

(A) #1170
(B) #1214
(C) #1432
(D) #1502

Questions 1-5 refer to the following brochure, card, and schedule.

난이도 ★★☆

Jewel Fitness Club

Jewel Fitness Club—New Member Special

❖ Basic Card–$20 per month
❖ Gold Card–$30 per month

You will find everything you want for your health and fitness regimen at Jewel Fitness Club. At all locations, we offer a complete array of workout equipment, fitness classes for all levels, and a full-size indoor swimming pool.

Jewel Fitness Club, a family-owned-and-operated business, is proud to have top-notch physical trainers on staff, customized fitness programs, and a full program of group classes. Our instructors must have at least five years of fitness industry experience before they are hired.

As a Basic Card member, you enjoy full access to exercise machines and equipment and group exercise classes. In our reception area every morning, you can find a selection of complimentary beverages until 11:00 A.M.

Gold Card members can take additional advantage of discounts on personal training sessions. They also have access to our indoor pool from 9:00 A.M. to 9:00 P.M., seven days a week.

To become a member of Jewel Fitness Club, visit our main location at 821 Duggan Boulevard, Old City, Montreal. Members must be 18 or older to join.

Jewel Fitness Club

Name: Joan Stanford
Jewel Fitness Club Member: 20256
Membership Type: Gold, Annual
Effective Date: September 15

Jewel Fitness Club

Duggan Boulevard branch
Class Schedule for Monday, October 1

Reminder: Classes are capped at fifteen participants.

Monday, October 1	Class	Instructor
7:30 A.M.	Aerobics for Beginners	Youhua D.
9:00 A.M.	Weightlifting	Annie P.
5:00 P.M.	Dance Cardio Workout	Antoine G.
6:30 P.M.	Aerobics Level 2	Sarah J.
7:00 P.M.	Chair Yoga and Gentle Stretch	Mark T.

1. What is suggested about Jewel Fitness Club?
   (A) It is introducing new classes to the schedule.
   (B) It is a national corporation.
   (C) It wants to increase its clientele.
   (D) It is expanding its branch locations.

2. According to the brochure, what is required of members?
   (A) They must attend at least two classes per week.
   (B) They must be at least eighteen years of age.
   (C) They must pay a one-time registration fee.
   (D) They must have approval to exercise from a doctor's office.

3. What membership benefit is available to Ms. Stanford?
   (A) A designated free parking area
   (B) Daily use of a swimming pool
   (C) Access to an open-air workout area
   (D) Free passes for guests

4. What is most likely true about the instructor named Sarah J.?
   (A) She has over five years of professional experience.
   (B) She is leading a beginner-level class.
   (C) She holds classes at more than one branch location.
   (D) She has recently been hired.

5. What is indicated on the schedule?
   (A) All classes cost an additional fee.
   (B) Some classes have been canceled.
   (C) Each class is offered twice during the day.
   (D) Two levels of difficulty are available for one of the classes.

To:　　All Employees
From:　Human Resources
Date:　10 September
Subject: Policy update

Free-and-Clear Accounting Employee Handbook

No-Gift Policy

To ensure fair and impartial treatment of all persons and organizations that employees have contact with, all employees of Free-and-Clear Accounting must abide by the following no-gift policy.

No gifts of any kind—no matter the value—offered by current or potential vendors, suppliers, or customers shall be accepted by any employee, at any time, on or off the work premises.

Examples of gifts include small items such as pens, hats, T-shirts, and key chains as well as items of greater value. This no-gift policy also applies to food or beverages. However, employees may use a company credit card to pay for a client's meal during a business meeting. Please direct any questions to Human Resources.

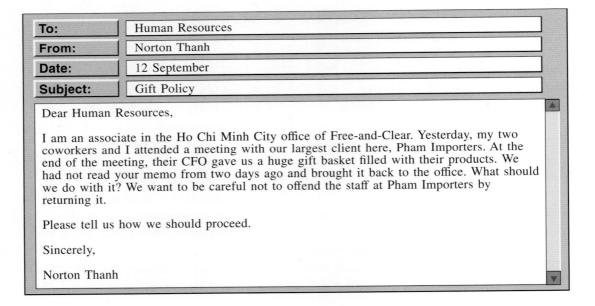

To:	Human Resources
From:	Norton Thanh
Date:	12 September
Subject:	Gift Policy

Dear Human Resources,

I am an associate in the Ho Chi Minh City office of Free-and-Clear. Yesterday, my two coworkers and I attended a meeting with our largest client here, Pham Importers. At the end of the meeting, their CFO gave us a huge gift basket filled with their products. We had not read your memo from two days ago and brought it back to the office. What should we do with it? We want to be careful not to offend the staff at Pham Importers by returning it.

Please tell us how we should proceed.

Sincerely,

Norton Thanh

15 September

Dear Mr. Thanh,

I had never heard of your company, so I was very surprised when your gift basket arrived. Then I saw the note you enclosed, explaining your predicament. I am sorry you could not keep it yourselves, but I can assure you that our residents are enjoying the fancy French and Italian food items very much.

Thank you for your thoughtfulness.

Sincerely,

Hanna Diep
Director, Golden Lotus Home for the Aged

6. What does the memo indicate about Free-and-Clear Accounting employees?
   (A) They are seeking new vendors and suppliers.
   (B) They must follow a dress code.
   (C) They often provide pens and key chains to clients.
   (D) They may take clients out to eat.

7. What is implied about Mr. Thanh?
   (A) He recently moved to Ho Chi Minh City.
   (B) He was unaware of a policy change.
   (C) He is the CFO of a company.
   (D) He sent a memo to all employees.

8. What is suggested about Pham Importers?
   (A) It has an office in Ho Chi Minh City.
   (B) It is a new client of Free-and-Clear Accounting.
   (C) It has locations in other countries.
   (D) It is the largest importer in the city.

9. What is the purpose of the card?
   (A) To request a service
   (B) To order food
   (C) To advertise a business
   (D) To express gratitude

10. What does Pham Importers most likely sell?
    (A) International foods
    (B) Greeting cards
    (C) Office supplies
    (D) T-shirts

Altadrive

10% OFF

Offer valid May 1–31 at the Encinitas location only on the following services:

1 – Oil change
2 – Brake repair
3 – Tire alignment
4 – Battery replacement

By appointment only. Schedule your service at www.altadrive.com/mayoffer.
Discount is in addition to 15%-off benefit for returning customers.

Open Monday to Friday, 7:00 A.M. to 6:00 P.M., Saturday, 7:00 A.M. to 5:00 P.M.

Altadrive

323 Main Street, Encinitas, CA 92024

(760) 555-0145

Name:	Kevin Kivelson	**Car Make:**	Netukar
Address:	137 Sagebrush Road	**Model:**	Speedy
	San Pedro, CA 92007	**Color:**	Silver

May 25

• Oil change	$35.00	
• Brake repair	$400.00	
Subtotal	$435.00	
10% discount	–$43.50	(coupon)
15% discount	–$65.25	(thank you!)
	$326.25	
• Patch tire	$25.00	
TOTAL	**$351.25**	

Technician's Notes: Customer reported that the tire pressure light was on. We found the customer's passenger-side front tire had a piece of metal lodged in it, which caused the tire to leak air. We removed the piece of metal, patched the tire, and reset the tire pressure light.

Schedule an appointment for June to enjoy discounts on windshield wiper replacements and air-conditioning service!

Altadrive

Customer Satisfaction Survey

Thank you for your recent visit to Altadrive. We love hearing from our customers! Please rate your service on the following, with 1 being "poor" and 5 being "excellent."

	1	2	3	4	5
Team knowledge					X
Team courtesy					X
Service speed					X
Service value					X

Any additional comments?

Thank you for the great service overall! The coupon made this service worth it. I brought my car in for service the day before a national holiday and you weren't fully staffed, but you still provided same-day service—and finished at 6:30 P.M. that day. I had scheduled only an oil change and brake repair, but my tire pressure light was on, and you managed to take care of that issue, too. Your waiting room is very comfortable and well lit, and I appreciated the complimentary refreshments. However, my favorite feature was the high tables, which made it easy for me to set up my laptop and get work done. Best of all, I was able to leave for my vacation the next morning.

Kevin Kivelson

11. What is suggested about Mr. Kivelson?

(A) He paid cash for his service repairs.

(B) He replaced his windshield wipers.

(C) He lives in the same town as Altadrive.

(D) He previously visited Altadrive.

12. According to the receipt, what problem did the technician find?

(A) A piece of metal was stuck in a tire.

(B) A leak was the result of a faulty tire patch.

(C) The tire pressure light was broken.

(D) Several tires needed to be replaced.

13. What does Altadrive indicate about air-conditioning service?

(A) It was recommended to Mr. Kivelson by a technician.

(B) It should be scheduled once a year.

(C) It will be discounted in June.

(D) It should be done regularly in Speedy models.

14. What feature of the waiting room does Mr. Kivelson like best?

(A) The beverages

(B) The tables

(C) The lighting

(D) The chairs

15. What is suggested about Mr. Kivelson's car repair?

(A) It was more expensive than he had anticipated.

(B) It was scheduled for early in the morning.

(C) It was done on a national holiday.

(D) It was completed after business hours.

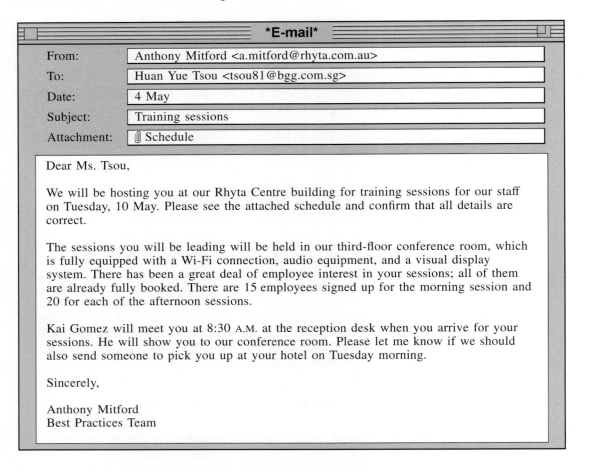

E-mail

From:	Anthony Mitford <a.mitford@rhyta.com.au>
To:	Huan Yue Tsou <tsou81@bgg.com.sg>
Date:	4 May
Subject:	Training sessions
Attachment:	📎 Schedule

Dear Ms. Tsou,

We will be hosting you at our Rhyta Centre building for training sessions for our staff on Tuesday, 10 May. Please see the attached schedule and confirm that all details are correct.

The sessions you will be leading will be held in our third-floor conference room, which is fully equipped with a Wi-Fi connection, audio equipment, and a visual display system. There has been a great deal of employee interest in your sessions; all of them are already fully booked. There are 15 employees signed up for the morning session and 20 for each of the afternoon sessions.

Kai Gomez will meet you at 8:30 A.M. at the reception desk when you arrive for your sessions. He will show you to our conference room. Please let me know if we should also send someone to pick you up at your hotel on Tuesday morning.

Sincerely,

Anthony Mitford
Best Practices Team

Training Schedule - Tuesday, 10 May
Huan Yue Tsou (BGG Solutions)

9:00–10:00 A.M.	Breakfast
10:00–Noon	"Selling Your Product Without Selling It: Ten Strategies for Using Social Media"
Noon–1:00 P.M.	Lunch
1:00–3:00 P.M.	"The Art of the Pitch: How to Describe Your Product in One Minute"
3:00–3:30 P.M.	Break
3:30–5:30 P.M.	"Managing Customer Expectations: How to Talk About Your Product's Limitations"
5:30–6:00 P.M.	Wrap up

```
┌─────────────────────────────────────────────────────────────────┐
│  *E-mail*                                                         │
├─────────────────────────────────────────────────────────────────┤
│  From:   Huan Yue Tsou <tsou81@bgg.com.sg>                        │
│  To:     Anthony Mitford <a.mitford@rhyta.com.au>                 │
│  Date:   5 May                                                    │
│  Re:     Training sessions                                        │
└─────────────────────────────────────────────────────────────────┘
```

Dear Mr. Mitford,

Thank you for the information. The schedule looks good to me, and I will arrive at 8:30 A.M. as requested. I will be glad of the extra time before the start of the first session to familiarize myself with your equipment. I plan to drive myself to your location in my own rental, so I will not need to be picked up. But could the employee who is planning to meet me at your building that morning please assist by printing out some handouts for me?

Best regards,

Huan Yue Tsou

16. What does Mr. Mitford mention about the upcoming training sessions?

(A) There is no more space for additional attendees.

(B) Participants will need to bring some materials with them.

(C) Some staff members have registered for multiple sessions.

(D) A computer workstation will be provided for each participant.

17. What is indicated about Ms. Tsou?

(A) She will train staff at Mr. Mitford's workplace.

(B) She has previously visited the Rhyta Centre building.

(C) She will colead a workshop with Mr. Mitford.

(D) She has been hired to provide technical support.

18. What is the main topic that will be addressed during the sessions?

(A) Legal issues

(B) Safety systems

(C) Sales techniques

(D) Management practices

19. How many people will attend the session about social media?

(A) 10

(B) 15

(C) 20

(D) 25

20. What will Mr. Gomez most likely do?

(A) Create copies of documents

(B) Arrange some transportation

(C) Arrive earlier than planned

(D) Change the start time of a session

Bartowsky Manufacturing ◈

Production Trial-Run Schedule

Product: <u>Guadiana Office Chair</u>

Date	Activity
Sunday 8 July	• David Mateja arrives in Biłgoraj
Monday 9 July	• Preproduction setup of machinery • Calibrating and adjusting equipment to designated specifications
Tuesday 10 July	• Production and assembly of parts
Wednesday 11 July	• Durability tests (weight, resistance, and material quality)
Thursday 12 July	• David Mateja departs for Bratislava

From:	dmateja@nostilde.sk
To:	thammond@nostilde.it
Subject:	Guadiana trial run
Date:	13 July

Dear Ms. Hammond,

I have an update about the Guadiana trial run at Bartowsky Manufacturing. I am happy to report that the factory is capable of manufacturing the chairs per our design specifications, and the estimated production costs suggest that this would be a viable partnership.

On Monday, I supervised the calibration of the equipment, and the next day, during the trial run, I noticed that the paint that was used to coat the metal elements did not meet our specifications. They were recoated immediately with the correct paint after I pointed out the problem. There were no other issues. The chair was tested on Wednesday and passed all tests.

Today, I discussed our production schedule by telephone with Martin Havranec, explaining that our distribution policy requires that the chairs be available at all retail locations on the release date. He assured me that Bartowsky Manufacturing was prepared to make a significant investment in order to meet our deadline.

David Mateja

Polish Firm Wins Nostilde Contract

22 July–Bartowsky Manufacturing, based in Biłgoraj, Poland, has secured a contract to produce office chairs for the international furniture brand Nostilde.

Nostilde plans to deliver an estimated 200,000 chairs to all its stores in the European Union. This is the largest order in Bartowsky's history. In order to meet the demand, the company pledged to invest in additional equipment to increase the factory's production capacity.

"We've been contemplating a large-scale equipment purchase for a couple of years," explained Bartowsky Manufacturing president Martin Havranec. "We have the space and an available labour pool. Once the new equipment is in place, we will be able to put many skilled applicants to work immediately."

21. According to the schedule, what happened on July 9?

    (A) Specifications were printed.
    (B) Machines were adjusted.
    (C) Personnel were trained.
    (D) Quality was tested.

22. What does Mr. Mateja suggest about production costs?

    (A) They will be confirmed by Mr. Havranec.
    (B) They were difficult to negotiate.
    (C) They have been revised.
    (D) They are acceptable.

23. When did Mr. Mateja most likely request a change to meet specifications?

    (A) On July 8
    (B) On July 10
    (C) On July 11
    (D) On July 12

24. What was Mr. Mateja promised on July 13?

    (A) That Bartowsky Manufacturing would purchase additional production equipment
    (B) That expedited delivery would be available for some customers
    (C) That production of the Nostilde chairs would start immediately
    (D) That most materials would be sourced in Poland

25. What does Mr. Havranec suggest about Bartowsky Manufacturing?

    (A) It has produced items for Nostilde before.
    (B) It designed a chair exclusively for Nostilde.
    (C) It will easily find qualified workers.
    (D) It will repair a section of the factory.

PART

7

CHAPTER

3

ETS
실전 모의고사

ETS 실전 모의고사 1회
ETS 실전 모의고사 2회
ETS 실전 모의고사 3회
ETS 실전 모의고사 4회
ETS 실전 모의고사 5회

ETS 실전 모의고사 01

PART 7

Directions: In this part you will read a selection of texts, such as magazine and newspaper articles, e-mails, and instant messages. Each text or set of texts is followed by several questions. Select the best answer for each question and mark the letter (A), (B), (C), or (D) on your answer sheet.

Questions 147-148 refer to the following advertisement.

Next Step: Success!

The Merriweather Convention Hall

8 June, 9:00 A.M. – 4:00 P.M.

Meet with human resources representatives!

Highlights

- Free admission
- Open positions with over 300 companies
- Résumé-writing help by appointment (a small fee applies)
- Professional placement services available
- Lectures and discussions on finding and keeping a job in today's competitive environment

Many different professions will be represented: office work, accounting, security, sales and marketing, shipping and receiving, and more.

147. What type of event is being publicized?

(A) A writing workshop
(B) An employment fair
(C) A computer networking seminar
(D) A human resources course

148. What is indicated about the event?

(A) It will take place over two days.
(B) It will be held at an office building.
(C) All activities and services are free of charge.
(D) Representatives from many companies will attend.

Go on to the next page

Questions 149-150 refer to the following text-message chain.

Serena Kitamura (7:15 P.M.)
Hi Alex, how did our colleagues do at Cycloquest today?

Alex Salinas (7:16 P.M.)
Well, Team Ridgeroad did great. Mika and Jonas tied for second in the downhill race, and Dylan came in third in cross-country. However, there were a few minor issues.

Serena Kitamura (7:16 P.M.)
Really? What happened?

Alex Salinas (7:17 P.M.)
Well, Mika had trouble with her brakes—we got them fixed before the next race. Besides that, Dylan pulled a muscle in his leg on one of the uphill climbs. He should be okay by tomorrow, though.

Serena Kitamura (7:18 P.M.)
Incidentally, this week we've seen a pretty significant bump in the online sales of our steel-frame bicycles. In fact, we sold over 30 units just today. I'm glad we at Ridgeroad Eagle decided to be a sponsor of this year's Cycloquest.

Alex Salinas (7:19 P.M.)
Yes, it really worked out well, didn't it?

149. What is Cycloquest?

(A) A corporate training program
(B) An exercise routine
(C) A sight-seeing tour
(D) A bicycle competition

150. At 7:19 P.M., what does Mr. Salinas most likely mean when he writes, "Yes, it really worked out well, didn't it"?

(A) The event has been enjoyable.
(B) The sponsorship has been successful.
(C) The group is in good physical shape.
(D) The sales team is trying hard.

14 February

Mr. Kurth Garibay
155 Cambridge Street
Tipperary E34 A039

RE: Case number 1253

Dear Mr. Garibay,

We sincerely regret the incident involving unapproved charges to your account.

As complaints like yours are ordinarily addressed by our Consumer Protection Department, I have turned over your case to Ms. Dina Legaspi. You can expect to receive a call from her within the next two business days.

Moreover, to prevent any further incidents, we have closed your account. You will be receiving a new account number as well as a new credit card within five to seven business days.

If at any time you need to contact us about your case, please use the case number found at the top of this letter.

Thank you for your continued business with Davao Bank.

Sincerely,

Armando Echeverria

Armando Echeverria
Accounts and Processing, Davao Bank

151. Why did the customer receive this letter?

(A) To report on a resolution to a problem
(B) To recommend adding security features
(C) To indicate that a policy has been updated
(D) To request that he visit the bank as soon as possible

152. What is suggested about Ms. Legaspi?

(A) She closed Mr. Garibay's account.
(B) She assigned Mr. Garibay a case number.
(C) She is in charge of issuing new credit cards.
(D) She works in the Consumer Protection Department.

Go on to the next page

Questions 153-154 refer to the following Web page.

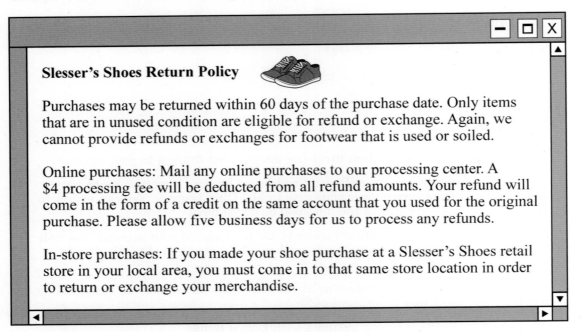

Slesser's Shoes Return Policy

Purchases may be returned within 60 days of the purchase date. Only items that are in unused condition are eligible for refund or exchange. Again, we cannot provide refunds or exchanges for footwear that is used or soiled.

Online purchases: Mail any online purchases to our processing center. A $4 processing fee will be deducted from all refund amounts. Your refund will come in the form of a credit on the same account that you used for the original purchase. Please allow five business days for us to process any refunds.

In-store purchases: If you made your shoe purchase at a Slesser's Shoes retail store in your local area, you must come in to that same store location in order to return or exchange your merchandise.

153. What is NOT stated in the return policy?

(A) A processing fee may be charged.
(B) Items must be returned within five days of purchase.
(C) A credit may be issued to the account charged.
(D) Items must be in new condition.

154. What is indicated about Slesser's Shoes?

(A) It sells footwear both online and at stores.
(B) It plans to update its Web page.
(C) It offers an overnight delivery option for orders.
(D) It sells its products in several countries.

FOR IMMEDIATE RELEASE

Media Contact: Layla Becker <lbecker@birdwingmedia.co.za>

PRETORIA (22 October) — [1] —. Birdwing Multimedia, one of the largest entertainment companies in South Africa and the producer of the hit movies *Night Rocket* and *The Beach of No Return*, made a surprising announcement on Wednesday. — [2] —. Jenetha Chikaonda, acting president, reported that company founder Frederick Vosloo was stepping down immediately from his position as president. Mr. Vosloo had hinted during an industry conference in March that he might retire within the year, but the timing of the announcement was unexpected. — [3] —. Ms. Chikaonda said that Mr. Vosloo wants to explore other avenues. She noted that Mr. Vosloo made his announcement as Birdwing Multimedia is preparing to move into its new headquarters in Cape Town next month. "With this change, the company is also ready for a change in leadership," she noted. — [4] —.

---

155. What is the subject of the press release?

(A) A new movie
(B) A promotion
(C) A retirement
(D) A conference

156. According to the press release, what will Birdwing Multimedia do in November?

(A) Host a leadership meeting
(B) Expand into other areas
(C) Relocate its headquarters
(D) Prepare for a merger

157. In which of the positions marked [1], [2], [3], and [4] does the following sentence best belong?

"Ms. Chikaonda will continue running Birdwing Multimedia until a new president is found."

(A) [1]
(B) [2]
(C) [3]
(D) [4]

E-mail

To:	All staff
From:	Gabriel Petrescu
Date:	Monday, May 3
Subject:	Important information

Dear staff:

I am happy to announce that we have found someone to fill our immediate need for a receptionist in our front office. Beginning today, Sina Ung will be joining our staff. Ms. Ung will be working three days a week on a temporary basis while we conduct a formal search for a permanent office receptionist.

Ms. Ung has extensive experience as a receptionist in the medical and pharmaceutical industries. Consequently, she is accustomed to answering busy phone lines, keeping track of appointments, and greeting visitors daily in a large office.

On Mondays, Tuesdays, and Wednesdays, Ms. Ung will be on duty at our reception desk during regular office hours, from 9:00 A.M. to 5:00 P.M. Until we hire a full-time receptionist, Ralph Nilsson will fill in on Thursdays. Jane Sim will fill in on the following day.

Please try to stop by our reception desk today to welcome Ms. Ung in person.

Gabriel Petrescu
Human Resources Manager

158. What is the purpose of the e-mail?

(A) To advertise a front office position
(B) To introduce a new employee
(C) To discuss a manager's duties
(D) To announce new office hours

159. The word "conduct" in paragraph 1, line 3, is closest in meaning to

(A) perform
(B) transport
(C) behave
(D) describe

160. Who will work at the reception desk on Fridays?

(A) Mr. Petrescu
(B) Ms. Ung
(C) Mr. Nilsson
(D) Ms. Sim

Canned Tomatoes Voluntary Recall Notice

September 25

Out of an abundance of caution, food production company Zeissmann Produce, Inc., is recalling some of its 28-ounce cans of diced tomatoes. This is a voluntary recall related to a defect in the structure of the cans. The problem was traced to a manufacturing defect. At this time, all affected cans have been removed from grocery store shelves.

We recommend that consumers check the code stamped on the bottom of 28-ounce cans of Zeissmann Produce, Inc., diced tomatoes to see if the product is affected by the recall. The product codes 803471 and 803472 are included in the recall. If you have a can with one of these codes, please return it to the original place of purchase for a refund. Additional information about the recall can be found on our Web site, www.zeissmannproduce.com/recall, or by calling 314-555-0183.

We apologize for any inconvenience this may cause you. We here at Zeissmann Produce, Inc., pride ourselves on the quality of our canned fruits, vegetables, and soups. Be assured that we are taking steps to prevent this from happening again.

Thank you for your loyalty.

Matilda Lim, CEO
Zeissmann Produce, Inc.

---

161. For whom is the notice intended?

(A) Grocery store clerks
(B) Grocery store owners
(C) Zeissmann Produce, Inc., employees
(D) Zeissmann Produce, Inc., customers

162. What is one action that Ms. Lim recommends?

(A) Returning a product for a refund
(B) Completing an online form
(C) Exchanging a product for another
(D) Contacting a customer service representative

163. What is mentioned about Zeissmann Produce, Inc.?

(A) It has a new Web site.
(B) It is an international company.
(C) Its products are organic.
(D) It sells canned soups.

Go on to the next page

CHAPTER 3

실전 모의고사 01

Questions 164-167 refer to the following e-mail.

To:	Leila Alizadeh
From:	Sara Kranmer
Date:	February 2
Subject:	Your request

Ms. Alizadeh,

I have made your business travel arrangements through May per your request. Your flight schedule is as follows.

March	Depart Boston March 1,11:20 A.M., Flight 23G Selangor Airlines	Arrive Kuala Lumpur March 2, 9:45 P.M.
	Depart Kuala Lumpur March 14, 2:20 P.M., Flight 54A, Selangor Airlines	Arrive Boston March 14, 5:25 P.M.
April	Depart Boston April 10, 11:55 A.M., Flight 3471, Rego Airlines	Arrive Beijing April 11,1:45 P.M.
	Depart Beijing April 22, 3:45 P.M., Flight 4498, Rego Airlines	Arrive Boston April 22, 5:30 P.M.
May	Depart Boston May 3, 6:40 A.M., Flight 117, Laurel Airlines	Arrive Philadelphia May 3, 8:10 A.M.
	Depart Philadelphia May 3, 8:55 P.M., Flight 109, Laurel Airlines	Arrive Boston May 3,10:15 P.M.

I can change any of the above flights through the travel agency without penalty until February 15. Regarding your return flight on March 14, you had requested that I book you a flight that leaves before noon. Unfortunately, there isn't one. The earliest flight I was able to book for you on that day departs at 2:20 P.M.

Finally, as we get closer to each of your travel dates, I will arrange your ground transportation to the airport.

Please let me know if this itinerary suits you.

Regards,
Sara Kranmer

164. Why did Ms. Kranmer write to Ms. Alizadeh?

(A) To suggest different dates for organizing a conference
(B) To provide an update on employees' vacation schedules
(C) To inform her of upcoming travel arrangements
(D) To remind her about changes to an airline policy

165. According to the schedule, when will Ms. Alizadeh take a one-day business trip?

(A) In February
(B) In March
(C) In April
(D) In May

166. From what city did Ms. Alizadeh want to leave before noon?

(A) Boston
(B) Kuala Lumpur
(C) Beijing
(D) Philadelphia

167. What is suggested about Ms. Alizadeh?

(A) She works at a travel agency.
(B) Her job is based in the Boston area.
(C) She is a preferred customer of Rego Airlines.
(D) Her assistant drives her to the airport.

Go on to the next page

Questions 168-171 refer to the following online chat discussion.

Lucy Pletsch (8:54 A.M.) Hello, everyone. Do you know anything about the time and location for Friday's management meeting?

Colleen Maeda (8:56 A.M.) It's at ten o'clock in Conference Room 6, as usual.

Lucy Pletsch (8:57 A.M.) Robert in Accounting told me that room is booked for a client meeting at that time.

Colleen Maeda (9:00 A.M.) Oh no! I have a slide presentation that requires use of the projector in that room. This is the second time this year Room 6 was double-booked. It's frustrating!

Lucy Pletsch (9:01 A.M.) Meeting space is at a premium around here. The only other spot I can think of is the cafeteria.

Colleen Maeda (9:02 A.M.) That can get noisy. And there are no projection capabilities, either. How about the corporate library?

Lucy Pletsch (9:03 A.M.) It's closed on Fridays during the summer.

Vincent Golding (9:04 A.M.) The employee break room? I can request a portable projector and screen from the audiovisual department.

Colleen Maeda (9:05 A.M.) Seating would be a bit tight.

Lucy Pletsch (9:06 A.M.) We can make that work.

---

168. Why did Ms. Pletsch start the online chat discussion?

(A) To request an alternate meeting time
(B) To inquire about a meeting location
(C) To report that some equipment has been repaired
(D) To request assistance from the audiovisual department

169. Where do the management meetings usually take place?

(A) In the library
(B) In the cafeteria
(C) In Conference Room 6
(D) In the employee break room

170. At 9:02 A.M., what does Ms. Maeda most likely mean when she writes, "That can get noisy"?

(A) There is a busy hallway near Conference Room 6.
(B) The management team is not usually quiet.
(C) The projector motor is very loud.
(D) It is hard to hear in the cafeteria.

171. What does Mr. Golding offer to do?

(A) Arrange to borrow some equipment
(B) Add some seats to the break room
(C) Update the agenda for a meeting
(D) Get a spare key to the library

Date: January 7
To: All new hires
From: Human Resources
Subject: Workshops

This is a reminder for all new hires regarding the HR workshop series. — [1] —. Please remember that attendance is mandatory. Workshops will be held on January 14, 16, and 18 in the large conference room on the third floor. — [2] —. An informal meet-and-greet breakfast will be served at 8:30 A.M., and sessions will run from 9:00 A.M. to 1:00 P.M., with a break for coffee and light refreshments between 10:45 A.M. and 11:15 A.M. — [3] —. Specific information about workshop topics will be sent to each of you shortly. — [4] —. The lunch hour starting at 1:00 P.M. will give new employees a chance to meet with their assigned mentors.

I look forward to seeing you all next week.

Francis Reggis, HR Manager

172. What is the purpose of the memo?

(A) To ask employees to submit their time sheets early
(B) To remind new employees about required training
(C) To recommend that mentors take some workshops
(D) To inform human resources staff about new policies

173. What is indicated about the workshop series?

(A) There will be time to socialize.
(B) There is an optional dinner.
(C) Instruction begins after lunch.
(D) Guest speakers will make presentations.

174. According to Mr. Reggis, what will recipients of the memo receive soon?

(A) Breakfast and lunch menus
(B) Agendas for mentoring sessions
(C) Detailed driving directions
(D) Details about workshop topics

175. In which of the positions marked [1], [2], [3], and [4] does the following sentence best belong?

"Look for signs pointing you to Conference Room C."

(A) [1]
(B) [2]
(C) [3]
(D) [4]

Go on to the next page

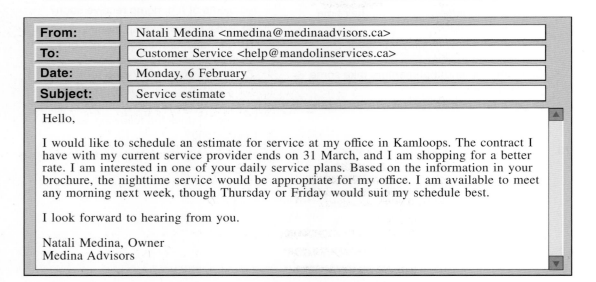

MANDOLIN SERVICES

Let us help you maintain a clean and inviting workspace that will impress your clients!

Our professionals can handle any office job. We specialise in removing dirt and grit from wood and tile floors. We also vacuum, empty garbage bins, dust and polish desks and chairs, and restock supplies. We will even replace light bulbs!

We offer a variety of service plans to accommodate your needs.

Mornings: For offices with medium traffic or that are infrequently visited by clients during regular Monday through Friday business hours. Recommended for offices with after-hours employees.

Nighttimes: For offices with heavy traffic and with regular client visits. Recommended for offices with tile floors (no carpeting or large area rugs) to allow for drying time after mopping.

Saturdays: For offices with low traffic or few client visits. Service can be scheduled on Saturday mornings or afternoons.

Please e-mail help@mandolinservices.ca or call us at (250) 555-0141 to schedule an estimate. The Mandolin Services team is ready to help you!

From:	Natali Medina <nmedina@medinaadvisors.ca>
To:	Customer Service <help@mandolinservices.ca>
Date:	Monday, 6 February
Subject:	Service estimate

Hello,

I would like to schedule an estimate for service at my office in Kamloops. The contract I have with my current service provider ends on 31 March, and I am shopping for a better rate. I am interested in one of your daily service plans. Based on the information in your brochure, the nighttime service would be appropriate for my office. I am available to meet any morning next week, though Thursday or Friday would suit my schedule best.

I look forward to hearing from you.

Natali Medina, Owner
Medina Advisors

176. What is NOT mentioned as receiving attention from the Mandolin Services team?

(A) Floors
(B) Furniture
(C) Windows
(D) Trash bins

177. What is indicated about Mandolin Services?

(A) It has won industry awards.
(B) It offers flexible scheduling.
(C) It is a family-operated business.
(D) It provides service seven days a week.

178. Why did Ms. Medina write the e-mail?

(A) She would like to reduce a service expense.
(B) She is unhappy with the quality of a current service.
(C) She learned that her service provider is going out of business.
(D) She is opening an office in a new town.

179. What is suggested about the office in Kamloops?

(A) It has carpeting.
(B) It has several rooms.
(C) It is scheduled to be renovated.
(D) It is regularly visited by clients.

180. In the e-mail, the word "suit" in paragraph 1, line 5, is closest in meaning to

(A) dress
(B) change
(C) fit
(D) describe

Go on to the next page

Questions 181-185 refer to the following article and e-mail.

DURBAN (4 August)—Home and Fashion Centre (HFC), the redesigned shopping plaza formerly known as the Northern Mall, features completely new stores. It boasts eight home-interior and clothing boutiques, a café, and an eight-screen cinema. The stores are all well known to online shoppers but have never had a physical location.

Cooper's Housewares, which is based in Johannesburg, is among the eight shops that have found a home at HFC. "We were filling so many orders from our online store that the choice to open a brick-and-mortar store here at HFC was obvious," said Denise Blay, vice president of marketing at Cooper's Housewares.

The stores at HFC are open from 9:30 A.M. to 8:30 P.M., Monday through Saturday, and from 12:30 P.M. to 5 P.M. on Sunday. The cinema is open from 10 A.M. to 11 P.M., seven days a week.

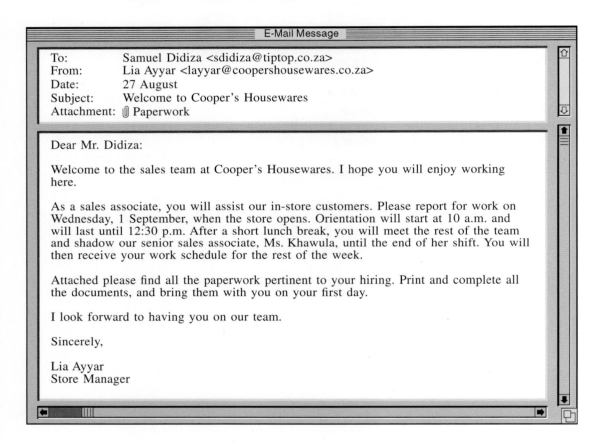

E-Mail Message

To: Samuel Didiza <sdidiza@tiptop.co.za>
From: Lia Ayyar <layyar@coopershousewares.co.za>
Date: 27 August
Subject: Welcome to Cooper's Housewares
Attachment: Paperwork

Dear Mr. Didiza:

Welcome to the sales team at Cooper's Housewares. I hope you will enjoy working here.

As a sales associate, you will assist our in-store customers. Please report for work on Wednesday, 1 September, when the store opens. Orientation will start at 10 a.m. and will last until 12:30 p.m. After a short lunch break, you will meet the rest of the team and shadow our senior sales associate, Ms. Khawula, until the end of her shift. You will then receive your work schedule for the rest of the week.

Attached please find all the paperwork pertinent to your hiring. Print and complete all the documents, and bring them with you on your first day.

I look forward to having you on our team.

Sincerely,

Lia Ayyar
Store Manager

181. What is one purpose of the article?

 (A) To list the stores available at a
 shopping mall
 (B) To highlight Durban's various shopping
 areas
 (C) To describe the items sold at Cooper's
 Housewares
 (D) To announce the redesign of a
 shopping plaza

182. What is suggested about Cooper's
 Housewares?

 (A) Its headquarters are in Durban.
 (B) It recently opened its first physical
 store.
 (C) It is closed on Saturdays and Sundays.
 (D) It is located next to a cafe.

183. What did Ms. Ayyar send to Mr. Didiza?

 (A) A map of the area
 (B) Sales reports
 (C) Employment forms
 (D) A customer survey

184. When does Mr. Didiza need to arrive at the
 store?

 (A) At 9:30 A.M.
 (B) At 10:00 A.M.
 (C) At 12:30 P.M.
 (D) At 5:00 P.M.

185. What will Mr. Didiza do on Wednesday
 afternoon?

 (A) Read some documents
 (B) Attend a class
 (C) Shop at Cooper's Housewares
 (D) Meet with Ms. Khawula

Go on to the next page

To:	Gavin Taggart <gtaggart@northdalebank.com>
From:	Olmo Family Dental <appt@olmofamilydental.com>
Date:	March 2
Subject:	Appointment reminder

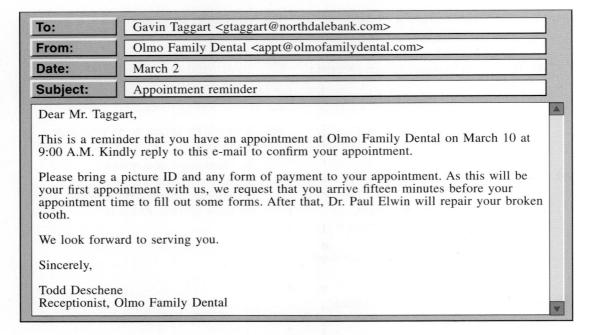

Dear Mr. Taggart,

This is a reminder that you have an appointment at Olmo Family Dental on March 10 at 9:00 A.M. Kindly reply to this e-mail to confirm your appointment.

Please bring a picture ID and any form of payment to your appointment. As this will be your first appointment with us, we request that you arrive fifteen minutes before your appointment time to fill out some forms. After that, Dr. Paul Elwin will repair your broken tooth.

We look forward to serving you.

Sincerely,

Todd Deschene
Receptionist, Olmo Family Dental

Olmo Family Dental
4428 San Amaro Blvd. NE
Albuquerque, NM 87109
info@olmofamilydental.com

Office hours: 10:00 A.M. to 6:00 P.M., Monday to Friday
8:00 A.M. to 1:00 P.M. on Saturday

Read about our office and staff at olmofamilydental.com.

For appointments or questions, call (505) 555-0114. To make online payments, visit olmofamilydental.com/pay.

https://www.olmofamilydental.com/reviews

I received dental care at Olmo Family Dental yesterday, and I was very pleased with the service provided by Dr. Marina Narvaez. She fixed a tooth that I broke earlier in the week, just one day after I moved to Albuquerque from Santa Fe. Dr. Narvaez is not only a great dentist, but she has an interesting background. Although she grew up in Albuquerque, she went to university and dental school in Detroit, Michigan. She returned to Albuquerque last year, when she was hired by Olmo Family Dental. According to Dr. Narvaez, even though Olmo Family Dental opened just five years ago, it is already one of the top dental practices in the city. And it is conveniently located just up the street from my new workplace.

I highly recommend Dr. Narvaez. I will certainly return to Olmo Family Dental when I need more dental work.

—Gavin Taggart, March 11

186. In the e-mail, what is Mr. Taggart asked to do?
(A) Bring completed forms
(B) Call Mr. Deschene
(C) Arrive early
(D) Use a credit card

187. When is Mr. Taggart's appointment?
(A) On Monday
(B) On Tuesday
(C) On Friday
(D) On Saturday

188. According to the business card, how should patients schedule an appointment with Olmo Family Dental?
(A) By completing an online form
(B) By sending an e-mail
(C) By calling the office
(D) By sending a text message

189. What is suggested about Dr. Narvaez?
(A) She specializes in dental care for children.
(B) She was not originally scheduled for Mr. Taggart's appointment.
(C) She has worked as a dentist at Olmo Family Dental for five years.
(D) She is not originally from Albuquerque.

190. What does the online review indicate about Mr. Taggart?
(A) He recently started a new job.
(B) He has been seeing Dr. Narvaez for several years.
(C) He has scheduled a follow-up appointment.
(D) He used to live in Detroit.

Go on to the next page

Welcome Home to Oval Orchard Rentals!

We operate two residential buildings centrally located in Westlands, Nairobi. All our flats feature a welcoming entrance hall, a study, a well-appointed kitchen, ample storage space, a laundry room, and a covered car park. Weekly cleaning services, electricity, Internet service, and satellite television are all included in the rent for each flat.

Our Lantana Road building has three-bedroom flats and is just a two-minute walk from the Lotus Business Complex and a bus stop. Our Rhapta Road building has four-bedroom flats and is pleasantly situated near the Japanese Embassy. Additionally, each Rhapta Road flat has a private outdoor garden equipped with a grill, a dining table, lounge furniture, and a hammock, making it a perfect retreat from the cosmopolitan rush of Westlands.

To view our beautiful flats, visit www.ovalorchardrentals.co.ke and register for one of our open house events, where one of our experienced agents will lead a tour and answer any questions you may have.

To:	Fredrick Makkink <f.makkink@quincemail.com>
From:	Hamida Chunga <hamida@ovalorchardrentals.co.ke>
Subject:	RE: Three-bedroom units
Date:	16 March
Attachment:	🔗 Open house information

Dear Mr. Makkink:

My name is Hamida Chunga, and I am an agent with Oval Orchard Rentals. Thank you for expressing interest in renting one of our lovely living spaces, and I am delighted to learn that you have recently moved to Nairobi. In your e-mail, you asked about our three-bedroom flats. We have just one three-bedroom unit available at Lantana Road for KSh 150,000 per month. I think you would appreciate being only a two-minute walk from your new workplace.

If you wish to see the unit in person, please attend our open house next week. Please find the schedule attached to this e-mail. I will be there to show you the flat.

All the best,

Hamida Chunga, Rental Agent

Oval Orchard Open House Showing Times, 20–23 March		
Day and Time		**Location**
Monday	8:30 A.M. to 11:00 A.M.	Rhapta Road Building, Unit #5
Tuesday	No showings	No showings
Wednesday	10:00 A.M. to 12:00 P.M.	Lantana Road Building, Unit #2
Thursday	8:30 A.M. to 11:00 A.M.	Rhapta Road Building, Unit #8

191. According to the advertisement, what is an additional feature of the flats in the Rhapta Road building?

(A) A weekly cleaning service
(B) A private garden
(C) A covered parking area
(D) A laundry room

192. What are interested individuals instructed to do before attending an open house?

(A) Register online
(B) Pay an agent fee
(C) Speak to an agent by phone
(D) Submit documents from an employer

193. What is the purpose of the e-mail?

(A) To request a refund
(B) To announce changes to a schedule
(C) To respond to an inquiry
(D) To provide transportation details

194. What does Ms. Chunga's e-mail suggest about Mr. Makkink?

(A) He has an appointment at the Japanese Embassy.
(B) He regularly takes the bus to work.
(C) He lived near Rhapta Road several years ago.
(D) He works in the Lotus Business Complex.

195. When most likely will Mr. Makkink attend an open house?

(A) On Monday
(B) On Tuesday
(C) On Wednesday
(D) On Thursday

Go on to the next page

http://www.tighesautopainting.ca/home_page

| **Home Page** | Services | Customer Comments | Contact Us |

Tighe's Auto Painting
Premium work at excellent prices

We provide painting, washing, and waxing for a wide variety of vehicles, including cars, vans, boats, and aircraft. And our detailing service is second to none—we can make your vehicle look like new inside and out!

We now offer mobile service. We come to your office or job site and provide care to your fleet on a regular schedule. This includes washing, waxing, and touching up paint chips. Our trucks carry all the necessary equipment, including power washers, towels, and vacuums. For more information about commercial accounts and to review contract options, contact Alison McCarthy at amccarthy@tighesautopainting.ca or 416-555-0146, Ext. 4.

Special promotion: sign a contract for weekly or monthly service by 4 December and receive 15% off!

E-mail

To:	Preston Warde <pwarde@polluxelectrical.ca>
From:	Ashok Dheer <adheer@polluxelectrical.ca>
Subject:	Update
Date:	22 November
Attachment:	Naboa_Affre_info

Dear Mr. Warde:

As we discussed, I've purchased the new vans for our fleet and signed up with Tighe's Auto Painting. They'll paint our logo on the vehicles. They can also touch up the paint on the vans we already own. After that, they'll come out every Thursday to wash and wax any vans that are in our lot. We can reevaluate the contract in six months and see whether we want to continue with them.

Also, I'm attaching the information regarding the electricians we are hiring: Max Naboa and Claude Affre. They both have driver's licenses and have driven vans like ours before.

Sincerely,

Ashok Dheer, Operations Supervisor

Home Page	Services	**Customer Comments**	Contact Us	▲

Hire Pollux Electrical and they will not disappoint you. I recently bought a bookstore, and the electrical system needed updating. After a telephone discussion, an appointment was booked. By the next day the system was fixed. The electrician, Max Naboa, was so polite and efficient. He had all the tools he needed in his van. The job only took a few hours. The cost was reasonable too.

– Sarah Ardenne, 20 December

196. According to the advertisement, what is new at Tighe's Auto Painting?

(A) A business name
(B) A type of service
(C) A brand of paint
(D) A set of appliances

197. Who most likely is Ms. McCarthy?

(A) The manager of the commercial accounts
(B) The scheduler of the detailing services
(C) A person who orders equipment and materials
(D) A marketing specialist who updates the Web page

198. What does the e-mail indicate about Mr. Dheer and Mr. Warde?

(A) They have previously spoken about vehicle services.
(B) They must arrange interviews for a job vacancy.
(C) They are planning to replace their old vans.
(D) They both work for a cleaning service.

199. What is most likely true about the contract Mr. Dheer mentions in his e-mail?

(A) It was for a two-year period.
(B) It will be renewed on Thursday.
(C) It finalized the purchase of new vans.
(D) It includes a discount on weekly service.

200. What is suggested about the service that Ms. Ardenne received?

(A) It was unsatisfactory.
(B) It involved a new employee.
(C) It took a long time to complete.
(D) It had to be rescheduled.

Stop! This is the end of the test. If you finish before time is called, you may go back to Parts 5, 6, and 7 and check your work.

ETS 실전 모의고사 02

PART 7

Directions: In this part you will read a selection of texts, such as magazine and newspaper articles, e-mails, and instant messages. Each text or set of texts is followed by several questions. Select the best answer for each question and mark the letter (A), (B), (C), or (D) on your answer sheet.

Questions 147-148 refer to the following Web page.

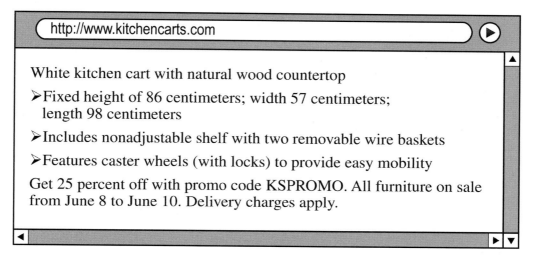

http://www.kitchencarts.com

White kitchen cart with natural wood countertop

➢Fixed height of 86 centimeters; width 57 centimeters; length 98 centimeters

➢Includes nonadjustable shelf with two removable wire baskets

➢Features caster wheels (with locks) to provide easy mobility

Get 25 percent off with promo code KSPROMO. All furniture on sale from June 8 to June 10. Delivery charges apply.

147. What feature of the kitchen cart is mentioned?

(A) It has a removable shelf.
(B) It can be moved around.
(C) It comes in a variety of colors.
(D) It can easily be adjusted with a tool.

148. What is indicated about the sale?

(A) It lasts for ten days.
(B) It is for a discontinued item.
(C) It requires a special code.
(D) It includes free delivery.

Go on to the next page

CHAPTER 3

실전 모의고사 02

MEMO

To: All Café Employees
From: Yvette Partridge, General Manager
Date: April 12
Subject: Daytime reservations

The following directives apply to all servers, counter staff, and managers. Please be advised that breakfast or lunch reservation requests must first be authorized by me before a confirmation is issued to a customer. Also, when a reservation request is received, be sure to take down the customer's first and last name, phone number, and the date and time for which the reservation is being requested. Then, inform the customer to expect a return call from us within 24 hours. Mr. Bradley and I are thrilled that breakfast and lunch reservations are becoming more popular. All the more reason why it is imperative to avoid mistakes such as overbookings; we certainly do not want to lose customers due to shortcomings on our part.

149. According to the memo, who can confirm breakfast and lunch reservations?

(A) Servers
(B) Ms. Partridge
(C) Managers
(D) Mr. Bradley

150. What is indicated about Ms. Partridge and Mr. Bradley?

(A) They used to be counter staff.
(B) They will hold a training session for all employees.
(C) They will extend the hours of breakfast and lunch service.
(D) They are pleased that the café is getting more reservation requests.

Questions 151-152 refer to the following job advertisement.

Curator of West African Art at Northfort Museum

The Curator of West African Art preserves, organizes, categorizes, displays, and makes recommendations for the acquisition of art primarily from Nigeria and Ivory Coast. The curator participates in strategic planning and collaborates with other museum personnel to further the institution's instructional, research, and public service events. The ability to read French, Igbo, and Dioula is essential. A reading knowledge of Hausa, Arabic, or other languages spoken in West Africa is desirable. Extensive knowledge is required of the interrelationships between West African history, cultures, and art as a basis for presenting the collection to the public. An advanced degree in art history or anthropology with a focus on West African cultures is required. To apply, please visit www.northfortmuseum.org/openpositions.

151. What is one of the curator's responsibilities?

(A) Consulting with museum staff
(B) Leading tours for visitors
(C) Selling works of art
(D) Promoting artists

152. What is NOT mentioned as a requirement for the position?

(A) Specialization in a relevant academic field
(B) Willingness to travel abroad
(C) Skillfulness in some languages
(D) Expertise in West African cultures

Go on to the next page

Questions 153-154 refer to the following online chat discussion.

James Rais 8:07 A.M.
Laura, I requested a repair for my air conditioner. Someone came by my office, but the problem has not been fixed.

Laura Xue 8:08 A.M.
I'm sorry to hear that. What is the issue?

James Rais 8:11 A.M.
My air conditioner is not cooling properly. It is set at a comfortable temperature, but the office is still too warm.

Laura Xue 8:13 A.M.
That sounds very frustrating. I will put in a recall notice and have the technician prioritize your office today.

James Rais 8:14 A.M.
That's great, but I don't want to pay twice. Is this a free service?

Laura Xue 8:16 A.M.
Absolutely. When a technician does not fix a problem on the first visit, any recall visit is complimentary.

---

153. Why does Mr. Rais contact Ms. Xue?

(A) He would like to rent an office.
(B) He has a maintenance issue.
(C) He wants to buy an air conditioner.
(D) He has a balance left on his account.

154. At 8:16 A.M., what does Ms. Xue most likely mean when she writes, "Absolutely"?

(A) A technician has made a repair.
(B) She will stop by Mr. Rais's office.
(C) A service fee will not be charged.
(D) She has not yet made a payment.

Questions 155-157 refer to the following chart.

TAMAGI ELECTRONIC MUSICAL INSTRUMENTS
Troubleshooting Tips for JZ-9M Keyboards

Thank you for purchasing the JZ-9M Tamagi keyboard with stand. If you experience problems with your instrument, please try to resolve them using this chart. Some problems can also be resolved by restoring your keyboard to factory settings (see page 16 of instruction manual). If problems persist, contact a Tamagi Service Center.

Issue	Suspected Cause	Solution
No sound is produced.	The instrument is switched off or unplugged.	Turn the on/off switch to the "ON" position.
Instrument turns off unexpectedly.	Automatic shut-off is enabled.	Press and hold the auto-off switch to deactivate this feature.
Low notes are weak or inaudible.	Both the main slider button and the octave slider button are engaged.	Lower the octave slider button to adjust the audio output.

155. Who is the intended audience for the information?

(A) Owners of the JZ-9M keyboard
(B) Employees of Tamagi
(C) Service center phone representatives
(D) Product assembly-line workers

156. What is mentioned as a reason to call a Tamagi Service Center?

(A) To restore a keyboard to factory settings
(B) To have a keyboard stand replaced
(C) To receive help with a recurring problem
(D) To obtain a refund on a purchase

157. Why should the user press and hold a switch?

(A) Because the instrument has turned off unexpectedly
(B) Because the sound is not playing loudly
(C) Because the octave slider switch is engaged
(D) Because the electrical cable will not detach

Go on to the next page

Questions 158-160 refer to the following e-mail.

To:	bella.mcintyre@cumulusmail.net
From:	customersupport@synchette.com
Date:	June 23
Subject:	Newest version

Dear Ms. McIntyre,

Thank you for choosing Synchette backup and recovery software for your business.

Our records indicate that you are currently using Version 8.0 of the software. As of August 1, we will no longer support that version. We advise you to update your software immediately. Between now and August 1, you can purchase Version 10.5, the current industry standard, at $15.00 off the list price.

Visit our Web site at www.synchette.com for more information about the powerful features of Synchette Version 10.5.

Sincerely,

Synchette Customer Support

158. Why did Synchette Customer Support send the e-mail?

(A) To notify a customer about a price increase
(B) To provide help with a technology problem
(C) To tell a customer to take immediate action
(D) To request feedback about a program's features

159. According to the e-mail, what will Synchette do on August 1 ?

(A) Stop supporting Version 8.0 of its software
(B) Release the latest version of its software
(C) Give an online demonstration of its software
(D) Send Ms. McIntyre an invoice for her new software

160. What does Synchette Customer Support recommend?

(A) Responding by e-mail
(B) Taking advantage of a low price
(C) Backing up all system files
(D) Contacting a representative

— [1] —. Every five years, engineers hired by Hartpool's town council inspect our sidewalks for damaged areas. A sidewalk inspection was completed last week.

Sidewalks that are slated to be repaired have been marked with red circles. They are also shown on a map on Hartpool's Web site, www.townofhartpool.gov. If your home or business is adjacent to a marked sidewalk, you will receive a letter notifying you of when the repairs will take place. The letter will include contact information in case you have questions about how the repairs might affect you. — [2] —. If your driveway connects to a marked sidewalk, you will be required to park on the street during the two-day repair period. — [3] —.

The town council is still taking bids from construction companies for the repair work. — [4] —. The project is expected to begin in early May and to take five weeks, weather permitting.

161. What is the purpose of the notice?

(A) To schedule driveway inspections
(B) To invite contractors to submit bids
(C) To inform town residents of construction work
(D) To explain how some sidewalks were damaged

162. According to the notice, what is one way that repair locations can be identified?

(A) By calling the town council
(B) By visiting the town's Web site
(C) By reading the local newspaper
(D) By looking for signs posted on buildings

163. In which of the positions marked [1], [2], [3], and [4] does the following sentence best belong?

"All residents will be advised when one has been selected."

(A) [1]
(B) [2]
(C) [3]
(D) [4]

Go on to the next page

Questions 164-167 refer to the following article.

TRENTON (April 4)—Lavender Skin Care Company CEO Donald McGrath has announced his company's intention to move its corporate base of operations from Hamilton, New Jersey, to Boise, Idaho. This shift is scheduled to take place early next year. The driving factor for this plan appears to be the need to reduce costs. Mr. McGrath noted that he hopes to accomplish this by moving to an area where the taxes on property tend to be lower.

Since his promotion from vice president of marketing last October, Mr. McGrath has made several changes to the company. Some of the changes include replacing the chief financial officer and discontinuing several underperforming products.

164. What is the article mainly about?

(A) A corporate executive appointment
(B) A company headquarters relocation
(C) A local firm's latest earnings report
(D) A company's workforce expansion

165. The word "driving" in paragraph 1, line 7, is closest in meaning to

(A) commuting
(B) operating
(C) motivating
(D) obsessing

166. What expense does Mr. McGrath hope to reduce?

(A) Taxes
(B) Utilities
(C) Salaries
(D) Training

167. What was Mr. McGrath's former position?

(A) Chief financial officer
(B) Vice president
(C) Financial advisor
(D) Town mayor

Questions 168-171 refer to the following information.

Noticeboard Space Available to Community Groups

Mooringtown Library is pleased to invite local community groups to use the free advertising space on its new noticeboard, located outside the front entrance of the library. Space on the board is available for up to four weeks at a time.

Notices must be approved in advance at the library's front desk and must meet the following requirements. All content must be suitable for public display. The notice must be written or printed on standard-quality paper with dimensions of either 8.5 in. x 11 in. or 5.5 in. x 8.5 in. The desired start and end date for display should be written in the front bottom right corner. — [1] —. Any notices that do not meet these requirements will not be considered and will be discarded. — [2] —.

— [3] —. Submissions are now being accepted at the Mooringtown Library front desk. Please have the actual notice, in the format in which you would like it to appear, with you when you arrive. Within one business day, you will receive a call confirming that your notice has been added to the board. — [4] —.

Mooringtown Library
www.mooringtownlib.co.au

---

168. What is indicated about advertising space on the Mooringtown Library notice board?

(A) It is available at no charge.
(B) It can be used for any length of time.
(C) It is open to all area businesses.
(D) It is intended mainly for sporting events.

169. What is NOT a stated requirement for a notice to be placed on the board?

(A) It must meet certain size requirements.
(B) It must be marked with posting dates.
(C) It must be reviewed beforehand.
(D) It must be signed by a librarian.

170. What should an advertiser bring to the library when making a submission?

(A) An outline of proposed content
(B) A final version of the notice
(C) A completed submission form
(D) A letter from an organization

171. In which of the positions marked [1], [2], [3], and [4] does the following sentence best belong?

"The name and telephone number of the person posting the notice must be clearly marked on the back."

(A) [1]
(B) [2]
(C) [3]
(D) [4]

Go on to the next page

Questions 172-175 refer to the following text-message chain.

Weilin Ying (9:07 A.M.) Hi, Shantoya. My flight out of Toronto has been delayed, so I won't be back in Boston in time to present my sales report.

Shantoya Blackwell (9:08 A.M.) Sorry to hear about your flight.

Weilin Ying (9:09 A.M.) It happens. Bassam Saeed and I worked on that report, so he can take over that presentation from me. Only, I haven't been able to reach him.

Shantoya Blackwell (9:10 A.M.) That is probably because he suddenly had to leave for Kuwait.

Weilin Ying (9:12 A.M.) He went home? Why?

Shantoya Blackwell (9:13 A.M.) Sorry, I don't know the details. Now, about your presentation, I suggest contacting Keiko Hayashi from our Chicago office.

Weilin Ying (9:13 A.M.) OK, I will.

Shantoya Blackwell (9:40 A.M.) Any word from Keiko?

Weilin Ying (9:41 A.M.) Yes. She said she would help, so the problem is solved.

Shantoya Blackwell (9:43 A.M.) Great. So how was that trade show in Toronto?

Weilin Ying (9:44 A.M.) Terrific. Lots of retailers have expressed interest in our kids' wear.

Shantoya Blackwell (9:45 A.M.) I'm not surprised. I see children wearing our apparel everywhere I go.

172. What is indicated about Mr. Ying?

(A) He recently joined the sales department.
(B) He first met Ms. Hayashi in Chicago.
(C) He is returning from a business trip.
(D) He regularly attends trade shows.

173. What is suggested about Mr. Saeed?

(A) He lives in Boston.
(B) He is from Kuwait.
(C) He is Ms. Blackwell's manager.
(D) He often visits his family.

174. At 9:41 A.M., what does Mr. Ying mean when he writes, "so the problem is solved"?

(A) He will be receiving a new ticket in the mail.
(B) A report was e-mailed to the management team.
(C) A coworker will take over his assignment.
(D) His flight departure was announced.

175. In what industry do the writers most likely work?

(A) Travel
(B) Clothing
(C) Entertainment
(D) Communication

Go on to the next page

TOWNER BOOKS
Receipt

Customer Information: Thomas Cabral, 8 Seaview Lane, Cardiff CF4

Thank you for shopping at our online bookshop! Here is your receipt for order #9207411.

Item Description	Quantity	Price
The Biography of Antonio Garcia by Erica Estes (final sale)	1	£15.00
A True Story of the World's Most Famous Chef by Samuel Ebsen	1	£18.50
Growing Up in Paris: A Memoir by Agnes Millot	1	£9.95
The History of Photography by Henry Salle	1	£21.25
TOTAL		£64.70

Note: Final sale items are not eligible for refunds or exchanges.

Order Status: Complete
Number of Shipments: 1

TOWNER BOOKS
Merchandise Return Policy and Procedure

Please complete all sections of this form and enclose a printed copy with the items you wish to return. Returns must be received within 90 days of the order date. Please allow 1–2 weeks for your return request to be processed. You will be notified via your preferred method of contact.

Order Number: 9207411

Customer Name/Address: Thomas Cabral, 8 Seaview Lane, Cardiff CF4

E-mail: tcabral@knet.co.uk

Phone: 029 5550 0161

How do you prefer to be contacted? Postal Mail ☐ E-mail ☐ Telephone ☐ Text Message ☑

Item Description	Reason for Return	Credit Type
The History of Photography	Front cover is torn	Refund ☑ Exchange ☐

176. What is suggested about the books purchased by Mr. Cabral?

(A) They were written by the same author.
(B) They were shipped from Cardiff.
(C) They were ordered online.
(D) They were hardcover books.

177. What is indicated about *The Biography of Antonio Garcia*?

(A) It cannot be exchanged.
(B) It is popular with customers.
(C) It is out of print.
(D) It was mailed separately.

178. Why did Mr. Cabral fill out the form?

(A) He was sent an item he did not order.
(B) He received a damaged item.
(C) He made a mistake when ordering.
(D) He wanted to update his contact information.

179. How much will Mr. Cabral be refunded?

(A) £9.95
(B) £15.00
(C) £18.50
(D) £21.25

180. How will the bookshop notify Mr. Cabral about the status of the return?

(A) By e-mail
(B) By telephone call
(C) By text message
(D) By postal mail

Go on to the next page

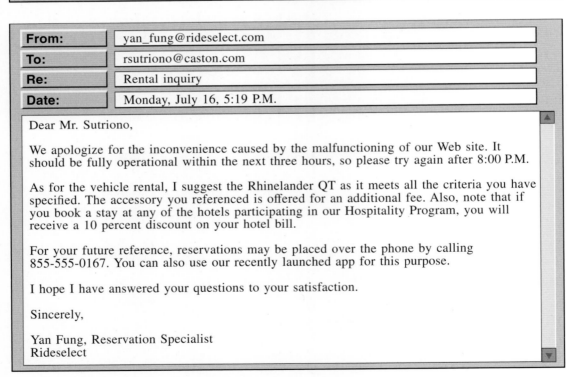

From:	rsutriono@caston.com
To:	reservations@rideselect.com
Subject:	Rental inquiry
Date:	Monday, July 16, 4:34 P.M.

Dear Reservation Specialist,

I am sending this e-mail because I am unable to make a reservation through your Web site: the page where I am supposed to select a vehicle consistently fails to load.

My family and I will be flying into Augusta next Thursday for a one-week vacation and would like to rent a car for the duration of our visit. I am looking for a vehicle that can comfortably seat five, has trunk space for three large bags, and costs no more than $250 per week.

When I used your service two years ago, I noticed that you offered various accessories, such as bicycle racks. Do you still offer these? Finally, are there any other services I might benefit from?

Thank you for your assistance.

Rachmat Sutriono

From:	yan_fung@rideselect.com
To:	rsutriono@caston.com
Re:	Rental inquiry
Date:	Monday, July 16, 5:19 P.M.

Dear Mr. Sutriono,

We apologize for the inconvenience caused by the malfunctioning of our Web site. It should be fully operational within the next three hours, so please try again after 8:00 P.M.

As for the vehicle rental, I suggest the Rhinelander QT as it meets all the criteria you have specified. The accessory you referenced is offered for an additional fee. Also, note that if you book a stay at any of the hotels participating in our Hospitality Program, you will receive a 10 percent discount on your hotel bill.

For your future reference, reservations may be placed over the phone by calling 855-555-0167. You can also use our recently launched app for this purpose.

I hope I have answered your questions to your satisfaction.

Sincerely,

Yan Fung, Reservation Specialist
Rideselect

181. What does the first e-mail indicate about Mr. Sutriono?

(A) He lives in Augusta.
(B) He is a first-time Rideselect customer.
(C) He needs a rental car for seven days.
(D) He recently purchased a bicycle.

182. What is true about the Rhinelander QT?

(A) It costs more than $250 per week to rent.
(B) Its trunk space can be expanded.
(C) It is Rideselect's most popular rental vehicle.
(D) It has room for five people.

183. What does Mr. Fung offer Mr. Sutriono?

(A) Free usage of a bicycle rack
(B) A complimentary bag
(C) A reduced price on a hotel stay
(D) A discount on a car rental fee

184. In the second e-mail, the word "placed" in paragraph 3, line 1, is closest in meaning to

(A) confirmed
(B) arranged
(C) estimated
(D) recommended

185. What does the second e-mail indicate about Rideselect?

(A) It has added a new way to make reservations.
(B) It scheduled routine maintenance of its Web site.
(C) It opened several more locations recently.
(D) It offers better rental rates than its competitors.

Go on to the next page

Questions 186-190 refer to the following Web page, e-mail, and customer review.

---

http://www.sportsol.com/products/detergent

SPORTSOL
Detergent

The deep-cleaning concentrate for tough stains

✓ Enzyme formula dissolves the most stubborn stains caused by grass and soil.

✓ Safe for use with both synthetic and natural fabrics.

✓ Citrus-based ingredients are biodegradable and environmentally safe.

Available in these convenient sizes:

PRODUCT NUMBER	DESCRIPTION	QUANTITY	WASH LOADS
A20	Sample Size	4-ounce bag	10
A30	Single Pack	1 bottle	20
A40	Twin Pack	2 bottles	40
A50	Super Pack	4 bottles	80

E-Mail Message

To: Liz Ingram
From: Dylan Campbell
Date: 6 October
Subject: RE: Information requested

Hello, Ms. Ingram,

Per your request, here are the most current marketing data about the Sportsol detergent.

Sales of the product have been growing steadily since we began selling it online last March; in fact, by the end of the current quarter we expect sales to have increased by 12 percent over last quarter. Wholly in line with this development, customer reviews have been quite positive, with the product scoring an average rating of 4.5 out of 5 stars.

There is, however, one problem. Following the most recent redesign of the bottle, we have been receiving reports that the product is leaking out, although in very small amounts. This issue has been brought to the attention of the packaging design team, which is currently investigating the problem so as to come up with a proper solution.

Sincerely,

Dylan Campbell, Leader
Marketing Team

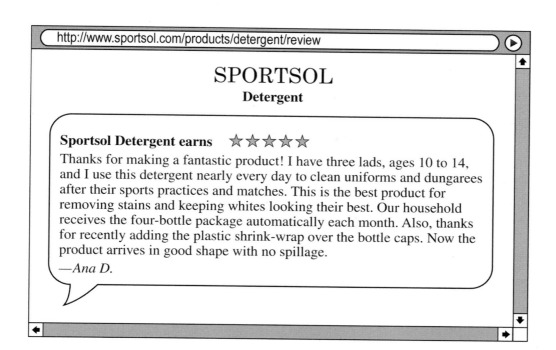

http://www.sportsol.com/products/detergent/review

SPORTSOL
Detergent

Sportsol Detergent earns ★★★★☆

Thanks for making a fantastic product! I have three lads, ages 10 to 14, and I use this detergent nearly every day to clean uniforms and dungarees after their sports practices and matches. This is the best product for removing stains and keeping whites looking their best. Our household receives the four-bottle package automatically each month. Also, thanks for recently adding the plastic shrink-wrap over the bottle caps. Now the product arrives in good shape with no spillage.

—Ana D.

186. What is indicated about Sportsol Detergent?

(A) It is sold in bottles only.
(B) It must be stored in a cool location.
(C) It cleans different fabric types safely.
(D) It is widely available in supermarkets.

187. What is a reason for Mr. Campbell's e-mail?

(A) To suggest advertising ideas for a new product
(B) To describe the sales status of a product
(C) To request assistance with package design
(D) To congratulate staff for developing a unique product

188. According to the customer review, what is true about Ana D.?

(A) She has several children.
(B) She wears uniforms to work.
(C) She plans to remove a stain on her carpet.
(D) She used Sportsol Detergent for the first time.

189. What is the number of the product that Ana D. generally purchases?

(A) A20
(B) A30
(C) A40
(D) A50

190. How did staff at Sportsol respond to a flaw affecting some of the customers?

(A) By changing a product's formula
(B) By adding material to secure bottle caps
(C) By increasing the size of product packaging
(D) By changing a shipping company

Go on to the next page

From:	Joanne Nagy <jnagy@sjs.com>
To:	Denny Smith <dsmith@doodlemail.com>
Date:	November 18
Subject:	Information
Attachment:	📎 Forms

Dear Mr. Smith,

My name is Joanne Nagy, and I am on the recruiting team at Seeger Jones Software (SJS). We have just created a new business development role that may suit you well. The position involves creating sales strategies to introduce our software tools to major institutions. In addition, the job requires providing input on product development to meet the needs of the marketplace.

At your earliest convenience, please advise me of your availability over the next week so that we can discuss this opportunity further. I have attached a few forms that all prospective employees must complete in advance. Please prioritize sending your current résumé to our employee compliance representative, whose e-mail address can be found at the bottom of the attached forms.

Thank you.

Joanne Nagy

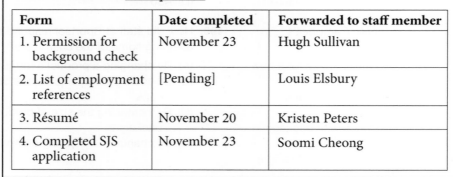

Seeger Jones Software: Personnel Office
File checklist for: Denny Smith

Form	Date completed	Forwarded to staff member
1. Permission for background check	November 23	Hugh Sullivan
2. List of employment references	[Pending]	Louis Elsbury
3. Résumé	November 20	Kristen Peters
4. Completed SJS application	November 23	Soomi Cheong

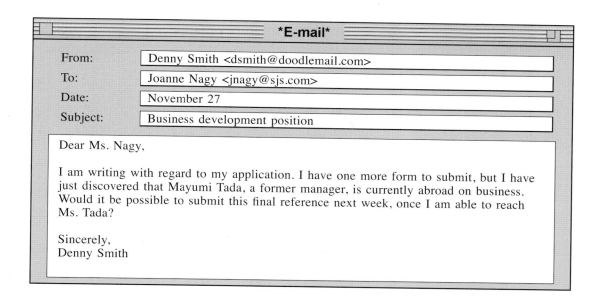

E-mail

From:	Denny Smith <dsmith@doodlemail.com>
To:	Joanne Nagy <jnagy@sjs.com>
Date:	November 27
Subject:	Business development position

Dear Ms. Nagy,

I am writing with regard to my application. I have one more form to submit, but I have just discovered that Mayumi Tada, a former manager, is currently abroad on business. Would it be possible to submit this final reference next week, once I am able to reach Ms. Tada?

Sincerely,
Denny Smith

191. What is one purpose of the first e-mail?

(A) To request feedback on a software program
(B) To ask for an opinion on a job applicant
(C) To arrange a meeting time
(D) To announce a promotion

192. What is indicated about the business development position?

(A) It will start next week.
(B) It was created recently.
(C) It was previously held by Ms. Nagy.
(D) It will be advertised online.

193. Who most likely is an employee compliance representative?

(A) Mr. Sullivan
(B) Mr. Elsbury
(C) Ms. Peters
(D) Ms. Cheong

194. What does the second e-mail indicate about Ms. Tada?

(A) She is unwilling to provide a reference.
(B) She will process some forms.
(C) She is a manager at SJS.
(D) She worked with Mr. Smith.

195. What form does Mr. Smith refer to in his e-mail to Ms. Nagy?

(A) Form 1
(B) Form 2
(C) Form 3
(D) Form 4

Go on to the next page

CHAPTER 3

실전 모의고사 02

Questions 196-200 refer to the following Web page, e-mail, and meeting notes.

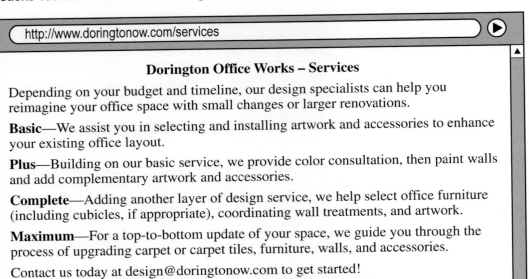

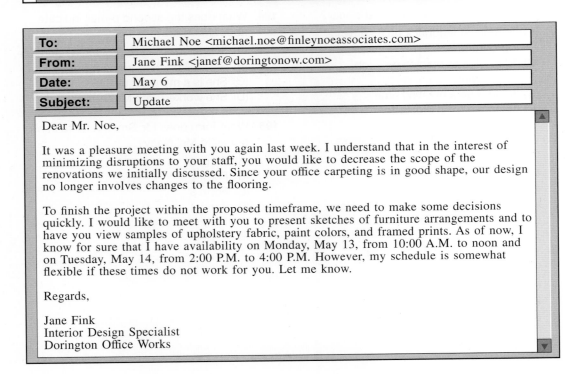

Meeting Notes by Jane Fink, Dorington Office Works
May 14, 4:00–6:00 P.M.
Project: Michael Noe, Finley and Noe Associates

The start date for the project was confirmed as June 17. All work is to be completed within four weeks of the start date.

Paint selections were finalized:
• "Seaside Tan" for the reception area and hallways
• "Warm Stone" for the offices
• "Pure Sage" for the break room

Other preliminary selections were made:
• "Arturo Grand" Series by Casual Craft Furniture. This furniture purchase will be bulk-pricing eligible, so a significant discount will be applied.

196. What does the Web page indicate about Dorington Office Works?

(A) It restores historic buildings.
(B) It creates original works of art.
(C) It manufactures furniture.
(D) It provides installation services.

197. What is a purpose of the e-mail?

(A) To request a detailed estimate
(B) To finalize the artwork selection process
(C) To acknowledge a change to a project
(D) To describe Ms. Fink's background in design

198. What service will Dorington Office Works likely provide to Mr. Noe?

(A) Basic
(B) Plus
(C) Complete
(D) Maximum

199. What is suggested about Mr. Noe?

(A) He requested a new project start date.
(B) He proposed an alternative meeting time.
(C) He did not have enough room to install cubicles.
(D) He decided on framed prints at the May 14 meeting.

200. According to the meeting notes, the cost of what selection will be reduced?

(A) "Seaside Tan"
(B) "Warm Stone"
(C) "Pure Sage"
(D) "Arturo Grand"

Stop! This is the end of the test. If you finish before time is called, you may go back to Parts 5, 6, and 7 and check your work.

ETS 실전 모의고사 03

PART 7

Directions: In this part you will read a selection of texts, such as magazine and newspaper articles, e-mails, and instant messages. Each text or set of texts is followed by several questions. Select the best answer for each question and mark the letter (A), (B), (C), or (D) on your answer sheet.

Questions 147-148 refer to the following coupon.

Brazilian Coffee Bean Company

10 percent off when you order two or more pounds

- Just $15 per pound for fresh coffee beans grown in Brazil's Bahia region!
- Free shipping in the United States for orders over $50

Coupon Code: LIKE-008; Valid through September 30.
Visit our Web site to order your coffee online.
www.braziliancoffeebean.com

---

147. What is indicated about the company?

(A) It is under new management.
(B) It sells coffee beans grown in a region of Brazil.
(C) It has opened several locations in Brazil.
(D) It ships coffee products to retail stores.

148. What could a customer buy for $15 ?

(A) A sample pack of two coffee varieties
(B) A 10 percent discount on the next order
(C) A single pound of coffee
(D) A coffee mug

Go on to the next page

Questions 149-150 refer to the following press release.

New Database to Facilitate Tracking of Archaeological Finds

Sectorsys, Ltd., is pleased to announce that it will soon team up with museums and archaeological societies worldwide to create an extensive database of artifacts discovered at archaeological sites. Says Eric Johannesen, CEO of Sectorsys, "Much of the information about treasures of the ancient world is not well documented and is not readily available. We plan on organizing an electronic database that will enable museums and professionals working in the field to access complete descriptions of artifacts." The database will initially contain information on 300,000 objects, and will be updated continually.

149. What product will Sectorsys offer?

(A) Supplies for archaeological digs
(B) Antitheft alarm systems for museums
(C) Software that holds information about artifacts
(D) Equipment for detecting fake artifacts

150. According to the press release, who will use the product?

(A) Dealers who buy and sell old objects
(B) Security guards at museums
(C) Companies that publish books on archaeology
(D) Museum employees and archaeologists

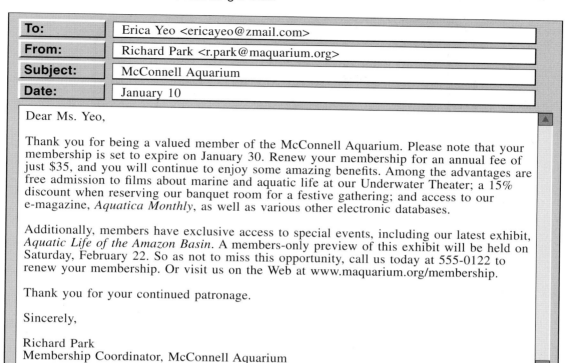

To:	Erica Yeo <ericayeo@zmail.com>
From:	Richard Park <r.park@maquarium.org>
Subject:	McConnell Aquarium
Date:	January 10

Dear Ms. Yeo,

Thank you for being a valued member of the McConnell Aquarium. Please note that your membership is set to expire on January 30. Renew your membership for an annual fee of just $35, and you will continue to enjoy some amazing benefits. Among the advantages are free admission to films about marine and aquatic life at our Underwater Theater; a 15% discount when reserving our banquet room for a festive gathering; and access to our e-magazine, *Aquatica Monthly*, as well as various other electronic databases.

Additionally, members have exclusive access to special events, including our latest exhibit, *Aquatic Life of the Amazon Basin*. A members-only preview of this exhibit will be held on Saturday, February 22. So as not to miss this opportunity, call us today at 555-0122 to renew your membership. Or visit us on the Web at www.maquarium.org/membership.

Thank you for your continued patronage.

Sincerely,

Richard Park
Membership Coordinator, McConnell Aquarium

151. What is NOT a benefit of being a member?
(A) Attending special events
(B) Watching films about sea life
(C) Accessing electronic materials
(D) Getting discounts on gift shop items

152. What is Ms. Yeo asked to do?
(A) Reserve the banquet room
(B) Write a magazine article
(C) Contact the McConnell Aquarium
(D) Attend a meeting

Go on to the next page

Questions 153-154 refer to the following text-message chain.

Garrett Jefferson (11:15 A.M.)
Hi, Divya. Can you remind me what time I am meeting with Carla today?

Divya Agarwal (11:19 A.M.)
Sure! Let me check.

Garrett Jefferson (11:21 A.M.)
Thanks. My schedule is not synching on my phone, and I am not sure why.

Divya Agarwal (11:23 A.M.)
It looks like you and Carla have two meetings today. One is with the chief editor from the local newspaper, and the other one is just you two about the 5-year plan.

Garrett Jefferson (11:24 A.M.)
Oh! I forgot about our meeting with Bruno Santamos. That's at 3:30 P.M., right?

Divya Agarwal (11:25 A.M.)
Yes, and the meeting about the 5-year plan is right after that at 4:30 P.M.

Garrett Jefferson (11:26 A.M.)
Got it. I'll see you in a couple of hours.

Divya Agarwal (11:27 A.M.)
See you in a bit.

153. At 11:19 A.M., what does Ms. Agarwal most likely mean when she writes, "Let me check"?

(A) She will see if a meeting has concluded.
(B) She will look at Mr. Jefferson's schedule.
(C) She will see if a client has arrived.
(D) She will try to reschedule a meeting.

154. What is indicated about Mr. Santamos?

(A) He will attend the 4:30 P.M. meeting.
(B) He shares an office with Mr. Jefferson.
(C) He works at the local newspaper.
(D) He has a very busy work schedule.

Sign up today for the third annual Hug the Shore 5K!

Saturday, June 20, at 10:00 A.M.

Hug the Shore is a five-kilometer footrace. The course starts and ends at the fountain in Sandy Mile Park. The registration fee is $25. All proceeds will be donated to Pure Ocean Promise. Runners will receive a T-shirt and are invited to celebrate after the event at Captain Kate's Grill, a popular local restaurant that is a five-minute walk away from the park.

Pure Ocean Promise is a nonprofit organization that strives to keep area beaches safe and pollution-free. It provides environmental education to area residents, hosts monthly beach clean-ups, and endorses ocean-friendly products. The event organizers will be including a complimentary reusable water bottle in the race packet.

155. The word "course" in paragraph 1, line 1, is closest in meaning to

(A) class
(B) route
(C) meal
(D) solution

156. What is suggested about Captain Kate's Grill?

(A) It gives away prizes.
(B) It is located in Sandy Mile Park.
(C) It serves healthy food.
(D) It is well liked.

157. According to the notice, what is one way that Pure Ocean Promise helps the community?

(A) By offering educational opportunities
(B) By offering recycling services
(C) By hosting a swim race every summer
(D) By making a swimming pool available in the summer

Go on to the next page

Questions 158-160 refer to the following e-mail.

To:	lynn.popal@camisat.net
From:	ckinsella@ubi.com
Re:	Inquiry
Date:	May 26

Dear Ms. Popal,

Thank you for your inquiry about Union Barbering Institute's four-week Master Barbering Program. — [1] —. You may sign up for one of any of the following periods: July 1 to July 26; September 9 to October 4; or November 4 to November 29.

— [2] —. Once you decide on your preferred time frame for taking the course, please contact our admissions coordinator, Mr. Farid Hazrati, at 555-0144 or at fhazrati@ubi.com so that he can enroll you and accept the first $50 of your tuition fee.

Please note that you are responsible for buying all course materials, including barbering tools. The complete list of necessary materials is available on the course Web site. — [3] —. Please bring the course textbook with you on the first day of class.

We look forward to seeing you and we trust you will find our program rewarding. — [4] —.

Sincerely,

Caren Kinsella
Assistant Program Director, Union Barbering Institute

158. Why is Ms. Popal advised to contact Mr. Hazrati?

(A) To set up a meeting with him
(B) To sign up for an educational program
(C) To update her contact information
(D) To obtain a list of course materials

159. What does the e-mail suggest about students?

(A) They should complete three separate courses.
(B) They must pay the whole cost of tuition before classes begin.
(C) They need to buy a textbook for use in the classroom.
(D) They can choose classes that meet in the evening.

160. In which of the positions marked [1], [2], [3], and [4] does the following sentence best belong?

"Our supply store is open weekdays from noon to 5:00 P.M."

(A) [1]
(B) [2]
(C) [3]
(D) [4]

198

Questions 161-163 refer to the following Web page.

---

https://www.jhpc.com.jm

| About Us | Contact Us | Upcoming Projects | Previous Projects | **News** |

Darius Lockyer, cofounder of the Jamaica Historical and Preservation Consortium (JHPC), is stepping down from his role as president. Mr. Lockyer made his announcement at a meeting on 7 April. "Stepping down from the work I love so much is difficult," he said. "But I am leaving JHPC in good hands. I plan to enjoy my time with my wife and grandchildren as well as in my garden." He is the second president of the organisation, having been promoted to the position after Gideon Morrison retired eight years ago. Mr. Lockyer's last official function will be to preside over JHPC's annual conference. This year it will be held at the Kingston Palm Swift Hotel from 3 to 5 June. Tia Alwood will serve as acting president beginning on 1 July. Ms. Alwood has been active in the organisation for many years.

---

161. What is the purpose of the Web page?

(A) To announce a retirement
(B) To propose a schedule change
(C) To welcome a partnership
(D) To report on a project

162. What is suggested about Mr. Morrison?

(A) He is the president of a hotel chain.
(B) He was at the meeting on April 7.
(C) He and Mr. Lockyer worked for JHPC at the same time.
(D) He and Ms. Alwood are planning an event in July.

163. According to the Web page, what will happen in June?

(A) Ms. Alwood will leave JHPC.
(B) A conference will be held.
(C) A new position will be created.
(D) Mr. Lockyer will travel with his family.

Go on to the next page

Questions 164-167 refer to the following schedule.

Thank you for booking a trip with Eccellenza Tours. Below please find the schedule for your group tour.

Day	Scheduled Events	Accommodations	Date
1	Arrive in Capri. Check into hotel.	Bellissima Capri	July 7
2	Sail along the Amalfi Coast and explore the Grotta Azzurra, a picturesque cave. **Optional morning excursion:** Tour the Augustus Gardens and dine at a charming local restaurant.	Same as above	July 8
3	Sail across the gulf and ride through Naples on our tour bus. Meet a popular chef and dine at his restaurant before checking in at the Napoli Inn. There is free time in the late afternoon and evening to explore the area on your own.	Napoli Inn	July 9
4	Travel to Venice and check in at the Crown Hotel. Take a walking tour of the city and visit a glass-blowing factory and store.	Crown Hotel	July 10
5	Spend the morning as you wish in Venice. The bus will leave from the Crown Hotel at 1:30 P.M. and will arrive in Florence in the evening. Check in at the Casa Pirello. **Optional morning excursion:** Travel the Venetian canals by gondola, a thin rowboat, operated by an entertaining gondolier.	Casa Pirello	July 11
6	Go on a guided tour of Florence, which includes visits to the most famous tourist attractions. End the day with a farewell dinner at the hotel restaurant.	Casa Pirello	July 12
7	A shuttle bus will depart from the hotel at 10:30 A.M. and will stop at the main train terminal and the airport.		July 13

Note: The tour includes transportation for the seven days, hotels, and the meals listed in the above itinerary. Each optional excursion that you choose to participate in, however, will incur an extra fee. Please see your tour guide for details.

164. What is scheduled for July 8 ?

(A) A tour of the city
(B) A visit to a cave
(C) A meal served in a garden
(D) A guided bus tour

165. Where will tour participants stay overnight on day five?

(A) In Capri
(B) In Naples
(C) In Venice
(D) In Florence

166. What is included in the price of the tour?

(A) A meal at Casa Pirello
(B) A cooking class
(C) A souvenir from a glass factory
(D) A boat ride on the canals

167. What is indicated about the optional excursions?

(A) They are available in Naples.
(B) They require advance reservations.
(C) They include museum tours.
(D) They take place in the morning.

Go on to the next page

Questions 168-171 refer to the following text-message chain.

Dirk Nelson [2:33 P.M.] Hello, Jeffrey and Lisa. I just heard from our linen supplier. They will not be able to deliver tablecloths in the color we requested until Saturday.

Jeffrey Lim [2:34 P.M.] But the grand opening event is this Friday evening. I thought we had confirmed the order. Didn't we receive a confirmation on Monday?

Lisa Cobb [2:35 P.M.] Yes, we did. I have it right here. We were expecting the delivery of two dozen large tablecloths in dark green.

Dirk Nelson [2:36 P.M.] Apparently there was a mix-up in the supplier's warehouse. They are now offering us a discount if we accept a different color.

Jeffrey Lim [2:37 P.M.] What other colors are available?

Lisa Cobb [2:38 P.M.] I'm looking at their Web site right now. There is a soft gold that I would go with.

Jeffrey Lim [2:39 P.M.] That will have to do. We can arrange to have contrasting floral centerpieces on all the tables.

Dirk Nelson [2:40 P.M.] That sounds good. I'll call the linen supplier and tell them that we will take the soft gold ones, and that they should be delivered this Thursday.

168. What type of work do the writers most likely do?

(A) Warehouse management
(B) Linens manufacturing
(C) Landscape design
(D) Event planning

169. When was an order confirmed?

(A) On Monday
(B) On Thursday
(C) On Friday
(D) On Saturday

170. At 2:35 P.M., what does Ms. Cobb most likely mean when she writes, "I have it right here"?

(A) She is looking at a message from a supplier.
(B) She is viewing a sample of the soft gold color online.
(C) She found an invoice for floral centerpieces on her desk.
(D) She has received a shipment of tablecloths.

171. What will Mr. Nelson most likely do next?

(A) Contact a restaurant
(B) Visit a company Web site
(C) Update a previous order
(D) Cancel a business relationship

Questions 172-175 refer to the following testimonial.

I am the marketing director at an architecture firm. I was looking for someone to take headshots of my colleagues and panoramas of our office space for our Web site, and I was struggling to find an experienced but affordable photographer. — [1] —. A friend recommended Katerina McMillan, who owns a photography business. I contacted her, and she quickly responded with a quote, her availability, and samples of her work. Her rates are reasonable, and she offers several discount packages for large jobs, including the office photo-shoot package, which we used. — [2] —. On the day of our session, Ms. McMillan set up a temporary portrait studio in one of our meeting rooms. — [3] —. She offers a photo-retouching service for an extra fee, but we declined that service, as we have a sizable graphic arts department on-site. Everyone was happy with Ms. McMillan's work, and she is the best photographer I've ever worked with. — [4] —.

— Eric Angler, June 3

172. According to the testimonial, why did Mr. Angler want photographs taken?

(A) To create products to sell
(B) To decorate his office building
(C) To add visual content to a Web site
(D) To satisfy a request from an architect

173. What is true about Mr. Angler's firm?

(A) It has a large portrait studio on-site.
(B) It operates out of multiple buildings.
(C) It employs a team of graphic artists.
(D) It was difficult for Ms. McMillan to find.

174. What is NOT indicated about Ms. McMillan?

(A) She offers volume discounts.
(B) She photographs landscapes.
(C) She is easy to work with.
(D) She retouches photos upon request.

175. In which of the positions marked [1], [2], [3], and [4] does the following sentence best belong?

"The package was perfect for our needs."

(A) [1]
(B) [2]
(C) [3]
(D) [4]

Go on to the next page

Appo Flavor Company
MEMO

From: Amy Girard
To: All Employees of Appo Flavor Company
Date: July 6
Subject: Office move

Next week, we will transition to our new offices. We think you will be pleased with the more spacious layout of these offices, as well as the abundance of natural light. Our relocation contractor will move one department each day. Take note of your area's move date as scheduled below.

Date	Department	Contact
July 11	Information Technology	Carly Morton
July 12	Research and Development	Alan Dubeck
July 13	Accounting	Brian Smith
July 14	Marketing	Nate Harbison
July 15	Human Resources	Amy Girard

On your move date, please remove all items from your desks, filing cabinets, and bookcases. Pack your things in boxes, then label each box with your name, department, and any notes—for example, if any of the boxes contain breakable objects. Reach out to the contact person listed for your department with any questions or concerns.

From:	Jayla Williams
To:	Alan Dubeck
Date:	July 7
Subject:	Moving day

Mr. Dubeck,

I will be presenting at the PEN Food Science conference in Lisbon next week, so I will not be in the office on the day of our department's scheduled move. I will return to the office on Thursday.

Would it be possible to have my things moved at the end of the week instead? Please let me know how to proceed.

Thanks,

Jayla Williams

176. What is suggested about the new office building?

(A) It has many windows.
(B) It has limited floor space.
(C) It is already furnished.
(D) It is located in another town.

177. What does Ms. Girard instruct staff to do?

(A) Stack boxes on top of desks
(B) Move fragile items personally
(C) Add identifying information to boxes
(D) Request a specific moving date by submitting a form

178. Whom should members of the accounting department contact with questions?

(A) Ms. Morton
(B) Mr. Dubeck
(C) Mr. Smith
(D) Ms. Girard

179. What is the purpose of the e-mail?

(A) To request time off
(B) To explain a scheduling conflict
(C) To ask to attend a conference
(D) To report on a special project

180. In what department does Ms. Williams most likely work?

(A) Information Technology
(B) Research and Development
(C) Marketing
(D) Human Resources

Go on to the next page

Questions 181-185 refer to the following form and e-mail.

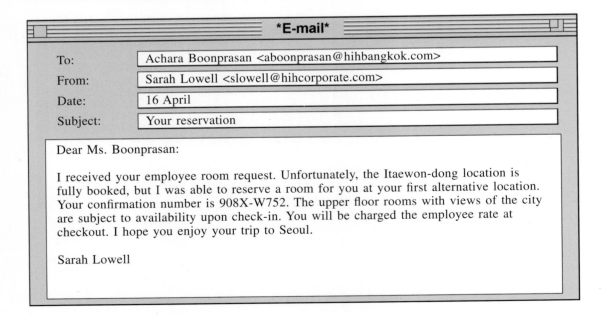

HIH – Hawthorne International Hotels

Employee Room Benefit Services – Booking Form

Employees who are eligible for the program must book reservations online using this form. Do not contact the hotel or the call centre directly.

Name: Achara Boonprasan

Location of the hotel you work for: Lumphini

City, country: Bangkok, Thailand

Today's date: 15 April

Employee ID: 7931-4782-0201

E-mail: aboonprasan@hihbangkok.com

Phone: 02-5861252

City, country you are visiting: Seoul, Republic of Korea

Requested dates: 22–27 August

Number of nights: 5

Hotel location: Itaewon-dong

Alternative choice 1: Insa-dong

Alternative choice 2: Hongdae

Special requests: This will be my first trip to Seoul, so I would like to request a room on an upper floor with a view.

Breakfast and, where available, access to our gym and pool are included in your reservation. You should receive an e-mail with information about your booking within 48 hours of submission. Please contact Global Support with questions or concerns.

E-mail

To:	Achara Boonprasan <aboonprasan@hihbangkok.com>
From:	Sarah Lowell <slowell@hihcorporate.com>
Date:	16 April
Subject:	Your reservation

Dear Ms. Boonprasan:

I received your employee room request. Unfortunately, the Itaewon-dong location is fully booked, but I was able to reserve a room for you at your first alternative location. Your confirmation number is 908X-W752. The upper floor rooms with views of the city are subject to availability upon check-in. You will be charged the employee rate at checkout. I hope you enjoy your trip to Seoul.

Sarah Lowell

181. What is indicated about Ms. Boonprasan?

  (A) She is being transferred to Korea.
  (B) She used to work at the call center.
  (C) She often travels to Seoul.
  (D) She is from Thailand.

182. What is indicated about the HIH employee room benefit program?

  (A) It is available to all employees.
  (B) Reservations may be made by calling a hotel directly.
  (C) Room reservations include breakfast.
  (D) All participating hotels have a gym and pool.

183. Where will Ms. Boonprasan most likely be staying on her trip?

  (A) In Lumphini
  (B) In Itaewon-dong
  (C) In Insa-dong
  (D) In Hongdae

184. What is suggested about Ms. Lowell?

  (A) She is a part-time employee at HIH.
  (B) She referred Ms. Boonprasan to HIH's Global Support department.
  (C) She is unable to honor the special request made by Ms. Boonprasan.
  (D) She has visited Bangkok.

185. In the e-mail, the word "rate" in paragraph 1, line 4, is closest in meaning to

  (A) price
  (B) class
  (C) quantity
  (D) evaluation

Go on to the next page

Questions 186-190 refer to the following product information and e-mails.

Fritz and Logan Furniture: The Contempo Collection
www.fritzlogan.com/contempocollection

Item Code	Description	Price
CC01	Four-seat cushion sofa	$680
CC02	Two-seat cushion sofa	$560
CC03	Armchair and matching ottoman	$430
CC04	Coffee table	$200
CC05	End table	$140

Product details:

- Sofas, armchairs, and ottomans are available in black or brown leather, or soft-grey microfiber fabric.
- Leather furniture should be vacuumed or wiped with a damp cloth.
- Microfiber fabric can be spot-cleaned with soap and water.
- All furniture is delivered preassembled.

If you have questions or would like to learn about special discounts, please contact sales@fritzlogan.com.

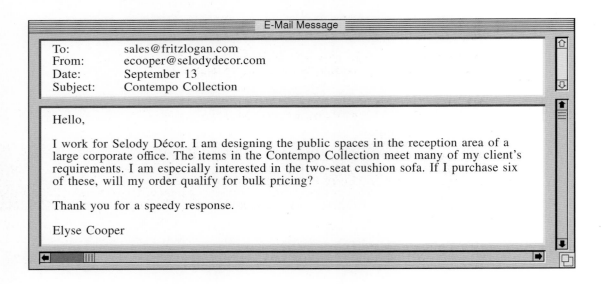

E-Mail Message

To: sales@fritzlogan.com
From: ecooper@selodydecor.com
Date: September 13
Subject: Contempo Collection

Hello,

I work for Selody Décor. I am designing the public spaces in the reception area of a large corporate office. The items in the Contempo Collection meet many of my client's requirements. I am especially interested in the two-seat cushion sofa. If I purchase six of these, will my order qualify for bulk pricing?

Thank you for a speedy response.

Elyse Cooper

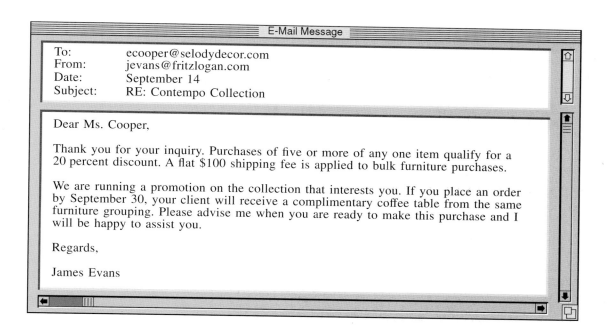

To: ecooper@selodydecor.com
From: jevans@fritzlogan.com
Date: September 14
Subject: RE: Contempo Collection

Dear Ms. Cooper,

Thank you for your inquiry. Purchases of five or more of any one item qualify for a 20 percent discount. A flat $100 shipping fee is applied to bulk furniture purchases.

We are running a promotion on the collection that interests you. If you place an order by September 30, your client will receive a complimentary coffee table from the same furniture grouping. Please advise me when you are ready to make this purchase and I will be happy to assist you.

Regards,

James Evans

---

186. What is indicated in the product information?

(A) More than one kind of table is available.
(B) Customers may transport items themselves.
(C) Preassembled items are subject to an extra fee.
(D) Fabric-covered pieces must be professionally cleaned.

187. Who most likely is Ms. Cooper?

(A) A furniture salesperson
(B) An office receptionist
(C) An interior decorator
(D) A corporate manager

188. In which item is Ms. Cooper most interested?

(A) CC01
(B) CC02
(C) CC03
(D) CC04

189. In the second e-mail, what is stated about bulk pricing?

(A) It is available for customers whose order totals more than $100.
(B) It is given to those who buy any of the items in the Contempo Collection.
(C) It qualifies for a reduced shipping fee.
(D) It is being offered for a limited time.

190. What is the listed price of the gift offered in the Fritz and Logan Furniture promotion?

(A) $140
(B) $200
(C) $430
(D) $560

Go on to the next page

To:	Simon Addington <saddington@happenings.co.uk>
From:	Ravi Tipanis <rtipanis@happenings.co.in>
Subject:	Information
Date:	22 March
Attachment:	📎 eng.report.doc

Dear Mr. Addington:

I just wanted to update you on the progress of the new campus in Hyderabad. The engineering inspections for each building went well, and we're on schedule for a mid-June opening. I've attached the reports for your reference. Let me know if you have any questions.

Sincerely,

Ravi Tipanis

www.globalbusinesswire.com

Happenings Corporation, the e-commerce company headquartered in London, finally opened its new campus in Hyderabad on 4 August. This is the company's first major campus outside of the UK, although it has a sorting center in Mumbai.

Simon Addington, the company's Senior Vice President of Global Facilities, flew in for the opening from Edinburgh. The event marked Mr. Addington's last official duty as he will be retiring on 31 August.

Other guests included Mr. Vineet Bapat, Vice President of Happenings Corporation India, and various government officials. The new campus will employ thousands of workers. The company is still hiring for a variety of positions—from software engineers to maintenance workers. For information on job openings, visit www.happenings.co.in/jobs.

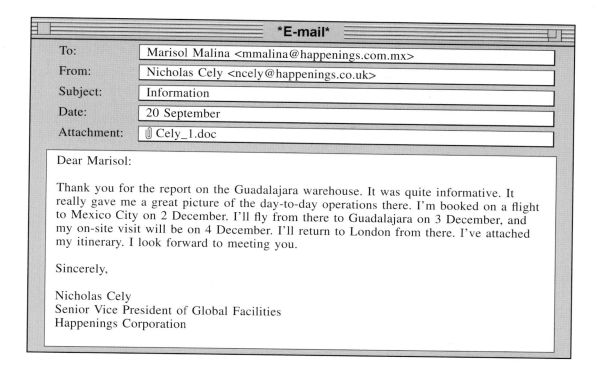

```
┌─────────────────────────────────────────────────────────────────────┐
│  ═══════════════════════════  *E-mail*  ═══════════════════════════  │
├──────────────┬────────────────────────────────────────────────────────┤
│  To:         │  Marisol Malina <mmalina@happenings.com.mx>            │
│  From:       │  Nicholas Cely <ncely@happenings.co.uk>                │
│  Subject:    │  Information                                           │
│  Date:       │  20 September                                          │
│  Attachment: │  📎 Cely_1.doc                                         │
└──────────────┴────────────────────────────────────────────────────────┘
```

Dear Marisol:

Thank you for the report on the Guadalajara warehouse. It was quite informative. It really gave me a great picture of the day-to-day operations there. I'm booked on a flight to Mexico City on 2 December. I'll fly from there to Guadalajara on 3 December, and my on-site visit will be on 4 December. I'll return to London from there. I've attached my itinerary. I look forward to meeting you.

Sincerely,

Nicholas Cely
Senior Vice President of Global Facilities
Happenings Corporation

191. What does the first e-mail suggest about the engineering reports?

(A) They were submitted in late April.
(B) They are incomplete.
(C) They were rejected by Mr. Tipanis.
(D) They do not indicate any major problems.

192. What can be concluded about the Hyderabad campus?

(A) It has been completely staffed.
(B) It opened later than expected.
(C) It is not as large as originally planned.
(D) It is not considered a major campus.

193. According to the article, where is the main office of Happenings Corporation located?

(A) In Mumbai
(B) In Hyderabad
(C) In Edinburgh
(D) In London

194. What is most likely true about Mr. Cely?

(A) He lives in Guadalajara.
(B) He is a friend of Ms. Malina.
(C) He replaced Mr. Addington.
(D) He attended the Hyderabad campus opening.

195. What did Mr. Cely send with the e-mail?

(A) His travel schedule
(B) Some pictures of Mexico
(C) A warehouse report
(D) Some tourist information

Go on to the next page ➡

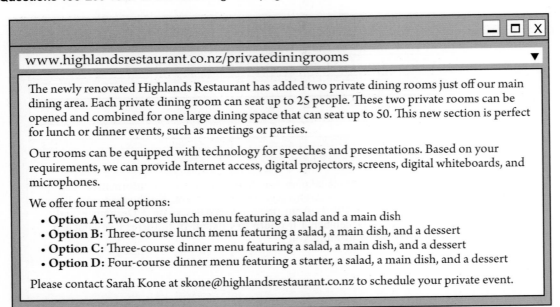

www.highlandsrestaurant.co.nz/privatediningrooms

The newly renovated Highlands Restaurant has added two private dining rooms just off our main dining area. Each private dining room can seat up to 25 people. These two private rooms can be opened and combined for one large dining space that can seat up to 50. This new section is perfect for lunch or dinner events, such as meetings or parties.

Our rooms can be equipped with technology for speeches and presentations. Based on your requirements, we can provide Internet access, digital projectors, screens, digital whiteboards, and microphones.

We offer four meal options:
- **Option A:** Two-course lunch menu featuring a salad and a main dish
- **Option B:** Three-course lunch menu featuring a salad, a main dish, and a dessert
- **Option C:** Three-course dinner menu featuring a salad, a main dish, and a dessert
- **Option D:** Four-course dinner menu featuring a starter, a salad, a main dish, and a dessert

Please contact Sarah Kone at skone@highlandsrestaurant.co.nz to schedule your private event.

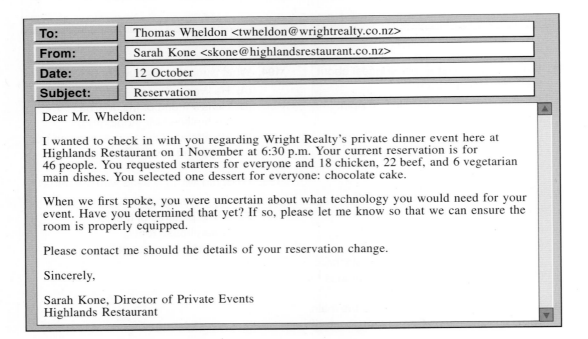

To:	Thomas Wheldon <twheldon@wrightrealty.co.nz>
From:	Sarah Kone <skone@highlandsrestaurant.co.nz>
Date:	12 October
Subject:	Reservation

Dear Mr. Wheldon:

I wanted to check in with you regarding Wright Realty's private dinner event here at Highlands Restaurant on 1 November at 6:30 p.m. Your current reservation is for 46 people. You requested starters for everyone and 18 chicken, 22 beef, and 6 vegetarian main dishes. You selected one dessert for everyone: chocolate cake.

When we first spoke, you were uncertain about what technology you would need for your event. Have you determined that yet? If so, please let me know so that we can ensure the room is properly equipped.

Please contact me should the details of your reservation change.

Sincerely,

Sarah Kone, Director of Private Events
Highlands Restaurant

```
+==============================================================================+
|  ≡≡≡≡≡≡≡≡≡≡≡≡≡≡≡≡≡≡≡≡≡≡≡        *E-mail*        ≡≡≡≡≡≡≡≡≡≡≡≡≡≡≡≡≡≡≡≡≡≡≡      |
+==============================================================================+
```

To: Sarah Kone <skone@highlandsrestaurant.co.nz>

From: Thomas Wheldon <twheldon@wrightrealty.co.nz>

Date: 14 October

Subject: RE: Reservation

Dear Ms. Kone:

Thank you for your e-mail. There have been some changes to my company's award
dinner on 1 November. We now have 48 people attending and need two additional
chicken main dishes added to our order. We have decided that we do not want to include
starters with our dinner. We plan to begin our award ceremony at 7:00 p.m. and would
like the meal service to begin at that time. We will need a digital projector, a screen,
and a microphone for our presentation.

Thank you for your assistance.

Thomas Wheldon
Real Estate Assistant
Wright Realty

196. What does the Web page indicate about Highlands Restaurant?

(A) It will be closing for renovations.
(B) It specializes in vegetarian food.
(C) It is a new restaurant.
(D) It has expanded.

197. What is a purpose of the first e-mail?

(A) To schedule a meeting
(B) To choose a place to eat
(C) To confirm details of an event
(D) To reserve a hotel room

198. What is suggested about the Wright Realty private event?

(A) It will be held in the combined space.
(B) Everyone will have vegetarian food.
(C) The entire office will attend.
(D) It is an annual event.

199. What meal option will most likely be served at the award dinner?

(A) Option A
(B) Option B
(C) Option C
(D) Option D

200. What equipment does Mr. Wheldon request?

(A) A music player
(B) A digital projector
(C) A computer
(D) A video camera

**Stop! This is the end of the test. If you finish before time is called, you may go
back to Parts 5, 6, and 7 and check your work.**

ETS 실전 모의고사 04

PART 7

Directions: In this part you will read a selection of texts, such as magazine and newspaper articles, e-mails, and instant messages. Each text or set of texts is followed by several questions. Select the best answer for each question and mark the letter (A), (B), (C), or (D) on your answer sheet.

Questions 147-148 refer to the following invitation.

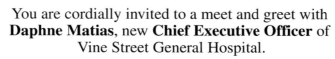

You are cordially invited to a meet and greet with
Daphne Matias, new **Chief Executive Officer** of
Vine Street General Hospital.

October 27, 4:00–5:30 P.M.

Main Conference Room, 2nd floor

Daphne Matias, a longtime hospital administrator at New Hope Hospital, has more than 25 years of experience working with medical centers.

You will have the opportunity to ask Ms. Matias about her vision for Vine Street General Hospital. Light refreshments will be served.

Interested guests can take a tour of Vine Street General Hospital's newly renovated clinics.

147. What is suggested about Ms. Matias?

(A) She works at New Hope Hospital.
(B) She plans to retire soon.
(C) She started a new job recently.
(D) She will be attending a conference on October 27.

148. What will guests be able to do?

(A) Ask questions
(B) Make an appointment
(C) Purchase snacks
(D) View some renovation plans

CHAPTER 3

실전 모의고사 04

Go on to the next page

Questions 149-150 refer to the following online review.

https://www.lakehouselodge.co.ke/reviews

What Our Guests Are Saying . . .

A friend and I traveled to Kenya and stayed at the Lake House Lodge for a few days. We had never been to Kenya before, and it was such a welcoming place. We joined a couple of half-day safaris to get a peek at some of the amazing animals in the region, including zebras and monkeys. From the windows of our room we could see the giraffes that wander freely around the lodge property. Some of the giraffes were so tame that they allowed us to hand-feed them treats. After spending the mornings taking photos of the wildlife, we enjoyed afternoon tea with other lodge visitors in the lovely garden. The lodge staff and our safari guides were kind and attentive. This was a unique vacation for us, and we hope to visit again.

—Walter Breyer, 2 February

149. What does Mr. Breyer indicate in his review?

(A) His trip to Kenya was very expensive.
(B) He was visiting Kenya for the first time.
(C) His vacation had to be shortened by a few days.
(D) He will be returning to Kenya for a business conference.

150. What is NOT an activity mentioned by Mr. Breyer?

(A) Observing local wildlife
(B) Relaxing with lodge guests
(C) Taking photos
(D) Camping outdoors

Jamal Knight [1:09 P.M.]
Hello, Min. I wanted to inform you that the meeting at 1:45 P.M. has been moved to Conference Room B. Your office door was closed, so I was not sure if you were in and if you had seen the e-mail.

Min Jia [1:13 P.M.]
Thanks for letting me know. I left the building earlier for lunch. I didn't see the message. Do you have a few minutes to discuss our presentation before the meeting?

Jamal Knight [1:14 P.M.]
Sure. I have all the printed materials with me now.

Min Jia [1:16 P.M.]
Great. I'm in my office.

Jamal Knight [1:17 P.M.]
OK. We can walk over to the conference room together after we talk.

151. Why did Mr. Knight contact Ms. Jia?

(A) To remind her to close an office door
(B) To invite her to a business lunch
(C) To ask her to reserve a conference room
(D) To inform her of a new meeting place

152. At 1:16 P.M., what does Ms. Jia most likely mean when she writes, "I'm in my office"?

(A) She thinks Mr. Knight has made a mistake.
(B) She can meet with Mr. Knight now.
(C) She is very busy with a project.
(D) She is reading her e-mail messages.

Go on to the next page

Questions 153-155 refer to the following e-mail.

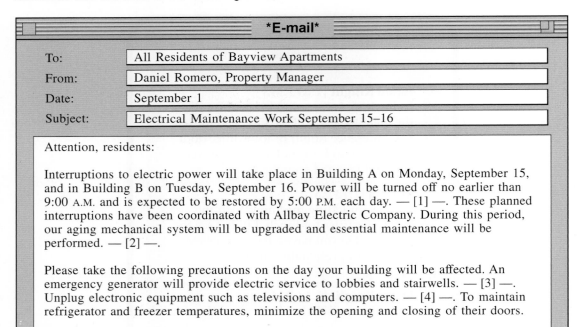

<table>
<tr><td>To:</td><td>All Residents of Bayview Apartments</td></tr>
<tr><td>From:</td><td>Daniel Romero, Property Manager</td></tr>
<tr><td>Date:</td><td>September 1</td></tr>
<tr><td>Subject:</td><td>Electrical Maintenance Work September 15–16</td></tr>
</table>

Attention, residents:

Interruptions to electric power will take place in Building A on Monday, September 15, and in Building B on Tuesday, September 16. Power will be turned off no earlier than 9:00 A.M. and is expected to be restored by 5:00 P.M. each day. — [1] —. These planned interruptions have been coordinated with Allbay Electric Company. During this period, our aging mechanical system will be upgraded and essential maintenance will be performed. — [2] —.

Please take the following precautions on the day your building will be affected. An emergency generator will provide electric service to lobbies and stairwells. — [3] —. Unplug electronic equipment such as televisions and computers. — [4] —. To maintain refrigerator and freezer temperatures, minimize the opening and closing of their doors.

Please reach out to me with questions at d.romero@bayviewapt.com. We appreciate your patience and understanding.

---

153. What is the purpose of the e-mail?

(A) To coordinate work between different contractors
(B) To announce a change in electric companies
(C) To explain a proposed billing increase
(D) To announce a planned service disruption

154. What are residents instructed to do?

(A) Purchase generators
(B) Unplug electronics
(C) Keep windows closed
(D) Meet with Mr. Romero

155. In which of the positions marked [1], [2], [3], and [4] does the following sentence best belong?

"Plan to use the stairs rather than the elevators."

(A) [1]
(B) [2]
(C) [3]
(D) [4]

Questions 156-158 refer to the following information.

Welcome to Cardona Town Suites!

Our accommodations are designed to provide our guests with the comforts of home and the conveniences of an office. We are sure that you will appreciate our many amenities.

A complimentary breakfast is served every morning in the Ivy Room from 7:00 to 10:00 A.M., and coffee, tea, and snacks can be enjoyed there throughout the day. A very reasonably priced dinner buffet is served on Tuesday and Thursday evenings, either on the patio or in the main conference room, depending on weather conditions. Laundry facilities are in the housekeeping building on the east side of the parking area. Coin-operated washers and dryers are available all day.

Our self-serve business center is stocked with essential office supplies and offers free Internet access and use of computers and printers. Front desk staff can reserve one of our meeting rooms for you with advance notice.

We hope that your stay with us is productive and enjoyable.

156. What type of guests would Cardona Town Suites mostly attract?

(A) Families with children
(B) Business travelers
(C) University students
(D) Tourists visiting local sites

157. Where can guests find a light snack during the day?

(A) At the front desk
(B) On the patio
(C) In the Ivy Room
(D) In a conference room

158. According to the information, what are guests NOT able to do themselves?

(A) Wash clothes
(B) Print documents
(C) Obtain food items
(D) Reserve a meeting room

Go on to the next page

Questions 159-161 refer to the following letter.

Avo Airlines Credit Card
178 Anderson Street
BRISBANE QLD 4001

Mr. John Lao
90 Banksia Court
DOTSWOOD QLD 4820

Dear Mr. Lao,

Did you know you could quickly earn 50,000 travel points as a new Avo Airlines credit card holder? Just for signing up, you will earn 20,000 travel points. Then, when you spend $1,000 within the first 3 months of using your Avo Airlines credit card, you will receive an additional 30,000 points. You also earn points when flying to any of our 75 national and international destinations. Your Avo Airlines credit card also entitles you to early boarding when flying with us. Moreover, you are eligible for discounts at any of our valued business partners. Enjoy access to all these benefits for an annual fee of just $99. For more information, visit www.avoairlines.com/cc.

Sincerely,

Debbie Urbano

Debbie Urbano, Member Services
Avo Airlines Credit Card

---

159. How many travel points can Mr. Lao automatically receive when he opens an Avo Airlines credit card?

(A) 10,000
(B) 20,000
(C) 30,000
(D) 50,000

160. What is stated about holders of an Avo Airlines credit card?

(A) They are offered a discount of $99 on airline tickets.
(B) They enjoy priority boarding on company flights.
(C) They do not pay an annual fee for the first year.
(D) They can use points to upgrade to a business class seat.

161. The word "benefits" in paragraph 1, line 7, is closest in meaning to

(A) advantages
(B) requests
(C) payments
(D) events

SEARCHING FOR A JOB?

Come to Barrington Public Library's series on conducting an effective job search!

Wednesdays, March 4, 11, 18, 25
6:30 P.M.–9:00 P.M.

Session 1: Identifying Job Opportunities
Session 2: Creating a Résumé
Session 3: Writing Cover Letters
Session 4: Interviewing Effectively

Join professional editor Catherine Troutman to learn the tricks of the trade for getting the job you want. She will teach you how to get your application noticed by developing an outstanding résumé and cover letter.

The event is free, but each session is limited to the first 40 respondents. To RSVP, e-mail Eitan Liebowitz at eliebowitz@bpl.org. Registration is available for the entire series or for an individual session.

162. What is indicated about the series?

(A) It will take place in several locations.
(B) It will happen in the morning.
(C) It will be offered every month.
(D) It will be held in the library.

163. What is mentioned as a benefit of attending the series?

(A) One-on-one help from several industry experts
(B) Tips for creating a cover letter
(C) Practice interviews with other participants
(D) Opportunities to network

164. What do participants need to do to sign up for a session?

(A) Send payment to Ms. Troutman
(B) Complete an online form
(C) Contact Mr. Liebowitz
(D) Submit a copy of their résumé

Go on to the next page

Questions 165-167 refer to the following e-mail.

```
========================  *E-mail*  ========================

From:      Marc Kuniya

To:        All employees

Subject:   Shannon White

Date:      May 9
```

To all staff:

It is my pleasure to announce that Shannon White will be joining Curry Light Fixtures, Inc., on May 12 as Chicago-based Sales Director for the central region. Prior to joining our team, Shannon served in a variety of roles at Energy Ambassadors Corporation (EAC). Shannon started her career as a sales associate at EAC right out of university to eventually become store manager at their Evanston location. Finally, Shannon spent the last five years working as a regional sales manager for EAC.

Shannon has a bachelor's degree in business and an MBA degree from East California University. During her studies, she conducted research in Singapore on sustainable growth. In her spare time, Shannon volunteers for a local charity that teaches art to young children. She also enjoys distance running and hopes to complete her first marathon by the end of this year.

Please help me welcome Shannon to the Curry Light Fixtures team!

Sincerely,

Marc Kuniya
Vice President of Sales
Curry Light Fixtures, Inc.

---

165. What is the purpose of the e-mail?

(A) To advertise a job opening
(B) To promote a university program
(C) To introduce a new employee
(D) To announce a relocation

166. What is true about Ms. White?

(A) She co-founded EAC.
(B) She holds two academic degrees.
(C) She has taught college classes.
(D) She has had several positions at Curry Light Fixtures, Inc.

167. What does Ms. White plan to do by the end of the year?

(A) Establish a local charity
(B) Find a job in Singapore
(C) Finish a research project
(D) Compete in a sports event

5 June, Weybridge—Chefs Roberto Bianchi and Antonio Conti have been preparing Italian cuisine for Londoners for the past ten years. — [1] —. Pomodoro, a bistro on Floortham Street in Weybridge, opened on 17 May to strong reviews. With the financial backing of Kenneth Mulgrew, a local investor, the restaurant occupies a beautiful two-story brick building with a contemporary interior décor. — [2] —. Open from 11:00 A.M. to 10:00 P.M., Pomodoro offers menu selections that fuse traditional Italian and British dishes. Mr. Bianchi comments, "Antonio and I are greatly influenced by British cuisine and London culture. We want to incorporate that into the dishes we serve in our restaurants."

This successful pair own three restaurants in the West End of London. Mr. Bianchi, who grew up near Capri, Italy, cites his father's cooking as his inspiration. "He carefully prepared dinner every night using old family recipes." After studying Italian cooking formally for two years and attending numerous workshops, Mr. Bianchi, together with his childhood neighbor Antonio Conti, came to London and opened Bella Ristorante. — [3] —. The duo have been successful restaurateurs ever since.

Conti explains, "We are trying to make our food accessible to those who don't live in the city so that they can enjoy it, too. — [4] —. Weybridge was a logical location because the local rail station makes it easy to get to and from surrounding towns."

Pomodoro takes reservations, but they should be made well in advance.

168. What did Mr. Mulgrew most likely provide to Mr. Bianchi and Mr. Conti?

(A) A list of properties
(B) Funding for their business
(C) Decorating services
(D) Menu ideas

169. What is suggested about Mr. Conti?

(A) He lives in Weybridge.
(B) He attended culinary school with Mr. Bianchi.
(C) He was raised in Italy.
(D) He took courses in British cooking.

170. Why was Weybridge chosen as a site for the restaurant?

(A) It is inexpensive to operate a business there.
(B) It is easy to get there from other towns.
(C) It is a heavily populated area.
(D) It is a very scenic seaside location.

171. In which of the positions marked [1], [2], [3], and [4] does the following sentence best belong?

"Now they have opened their first restaurant outside the city."

(A) [1]
(B) [2]
(C) [3]
(D) [4]

Go on to the next page

Questions 172-175 refer to the following online chat discussion.

Leticia Clark (1:15 P.M.)	Hello, Ana. Do you know what the issue is with the Fonte Books sales page?
Ana Weiser (1:17 P.M.)	Sorry, I wasn't aware there is one. Let me look at it.
Leticia Clark (1:18 P.M.)	I started getting calls about it on the help line about 25 minutes ago. Now they are getting more frequent.
Ana Weiser (1:19 P.M.)	I see it now. When a customer clicks on the "BUY NOW" button, the books in the shopping cart disappear.
Leticia Clark (1:20 P.M.)	Exactly.
Ana Weiser (1:21 P.M.)	Hi, Joseph. It seems we have a problem with the Fonte Books online order form. Can you post a "Page down for maintenance" message while I get everything sorted out?
Joseph Ilomo (1:22 P.M.)	Sure thing. How long do you think you'll need?
Ana Weiser (1:23 P.M.)	Maybe about 40 minutes.
Joseph Ilomo (1:24 P.M.)	Sounds good.
Leticia Clark (1:25 P.M.)	Thanks, Ana.
Ana Weiser (1:26 P.M.)	Sure. I'll get things running smoothly again as quickly as possible and notify you both when I'm done.

172. What problem is identified in the chat discussion?

(A) A call center is understaffed.
(B) A popular book has sold out.
(C) An online shopping portal cannot process orders.
(D) A technical support crew cannot fix a connectivity issue.

173. From whom is Ms. Clark receiving calls?

(A) Book authors
(B) Office staff
(C) Customers
(D) Sales representatives

174. What is Mr. Ilomo asked to do?

(A) Complete a sales transaction
(B) Contact a branch office
(C) Display a temporary message
(D) Postpone a maintenance task

175. At 1:24 P.M., what does Mr. Ilomo most likely mean when he writes, "Sounds good"?

(A) He accepts a proposed plan.
(B) He will meet with colleagues shortly.
(C) He thinks that a marketing idea will be successful.
(D) He is glad that Ms. Weiser will keep meeting notes.

Go on to the next page

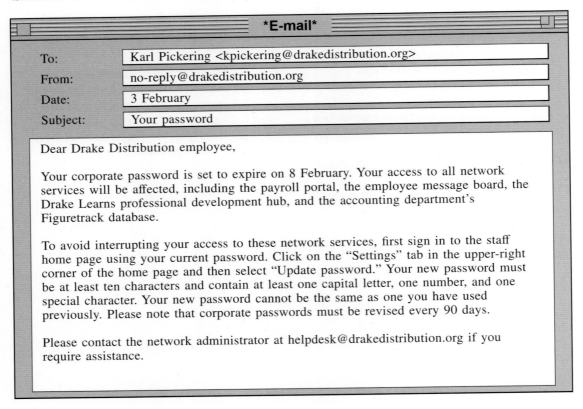

E-mail

To: Karl Pickering <kpickering@drakedistribution.org>

From: no-reply@drakedistribution.org

Date: 3 February

Subject: Your password

Dear Drake Distribution employee,

Your corporate password is set to expire on 8 February. Your access to all network services will be affected, including the payroll portal, the employee message board, the Drake Learns professional development hub, and the accounting department's Figuretrack database.

To avoid interrupting your access to these network services, first sign in to the staff home page using your current password. Click on the "Settings" tab in the upper-right corner of the home page and then select "Update password." Your new password must be at least ten characters and contain at least one capital letter, one number, and one special character. Your new password cannot be the same as one you have used previously. Please note that corporate passwords must be revised every 90 days.

Please contact the network administrator at helpdesk@drakedistribution.org if you require assistance.

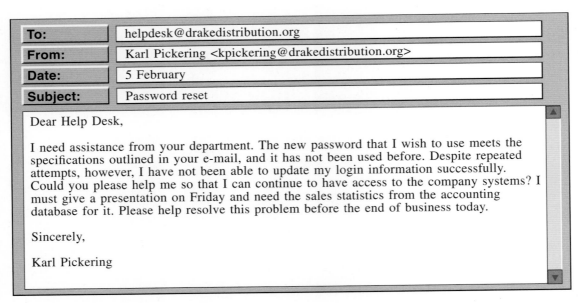

To: helpdesk@drakedistribution.org

From: Karl Pickering <kpickering@drakedistribution.org>

Date: 5 February

Subject: Password reset

Dear Help Desk,

I need assistance from your department. The new password that I wish to use meets the specifications outlined in your e-mail, and it has not been used before. Despite repeated attempts, however, I have not been able to update my login information successfully. Could you please help me so that I can continue to have access to the company systems? I must give a presentation on Friday and need the sales statistics from the accounting database for it. Please help resolve this problem before the end of business today.

Sincerely,

Karl Pickering

176. What is a purpose of the first e-mail?

(A) To announce a new company policy
(B) To notify an employee of a deadline
(C) To introduce a new professional development course
(D) To explain why an account has been deleted

177. What is indicated in the first e-mail?

(A) Login information must be changed periodically.
(B) The staff home page has recently been redesigned.
(C) Some databases are offline for maintenance.
(D) Each staff member must contact the help desk.

178. In the second e-mail, the word "meets" in paragraph 1, line 1, is closest in meaning to

(A) encounters
(B) locates
(C) appears
(D) satisfies

179. What problem is Mr. Pickering having?

(A) His call to the help desk was not returned.
(B) His access to the staff home page has been suspended.
(C) He is unable to reset his password.
(D) He has lost a link to a Web page.

180. Where will Mr. Pickering most likely find the information he needs for his presentation?

(A) In the payroll portal
(B) In Drake Learns
(C) In Figuretrack
(D) On the employee message board

Go on to the next page

Rental Agreement

This agreement is made on _November 20_ between _Alex Edwards_ (landlord) and _Joshua and Maisie Adler_ (renters) to rent the dwelling at _42 Oak Place_ under the following terms and conditions:

Section 1: Occupancy
The renters may occupy the premises _from January 1 through December 31_. Occupancy of this property will be limited to _Joshua and Maisie Adler and their children_. Guests of the renters may stay on the premises for no longer than ten consecutive days per visit.

Section 2: Payment
The renters agree to pay $1,500 per month. The rent is due on or before the first of every month.

Section 3: Security deposit
The renters will pay a security deposit equal to one month's rent. This is intended to cover any damages that might occur during the period of the occupancy. If the renters leave the premises in the same condition as when they moved in, the entire security deposit will be returned. The landlord may also use the security deposit to cover any unpaid rent.

Section 4: Utilities
The renters must pay electricity, gas, and Internet fees directly to the supplier. The landlord will be responsible for fees associated with weekly trash pickup and water.

Landlord: _Alex Edwards_
Alex Edwards

Renters: _Joshua and Maisie Adler_
Joshua and Maisie Adler

Date: _November 20_

E-mail

From:	Maisie Adler
To:	Alex Edwards
Date:	June 20
Subject:	Rental agreement

Dear Mr. Edwards,

I have a request of you. Would it be possible for my mother to stay with us for two weeks? She has a construction project planned for her house at the beginning of August and does not have other housing options during that period.

Also, I have just mailed the check for next month's rent, so you should receive it before July 1st. Please note that I have sent it to your new address, as you directed.

Thanks for your consideration,

Maisie Adler

181. What is indicated about the rental agreement?

(A) It is for one renter.
(B) It was signed at 42 Oak Place.
(C) It is for one year.
(D) It can be renewed.

182. What is stated about the security deposit?

(A) It is the same amount as a month's rent.
(B) It must be paid by check.
(C) It covers the first month's rent.
(D) It can be applied to unpaid utilities.

183. For what service does the landlord pay?

(A) Electricity
(B) Gas
(C) Internet
(D) Water

184. For what part of the rental agreement does Ms. Adler request an exception?

(A) Section 1
(B) Section 2
(C) Section 3
(D) Section 4

185. What does Ms. Adler imply about the rent check?

(A) It was sent to the wrong address.
(B) It will arrive on time.
(C) It is from a new account.
(D) It may have been lost in the mail.

Go on to the next page

To:	faisal-ali@znetmail.com
From:	a.skartsi@tourism.lavidas.gov
Date:	24 July
Subject:	RE: Final details

Dear Mr. Ali,

Thank you for your e-mail about the welcome dinner on 30 July for the Reviving Tourism in Lavidas conference. I've added your name to the list of guests who will receive a vegetarian meal.

The conference will be held at the Iris Hotel. If you use public transportation, you can take either the Route 3 bus or the Route 5 bus from the Port James depot. The Iris Hotel is conveniently located right across from the final stop. The town's two other hotels are both visible from the entrance to the Iris Hotel, so you can easily reach whichever one you'll be staying in.

Please let me know if you have any further questions or concerns.

Best wishes,

Alicia Skartsi

Lavidas Island Bus Schedule
Monday–Sunday, May through August

#	Route	Departure Times	
		From Port James	*To Port James*
1	Port James–Mela–Ampra	12:30 P.M., 7:30 P.M.	8:00 A.M., 11:30 A.M.
2	Port James–Kanisi	6:45 P.M.	8:15 A.M.
3	Port James–Plata–Elodia	4:30 P.M.	7:45 A.M.
4	Port James–Samirola	8:15 A.M., 6:30 P.M.	7:00 A.M., 6:00 P.M.
5	Port James–Mela–Elodia	12:45 P.M., 6:45 P.M.	9:30 A.M., 11:45 A.M.
6	Port James–Airport	9:30 A.M., noon, 3:15 P.M.	10:30 A.M., 1:00 P.M., 5:00 P.M.

LAVIDAS ISLAND BUSES

We are sorry to inform you that today (**30 July**) there will be **no** buses running to Samirola. This is due to a temporary road closure. For alternative transportation options, speak to someone in the main office.

Please be advised that, as always, tickets **must** be purchased before you board any bus. Tickets are available here in Port James at the Lavidas Buses main office or in the airport. They are also for sale in restaurants and shops across the island.

---

186. For what purpose is Mr. Ali traveling to Lavidas Island?

(A) To teach a class about the local cuisine
(B) To learn about tourism on the island
(C) To attend a transportation seminar
(D) To perform hotel inspections

187. What information does Ms. Skartsi most likely know about Mr. Ali?

(A) His time of arrival on the island
(B) His dietary requirements
(C) The hotel in which he will be staying
(D) The country in which he lives

188. In what town is the Iris Hotel located?

(A) Port James
(B) Mela
(C) Samirola
(D) Elodia

189. What bus route has been canceled for July 30 ?

(A) Route 1
(B) Route 2
(C) Route 4
(D) Route 6

190. What does the notice indicate about the restaurants on the island?

(A) They sell bus tickets.
(B) They are located near bus stations.
(C) They have extended hours during the tourist season.
(D) They sell souvenirs to tourists.

Go on to the next page

Questions 191-195 refer to the following Web page, memo, and e-mail.

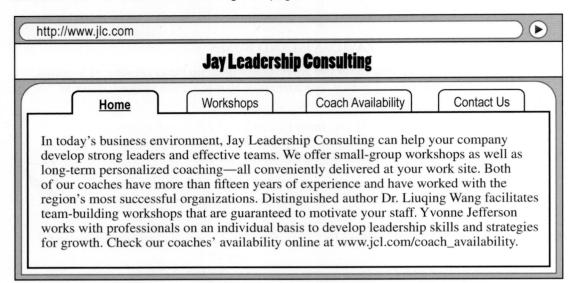

http://www.jlc.com

Jay Leadership Consulting

| Home | Workshops | Coach Availability | Contact Us |

In today's business environment, Jay Leadership Consulting can help your company develop strong leaders and effective teams. We offer small-group workshops as well as long-term personalized coaching—all conveniently delivered at your work site. Both of our coaches have more than fifteen years of experience and have worked with the region's most successful organizations. Distinguished author Dr. Liuqing Wang facilitates team-building workshops that are guaranteed to motivate your staff. Yvonne Jefferson works with professionals on an individual basis to develop leadership skills and strategies for growth. Check our coaches' availability online at www.jcl.com/coach_availability.

MEMO

To: SRT Division professional staff
From: Kendall Harkin, Divisional Director
Date: October 12
Re: Workshops

Narlan Enterprises is pleased to welcome back Dr. Liuqing Wang for two days next week. Dr. Wang will be leading workshops that I hope many of you will be able to attend. Feedback on these workshops has always been very positive, so I highly recommend that you attend if possible.

| *Building Strong Teams* | October 18, 9:30 a.m. to 11:30 a.m. | 3rd Floor, Lounge B |
| *Ideas into Action* | October 19, 10:00 a.m. to 11:30 a.m. | Weston Room |

Seating is limited, so register as soon as possible using Narlan's online event portal. As usual, check with your manager beforehand to make sure business responsibilities will be met while you are attending the workshop.

To:	info@jlc.com
From:	Alex Worley
Date:	October 22
Subject:	Next step

Hello,

A couple of days ago, I participated in one of Dr. Wang's workshops at Narlan Enterprises. I signed up based on the positive comments my colleagues made about the previous day's workshop. I was lucky to get the last available seat in that very inspiring and interactive workshop. The group work we did was very beneficial.

At one point, Dr. Wang mentioned that Jay Leadership Consulting also provides one-on-one coaching. I spoke with my boss, Ms. Harkin, about the possibility, and she supported the idea. Can you tell me more about the options?

Thank you,

Alex Worley

191. Where are Jay Leadership Consulting workshops usually conducted?

(A) In hotel ballrooms
(B) Over the Internet
(C) At its headquarters
(D) At its clients' offices

192. What does the memo instruct workshop attendees to do?

(A) Consult their supervisors
(B) Develop new business ideas
(C) Recommend the workshops to others
(D) Provide feedback about the workshop

193. Why did Mr. Worley send the e-mail?

(A) To provide a reference
(B) To inquire about a program
(C) To postpone an appointment
(D) To complain about a workshop

194. What is probably true about the Ideas into Action workshop?

(A) It was delivered to a full room.
(B) It was postponed to a later date.
(C) It was held late in the afternoon.
(D) It received poor feedback from attendees.

195. What will the recipient of Mr. Worley's e-mail most likely do in response?

(A) Send a refund to Mr. Worley
(B) Complete a registration form
(C) Offer Ms. Jefferson's services
(D) Provide information about team-building opportunities

Go on to the next page

FOR IMMEDIATE RELEASE
13 October

Contact: Ruby Raymond, rraymond@sunnyplazahotel.com.jm

(Kingston)—The Sunny Plaza Hotel on St. Lucia Avenue in Kingston announced today that it will reopen its restaurant, Sunshine Grill, on 28 October. The restaurant has gone through extensive remodeling, which includes the addition of a banquet space that will be reserved for groups of 30 or more guests. Marc Silva remains as Executive Chef, overseeing all restaurant operations, but Leica Ellison will assume the role of Head Chef for the banquet and catering side.

Sunny Plaza Manager Derek Cordova said, "We're excited about these changes. The Sunny Plaza has always offered a top-notch experience for overnight guests. Now we can provide a setting for business and social events as well." The Sunny Plaza Hotel offers 70 guest rooms, a fitness area, a business centre, and a meeting space.

To:	Derek Cordova
From:	Leica Ellison
Date:	20 October
Subject:	Reservation request

Hi, Derek.

Thank you for forwarding the request from the Kingston Science Association (KSA) to hold their annual dinner event in our banquet space here at the Sunny Plaza Hotel. If it is acceptable to you, I would like to wait until 31 October before confirming the KSA event date of 25 November. While our kitchen is now fully staffed, we still have some gaps in our service staff. We will need a minimum of twelve servers to handle a group as large as the KSA. I would like to have these positions filled before we commit so that we can be confident that the staff will be fully trained by the event date. Please let me know if this slight delay will be a problem.

Thank you,

Leica

The Kingston Science Association (KSA) is proud to recognise Leonel Avila as the first recipient of the Unger Technology and Innovation Award. Please join us in celebrating this achievement at the association's annual dinner.

Friday, 29 December, 6:30 P.M.
Opal Room, Northern View Conference Centre
130 Seymour Avenue, Kingston

KSA President Vondra Stephens will present the award, which has been made possible by the generous sponsorship of Kingston business leader Edward Unger.

Please respond to event coordinator Janine Blissett at jblissett@ksa.com.jm by 20 December.

196. What does the press release announce?

(A) The construction of a new hotel
(B) The completion of a renovation project
(C) The hiring of an executive chef
(D) The updating of a restaurant's menu

197. According to the press release, what does the Sunny Plaza Hotel offer?

(A) Discounts for large groups
(B) A dry cleaning service
(C) A swimming pool
(D) Exercise equipment

198. What is suggested about the reservation request Ms. Ellison received?

(A) It will be confirmed right away.
(B) It is for twelve rooms.
(C) It is for an event with at least 30 guests.
(D) It will be handled by Ms. Raymond.

199. According to the invitation, who will receive a prize?

(A) Mr. Avila
(B) Ms. Stephens
(C) Ms. Blissett
(D) Mr. Unger

200. What is suggested about the KSA event?

(A) It is being held for the first time.
(B) It will end at 6:30 P.M.
(C) It will take place at the Sunny Plaza Hotel.
(D) It has been moved to a different date.

Stop! This is the end of the test. If you finish before time is called, you may go back to Parts 5, 6, and 7 and check your work.

ETS | 실전 모의고사 05

PART 7

Directions: In this part you will read a selection of texts, such as magazine and newspaper articles, e-mails, and instant messages. Each text or set of texts is followed by several questions. Select the best answer for each question and mark the letter (A), (B), (C), or (D) on your answer sheet.

Questions 147-148 refer to the following flyer.

Hollandville Public Library
Annual Book Sale
Friday, October 12, to Tuesday, October 16

- Purchase used books of all genres at bargain prices!
- Book donations accepted September 15 to October 7.
  To donate, bring your gently used books to the front desk.
- The sale will be held in room B, outside the library café.
- All proceeds will go toward updating the children's collection.
- A flat fee of $5 includes admission and a stylish engraved bookmark.

---

147. What is indicated about the Hollandville Public Library?

(A) It is hosting its first book sale.
(B) It accepts book sale donations throughout the year.
(C) Its children's section will be improved.
(D) It is looking for volunteers to work at its book sale.

148. What does the cost of entry include?

(A) A book
(B) A café voucher
(C) A membership discount
(D) A bookmark

Go on to the next page

Questions 149-150 refer to the following text-message chain.

Shadia Alotaibi [10:15 A.M.] Rocio, thanks again for chatting with me at the career fair last week. Your tips on résumé writing helped. Are you still able to meet to review mine?

Rocio Souza [10:16 A.M.] Of course. Can you stop by my office downtown? Any time after 4:00 P.M. is good.

Shadia Alotaibi [10:18 A.M.] Sorry, I can't today. My car will be in the auto shop all day.

Rocio Souza [10:19 A.M.] I live in the southeast part of town. Isn't that close to you? We could meet somewhere in the vicinity after work hours.

Shadia Alotaibi [10:20 A.M.] That might be easier. Do you know the Lemon Tree Café? Say, 6:30 this evening?

Rocio Souza [10:22 A.M.] I just checked my schedule — and yes, I know where that is. See you then!

149. Why is Ms. Alotaibi contacting Ms. Souza?

(A) To arrange a follow-up job interview
(B) To report on an auto shop service
(C) To request professional guidance
(D) To apologize for missing an appointment

150. At 10:20 A.M., what does Ms. Alotaibi most likely mean when she writes, "That might be easier"?

(A) Her neighborhood has many cafés.
(B) Ms. Souza's office building is familiar.
(C) Many bus routes go downtown.
(D) A suggested meeting is convenient.

ADDERSON INDUSTRIAL

Security Alarm Systems

Adderson Industrial alarms are designed for areas of a building in which early detection is critical to security. They are typically installed in laboratories, industrial buildings, and archives and can be adjusted for the specific environments in which they are installed. In addition to the newest camera technology, options include infrared temperature sensors and 24–7 monitoring.

Using state-of-the-art wireless and automation technology, the system sends notifications to the central monitoring station within seconds of detecting movement or a change in temperature. Contracts for monitoring on a monthly or annual basis are available.

---

151. What is stated about the product?

(A) It is intended for residential buildings.
(B) It sends text-message notifications.
(C) It is suitable for outdoor use.
(D) It has sensors to detect changes in heat.

152. What option is available to customers?

(A) A camera upgrade
(B) Additional telephone lines
(C) Yearly monitoring contracts
(D) Free installation

Go on to the next page

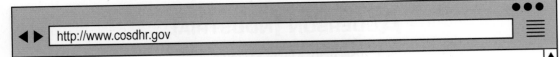

CITY OF STEELESVILLE
DEPARTMENT OF HUMAN RESOURCES
Notice of Revised Job Application Process

Effective June 1, the Department of Human Resources (DHR) of the City of Steelesville will only accept employment applications submitted electronically. Paper-based applications will be declined.

To start the process, go to www.cosdhr.gov/sign-up and create a personal profile. Next, click the Submit button and then set up a username and password. Your log-on credentials will enable you to search our employment database for a position that matches your interests and abilities. Once you have found an appropriate position, click on the name, complete the application form, and upload your résumé and cover letter. Please include the position's reference number, located at the top of the application form, in your cover letter. **Please note: applications without these two documents will not be reviewed.**

If you have any problems with the Web site, please call our 24-hour technical support center at 555-0125 or e-mail techsupport@cosdhr.gov.

153. What does the announcement indicate about DHR?

(A) It will no longer require résumé submission.

(B) It updates its employment database weekly.

(C) It will refuse job applications submitted on paper.

(D) It responds to employment inquiries within 24 hours.

154. What are job seekers asked to do?

(A) Change their username regularly

(B) Indicate a reference number in their cover letter

(C) List their career goals on the application form

(D) Submit two letters of reference with each application

Questions 155-157 refer to the following news article.

MUMBAI, India, June 3 — Star Airways, Mumbai's dominant airline for the past five years, has reported it is planning to replace its entire aircraft fleet with European-produced Skystream jets. Starting with an initial purchase of 90 jets, Star Airways expects the changeover to take a decade to complete. The new planes will enable the airline to expand its international routes as well as provide replacements for its aging fleet of jet planes. Star Airways and Skystream, in a joint announcement at the Brussels Air Show on Thursday, said that the order included seventeen of the new AWB850 aircraft. This will make Star Airways the first Indian carrier to fly the AWB850, an aim it has had since the powerful jets were first produced.

155. What is the purpose of the article?

(A) To describe recent renovations at an airport
(B) To announce a new business agreement
(C) To inform investors of updated project plans
(D) To report on the merger of two airlines

156. How long is the change expected to take?

(A) Three years
(B) Five years
(C) Ten years
(D) Seventeen years

157. What is NOT reported as a goal of Star Airways?

(A) To relocate its international headquarters
(B) To be among the first to use a new aircraft
(C) To replace the older planes in its fleet
(D) To increase its number of flight destinations

Go on to the next page

Questions 158-160 refer to the following e-mail.

From:	omtproject@avhmuseum.org
To:	khandzlik@mediomail.com
Date:	September 23
Subject:	OMT Project

Dear Ms. Handzlik,

We would like to express our appreciation for your contribution of $100 to the Online Museum Translation Project. Support from community members like you is helping to finance the translation of our Museum Web portal into Spanish and French, a project that is now nearing completion. The importance of such contributions cannot be stressed enough; without them, we would not be able to pay our translators for their services.

With best regards,

Albuquerque Valley History Museum

158. Why was the e-mail sent to Ms. Handzlik?

(A) To ask her to provide a service
(B) To inquire about a recent visit
(C) To thank her for a donation
(D) To offer a museum ticket

159. The word "stressed" in paragraph 1, line 4, is closest in meaning to

(A) exhausted
(B) emphasized
(C) forced
(D) worried

160. What project is the museum currently involved in?

(A) Organizing a community event
(B) Renovating its old building
(C) Purchasing new exhibits
(D) Creating new language versions of its Web site

Staff Recognition Programme

Have you experienced an especially noteworthy level of service from a city employee? The Staff Appreciation Programme is designed to recognise Brisbane city government employees who excel in service to the public. — [1] —. Nominations may be made by fellow employees as well as members of the public. Persons submitting nominations need not be residents of Brisbane. — [2] —. Nominators are asked to submit commentary or documentary evidence of the employee's exemplary performance and professionalism. — [3] —. Submissions are considered during each quarterly meeting of the city's executive committee, and a candidate is selected. The recipient is announced soon afterwards and receives a plaque during a brief ceremony at the city hall. — [4] —.

161. What is the purpose of the program?

(A) To acknowledge staff who have served for many years

(B) To reward staff who have done a job well

(C) To remember staff who have retired

(D) To recommend staff for new assignments

162. Who is in charge of the selection process?

(A) Members of a committee

(B) Employee supervisors

(C) Brisbane business executives

(D) The mayor of Brisbane

163. In which of the positions marked [1], [2], [3], and [4] does the following sentence best belong?

"The honoree is also featured in local media reports."

(A) [1]

(B) [2]

(C) [3]

(D) [4]

Go on to the next page

Gina Kwon (1:09 P.M.) Hello, Jim. I think I left my USB drive in Ludmilla's office. Our presentation to the board of directors of Snackerlandia is on it. Can you get it and bring it with you?

Jim Smith (1:10 P.M.) Sure. Are you at their location already?

Gina Kwon (1:12 P.M.) No, I'm at Conchita's Coffee House. I wanted to go over the key elements of that presentation one last time when I noticed that I did not have the drive with me.

Jim Smith (1:13 P.M.) Don't worry. We'll do just fine. After all, we have been designing that digital advertising campaign every day for the last two months. I'm going over to Ludmilla's office now.

Gina Kwon (1:17 P.M.) And? Did you get it?

Jim Smith (1:18 P.M.) Sorry, Gina. It seems Ludmilla has left for the day and has locked her office. I can call the security desk to come and open the door to her office.

Gina Kwon (1:19 P.M.) That won't be necessary. You'll find the document on the shared drive in the "New Projects" folder under the name "Snackadcamp." Just copy it on a USB drive.

Jim Smith (1:22 P.M.) Alright. Is it password protected?

Gina Kwon (1:23 P.M.) No, it's not.

Jim Smith (1:25 P.M.) Okay, I'll get right to it. Anything else?

Gina Kwon (1:26 P.M.) No, thanks. See you there.

164. What type of business are the writers in?

    (A) Computer technology
    (B) Building security
    (C) Advertising
    (D) Food service

165. What is suggested about Mr. Smith?

    (A) His presentation to Snackerlandia officials was well received.
    (B) He regularly gives presentations with Ms. Kwon.
    (C) His office is next to Ludmilla's office.
    (D) He will be attending a meeting soon.

166. At 1:18 P.M., what does Mr. Smith mean when he writes, "Sorry, Gina"?

    (A) He feels bad that Ms. Kwon has to redo the presentation.
    (B) He is apologetic that he is unable to get Ms. Kwon's USB drive.
    (C) He is upset that Ms. Kwon is not yet at Snackerlandia's office.
    (D) He regrets that it took Ms. Kwon two months to work on the project.

167. What will most likely happen next?

    (A) A file will be copied.
    (B) A password will be changed.
    (C) Some folders will be created.
    (D) Some software will be installed.

Go on to the next page

WYB Technologies, Inc.

456 W. 45th St.
New Hope, TX 75009

January 5
Simon Kwan
PO Box 352
McKinney, TX 75071

Dear Mr. Kwan:

This letter is to confirm our agreement for your services as a software-training consultant for WYB Technologies, Inc.

Your assignment will begin on February 15 and end on June 15. This includes conducting training sessions at each of our three regional offices and attending all regular monthly meetings.

As we discussed, you will be compensated a total of $1,400.00 for your services. Payment will be disseminated as follows:

March 15: $350   April 15: $350   May 15: $350   June 15: $350

Because this is a part-time temporary assignment, you are not entitled to holiday or vacation pay, nor will you be compensated for time spent preparing for the assignment outside of working hours.

To confirm your acceptance of this appointment, please sign and return this letter to the office of human resources.

I am pleased that you will be joining us to help with our software training needs, and I welcome you to our WYB community. We look forward to working with you.

If I can be of any assistance to you, please contact me at 839-555-0392.

Sincerely,

Christine DeGenero

Christine DeGenero
Director of Human Resources

Employee signature: _*Simon Kwan*_   Date: _*January 11*_
                     Simon Kwan

168. What is the purpose of the letter?

    (A) To advertise a job opening
    (B) To confirm an offer of employment
    (C) To discuss training for a new employee
    (D) To announce a salary increase

169. Who is the recipient of the letter?

    (A) A human resources director
    (B) A salesperson
    (C) A consultant
    (D) A company president

170. What is NOT listed as a job requirement?

    (A) Attending meetings
    (B) Submitting weekly work plans
    (C) Visiting several WYB offices
    (D) Conducting training sessions

171. What is stated in the letter?

    (A) Meetings take place on the 15th of each month.
    (B) Employees will receive holiday and vacation pay after three months of employment.
    (C) The letter should be signed by the recipient.
    (D) Job applicants will be interviewed by telephone.

Go on to the next page

To:	hmuranaka@myemail.com
From:	tours@mammothcanyonpark.org
Date:	January 2
Subject:	Tour confirmation
Attachment:	📎 Map with directions

Dear Mr. Muranaka,

Thank you for booking our Hidden Pathway Tour at Mammoth Canyon Park. Note that this e-mail does not serve as your admission ticket. — [1] —. You must pick up your tickets in person at our Visitor Center and must produce photo identification at that time. A map with directions is attached.

Also note that during the winter, some roads may be closed. — [2] —. Before you leave home, be sure to call our Visitor Center at (208) 555-0136 to ask about road closures and detours.

Please review the details of your order below to ensure that all the information is correct. — [3] —. The Hidden Pathway Tour lasts approximately three hours, so we advise that you dress warmly, wear proper boots, and bring enough water and a snack for the hike.

Confirmation code: HPT010201	Tour date and time: January 10, 10:00 A.M.
Purchase date: January 2	Quantity: 5
Payment type: Credit card	Total: $50.00

Speak to a park ranger to learn how you can apply this purchase to an annual membership!

Thank you for considering Mammoth Canyon Park for your adventures. — [4] —. We look forward to hosting you and hope you enjoy your visit.

172. According to the e-mail, why would a customer call the Visitor Center?

(A) To check the road conditions
(B) To ask about the hours of operation
(C) To request directions to Mammoth Canyon Park
(D) To inform the tour guide about a late arrival

173. What must Mr. Muranaka provide when he picks up his tickets?

(A) A park membership card
(B) Photo identification
(C) A confirmation e-mail
(D) His credit card number

174. What is Mr. Muranaka advised to bring on the trip?

(A) Hiking poles
(B) A flashlight
(C) Refreshments
(D) A raincoat

175. In which of the positions marked [1], [2], [3], and [4] does the following sentence belong?

"You can make changes to your reservation by visiting mammothcanyonpark.org/tours."

(A) [1]
(B) [2]
(C) [3]
(D) [4]

Go on to the next page

```
══════════════════════ *E-mail* ══════════════════════
```

To:	Julianne Reid <juliannereid@farlanduniversity.ac.uk>
From:	Eva MacLean <emaclean@sandington.gov.uk>
Date:	26 July
Subject:	August Event

Dear Ms. Reid,

I am delighted that you have agreed to speak at our celebration on 25 August, when we will reopen the doors to community members and introduce them to the results of our library restoration and renovation project. The historical perspective provided by your presentation will complement the technical elements of the talk to be given by the architect responsible for the building's redesign. Please let us know of your technology needs so that we may have everything ready for you. Guests will begin arriving in the morning at 9:30, when a light breakfast will be served. You are the first speaker of the day, so please plan to arrive by 9:00. The library is just a short walk from the Sandington train station.

We appreciate your willingness to share with our patrons the history of the town of Sandington and its library. After so many months of limited access to our collections and facilities, they eagerly anticipate their return to this community space.

Sincerely,

Eva MacLean

Passenger Rail System—Farland Line

Train Number	Stations and Arrival Times				
	Farland University	Baldwin	Ramsey Centre	Normont	Sandington
22	08:10	08:22	08:31	08:36	08:45
34	08:55	09:07	09:16	09:21	09:30
75	09:30	09:42	09:51	09:56	10:05
96	10:05	10:17	10:26	10:31	10:40

Notice: Please be advised that the ticket machine at Baldwin Station is out of order at this time. Passengers who board at Baldwin Station must purchase their tickets on the train.

176. What event is being held on August 25 ?

(A) A book signing
(B) An exhibit of historical photos
(C) The reopening of a building
(D) The presentation of an award

177. Who most likely is Ms. Reid?

(A) A librarian
(B) An architect
(C) A news reporter
(D) A historian

178. What information does Ms. MacLean request from Ms. Reid?

(A) Her travel details
(B) Her technology requirements
(C) Her dietary preferences
(D) Her speaking fee

179. What train will Ms. Reid most likely take in order to arrive on time?

(A) Number 22
(B) Number 34
(C) Number 75
(D) Number 96

180. At what station are tickets currently unavailable for purchase?

(A) Baldwin
(B) Ramsey Centre
(C) Normont
(D) Sandington

Go on to the next page

Rome: Mystery in a Minor Key **by Martina Hansen**
Reviewed by Michael Shura

Rome: Mystery in a Minor Key, Martina Hansen's best-selling novel, was inspired by a true story Hansen read in a local magazine. The novel tells the story of Eva Lombardo, a young woman of Italian descent, born and raised in Denmark. The family is estranged from Eva's grandmother, a famous composer who refuses to have any contact with them. When a newspaper article brings some unexpected news, Eva goes to Rome to confront her grandmother but finds that the situation is far more complicated than she had imagined. Although the ending is somewhat dark and bleak, many readers will find the story moving, and the main characters are skillfully drawn.

E-mail

To:	Martina Hansen <mhansen@inkwell.com>
From:	Peter Keo <keo.p@sturbridge.edu>
Date:	February 15
Re:	Invitation

Dear Ms. Hansen,

Thank you for agreeing to visit Sturbridge University on Thursday, March 6, to speak to the students in my creative writing class. These are all advanced students with some knowledge of fictional technique. They have many questions about the way you organized your material and developed your characters. Everybody wants to know if you based the composer on a real person!

I understand that you will be coming to campus on the number twelve bus. It stops directly in front of the library. I will meet you there at two o'clock, and we will walk over to Cayuga Hall together.

Yours,

Peter Keo

181. What is indicated about Ms. Hansen's novel?

(A) It was written in Denmark.
(B) It has not sold many copies.
(C) It is based on real events.
(D) It has a joyful ending.

182. In the book review, the word "drawn" in paragraph 1, line 8, is closest in meaning to

(A) pulled
(B) described
(C) understood
(D) acted

183. What is suggested about the students in a creative writing class?

(A) They have read *Rome: Mystery in a Minor Key*.
(B) They are beginning writers.
(C) They are planning to travel to Rome.
(D) They are enrolled in an evening class.

184. Who most likely is Mr. Keo?

(A) A book reviewer
(B) A bus driver
(C) A university professor
(D) A library assistant

185. What does the e-mail imply about Ms. Hansen?

(A) She will ride public transportation on March 6.
(B) She graduated from Sturbridge University.
(C) She works in Cayuga Hall.
(D) She did not accept an invitation.

Go on to the next page

Kimberly Arboretum

Our 20-acre property is a sanctuary for trees from many regions. Our pleasant local weather and greenhouse technology make it possible for us to care for noninvasive trees from around the world.

We are currently looking for five volunteers to help with our programs. Volunteers will have an opportunity to learn more about the trees we tend and to provide guided tours for visitors. Some volunteers will also help tend trees in the arboretum. Applicants must be high school or college students with an interest in botany and education, and they should be able to communicate effectively with the public. No previous experience is necessary, and applicants should be willing to commit to six or more hours per week. For more information and to submit an application, please contact Ms. Jin Hou, our administrative assistant, at jhou@kimberlyarboretum.org.

Weekly Volunteer Log for Kimberly Arboretum

Name: **Stephanie Cross**   Weekly Total: **8 hours**

	Time In	Time Out	Time In	Time Out	Total Hours
Monday	—	—	—	—	—
Tuesday	10 A.M.	11 A.M.	—	—	1
Wednesday	9 A.M.	11 A.M.	2 P.M.	4 P.M.	4
Thursday	10 A.M.	12 P.M.	6 P.M.	7 P.M.	3
Friday	—	—	—	—	—

```
╔══════════════════════ *E-mail* ══════════════════════╗

   To:        │ Jin Hou                                      │
   From:      │ Stephanie Cross                              │
   Subject:   │ Question                                     │
   Date:      │ March 9                                      │
```

Hello Ms. Hou,

I have really enjoyed working here over the past month, especially seeing and working around the trees I have been studying at university.

I recently spoke with Edward Nims in the African tree section, and he said he needs help with the care of the trees there. It was also interesting to hear about the knowledge of trees he gained while working in a wildlife sanctuary in Tanzania and how he is now applying that knowledge to the care of the arboretum.

I have been guiding tours on Tuesday, Wednesday, and Thursday mornings. Now that the South American tree exhibit has two additional volunteers, I was wondering if I could help Mr. Nims in the evening, on the day when I have been working in the South American section. Please let me know if you approve of this adjustment.

Sincerely,

Stephanie Cross

186. What is required of applicants for the volunteer position?

(A) A university degree
(B) Good communication skills
(C) A driver's license
(D) Significant knowledge of trees

187. How many hours does Ms. Cross usually work on Wednesdays?

(A) One hour
(B) Three hours
(C) Four hours
(D) Eight hours

188. To whom did Ms. Cross send her e-mail?

(A) An administrative assistant
(B) An arboretum volunteer
(C) A college professor
(D) A payroll manager

189. According to the e-mail, what is Mr. Nims responsible for?

(A) Writing recruitment notices
(B) Providing specialized care for trees
(C) Leading overseas trips to Africa
(D) Creating lesson plans for free classes

190. When does Ms. Cross want to work with Mr. Nims?

(A) On Mondays
(B) On Tuesdays
(C) On Wednesdays
(D) On Thursdays

Go on to the next page ➡

Questions 191-195 refer to the following product description, review, and e-mail.

The Cool Compact System 3 is a window-mounted, mini-compact air conditioner designed to quickly cool a small room up to 14 square meters in size. Our state-of-the-art technology keeps you cool with no unnecessary noise. Its washable mesh filter helps clean the air by trapping dirt and dust, and its low-power start-up conserves energy.

http://www.coolcompact.com/reviews

Review by David Thompkins, July 8

I purchased four System 3 units last year directly from the Cool Compact Web site, one for each bedroom in my house. They quickly cooled my bedrooms all last summer, although they were louder than I had expected. They made an unpleasant humming sound. I stored them in a closet during the winter and when I took them out last week, three out of the four did not work.

I called customer service, but I could not get in touch with anyone because of a national holiday. When I was finally able to speak with a representative the next day, I was informed that the warranty was for one year and had expired the day before. The representative refused to replace the units even after I explained the holiday situation. I am very disappointed in this company.

```
    ┌─────────────────────────────────────────────────────────────────┐
    │══════════════════════════  *E-mail*  ═══════════════════════════ │
    ├─────────────────────────────────────────────────────────────────┤
    │  To:       │ David Thompkins <dthompkins@rmail.com>              │
    │  From:     │ Lana Gray <lgray@coolcompact.com>                   │
    │  Subject:  │ Cool Compact System 3                               │
    │  Date:     │ July 10                                             │
    └─────────────────────────────────────────────────────────────────┘
```

Dear Mr. Thompkins,

We just read the review you posted on our Web site, and we would like to extend our apologies for your experience with Cool Compact System 3 units and our customer service. Our technology has improved recently, so our new units are now much quieter than the ones you purchased last year. Because we want our customers to be comfortable and to have some peace of mind, all our air conditioners have always come with a two-year warranty.

I would like to address your issue right away to restore your trust in Cool Compact. We will replace your three defective air conditioners as well as the functional one. Please call me so that we can arrange for delivery of the units to your home.

Regards,

Lana Gray
Customer Service Manager
(609) 555-0143

---

191. What does the product description indicate about the Cool Compact System 3 ?

(A) It features a washable filter.
(B) It cools any room in an hour.
(C) It can blow air in only one direction.
(D) It is battery-operated.

192. What does Mr. Thompkins indicate in his review about the products he purchased?

(A) He already returned some of them.
(B) He received a discount on them.
(C) He ordered them from a Web site.
(D) He bought them for a friend.

193. What is suggested about the bedrooms in Mr. Thompkins' home?

(A) They are no bigger than 14 square meters.
(B) They face a noisy street.
(C) They stay cool naturally in the summer.
(D) They have large windows.

194. What incorrect information did Mr. Thompkins receive during a customer service call?

(A) That customer service was available on holidays
(B) That his air conditioners could be stored safely in closets
(C) That Ms. Gray responds to all customer reviews
(D) That the warranty on his air conditioners had expired

195. What does Ms. Gray offer Mr. Thompkins?

(A) A full refund
(B) Four new cooling units
(C) Some gift certificates
(D) A warranty extension

Go on to the next page

https://www.karisblog.com.au

5 September

Calling Marina is expected to be released on 10 October, just in time for consideration for the Hanny Awards. The movie was supposed to be out in June but suffered a series of setbacks. First, Jakub Vítek stepped in to replace Marcus Blane as director. Then there was unexpected rainy weather at the filming location in France. One of the actors, rising star Alice Moreau, discovered that all of her costumes were water damaged and unusable. The wardrobe staff had quite a job to do to fix that problem! The film clips I've seen, however, look great, and this is one movie I plan to see!

In my next post, I'll discuss the latest action movies being filmed in China.

Thanks for visiting my site!

—Kari

Around Adelaide

12 October

The Kimber Cinema reopens today after an eight-month renovation. To celebrate the reopening, the theatre will be showing three new movies, including the thriller *Calling Marina*. Admission will be half-price today and tomorrow.

Manager Ena Piripi said she is delighted to have the theatre open again, and she knows other businesses in the Hartsland Street Shopping Centre are pleased also. Road detours and construction vehicles in the parking area made it difficult to get into the shopping centre. Enzo Laurita, owner of Rosa's Café, said business was slow while the construction was going on. In fact, he decided it was a good time to temporarily close his Italian restaurant to renovate the kitchen and install a new pizza oven. He and co-owner Johana Stace expect to see a boom in business and are hiring additional staff now that they have reopened.

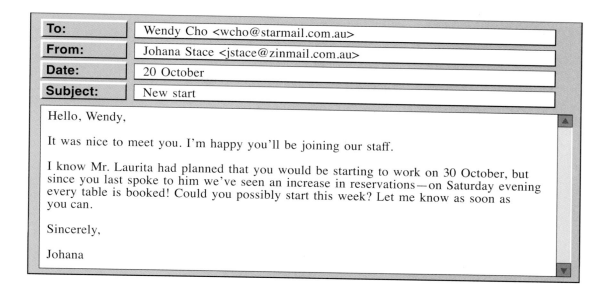

To:	Wendy Cho <wcho@starmail.com.au>
From:	Johana Stace <jstace@zinmail.com.au>
Date:	20 October
Subject:	New start

Hello, Wendy,

It was nice to meet you. I'm happy you'll be joining our staff.

I know Mr. Laurita had planned that you would be starting to work on 30 October, but since you last spoke to him we've seen an increase in reservations—on Saturday evening every table is booked! Could you possibly start this week? Let me know as soon as you can.

Sincerely,

Johana

196. What is the purpose of the blog post?

(A) To announce film award recipients
(B) To provide news about movies
(C) To report on weather conditions
(D) To review popular film-making locations

197. What does the blog post suggest about Ms. Moreau?

(A) She was born in France.
(B) She is a well-known movie director.
(C) Her flight was delayed by weather.
(D) Her wardrobe for a film had to be replaced.

198. What does the article indicate about Kimber Cinema?

(A) It will reopen in eight months.
(B) Its parking area is under construction.
(C) It will offer half-price tickets every week.
(D) It will show a movie that experienced production delays.

199. In the article, what does Mr. Laurita mention about his business?

(A) It was closed for a brief time.
(B) It is offering fewer pizza options.
(C) It has benefited from a new location.
(D) It has raised prices on its menu items.

200. What does Ms. Stace request that Ms. Cho do?

(A) Reserve a special event room
(B) Attend a staff training on Saturday
(C) Begin work at Rosa's Café earlier than expected
(D) Introduce herself to the manager

Stop! This is the end of the test. If you finish before time is called, you may go back to Parts 5, 6, and 7 and check your work.

ANSWER SHEET

실전 모의고사

수험번호

응시일자 : 20   년   월   일

성명 한글 / 한자 / 영자

READING (Part V ~ VII)

101 102 103 104 105 106 107 108 109 110 111 112 113 114 115 116 117 118 119 120
121 122 123 124 125 126 127 128 129 130 131 132 133 134 135 136 137 138 139 140
141 142 143 144 145 146 147 148 149 150 151 152 153 154 155 156 157 158 159 160
161 162 163 164 165 166 167 168 169 170 171 172 173 174 175 176 177 178 179 180
181 182 183 184 185 186 187 188 189 190 191 192 193 194 195 196 197 198 199 200

READING (Part V ~ VII)

101 102 103 104 105 106 107 108 109 110 111 112 113 114 115 116 117 118 119 120
121 122 123 124 125 126 127 128 129 130 131 132 133 134 135 136 137 138 139 140
141 142 143 144 145 146 147 148 149 150 151 152 153 154 155 156 157 158 159 160
161 162 163 164 165 166 167 168 169 170 171 172 173 174 175 176 177 178 179 180
181 182 183 184 185 186 187 188 189 190 191 192 193 194 195 196 197 198 199 200

ANSWER SHEET

실전 모의고사

수험번호

응시일자 : 20   년   월   일

성 명
한글
영자

READING (Part V ~ VII)

101 102 103 104 105 106 107 108 109 110 111 112 113 114 115 116 117 118 119 120
121 122 123 124 125 126 127 128 129 130 131 132 133 134 135 136 137 138 139 140
141 142 143 144 145 146 147 148 149 150 151 152 153 154 155 156 157 158 159 160
161 162 163 164 165 166 167 168 169 170 171 172 173 174 175 176 177 178 179 180
181 182 183 184 185 186 187 188 189 190 191 192 193 194 195 196 197 198 199 200

READING (Part V ~ VII)

101 102 103 104 105 106 107 108 109 110 111 112 113 114 115 116 117 118 119 120
121 122 123 124 125 126 127 128 129 130 131 132 133 134 135 136 137 138 139 140
141 142 143 144 145 146 147 148 149 150 151 152 153 154 155 156 157 158 159 160
161 162 163 164 165 166 167 168 169 170 171 172 173 174 175 176 177 178 179 180
181 182 183 184 185 186 187 188 189 190 191 192 193 194 195 196 197 198 199 200

ANSWER SHEET

실전 모의고사

수험번호

응시일자 : 20   년   월   일

성명	
	한글
	한자
	영자

READING (Part V ~ VII)

101 102 103 104 105 106 107 108 109 110 111 112 113 114 115 116 117 118 119 120

121 122 123 124 125 126 127 128 129 130 131 132 133 134 135 136 137 138 139 140

141 142 143 144 145 146 147 148 149 150 151 152 153 154 155 156 157 158 159 160

161 162 163 164 165 166 167 168 169 170 171 172 173 174 175 176 177 178 179 180

181 182 183 184 185 186 187 188 189 190 191 192 193 194 195 196 197 198 199 200

READING (Part V ~ VII)

101 102 103 104 105 106 107 108 109 110 111 112 113 114 115 116 117 118 119 120

121 122 123 124 125 126 127 128 129 130 131 132 133 134 135 136 137 138 139 140

141 142 143 144 145 146 147 148 149 150 151 152 153 154 155 156 157 158 159 160

161 162 163 164 165 166 167 168 169 170 171 172 173 174 175 176 177 178 179 180

181 182 183 184 185 186 187 188 189 190 191 192 193 194 195 196 197 198 199 200

ANSWER SHEET

실전 모의고사

응시일자 : 20   년   월   일

수험번호

READING (Part V ~ VII)

101	121	141	161	181
102	122	142	162	182
103	123	143	163	183
104	124	144	164	184
105	125	145	165	185
106	126	146	166	186
107	127	147	167	187
108	128	148	168	188
109	129	149	169	189
110	130	150	170	190
111	131	151	171	191
112	132	152	172	192
113	133	153	173	193
114	134	154	174	194
115	135	155	175	195
116	136	156	176	196
117	137	157	177	197
118	138	158	178	198
119	139	159	179	199
120	140	160	180	200

성   명
한글
한자
영자

READING (Part V ~ VII)

101	121	141	161	181
102	122	142	162	182
103	123	143	163	183
104	124	144	164	184
105	125	145	165	185
106	126	146	166	186
107	127	147	167	187
108	128	148	168	188
109	129	149	169	189
110	130	150	170	190
111	131	151	171	191
112	132	152	172	192
113	133	153	173	193
114	134	154	174	194
115	135	155	175	195
116	136	156	176	196
117	137	157	177	197
118	138	158	178	198
119	139	159	179	199
120	140	160	180	200

*toeic.

토익
단기공략
PART

정답과 해설

INTRODUCTION

패러프레이징

PRACTICE

본책 p.020

프리미엄 제품 계열, 가정용 냉장고 모델 770~850번

냉장고의 일반적인 많은 문제들은 쉽게 해결할 수 있고, 그럼으로써 방문 서비스 비용을 절약할 수 있습니다. 수리 기사의 서비스를 받으려고 전화하기 전에 스스로 문제를 해결할 수 있는지 알아보려면 다음과 같은 권고사항들을 시도해 보세요.

어휘 | premium 고급의 solve 해결하다, 풀다 save 절약하다
repair technician 수리 기사

1 사용 설명서는 누구를 대상으로 하는가?

(A) 수리 기사
(B) 가전제품 소유자

패러프레이징
지문의 refrigerator → 보기의 appliance

아래의 수영장 안전 예방책을 다시 한 번 숙지해 주세요. 여러분은 휴양 관리자로서 이 규정들을 다음 번 주간 회의 때 직원들과 논의해야 할 의무가 있습니다.

어휘 | refamiliarize oneself with ~을 다시 숙지하다 safety
precaution 안전 예방책 regulation 규정

2 공지의 목적은?

(A) 관리 직원들이 규정을 확실히 준수하도록 하기 위하여
(B) 이용객들에게 수영장 사용에 관해 교육하기 위하여

패러프레이징
지문의 a recreation manager
→ 보기의 management staff
지문의 precautions → 보기의 regulations

모니카 슬라바 [오후 3시 19분] 노던 필즈 대학 육상부 선수 몇 명에게 그 회사 신발을 신고 달리기 경주를 시켜 볼 수 있겠는데요. 그런 다음 그 신발에서 나오는 통계수치를 관중들이 볼 수 있는 대형 스크린에 실시간으로 전송하고요.

린 잰 [오후 3시 20분] 짚 스트링스가 우리에게 견본 몇 켤레 줄 수 있을까요? 달리기가 끝나면 상으로 그 신발을 나눠줄 수 있을 거예요.

어휘 | track team 육상팀 foot race 경주 transmit
전송하다 statistics 통계 generate 만들어 내다 give away
무료로 주다

3 노던 필즈 대학에 대해 암시된 것은?

(A) 학생 육상부가 있다.
(B) 그 대학의 많은 학생들이 짚 스트링스 신발을 갖고 있다.

패러프레이징
지문의 track team → 보기의 organization of student runners

바그너 씨는 4층에 경비원 한 명을 더 고용할 것을 요청했다. 최근 그리스 조각품의 소장 규모가 확대되어 이곳을 찾는 방문객의 수가 증가했다고 그녀는 설명했다.

어휘 | additional 추가의 security guard 경비원
expansion 확장 sculpture 조각품 collection 수집품

4 바그너 씨는 왜 추가적인 경비를 요청하는가?

(A) 귀중한 그림을 보호하기 위해
(B) 늘어난 방문객들을 관리하기 위해

어휘 | monitor 감시하다 traffic (차, 사람 등의) 교통량

패러프레이징
지문의 the number of visitors to this area has increased → 보기의 increased visitor traffic

---

올리버 씨께:

4월 2일에 논의한 내용에 대한 후속 조치로서 아래 품목들을 수입하고자 합니다. 이 가격이 정확한지, 해당 품목의 재고가 있는지 확인해 주십시오. 그리고 이 제품들을 언제 발송할 수 있는지 알려 주십시오.

어휘 | follow up on ~의 후속 조치를 하다 import 수입하다
in stock 재고가 있는

5 올리버 씨는 무엇을 요청받았는가?

(A) 확인 편지를 우편으로 보낼 것
(B) 상품 구매 가능 여부를 확인해 줄 것

어휘 | confirmation 확인 verify 확인하다, 증명하다
availability 구매 가능성, 이용 가능성

패러프레이징
지문의 confirm → 보기의 Verify
지문의 the items are in stock
→ 보기의 product availability

저희 온라인 비즈니스 프로그램에서 강의하시는 데 관심을 가져 주셔서 감사합니다. 지원 서류를 검토한 결과 저희는 귀하께 다가오는 학기를 위한 강사직을 제안드리고자 합니다.

어휘 | application material 지원 서류 instructor 강사

6 이메일을 보낸 이유는?

(A) 대학에서 채용 제안을 하기 위해
(B) 비즈니스 수업에 대한 정보를 제공하기 위해

패러프레이징
지문의 offer you an instructor's position
→ 보기의 offer employment

매표소에서 표와 함께 나이를 증명할 수 있는 신분증을 제시하십시오. 행사일 48시간 전 혹은 그 이전에 예약을 취소하면 표 가격을 전액 환불 받을 수 있습니다. 예약을 변경하거나 환불 받으려면 저희 고객 서비스 전화 +64 3 555 0199번으로 연락주십시오.

어휘 | identification 신분증 proof 증거, 증명 ticket booth 매표소 full refund 전액 환불 reschedule 일정을 변경하다

7 티켓 소지자는 왜 고객 서비스에 전화하겠는가?

(A) 표를 추가로 구입하기 위해
(B) 예약일을 변경하기 위해

패러프레이징
지문의 reschedule → 보기의 change a reservation date

수신: 전 직원
발신: 하미드 아마리
제목: 점검

메인 이메일 서버가 이번 주 토요일인 10월 22일 오전 7시부터 오전 11시까지 정기 점검을 위해 다운됩니다. 금요일 밤에 퇴근하실 때는 점검이 원활하게 이뤄질 수 있도록 컴퓨터 전원을 꺼 주시기 바랍니다.

어휘 | maintenance 점검, 보수 관리 down (컴퓨터 시스템이) 다운된 routine 정기적인, 정례적인 reliability 믿음직함, 신뢰도 shut down (컴퓨터를) 끄다 accommodate (요구 등에) 부응하다 procedure 절차

8 아마리 씨는 직원들에게 무엇을 해달라고 요청하는가?

(A) 컴퓨터를 끌 것
(B) 업무 지원 센터에 예약을 할 것

패러프레이징
지문의 shut down your computer
→ 보기의 Turn off their computers

CHAPTER 1 문제 유형별 전략

UNIT 01 주제 / 목적 문제

기출 예제

본책 p.024

Q 이메일을 보낸 목적은?

(A) 신임 축제 담당자를 소개하려고
(B) 요청이 승인되었음을 확정해주려고
(C) 선퀴스트 공원에서 열릴 음악 행사를 알리려고
(D) 계약 기간을 연장하려고

어휘 | grant 승인하다, 인정하다 extend 연장하다 contract 계약

수신: saul.abramov@urkmagazine.com
발신: b.perkins@yeloyamusicfestival.org
제목: 옐로야 음악 축제

귀하께서 올해 선퀴스트 공원에서 열릴 옐로야 음악 축제의 공식 사진작가로 승인되셨음을 알려드리게 되어 기쁩니다. 언론팀에 들어오시게 된 것을 환영합니다!

언론 출입증 찾는 방법과 관련해 축제 언론실에서 곧 연락을 드릴 것입니다. 그동안 질문이 있으시면 주저하지 마시고 952-555-0183으로 연락 주세요.

벨린다 퍼킨스, 행사 담당자

- - -

어휘 | approve 승인하다, 인가하다 photographer 사진작가 press 언론, 신문 in the meantime 그동안에, 당분간 hesitate 주저하다

기출 ETS PRACTICE

본책 p.025

1 (B) **2** (D)

원 씨께,

네이온테크에서는 귀사의 컴퓨터, 휴대전화 및 기타 전자제품을 책임감 있게 재활용하는 데 전념하고 있습니다. 저희 효율적인 수집망을 통해 비용은 낮게, 서비스는 합리적인 가격으로 유지합니다. 4개국에 시설을 갖추고 있어 선적 거리 및 연료 소비를 최소화할 수 있습니다.

한국에서 가장 빠르게 확장되는 업체들 중 하나의 지속가능경영책임자로서 귀하의 재활용 장소 및 대상에 관한 결정은 큰 영향을 미칩니다. **재활용 가능한 전자 폐기물을 보낼 곳을 선택하실 때, 동봉된 네이온테크 안내 책자를 봐 주셨으면 합니다.** 저희 서비스 품질에 대해 더 확신이 필요하시다면 안내 책자 뒷장에 명시된 고객사 중 어느

곳이든 전화를 하거나 서신을 보내 보시기 바랍니다. 귀사의 특정 요구 사항에 대해 논의하고 싶으시다면 저에게 연락하시거나 원하실 경우 저희 서울 지사에 있는 박우진 씨와 말씀 나누십시오.

브렌던 딜크스
수석 고객 관리자

- - -

어휘 | be dedicated to ~에 전념하다 affordable (가격이) 적당한, 감당할 수 있는 consumption 소비 assurance 확언, 장담 specific 구체적인, 특정한 requirement 요건, 필요조건

---

1 편지의 목적은?

(A) 새로운 환경 규정을 설명하려고
(B) 재활용 서비스를 홍보하려고
(C) 충성 고객에게 할인을 제공하려고
(D) 전자제품 브랜드를 추천하려고

해설 | 주제 / 목적

편지의 첫 단락 첫 문장에서 '네이온테크에서는 귀사의 컴퓨터, 휴대전화 및 기타 전자제품을 책임감 있게 재활용하는 데 전념하고 있다(At Nayontech, we are dedicated to responsibly recycling your computers, mobile phones, and other electronics)'고 재활용 서비스를 소개한 후, 두 번째 단락 두 번째 문장에서 '재활용 가능한 전자 폐기물을 보낼 곳을 선택하실 때, 동봉된 네이온테크 안내 책자를 봐 주셨으면 한다(I hope you will consider the enclosed brochure ~ send your recyclable electronic waste)'면서 홍보물 안내 책자에 대해 언급하고 있으므로 (B)가 정답이다.

어휘 | regulation 규정, 규제 promote 홍보하다

패러프레이징

지문의 recycling your computers, mobile phones, and other electronics → 보기의 a recycling service

---

완벽한 선물

친구들, 사랑하는 이들과 1년 내내 날마다 새롭고 특별한 사진을 공유한다고 상상해보십시오! **골드 코스트 이매지네이션 사는 귀가가 보내 주신 이미지를 이용하여 특별한 사람들, 인상적인 장소들, 중요한 행사들의 이미지를 사용한 맞춤형 달력을 제작해 드립니다.**

사진첩을 훑어보시고 넣고 싶은 사진들을 고르기만 하세요. 귀하의 디지털 이미지나 전통적인 인화 사진을 이용하여 맞춤 선물을 제작해 드리겠습니다. 생일, 기념일, 특별 행사일 등도 추가 비용 없이 표시할 수 있습니다!

저희 상담원이 수십 가지 형태와 스타일 중에서 선택하실 수 있도록 도와 드릴 것입니다. 더 많은 정보를 원하시면 (07) 7010 2390으로 전화 주시거나 저희 웹사이트 www.gci.co.au를 방문하여 주십시오.

어휘 | **personalize** 고객의 요구에 맞게 제작하다 **memorable** 기억할 만한, 인상적인 **go through** 검토하다 **anniversary** 기념일 **indicate** 나타내다, 표시하다 **additional fee** 추가 비용 **consultant** 상담원, 컨설턴트 **dozens of** 수십의 **format** 포맷, 형(型)

2 무엇이 광고되고 있는가?

(A) 여행 우편 엽서   (B) 사진첩
(C) 생일 카드   (D) 맞춤 달력

해설 | **주제 / 목적**
광고의 주제를 이해하고 있는지를 묻는 문제이다. 첫 번째 단락 두 번째 문장에서 '고객이 제공하는 이미지를 이용한 맞춤형 달력 제작 서비스를 제공한다(Gold Coast Imagination, Inc., will use images that you provide to create a personalized daily calendar)'고 했으므로 정답은 (D)이다.

기출 ETS TEST   본책 p.026

1 (C) **2** (A) **3** (D) **4** (C) **5** (C) **6** (B)
7 (A) **8** (D) **9** (A) **10** (C) **11** (B) **12** (D)

[1-2] 편지

키플러 스타 은행
660 센츄리 가
빌링스, MT 59102

3월 27일

세실리아 페리디노
90 영 가
빌링스, MT 59107

제목: 850981-591 계좌

페리디노 씨께,

¹귀하의 새 연락처 정보에 대해 서신으로 알려 주셔서 감사합니다. 귀하의 계좌 정보를 새롭게 변경했으며 이후 입출금 내역서 및 서신은 현재 주소로 발송될 것입니다.

귀하의 서신을 오늘 받아서, 최근 입출금 내역서는 이전 주소로 이미 발송되었음을 알려드립니다. 단, **²온라인으로 계좌에 접속하시면 언제든 계좌 세부 사항(계좌 잔고, 최근 청구사항, 지급액 등)을 확인하실 수 있습니다.**

이용해 주셔서 감사합니다.

칼 델가도
고객 서비스 담당자

어휘 | **subsequent** 그 이후의, 차후의 **statement** 입출금 내역서, 명세서 **correspondence** 서신 **current** 현재의 **account balance** 계좌 잔고, 잔액

1 편지는 무엇에 관한 내용인가?

(A) 결제 연체   (B) 신규 계좌
(C) 주소 변경 요청   (D) 잘못된 계좌 잔고

해설 | **주제 / 목적**
편지 첫 단락 첫 문장에서 '새 연락처 정보(your new contact information)를 알려줘서 감사하다'고 하면서, 이후 '입출금 내역서 및 서신은 현재 주소로 발송될 것이라(all subsequent statements and correspondence will be sent to your current address)'고 했으므로 주소 변경을 요청받았다는 것을 알 수 있다. 따라서 (C)가 정답이다.

어휘 | **overdue** 기한이 지난

2 델가도 씨는 페리디노 씨에게 무엇을 하라고 제안하는가?

(A) 웹사이트 방문   (B) 고객 서비스 센터에 전화
(C) 송금   (D) 서식 작성

해설 | **세부 사항**
두 번째 단락 마지막 문장에서 '온라인으로 계좌에 접속하면 (by accessing your account online) 언제든 계좌 세부 사항을 확인할 수 있다'고 했으므로 (A)가 정답이다.

어휘 | **fill out a form** 서식을 작성하다

패러프레이징
지문의 accessing your account online
→ 보기의 Visit a Web site

[3-4] 이메일

수신: 티나 셔마 <tinas@writersworld.com>
발신: 크리스토퍼 로테 <christopher_lote@wtj.com>
날짜: 10월 1일
제목: 글 제출
첨부: ⬀ 로테의 에세이

셔마 씨께:

당신의 전 보조인 데릴 브라운에게서 이메일 주소를 받았습니다. 그는 마침 제 예전 동료이기도 합니다. 우리는 <투자 다이제스트>에서 편집자로 일했었습니다.

⁴저는 수년간 당신의 소설과 시를 읽어왔고 당신이 <작가의 세상>의 새 편집장이라는 것을 알고 기뻤습니다. ³,⁴이 이메일에 첨부한 저의 짧은 에세이를 향후 잡지의 논픽션 부문에 사용하는 것을 고려해 주시기 바랍니다. 이 글은 기술 시대의 우정에 관한 것입니다. 저는 5년 넘게 단편소설과

에세이를 출간해 왔으며 <바스켓 하우스 리뷰>, <고독한 오늘>을 포함해 다양한 출판물에 제 작품을 게재했습니다.

시간 내주셔서 감사합니다.

크리스토퍼 로테

어휘 | submission 제출 essay (짧은) 글 former 이전의 assistant 보조원 colleague 동료 editor 편집자 investment 투자 digest 요약(문) fiction 소설 poetry 시 nonfiction 비소설 section 부문 age 시대 publish 출판하다 appear 나타나다 various 다양한 publication 출판물 including ~을 포함하여 solitude 고독

3 로테 씨가 이메일을 보낸 이유는?

(A) 작문 샘플을 요청하려고
(B) 신입 사원을 소개하려고
(C) 이전 동료에 대해 문의하려고
(D) 원고 채택 검토를 요청하려고

해설 | 주제 / 목적
두 번째 단락의 두 번째 문장에서 로테 씨가 '이 이메일에 첨부한 저의 에세이를 향후 잡지의 논픽션 부문에 사용하는 것을 고려해 주시기 바란다(I hope you will consider ~ journal's nonfiction section)'고 했으므로 (D)가 정답이다.

4 <작가의 세상>에 대해 암시된 것은?

(A) 편집 직원이 많다.
(B) 공공 정책 문제에 초점을 맞추고 있다.
(C) 다양한 종류의 글쓰기를 포함한다.
(D) 전국적으로 유통된다.

해설 | 추론
키워드 *Writer's World*가 나오는 부분을 찾아야 한다. 두 번째 단락의 첫 문장에서 로테 씨가 '수년간 당신의 소설과 시를 읽어왔고 당신이 <작가의 세상>의 새 편집장이라는 것을 알고 기뻤다(I have been a reader ~ editor of *Writer's World*)'고 했고, 이어서 '이메일에 첨부한 에세이를 향후 잡지의 논픽션 부문에 사용하는 것을 고려해 주시기 바란다(I hope you will consider ~ journal's nonfiction section)'고 했다. 로테 씨가 <작가의 세상>에 자신의 에세이를 써 달라고 요청하며 논픽션 부문을 특정해 언급한 것으로 보아 해당 잡지는 여러 종류의 글로 구성된다는 것을 짐작할 수 있다. 따라서 정답은 (C)이다.

어휘 | editorial 편집의 focus on ~에 초점을 맞추다 issue 문제 public 공공의 policy 정책 circulate 유포하다

[5-8] 공지

커머스 센터 플라자 임차인께 알려드립니다

5,6에너지 절약 및 공공요금 절감을 위해, 돌아오는 국경일 주간인 3월 15일부터 22일까지 전 사무실의 난방을 저온

설정으로 낮출 예정입니다. 본 조치는 3월 한 달간 저희 사무실 단지의 에너지 사용량을 크게 줄일 가능성이 있는 시범 프로그램의 일환입니다. 절약된 금액은 3월 관리비에서 차감되는 형식으로 모든 임차인께 돌아갈 것입니다. 성공할 경우 야간과 주말뿐 아니라 다른 공휴일 기간에도 난방 및 냉방 최소 설정을 하는 것으로 시범 프로그램이 연장될 예정입니다.

6**3월 공휴일 기간에 공식적으로는 전 사무실이 문을 닫지만 일부 직원들이 건물에서 근무할 수도 있음을 건물 관리소에서도 잘 알고 있습니다.** 7**연휴 주간 중 언제든 사무실을 사용할 계획이 있으시면 랄프 스나이더에게 627-5899 내선 번호 234번으로 연락 주십시오.** 명시하신 날짜와 시간 동안 사무실을 사용하실 수 있도록 준비하겠습니다.

시범 프로그램 기간 동안 여러분의 의견을 받습니다. 의견 및 문의 사항은 건물 관리소장인 제럴딘 텔러에게 627-5899 내선 번호 200번으로 전달 바랍니다. 8**3월 23일에는 프로그램 경험에 관한 자료를 수집하는 데 도움이 될 설문지가 건물 내 전원에게 배부될 예정입니다.** 시간을 내셔서 설문을 작성하고 텔러 씨에게 그때 회신해 주시면 감사하겠습니다.

건물 관리소
커머스 센터 플라자 사무실 단지

어휘 | tenant 임차인 in an effort to ~을 위한 노력으로 utilities 공공요금, 공과금 upcoming 다가오는, 곧 있을 pilot program 시범 프로그램 potential 가능성 significant 중요한, 커다란 maintenance cost 유지비, 관리비 occupy 사용하다, 차지하다 specify 명시하다 distribute 배부하다, 나누어 주다 complete the survey 설문을 작성하다

5 공지의 목적은?

(A) 공공요금 상승에 대해 설명하려고
(B) 임차인들을 건물 위원회 회의에 초대하려고
(C) 에너지 절약 프로그램에 대해 알리려고
(D) 곧 있을 공사 프로젝트에 관해 설명하려고

해설 | 주제 / 목적
공지의 첫 단락 첫 문장에서 '에너지 절약 및 공공요금 절감을 위해(In an effort to save energy and reduce the cost of utilities) 돌아오는 국경일 주간인 3월 15일부터 22일까지 전 사무실의 난방을 저온 설정으로 낮출 예정'이라고 했으므로 (C)가 정답이다.

어휘 | conservation 보존

패러프레이징
지문의 save energy → 보기의 energy conservation

6 건물 관리소는 어떻게 비용을 감축할 계획인가?

(A) 필요할 때만 수리해서
(B) 사무실을 사용하지 않을 때 난방을 줄여서

(C) 더 효율적인 최신 장비를 설치해서
(D) 전문가의 조언을 따라서

해설 | 세부 사항
첫 단락 첫 문장에서 '에너지 절약 및 공공요금 절감을 위해 3월 15일부터 22일까지 국경일 주간에 전 사무실의 난방을 저온 설정으로 낮출 예정(the heating in all offices will be turned down to a low temperature setting)'이라고 했으며, 두 번째 단락 첫 문장에서 '3월 공휴일 기간에 공식적으로는 전 사무실이 문을 닫는다(all offices will be officially closed)'고 했으므로 사무실을 사용하지 않을 때 난방을 줄인다는 것을 알 수 있다. 따라서 (B)가 정답이다.

어휘 | install 설치하다 efficient 효율적인 expert 전문가

패러프레이징
지문의 the heating in all offices will be turned down to a low temperature setting → 보기의 reducing heat
지문의 all offices will be officially closed
→ 보기의 offices are not in use

7 스나이더 씨에게 연락을 취할 이유로 공지에 명시된 것은?

(A) 3월 15일 주간 동안 건물 사용을 준비하기 위해
(B) 제안된 개조 프로그램에 대해 제의하기 위해
(C) 공과금 변동 사항을 알리기 위해
(D) 사무실 추가 공간 요청서를 제출하기 위해

해설 | Not / True
두 번째 단락 두 번째 문장에서 '연휴 주간 중 언제든 사무실을 사용할 계획이 있으면(If you are planning to occupy your office at any time during the holiday week) 랄프 스나이더에게 연락하라'고 했고, 연휴 기간이 3월 15일부터 22일까지이므로 (A)가 정답이다.

어휘 | renovation 개조, 보수 submit 제출하다

패러프레이징
지문의 occupy your office → 보기의 use the building
지문의 during the holiday week
→ 보기의 during the week of March 15

8 공지에 따르면, 임차인들은 3월 22일 이후에 무엇을 하라고 요청받겠는가?

(A) 불필요한 조명 끄기
(B) 추가 근무 자원하기
(C) 건물 관리소장 새로 선출하기
(D) 설문지 작성하기

해설 | 세부 사항
마지막 단락 후반부에서 '3월 23일에는 설문지가 건물 내 전원에게 배부될 예정'이라고 한 후, '시간을 내서 설문을 작성하고(please take the time to complete the survey) 텔러 씨에게 회신해주면 감사하겠다'고 하므로 (D)가 정답이다.

어휘 | elect 선출하다 questionnaire 설문지

패러프레이징
지문의 On March 23 → 질문의 after March 22
지문의 survey → 보기의 questionnaire

[9-12] 기사

멜퀼라 고객들의 승리
조슬린 길모어

⁹다양한 천연 유제품 제조업체인 멜퀼라가 5월 15일자로 뚜껑을 돌려서 여닫는 유리병에 요거트를 제공한다. 지금까지 해당 제품은 플라스틱 컵으로만 판매됐다. ¹⁰이러한 행보는 제품을 개봉한 후 컵을 냉장고에 두면 맛이 없어진다는 고객의 불만 사항에 어느 정도 대응한 것이다. 많은 구매자들은 업체 웹사이트에 의견을 올리며 유리 용기에 포장된 제품이 플라스틱에 포장된 제품보다 맛을 더 오래 유지한다는 연구 결과를 언급했다.

¹¹멜퀼라의 수석 영업부장은 전국의 주요 소비자 단체 중 하나인 푸드 소스가 소비자들이 제기한 우려를 지지하고 나서야 해당 변경 사항을 시행하기로 결정한 것이 아닌지 묻는 질문에 놀랄 만큼 솔직하게 답했다. "지난 5년간 판매가 꾸준히 성장했습니다." ¹¹제프 폴라드가 설명했다. "그래서 약간 자만했을 테고 주의 환기가 필요했을 겁니다." 그러나 그는 새로운 조치가 전 세계 유제품 업체들의 혁신적인 제조 기술과 마케팅 전략을 더 많이 채택하면서 이뤄진 것이기도 하다는 사실을 지적했다. "멜퀼라가 시장 점유율을 유지하고 확대하고자 한다면, 분명 이러한 발전을 받아들여야 합니다"라고 말했다.

멜퀼라는 소비 심리가 재무 성과에 미칠 수 있는 엄청난 영향을 잘 알고 있다. 2년 전 멜퀼라는 시나몬 헤이즐넛 아이스크림으로 낙농업연구기관 최우수상을 수상했다. 낙농업연구기관은 약 3천 5백 명의 아이스크림 애호가들을 대상으로 조사를 실시했는데 대다수가 멜퀼라 제품의 부드러운 식감과 풍부한 맛, 저지방 및 저칼로리 함량 등을 칭찬했다. ¹²수상 직후 몇 개월 만에 멜퀼라는 거의 모든 제품의 수요가 급증했고 수익의 33퍼센트 상승으로 이어졌다. 이에 따라 자신들의 성패는 소비자에게 달렸으며 소비자 요구를 무시하면 회사에 상당한 재정적 위험이 따르게 된다는 사실을 깊이 깨닫게 되었다.

어휘 | dairy product 유제품 to date 지금까지 retain 유지하다 implement 시행하다 measure 조치 adoption 채택, 선정 strategy 전략 embrace 받아들이다 market share 시장 점유율 profound 심오한, 엄청난 consumer sentiment 소비 심리 virtually 사실상, 거의 soar 급증하다 revenue 수익, 수입 considerable 상당한

9 기사를 쓴 목적은?

(A) 제품 포장의 변화에 대해 알리려고
(B) 업체가 제공하는 다양한 제품을 홍보하려고

(C) 소비자들이 온라인으로 제품을 조사한다는 것을
　　보여주려고
(D) 소비자들의 구매 습관에 대해 이야기하려고

해설 | 주제 / 목적

기사 첫 단락 첫 문장에서 '다양한 천연 유제품 제조업체인 멜퀼라가 5월 15일자로 뚜껑을 돌려서 여닫는 유리병에 요거트를 제공할 것(will be offering its yogurt in screw-top glass jars)'이라고 했고, '지금까지 해당 제품은 플라스틱 컵으로만 판매됐다(the product is sold only in plastic cups)'고 했으므로 요거트 용기의 변경을 알리는 내용이다. 따라서 (A)가 정답이다.

어휘 | promote 홍보하다 purchasing habit 구매 습관

패러프레이징
지문의 in screw-top glass jars / in plastic cups
→ 보기의 a change in the packaging

10 고객들이 멜퀼라 요거트에 불만을 제기한 이유는?

(A) 큰 슈퍼마켓에서만 판매됐다.
(B) 맛의 종류가 제한되어 있었다.
(C) 신선함이 오래 유지되지 않았다.
(D) 저지방 제품이 아니었다.

해설 | 세부 사항

첫 단락 두 번째 문장에서 '제품을 개봉한 후 컵을 냉장고에 두면 맛이 없어진다는 고객의 불만 사항(complaints from customers who argue that the product loses its flavor)'을 제시한 후, '많은 구매자들은 유리 용기에 포장된 제품이 플라스틱에 포장된 제품보다 맛을 더 오래 유지한다(products packaged in glass containers retain their flavor longer than those packaged in plastic)는 연구 결과를 언급했다'고 했다. 따라서 플라스틱 컵에서는 신선함이 오래 유지되지 않았다는 (C)가 정답이다.

패러프레이징
지문의 retain their flavor longer
→ 보기의 stay fresh for very long

11 폴라드 씨는 누구인가?

(A) 멜퀼라 경쟁업체 소유주　(B) 멜퀼라 영업부장
(C) 푸드 소스 관리자　(D) 낙농업연구기관 대변인

해설 | 세부 사항

두 번째 단락 첫 문장에서 멜퀼라의 수석 영업부장(Melquila's senior director of sales)을 언급하면서 제프 폴라드가 설명했다고 했으므로 (B)가 정답이다.

어휘 | competitor 경쟁자 spokesperson 대변인

패러프레이징
지문의 senior director → 보기의 head

12 멜퀼라에 대해 명시된 것은?

(A) 2년 전 광고 활동을 확대했다.
(B) 경쟁업체들에게 고객을 계속 빼앗기고 있었다.
(C) 많은 고객 설문조사를 실시했다.
(D) 수상 이후 수익 증가가 있었다.

해설 | Not / True

마지막 단락 후반부에서 '수상 직후 몇 개월 만에 멜퀼라는 거의 모든 제품의 수요가 급증했고 수익의 33퍼센트 상승으로 이어졌다(In the months immediately following receipt of the award, Melquila saw demand for virtually all of its products soar, resulting in a 33 percent jump in revenue)'고 했으므로 (D)가 정답이다.

어휘 | advertising effort 광고 활동 earnings 수익, 소득

패러프레이징
지문의 a 33 percent jump in revenue
→ 보기의 an increase in earnings
지문의 following receipt of the award
→ 보기의 after receiving an award

UNIT 02 　세부 사항 문제

본책 p.030

기출 예제

Q 폐쇄 사유는?

(A) 특별 행사　　　　　(B) 기상 조건
(C) 건설 프로젝트　　　(D) 도로 보수

회람

발신: 에이딘 하란, 운영 책임자
수신: 베이뷰 가 전 직원
날짜: 7월 26일 금요일

7월 30일 화요일부터 베이뷰 가의 당사 사옥을 방문하는 차량들은 추후 통지가 있을 때까지 빌라 로를 따라 우회해야 한다는 점을 알고 계십시오. **이 폐쇄는 시의 새로운 스포츠 경기장 부지 개발을 위해 필수적입니다.** 운전해서 출근하는 직원들은 추가적인 이동 시간을 감안해야 합니다. 평소 린 가에서 시내버스를 타는 통근자들은 대체 버스 정류장을 이용해야 할 것입니다.

- -

어휘 | vehicular 차량의 detour 우회로 further 추가의
notice 공지 closure 폐쇄 necessary 필수적인 site 부지
development 개발 stadium 경기장 commuter 통근자
normally 보통 때 alternate 대체의

1 (C)   **2** (A)

캉 카펫 스토어

2987 클레어몬트 대로 할리팩스, NS

902-555-0145 www.kangcarpet.ca

5월 2일 토요일 특별 행사가 열립니다!

획기적인 새 카펫 섬유를 넣어 만든 신제품 카펫 마바클린 출시 기념 특별 행사에 저희 최고의 고객이신 귀하를 초대합니다. 마바클린 카펫이 비슷한 가격대의 카펫들보다 먼지를 최대 25% 덜 타고 더 오래 지속된다는 사실이 공장 테스트로 밝혀졌습니다. **5월 2일 저희 매장에서 마바클린 카펫을 구매하시면 최대 정가의 40%까지 할인 받으실 수 있습니다.** 5월 2일에 본 공지문을 저희 매장으로 가져오셔서 매장 직원에게 제시하시고 마바클린 전시장 입장 권한을 받으세요. 만나 뵙기를 고대합니다!

어휘 | revolutionary 혁명적인, 획기적인 trap (덫으로) 잡다, 끌어모으다 comparably priced 비슷하게 가격이 매겨진 regular price 정가 gain admission to ~에 입장 허가를 받다

---

1 고객은 어떻게 마바클린 카펫의 할인 자격을 얻는가?

(A) 온라인으로 카펫을 주문한다.

(B) 캉 카펫 스토어를 친구에게 추천한다.

(C) 매장 행사에 참석한다.

(D) 고객 설문조사를 작성한다.

해설 | 세부 사항

discount를 키워드로 잡고 discount가 언급되는 부분에서 답을 찾아야 한다. 세 번째 문장에서 '5월 2일 매장에서 마바클린 카펫을 구매하면 최대 정가의 40%까지 할인 받을 수 있다(And if you purchase a Marvaclean carpet at our store on May 2, you can save up to 40% off the regular price)'고 하면서 할인을 받을 수 있는 자격에 대해 언급하였으며, 제목에서 '5월 2일 토요일 특별 행사가 열린다(Special event on Saturday, May 2)'고 했으므로 (C)가 정답이다.

어휘 | qualify for ~의 자격을 얻다 complete a survey 설문을 작성하다

패러프레이징

지문의 40% off the regular price → 질문의 a discount

탕 씨께:

저희의 기록에 따르면 귀하의 산업 디자이너 단체 회원권이 만료되려고 합니다. 귀하께서 이 사실을 잊으신 것에 불과하길 바라며, 회원 자격이 소멸되기 전에 갱신하실 것을 권하고 싶습니다.

지난해는 저희 산업 디자이너 단체가 새 잡지 <빛과 형체>를 창간한 흥미로운 시기였습니다. 올해 저희는 웹사이트 개선을 시작할 것입니다. 이 변경 작업들이 완료되면 귀하는 온라인 상에서 연락처 정보를 최근의 것으로 갱신하고, 회의 등록을 하고, 회비를 지불하실 수 있을 것입니다.

지금 회원권을 갱신하시려면 동봉된 양식을 기입하여 제공된 봉투에 넣어 우편으로 보내 주세요. 귀하의 회원권 현황이 레벨 A에 있는 것으로 기록되어 있습니다. 혹시 회원 등급이 바뀌었다면 표시해주십시오. 최근에 회원권을 갱신하셨다면 이 안내문은 무시하여 주시기 바랍니다.

올루지미 오두야

회원관리 책임자

어휘 | industrial designer 산업 디자이너 expire 만료되다 renew 갱신하다 lapse 소멸되다 launch 출시하다, 창간하다 update 최신의 것으로 갱신하다 register for ~에 등록하다 due 회비, 요금 fill out (양식 등을) 기입하다 enclosed 동봉된 envelope 봉투 status 상황 indicate 표시하다, 명시하다 disregard 무시하다, 묵살하다

---

2 탕 씨는 무엇을 하라고 요청받는가?

(A) 양식 기입

(B) 이메일 메시지 전송

(C) 웹사이트 방문

(D) 산업 디자이너 단체 사무실로 전화

해설 | 세부 사항

편지의 세 번째 단락에서 요청의 표현 please를 사용하여 '동봉된 양식을 작성해서 우편으로 보내 달라(To renew your membership now, please fill out the enclosed form and mail it in the envelope provided)'고 요청하고 있으므로 정답은 (A)이다.

기출 ETS TEST   본책 p.032

1 (C)	**2** (A)	**3** (A)	**4** (D)	**5** (D)	**6** (C)
7 (B)	**8** (D)	**9** (D)	**10** (C)	**11** (C)	**12** (A)

[1-2] 이메일

수신: 마케팅팀

발신: 존 메타

날짜: 1월 21일 목요일

제목: 명함

안녕하세요, 여러분.

¹다음 주 수요일 오전에 명함이 인쇄되어 이튿날 오후 사무실로 배송될 예정입니다. 몇 분은 최근에 업무가 바뀐

것으로 알고 있습니다. 그래서 모든 분의 정보가 정확한지 확인하고자 합니다. **²직책이 변경됐다면 늦어도 내일 오후 5시까지 성함과 새 직책을 적어 본 이메일에 회신해 주십시오.** 말씀이 없으시면 기존 명함의 정보가 여전히 정확하다는 뜻으로 알겠습니다.

각 직원 여러분은 300장이 든 상자 하나씩 받으실 겁니다. 다음 주 금요일까지 제 사무실에서 찾아가 주세요.

감사합니다.

존 메타
관리 비서

어휘 | no later than 늦어도 ~까지 assume 추정하다
administrative 행정의, 관리의

1 새 명함은 언제 메타 씨의 사무실에 도착할 것인가?

(A) 화요일   (B) 수요일

(C) 목요일   (D) 금요일

해설 | 추론
이메일 첫 단락 첫 문장에서 '다음 주 수요일 오전에 명함이 인쇄되어 이튿날 오후 사무실로 배송될 예정(Business cards will be printed next Wednesday morning and delivered to my office the following afternoon)'이라고 했으므로 새 명함은 목요일에 사무실에 도착할 예정이라는 것을 짐작할 수 있다. 따라서 (C)가 정답이다.

2 누구에게 이메일 회신 요청을 하는가?

(A) 직책이 변경된 직원
(B) 최근 새 주소로 이사한 직원
(C) 새 명함이 배송될 때 자리를 비울 예정인 직원
(D) 300장 이상의 명함이 필요한 직원

해설 | 세부 사항
첫 단락의 세 번째 문장에서 '직책이 변경됐다면(If your position has changed) 늦어도 내일 오후 5시까지 성함과 새 직책을 적어 본 이메일에 회신해 달라'고 했으므로 (A)가 정답이다.

[3-5] 공지

도서관 6월 행사

보드 게임의 밤: 매주 금요일 오후 6시-10시
도서관 회의실에서 매주 열리는 게임의 밤에 참여해 좋아하는 보드 게임을 즐기거나 새로운 보드 게임을 배우며 보드 게임 애호가 친구를 사귀어 보세요. 본인의 게임을 가져오시거나 도서관에 소장된 게임으로 즐겨보세요. 아동 및 성인을 위한 게임이 제공됩니다.

그림의 기초: 6월 12일 오후 2시-4시
10대 청소년 및 성인이 연필과 잉크를 사용해 초상화와 사물 그리기 기법을 배울 수 있습니다. 재료는 제공됩니다. **³공간이 한정되어 있습니다.** 도서관이나 도서관 웹사이트에서 등록해 주세요.

비전문가를 위한 조류 관찰: 6월 16일 오후 1시-3시
새 애호가들은 **⁴올림피아 대학교 생물학자이자 <당신 주위에 있는 새들>의 저자인 메르세데스 오티즈**와 함께 도서관 마당에서 열리는 새 관찰 활동에 참여할 수 있습니다. 오티즈 씨가 새들의 겉모습을 보고 어떤 새인지 알 수 있도록 참여자들을 도와드립니다.

음악의 시간: 6월 20일 오전 10시-11시
인기 있는 아동 음악가 태미 린데일과 함께 한 시간 동안 음악과 연극으로 상호 작용을 펼쳐보세요. 악기와 장난감이 제공됩니다. 3-6세 아동에게 적합합니다. **⁵등록은 하지 않아도 되지만 앞 좌석과 가운데 좌석은 아동 30명으로 제한되니 일찍 도착해 주세요.**

책 애호가들의 모임: 6월 28일 오후 6시-8시
도서관에서 매월 열리는 북클럽 모임에 함께해 보세요. 이번 달에는 알프레드 페더슨의 새 소설 <도시의 삶>에 관해 이야기 나눌 예정입니다.

어휘 | enthusiast 애호가, 열렬한 지지자 register 등록하다
biologist 생물학자 observe 관찰하다 appearance 외모,
외관 interactive 상호작용을 하는, 상호적인

3 참가자들은 어떤 행사에 미리 신청해야 하는가?

(A) 그림의 기초
(B) 비전문가를 위한 조류 관찰
(C) 음악의 시간
(D) 책 애호가들의 모임

해설 | 세부 사항
두 번째 행사 그림의 기초(Basics of Drawing)에서 '공간이 한정되어 있다(Space is limited.)'고 하므로 (A)가 정답이다.

어휘 | in advance 미리

패러프레이징
지문의 register → 질문의 sign up

4 오티즈 씨는 누구이겠는가?

(A) 도서관 직원   (B) 동물원 사육사
(C) 화가   (D) 과학자

해설 | 추론
Ortiz를 키워드로 잡고 Ortiz가 언급되는 부분에서 답을 찾아야 한다. 세 번째 행사인 비전문가를 위한 조류 관찰(Bird-Watching for Amateurs)에서 '올림피아 대학교 생물학자이자 <당신 주위에 있는 새들>의 저자인 메르세데스 오티즈(University of Olympia biologist and

author of *Birds in Your Neighborhood* Mercedes Ortiz)'라고 했으므로 오티즈 씨는 과학자라는 것을 짐작할 수 있다. 따라서 정답은 (D)이다.

패러프레이징
지문의 biologist → 보기의 scientist

5 음악의 시간 참가자들에게 무엇을 하라고 권하는가?

(A) 온라인으로 비용 지불하기
(B) 악기 가져오기
(C) 의자 가져오기
(D) 일찍 도착하기

해설 | 세부 사항
Music Hour가 언급된 항목에서 답을 찾아야 한다. 음악의 시간에 대해 설명한 마지막 문장에서 '등록은 하지 않아도 되지만 앞 좌석과 가운데 좌석은 아동 30명으로 제한되니 일찍 도착하라(get there early)'라고 했으므로 (D)가 정답이다.

패러프레이징
지문의 get there early → 보기의 Arrive early

[6-8] 웹페이지

```
http://www.t-note.com/aboutus
```

⁶번역업계에 종사하거나 입문하고자 하는 분만을 위해 제공되는 유일한 구직 웹사이트 t-note.com에 오신 것을 환영합니다. ⁷하단의 양식을 제출하고 적합한 일자리가 게시될 때마다 이메일을 받아보세요. 웹사이트의 다른 부분에서 다가오는 취업박람회, 사용자 추천의 글, 이력서 작성 요령, 번역 전문가들에게 듣는 구직 조언 등도 살펴보세요.

해당하는 모든 란을 클릭하세요. 오늘 바로 등록하고 보람 있는 번역가로서의 여정을 시작하세요!

이름: _____

이메일 주소: _____

언어: ◎영어 ◎스페인어 ◎프랑스어 ◎독일어 ◎이탈리아어
◎러시아어 ◎일본어 ◎중국어 ◎광둥어 ◎한국어 ◎아랍어
◎우르두어 ◎힌디어 ◎페르시아어 ◎인도네시아어
◎기타 _____

번역 경력 유형, 경력이 있는 경우:
◎행정 ◎상업 ◎금융 ◎법률 ◎의학
◎기술 ◎기타 _____

⁸선호 고용 형태:
◎현장 근무—도시 또는 국가를 명시하세요. _____
◎원격 근무

제출

어휘 | dedicated to ~에 전념하는 exclusively 독점적으로, 오로지 suitable 적합한 job fair 취업박람회 testimonial 추천의 글, 추천사 fulfilling 성취감을 주는 off-site 원격의, 현장 밖의

6 웹페이지에 따르면, t-note.com은 다른 구직 웹사이트와 어떻게 다른가?

(A) 구인 목록이 매우 상세하다.
(B) 내용이 매일 업데이트된다.
(C) 특별히 번역 일자리를 구하는 사람들을 위한 것이다.
(D) 다양한 언어로 볼 수 있다.

해설 | 세부 사항
웹페이지 첫 단락 첫 문장에서 '번역업계에 종사하거나 입문하고자 하는 분만을 위해 제공되는 유일한 구직 웹사이트(the only job-search Web site dedicated exclusively to those working in or looking to join the field of translation)'에 오신 것을 환영한다고 했으므로 (C)가 정답이다.

어휘 | extremely 극히, 극도로 specifically 특별히

7 t-note.com이 제공하는 것은?

(A) 월간 소식지
(B) 개인 맞춤형 일자리 알림
(C) 취업박람회 무료 입장권
(D) 전문가 이력서 검토 서비스

해설 | 세부 사항
첫 단락 두 번째 문장에서 '하단의 양식을 제출하고 적합한 일자리가 게시될 때마다 이메일을 받아보라(receive an e-mail whenever a suitable job is posted)'고 했으므로 (B)가 정답이다.

어휘 | notification 알림, 통지

패러프레이징
지문의 an e-mail → 보기의 notifications

8 서식에서 요청하는 정보는?

(A) 경력 연수
(B) 급여 요건
(C) 최근 작업물 견본
(D) 선호하는 근무 장소

해설 | 세부 사항
웹페이지 하단의 선호 고용 형태(Desired employment type)에서 '현장 근무 - 도시 또는 국가를 명시하라(On-site —list city or country)'고 했으므로 (D)가 정답이다.

어휘 | requirement 요건

패러프레이징
지문의 Desired → 보기의 Preferred
지문의 city or country → 보기의 location

[9-12] 편지

5월 16일

토마스 르노 박사
11경제학과
맥그루더 대학교
543 쇼어라인 로
보스턴, MA 02243

르노 박사님께,

저는 투자 및 재무 계획 제반 서비스 업체인 이스트필드 사의 운영 담당 부사장입니다. **9지난 목요일 저녁, 소셜미디어가 소비자 신뢰 지수에 미치는 영향에 관한 박사님의 강의를 들었습니다.** 소셜 미디어의 확장이 단기적으로 경제 성장에 어떤 영향을 미치는지에 관한 박사님의 분석이 인상 깊었습니다.

10저희 이스트필드에서는 직원 전문성 개발 노력의 일환으로 직원들에게 지속적인 사내 교육 워크숍 프로그램을 제공하고 있는데요. 강연하신 것과 같은 주제로 워크숍 하나를 맡아 주실 의향이 있으신지요? 강의는 질의응답을 포함해 90분간 진행되며 보통 약 25명의 참가자가 모입니다. **11작년에는 같은 학과에 계신 카터 박사님이 오셔서 진행해 주셨고 매우 성공적이었습니다.**

12의향이 있으시다면 제 비서 다니엘 윙에게 617-555-0172로 연락 주셔서 보수에 대해 말씀 나누십시오. 답장 기다리겠습니다.

아나냐 파텔
운영 부사장

- -

어휘 | investment 투자 audience 청중 consumer confidence 소비자 신뢰 analysis 분석 expansion 확장 in the short term 단기적으로 commitment 헌신, 전념 typically 보통, 일반적으로 compensation 보상, 보상금

9 파텔 씨는 르노 박사의 의견에 대해 어떻게 알았는가?

(A) 라디오 프로그램에서 강연하는 것을 들었다.
(B) 맥그루더 대학교의 동료였다.
(C) 박사에 관한 신문 기사를 읽었다.
(D) 박사의 강연에 참석했다.

해설 | 세부 사항
편지 첫 단락 두 번째 문장에서 '목요일 저녁, 소셜미디어가 소비자 신뢰 지수에 미치는 영향에 관한 박사님의 강의를 들었다(I was in the audience last Thursday evening when you spoke about the effects of social media on measures of consumer confidence)'고 했으므로 (D)가 정답이다.

어휘 | colleague 동료 article 기사

패러프레이징
지문의 was in the audience → 보기의 attended

10 이스트필드 사 직원에 대해 암시된 것은?

(A) 근무 일정이 유연하다.
(B) 대학 강의에 등록하도록 권장받는다.
(C) 사내 교육 수업에 참석할 수 있다.
(D) 업무 성과가 향상되면 보너스를 받는다.

해설 | 추론
두 번째 단락 첫 문장에서 '이스트필드에서는 사내 교육 워크숍 프로그램을 제공하고 있다(Eastfield offers an in-house program of continuing education workshops for our staff members)'고 했으므로 (C)가 정답이다.

어휘 | flexible 유연한, 탄력적인 enroll in ~에 등록하다 on-site 현장의

패러프레이징
지문의 an in-house program of continuing education workshops → 보기의 on-site learning sessions

11 편지에 따르면, 이전에 이스트필드 사를 방문한 사람은?

(A) 연구를 시행하는 연구원들
(B) 소비자 단체장
(C) 경제학 교수
(D) 경제 소식지 기자

해설 | 세부 사항
두 번째 단락 마지막 문장에서 '작년에는 같은 학과에 계신 카터 박사님이 오셔서 진행해 주셨다(Last year we had another member of your department, Dr. Carter, come to lead a group)'고 했고, 수신자 정보에서 르노 박사가 경제학과(Department of Economics) 소속으로 제시되어 있으므로 카터 박사도 경제학과 교수임을 알 수 있다. 따라서 (C)가 정답이다.

어휘 | conduct 하다

12 르노 박사가 윙 씨에게 연락을 취해야 하는 이유는?

(A) 강의료에 대해 논의하기 위해
(B) 워크숍 주제를 선정하기 위해
(C) 회사에 가는 길을 물어보기 위해
(D) 투자 관련 안내 책자를 요청하기 위해

해설 | 세부 사항
마지막 단락 첫 문장에서 '의향이 있으시다면 비서 다니엘 윙에게 연락 주셔서 보수에 대해 논의하라(please call my assistant, Daniel Wong, at 617-555-0172 to discuss compensation)'고 했으므로 (A)가 정답이다.

패러프레이징
지문의 compensation
→ 보기의 the amount of a payment

UNIT 03 Not / True 문제

기출 예제

본책 p.036

Q 그린게이지 콘퍼런스 센터에서 이용할 수 있는
것으로 언급되지 않은 것은?

(A) 무료 인터넷 접속
(B) 프레젠테이션 소프트웨어
(C) 식당 시설
(D) 현지의 호텔 객실들

그린게이지 콘퍼런스 센터

샬럿 공항에서 불과 40분 거리에 위치한 그린게이지
콘퍼런스 센터는 귀사가 다음 사내 행사를 개최할 장소로
더할 나위 없는 곳입니다. 아름답게 굽이치는 능선들과 삼림
속에 자리잡고 있는 저희 센터는 조용한 전용 휴식처를
제공합니다. 저희는 멀티미디어 프레젠테이션에 필요한
모든 장비가 구비된 회의 시설과 회의실들을 제공합니다.
또한 (B)사무 생산성 소프트웨어 일체와 (A)무료 무선 인터넷
접속, (C)두 개의 식당, 연회장이 완비된 비즈니스 센터도
제공합니다.

어휘 | corporate 기업의, 회사의 woodland 삼림 지대
serene 평화로운, 고요한 retreat 피난처, 휴식처 facility 시설,
설비 suite (관련 프로그램들의) 묶음, 세트 complimentary
무료의 wireless 무선

기출 ETS PRACTICE

본책 p.037

1 (D) **2** (B)

2월 20일

구인 광고

포트 멜버른의 새 향신료 가게에서 정규직 계산대 직원을
구합니다. 식료품점 또는 소매점에서 일을 한 경험이
요구됩니다. 다음 달 개장에 맞춰 일을 시작할 수 있어야
합니다. **4개월 근무 후 직원 할인이 가능합니다.** 이력서와
자기소개서를 월터 머헌에게 wmaughan@pmhs.com.au로
2월 25일까지 보내십시오.

어휘 | help wanted 구인 광고 cashier 출납원 grocery
식료품 잡화점 retail 소매 require 요구하다 grand opening
개장 CV 이력서 cover letter 자기소개서

---

1 광고된 일자리에 대해 명시된 것은?

(A) 관리직이다.   (B) 파트타임직이다.
(C) 4개월짜리 일자리이다. (D) 직원 할인이 주어진다.

해설 | Not / True
광고의 네 번째 문장에서 '4개월 근무 후 직원 할인이
가능하다(Employee discount available after four
months on the job)'고 했으므로 (D)가 정답이다.

어휘 | managerial 관리의

에크만 마켓

• (D)건강 목표를 세우는 데 조언이 필요하십니까?
• 좋아하는 음식을 좀 더 영양가 있게 만들고 싶으십니까?
• 당신과 가족을 위한 건강한 간식을 찾고 계십니까?

에크만 마켓이 돕겠습니다! 저희가 (A)현장 요리 수업과
(C)개인 쇼핑 투어, (D)일대일 상담을 제공해 드립니다.

오셔서 에크만 마켓 퍼스 지점의 공인 영양사인 제니퍼
요시무라를 만나보세요. 건강식에 대한 요시무라의 블로그를
이미 읽으신 적이 있거나 그녀가 지역 텔레비전에 출연하여
인터뷰하는 모습을 보신 적이 있을 수도 있습니다. www.
eckmanmarkets.com.au/nutritionist 혹은 정문 옆에 있는
요시무라의 테이블에 들르셔서 좀 더 알아보세요.

어휘 | goal 목표 nutritious 영양가 있는 on-site 현장의
one-on-one consultation 일대일 상담 accredited 공인된,
인가 받은 practising 개업 중인(= practicing) dietitian 영양사

---

2 에크만 마켓이 제공하는 것으로 공지에 언급되지 않은 것은?

(A) 요리 강좌
(B) 제품 견본
(C) 매장 투어
(D) 목표 달성을 위한 도움

해설 | Not / True
광고의 첫 단락 '현장 요리 수업과 개인 쇼핑 투어를
제공한다(We provide on-site cooking classes,
personal shopping tours)'는 말에서 (A)와 (C)가
언급되었다. 바로 그 뒤의 '일대일 상담(one-on-one
consultations)을 제공한다'는 말과, 제목 아래 첫 문장에서
'건강 목표를 세우는 데 조언이 필요한지(Need advice on
setting health goals)' 묻고 있으므로 (D)도 언급되었다.
하지만 제품 견본을 제공한다는 말은 없으므로 (B)가
정답이다.

패러프레이징
지문의 provide → 질문의 offer
지문의 on-site cooking classes
→ 보기의 Lessons in cooking
지문의 shopping tours
→ 보기의 Tours of the store
지문의 advice, one-on-one consultations
→ 보기의 Help

1 (D)	2 (B)	3 (C)	4 (B)	5 (D)	6 (B)
7 (D)	8 (C)	9 (C)	10 (B)	11 (A)	12 (C)

[1-2] 안내 책자

NLG 컴퓨터 수리 회사
25년 이상 러틀랜드 카운티에 서비스 제공

컴퓨터 서비스
- 바이러스, 악성 프로그램 및 기타 유해 프로그램을 제거합니다.
- 시스템 충돌 또는 하드웨어 손상으로 인해 손실된 데이터를 복구합니다.
- 가정 또는 회사의 무선 네트워크 환경을 설정합니다.
- **¹러틀랜드 카운티 어디에서나 귀하의 컴퓨터를 수거, 수리 및 반환해 드리며 경쟁업체와는 달리 이 서비스는 요금에 포함되어 있습니다.**

IT 교육
귀사에 컴퓨터 문제가 반복되어 발생할 경우, **²저희의 대면 교육에 대해 문의하세요. 시간당 80파운드의 저렴한 비용으로 귀사 직원들의 요구사항 해결과 IT 역량 구축을 위해 특별히 교육과정을 맞춰드릴 수 있습니다.**

자세한 정보를 원하시면 저희 웹사이트 www.nlgcomputer repairs.co.uk를 방문하시거나 01632 960547로 전화 주십시오.

어휘 | repair 수리 serve 서비스를 제공하다 remove 제거하다 malware 악성 소프트웨어 harmful 해로운 recover 복구하다 as a result of ~의 결과로 crash 충돌 damage 손상 configure (컴퓨터의) 환경을 설정하다 competition 경쟁사 charge 요금 recurring 되풀이하여 발생하는 in-person 직접의 session (특정 활동) 시간 per ~당 tailor 맞추다 specially 특히 address 해결하다 skill 기술

1 안내 책자에 따르면, 이 업체의 독특한 점은?

(A) 온라인 데이터 저장소를 제공한다.
(B) 컴퓨터를 주문 제작해 준다.
(C) 러틀랜드 카운티에 많은 지점이 있다.
(D) 고객 물품 운송에 대해 추가 요금을 청구하지 않는다.

해설 | 세부 사항
컴퓨터 서비스의 마지막 항목에서 '러틀랜드 카운티 어디에서나 귀하의 컴퓨터를 수거, 수리 및 반환해 드리며 경쟁업체와는 달리 이 서비스는 요금에 포함되어 있다(We collect, repair ~ included in the charge)'고 했다. 따라서 컴퓨터 배송에 대한 요금을 추가로 청구하지 않는다는 점이 타사와 구별되므로 (D)가 정답이다.

어휘 | storage 저장(소) customized 주문 제작된 location 지점 charge 청구하다 additional 추가의 fee 요금 transport 운송하다

패러프레이징
지문의 included in the charge
→ 보기의 does not charge an additional fee

2 교육 세션에 대해 언급된 것은?

(A) 상급 학습자를 대상으로 한다.
(B) 합리적인 가격이다.
(C) 인터넷으로 이용할 수 있다.
(D) 월 단위로 열린다.

해설 | Not / True
IT 교육 설명에서 '저희의 대면 교육에 대해 문의하라 (ask us about our in-person training sessions)'면서 '시간당 80파운드의 저렴한 비용으로 직원들의 요구사항 해결 및 IT 역량 구축을 위해 교육과정을 맞춰줄 수 있다(At the low cost ~ build their IT skills)'고 했으므로 (B)가 정답이다.

어휘 | intend 의도하다 advanced 상급의 reasonably 합리적으로 priced 가격이 책정된 available 이용 가능한 basis 기준

패러프레이징
지문의 At the low cost → 보기의 reasonably priced

[3-5] 이메일

발신: 카트야 스보보도바 <katya@casalopez.net>
수신: 앨런 제이 <anjay@santorolaw.com>
제목: 카사 로페즈 예약
날짜: 8월 8일
첨부: 🖇 보증금 영수증

제이 씨께,

곧 있을 산토로 앤 라몬트 합동 법률사무소의 기념 행사 장소로 카사 로페즈를 선택해 주셔서 감사합니다. 10월 16일 오후 7시부터 9시까지 좌석 정원 108명으로 코르도바 실 예약을 확정하고자 메일 드립니다. **⁵⁽ᶜ⁾말씀드린 대로 해당 참석자 수로는 6명씩 앉을 수 있는 원형 테이블을 추천합니다만, 다른 테이블 형태도 쉽게 설치 가능합니다.** 우리가 논의한 대로 **³,⁵⁽ᴮ⁾회사 퇴임을 기념하는 직원 세 분에 관한 슬라이드쇼를 보여주실 수 있도록 코르도바 실에 프로젝터를 설치해 드리겠습니다.**

⁴저희 웹사이트 www.casalopez.net에서 파티 메뉴 링크를 보실 수 있습니다. 100여 가지 음식 및 음료 메뉴에서 선택하시면 됩니다. 어떤 메뉴이든 클릭하셔서 해당 메뉴에 들어있는 재료와 준비되는 과정을 확인하세요. **⁵⁽ᴬ⁾메뉴 선택에 도움이 필요하시면 이메일을 보내주시거나 555-0174로 전화 주십시오. 9월 15일까지 메뉴를 선택해 주시기** 바랍니다.

아울러 본 이메일로 500달러의 보증금을 수령했음을 확인해 드립니다. 영수증이 첨부되어 있습니다. 메뉴를 선택하시면 총 금액에 대한 청구서를 받으실 것입니다.

카트야 스보보도바
행사 관리자
카사 로페즈

어휘 | reservation 예약 seating accommodation 좌석 정원, 좌석 수용 인원 retirement 은퇴, 퇴직 ingredient 재료 deposit 보증금, 착수금

---

3 10월 16일에 행사가 열리는 이유는?

(A) 신규 채용된 직원들을 환영하려고
(B) 산토로 앤 라몬트의 새 사무실 개소를 축하하려고
(C) 직원들의 퇴임을 기념하려고
(D) 회사의 신임 회장 임명을 알리려고

해설 | 세부 사항
이메일 첫 단락 마지막 문장에서 '회사 퇴임을 기념하는 직원 세 분(the three employees whose retirement from your company will be celebrated)에 관한 슬라이드쇼를 보여줄 수 있도록 코로도바 실에 프로젝터를 설치해주겠다'고 했으므로 (C)가 정답이다.

어휘 | appointment 임명, 지명

4 이메일에 따르면, 제이 씨가 카사 로페즈 웹사이트에서 찾을 수 있는 것은?

(A) 주문 건에 대한 청구서
(B) 음식 설명
(C) 출력해서 서명해야 하는 계약서
(D) 코르도바 실의 좌석 배치도

해설 | 세부 사항
Web site를 키워드로 잡고, Web site가 언급된 항목에서 답을 찾아야 한다. 두 번째 단락 첫 문장에서 '웹사이트에서 파티 메뉴 링크(On the home page of our Web site ~ you will find the link for party menus)'를 볼 수 있으며, 100여 가지 음식 및 음료 메뉴에서 선택하면 된다(There, you may choose from over 100 food and beverage options)'고 하므로 (B)가 정답이다.

어휘 | invoice 청구서 contract 계약서

패러프레이징
지문의 food and beverage options → 보기의 food items

5 카사 로페즈가 제공할 수 있는 서비스로 언급되지 않은 것은?

(A) 메뉴 선택에 관한 조언 제공
(B) 슬라이드 쇼를 위한 프로젝터 설치
(C) 제안된 탁자 배열 변경
(D) 행사 구역 장식

해설 | Not/True
첫 단락 세 번째 문장에서 '해당 참석자 수로는 6명씩

앉을 수 있는 원형 테이블을 추천하지만, 다른 테이블 형태도 쉽게 설치 가능하다(I would recommend round tables that each seat six people; however, other table setups can easily be arranged)'면서 (C)를 언급했고, 이어서 '회사 퇴임을 기념하는 직원 세 분에 관한 슬라이드쇼를 위한 프로젝터를 설치해주겠다(I will have a projector set up in the Córdoba Room so that you can present a slide show)'며 (B)를 언급했다. 두 번째 단락 세 번째 문장에서 '메뉴 선택에 도움이 필요하면(Should you need assistance making menu choices) 이메일을 보내거나 전화를 달라'고 했으므로 (A)가 언급되었다. 하지만 행사 구역 장식에 대한 이야기는 없으므로 (D)가 정답이다.

어휘 | decorate 장식하다

패러프레이징
지문의 recommend round tables that each seat six people → 보기의 the suggested arrangement of tables
지문의 assistance making menu choices → 보기의 advice in making menu selections

---

[6-8] 보고서

검색 업데이트: 밸브콤프 웨스트 코스트 센터

부지검색위원회는 미국과 캐나다 전역 15개 도시의 기반 시설 및 접근성을 검토한 후 12개의 장소를 제외시켰다. **[6]포틀랜드, 시애틀, 밴쿠버는 밸브콤프의 웨스트 코스트 센터를 세울 수 있는 부지로 여전히 고려 중이다.** 위원회는 최종 결정을 내리기 전 해당 3개 도시를 방문해 각 시의회와 면담하고 있다.

위원회는 오리건 주 포틀랜드를 검토한 결과 포틀랜드가 신규 업체와 성장 중인 업체를 환영한다는 점에 주목했다. **[7]포틀랜드는 밸브콤프 본사와는 거리가 멀지만 엔진 부품 생산업체인 마톤 모터 사와 가깝다. 밸브콤프의 웨스트 코스트 센터를 포틀랜드에 두면 주요 고객사인 해당 업체 주문이 효율적이고 비용 효율성 높게 이루어질 수 있다.**

웨스트 코스트 센터를 포틀랜드의 항구 지역과 가까운 곳에 세우면 밸브콤프가 모든 운송수단을 이용해 선적을 진행할 수 있다. 컬럼비아강에는 해상 터미널 세 곳이 있으며 포틀랜드 공항이 부두와 인접한 거리에 있다. **[8]현재 보수 중인 철도망은 내년부터 증가할 화물을 처리할 수 있다. 현재는 12월까지 여객 열차만 운행 중이다.** 마지막으로 주요 고속도로가 항구와 포틀랜드 도심 지역을 지나가므로 트럭 운송은 믿을 만한 교통수단이 될 수 있다.

어휘 | accessibility 접근, 접근 가능성 eliminate 제거하다, 탈락시키다 under consideration 고려 중인 viable 실행 가능한 respective 각각의 component 부품 cost effective 비용 효율적인 transportation mode 운송수단 adjacent to ~에 인접한 freight 화물 reliable 믿을 만한, 신뢰할 수 있는

6 위원회는 현재 몇 개의 장소를 고려하고 있는가?

(A) 1 (B) 3 (C) 12 (D) 15

해설 | 세부 사항
보고서 첫 단락 두 번째 문장에서 '포틀랜드, 시애틀, 밴쿠버는 밸브콤프의 웨스트 코스트 센터를 세울 수 있는 부지로 여전히 고려 중(Portland, Seattle, and Vancouver remain under consideration as viable locations for Valvecomp's west coast center)'이라고 했으므로 (B)가 정답이다.

7 마톤 모터 사에 대해 암시된 것은?

(A) 포틀랜드 중심부로 시설을 이전한다.
(B) 대표를 새로 임명했다.
(C) 밸브콤프가 좀 전에 매입했다.
(D) 밸브콤프의 주요 고객사이다.

해설 | 추론
Martone Motor Company를 키워드로 잡고, Martone Motor Company가 언급된 부분에서 답을 찾아야 한다. 두 번째 단락에서 '엔진 부품 생산업체인 마톤 모터 사와 가깝다(it is close to the Martone Motor Company, a manufacturer of engine components)'고 했고 '밸브콤프의 웨스트 코스트 센터를 포틀랜드에 두면 주요 고객사(this major client)인 해당 업체 주문이 효율적이고 비용 효용성 높게 이루어질 수 있다'고 했다. 여기서 주요 고객사는 마톤 모터 사를 가리키므로 (D)가 정답이다.

어휘 | facility 시설 appoint 임명하다, 지명하다

패러프레이징
지문의 major client → 보기의 important client

8 보고서에 따르면, 포틀랜드에 대해 사실인 것은?

(A) 공항이 너무 작아서 화물 처리가 불가능하다.
(B) 교통 기반 시설이 시애틀과 비슷하다.
(C) 새해에는 철도 교통으로 화물 운송을 시작할 수 있다.
(D) 광범위한 고속도로망은 보수를 해야 한다.

해설 | Not / True
마지막 단락 세 번째 문장에서 '현재 보수 중인 철도망은 내년부터 증가할 화물을 처리할 수 있으며 현재는 12월까지 여객 열차만 운행 중(The rail network, which is undergoing some renovation, will be able to handle increased freight starting in the new year — currently only passenger trains are operating through December)'이라고 했으므로 (C)가 정답이다.

어휘 | extensive 광범위한 in need of ~을 필요로 하는

패러프레이징
지문의 handle increased freight
→ 보기의 carrying freight

[9-12] 편지

블랙 크릭 네트워킹 협회
15 사우스 월넛 가
블랙 크릭, NE 68897

BCNA 회원 여러분께,

기다려 주셔서 감사합니다. 블랙 크릭 네트워킹 협회 안내 책자를 동봉합니다. 보통 연간 회원 자격을 갱신하실 때 받으시는 책자입니다. 올해는 늦어져서 죄송합니다. **9**사무실 이전 절차를 진행하느라 평상시의 안내 책자 출간 마감일을 맞출 수가 없었습니다. **10**책자를 한 권 더 원하시면 패티 그린왈드에게 membership@BCNA.net으로 요청사항을 전달해 주십시오.

11(C)저희 웹사이트에서 BCNA의 아이디와 비밀번호로 전자책 버전을 이용하실 수 있습니다. 본문에서 검색이 가능해 다른 BCNA 회원의 주소 및 전화번호를 찾기 쉽습니다.

여러분이 목록에 어떻게 기재되어 있는지 확인해 주시기 바랍니다. 등재된 내용이 예전 정보이거나 잘못된 경우 **11(B)**로그인하셔서 '내 계정' 버튼을 클릭하시고 연락처 정보를 수정하세요. 같은 페이지에서 **11(D)**회원 자격 현황 확인 및 만료 전 갱신도 가능합니다.

12웹사이트에서 대화형 회원 지도를 제작하려고 준비 중입니다. **11(A)**최신 기술에 능숙하고 도움을 주실 의향이 있는 자원봉사자는 론 샌덜링에게 전화 바랍니다.

프랜신 쿠퍼
협회장

연락처:
패티 그린왈드: 308-555-0147
론 샌덜링: 308-555-0122

어휘 | enclosed 동봉된 relocate 이전하다 publishing 출간, 출판 out-of-date 구식의, (더 이상) 쓸모없는 verify 확인하다 expire 만료되다 interactive 대화형의, 상호적인 tech-savvy 최신 기술에 능통한

9 지연된 이유는?

(A) 프린터에 오류가 생겼다.
(B) 수송품이 분실됐다.
(C) BCNA 사무실이 이전했다.
(D) BCNA가 예상보다 빠르게 성장했다.

해설 | 세부 사항
첫 단락 네 번째 문장에서 '사무실 이전 절차를 진행하느라(We were in the process of relocating our office) 평상시의 안내 책자 출간 마감일을 맞출 수가 없었다'고 했으므로 (C)가 정답이다.

어휘 | than expected 예상했던 것보다

패러프레이징
지문의 We were in the process of relocating our office
→ 보기의 The BCNA office was being moved.

10 편지에 따르면, 그린왈드 씨의 책무는?

(A) 급여 배분
(B) 안내 책자 추가 제공
(C) BCNA 행사 기획
(D) BCNA 공식 기록 작성

해설 | 세부 사항
Ms. Greenwald를 키워드로 잡고, Ms. Greenwald가
언급된 부분에서 답을 찾아야 한다. 첫 단락 마지막
문장에서 '책자를 한 권 더 원하시면(If you would
like another copy) 패티 그린왈드에게 요청사항을
전달해달라'고 했으므로 안내 책자를 추가로 제공하는 것은
그린왈드 씨의 책무임을 알 수 있다. 따라서 정답은 (B)이다.

어휘 | distribute 분배하다, 나누어 주다 paycheck 급료

패러프레이징
지문의 another copy → 보기의 additional directories

11 회원들이 온라인에서 할 수 있는 사항으로 언급되지 않은
것은?

(A) 론 샌덜링에게 연락하기
(B) 안내 책자 기재 사항 업데이트하기
(C) 전화번호 검색하기
(D) 회원 자격 갱신하기

해설 | Not / True
두 번째 단락에서 '웹사이트에 있는 전자책에서 검색이
가능해 다른 BCNA 회원의 주소 및 전화번호를 찾기
쉽다(The text is searchable, making it easy to find
the addresses and phone numbers of other BCNA
members)'고 했으므로 (C)는 온라인에서 가능하다. 세
번째 단락 두 번째 문장에서 '로그인해서 연락처 정보를
수정하라(correct your contact information)'고
했으므로 (B) 역시 온라인에서 가능하다. 세 번째 단락
마지막 문장에서 '회원 자격 현황 확인 및 만료 전 갱신도
가능하다(On that same page, you can also verify
the status of your membership and renew it before
it expires)'고 했으므로 (D)도 가능하다. 편지 마지막
문장에서 '최신 기술에 능숙하고 도움을 주실 의향이 있는
자원봉사자는 론 샌덜링에게 전화 바란다(Tech-savvy
volunteers ~ call Ron Sandering)'고 했다. 전화는
온라인에서 할 수 있는 사항이 아니므로 (A)가 정답이다.

12 BCNA가 자원봉사자를 찾는 목적은?

(A) 잠재 회원을 찾으려고
(B) 자료 배분을 도우려고
(C) 웹사이트 신규 기능을 생성하려고
(D) 신규 서비스에 대해 회원들에게 설문 조사를 하려고

해설 | 세부 사항
volunteers를 키워드로 잡고, volunteers가 언급된
부분에서 답을 찾아야 한다. 마지막 단락에 봉사자들에
대해 언급되어 있다. '웹사이트에서 대화형 회원 지도를
제작하려 준비 중(We are preparing to make an
interactive map of our membership for the Web
site)'이라고 했으므로 (C)가 정답이다.

어휘 | potential 잠재적인, 가능성이 있는 feature 특색, 기능

패러프레이징
지문의 make an interactive map of our membership
for the Web site → 보기의 create a new feature for its
Web site

UNIT 04 추론 문제

기출 예제   본책 p. 042

Q 얼햄 씨는 누구일 것 같은가?

(A) 변호사   (B) 부동산 중개사
(C) 세미나 진행자   (D) 행정 보조

얼햄 씨께,

**사비노 부동산 세미나 "아파트 분양을 위한 타겟 마케팅"을
수료하신 것을 축하드립니다. 귀하의 경력에 도움이 되는
소중한 정보를 얻으셨기를 바랍니다.**

다음 세미나는 8월 8일 토요일에 열릴 예정입니다. 상업용
부동산법의 최근 개정 사항에 초점을 맞출 것입니다.
7월 20일까지 등록하시면 모든 강좌 교재를 30%
할인해드립니다. www.savinorealestate.com에서
온라인으로 등록하세요. 함께해 주시기를 바랍니다!

안톤 사비노

어휘 | complete 완료하다 condominium 아파트 valuable
소중한 focus on 초점을 맞추다 recent 최근의 commercial
상업의 law 법 sign up 등록하다 material 자료 register
등록하다

기출 **ETS PRACTICE**   본책 p. 043

1 (C)   **2** (D)

주목해 주세요!

이 화물 엘리베이터는 직원 전용입니다. 일반인이 사용하는
용도가 아닙니다. **고객들은 매장 뒤편 탈의실 오른쪽에 있는
승객용 엘리베이터를 이용하셔야 합니다.**

고객님의 협조에 감사드리며 즐거운 쇼핑 되십시오!

– 관리 사무실

- -

어휘 | freight 화물 intend 의도하다 general public
일반 대중 fitting room 탈의실 cooperation 협력
management 경영진, 관리

1 이 공지는 어디에서 발견되겠는가?

    (A) 박물관   (B) 창고
    (C) 백화점   (D) 사무실 건물

해설 | 추론
공지의 세 번째 문장에서 '고객들은 매장 뒤편 탈의실
오른쪽에 있는 승객용 엘리베이터를 이용해야
한다(Customers should use the passenger
elevators to the right of the fitting rooms at the
back of the store)'고 한 후, '고객님의 협조에 감사드리며
즐거운 쇼핑이 되길 바란다(enjoy your shopping
experience)'고 했으므로 공지 장소는 백화점이라는 것을
짐작할 수 있다. 따라서 (C)가 정답이다.

- -

수신: 이경빈 <kyi@moto.net>
발신: 미구엘 에르난데스 <mhernandez@mintner_mag.com>
날짜: 1월 3일
제목: 귀하의 응모작

좋은 소식을 알려 드리고자 메일 드립니다. **귀하의 사진
'겨울의 해안선'이 〈민트너 포토그래피 매거진〉에서 후원한
풍경 사진 콘테스트 '우리 세상의 풍경'에서 3위 수상작으로
선정되었습니다.**

귀하의 사진은 다른 수상작들과 함께 〈민트너 포토그래피
매거진〉 3월호에 실릴 예정입니다. 더불어 5월 9일부터 5월
21일까지 버밍엄의 페리베일 미술관에서 열릴 특별 풍경
사진전에도 특별 전시될 예정입니다.

귀하는 400파운드의 상금과 〈민트너 포토그래피 매거진〉
2년 정기 구독권을 받게 됩니다.

귀하의 성공을 진심으로 축하드립니다. 저희는 귀하의 작품을
세계 독자들과 공유하기를 고대하고 있으며 앞으로 귀하의
작품을 더 많이 보게 되기를 희망합니다.

어휘 | submission 제출, 응모작 third-place 3위
landscape 풍경 issue (정기 간행물의) 호 exhibit 전시회
look forward to ~하기를 고대하다 readership 독자 수

2 이 씨의 사진에 대해 암시된 것은?

    (A) 흑백 사진이다.
    (B) 이전에 발표된 적이 있다.
    (C) 잡지사에서 판권을 사들였다.
    (D) 풍경을 묘사하고 있다.

해설 | 추론
지문 첫 번째 단락에서 '이 씨의 해안선 사진이 풍경
사진 콘테스트에서 3위 수상작으로 선정되었다(Your
photograph *Coastline in Winter* has been chosen ~
landscape photography contest)'고 했으므로 정답은
(D)이다.

어휘 | previously 이전에 publish 발표하다, 발행하다
depict 묘사하다

기출 ETS TEST   본책 p.044

1 (C)	**2** (D)	**3** (B)	**4** (C)	**5** (D)
6 (C)	**7** (B)	**8** (D)	**9** (C)	**10** (B)
11 (C)	**12** (D)	**13** (D)		

[1-2] 온라인 채팅

- -

티모시 리더 [오후 1시 9분]
안녕하세요, 루시아. 지금 자리로 돌아왔으니 아까 요청하신
수치를 찾아볼 수 있습니다. 원하시는 바를 정확히
알려주세요.

루시아 브릴 [오후 1시 12분]
¹,²우리 화장품 제품군별로 최근 마감된 분기에 해당하는
최신 매출액 수치가 필요합니다. 제가 갖고 있는 수치는
5월말까지만 나와 있어요. ²제 컴퓨터가 데이터베이스에
접속하는 데 문제가 생긴 것 같아요.

티모시 리더 [오후 1시 14분]
알겠습니다. 어렵지 않을 겁니다. ²이메일로 될 것 같아요.

루시아 브릴 [오후 1시 15분]
네, 좋습니다. 도와주셔서 감사합니다.

- -

어휘 | sales figure 매출액 assume 추정하다

1 리더 씨에 대해 암시된 것은?

    (A) IT 부서에서 일한다.
    (B) 브릴 씨를 교육하고 있다.
    (C) 화장품 회사에서 일한다.
    (D) 회의를 잡으려고 한다.

해설 | 추론
1시 12분에 루시아 브릴이 '화장품 제품군별로(each of our
cosmetic lines) 최근 마감된 분기에 해당하는 최신 매출액
수치가 필요하다'고 했으므로 리더 씨도 화장품 회사에서
근무한다고 짐작할 수 있다. 따라서 정답은 (C)이다.

2 오후 1시 14분에 리더 씨가 "어렵지 않을 겁니다"라고 쓴
의도는 무엇이겠는가?

    (A) 브릴 씨의 컴퓨터를 쉽게 고칠 수 있다.
    (B) 제품을 빠르게 선적할 수 있다.

(C) 마감을 연장할 수 있다.
(D) 매출 정보를 제공할 수 있다.

해설 | 의도 파악
1시 12분에 루시아 브릴이 '최신 매출액 수치가 필요하다(I need the updated sales figures)'고 하면서 컴퓨터가 데이터베이스에 접속하는 데 문제가 생긴 것 같다'고 어려움에 대해 언급하자, 1시 14분에 리더 씨는 '어렵지 않을 겁니다(That shouldn't be difficult to do)'라고 답한 뒤 '이메일로 될 것 같다(I assume that e-mail is OK)'고 덧붙였다. 따라서 '어렵지 않을 겁니다'라는 말은 리더 씨가 최신 매출 정보를 이메일로 제공할 수 있다는 뜻이므로 (D)가 정답이다.

어휘 | extend a deadline 기한을 연장하다

패러프레이징
지문의 sales figures → 보기의 sales information

[3-5] 편지

메디프로 얼라이언스
코닝스트라트 251
6511 LA, 네이메헌
네덜란드
전화: 024 217 9961

엘레니 카트산토니스
842 아타라시스 가
2221 니코시아
키프로스

카트산토니스 씨께,

오늘날 전 세계 비즈니스 환경은 극도로 상호 연결되고 상호 의존적이므로 국내외 동료들과 직업적인 유대를 맺는 것이 어느 때보다도 중요합니다. **⁴이러한 이유로 메디프로 얼라이언스에서는 42개국 의학 연구소 과학자 4만 명 이상의 정보를 담은 광대한 데이터베이스를 만들었습니다. ³,⁴지금 메디프로 얼라이언스에 가입하셔서 동료 관계를 넓혀보세요.**

⁵저희 스탠다드 비즈니스 리스팅 가입자가 되시면 가입된 각 개인의 이름, 직함, 연락처 정보와 의사, 간호사, 물리치료사를 대상으로 하는 당사의 다른 의료 전문가 데이터베이스에 접속하실 수 있습니다. 또한 프리미엄 비즈니스 리스팅에 가입하시면 앞서 언급한 정보뿐 아니라 공개 승인을 받은 상세 데이터에도 접속 가능합니다.

본 서비스가 귀하께 매우 유용하리라고 확신하기에 30일 무료 이용권을 제공해 드립니다. 무료 이용권을 등록하시거나 가입하시려면 저희 웹사이트 www.mpalliance.com.nl/subscription을 방문하세요.

마르욜레인 블루멘벨트
수석 마케팅 담당자

어휘 | profoundly 깊이, 극심하게 **interconnected** 상호 연결된 **interdependent** 상호 의존적인 **colleague** 동료 **compile** 편집하다, 편찬하다 **extensive** 광범위한 **physical therapist** 물리치료사 **subscribe to** ~에 가입하다, ~을 구독하다 **aforementioned** 앞서 언급한 **disclose** 밝히다, 드러내다 **invaluable** 매우 유용한, 귀중한 **sign up for** ~을[에] 등록하다, 신청하다

3 편지의 목적은?
(A) 최신 정보를 요청하려고
(B) 신규 고객을 유치하려고
(C) 행사 등록 방법을 설명하려고
(D) 의료진을 추천하려고

해설 | 주제 / 목적
편지 첫 단락 마지막 문장에서 '지금 메디프로 얼라이언스에 가입하셔서 동료 관계를 넓혀보라(Join Medipro Alliance today and broaden your peer-to-peer connections)'고 했으므로 (B)가 정답이다.

어휘 | register 등록하다

4 카트산토니스 씨는 누구이겠는가?
(A) 의사   (B) 간호사
(C) 연구소 과학자   (D) 물리치료사

해설 | 추론
첫 단락 두 번째 문장에서 '메디프로 얼라이언스에서는 42개국 의학 연구소 과학자 4만 명 이상의 정보를 담은 광대한 데이터베이스를 만들었으며(That is why Medipro Alliance ~ 40,000 medical laboratory scientists located in 42 countries), 지금 메디프로 얼라이언스에 가입하셔서 동료 관계를 넓혀보라(Join Medipro Alliance ~ peer-to-peer connections)'고 했으므로 편지의 수신자인 카트산토니스 씨 또한 의학 연구소 과학자라는 것을 짐작할 수 있다. 따라서 (C)가 정답이다.

5 메디프로 얼라이언스는 어떤 서비스를 제공하는가?
(A) 웹사이트 디자인
(B) 분실 데이터 복구
(C) 의료 교육 제공
(D) 직업상의 커뮤니케이션 촉진

해설 | 세부 사항
두 번째 단락 첫 문장에서 '스탠다드 비즈니스 리스팅 가입자가 되면 가입된 각 개인의 이름, 직함, 연락처 정보와 다른 의료 전문가 데이터베이스에 접속할 수 있다(you will have access to the name, title, and contact information of each individual included in this and any of our other databases of medical professionals)'고 했으므로 (D)가 정답이다.

어휘 | facilitate 가능하게 하다, 용이하게 하다

에스터월 (4월 5일) – 하버 가를 따라 구도심 지역 개발을 기대하는 부동산 투자자들은 곧 에스터월 재개발 위원회 (ERC)가 제안한 엄격한 새 기준을 따라야 할 수도 있다.

위원회는 지역의 고색창연한 건물을 적절하게 재사용하는 것에 대한 주민들의 우려를 고려하여 최근 하버 가 인근 지역 내 향후 개발 프로젝트를 구체화하기 위한 설계 지침의 초안을 작성했다.

6다소 방치되었지만 역사적인 지역 중심부에 위치한 하버 가는 이익을 얻을 기회를 감지한 투자자들에게 점점 주목을 받아왔다. 최근에는 노후된 건물을 새 상점과 주거용 건물로 교체하자는 제안이 여섯 차례 있었다.

위원회는 이에 대응하여 유산 보존이라는 강경한 입장을 취하고 있다. "저희 생각은 지역에 다시 활력을 불어넣는 것이지만 원래 특성을 보여주면서 그렇게 하는 것입니다." ERC 대변인 브래드 나이트가 설명한다. 제안된 지침에 따르면 건축학적 또는 역사적인 가치를 지닌 것으로 인정된 구조물들은 복원되어야 하며 새로운 건축물은 양립 가능한 설계 원칙을 따라야 한다.

7ERC의 초안은 웹사이트 esterwallrc.org.uk에서 확인 가능하다. 인쇄물은 디턴 공립 도서관에서 볼 수 있다.

8ERC는 4월 8일 오후 1시 30분, 하버 가 커뮤니티 센터에서 대중 집회를 개최할 예정이다. 8,9ERC 위원들은 집회에서 제안서 관련 질문에 답할 것이며 시민들은 자신의 견해를 밝힐 수 있다. 9참석이 불가능한 사람은 로나 후에게 lhu@esterwallrc.org.uk로 피드백을 보내면 된다.

어휘 | investor 투자자 in light of ~에 비추어, ~을 고려하여 appropriate 적절한 venerable 존경할 만한, 훌륭한 increasingly 점점 더 of late 최근에 replace 대체하다, 교체하다 in response 이에 대응하여 take a strong stand 강경한 입장을 취하다 heritage 유산 preservation 보존, 보호, 유지 revitalize 새로운 활력을 주다 spokesperson 대변인 restore 복원하다 conform to ~을 따르다 compatible 양립할 수 있는 public assembly 대중 집회, 일반 집회 voice one's opinions 견해를 밝히다

6 하버 가에 대해 명시된 것은?

(A) 디턴 공립 도서관 옆에 있다.
(B) 주차 공간이 충분하다.
(C) 역사적 의의가 있다.
(D) 인기 많은 쇼핑 장소이다.

해설 | Not / True
기사의 세 번째 단락 첫 문장에서 '다소 방치되었지만 역사적인 지역 중심부에 위치한 하버 가(located at the heart of a somewhat neglected but historic area)'라고 했으므로 (C)가 정답이다.

어휘 | ample 충분한 significance 중요성, 의의

7 기사에 따르면, 독자들은 왜 ERC 웹사이트를 방문해야 하는가?

(A) 설계에 관해 투표하기 위해
(B) 문서를 보기 위해
(C) 도서관 운영시간을 확인하기 위해
(D) 건설 허가를 받기 위해

해설 | 세부 사항
Web site를 키워드로 잡고 Web site가 언급되는 부분에서 답을 찾아야 한다. 다섯 번째 단락에서 'ERC의 초안은 웹사이트 esterwallrc.org.uk에서 확인 가능하다(The ERC's draft is available online at their Web site, esterwallrc.org.uk)'고 했으므로 (B)가 정답이다.

어휘 | permit 허가(증)

패러프레이징
지문의 The ERC's draft → 보기의 a document

8 ERC 위원들은 왜 하버 가 커뮤니티 센터에 갈 것인가?

(A) 곧 있을 문화 행사를 기획하려고
(B) 새 주민들을 환영하려고
(C) 교육 프로그램을 시작하려고
(D) 제안된 규정에 관해 논의하려고

해설 | 세부 사항
마지막 단락 첫 문장에서 'ERC는 4월 8일 오후 1시 30분, 하버 가 커뮤니티 센터에서 대중 집회를 개최할 예정(The ERC will hold a public assembly at the Harbour Street Community Centre ~)'이라고 했다. 이어서 'ERC 위원들은 집회에서 제안서 관련 질문에 답할 것이며 시민들은 자신의 견해를 밝힐 수 있다(ERC officials will answer questions about the proposal and the citizens will be able to voice their opinions)'고 했으므로 제안서에 관해 논의하려는 것을 알 수 있다. 따라서 (D)가 정답이다.

어휘 | upcoming 곧 있을, 다가오는 regulation 규정

패러프레이징
지문의 answer questions, voice their opinions → 보기의 discuss

9 후 씨는 무엇을 하겠는가?

(A) 미디어 질문에 응답
(B) 개발 프로젝트 점검
(C) 주민 의견 수집
(D) 도급업체 제안서 검토

해설 | 추론
마지막 단락에서 'ERC 위원들은 집회에서 제안서 관련 질문에 답할 것이며 시민들은 자신의 견해를 밝힐 수 있다(the citizens will be able to voice their

opinions)'고 한 후, '참석이 불가능한 사람은 로나 후에게 lhu@esterwallrc.org.uk로 피드백을 보내면 된다(Those unable to attend can e-mail feedback to Lorna Hu ~)'고 했으므로 후 씨는 주민 의견을 수집하는 것으로 짐작할 수 있다. 따라서 (C)가 정답이다.

어휘 | inspect 점검하다, 검사하다   gather 모으다

<u>패러프레이징</u>
지문의 opinions, feedback → 보기의 comments

[10-13] 이메일

수신: 알리나 고메즈 <agomez@galleonair.com>
발신: 토모코 오노 <tono@szmail.net>
제목: 2월 경유
날짜: 3월 3일

고메즈 씨께,

[11]귀사의 품격 있는 서비스에 익숙한 고객으로서 제가 최근 경유지에서 겪은 불만족스러운 경험에 대해 말씀드려야 할 것 같습니다. 2월 25일, 뉴어크발 댈러스행 항공편(GL115)이 기계적 문제로 연착되었습니다. 결국 댈러스에 도착했을 때 오스틴으로 가는 연결편을 놓쳤고 숙박할 방이 필요했어요. [10]갈레온 항공 고객 서비스 상담원이 교통편을 마련해주고 위클리프 인에서 사용할 쿠폰을 주었습니다.

[10]위클리프 인에서의 짧은 투숙은 불만족스럽고 불쾌했습니다. [12](C)호텔 식당에서 식사를 주문했는데 항공사에서 준 식사 쿠폰으로 계산하려고 하자 코드가 유효하지 않다고 했습니다. 제 사비로 저녁 식사 비용 19.78달러를 계산하고 난 후 [12](A)위층으로 올라가 피트니스 센터를 찾았는데 보수 공사로 문을 닫았더군요. 마지막으로 방이 너무 더웠지만 [12](B)온도 조절 장치가 고장 나 난방을 줄일 수가 없었습니다.

[11]이번 일이 있기 전까지 갈레온 항공은 제가 선호하는 항공사였어요. 부디 위클리프 인과의 계약은 갱신하지 마시고 향후에는 승객들을 다른 곳으로 보내셨으면 합니다. 위클리프 인의 총지배인인 알린 찰스에게도 메일을 써서 제 경험에 대해 얘기했습니다.

[13]쿠폰(#8892730)을 쓸 수 없었으니 저녁 식사 비용을 보상해 주시기 바랍니다. 다음번에 갈레온 항공을 이용할 때는 제가 평상시 받았던 모범적인 서비스를 받았으면 합니다. 추가 정보가 필요하시면 연락 주세요.

토모코 오노
788 하이포인트 테라스
케리빌, NJ 08001
856-555-0195

어휘 | stopover 경유, 기착   mechanical 기계적인 frustrating 불만족스러운   invalid 무효한, 효력이 없는 thermostat 온도 조절 장치   carrier 항공사   incident 일, 사건 compensate 보상하다   exemplary 모범적인

10 오노 씨가 이메일을 보낸 목적은?

(A) 예약을 확정하려고
(B) 불만을 제기하려고
(C) 발권 문제를 해결하려고
(D) 서비스에 대해 문의하려고

해설 | 주제/목적
이메일 첫 단락 마지막 문장에서 '갈레온 항공 고객 서비스 상담원이 교통편을 마련해주고 위클리프 인에서 사용할 쿠폰을 주었다(The Galleon Airways customer service representative arranged ~ at the Wycliff Inn)'고 한 후, 두 번째 단락 첫 문장에서 '위클리프 인에서의 짧은 투숙은 불만족스럽고 불쾌했다(My brief stay at the Wycliff Inn was frustrating and unpleasant)'고 했으므로 정답은 (B)이다.

어휘 | reservation 예약   settle 해결하다

11 오노 씨가 이메일에서 암시하는 것은?

(A) 여행사를 통해 정기적으로 여행 준비를 한다.
(B) 곧 휴가를 갈 계획이다.
(C) 갈레온 항공을 자주 이용한다.
(D) 현재 호텔업계에 종사한다.

해설 | 추론
첫 단락 첫 문장에서 오노 씨는 본인을 '귀사의 품격 있는 서비스에 익숙한 고객(As a customer familiar with your usual high standards)'이라고 밝혔으며, 세 번째 단락 첫 문장에서 '이번 일이 있기 전까지 갈레온 항공은 내가 선호하는 항공사였다(Galleon Airways had been my preferred carrier until this incident)'고 하였으므로 오노 씨는 갈레온 항공을 자주 이용한다는 것을 짐작할 수 있다. 따라서 정답은 (C)이다.

어휘 | routinely 정례적으로   frequently 자주

12 오노 씨가 위클리프 인에 대해 언급하지 않은 것은?

(A) 운동 시설   (B) 난방장치
(C) 음식 서비스   (D) 객실 담당 직원

해설 | Not/True
두 번째 단락에서 위클리프 인에 대해 주로 언급되었다. '호텔 식당에서 식사를 주문했다(I ordered a meal at the hotel's restaurant)'고 했으므로 (C)가 언급되었으며, '위층으로 올라가 피트니스 센터를 찾았다(I went upstairs to visit the fitness center)고 했으므로 (A)가 언급되었다. '온도 조절 장치가 고장 나 난방을 줄일 수가 없었다(I was

unable to turn down the heat because the thermostat was broken)'며 (B)도 언급했지만, 객실 담당 직원에 대한 이야기는 없으므로 (D)가 정답이다.

어휘 | facility 시설

패러프레이징
지문의 meal → 보기의 food
지문의 fitness center → 보기의 exercise facility
지문의 thermostat → 보기의 heating system

13 오노 씨가 고메즈 씨에게 요청한 것은?

(A) 영수증　　　　　　　(B) 항공편 시간표
(C) 호텔 추천　　　　　　(D) 식사 비용 상환

해설 | 세부 사항
마지막 단락 첫 문장에서 오노 씨가 '쿠폰을 쓸 수 없었으니 저녁 식사 비용을 보상해 줄 것(I hope that you will compensate me for my dinner)'을 요청했으므로 (D)가 정답이다.

어휘 | recommendation 추천　reimbursement 상환, 변제

패러프레이징
지문의 compensate me for my dinner
→ 보기의 Reimbursement for a meal

UNIT 05　문장 삽입 문제

기출 예제　　　　　　　　　　　　본책 p.048

Q [1], [2], [3], [4]로 표시된 곳 중에서 다음 문장이 들어가기에 가장 적합한 곳은?

"탑승 전에 여행 가방을 수하물로 맡길 필요 없이 돈과 시간을 절약하세요."

(A) [1]　　(B) [2]　　(C) [3]　　(D) [4]

카릴의 슬릭롤 기내 휴대용 가방으로
출장을 편하게 다니세요.

소형 디자인의 가볍고 내구성이 좋은 이 가방은 모든 주요 항공사의 기내 수하물 요건을 충족합니다. 탑승 전에 여행 가방을 수하물로 맡길 필요 없이 돈과 시간을 절약하세요. 크기가 21 x 34 x 55센티미터에 무게는 2킬로그램이 약간 넘는 슬릭롤 기내용 가방은 찌그러짐 방지 외피로 만들어졌습니다. 바퀴는 360도 회전하고 접이식 손잡이는 누르는 버튼으로 작동되어 공항과 좁은 비행기 통로에서도 쉽게 조종할 수 있습니다.

모든 카릴 제품에는 파손에 대한 2년 보증이 포함됩니다. 슬릭롤 기내용 가방이 비행 중에 손상될 경우, 저희에게 반송해주시기만 하면 교체해 드립니다.

어휘 | carry-on bag (기내) 휴대용 가방　compact 소형의 lightweight 경량의　durable 내구성 있는　requirement 요건 luggage 수하물　measure (치수가) ~이다　weigh 무게가 ~이다　crush-proof 찌그러지지 않는　shell 외피　rotate 회전하다　collapsible 접을 수 있는　enable 가능하게 하다 maneuver 조종하다　aisle 통로　breakage 파손　damaged 훼손된　replacement 교체

기출　ETS PRACTICE　　　　　　본책 p.049

1 (C)　**2** (C)

역사의 날을 달력에 표시하세요!

셰도나 역사학회(HSS)가 할스턴 필드에서 9월 20일 오전 10시부터 오후 6시까지 연례 행사인 역사의 날을 개최합니다. 이 행사는 역사학자 에드 토팡가의 강연을 포함해 HSS 회원들이 이끄는 다양한 활동으로 구성됩니다. <셰도나: 첫 100년>의 저자인 토팡가 씨는 우리 마을 설립에 대한 개요를 발표할 예정입니다. 린다 오거스 씨가 이끄는 가구 복원 워크숍도 열릴 예정입니다. 그녀는 골동품 가구 복원을 전문으로 하는 리쥬브네이션의 사장입니다. 또한 박람회 방문객들은 셰도나 마을에서 가장 오래된 집 세 채를 둘러볼 수 있도록 초대됩니다. 여러분의 나이와 관심사가 무엇이든, 원하는 것을 찾을 수 있을 것입니다. **행사의 전체 일정을 보시려면 HSS 웹사이트 www.hss.org를 방문하세요.** 행사 입장료는 무료이지만 기부가 권장됩니다.

할스턴 필드에는 방문객 주차장이 없습니다. 그러므로 참석자는 메이슨 로에 있는 주차 구역을 이용해야 합니다.

어휘 | historical 역사의　annual 연례의　feature 특별히 포함하다　various 다양한　lecture 강의　historian 사학자 author 저자　present 발표하다　overview 개요　founding 설립　restoration 복원　rejuvenation 회생　specialize in ~을 전문으로 하다　restore 복원하다　fair 박람회　admission 입장　donation 기부　encourage 장려하다　attendee 참석자

1 [1], [2], [3], [4]로 표시된 곳 중에서 다음 문장이 들어가기에 가장 적합한 곳은?

"여러분의 나이와 관심사가 무엇이든, 원하는 것을 찾을 수 있을 것입니다."

(A) [1]　　(B) [2]　　(C) [3]　　(D) [4]

해설 | 문장 삽입
제시된 문장에서 '원하는 것을 찾을 수 있을 것이다'라는 말을 보면 이 행사에서 여러 가지 다양한 활동이 진행된다는 것을 알 수 있다. 따라서 '행사의 전체 일정을 보시려면 HSS 웹사이트 www.hss.org를 방문하라(For a full schedule of events, visit the HSS Web site at www.hss.org)'며

행사에 어떤 활동들이 있는지 확인할 수 있는 방법을
알려주는 문장 앞에 들어가는 것이 글의 흐름상 자연스럽다.
그러므로 (C)가 정답이다.

브리검 앤 존스 자물쇠

정부 기관, 보석회사, 전자제품 소매업체들은 모두 수십
년간 브리검 앤 존스에 그들의 소중한 물품과 데이터의
관리를 맡겨 왔습니다. 저희는 이제 귀사도 그렇게 해주시길
바랍니다.

가장 작은 귀중품까지도 안전하게 지킬 수 있는 견고하고
매력적인 자물쇠를 만드는 것이 저희의 사명입니다. 모든
자물쇠는 단단한 강화 놋쇠로 수작업을 통해 만들어지며,
광범위한 응력 검사를 거칩니다. 품질 관리 공정을 거치는
동안 자물쇠를 매우 뜨거운 온도에 놓고, 망치로 때리는 것은
물론 다이아몬드 날이 달린 칼로 썰기도 합니다. **자물쇠가
이러한 검사에 통과하지 못하면, 저희는 가능한 한 가장
안전한 자물쇠를 만들어 내도록 디자인과 생산 공정을
재검사합니다.** 이러한 우수한 장인정신 덕분에 브리검 앤
존스는 80년간 자물쇠 산업을 선도해 왔습니다.

당사의 창립 80주년을 기념하기 위해 단골고객 여러분께만
독점적인 할인을 제공하고 있습니다. 5월 말일까지 모든
재주문에 대해 5퍼센트 가격 할인을 해드리며, 100달러
이상의 주문에 대해 배송비를 면제해 드립니다.

어휘 | government agency 정부 기관 jeweler 보석회사
electronics 전자제품 retailer 소매회사 inventory 재고
mission 사명 durable 견고한 secure 안전하게 지키다
solid 단단한 reinforced 보강된 brass 놋쇠 undergo 겪다
extensive 광범위한 stress 응력 quality control process
품질 관리 공정 chop 썰다, 다지다 ensure 확실하게 하다
exclusive 독점적인, 배타적인 loyal customer 단골고객
recurring order 재주문 reduction 감소, 할인 waive
면제하다

2 [1], [2], [3], [4]로 표시된 곳 중에서 다음 문장이 들어가기에
가장 적합한 곳은?

"이러한 우수한 장인정신 덕분에 브리검 앤 존스는 80년간
자물쇠 산업을 선도해 왔습니다."

(A) [1] (B) [2] (C) [3] (D) [4]

해설 | 문장 삽입
제시된 문장에서 '이러한 우수한 장인정신 덕분에(Because
of this fine craftsmanship)'라고 했으므로 장인정신을
설명하는 문장 뒤에 제시된 문장이 들어가야 한다. [3]번
앞에서 '자물쇠가 이러한 검사에 통과하지 못하면 저희는
가능한 한 가장 안전한 자물쇠를 만들어 내도록 디자인과
생산 공정을 재검사합니다(If any locks fail these trials,
we reexamine their design and our production
process to ensure we are making the most secure

locks possible)'라고 했으므로 장인정신을 보여주는
예라고 할 수 있다. 따라서 정답은 (C)이다.

어휘 | craftsmanship 장인정신, 장인 기술 padlock 자물쇠

기출 **ETS TEST**   본책 p. 050

1 (D)	**2** (B)	**3** (D)	**4** (B)	**5** (A)
6 (C)	**7** (B)	**8** (B)	**9** (C)	**10** (D)
11 (C)	**12** (D)	**13** (B)	**14** (C)	**15** (C)

[1-3] 이메일

수신: staff@tenoriopublications.co.nz
발신: amir.hassan@tenoriopublications.co.nz
날짜: 1월 15일
제목: 새해의 새로운 시작

팀 여러분께,

작년 말부터 저는 우리 회사가 좀 더 능률적으로 일하는
데 도움이 될 방안을 고민해 왔습니다. 그러기 위해 **1저는
우리가 정기적으로 수행하는 모든 업무를 재검토하고 각
단계를 기록하는 데 많은 시간을 보냈습니다.** 그렇게 하면
혹시 누군가가 갑작스럽게 결근할 경우 다른 팀원이 쉽게 그
업무에 뛰어들 수 있습니다.

제가 만든 온라인 문서 링크가 들어 있는 별도의 이메일을
받으셨을 겁니다. 거기에서 섹션별 각각의 프로그램과 함께
각 주요 활동이 수행되는 방법에 대한 세분화된 설명을
찾으실 수 있을 겁니다. **3제가 적은 것이 최종 버전이
아니라는 것을 알아 주십시오.** 이것들은 단지 시작점일
뿐입니다. 여러분 중 일부는 특정 분야에 더 많은 전문
지식을 보유하고 있고 일을 하는 데 있어 자신만의 더 좋은
방법을 가지고 있을 것입니다. 물론 여러분의 통찰력을
환영합니다. 사실, **2제안 사항이 있는 사람은 누구라도 이
문서에 본인의 의견을 추가해 달라고 권하는 바입니다.**

여러분의 도움에 감사드립니다.

아미르 하산

어휘 | efficiently 능률적으로 to that end 그 목적을 위해
reexamine 재검토하다 task 업무 perform 수행하다
on a regular basis 정기적으로 step 단계 absent 결근한
jump in 뛰어들다 separate 별도의 section 부문
breakdown 명세, 분석 major 주요한 intend 의도하다
expertise 전문 지식 certain 특정한 method 방법
certainly 분명히 insight 통찰력 encourage 장려하다
suggestion 제안 add 더하다 comment 논평

1 하산 씨가 진행해 온 프로젝트는?

(A) 새로운 마케팅 자료 작성
(B) 회사의 임무 재평가
(C) 일부 작업장 재배치
(D) 회사 업무 절차 문서화

해설 | 세부 사항
첫 단락의 두 번째 문장에서 하산 씨가 '나는 우리가 정기적으로 수행하는 모든 업무를 재검토하고 각 단계를 기록하는 데 많은 시간을 보냈다(I have spent a lot of time reexamining all the tasks ~ each step is written down)'고 했으므로 회사 업무를 검토하여 문서화하는 일을 했음을 알 수 있다. 따라서 (D)가 정답이다.

어휘 | material 자료 reevaluate 재평가하다 mission 임무 rearrange 재배치하다 workstation 작업장 document 기록하다 process 절차

패러프레이징
지문의 each step is written down
→ 보기의 Documenting a company's processes

2 직원들은 무엇을 하라고 권장받는가?

(A) 소프트웨어 시험 사용
(B) 의견 제공
(C) 더 많은 시간 근무
(D) 새로운 기술 습득

해설 | 세부 사항
두 번째 단락의 마지막 문장에서 '제안 사항이 있는 사람은 누구라도 이 문서에 본인의 의견을 추가해 주길 권한다(I would like to encourage ~ to add their comments to the document)'라고 했으므로 (B)가 정답이다.

패러프레이징
지문의 add their comments
→ 보기의 Provide feedback

3 [1], [2], [3], [4]로 표시된 곳 중에서 다음 문장이 들어가기에 가장 적합한 곳은?

"이것들은 단지 시작점일 뿐입니다."

(A) [1]   (B) [2]   (C) [3]   (D) [4]

해설 | 문장 삽입
제시된 문장의 They가 문제 해결의 단서로, 주어진 문장 앞에 they로 받을 수 있는 복수 명사가 있어야 한다. 또한 '시작점일 뿐이다'라고 했으므로 어떤 일의 단계나 과정에 대해 언급하는 내용이 앞에 와야 자연스럽게 연결될 수 있다. 따라서 my notes라는 복수 명사가 있고 '내가 적은 것이 최종 버전이 아니라는 것을 알아 달라(Please know that my notes are not intended to be a final version)'고 한 문장 뒤인 (D)가 정답이다.

[4-7] 기사

<델맥스 시티 타임스>
9월 2일

개인 트레이너가 인기 체육관에서 지역 주민 건강 도모

3년 전 개인 트레이너 캐롤 유 씨가 프리즘 체육관을 열기 위해 평생 모은 돈을 투자했을 때 친구들은 우려했다. "당신은 큰 모험을 하고 있어요."라고 한 동료는 그녀에게 말했다. 하지만 투자는 가치 있는 일로 드러났다.

현재 프리즘 체육관은 350명의 회원과 21명의 직원을 두고 있다. **4**이 시설은 24시간 운영되며, 12명의 개인 트레이너가 있다. 현재 맨델 빌딩 2층에 2,200제곱피트 공간을 차지하고 있지만, 다음 달에는 같은 건물 1층에 있는 더 넓은 공간으로 이전할 예정이다. **7**"이렇게 빨리 더 넓은 공간이 필요하리라고는 생각도 못 했어요."라고 유 씨는 말했다. 하지만 사업이 제가 예상한 것보다 더 빨리 성장했죠.

5델맥스 시 토박이인 유 씨는 중심가에 있는 웰니스 체육관에서 개인 트레이너로 근무한 적이 있다. 그녀는 플러스 피트니스 사가 그 시설을 인수한 후 그녀의 근무시간을 줄이자 그곳을 그만두고는 곧 바로 초기 장비 구매 비용 5만 달러를 투자해 프리즘 체육관을 창업했다. "3만 달러는 선금으로 냈고, 나머지는 할부로 했습니다. 놀랍도록 빠른 성장 덕분에 남은 2만 달러를 예상보다 빨리 갚았죠."라고 그녀는 말했다.

유 씨는 체육관을 연 후에 무홍보 전략을 택했다. **6**"모든 회원이 델맥스 시 주민으로 다른 회원들로부터 긍정적인 입소문을 듣고 가입했죠."라고 그녀는 말했다. 주를 이루는 회원들은 체육관을 다닌 경험이 거의 없는 초보자들이라고 그녀는 설명했다. 그래서 프리즘 체육관의 전 직원은 "우호적이고 상냥하다."

어휘 | keep fit 건강을 유지하다 invest 투자하다 savings 저축한 돈 concerned 걱정하는 risk 위험 investment 투자 prove 판명되다 worth ~할 가치가 있는 facility 시설 access 접속, 접근 occupy 차지하다 quit 그만두다 reduce 줄이다 initial 초기의 equipment 장비 purchase 구매 up front 사전에, 미리 on installments 할부로 rapid 빠른 growth 성장 remaining 남아 있는 positive 긍정적인 word of mouth 입소문 typical 전형적인, 대표적인 friendly 우호적인 approachable 가까이하기 쉬운

4 기사에 따르면, 프리즘 체육관에 대해 사실인 것은?

(A) 옥외 피트니스 강습을 운영한다.
(B) 하루에 24시간 문을 연다.
(C) 2,200명의 회원이 있다.
(D) 여러 지점이 있다.

해설 | Not / True
두 번째 단락 두 번째 문장에서 '이 시설은 24시간 운영된다(The facility offers 24-hour access)'라고 했으므로 정답은 (B)이다.

패러프레이징

지문의 offers 24-hour access

→ 보기의 is open 24 hours a day

5 유 씨에 대해 명시된 것은?

(A) 델맥스 시에서 태어났다.

(B) 2개의 체육관을 소유하고 있다.

(C) 플러스 피트니스 사를 경영한 적이 있다.

(D) 자신만의 운동기구 제품군을 판매한다.

해설 | Not / True

세 번째 단락 첫 문장에서 '델맥스 시 토박이인 유(Yoo, a Delmax City native)'라고 했으므로 정답은 (A)이다.

패러프레이징

지문의 a Delmax City native

→ 보기의 born in Delmax City

6 유 씨가 프리즘 체육관의 회원들에 대해 언급한 것은?

(A) 다른 체육관에서 옮겨왔다.

(B) 마케팅 동영상에 곧 나올 것이다.

(C) 체육관에 서로를 소개했다.

(D) 델맥스 시 외곽에 산다.

해설 | 세부 사항

네 번째 단락 두 번째 문장에서 '모든 회원이 델맥스 시 주민으로 다른 회원들로부터 긍정적인 입소문을 듣고 가입했다(All of our members ~ via positive word of mouth from other clients)'고 했으므로 정답은 (C)이다.

7 [1], [2], [3], [4]로 표시된 곳 중에서 다음 문장이 들어가기에 가장 적합한 곳은?

"하지만 사업이 제가 예상한 것보다 더 빨리 성장했죠."

(A) [1]   (B) [2]   (C) [3]   (D) [4]

해설 | 문장 삽입

제시된 문장에 '하지만(But)'이라는 말이 있으므로 그 앞 문장은 제시된 문장과 의미상 반대되는 내용이 되어야 한다. [2]번 앞에서 '이렇게 빨리 더 넓은 공간이 필요하리라고는 생각도 못 했다(I didn't think I would need more space so soon)'고 했는데 이는 제시된 문장과 반대되는 내용이므로 정답은 (B)이다.

[8-11] 편지

암보스 퍼니처 플러스

락손 가 247번지

3월 19일

산달리오 위 씨

리가야 가 917번지 아파트 3B

마닐라, PH 1000

위 씨께,

8귀하의 주문품이 배송 중에 손상되었다는 소식을 들었습니다. 암보스 퍼니처 플러스를 대신해 이 일로 끼친 불편에 사과 말씀을 드립니다. **9**저희는 모든 상품을 세 겹의 비닐 충전재로 포장합니다. 하지만 분명 이번 경우에는 충분하지 못했습니다. 이런 일이 발생해서 재차 죄송하다는 말씀을 드립니다.

배송기사가 귀하께서 편리한 시간에 가구를 회수할 예정이며 물론 무료입니다. 배송기사로부터 상품이 회수되었다는 확인을 받는 즉시 저희는 교환해드릴 의자를 배송할 것입니다. **11**안타깝게도 주문하신 탁자는 마지막 재고품이었습니다. 따라서 저희는 그 제품을 교환해 드릴 수 없습니다. 다른 탁자를 주문하기를 원하시면 고객지원부로 전화주십시오. 원치 않으시면 탁자의 금액을 파일에 있는 신용카드로 환불해 드리겠습니다.

8이러한 조치로 문제가 만족스럽게 해결되기를 바랍니다. 암보스 퍼니처 플러스를 선택해 주신 데 대한 감사의 표시로 **10**향후 주문에 사용할 수 있는 무료 배송 쿠폰을 동봉합니다. 양해해 주셔서 감사드리며, 앞으로도 계속 저희를 찾아주시기를 기대합니다.

암보스 퍼니처 플러스 일동

첨부 재중

어휘 | damaged 손상된 delivery 배달 triple 세 개의 padding 충전재 at no charge 무료로 confirmation 확인 ship out (상품을) 출하하다 replacement 교체 in stock 재고가 있는 support line 고객지원부 measure 조치 resolve 해결하다 a token of ~의 표시 gratitude 감사

8 편지의 주목적은?

(A) 한 물품의 재고가 있음을 알리기 위해

(B) 배송된 물건의 문제를 해결하기 위해

(C) 단골고객에게 신제품을 광고하기 위해

(D) 고객에게 연락처를 알려 주기 위해

해설 | 주제 / 목적

편지의 맨 처음에서 '고객의 주문품이 배송 중에 손상되었다는 말을 들었다(We have received news that your order was damaged upon delivery)'며 회사를 대표하여 사과한다는 말이 나온다. 그리고 세 번째 단락에서 '이러한 조치로 문제가 만족스럽게 해결되기를 바란다(We hope these measures will satisfactorily resolve the matter)'고 했으므로 정답은 (B)이다.

어휘 | market (상품을) 광고하다 repeat customer 단골고객

9 암보스 퍼니처 플러스에 대해 명시된 것은?

(A) 대량 주문 시 배송은 무료다.

(B) 가구는 광범위한 품질 보증을 제공한다.

(C) 물품은 여러 겹의 충전재에 싸여 배송된다.

(D) 반품을 하려면 고객이 가구를 가게로 들고 와야 한다.

해설 | Not / True

첫 번째 단락 세 번째 문장에서 '저희는 모든 상품을 세 겹의 비닐 충전재로 포장합니다(We package all of our goods in a triple layer of plastic padding)'라고 했으므로 정답은 (C)이다.

어휘 | extensive 광범위한 warranty 품질 보증

<u>패러프레이징</u>
지문의 a triple layer of plastic padding
→ 보기의 multiple layers of padding

10 편지에 들어 있는 것은?

(A) 주문서   (B) 사용 설명서
(C) 제품 카탈로그   (D) 배송 쿠폰

해설 | 세부 사항
세 번째 단락 두 번째 문장에서 '향후 주문에 사용할 수 있는 무료 배송 쿠폰을 동봉합니다(we are including a coupon for free shipping on a future order)'라고 했으므로 정답은 (D)이다.

어휘 | voucher 상품권, 쿠폰

<u>패러프레이징</u>
지문의 a coupon for free shipping
→ 보기의 A shipping voucher

11 [1], [2], [3], [4]로 표시된 곳 중에서 다음 문장이 들어가기에 가장 적합한 곳은?

"따라서 저희는 그 제품을 교환해 드릴 수 없습니다."

(A) [1]   (B) [2]   (C) [3]   (D) [4]

해설 | 문장 삽입
제시된 문장에 '따라서(Therefore)'라는 말이 있으므로 그 전에 원인에 대한 언급이 있어야 한다. [3]번 앞 문장에서 '안타깝게도 주문하신 탁자는 마지막 재고품이었다(Unfortunately, the table you ordered was the last one in stock)'고 하면서 제품 교환이 안 되는 이유를 언급했으므로 정답은 (C)이다.

[12-15] 기사

메헬렌의 긍정적 변화

12유럽 전역에서 풍력 터빈과 풍력 에너지 기술을 생산하는 선두업체인 윈드 다이나믹스가 벨기에 메헬렌에 생산 공장을 열겠다는 계획을 발표했다. **13**이 네덜란드 회사는 버려진 캔텍 전화 공장을 매입해서 보수하고 장비를 갖추는 데 1,500만 유로 이상을 쓰고 있다. 이번 사업은 향후 2년간 대략 200개의 신규 생산직과 50개의 사무직 일자리를 창출하리라 예상된다. 이것은 최근 공장 폐쇄와 실직으로 큰 타격을 입은 공업 지역인 메헬렌으로서는 기쁜 소식이다. **15**바텔 빌더스는 이미 공장 전환 작업을 맡는 계약을 체결했다.

<u>또한 공사 프로젝트를 완료하기 위해 직원을 추가로 더 고용할 예정이다.</u>

공장은 주로 회사의 풍력 터빈에 들어가는 기어 구동장치의 조립 및 테스트 용도로 활용될 것이다. 윈드 다이나믹스는 **14**메헬렌 사업 개발 협회(MBDA)와 협력하여 개발 보조금을 지급해 입사 직원들에게 녹색 기술을 교육시킬 것이다. **14**MBDA 제인 아렌스 회장은 "메헬렌이 에너지 절약과 지역 경제 발전에 일조하게 되어 자랑스럽습니다"라고 말한다.

어휘 | leading 선두의 wind turbine 풍력 터빈 wind energy 풍력 에너지 production plant 생산 공장 Dutch 네덜란드의 equip 장비를 갖추다 abandoned 버려진 industrial area 공업 지역 be hit hard 큰 타격을 입다 closure 폐쇄 job loss 실직 contract 계약을 맺다 undertake 착수하다, 맡다 transformation 변환, 전환 primarily 주로 assembly 조립 gear drive 기어 구동장치 incorporate 포함시키다 in cooperation with ~와 협력하여 development grant 개발 보조금 incoming workforce 입사 직원 green technology (환경 보존을 위한) 녹색 기술 be proud to ~하게 되어 자랑스럽다 contribute to ~에 기여하다 conservation 보존, 절약 economic growth 경제 성장

12 기사의 주요 내용은?

(A) 신임 회사 CEO 임명   (B) 두 기업의 합병
(C) 풍력 터빈 생산 과정   (D) 시설 개설

해설 | 주제 / 목적
기사 맨 처음에 '유럽 전역에서 풍력 터빈과 풍력 에너지 기술을 생산하는 선두업체인 윈드 다이나믹스가 벨기에 메헬렌에 생산 공장을 열겠다는 계획을 발표했다(Wind Dynamics, the leading producer ~ open a production plant in Mechelen, Belgium)'고 했으므로 정답은 (D)이다.

<u>패러프레이징</u>
지문의 open a production plant
→ 보기의 The opening of a facility

13 캔텍 전화 공장에 무슨 일이 있겠는가?

(A) 유적지로 복원될 것이다.
(B) 다른 산업체에 의해 사용될 것이다.
(C) 새로운 장소로 옮겨 갈 것이다.
(D) 빈 공간을 만들기 위해 철거될 것이다.

해설 | 세부 사항
기사 첫 단락 두 번째 문장에서 '이 네덜란드 회사는 버려진 캔텍 전화 공장을 매입해서 보수하고 장비를 갖추는 데 1,500만 유로 이상을 쓰고 있다(The Dutch company is spending ~ Cantek Telephone factory)'고 했다. 이를 통해 캔텍 전화 공장이 윈드 다이나믹스 사의 생산 공장으로 전환될 것임을 알 수 있으므로 정답은 (B)이다.

14 아렌스 씨는 누구인가?

(A) 윈드 다이나믹스 직원　　(B) 신문 기자
(C) 협회 회장　　(D) 벨기에의 한 도시 시장

해설 | 세부 사항
지문 마지막 문장에서 'MBDA 제인 아렌스 회장(Jane
Arens, MBDA president)'이라고 했고 MBDA는 the
Mechelen Business Development Association을
말하므로 정답은 (C)이다.

15 [1], [2], [3], [4]로 표시된 곳 중에서 다음 문장이 들어가기에
가장 적합한 곳은?

"또한 공사 프로젝트를 완료하기 위해 직원을 추가로 더
고용할 예정이다."

(A) [1]　　(B) [2]　　(C) [3]　　(D) [4]

해설 | 문장 삽입
제시된 문장에서 It이 가리키는 것이 무엇인지 찾아야 한다.
그리고 also라는 말이 있으므로 의미상 추가 계획임을
알 수 있다. [3]번 앞 문장에서 '바텔 빌더스는 이미 공장
전환 작업을 맡는 계약을 체결했다(Battel Builders has
already been contracted to undertake the plant's
transformations)'고 했다. 제시된 문장에서 Battel
Builders가 대명사 It으로 바뀐 것이고, 계약 체결에 더하여
직원도 또한(also) 추가로 고용할 것이라고 하므로 정답은
(C)이다.

UNIT 06　동의어 문제

기출 예제
본책 p.054

Q 첫 번째 단락 4행에 쓰인 단어 "yield"와 의미상
가장 가까운 것은?

(A) 허락하다　　(B) 실패하다
(C) 따라가다　　(D) 생산하다

알마, 성장을 위한 준비가 되다

이달 아르헨티나에서 콘도르 PX 브랜드의 밀 씨앗 판매가
크게 증가했다. 지난해 아르헨티나의 많은 지역에서
평년보다 높은 기온과 평균 이하의 강우량으로 전반적으로
밀 **생산**량이 크게 줄었다. 그러나 불리한 기상 조건에도
불구하고 콘도르 PX 밀의 생산량은 비교적 좋았다.

콘도르 PX는 브라질의 알마 종묘 회사가 재배했다. 알마는
몇 년 동안 아르헨티나 유통업체를 통해 콘도르 PX를
판매해왔지만 지금까지는 그다지 인기를 끌지 못했다.
투자자들 또한 알마의 가파른 수익 증가에 주목했다.

어휘 | poised for ~할 태세를 갖춘　growth 성장　huge
거대한　wheat seed 밀종자, 밀 씨앗　above-average 평균
이상의　temperature 기온　below-average 평균 이하의
rainfall 강우(량)　cause A to A가 ~하도록 시키다　yield
산출하다, 내다　sharply 급격히　overall 전반적으로　adverse
불리한　comparatively 비교적　distributor 유통업체,
배급업자　catch on 인기를 얻다, 유행하다　investor 투자자
take notice of ~을 알아차리다, 주목하다　rapidly 빠르게
fortune 재산

기출 **ETS PRACTICE**
본책 p.055

1 (A)　**2** (C)　**3** (C)

<동전에서 신용카드까지: 여러 시대에 걸쳐 변화된
금융업>은 고대에서부터 현재에 이르기까지 은행과
금융업의 역사를 간결히 다루고 있다. 여러 신문사에서 경제
뉴스를 취재하면서 경력을 쌓아 온 제임스 갤러거 씨는
자신의 주제에 대해 면밀히 조사했다. 갤러거 씨는 사실들을
신중히 제시하는 동시에, **무미건조할** 수도 있었을 이 책을
흥미롭고 재미있는 책으로 만들었다. 그는 역사적 인물들에
대한 재미있는 일화들을 이야기함으로써 그들이 마치 살아
숨쉬는 것처럼 만든다. 이 주제에 별로 흥미가 없는 사람들도
이 책에서 눈을 뗄 수 없을 것이다.

어휘 | banking 금융업, 은행 업무　concise 간결한　ancient
고대의　career 경력　cover 보도[방송]하다, 취재하다
financial 금융의, 재무의　investigate 조사하다　subject
과목, 주제　present 제시하다, 발표하다　amusing 재미있는,
신나는　anecdote 일화, 기담　figure 인물, 모습　particularly
특별히　attracted to ~에 매혹된　matter (책 등의) 내용
engrossing 마음을 사로잡는, 열중하게 하는

---

1 5행에 쓰인 단어 "dry"와 의미상 가장 가까운 것은?

(A) 지루한　　(B) 비어 있는
(C) 불모의　　(D) 유머가 넘치는

해설 | 동의어
dry는 명사 book을 수식하고 있다. dry는 보통 '물기가
없는, 건조한'이란 뜻으로 쓰이지만, 지문에서와 같이 dry
book이라고 할 때 dry는 '무미건조한, 지루한'이란 의미를
갖게 되므로 정답은 (A)이다.

에머리 씨께,

귀하가 매니저로 남을 수 있게 되었고 대부분의 매장
직원들도 남게 되어 대단히 기쁩니다. 여러분은 헌신적인
팀이어서, 그곳 매장에서 귀하와 귀하의 팀과 함께 일하는
게 즐거웠습니다. 저는 덴버와 샌프란시스코에서도 여러
상점들이 변화를 꾀하는 과정을 도왔는데요, 귀하의 상점만큼
변화가 원활하게 이루어진 곳은 없었습니다. 일을 잘 수행해

주셔서 감사드립니다.

모든 일이 계속 잘 **진행될** 것이라고 확신합니다. 질문이나 문제가 있으면 언제든지 연락주시기 바랍니다.

어휘 | stay on 계속 남아 있다 dedicated 헌신적인 transition 이행, 변천, 전환 go smoothly 원활하게 돌아가다 confident 확신하는 run 잘 움직이다, 작동하다 concerns 걱정거리, 관심사

2 두 번째 단락 1행에 쓰인 단어 "run"과 의미상 가장 가까운 것은?

(A) 이해하다   (B) 질주하다
(C) 진행되다   (D) 열리다

해설 | 동의어
run은 문맥상 '진행되다'라는 의미로 쓰였는데, function이 '기능하다, 진행되다'라는 의미이므로 정답은 (C)이다.

TU 온라인 수업 제공

8월 12일 – 지난달, 티루파티 대학은 온라인 비즈니스 수업을 제공하는 지역 내 최신 기관이 되었다. 학생들은 전적으로 인터넷으로만 제공되는 다양한 전체 인정 학점 수업들 중에서 선택할 수 있다.

부총장 R. D. 메타 박사는 "저희는 이런 새로운 방향에 기대감이 크며 학생들도 마찬가지입니다. 학생들은 편리함과 유연성을 마음에 들어 합니다"라고 **말했다**. 티루파티의 기존 수업과 마찬가지로, MBA나 관련 분야에서 고급 학위 소지 요건을 갖춘 매우 우수한 강사들이 모든 온라인 수업을 진행한다. 메타 박사에 따르면 티루파티 대학은 봄에 온라인 강의 과목을 확장할 계획이다.

어휘 | institution 기관 a range of 다양한 chancellor 총장 direction 방향 flexibility 유연성, 융통성 advanced degree (석사·박사) 고급 학위 expand 확장하다

3 두 번째 단락 1행에 쓰인 단어 "noted"와 의미상 가장 가까운 것은?

(A) 적어 두었다   (B) 기억했다
(C) 말했다   (D) 보았다

해설 | 동의어
noted 뒤에 인터뷰한 인용문이 나오고 있으므로 문맥상 noted는 '언급하다, 말하다'라는 뜻으로 쓰였다. 따라서 정답은 (C)이다.

기출 ETS TEST   본책 p.056

1 (B)	**2** (A)	**3** (C)	**4** (B)	**5** (C)
6 (A)	**7** (D)	**8** (D)	**9** (B)	**10** (B)
11 (D)	**12** (D)	**13** (B)	**14** (A)	**15** (B)

[1-3] 이메일

수신: <subscriber@infoapp.com>
발신: <service@nicholsfinest.com>
제목: 용역업체가 필요하십니까?
날짜: 5월 25일

이웃 주민 여러분께,

¹물이 새는 수도꼭지를 고치고, 여러분 집에 있는 방을 페인트칠하고, 가전제품을 수리하고, 새로운 창문이나 문을 설치할 적임자를 찾는 데 어려움을 겪어 보신 적이 있나요? 그렇다면 니콜스 파이니스트가 바로 여기 있습니다. 니콜스 파이니스트는 전화나 컴퓨터로 이용하실 수 있습니다. **¹우리는 특별한 ²방식을 사용해 여러분이 계신 지역의 용역업체와 수리 서비스를 평가합니다.**

당사 전유의 점수 평가 시스템은 사업 인허가 증명, 사업체 운영 기간, 소비자 후기 등을 고려합니다. 저희 웹사이트에서 서비스 업체를 찾기 위한 간단한 질문지를 작성하기만 하면 최대 6명의 관련 전문가에 대한 순위와 후기를 제공해 드립니다. 저희 서비스는 무료입니다. 하지만 **³당사를 통해 고용하게 되는 서비스 공급업체에 대한 후기를 제출해 주시기를 부탁드립니다.**

오늘 www.nicholsfinest.com을 방문해 양질의 서비스 공급업체들을 만나 보세요.

여러분의 친구 니콜스 파이니스트

어휘 | contractor 용역업체, 계약자 neighbor 이웃 trouble 곤란 leaky 새는 faucet 수도꼭지 appliance 가전제품 install 설치하다 access 이용하다 formula 공식 rate 평가하다 proprietary 전유의 scoring 점수 take into account ~을 고려하다 proof 증명 licensing 인허가 operation 영업 consumer 소비자 review 논평 simply 간단히 fill out 작성하다 brief 간단한 questionnaire 설문지 relevant 관련 있는 professional 전문가 end up 결국 ~하게 되다

1 이메일의 목적은?

(A) 집수리 업계에 교육 프로그램을 홍보하는 것
(B) 집수리 서비스 업자들에 대한 정보 업체를 홍보하는 것
(C) 사업주들에게 회사 등록을 장려하는 것
(D) 명단에 올릴 새 용역업체들을 초대하는 것

해설 | 주제/목적
첫 문장에서 '물이 새는 수도꼭지를 고치고, 집에 있는 방을 페인트칠하고, 가전제품을 수리하고, 새로운 창문이나 문을 설치할 적임자를 찾는 데 어려움을 겪은 적이 있는지(Have you ever had ~ new windows or doors?)'를 물으며 '그렇다면 니콜스 파이니스트가 바로 여기 있다(Then Nichols' Finest is for you)'고 했고, 네 번째 문장에서 '우리는 특별한 방식을 사용해 여러분이 계신 지역의 용역업체와 수리 서비스를 평가한다(We use a special

---

~ in your local area)'고 했다. 따라서 주민들에게 집수리 업자에 대한 정보 공급업체인 니콜스 파이니스트를 홍보하려는 목적으로 이메일을 작성한 것이므로 (B)가 정답이다.

어휘 | advertise 광고하다 industry 산업 promote 홍보하다 resource 자원 encourage 장려하다 register 등록하다 directory 명단, 안내 책자

2 첫 번째 단락 4행에 쓰인 "formula"와 의미상 가장 가까운 것은?

(A) 방법   (B) 방향
(C) 노력   (D) 표현

해설 | **동의어**
의미상 용역업체와 수리 서비스를 평가하기 위한 특별한 '방식'이라는 뜻으로 쓰인 것이므로 정답은 (A) method이다.

3 니콜스 파이니스트를 이용하는 소비자들은 무엇을 요청받는가?

(A) 등록비 지불   (B) 주택 소유자 보험 증명
(C) 서비스 후기   (D) 친구 추천

해설 | **세부 사항**
두 번째 단락의 마지막 문장에서 '당사를 통해 고용하게 되는 서비스 공급업체에 대한 후기를 제출해 주시기를 부탁드린다(we kindly request that ~ end up hiring through us)'고 했으므로 (C)가 정답이다.

[4-7] 기사

방갈로르 (11월 3일) – **4,5DPQR 주식회사는 6년 전 작은 스타트업 기술업체로 창립되었다. 4현재는 20억 파운드 이상의 가치로 추산되며 회사 주식을 최초 상장하려는 참이다.** 이렇게 빠른 변모는 대중이 최근 DPQR의 게임 <퀸시>에 크게 몰입한 덕분이다.

6<퀸시>는 지난 몇 년간 DPQR이 제작하고 시장에 내놓은 8개 게임 중 하나이지만, 아주 많은 팬을 거느린 유일한 게임이다. DPQR의 CEO 사트야 바반에 따르면 <퀸시>는 거의 2천만 대의 모바일 기기에서 다운로드 되었다고 한다. "지금까지 사람들의 관심이 수그러들 기미가 보이지 않아요."라고 바반 씨는 말한다.

"기본 게임은 무료지만 수익의 많은 부분은 게임 향상을 위한 특별 가상 아이템 구입과 업그레이드에서 창출됩니다." 피니언 그룹의 시장 분석가인 마크 롤로가 밝혔다. "이러한 매출 개념이 새로운 것은 아니지만 이 특정 제품에 대한 소비의 7정도는 업계에서 유례없는 일입니다." 투자자들은 게임의 인기가 계속 올라갈 것이고 유사한 게임 개발에 사용할 회사 수익을 증가시킬 것이라고 생각한다.

어휘 | found 설립하다 estimate 추산하다, 추정하다 on the verge of ~하기 직전의 be attributed to ~의 덕분으로 여겨지다, ~에 기인하다 obsession 집착 handheld 손에 쥐고 쓸 수 있는, 소형의 to date 지금까지 tremendous 엄청난, 굉장한 revenue 수익, 수입 generate 만들어 내다, 발생시키다 virtual 가상의 enhance 높이다 unprecedented 유례없는 investor 투자자

4 기사는 무엇을 발표하는가?

(A) 신임 CEO 채용
(B) 회사 가치 상승
(C) 새 기기 출시
(D) 성공적인 제품의 출시 기념일

해설 | **주제 / 목적**
기사 첫 부분에서 'DPQR 주식회사는 6년 전 작은 스타트업 기술업체로 시작하여 현재는 20억 파운드 이상의 가치로 추산되며(Today, it is estimated to be worth over £2 billion) 회사 주식을 최초 상장하려는 참'이라고 회사 가치 상승을 알리고 있으므로 (B)가 정답이다.

패러프레이징
지문의 worth over £2 billion
→ 보기의 The increase in a company's value

5 DPQR에 대해 명시된 것은?

(A) 이전에 피니언 그룹에서 소유했다.
(B) 최초의 제품은 <퀸시>였다.
(C) 6년간 운영되고 있다.
(D) 모바일 기기 판매가 늘었다.

해설 | **Not / True**
첫 단락 첫 문장에서 'DPQR 주식회사는 6년 전 작은 스타트업 기술업체로 창립되었다(Six years ago, DPQR Ltd. was founded as a tiny start-up technology firm)'고 했으므로 (C)가 정답이다.

어휘 | formerly 이전에, 예전에

패러프레이징
지문의 Six years ago, DPQR Ltd. was founded
→ 보기의 It has been in business for six years.

6 DPQR 제품 대다수에 대해 사실인 것은?

(A) <퀸시>보다 인기가 없다.
(B) 계속 업데이트된다.
(C) 사용하기에 쉽다.
(D) 제작 비용이 매우 많이 든다.

해설 | **Not / True**
두 번째 단락 첫 문장에서 <퀸시>는 지난 몇 년간 DPQR이 제작하고 시장에 내놓은 8개 게임 중 하나이지만, 많은 팬을 거느린 유일한 게임(Quincey is one of eight

games that DPQR has produced and marketed over years, yet it is the only one to have gained such a following)'이라고 했으므로 DPQR 제품 대다수는 <퀸시>보다 인기가 없다는 것을 알 수 있다. 따라서 (A)가 정답이다.

7 세 번째 단락 7행에 쓰인 "degree"와 의미상 가장 가까운 것은?

(A) 업적　　　　　　　(B) 요금
(C) 온도　　　　　　　(D) 정도

해설 | 동의어
degree of spending은 의미상 '소비의 정도'라는 뜻으로 쓰인 것으로 '정도'를 뜻하는 (D) extent가 정답이다.

[8-11] 이메일

발신: 제레미 장
수신: 앤 두갈; 에밀리 박; 오스카 멘데즈
날짜: 3월 29일
8제목: 오늘 교육 연기

교육 참가자들께,

8본 지출 품의 교육에 등록해 주셔서 감사합니다. 8,9교육장의 기술적 문제로, 아쉽게도 오늘은 교육이 열리지 않습니다. 다시 일정을 잡고 있으며 세부 사항이 확정되면 이메일을 보내드리겠습니다.

본 교육에서 **10다루는** 주제는 부서 예산 편성, 업무비 카드, 회사 상환 정책 등이 포함됩니다. **11새로운 급여 시스템에 관한 정보는 포함되지 않으며, 해당 주제는 전 직원에게 이메일로 발송될 문서에서 따로 다뤄질 예정입니다.**

문의 사항이 있으시면 저에게 이메일을 보내주세요. 다음 주 효과적인 설문 조사 개발 교육을 비롯해 직원들이 이용할 수 있는 기타 교육 목록을 보시려면 저희 웹사이트 www.zurergroup.net/train을 방문하세요.

불편을 드려 죄송합니다. 곧 만나 뵙게 되길 바랍니다.

제레미 장

- -

어휘 | register 등록하다 take place 개최되다, 열리다 finalize 확정하다, 마무리하다 budgeting 예산 편성 reimbursement 상환, 변제 separately 따로, 별도로 effective 효과적인

8 장 씨는 누구이겠는가?

(A) 재무 상담가　　　　(B) 급여 전문가
(C) 수리 기술자　　　　(D) 교육 담당자

해설 | 추론
제목에서 '오늘 교육 연기(Today's session

postponed)'를 언급했고 이메일 첫 단락 첫 문장에서 '지출 품의 교육에 등록해 주셔서 감사하다(Thank you for registering for the session on expense reporting)'고 했다. 또한 '오늘은 교육이 열리지 않는다(this session will not take place today)'면서 교육 관련 내용을 지속적으로 알리고 있으므로 발신자인 장 씨는 교육 담당자라는 것을 짐작할 수 있다. 따라서 (D)가 정답이다.

9 연기하는 이유로 거론된 것은?

(A) 직원들의 낮은 관심도
(B) 기술적 문제
(C) 교육 내용 변경
(D) 강연자의 겹치는 일정

해설 | 세부 사항
첫 단락 두 번째 문장에서 '교육장의 기술적 문제로 (because of technical issues in our training room), 아쉽게도 오늘은 교육이 열리지 않다'고 했으므로 (B)가 정답이다.

어휘 | scheduling conflict 일정 겹침

패러프레이징
지문의 technical issues → 보기의 Technical problems

10 두 번째 단락 1행에 쓰인 "covered"와 의미상 가장 가까운 것은?

(A) 보호되는
(B) 다루어진
(C) 지불된
(D) 숨겨진

해설 | 동의어
교육에서 다루는 주제에 대해 말하고 있으므로 '다루다'는 뜻으로 쓰인 (B) dealt with가 정답이다.

11 직원들은 이메일로 무엇을 받을 수 있을 것인가?

(A) 신청서
(B) 직원 만족도 설문 조사
(C) 온라인 교육 목록
(D) 회사 시스템에 관한 문서

해설 | 세부 사항
두 번째 단락 마지막 문장에서 '새로운 급여 시스템에 관한 정보는 포함되지 않으며, 해당 주제는 전 직원에게 이메일로 발송될 문서에서 따로 다뤄질 예정(This session does not include information about our new payroll system; that will be covered separately in a document to be emailed to all staff)'이라고 했으므로 (D)가 정답이다.

패러프레이징
지문의 our new payroll system
→ 보기의 a company system

[12-15] 편지

고든 파이낸셜 서비스

3월 25일

라리타 카푸어
4200 유니버시티 플레이스
포틀랜드, ME 04146

카푸어 씨께,

고든 파이낸셜 서비스가 6월 2일부터 6월 4일까지 텍사스 주 휴스턴에서 개최하는 세미나에 귀하의 참석을 확정하기 위해 메일 드립니다. **14(D)귀하는 6월 3일에 발표하기로** 되어 있습니다.

또한 **14(B)마지막 날 연회와 출장 요리 저녁 식사**에도 **12초청**하고 싶습니다. **13행사는 오후 6시 제럴드 애덤스 컨퍼런스 센터, 세미나 장소 위층에서 시작됩니다.**

휴스턴에서의 숙박 세부 사항은 제 비서인 팻 고먼이 준비했습니다. **14(C)그랜드 리젠트 호텔이 매우 편안하실 겁니다.** 저희 세미나 장소에서도 도보로 가까운 거리입니다. 시설에 관한 문의사항은 호텔로 직접 연락해 주십시오.

발표 내용은 저희 법무 및 공보처에서 미리 승인이 이뤄져야 합니다. 따라서 발표 자료 전체 사본 및 관련 자료를 되도록 빨리 저희에게 보내주시기 바랍니다.

15수많은 동료들이 포트폴리오 다각화 부문의 전문성을 토대로 귀하를 강력히 추천했습니다. 만나 뵙고 귀하의 전문 경력에 대해 더 듣길 고대합니다.

자말 핫산
부사장, 전문성 개발 전략

어휘 | give a presentation 발표하다 extend an invitation 초대하다 proceeding 행사, 일련의 행위들 in advance 미리 public affairs 공무, 공보 related 관련된 at one's earliest convenience 되도록 빨리 expertise 전문 지식 diversification 다각화, 다양성

---

12 두 번째 단락 1행에 쓰인 "extend"와 의미상 가장 가까운 것은?

(A) 연기하다   (B) 늘이다
(C) 도달하다   (D) 제공하다

해설 | 동의어

목적어 an invitation과 함께 '초대하다'라는 뜻으로 쓰인 것으로 정답은 (D) offer이다.

13 카푸어 씨는 어디서 발표를 할 예정인가?

(A) 호텔
(B) 컨퍼런스 센터
(C) 회사 본사
(D) 법률사무소

해설 | 세부 사항

두 번째 단락에서 '마지막 날 연회와 출장 요리 저녁 식사 행사는 오후 6시 제럴드 애덤스 컨퍼런스 센터, 세미나 장소 위층에서 시작된다(This event will begin at 6:00 P.M. in the Gerald Adams Conference Center, upstairs from where our seminar proceedings have been scheduled)'고 했으므로 세미나도 같은 제럴드 애덤스 컨퍼런스 센터에서 열린다는 것을 알 수 있다. 따라서 정답은 (B)이다.

어휘 | headquarters 본사, 본부

패러프레이징
지문의 seminar proceedings → 질문의 presentation

14 편지에서 언급되지 않은 것은?

(A) 세미나 시간   (B) 친목 모임
(C) 현지 숙소   (D) 발표 일자

해설 | Not / True

첫 단락 마지막 문장 '6월 3일 발표 일정이 잡혀 있다(You have been scheduled to give your presentation on June 3)'에서 (D)를 언급하였고, 두 번째 단락의 첫 문장 '마지막 날 연회와 출장 요리 저녁 식사(a reception and catered dinner)'에서 (B)를 언급했음을 알 수 있다. 세 번째 단락에서 '그랜드 리젠트 호텔이 매우 편안할 것(you will find the Grand Regent Hotel very comfortable)'이라고 했으므로 (C)도 언급되었지만 세미나 시간에 대한 이야기는 없으므로 (A)가 정답이다.

패러프레이징
지문의 your presentation on June 3
→ 보기의 A presentation date
지문의 a reception and catered dinner
→ 보기의 A social gathering
지문의 the Grand Regent Hotel
→ 보기의 Local accommodations

15 핫산 씨는 카푸어 씨에 대해 어떻게 알았는가?

(A) 출판물을 통해
(B) 직업적인 평판을 통해
(C) 이전 세미나 참석을 통해
(D) 구직 활동을 통해

해설 | 세부 사항

마지막 단락 첫 문장에서 '수많은 동료들이 포트폴리오 다각화 부문의 전문성을 토대로 핫산 씨를 강력히 추천했다(Numerous colleagues have highly recommended you based on your expertise in portfolio diversification)'고 했으므로 (B)가 정답이다.

어휘 | publication 출판물 reputation 명성, 평판 attendance 참석

패러프레이징
지문의 based on your expertise → 보기의 professional

UNIT 01 이메일/편지

기출 예제 본책 p.062

수신: 다이애나 로페즈
발신: 실비오 구아르다
날짜: 8월 28일
제목: 인사 파일

로페즈 씨께,

GHT 내셔널 직원 파일을 업데이트했고 올해 귀하의 파일을 완료하는 데 필요한 서류 몇 가지가 없다는 것을 알았습니다. 회사 규정을 준수하기 위해 **¹편집국 전 직원은 파일에 다음의 항목을 갖춰야 합니다.**

• 최근 연례 인사 고과 사본
• 현재 이력서
• 작성 및 서명한 직원 데이터 양식

²9월 3일 월요일까지 본 서류를 제출해주시겠습니까?

문의사항이나 우려가 있으시다면 저에게 이메일을 보내주시거나 제 비서에게 내선 번호 241번으로 전화 주십시오.

실비오 구아르다
인사부장
GHT 내셔널

─────────────────────

어휘 | comply with 준수하다 regulation 규정, 규제 editorial 편집의, 편집과 관련된 current 현재의 submit 제출하다 extension 내선 번호

기출 ETS TEST 본책 p.064

1 (C)	**2** (B)	**3** (D)	**4** (C)	**5** (D)
6 (D)	**7** (D)	**8** (B)	**9** (C)	**10** (D)
11 (C)	**12** (A)	**13** (B)	**14** (C)	**15** (B)
16 (A)	**17** (D)	**18** (C)	**19** (D)	**20** (B)
21 (A)	**22** (B)	**23** (D)	**24** (A)	**25** (A)
26 (A)	**27** (C)	**28** (B)	**29** (D)	

[1-3] 이메일

수신: 아룹 찬드라 <achandra@arvindatech.co.in>
발신: announcements@iags.org.in

─────────────────────

제목: 안내 사항
날짜: 1월 12일

찬드라 씨께,

¹인도 지질과학 아카데미(IAGS)에서는 저희 아카데미가 후원하는 온라인 강연 시리즈를 회원 여러분께 최초로 알려드리고자 합니다. ²IAGS는 전국 최고의 학자 및 기업가들과 제휴하여 저희 분야에 관련된 주제로 온라인 강연을 제공해 왔습니다. 강연은 2개월마다 개최되며 약 2시간 동안 이뤄집니다. 각 강연이 끝나면 참석자는 30분간 열리는 상호 질의응답 시간에 참여할 수 있습니다.

지식을 넓히고 업계에 관한 귀중한 통찰력을 얻게 될 이 멋진 새로운 기회에 참여를 원하시면 저희 웹사이트 www.IAGS. org.in을 방문하세요. **³(A),(B)올해 여섯 개 강연의 날짜와 시간 및 주제를 보실 수 있습니다.** 아울러 참여를 위한 기술적 요건에 관한 정보뿐 아니라 **³(C)등록 및 결제 안내도 확인 가능합니다.**

12월 14일 강연자를 구하고 있음을 알려드립니다. 관심이 있으시면 강연 담당자 바수 쿠마르에게 vkumar@iags.org. in으로 연락해 주십시오.

─────────────────────

어휘 | geological science 지질과학 scholar 학자 relevant to ~에 관련된 every other 하나 걸러 approximately 거의, ~가까이 interactive 상호적인, 대화형의 expand 확장시키다, 확대하다 valuable 귀중한 registration 등록 requirement 요건

1 찬드라 씨가 이메일을 받은 이유는?

(A) 지질학 연구에 지원하고 있어서
(B) 강연을 할 예정이어서
(C) IAGS의 회원이어서
(D) 강연 시리즈를 준비하고 있어서

해설 | 세부 사항
이메일의 첫 단락 첫 문장에서 '인도 지질과학 아카데미(IAGS)에서는 아카데미가 후원하는 온라인 강연 시리즈를 회원 여러분께 최초로 알려준다(The Indian Academy of Geological Science (IAGS) wants its members to be among the first to know about our academy-sponsored online lecture series)'고 했으므로 수신자인 찬드라 씨가 IAGS 회원임을 알 수 있다. 따라서 (C)가 정답이다.

어휘 | geology 지질학 organize 준비하다, 조직하다

2 강연에 대해 명시된 것은?

(A) 매월 개최된다.
(B) 특정 직종에 초점을 두고 있다.

(C) 무료이다.

(D) IAGS 본부에서 개최될 것이다.

해설 | Not / True

첫 단락 두 번째 문장에서 'IAGS는 IAGS 분야에 관련된 주제로 온라인 강연을 제공해 왔다(give online lectures on topics relevant to our field)'고 했으므로 (B)가 정답이다. 세 번째 문장에서 '강연은 2개월마다 개최된다(The lectures will take place every other month)'고 했으므로 (A)는 오답이다.

어휘 | profession 직업, 직종 **free of charge** 무료로

패러프레이징

지문의 topics relevant to our field
→ 보기의 a specific profession

3 IAGS 웹사이트에서 확인할 수 있는 것으로 언급되지 않은 것은?

(A) 강연 날짜 및 시간

(B) 강연 주제 목록

(C) 등록 안내

(D) 강연자 프로필

해설 | Not / True

IAGS Web site를 키워드로 IAGS Web site가 언급되는 부분에서 답을 찾아야 한다. 두 번째 단락 두 번째 문장에서 '올해 여섯 개 강연의 날짜와 시간 및 주제를 보실 수 있다(There you will find the dates, times, and topics for this year's six lectures)'고 했으므로 (A)와 (B)가 언급되었다. 두 번째 단락 마지막 문장에서 '등록 및 결제 안내도 확인 가능하다(You will also find registration and payment instructions)'고 했으므로 (C)가 언급되었다. 하지만 강연자 프로필에 대한 이야기는 없으므로 (D)가 정답이다.

패러프레이징

지문의 topics for this year's six lectures
→ 보기의 A list of lecture topics

[4-6] 편지

> <해슬리 매거진>
> 43 브로드 가
> 프레이밍햄, MA 01701
>
> 12월 1일
>
> 제임스 조 씨
> 262 사우스 가
> 노먼, OK 73070
>
> 조 씨께,
>
> **4<해슬리 매거진>의 충실한 독자가 되어 주셔서 감사합니다.**
> 아시다시피 매월 발행되는 잡지는 수상작가들의 분별력 있는 기사로 가득합니다. 저희는 독자들에게 정보를 알리고

> 즐거움을 주기 위해 정치, 과학, 문화, 세계 여행을 포함해 이례적일 정도로 다양한 주제를 다룹니다.
>
> 서비스를 중단 없이 받으시려면 지금 구독 갱신을 고려하십시오. <해슬리 매거진>의 구독료는 보통 연간 39.99달러입니다. 하지만 1월 1일 이전에 이 편지에 답장해 주신다면 **6연간 29.99달러의 가격을 보장해드릴 수 있습니다.** 사실 이는 저희가 제공해 드리는 최상의 구독료입니다.
>
> 저희는 계속해서 귀하께 인쇄 간행물을 보내드릴 예정입니다. 저희 웹사이트 www.hathleymagazine.com에서 디지털 버전 또한 읽으실 수 있습니다. **5최근 모바일 앱을 출시하여 저희 잡지의 내용을 휴대폰이나 다른 모바일 기기로도 읽으실 수 있습니다.**
>
> 곧 귀하의 답장을 받아 보기를 바랍니다.
>
> 로셀 구스타브
> 구독 서비스

어휘 | loyal 충실한 **issue** (간행물의) 호 **thoughtful** 사려 깊은 **award-winning** 상을 받은 **cover** 다루다, 취재하다 **exceptional** 특출한 **range** 범위 **politics** 정치 **inform** 알리다 **entertain** 즐겁게 하다 **ensure** 보장하다 **uninterrupted** 중단 없는 **renew** 갱신하다 **subscription** 구독(료) **normally** 보통 **guarantee** 보장하다 **continue** 계속하다 **recently** 최근에 **launch** 출시하다 **content** 내용물

4 조 씨에 대해 암시된 것은?

(A) <해슬리 매거진>에 글을 기고한다.

(B) 주로 과학 주제에 관심이 있다.

(C) 현재 <해슬리 매거진>을 받아보고 있다.

(D) 주소 변경 양식을 제출했다.

해설 | 추론

첫 문장에서 '<해슬리 매거진>의 충실한 독자가 되어 주셔서 감사하다(Thank you for being a loyal reader of Hathley Magazine)'고 했으므로 조 씨가 <해슬리 매거진>을 꾸준히 구독해 왔음을 알 수 있다. 따라서 (C)가 정답이다.

어휘 | interested 관심 있는 **submit** 제출하다 **form** 양식

5 <해슬리 매거진> 구독 혜택으로 언급된 것은?

(A) 온라인 토론방 이용

(B) 오락시설 할인

(C) 보너스 세계지도책

(D) 기사에 대한 모바일 접근

해설 | Not / True

세 번째 단락의 마지막 문장에서 '최근 모바일 앱을 출시하여 잡지의 내용을 휴대폰이나 다른 모바일 기기로도 읽을 수 있다(We recently launched ~ read our magazine's content on your phone or any mobile device)'고 했으므로 (D)가 정답이다.

어휘 | access 이용, 접근 venue 장소 atlas 지도책

패러프레이징
지문의 read our magazine's content on your phone or any mobile device → 보기의 Mobile access to articles

6 [1], [2], [3], [4]로 표시된 곳 중에서 다음 문장이 들어가기에 가장 적합한 곳은?

"사실 이는 저희가 제공해 드리는 최상의 구독료입니다."

(A) [1]　　　(B) [2]　　　(C) [3]　　　(D) [4]

해설 | 문장 삽입
제시된 문장의 '이것이 최상의 구독료이다(this is the best subscription price)'라고 한 부분이 문제 해결의 단서이다. 앞에서 언급된 명사를 this로 받아 가장 좋은 가격이라고 했으므로, 제시된 문장 앞에는 가격을 나타내는 명사가 와야 한다. 따라서 연간 29.99달러의 가격을 보장해 줄 수 있다며 가격을 제시한 문장 뒤인 (D)가 정답이다.

[7-9] 이메일

수신: 안나 첸
발신: 엔리케 살가도
날짜: 4월 22일
제목: 면담

첸 씨께,

지난주에 저를 만나 주셔서 감사합니다. 제가 그토록 존경하는 디자이너께 피드백을 받을 수 있다는 건 무척 신나는 일입니다. 귀중한 시간을 내신다는 것을 잘 알기에 한 시간 이상 저와 얘기 나눠 주셔서 정말 영광이었습니다. 저의 프랑스 방문 일정 중 가장 좋았습니다.

⁸제 디자인 포트폴리오를 검토하시면서 특히 두꺼운 직물 사용에 관해 말씀해 주신 내용이 놀라웠습니다. 두꺼운 직물로 작업하는 것에 대해 오랫동안 확신이 없었는데, 격려해 주셔서 더 자주 사용해야겠다는 생각이 듭니다.

⁹제가 향후 시간제 인턴으로 선생님과 함께 일할 수 있다고 언급하셨는데요. ⁷마드리드에서 패션학교를 최근 막 졸업한 제 경력상, 직장생활을 시작하기에 선생님의 파리 패션 디자인 사무실만한 곳이 없다고 말씀드리고 싶습니다. 상황이 바뀌고 제 도움을 원하시면 바로 알려주십시오.

엔리케 살가도

어휘 | devote 바치다, 쏟다, 기울이다 encouragement 격려 prompt (어떤 일이 일어나도록) 하다, 유도하다 recently 최근 circumstances 사정, 상황 assistance 도움, 보조

7 살가도 씨에 대해 암시된 것은?

(A) 유명 디자이너이다.
(B) 대학교 학위 과정을 마치지 못했다.

(C) 첸 씨의 이메일에 답장하고 있다.
(D) 디자인 업무를 해본 적이 없다.

해설 | 추론
이메일의 마지막 단락 두 번째 문장에서 '마드리드에서 패션학교를 최근 막 졸업한 경력상, 직장생활을 시작하기에 첸 선생님의 파리 패션 디자인 사무실만한 곳이 없다(having only recently graduated from the School of Fashion in Madrid, there is no place I would rather begin my professional life than at your fashion design office in Paris)'고 했으므로 살가도 씨는 디자인 업무를 해본 적이 없다는 것을 알 수 있다. 따라서 (D)가 정답이다.

어휘 | degree 학위

8 살가도 씨가 놀란 이유는?

(A) 첸 씨가 그의 디자인을 구매하겠다고 제안했다.
(B) 첸 씨가 그의 직물 사용에 대해 칭찬했다.
(C) 첸 씨가 그의 디자인에 쓰인 일부 직물을 탐탁치 않게 여겼다.
(D) 첸 씨는 색을 더 많이 써야 그의 작품이 나아질 것이라고 느꼈다.

해설 | 세부 사항
surprised를 키워드로 잡고 surprised가 언급되는 부분에서 답을 찾아야 한다. 두 번째 단락에서 '디자인 포트폴리오를 검토하시면서 특히 두꺼운 직물 사용에 관해 말씀해 주신 내용이 놀라웠다(I was surprised by what you said while reviewing my design portfolio, especially about my use of heavy fabrics)'고 하면서 '두꺼운 직물로 작업하는 것에 대해 오랫동안 확신이 없었는데, 격려해 주셔서 더 자주 사용해야겠다는 생각이 든다(I now feel that your encouragement will prompt me to use them more often)'고 했으므로 (B)가 정답이다.

어휘 | compliment 칭찬하다 disapprove of ~을 못마땅해하다 texture 직물, 질감

패러프레이징
지문의 encouragement → 보기의 compliment

9 면담 결과로 암시된 것은?

(A) 살가도 씨는 정규직 일자리만 수락할 것이다.
(B) 살가도 씨는 마드리드로 돌아갈 것이다.
(C) 첸 씨에게는 현재 인턴 공석이 없다.
(D) 첸 씨는 살가도 씨를 누군가에게 추천할 것이다.

해설 | 추론
마지막 단락 첫 문장에서 '향후 시간제 인턴으로 함께 일할 수 있다고 첸 씨가 언급하였다(You mentioned that you would be open to my working with you as a part-time intern in the future)'고 했으므로 현재는 인턴 공석이 없다는 것을 짐작할 수 있다. 따라서 (C)가 정답이다.

어휘 | currently 현재 refer A to B A를 B에게 추천하다[소개하다]

[10-13] 편지

> **11로치 앤 그린, 변호사 사무소**
> 121-125 커머셜 로
> 런던 E1 3LP
>
> 2월 28일
>
> 사라 루스, 소유주
> 힐러리 오브 그리니치
> 198-200 그리니치 하이 로
> 런던 SE10 1FN
>
> 루스 씨께,
>
> **11**2월 24일 개최해 주신 은퇴 기념 파티에 관해 서신 드립니다. 제가 귀하의 식당에 방문한 것은 처음이었지만 그날 저녁 저희가 퇴직을 기념해 준 전 전무이사 파드마 파텔이 가장 좋아하는 곳입니다. **10**파텔 씨가 종종 음식 맛을 칭찬했어요. 그리고 사실 저녁 식사의 모든 음식이 완벽하더군요. **13**음식이 너무 맛있어서 곧 저녁식사 하러 친구들, 가족들을 데려올 계획을 이미 세웠습니다.
>
> 또한 직원들이 보여주신 전문성 **12**수준에도 감동을 받았습니다. 서빙 직원들은 신속하고 공손했으며 메뉴에 대한 저희의 모든 질문에 답변이 가능했습니다.
>
> 즐거운 경험을 갖게 해 주셔서 정말 감사합니다! 힐러리 오브 그리니치에서 파티를 여는 것이 로치 앤 그린의 새 전통이 되길 기대합니다.
>
> 앨런 로치, 상무

어휘 | solicitor 변호사 in reference to ~에 관해 retirement 퇴직, 은퇴 establishment 시설, 식당 former 이전의, 전 indeed 사실, 실은 to perfection 완벽히, 완전히 demonstrate 보여주다, 입증하다 prompt 신속한, 즉각적인 courteous 공손한, 정중한 tradition 전통

10 힐러리 오브 그리니치는 무엇인가?

(A) 요리 학교
(B) 파티용품점
(C) 법률사무소
(D) 식당

해설 | 세부 사항
편지의 첫 단락 세 번째 문장에서 '파텔 씨가 종종 음식 맛을 칭찬했고 사실 저녁 식사의 모든 음식이 완벽했다 (Ms. Patel has often praised the quality of your food, and indeed, for our dinner, each dish was cooked

to perfection)'고 했으므로 힐러리 오브 그리니치는 파텔 씨가 자주 방문하는 식당이라는 것을 알 수 있다. 따라서 (D)가 정답이다.

패러프레이징
지문의 your establishment → 보기의 A restaurant

11 2월에 파텔 씨가 축하받은 이유는?

(A) 전무로 승진했다.
(B) 법률사무소를 새로 개업했다.
(C) 로치 앤 그린에서 퇴직했다.
(D) 로스쿨을 졸업했다.

해설 | 세부 사항
Ms. Patel과 February를 키워드로 잡고 Ms. Patel과 February가 언급되는 부분에서 답을 찾아야 한다. 첫 단락 첫 문장에서 '2월 24일 개최해 주신 은퇴 기념 파티에 관해 편지를 쓴다(I'm writing in reference to the retirement party that you hosted for us on 24 February)'고 한 후 '그날 저녁 퇴직을 기념해 준 전 전무이사 파드마 파텔(Padma Patel, who was honored that night by our firm)이 가장 좋아하는 곳'이라고 했기에 파텔 씨가 퇴직했다는 것을 알 수 있다. 또한 편지 맨 위에서 이 회사 이름을 알 수 있으므로 (C)가 정답이다.

어휘 | promote 승진시키다 graduate from ~를 졸업하다

12 두 번째 단락 1행에 쓰인 "degree"와 의미상 가장 가까운 것은?

(A) 정도   (B) 자격
(C) 지위   (D) 요약

해설 | 동의어
'직원들이 보여주신 전문성 수준에도 감동을 받았다(I was equally impressed by the degree of professionalism demonstrated by your staff)'는 의미로 '수준, 정도'를 뜻하는 (A) level이 정답이다.

어휘 | qualification 자격, 자질 position 직급, 지위

13 로치 씨가 편지에서 암시한 것은?

(A) 신입 직원을 채용하는 과정을 진행 중이다.
(B) 힐러리 오브 그리니치와 다시 거래할 것이다.
(C) 가족에게서 힐러리 오브 그리니치에 대해 처음 들었다.
(D) 루스 씨가 그가 한 문의에 관해 연락을 주기를 기대한다.

해설 | 추론
첫 단락 마지막 문장에서 '음식이 너무 맛있어서 곧 저녁식사 하러 친구들, 가족들을 데려올 계획을 이미 세웠다(I have already made plans to bring a group of friends and family for dinner soon)'고 했으므로 (B)가 정답이다.

어휘 | in the process of ~의 과정에서, ~ 진행 중인

패러프레이징
지문의 bring a group of friends and family for dinner
→ 보기의 do business

[14-17] 이메일

수신: 아르노 레이트너 <aleitner@packfuse-europe.com>
발신: 몬세라트 페레르 <mferrer@lintenapharma.es>
제목: 에이팩스 2000 기계의 추가 문제
날짜: 3월 6일

레이트너 씨께,

**15 2월 13일에, 팩퓨즈는 바르셀로나에 있는 린테나
파르마 공장에 새로운 에이팩스 2000 포장 기계 여러 대를
설치했습니다.** 처음에는, 모든 기계가 원활하게 작동했으며
각 기계는 모양과 크기가 다른 약병을 분류하고 방향을 잡고
세척했습니다.

**14 2월 25일에 가장 큰 병을 처리하는 기계가 오작동하기
시작했습니다.** 병을 잘못된 방향으로 돌리고 있었습니다.
**15 2월 28일에 팩퓨즈 엔지니어들이 이 문제 해결을 위해
다시 방문했습니다. 14 그 이후로 이 기계의 세척 과정의
효과가 좀 떨어지는 것을 알아차렸습니다.** 3월 2일에 우리측
품질관리팀은 이 기계를 통과한 병의 80%만이 우리의 위생
기준을 충족한다는 것을 발견했습니다. 또한 기계를 통과하는
동안 일부 병이 긁혔습니다.

어제 저는 우리 공장을 방문했던 팩퓨즈 엔지니어들에게
연락했습니다. 그들은 세척 문제에 대해 전화 상담을
제안했습니다. 우리가 이미 사용 설명서의 모든 조언을
시도했지만 효과가 없었기 때문에 이는 만족스럽지 않네요.
이러한 오작동으로 생산 기한이 크게 지연되고 있으므로
기계를 수리하거나 교체해야 합니다. **16 문제가** 시급하므로
**17 엔지니어들이 가능한 한 빨리 여기 공장에 와서 수리
작업을 수행할 수 있도록 주선해 주시기를 부탁드립니다.**

몬세라트 페레르
운영 이사, 린테나 파르마

어휘 | install 설치하다 initially 초기에는 smoothly
순조롭게 sort 분류하다 orient 방향을 잡다[맞추다]
medicine 의학 malfunction 제대로 작동하지 않다
effective 효과적인 quality control 품질 관리 hygiene 위생
scratch 긁다 disruption 중단, 지장 arrange for A to A가
~을 하도록 주선하다

14 오작동하는 기계의 문제점은?

(A) 가장 큰 병에 라벨을 잘못 붙이고 있다.
(B) 더 작은 병은 분류하지 못하고 있다.

(C) 병을 잘 닦아내지 못하고 않다.
(D) 전체 병의 80%를 깨고 있다.

해설 | 세부 사항
malfunction을 키워드로 잡고 malfunction이 언급되는
부분에서 답을 찾아야 한다. 두 번째 단락 첫 문장에서
'2월 25일에 가장 큰 병을 처리하는 기계가 오작동하기
시작했다(the machine that processes our largest
bottles began to malfunction)'고 한 후, 세 번째
문장에서 '그 이후로 이 기계의 세척 과정의 효과가 좀
떨어지는 것(the cleaning process on this machine is
less effective)을 알아차렸다'고 했으므로 (C)가 정답이다.

어휘 | mislabel ~에 라벨을 잘못 붙이다

패러프레이징
지문의 the cleaning process on this machine is less
effective → 보기의 It is not cleaning bottles well.

15 팩퓨즈 엔지니어들에 대해 암시된 것은?

(A) 대부분의 에이팩스 2000 기계를 잘못 설치했다.
(B) 2월에 린테나 파르마 공장을 두 번 방문했다.
(C) 3월에 페레르 씨와 연락을 시작했다.
(D) 린테나 파르마 제품에 대한 연례 품질 관리 검사를
    수행한다.

해설 | 추론
Packfuse engineers를 키워드로 잡고 Packfuse
engineers가 언급되는 부분에서 답을 찾아야 한다. 두 번째
단락 두 번째 문장에서 '2월 28일에 팩퓨즈 엔지니어들이
이 문제 해결을 위해 다시 방문했다(The Packfuse
engineers came back to fix this on 28 February)'고
했으며, 첫 단락 첫 문장에서 '2월 13일에, 팩퓨즈는 린테나
파르마 공장에 새로운 에이팩스 2000 포장 기계 여러 대를
설치했다(On 13 February, Packfuse installed several
new Apax 2000 packaging machines in our Lintena
Parma factory ~)'고 했으므로 2월에 린테나 파르마
공장을 두 번 방문했다는 것을 짐작할 수 있다. 따라서 (B)가
정답이다.

어휘 | initiate 개시하게 되다

패러프레이징
지문의 came back to fix this on 28 February
→ 보기의 visited ~ twice in February

16 세 번째 단락 5행에 쓰인 "matter"와 의미상 가장 가까운
것은?

(A) 상황   (B) 중요성
(C) 재료   (D) 액수

해설 | 동의어
Because of the urgency of this matter는 '문제가
시급하므로'라는 의미로 쓰였기에 '상황'을 뜻하는 (A)
situation이 정답이다.

17 페레르 씨가 요청하는 것은?

(A) 사용 설명서   (B) 마감일 연장
(C) 환불   (D) 서비스 예약

해설 | 세부 사항
마지막 단락 마지막 문장에서 '엔지니어들이 가능한 한 빨리 여기 공장에 와서 수리 작업을 수행할 수 있도록 주선해 주길 부탁한다(I ask that you arrange for engineers to carry out repairs here ~)'고 했으므로 (D)가 정답이다.

어휘 | extend 연장하다 service (차량, 기계의) 점검

패러프레이징
지문의 ask → 질문의 request
지문의 arrange for engineers to carry out repairs
→ 보기의 A service appointment

[18-21] 편지

5월 1일

자넷 그레고리
143 터드웰 가
율라, ID 83879

그레고리 씨께,

축하합니다! **18**제4회 연례 '테이스트 오브 이탈리아' 요리 경연대회에서 6인의 결선 진출자 중 한 명으로 선발되신 것을 알려드리게 되어 기쁩니다. 귀하의 스파게티 베르데 조리법은 이탈리아 정통 재료를 창의적으로 이용해 100여 개 참가작 중 심사위원들이 가장 좋아한 조리법 중 하나로 선정됐습니다. **18**귀하는 결선 진출자로서 저희 경연대회의 주요 후원업체인 퀸디치 레스토랑 100달러 상품권을 수상하셨습니다.

아울러 젬머 시의 연례 이탈리아 페스티벌 동안 심사위원단을 위한 조리법을 준비해 주십시오. **19**올해 축제는 5월 31일 금요일부터 6월 2일 일요일까지 개최될 예정입니다. 결선 참가자들은 일요일 오후 2시, 퀸디치 바로 밖 천막이 있는 곳에서 요리를 시작하게 됩니다. 심사는 오후 3시 30분에 열리며 시상식이 바로 이어질 예정입니다. **20**우승자는 퀸디치의 유명 요리사이자 TV 명사인 아만도 콘티가 제공하는 요리 지도를 1주일간 받게 됩니다. 콘티 씨가 5일간 매일 자신의 요리법에 관해 직접 설명해 주실 것입니다.

21결승전에 참가를 원하신다고 알려주시면 귀하의 자리를 확보하는 서식을 작성해 회신하실 수 있도록 안내해 드립니다. 늦어도 5월 16일 목요일까지는 저희 사무실 (208) 555-0157로 전화하셔서 확정해 주십시오.

답장을 기다리겠습니다!

바르톨로메오 파그노토

'테이스트 오브 이탈리아' 담당자
퀸디치

어휘 | finalist 결선 진출자 authentic 정통의 ingredient 재료 venue 장소 award ceremony 시상식 immediately 즉시, 즉각 culinary 요리의 celebrated 유명한 personality 유명인 hands-on 직접 해 보는 final competition 결승전 secure 확보하다 no later than 늦어도 ~까지

18 파그노토 씨가 그레고리 씨에게 편지를 쓴 이유는?

(A) 그레고리 씨를 요리 강사로 채용하려고
(B) 그레고리 씨의 이력서를 받았음을 알려주려고
(C) 그레고리 씨가 수상자임을 밝히려고
(D) 대회 심사를 맡아 달라고 부탁하려고

해설 | 주제 / 목적
편지의 첫 단락 첫 문장에서 '요리 경연대회에서 6인의 결선 진출자 중 한 명으로 선발되신 것을 알려드린다(announce your selection as one of six finalists in ~ cooking contest)'라고 한 후, 첫 단락 마지막 문장에서 '결선 진출자로서 경연대회의 주요 후원업체인 퀸디치 레스토랑 100달러 상품권을 수상하셨다(you have been awarded a $100 gift certificate)'고 했으므로 (C)가 정답이다.

어휘 | recipient 받는 사람, 수령인

패러프레이징
지문의 been awarded a $100 gift certificate
→ 보기의 an award recipient

19 대회 참가자들은 언제 시간을 내야 하는가?

(A) 5월 16일   (B) 5월 31일
(C) 6월 1일   (D) 6월 2일

해설 | 세부 사항
두 번째 단락에서 '올해 축제는 5월 31일 금요일부터 6월 2일 일요일까지 개최될 예정(This year's festival will take place Friday, May 31, through Sunday, June 2)'이라고 한 후, '결선 참가자들은 일요일 오후 2시, 퀸디치 바로 밖 천막이 있는 곳에서 요리를 시작하게 된다(Finalists will begin cooking at 2:00 P.M. on Sunday in a tented venue just outside Quindici)'고 했으므로 대회 참가자들은 일요일인 6월 2일 시간을 내야 한다는 것을 알 수 있다. 따라서 (D)가 정답이다.

어휘 | available 시간이 되는

패러프레이징
지문의 Finalists → 질문의 contest participants

20 '테이스트 오브 이탈리아' 요리 경연대회에서 우승하면 무엇을 상으로 받는가?

(A) 레스토랑 일자리   (B) 요리 수업
(C) 수료증   (D) TV 프로그램 출연

해설 | 세부 사항

두 번째 단락 다섯 번째 문장에서 '우승자는 퀸디치의 유명 요리사이자 TV 명사인 아만도 콘티가 제공하는 요리 지도를 1주일간 받게 된다(The winner will receive one week of culinary instruction ~)'고 했으므로 (B)가 정답이다.

어휘 | certificate of achievement 수료증 appearance 출연

패러프레이징

지문의 culinary instruction → 보기의 cooking lessons

21 그레고리 씨는 무엇을 확정하라고 요청받는가?

(A) 행사 참여 결정
(B) 우편물 발송 주소
(C) 레스토랑 예약
(D) 요리사와의 교육 일정

해설 | 세부 사항

마지막 단락 첫 문장에서 '결승전에 참가를 원하신다고 알려주시면(Once you notify us that you intend to join us for the final competition) 귀하의 자리를 확보하는 서식을 작성해 회신하실 수 있도록 안내해 드린다'고 했으므로 (A)가 정답이다.

어휘 | reservation 예약

패러프레이징

지문의 join us for the final competition → 보기의 participate in an event

[22-25] 이메일

수신: 크리틴트 직원들
발신: <jose.palermo@krytint.com>
날짜: 11월 22일 월요일
제목: 도움에 감사드립니다
첨부: 프로젝트 보기

안녕하세요 여러분,

22사무실에서 계속 도와주시는 여러분께 감사드리고 여러분의 노력을 알고 있다는 말씀을 드리고 싶습니다. 많은 분들이 청소가 이뤄진 것을 알아차렸고 깔끔한 사무실이 큰 변화를 낳는다고 언급해 주셨습니다. 앞으로도 계속 잘해 나갑시다!

23새 건물이 지난달 처음 이사 들어왔을 때보다 훨씬 더 좋아 보이지만 다음 주 그래프톤에서 고객들이 오시기 전에 정리해야 할 일이 아직 많습니다. 이를 위해 가급적 빨리 여러분의 도움이 필요한 프로젝트를 적었습니다. **24첨부된 문서를 보시고 작업 중인 곳에 여러분의 이름을 적어 주십시오.** 여러분의 도움에 깊은 감사를 드립니다. 신청하신 작업은 금요일까지 완료해 주십시오.

아울러 청소업체가 일주일에 세 번만 오도록 예산을 편성했습니다. 그러니 사무실 정돈을 계속 열심히 해 주시기 바랍니다. 특히 업체가 오지 않는 화요일과 목요일에요. 청소업체 직원에게 매주 금요일 냉장고 안을 치워 달라고 요청했습니다. **25냉장고에 남겨두고 싶은 물품이 있으시면 성함과 날짜를 쓰셔서 버리지 않는다는 것을 알 수 있도록 해 주십시오.** 이를 위해 컬러 견출지가 준비되어 있습니다. 물품 보관함 맨 위 칸에 있습니다.

이전 기간 동안 도와주셔서 감사합니다!

호세 팔레르모
크리틴트 인더스트리즈
사무장

어휘 | unrecognized 자각하지 못하는, 인식하지 못하는 to this end 이것을 위해 chore 일 appreciate 감사하다 complete 완료하다 sign up for ~을 신청하다 budget 예산을 세우다 available 이용 가능한 transition 이전, 이행

22 직원들에게 무엇 때문에 감사하는가?

(A) 실수 정정
(B) 사무실 깨끗이 유지
(C) 사무용품 보충
(D) 신규 고객 영입

해설 | 세부 사항

thank를 키워드로 잡고 thank가 언급되는 부분에서 답을 찾아야 한다. 이메일의 첫 단락 첫 문장에서 '사무실에서 계속 도와주시는 여러분께 감사드린다(I would like to thank those of you who continually help out around the office ~)'고 한 후, '청소가 이뤄진 것을 알아차렸고 깔끔한 사무실이 큰 변화를 낳는다(they notice when things get cleaned and that a tidy office makes a big difference)고 많은 분들이 언급해 주었다'고 했으므로 사무실을 깨끗이 유지하는 것에 감사한다는 것을 알 수 있다. 따라서 (B)가 정답이다.

어휘 | restock 다시 채우다 obtain 얻다, 구하다

패러프레이징

지문의 things get cleaned → 보기의 Keeping the office clean

23 크리틴트 인더스트리즈는 지난달에 무엇을 했는가?

(A) 청소 서비스업체 새로 고용
(B) 사무용품 구입
(C) 운영 요일 변경
(D) 새 사무실로 이전

해설 | 세부 사항

last month를 키워드로 잡고 last month가 언급되는 부분에서 답을 찾아야 한다. 두 번째 단락 첫 문장에서 '새 건물이 지난달 처음 이사 들어왔을 때보다 훨씬 더 좋아 보인다(While the new building is looking much nicer than it did last month when we first moved in, ~)'고 했으므로 (D)가 정답이다.

어휘 | purchase 구매하다 relocate 이전하다

패러프레이징
지문의 moved in → 보기의 Relocate to
지문의 the new building → 보기의 a new workspace

24 이메일에 포함된 것은?

(A) 작업 목록
(B) 업무 일정
(C) 분기별 예산
(D) 고객 명부

해설 | 세부 사항
두 번째 단락 세 번째 문장에서 '첨부된 문서를 보시고 작업 중 한 곳에 여러분의 이름을 적어달라(Please view the attached document and put your name down for one of these chores)'고 했으므로 (A)가 정답이다.

어휘 | quarterly 분기별의 directory 안내 책자, 명부

패러프레이징
지문의 attached → 질문의 included
지문의 chores → 보기의 tasks

25 직원들은 왜 컬러 견출지를 사용해야 하는가?

(A) 음식물에 라벨을 붙이려고
(B) 이사업체를 위해 상자에 표시하려고
(C) 공간 청소를 요청하려고
(D) 중요 문서를 변경하려고

해설 | 세부 사항
colored tags를 키워드로 잡고 colored tags가 언급되는 부분에서 답을 찾아야 한다. 마지막 단락 세 번째 문장에서 '냉장고에 남겨두고 싶은 물품이 있으시면 성함과 날짜를 쓰셔서 버리지 않는다는 것을 알 수 있도록 해달라(If you have anything in there that you would like to be saved, please mark it ~)'고 한 후, '이를 위해 컬러 견출지가 준비되어 있다(Colored tags are available for this purpose)'고 했으므로 (A)가 정답이다.

어휘 | request 요청하다

패러프레이징
지문의 mark → 보기의 label

[26-29] 편지

우드포드 그로서리
63 길드리 가
슈루즈버리, 슈롭셔, SY2 1UQ
01743 499955

4월 1일

고객 여러분께,

우드포드 그로서리에 신나는 변화가 일고 있습니다! **26**이번 달 하순에 방문하셔서, 여러분의 쇼핑 경험을 더욱 즐겁게 만들 수 있도록 진행 중인 개선 사항을 확인하시기 바랍니다.

아시다시피 **26,29(B)**저희 매장을 5,000평방미터 정도 더 늘리는 큰 개조 공사를 진행하고 있습니다. 4월 10일부터 농산물 구역은 두 배 가까이 넓어져 **29(A)**더욱 다양한 과일 및 채소를 제공해 드릴 수 있으며 여러분이 매장 내에서 더 쉽게 이동하실 수 있습니다. 아울러 제과 구역도 확장하여 여러분이 사랑해 주신 갓 구운 빵과 제과류를 더 많이 제공해 드릴 수 있게 됩니다.

274월 20일 토요일에 고객 감사의 날로 개조 공사를 기념할 예정입니다. 제과부와 조리식품부에서 진행하는 요리 시연 및 무료 시식이 있습니다. 또한 **29(C)**이 날부터는 매주 토요일 오전 7시가 아닌 오전 6시에 매장을 열어 쇼핑을 더 일찍 마치실 수 있습니다.

새로운 우드포드 그로서리 방문을 장려하고자 시리얼, 청소용품을 비롯해 다양한 제품에 사용 가능한 할인 쿠폰을 동봉해 드립니다. 쿠폰은 4월 30일까지 유효합니다. **28**특별 할인 날짜와 제품 설명회가 명시된 달력도 들어 있습니다. 이번 달에 들러 보세요. 여러분과 가족을 위한 맛있는 요리를 만드실 수 있도록 도와드리겠습니다.

세실리 왓킨스
매장 관리자

동봉

어휘 | improvement 개선 enjoyable 즐거운 undergo 겪다 significant 중요한, 커다란 approximately 거의, 가까이 expand 확장시키다, 확대하다 appreciation 감사 enclose 동봉하다 a range of 다양한 demonstration 시연, (시범) 설명

26 편지의 목적은?

(A) 매장 확장 완료를 알리려고
(B) 제과 제품 맞춤 브랜드를 광고하려고
(C) 매장 소유권 변경을 소개하려고
(D) 새 매장 지점을 홍보하려고

해설 | 주제/목적
편지의 첫 단락 두 번째 문장에서 '이번 달 하순에 방문하셔서, 쇼핑 경험을 더욱 즐겁게 만들 수 있도록 진행 중인 개선 사항을 확인하라(We hope you will visit us later this month and see the improvements ~ your shopping experience more enjoyable)'고 한 후, 두 번째 단락 첫 번째 문장에서 '매장을 5,000평방미터 정도 더 늘리는 큰 개조 공사를 진행하고 있다(we have been undergoing a significant renovation that is adding approximately 5,000 square metres to our store)'고 했으므로 (A)가 정답이다.

어휘 | announce 알리다, 발표하다 completion 완료, 완공
advertise 광고하다 ownership 소유권 promote 홍보하다

패러프레이징

지문의 a significant renovation that is adding
approximately 5,000 square metres to our store
→ 보기의 a store expansion

27 우드포드 그로서리는 언제 특별 행사를 개최할 것인가?

(A) 4월 1일　　　　　(B) 4월 10일
(C) 4월 20일　　　　(D) 4월 30일

해설 | 세부 사항

세 번째 단락 첫 문장에서 '4월 20일 토요일에 고객 감사의
날로 개조 공사를 기념할 예정(We will be celebrating
the renovations with a customer appreciation day
on Saturday, 20 April)'이라고 했으므로 (C)가 정답이다.

패러프레이징

지문의 a customer appreciation day
→ 질문의 a special event

28 편지에 포함된 것은?

(A) 설문지
(B) 행사 일정
(C) 제품 목록
(D) 제품 견본

해설 | 세부 사항

마지막 단락에 편지에 포함된 것이 언급되어 있다. 세 번째
문장에서 '특별 할인 날짜와 제품 설명회가 명시된 달력도
들어 있다(You will also find a calendar indicating
special sale days and product demonstrations)'고
했으므로 (B)가 정답이다.

어휘 | questionnaire 설문지

패러프레이징

지문의 a calendar indicating special sale days and
product demonstrations
→ 보기의 A schedule of events

29 우드포드 그로서리의 변화로 언급되지 않은 것은?

(A) 제품 품목 확대
(B) 매장 면적 증가
(C) 운영시간 연장
(D) 출납원 추가

해설 | Not / True

두 번째 단락 두 번째 문장에서 '4월 10일부터 농산물
구역은 두 배 가까이 넓어져 더욱 다양한 과일 및 채소를
제공해 드릴 수 있다(which will allow us to offer a
greater variety of fruits and vegetables)'고 했으므로
(A)가 언급되었고, 두 번째 단락 첫 문장에서 '매장을

5,000평방미터 정도 더 늘리는 큰 개조 공사를 진행하고
있다(we have been undergoing a significant
renovation that is adding approximately 5,000
square metres to our store)'고 했으므로 (B)가
언급되었다. 세 번째 단락 세 번째 문장에서 '매주 토요일
오전 7시가 아닌 오전 6시에 매장을 열어(we will start
opening on Saturdays at 6:00 A.M. instead of 7:00
A.M) 쇼핑을 더 일찍 마칠 수 있다'고 했으므로 (C)가
언급되었다. 하지만 출납원 추가에 대한 이야기는 없으므로
(D)가 정답이다.

어휘 | floor space 건평, 매장 면적 extend 연장하다
additional 추가의

패러프레이징

지문의 a greater variety of fruits and vegetables
→ 보기의 A wider selection of products
지문의 adding approximately 5,000 square metres
→ 보기의 Increased floor space
지문의 start opening on Saturdays at 6:00 A.M.
instead of 7:00 A.M.
→ 보기의 Extended hours of operation

UNIT 02　공지 / 회람

기출 예제　　　　　　　　　　　　　　　　　本책 p.072

회원들에게 알립니다

다음 주 국경일을 기념하여 그리솜 피트니스 클럽의
이용시간이 다음과 같이 제한됨을 알려드립니다.

5월 4일 월요일: 평소와 같이 오전 8시에 문을 열지만 오후
　　　　　　　　 8시에 일찍 문을 닫습니다. **1이날 보육
　　　　　　　　 서비스는 영향을 받지 않습니다.** 하지만
　　　　　　　　 **2회원님의 그룹 피트니스 강사에게 문의해
　　　　　　　　 수업이 예정대로 진행되는지 확인해
　　　　　　　　 보십시오.**

5월 5일 화요일: 종일 폐관될 예정입니다.

3월 6일 수요일부터 정규 개폐관 시간을 재개합니다. 문의
사항이 있으시면 ktripper@grissomfitness.com으로 케빈
트리퍼 매니저에게 연락 주십시오.

- -

어휘 | attention 알립니다 in observance of ~을 기념하여
national holiday 국경일 limited 제한된 drop-in 예약이
필요 없는 childcare 보육 affect 영향을 미치다 instructor
강사 resume 재개하다 regular 정기적인

---

1 (C)	**2** (A)	**3** (B)	**4** (B)	**5** (A)	**6** (B)
7 (D)	**8** (A)	**9** (B)	**10** (C)	**11** (D)	**12** (B)
13 (D)	**14** (A)	**15** (A)	**16** (D)	**17** (A)	**18** (A)
19 (B)	**20** (D)	**21** (D)	**22** (B)	**23** (A)	**24** (C)

[1-2] 회람

발신: 제인 무산테, 인사부장
수신: 회장실 직원, 연구개발실 직원
제목: 인사 이동 알림
날짜: 3월 7일 수요일 오후 4시 19분

홍 한 팜이 회장실에서 연구개발실로 직무 이동을
수락했음을 알려드리게 되어 기쁩니다. 홍 한은 다음 주에
버논 웨스트와 교육을 시작하게 되며, **¹버논이 월말에
퇴직하고 나면** 연구개발실 사무 비서직을 맡을 예정입니다.

**²인사부서 동료인 존 루셀이 회장실 사무 비서직의 직무
기술서를 업데이트하고 있으며 내일 공석을 게시할
것입니다.** 월말까지 해당 직책을 충원할 것으로 예상합니다.

회사에 30년 이상 재직 후 은퇴하는 버논을 축하해 주시고
홍 한의 새 직책 이동이 잘 이뤄지기를 바랍시다.

어휘 | transfer 이동, 전근 take over as ~직을 맡다, 인계하다
administrative 관리의, 행정의 colleague 동료 fill the
position 공석을 충원하다 retirement 은퇴, 퇴직

1 누가 회사를 떠나는가?

(A) 제인 무산테　　　　(B) 홍 한 팜
(C) 버논 웨스트　　　　(D) 존 루셀

해설 | 세부 사항
회람의 첫 단락 마지막 문장에서 '버논이 월말에 퇴직하고
난 후(after Vernon retires at the end of the
month)'라고 했으므로 (C)가 정답이다.

패러프레이징
지문의 retires → 질문의 is leaving the company

2 월말에 어떤 일이 있을 것인가?

(A) 새로운 사무 비서가 올 것이다.
(B) 회장이 퇴임할 것이다.
(C) 직무 기술서가 수정될 것이다.
(D) 인사부서 사람이 승진할 것이다.

해설 | 세부 사항
the end of the month를 키워드로 잡고 the end of the
month가 언급되는 부분에서 답을 찾아야 한다. 두 번째
단락에서 '존 루셀이 회장실 사무 비서직의 직무 기술서를
업데이트하고 있다(John Roussel ~ is updating the job

description for the administrative assistant position
in the President's office)'고 한 후, '월말까지 해당
직책을 충원할 것으로 예상한다(We expect to have the
position filled by the end of the month)'고 했으므로
(A)가 정답이다.

어휘 | revise 수정하다, 변경하다 promote 승진시키다

[3-5] 공지

던포트 경전철

1월 20일

승객 여러분께,

던포트 경전철은 운영비 상승으로 인해 3월 1일부터
여객운임을 인상할 예정입니다. **⁴성인, 대학생, 학생 요금이
5퍼센트 인상됩니다.** 5세 이하 아동은 계속 무료로 탑승할 수
있습니다.

고객 여러분께 불편을 드려 죄송합니다. **³저희 던포트
경전철이 7년만에 처음 운임을 인상한다는 점을 말씀드리고
싶습니다. ⁵여객운임 수익은 직원 급여 및 전반적인 열차
유지 보수에 사용됩니다.**

기대하시는 수준의 서비스를 계속 제공해 드리겠습니다.
던포트 경전철을 이용해 주셔서 감사합니다.

어휘 | operating cost 운영비 free of charge 무료로
inconvenience 불편 revenue 수익, 수입 maintenance
유지 보수

3 던포트 경전철에 대해 명시된 것은?

(A) 신규 노선을 추가한다.
(B) 7년 전 운임을 인상했다.
(C) 고객 불만사항에 응대하고 있다.
(D) 승객 수 감소를 겪고 있다.

해설 | Not / True
공지의 두 번째 단락 두 번째 문장에서 '던포트 경전철이
7년만에 처음 운임을 인상한다(this is the first fare
increase for Dunnport Light Rail service in seven
years)'고 했으므로 (B)가 정답이다.

어휘 | decrease 감소

패러프레이징
지문의 fare increase → 보기의 raised its fares

4 대학생에 대해 암시된 것은?

(A) 열차 월간 탑승권을 할인된 가격으로 구매할 수 있다.
(B) 운임이 성인 운임과 같은 비율로 오를 것이다.
(C) 3월 1일까지 학생증을 갱신해야 한다.
(D) 한때 던포트 경전철을 무료로 이용할 수 있었다.

해설 | 추론
university students를 키워드로 잡고 university students가 언급되는 부분에서 답을 찾아야 한다. 첫 단락 두 번째 문장에서 '성인, 대학생, 학생 요금이 5퍼센트 인상된다(The cost of tickets for adults, university students, and school-aged children will go up by 5 percent)'고 했으므로 (B)가 정답이다.

어휘 | purchase 구매하다 renew 갱신하다

패러프레이징
지문의 The cost of tickets ~ will go up by 5 percent
→ 보기의 Their fare will increase

5 공지에 따르면, 운임으로 얻는 수익이 사용되는 곳은?

(A) 직원 급여 지급
(B) 열차편 확대
(C) 역 개조
(D) 광고 개선

해설 | 세부 사항
revenue를 키워드로 잡고 revenue가 언급되는 부분에서 답을 찾아야 한다. 두 번째 단락 세 번째 문장에서 '여객운임 수익은 직원 급여 및 전반적인 열차 유지 보수에 사용된다(Revenue from passenger fares is used for employee salaries and general train maintenance)'고 했으므로 (A)가 정답이다.

어휘 | advertising 광고

패러프레이징
지문의 for employee salaries
→ 보기의 To pay employees

[6-8] 회람

```
회람

수신: 디자인 팀원들
발신: 그레타 폴슨, CEO
날짜: 6월 9일
제목: 수고했습니다!

콘트레라스 크리에이티브는 만족한 고객으로부터 꾸준하게 일을 받으면서 엄청난 한 해를 보냈고 여러분이 그 성공의 중요한 일부분이었습니다. ⁶감사의 표시로 이번 달에 모두의 계좌에 1,200달러를 추가로 입금할 예정입니다.

수년에 걸쳐 여러 디자인 팀과 함께 일을 해봤지만 팀이 이렇게 호의적인 경우는 드물었습니다. ⁷여러분은 기한을 잘 준수하고 건설적인 비판을 수용하며 전략적이고 효과적인 방식으로 결과물을 생성합니다.

매년 얼마나 많은 프로젝트를 받게 될지 예측하기가 쉽지
```

않기 때문에 보너스가 항상 ⁸정기적으로 주어질 수는 없습니다. 그러나 우리가 여러분의 노력과 전문성을 매우 높이 평가하고 있다는 것을 알아주시기 바라며, 앞으로도 여러분의 기여를 기대하겠습니다!

어휘 | tremendous 엄청난 steady 꾸준한 integral 필수적인 appreciation 감탄, 감사 deposit 예치하다 account 계좌 occasion 때, 경우 agreeable 기분 좋은, 선뜻 동의하는 receptive 수용적인 constructive 건설적인 criticism 비판 deliverable 결과물 forecast 예측하다 professionalism 전문성 look forward to ~을 기대하다 contribution 기여

6 회람의 목적은?

(A) 경비 보고서 검토
(B) 곧 지급될 보너스 발표
(C) 계약 요건 요약
(D) 잠재 신규 고객에 대한 소식 공유

해설 | 주제 / 목적
회람의 첫 단락 마지막 문장에서 '감사의 표시로 이번 달에 모두의 계좌에 1,200달러를 추가로 입금할 예정(To show our appreciation, we will be depositing an extra $1,200 into each of your accounts this month)'이라고 했으므로 (B)가 정답이다.

어휘 | expense 경비, 비용 upcoming 앞으로 다가오는 summarize 요약하다 requirement 필요조건 potential 잠재적인

패러프레이징
지문의 an extra $1,200 → 보기의 an upcoming bonus

7 디자인 팀원들에 대해 명시된 것은?

(A) 종종 해외 고객과 직접 일한다.
(B) 제품을 배송하는 새로운 방법을 개발했다.
(C) 비교적 최근에 고용되었다.
(D) 피드백을 받는 것에 열린 마음이다.

해설 | Not / True
회람의 수신자가 디자인 팀원들이고 두 번째 단락 마지막 문장에서 '여러분은 기한을 잘 준수하고 건설적인 비판을 수용한다(You meet your deadlines, are receptive to constructive criticism ~)'고 했으므로 디자인 팀원들이 피드백을 잘 수용한다는 것을 알 수 있다. 따라서 (D)가 정답이다.

어휘 | relatively 비교적 open (생각, 태도가) 열려 있는, (새로운 생각에) 귀 기울이는

패러프레이징
지문의 receptive to constructive criticism
→ 보기의 open to receiving feedback

8 세 번째 단락 2행에 쓰인 "regular"와 의미상 가장 가까운 것은?

(A) 고정된
(B) 정돈된, 질서 있는
(C) 비공식의
(D) 자격을 갖춘

해설 | **동의어**

on a regular basis는 '정기적으로'의 의미로 '보너스가 항상 정기적으로 주어질 수는 없다(bonuses cannot always be given on a regular basis)'는 것은 보너스 지급이 고정된 것이 아니라는 것을 의미한다. 따라서 '고정된'을 뜻하는 (A) fixed가 정답이다.

[9-11] 공지

로렌조 키친
퍼펙트 피자 콘테스트

로렌조 키친에서 **10(A)제1회 퍼펙트 피자 콘테스트** 개최를 알립니다. 지역 내 피자 애호가들은 완벽한 피자 토핑 조합에 관한 독창적인 아이디어를 제출해 주십시오. 저희 피자 요리사들이 모여서 피자를 만들면, **99번 채널의 <우드 파이어 그릴> 진행자인 폴렛 푸치니를 비롯한 10(B)'피자 전문가' 판정단과 지역 토크쇼 고정 게스트가 심사합니다.** 아래와 같이 3위까지 상을 드립니다.

• 1위: 로렌조 키친 50달러 상품권 및 시상하신 피자를 고정 메뉴에 포함
• 2위: 로렌조 키친 30달러 상품권 및 시상하신 피자를 2개월간 월간 특선 메뉴에 포함
• 3위: 로렌조 키친 20달러 상품권 및 시상하신 피자를 1개월간 월간 특선 메뉴에 포함

콘테스트 참가를 원하는 분은 정문 근처 진열대에서 참가 신청서를 가져가시면 됩니다. 신청서에는 성과 이름, 전화번호, 제안하시는 토핑 목록, 선호하는 소스(레드 또는 화이트)가 포함되어야 합니다. 신청서는 7월 15일까지 입구의 지정된 박스에 넣어 주시면 됩니다.

10(C)참가자는 길포드 시에 거주해야 하며 식품업계에 종사하면 안 됩니다. **10(D)1인당 1회만 참여해 주십시오.** 우승자는 7월 25일까지 전화로 연락 드립니다. **118월 3일 토요일부터 오셔서 우승 피자를 맛보세요.**

- -
어휘 | enthusiast 애호가, 열광적인 팬 assemble 모이다
as follows 다음과 같이 permanent 영구적인 entry form
참가 신청서 preference 선호 designated 지정된 reside
거주하다

---

9 푸치니 씨는 누구이겠는가?

(A) 이전 대회 우승자
(B) TV 출연 명사
(C) 레스토랑 주인
(D) 요리책 저자

해설 | **추론**

Puccini를 키워드로 잡고 Puccini가 언급되는 부분에서 답을 찾아야 한다. 공지의 첫 단락 세 번째 문장에서 '9번 채널의 <우드 파이어 그릴> 진행자인 폴렛 푸치니(Paulette Puccini, host of Channel 9's *Wood Fire Grill*)'라고 했으므로 (B)가 정답이다.

어휘 | celebrity 명사, 유명 인사

패러프레이징
지문의 host of Channel 9
→ 보기의 A television celebrity

10 퍼펙트 피자 콘테스트에 대해 언급된 것은?

(A) 매년 개최된다.
(B) 로렌조 키친 요리사가 심사할 것이다.
(C) 지역 거주자들만 출전할 수 있다.
(D) 여러 번 참가할 수 있다.

해설 | **Not / True**

첫 단락 첫 문장에서 '제1회 퍼펙트 피자 콘테스트(its first ever Perfect Pizza contest)'라고 했으므로 (A)는 오답이다. 첫 단락 세 번째 문장에서 '피자 전문가 판정단과 지역 토크쇼 고정 게스트가 심사한다(which will then be judged by a panel of "pizza experts" ~ and a regular guest on local talk shows)'고 했으므로 (B)도 오답이다. 마지막 단락 두 번째 문장에서 '1인당 1회만 참여해 달라(Limit one entry per person)'고 했으므로 (D)도 오답이다. 마지막 단락 첫 문장에서 '참가자는 길포드 시에 거주해야 한다(Entrants must reside in Guilford City)'고 했으므로 (C)가 정답이다.

어휘 | compete in 출전하다, 참가하다

패러프레이징
지문의 reside in Guilford City → 보기의 local residents

11 공지에 따르면, 8월에 무슨 일이 있을 것인가?

(A) 두 번째 대회가 시작될 것이다.
(B) 심사위원들이 대회 우승자 선정을 위해 만날 것이다.
(C) 레스토랑이 기념식에서 우승자들을 시상할 것이다.
(D) 레스토랑에서 몇 가지 새로운 메뉴를 제공할 것이다.

해설 | **세부 사항**

August를 키워드로 잡고 August가 언급되는 부분에서 답을 찾아야 한다. 마지막 단락 마지막 문장에서 '8월 3일 토요일부터 오셔서 우승 피자를 맛보라(Come and try the winning creations starting Saturday, August 3)'고 했으므로 (D)가 정답이다.

어휘 | recognize (공로를) 인정하다, 표창하다

패러프레이징
지문의 winning creations → 보기의 new menu items

수신: 전 직원
발신: 매튜 베넷, 운영책임자
날짜: 10월 4일
제목: 신분증

1210월 10일, 다음 주 월요일에 새로운 보안 시스템이 설치될 예정입니다. 이 시스템이 완전히 활성화되면 왓틀리 직원은 항상 신분증을 가지고 다녀야 합니다. 이 플라스틱 카드에는 디지털 신분 확인 코드가 내장되어 있어 왓틀리 구내 모든 건물에 전자 출입이 가능해집니다.

13신분증은 10월 7일 금요일 인사부서에서 받으실 수 있습니다. 전 부서 관리자가 일정표를 받으셨으니 신분증을 언제 받을 수 있는지 부서원들에게 알려주실 겁니다. 직원 여러분은 10월 12일 이후 새 신분증 없이는 왓틀리의 어떤 시설에도 출입하실 수 없습니다. **14**문의나 우려사항이 있으신 경우 관리자에게 말씀하십시오.

어휘 | security 보안 install 설치하다 activate 활성화시키다 be embedded with ~가 내장되다 obtain 얻다, 구하다

12 회람을 쓴 목적은?

(A) 직원들에게 부서의 새 위치를 알리려고
(B) 회사 정책을 소개하려고
(C) 건물 임시 폐쇄를 알리려고
(D) 최근 보안 위반에 대해 신고하려고

해설 | 주제/목적
맨 첫 문장에서 '10월 10일, 다음 주 월요일에 새로운 보안 시스템(A new security system)이 설치될 예정'이라고 한 후, '이 시스템이 완전히 활성화되면 왓틀리 직원은 항상 신분증을 가지고 다녀야 한다(it will require that Wattley employees carry identification badges at all times)'고 했으므로 (B)가 정답이다.

어휘 | temporary 임시의, 일시적인 report 알리다, 보도하다 violation 위반

13 직원들은 무엇을 하라고 요청받는가?

(A) 회의 참석
(B) 다른 입구 이용
(C) 서식에 서명
(D) 신분증 수령

해설 | 세부 사항
두 번째 단락 첫 문장에서 '신분증은 10월 7일 금요일 받을 수 있다(Badges will be available on Friday, October 7, ~)'고 한 후, '전 부서 관리자가 신분증을 언제 받을 수 있는지 부서원들에게 알려주실 것(The supervisors ~ will advise their staff about when their badges can be obtained)'이라고 했으므로 직원들은 신분증 수령을 요청받았다고 할 수 있다. 따라서 (D)가 정답이다.

어휘 | alternate 대체하는, 교대의

패러프레이징
지문의 be obtained → 보기의 Get
지문의 badges → 보기의 identification card

14 직원들은 우려사항에 대해 누구와 연락하라는 지시를 받는가?

(A) 부서장
(B) 보안 요원
(C) 인사부 직원
(D) 운영책임자

해설 | 세부 사항
concerns를 키워드로 잡고 concerns가 언급되는 부분에서 답을 찾아야 한다. 마지막 단락 마지막 문장에서 '문의나 우려사항이 있는 경우 관리자에게 말씀해달라(Please direct any questions or concerns to your manager)'고 했으므로 (A)가 정답이다.

어휘 | personnel 직원들, 부서 인원

**스튜어즈 베이 예술 위원회에서
스프링 플링 기념 행사를 개최합니다**

스튜어즈 베이 예술 위원회에서 기쁜 소식을 알려드립니다. 시 소유 신문사인 <스튜어즈 베이 저널>이 올해 스프링 플링 기념 행사를 후원할 예정입니다. **15**올해 기념 행사는 다른 해보다 많은 행사가 열립니다. 3월 20일 주간 내내 개최될 행사 중 몇 가지만 안내합니다.

주요 행사는 다음과 같습니다:
셰프의 베스트 브런치 – **16(A)**본 연례 인기 행사에는 지역 레스토랑의 요리사들이 참여합니다. 올해는 오테리아 레스토랑의 루이자 레예스가 요리사팀을 이끌어 커뮤니티 센터에서 맛있는 브런치 뷔페를 준비합니다. 표는 1인당 25달러입니다. **16(B)**수익금은 스튜어즈 베이 커뮤니티 센터에서 열리는 위원회 미술 교육 프로그램에 바로 전달됩니다. 예약하시려면 267-555-0122로 전화해 주세요. 표가 500장밖에 없으며 **16(C)**본 행사는 매번 매진됩니다.

닷 솔리 재즈 밴드 – 토요일 저녁 7시 30분부터 테라핀 파크 파빌리온에서 재즈 트리오가 무료 콘서트를 펼칩니다. 가벼운 간식을 구매할 수 있습니다. 비가 올 경우 콘서트는 타운홀 강당에서 개최될 예정입니다.

타운홀 미술전 및 경연대회 – 본 전시는 일주일 내내 타운홀 건물 정규 운영시간 동안 대중에게 개방됩니다. 주말에 있을 시상식에서는 작년 수상자 칼리브 마틴이 시상할 예정입니다.

17다음 주 <스튜어즈 베이 저널>에서 스프링 플링 기념 행사 프로그램 전체를 찾아보세요.

어휘 | feature 특별히 포함하다 scrumptious 아주 맛있는 proceeds 수익금 make a reservation 예약하다 refreshment 간식 comprehensive 종합적인, 포괄적인

15 스프링 플링 기념 행사에 대해 암시된 것은?

(A) 작년보다 더 많은 행사를 제공할 예정이다.
(B) 지역 업체 소유주가 주최한 것이다.
(C) 음악 공연이 며칠간 저녁에 열린다.
(D) 지역 관광을 증대하기 위해 계획됐다.

해설 | **추론**
공지의 첫 단락 두 번째 문장에서 '올해 기념 행사는 다른 해보다 많은 행사가 열린다(This year's celebration will feature more events than any other year)'고 했으므로 작년보다 더 많은 행사를 제공할 예정이라는 것을 짐작할 수 있다. 따라서 (A)가 정답이다.

어휘 | organize 준비하다, 조직하다 tourism 관광, 관광업

패러프레이징
지문의 than any other year → 보기의 than last year

16 셰프의 베스트 브런치에 대해 사실이 아닌 것은?

(A) 매년 개최된다.
(B) 예술 위원회를 위한 모금을 한다.
(C) 보통 많은 사람들이 참석한다.
(D) 객원 연설자가 나올 것이다.

해설 | **Not / True**
The Chef's Best Brunch가 언급된 부분에서 답을 찾아야 한다. 첫 문장에서 '본 연례 인기 행사(This yearly favorite)'라고 했으므로 (A)가 언급되었고, 네 번째 문장에서 '수익금은 스튜어즈 베이 커뮤니티 센터에서 열리는 위원회 미술 교육 프로그램에 바로 전달된다(The proceeds go directly to support the council's art education programs ~)'고 했으므로 (B)가 언급되었다. 마지막 문장에서 '본 행사는 매번 매진된다(this event always sells out)'고 했으므로 (C)도 언급되었다. 하지만 객원 연설자가 나올 것이라는 이야기는 없으므로 (D)가 정답이다.

어휘 | raise funds 모금하다, 자금을 조성하다 well attended 많은 사람이 참석한

패러프레이징
지문의 yearly → 보기의 annually
지문의 proceeds → 보기의 funds
지문의 always sells out → 보기의 usually well attended

17 공지에 따르면, 지역 신문에 게재될 것은?

(A) 축제 전체 일정표
(B) 요리 경연대회 관련 세부 사항
(C) 미술전 우승자의 간단한 약력
(D) 테라핀 파크 지도

해설 | **세부 사항**
공지의 마지막 문장에서 '다음 주 <스튜어즈 베이 저널>에서 스프링 플링 기념 행사 프로그램 전체를 찾아보라(Look for a comprehensive Spring Fling Celebration program in next week's *Stewards Bay Journal*)'고 했으므로 (A)가 정답이다.

어휘 | culinary 요리의 biography 전기

패러프레이징
지문의 in next week's *Stewards Bay Journal*
→ 질문의 in the local newspaper
지문의 a comprehensive Spring Fling Celebration program → 보기의 A complete schedule of the festival

[18-20] 회람

발신: 리암 페리, 마케팅 이사
수신: 마케팅부 전 직원
날짜: 8월 5일
제목: 주스 신제품 군

지난주는 새로 출시된 과일 주스 제품군의 무료 샘플 프로그램의 마지막 주였습니다. 잠재 고객들은 **19(C)무료 음료**와 향후 구매를 위한 **19(A)15퍼센트 할인 쿠폰**을 받았습니다. 그 다음에 그들은 **19(D)설문지** 작성을 요청받았습니다. 본 프로그램은 7월 15일부터 7월 31일까지 진행되었으며, 할인 쿠폰은 우리의 전 제품에 적용되는 것으로 10월 1일까지 유효합니다.

18본 프로그램을 통해 수집한 정보를 간략히 요약하면 다음과 같습니다:

• 세 가지 종류의 주스가 조사되었으며, 고객 선호도가 높은 순서대로 나열하면 망고 마운틴, 그레이트 구아바, 얌 코코플럼 순입니다.
• 설문 조사 분석에 따르면, **20고객들은 얌 코코플럼에 설탕이 너무 많이 들어 있다고 느꼈습니다.** (어떤 상품에도 인공감미료를 넣지 않았으며, 모두 주재료가 되는 과일 본연의 맛을 살렸기 때문에 이는 놀라운 결과입니다.)
• 많은 고객이 망고 마운틴과 그레이트 구아바의 맛의 조화를 "매우 뛰어나다"라고 평가했습니다.

다음 주에 회의를 열어 여러분과 이러한 점들에 대해 좀더 상세히 논의하고자 합니다. 제스 브론스키 씨가 본 회의의 의제를 정리하고 있으며, 곧 시간과 장소를 여러분에게 공지할 것입니다.

어휘 | line 제품군 potential 잠재적인 complimentary 무료의 questionnaire 설문지 apply to ~에 적용하다, 해당하다 full range of 전 범위의 following 다음에 말하는 것 briefly 간략히 summarize 요약하다 variety 종류, 품종 measure 측정하다 in descending order (큰 수에서 작은 수로의) 하향 순서로 contain 포함하다 artificially 인공적으로

flavor 맛을 내다; 맛 preserve 보존하다 be based on ~에 기반하다, 기초를 두다 rate 평가하다 combination 조화 superb 매우 뛰어난 put together 모으다, 편집하다 agenda 의제, 협의 사항 notify 통보하다

18 회람의 목적은?

(A) 조사 결과를 보고하는 것
(B) 마감의 연기를 요청하는 것
(C) 신제품의 이름을 추천하는 것
(D) 새로운 할인을 제안하는 것

해설 | 주제 / 목적
두 번째 단락 첫 문장에서 '프로그램을 통해 수집한 정보를 간단히 요약하면 다음과 같다(The following briefly summarizes information gathered through the program)'고 했으므로 정답은 (A)이다.

어휘 | extension 연장 recommend 추천하다

패러프레이징
지문의 information gathered through the program
→ 보기의 the results of a study

19 잠재 고객들이 받지 않은 것은?

(A) 할인권
(B) 성분 목록
(C) 주스의 무료 샘플
(D) 피드백 서식

해설 | Not / True
첫 번째 단락의 두 번째 문장과 세 번째 문장에서 (A), (C), (D)의 내용이 언급되었다. (A)는 15퍼센트 할인 쿠폰(15% discount coupons)을, (C)는 무료 음료(complimentary bottles of the drinks)를, (D)는 설문지(feedback questionnaires)를 바꿔 표현한 것이며, 성분 목록은 전혀 언급된 바 없으므로 정답은 (B)이다.

어휘 | certificate 증명서 ingredient 성분, 구성 요소

패러프레이징
지문의 discount coupons
→ 보기의 A discount certificate
지문의 complimentary bottles of the drinks
→ 보기의 A free sample of juice
지문의 feedback questionnaires
→ 보기의 A feedback form

20 잠재 고객들은 어떤 점을 지적하였는가?

(A) 인공 재료가 사용되었다.
(B) 할인 절차가 혼란스럽다.
(C) 주스의 양이 너무 적다.
(D) 주스 중 하나가 너무 달다.

해설 | 세부 사항
설문 조사의 결과가 제시된 두 번째 단락을 살펴봐야 한다. 나열된 결과 중 두 번째 내용 '고객들은 얌 코코플럼에 설탕이 너무 많이 들어 있다고 느꼈다(customers felt Yum Cocoplum contained too much sugar)'고 했으므로 정답은 (D)이다.

어휘 | artificial 인공의 procedure 절차, 진행

패러프레이징
지문의 contained too much sugar → 보기의 too sweet

[21-24] 공지

로저 윌킨슨, 페이스 앤 브라운 아키텍츠 사 합류

²¹금요일 회사 전체 회의에서 신시아 후 회장 겸 CEO는 오랜 물색 끝에 페이스 앤 브라운 사의 복원 프로젝트를 총괄할 신임 이사로 로저 H. 윌킨슨 씨를 선발했다고 발표했다. 5월 1일부터 ²²윌킨슨 씨는 지난 1월 3일 퇴직한 키이라 파웰스 씨의 후임 자리를 맡게 된다. 윌킨슨 씨는 런던에 있는 버셔 블레이크번스 사에서 수석 프로젝트 설계사로 근무하다가 이번에 페이스 앤 브라운 사로 옮기게 됐다. ²³런던에서는 지난 10년간 거주했다.

윌킨슨 씨는 대외적으로 회사를 대표하고 복원과 사적 보존으로 사업 영역을 확장하면서 회사의 명확한 전략적 방향을 설정하는 책임을 맡을 예정이다. 그는 아주 다양한 재능과 25년 이상의 설계 및 프로젝트 관리 경력을 자랑하는 인물이다. ²⁴멜버른에 소재한 32층짜리 유서 깊은 호텔인 스타샴 호텔의 복원 공사를 진행한 것으로 가장 유명하며, 이 건축물로 호주에서 가장 권위 있는 설계상인 쉴즈 메달을 받은 바 있다.

- - - - - - - - - -

어휘 | lengthy 긴 select 선택하다 restoration 복구, 복원 succeed 성공하다, 계승하다 retire 퇴직하다 be responsible for ~에 책임을 지다 represent 대표하다 externally 외부적으로 ensure 반드시 ~하게 하다, 보증하다 strategic 전략적인 direction 방향 expand 확장하다 historic preservation 사적·문화재 보존 diverse 다양한 talent 재능 prestigious 권위 있는, 명망 있는
---

21 이 공지는 어디에서 볼 수 있을 것 같은가?

(A) 신문 광고
(B) 경영학 교재
(C) 전화번호부
(D) 사보

해설 | 추론
첫 번째 단락의 핵심 내용은 금요일 회사 전체 회의에서 신임 이사로 로저 H. 윌킨슨 씨를 선발했다는 내용이며 이후 윌킨슨 씨가 맡을 책임과 개인 이력 소개로 이어지므로 사내 소식을 전달하는 사보에 어울릴 만한 글이다. 따라서 정답은 (D)이다.

22 키이라 파웰스 씨는 누구인가?

(A) 회사의 전임 회장
(B) 회사의 전임 이사
(C) 성공한 의류 디자이너
(D) 유명한 역사가

해설 | 세부 사항
첫 번째 단락에서 '윌킨슨 씨가 1월 3일 퇴직한 키이라 파웰스 씨의 후임이 된다(Mr. Wilkinson will succeed Keira Powells, who retired on January 3)'는 것을 알 수 있는데 앞서 윌킨슨 씨가 신임 이사로 선출되었다고 했으므로 정답은 (B)이다.

어휘 | former 이전의, 과거의 well-known 유명한 historian 역사가

23 로저 윌킨슨 씨는 런던에서 얼마나 오랫동안 살았는가?

(A) 10년
(B) 15년
(C) 25년
(D) 32년

해설 | 세부 사항
London을 키워드로 잡고 찾아보면, 지문 첫 번째 단락 마지막 문장에서 '윌킨슨 씨가 런던에 있는 회사에서 근무했는데, 런던에서는 지난 10년간 거주했다(Wilkinson ~ in London, where he has lived for the last ten years)'고 했다. 따라서 정답은 (A)이다.

24 공지에 따르면, 로저 윌킨슨 씨는 무엇으로 유명한가?

(A) 페이스 앤 브라운 사에서 복원 프로젝트를 총괄한 것
(B) 버셔 블레이크번스 사에서 가장 오래 근무한 이사인 것
(C) 멜버른에서 유서 깊은 건물을 새단장한 것
(D) 런던에서 유수의 디자인상을 받은 것

해설 | 세부 사항
두 번째 단락 중간에 '멜버른에 소재한 32층짜리 유서 깊은 호텔인 스타샴 호텔의 복원 공사를 진행한 것으로 가장 유명하다(He is probably best known for his restoration work ~ in Melbourne)'고 언급되어 있으므로 (C)가 정답이다. (A)는 이번에 부임해서 앞으로 할 일이며, (B)는 버셔 블레이크번스 사에서 근무한 것은 맞지만 가장 오래 근무했는지는 알 수 없으므로 오답이다. 또한 그는 런던이 아닌 호주에서 상을 받았으므로 (D)도 오답이다.

어휘 | direct 지휘하다, (길을) 안내하다 renovate 보수하다

패러프레이징
지문의 restoration work → 보기의 Renovating

UNIT 03 광고/안내문

기출 예제   본책 p.082

윈스턴 아이스크림
19 마켓 가, 돌린턴
792-555-0197

일단 저희 프리미엄 아이스크림과 케이크를 맛보시면 계속해서 다시 찾게 되실 겁니다. 윈스턴은 오시기 편리한 곳에 위치한 온 가족을 위한 디저트 가게이며, 시에서 유일하게 개별 파티룸을 갖춘 아이스크림 매장입니다.

저희는 제공합니다:
- 15가지 다양한 아이스크림 - **¹지역 생산 재료를 이용해 매장에서 직접 제조**
- 다양한 과일 및 견과류 토핑
- 주문 제작 아이스크림 케이크
- 고객을 위한 무료 무선 인터넷

영업시간: 화요일-일요일 오전 11시-오후 8시
²하계 (5-10월): 밤 10시까지 영업

³수요일은 키즈 데이로, 모든 어린이 사이즈 아이스크림을 50퍼센트 할인해드립니다.

어휘 | conveniently located 편리한 위치에 있는, 위치가 좋은 ingredient 재료, 성분 made to order 주문 제작된 complimentary 무료의 patron 고객, 후원자

기출 ETS TEST   본책 p.084

1 (D)	**2** (B)	**3** (D)	**4** (B)	**5** (B)	**6** (C)
7 (D)	**8** (D)	**9** (B)	**10** (B)	**11** (B)	**12** (D)
13 (B)	**14** (C)	**15** (C)	**16** (A)	**17** (D)	**18** (B)
19 (D)	**20** (B)	**21** (B)	**22** (C)	**23** (B)	**24** (A)

[1-2] 웹사이트 안내문

돌로미노

홈페이지	**돌로미노 뉴스**	회사 소개	지점 안내

게시일: 10월 1일 화요일

다음에 쇼핑하러 가실 때 돈을 절약하고 싶으신가요? **¹돌로미노에서 오늘부터 시작되는 시즌 종료 세일을 이용해 보세요.** 폭넓은 상품을 경쟁력 있는 가격에 판매합니다. **²(A),(C),(D)신발, 재킷, 셔츠, 시계, 전자레인지, 선풍기** 등 매우 다양한 제품을 정가에서 최대 60%까지 할인 판매합니다. 저희 온라인 상점 www.dolominos.com을 통해 주문하시는 상품에도 할인이 똑같이 적용됩니다.

이번 행사에는 다른 할인 행사나 할인 쿠폰과 중복으로 사용될 수 없습니다. 세일은 10월 10일에 끝납니다.

어휘 | end-of-season sale 시즌 종료 세일 extensive 광범위한, 폭넓은 inventory 재고(품) a wide assortment of 매우 다양한 offer 할인 행사 be combined with ~와 결합되다

1 광고되고 있는 것은?

(A) 신제품 구입 가능
(B) 신규 매장 오픈
(C) 단골 고객을 위한 경연 대회
(D) 제품 가격 할인

해설 | 주제 / 목적
지문 초반에서 '오늘부터 시작되는 시즌 종료 세일을 이용해 보라(Take advantage of the end-of-season sale at Dolomino's, starting today)'고 하면서 할인 폭, 할인 제품, 세일 기간 등에 관해 안내하고 있다. 따라서 정답은 (D)이다.

어휘 | frequent customer 단골 고객

2 상점에서 구입 가능한 상품으로 언급되지 않은 것은?

(A) 가전제품   (B) 원예 도구
(C) 신발류   (D) 의류

해설 | Not / True
지문 중반에 할인 품목이 열거되어 있다. microwave ovens와 fans는 (A)에 해당하고, shoes는 (C), jackets와 shirts는 (D)에 해당한다. 원예 도구는 언급되지 않았으므로 정답은 (B)이다.

어휘 | gardening 원예 footwear 신발류

[3-4] 광고

> ### 취업 박람회
> 메츠거 항공
>
> 메츠거 항공에서는 국제선 승무원을 찾고 있으며 마이애미의 메츠거 항공사 센터에서 3월 1일 화요일 오전 9시부터 취업 박람회를 개최합니다.
>
> 자격 요건:
> - 야간, 주말, **3(A)휴일 근무 가능자**
> - **3(C)21세 이상자**
> - **3(B)이주 가능자**
> - 우수한 의사소통 능력 소유자
> - 스트레스가 많은 상황에서도 역할을 잘 수행하는 자
> - 타인과 협업 가능한 자
>
> 메츠거 항공은 전 직원에게 유급 휴가, 연2회 임금 인상, 전문성 개발 과정 등 많은 혜택을 제공합니다.

관심 있는 분들은 제출할 이력서를 준비하고 취업 박람회에서 지원서를 작성하여야 합니다. 1차 면접은 오후 동안 진행됩니다.

4합격자들은 도쿄에 있는 메츠거 항공 교육 시설에서 6주간 보내게 됩니다. 교육 프로그램을 이수한 신규 승무원들은 바르셀로나 또는 밀라노에서 근무하게 됩니다.

어휘 | flight attendant 승무원 requirement 요건, 필요조건 superior 우수한 function 기능하다 paid vacation 유급 휴가 semi-annual 반년의 raise 임금 인상 initial 초기의 successful candidate 합격자 certified 공인된

3 메츠거 항공의 승무원이 되는 데 필요한 요건으로 언급되지 않은 것은?

(A) 휴일 근무 의향
(B) 새로운 도시로 이주할 의향
(C) 최저 연령 21세
(D) 최소 1년 경력

해설 | Not / True
Requirements로 나열된 부분을 읽고 오답을 지워 나간다. (A)는 첫 번째 요건인 휴일 근무 가능자(Must be able to work nights, weekends, and holidays)에 포함되어 있고, (B)는 세 번째 자격 요건인 이주 가능자(Must be prepared to relocate)이고, (C)는 두 번째 자격인 21세 이상자(Must be at least 21 years old)이므로 정답은 (D)이다.

어휘 | willingness 의향 minimum 최소한의

패러프레이징
지문의 at least → 보기의 minimum
지문의 relocate → 보기의 move to a new city

4 합격자는 어디에서 승무원 교육을 받는가?

(A) 마이애미
(B) 도쿄
(C) 바르셀로나
(D) 밀라노

해설 | 세부 사항
마지막 단락에서 '합격자는 도쿄의 메츠거 항공 교육 시설에서 6주를 보낸다(Successful candidates will spend ~ Training Facility in Tokyo)'고 하므로 정답은 (B)이다. (A) Miami는 취업 박람회가 열리는 곳이다.

[5-7] 안내문

> ### 5그레이디 가스 회사 요금 설명
>
> **5월 배달료:** 그레이디 및 인근 지역의 거주 고객 및 기업 고객에게 매월 천연 가스를 배달하는 요금입니다.
>
> **5서비스 개시 수수료:** **6거주 고객 또는 기업 고객 계정을**

신규로 개설하여 서비스를 개시하면 20달러의 요금이 부과됩니다. 이것은 고객의 첫 번째 청구서에 표시될 일회성 요금입니다.

⁵신용카드 결제: 신용카드 결제 시 1퍼센트의 카드 수수료가 부과됩니다. 은행 계좌에서 월 자동 이체로 등록하면 해당 수수료를 내지 않아도 됩니다.

⁵연체료 부과: 청구 기간 종료 후 21일 내에 결제가 이뤄져야 합니다. 청구 기간 및 결제 기일은 모든 고객 청구서의 첫 페이지에 명확히 명시되어 있습니다. 총 지불액 결제가 기일에서 10일 이상 지나고 이뤄질 경우 25달러의 연체 수수료가 다음 달 청구서에 추가됩니다.

⁵서비스 복구 수수료: 청구서 미납으로 인해 서비스가 종료될 경우, 서비스 복구 시 15달러의 수수료가 부과됩니다. 해당 수수료는 부가되는 연체료와 별도입니다. 요청 당일 서비스가 복구되려면, 당일 오전 11시까지 결제가 이뤄져야 합니다. **⁷그레이디 가스 회사 555-0141로 전화하셔서 신용카드로 결제하시거나** 주니퍼 길 514번지에 있는 고객 서비스 센터를 방문하시면 됩니다.

어휘 | charge 요금; 청구하다 residential 거주의 surrounding 인근의, 주위의 initiation 개시, 시작 convenience fee 카드 결제 시 내는 소액의 수수료 assess (요금을) 부과하다 electronic transfer 온라인 이체 reinstatement 복구, 회복 in addition to ~ 이외에

---

5 안내문의 목적은?

(A) 천연 가스 배달료가 곧 인상된다는 것을 알리려고
(B) 가스 서비스 요금이 어떻게 결정되는지 세부 사항을 알려주려고
(C) 고객의 요금 자동이체 요청을 확정하려고
(D) 고객 서비스 센터가 영업시간을 연장했음을 언급하려고

해설 | 주제 / 목적
안내문 제목에서 그레이디 가스 회사 요금 설명(Explanation of Grady Gas Company's fees)이라고 했고, 월 배달료(Monthly Delivery Charge), 서비스 개시 수수료(Service Initiation Fee), 신용카드 결제(Payments by Credit Card), 연체료 부과(Late Payment Charge), 서비스 복구 수수료(Service Reinstatement Fee)에 대해 세부적으로 설명하고 있으므로 (B)가 정답이다.

어휘 | determine 결정하다 funds 자금, 돈 extend 늘리다, 연장하다

6 안내문에 따르면, 고객의 첫 번째 청구서에 항상 표시되는 요금은 얼마인가?

(A) 10달러
(B) 15달러
(C) 20달러
(D) 25달러

해설 | 세부 사항
a customer's first bill을 키워드로 잡고 a customer's first bill이 언급되는 부분에서 답을 찾아야 한다. 서비스 개시 수수료(Service Initiation Fee)에 대한 설명에서 '거주 고객 또는 기업 고객 계정을 신규로 개설하여 서비스를 개시하면 20달러의 요금이 부과된다(A fee of $20 will be charged to open a new residential or business account with the company and initiate service)'고 한 후, '이것은 고객의 첫 번째 청구서에 표시될 일회성 요금(This is a one-time fee that will appear on a customer's first bill)'이라고 했으므로 (C)가 정답이다.

패러프레이징
지문의 a one-time fee → 질문의 a charge

7 그레이디 가스 회사에 대해 명시된 것은?

(A) 주니퍼 길에 있는 지점을 폐쇄한다.
(B) 고객 요청 당일에는 서비스를 복구할 수 없다.
(C) 기업 고객에게만 서비스를 제공한다.
(D) 전화로 신용카드 결제가 가능하다.

해설 | Not / True
서비스 복구 수수료(Service Reinstatement Fee)에 대한 설명에서 '그레이디 가스 회사 555-0141로 전화하셔서 신용카드로 결제하라(by telephoning Grady Gas Company at 555-0141 to make a credit card payment)'고 했으므로 (D)가 정답이다.

어휘 | reinstate 복구하다, 회복하다

패러프레이징
지문의 by telephoning → 보기의 over the phone

[8-10] 광고

아파트 매물: 오싱턴에 있는 밝은 침실 하나짜리 아파트
임대료: 1,700달러 / 월, 공과금 포함
상세 소개: 이제 운영 4년째를 맞는 퍼널드 부동산은 토론토에서 가장 혁신적인 부동산 관리회사 중 하나입니다. **¹⁰지난 2년간 저희는 역사적인 시가지에 있는 ⁸여섯 개의 빈티지한 아파트 건물을 사들여 보수했습니다.** 저희는 회사를 키우면서 계속 그런 전도유망한 부동산을 훌륭한 임대 아파트 단지로 변화시킬 계획입니다. **⁸현재 고색창연한 ⁹⁽ᴬ⁾12층 건물인 더 트레이던의 3층에 침실 하나짜리 아파트 한 채가 비어 있습니다. ⁹⁽ᶜ⁾새롭게 보수되었으며** 인기 있는 오싱턴 동네에 위치한 더 트레이던은 "도시 속의 풍요로운 삶"이라는 모토를 구현하고 있습니다. 더 트레이던의 로비 입구에서 바로 길 건너편에 있는 유명한 가스파로 카페에서 갓 구운 페이스트리를 즐기세요. 그런 다음 초과된 칼로리는 **⁹⁽ᴰ⁾건물 지하에 있는 무료 24시간 체력단련실**에서 운동으로 태우세요. 아니면 입주자 라운지에서 그냥 편안히 쉬세요. 이 호화로운 아파트는

커다란 수납장도 딸려 있고 쇼 공원도 보입니다. 집을 보고 싶으시면 555-0127번으로 연락 주십시오.

어휘 | utilities 공과금 operation 운영 realty 부동산 innovative 혁신적인 property management firm 부동산 관리회사 vintage 빈티지한(오래되어도 새롭고 가치 있는) historical 역사적인 vacant 비어 있는 venerable 고색 창연한 embody 상징하다, 구현하다 motto 모토, 좌우명 fitness center 체력단련실, 헬스클럽 basement 지하실 tenant 입주자 closet 수납장, 벽장 viewing (집) 둘러보기

8 퍼널드 부동산에 대해 암시된 것은?

(A) 다른 회사와 합병할 계획이다.
(B) 나무 수납장도 디자인한다.
(C) 이 회사의 계약은 2년간 지속된다.
(D) 이 회사의 임대 아파트는 오래된 건물에 있다.

해설 | 추론
광고 중간에 보면 '여섯 개의 빈티지한 아파트 건물을 사들여 보수했으며(we have acquired and renovated six vintage apartment buildings)', '현재 고색창연한 12층 건물 3층에 아파트 한 채가 비어 있다(We now have a vacant 1-bedroom, third-floor apartment ~ building)'는 내용이 있으므로 정답은 (D)이다.

패러프레이징
지문의 six vintage apartment buildings
→ 보기의 older buildings

9 더 트레이던에 대해 언급되지 않은 것은?

(A) 12층짜리이다.
(B) 로비에 카페가 있다.
(C) 최근에 보수되었다.
(D) 그 건물에 체력단련실이 있다.

해설 | Not / True
(A)는 지문 중간의 in the venerable 12-story building 에서, (C)는 그 다음 문장의 Newly renovated에서, (D)는 지문 후반부의 fitness center in the building's basement에서 각각 언급되었다. 카페는 로비에 있는 것이 아니라 로비 정문의 건너편(just across the street from The Traydan's lobby entrance)에 있으므로 정답은 (B)이다.

10 [1], [2], [3], [4]로 표시된 곳 중에서 다음 문장이 들어가기에 가장 적합한 곳은?

"저희는 회사를 키우면서 계속 그런 전도유망한 부동산을 훌륭한 임대 아파트 단지로 변화시킬 계획입니다."

(A) [1]　　(B) [2]　　(C) [3]　　(D) [4]

해설 | 문장 삽입
제시된 문장에서 정답의 단서는 such promising properties(그런 전도유망한 부동산)이므로 지문에서 이와

관련된 부분을 찾아야 한다. 첫 번째 단락의 '지난 2년간 역사적인 시가지에 있는 여섯 개의 빈티지한 아파트 건물을 사들여 보수했다(Over the past two years, we have acquired and renovated six vintage apartment buildings in historical city neighborhoods)'에서 six vintage apartment buildings라는 부분이 의미상 such promising properties와 연결되므로 제시된 문장은 [2]에 들어가야 한다. 따라서 정답은 (B)이다.

[11-14] 안내문

데미 NX-작동법　　　　　　　　　　p.4

11데미 NX 무선 전기 드릴 구매를 축하드립니다! 다음 몇 페이지에 걸쳐 이 최첨단 전동 공구를 작동시키는 데 필요한 기본 지침들이 설명되어 있습니다.

배터리
귀하의 데미 NX 무선 전기 드릴은 두 개의 충전용 18볼트 배터리(제품 패키지에 포함)로 작동됩니다. **12배터리는 NX 무선 전기 드릴과 데미 18볼트 배터리 충전기(제품 패키지에 포함)와 호환되도록 특별히 고안된 것입니다.** 처음에 드릴을 사용하기 전에 배터리를 충전기에 넣고 적어도 6시간 동안 충전하십시오. 그리고 배터리를 드릴의 배터리 장착부에 넣으십시오(7페이지 상세 그림 참조).

데미 18볼트 배터리 충전기는 최신 배터리 충전 기술을 사용하기 때문에 **13배터리를 쓰지 않을 때는 항상 충전기에 넣어 두어야 합니다.** 그러면 NX 무선 전기 드릴을 필요할 때마다 즉시 사용할 수 있습니다. 데미 충전용 18볼트 배터리의 평균 수명은 사용 정도에 따라 다릅니다. **14충전기나 드릴이 손상되는 걸 막기 위해 데미 배터리만을 사용하십시오.**

어휘 | Congratulations on ~을 축하드립니다 cordless (전기 기구가) 무선의 electric drill 전기 드릴 guideline 지침 state-of-the-art 최첨단의, 최신식의 power tool 전동 공구 power 동력을 공급하다 rechargeable 재충전되는 specifically 특별히 be designed for ~을 위해 고안되다 compatibility 호환성, 양립성 charger 충전기 insert 삽입하다 compartment 구획 diagram 도표, 도해 make use of ~을 이용하다 indefinitely 무기한으로 at a moment's notice 당장에, 즉석에서 average life 평균 수명 depending on ~에 따라 brand 상표

11 안내문은 어디에서 볼 수 있겠는가?

(A) 데미 제품 광고에서
(B) 전동 공구 사용설명서에서
(C) 주택 개량 기술에 관한 책에서
(D) 인기 브랜드 공구 제품 후기에서

해설 | 추론
지문의 첫 문장에서 '전기 드릴 구매를 축하한다'고 말한

후 그 다음 문장에서 '다음 몇 페이지에 걸쳐 전동 공구를 작동시키는 데 필요한 기본 지침들이 설명되어 있다(The following pages will explain the basic guidelines for operating this state-of-the-art power tool)'고 했으므로 (B)가 정답이다.

어휘 | advertisement 광고 instruction manual 사용설명서, 취급설명서 home improvement 주택 개조[개량]

12 배터리에 대해 명시된 것은?

(A) 2주마다 충전해야 한다.
(B) 공장에서 충전되었다.
(C) 한정된 품질 보증을 받는다.
(D) 이 제품에 사용하도록 고안되었다.

해설 | Not/True
배터리 항목의 첫 단락 두 번째 문장에서 '배터리는 NX 무선 전기 드릴과 데미 18볼트 배터리 충전기와 호환되도록 특별히 고안되었다(These are specifically designed ~ with the Demy 18-Volt Battery Charger)'고 하므로 (D)가 정답이다. (A), (B), (C) 모두 지문에 언급되어 있지 않다.

어휘 | limited warranty (일부 항목에 한해서만 보증해 주는) 한정된 품질 보증

13 안내문에 따르면, 배터리는 어디에 보관해야 하는가?

(A) 에어컨이 설치된 장소
(B) 배터리 충전기 안
(C) 전동 공구 안
(D) 보호 케이스

해설 | 세부 사항
배터리 항목의 두 번째 단락에서 '배터리를 쓰지 않을 때는 항상 충전기에 넣어 두어야 한다(you should leave your batteries in the charger indefinitely between uses)'고 하므로 (B)가 정답이다.

어휘 | air-conditioned 에어컨이 있는, 냉방장치가 된

14 이 안내문에서는 무엇을 하지 말라고 주의를 주는가?

(A) 약하게 충전된 배터리를 사용하는 것
(B) 2주 동안 배터리를 한 번 이상 충전하는 것
(C) 다른 제조업체가 만든 배터리를 사용하는 것
(D) 배터리를 충분히 충전하기 전에 충전기를 여는 것

해설 | 세부 사항
맨 마지막 문장에서 '충전기나 드릴이 손상되는 걸 막기 위해 데미 배터리만 사용하라(To avoid possible damage to your charger or drill, use only Demy brand batteries)'고 권장하고 있다. 이는 곧 다른 업체의 배터리를 사용하지 말라는 의미이므로 (C)가 정답이다.

어휘 | manufacturer 제조업자[업체]

[15-17] 안내 책자

써모제스트로 난방하세요!

올 겨울, 써모제스트 난방 시스템으로 집이나 사무실을 더욱 편안한 장소로 만들어 보세요! 전통적인 실내 난방기는 방의 한 부분에만 열을 집중시켜 추운 부분이 많습니다. 이와 대조적으로 써모제스트 난방 시스템은 모든 공간을 고르게 데워 구석구석 온도가 쾌적해집니다. 또한 사용 중인 방만 난방하므로 **15(B)에너지 소비량을 줄여줍니다.**

써모제스트에는 회전 바퀴 및 견고하지만 경량의 핸들 세트가 함께 들어 있어 **15(D)자리 이동이 수월합니다.** **15(A)공기를 건조하게 하는 대부분의 실내 난방기와 달리 저희 특허 시스템은 정상 습도를 유지할 수 있도록 돕습니다.**

1612월 31일까지 우편 또는 온라인으로 접수된 주문 건은 25퍼센트 할인에 무료 배송까지 받으실 수 있습니다. **17해당 일자 이후에는 정상 소매가와 1대당 35달러의 배송비가 청구될 예정입니다.** 어떠한 이유로든 저희 제품에 만족하지 못하신다면 60일 이내에 배송비를 포함해 전액 환불을 받으시고 반품하시면 됩니다.

- - - - - - - - - -

네! 절감하고 싶습니다. _____ 대 보내주세요.

☐ 12월 31일까지 주문하겠습니다. 25% 할인을 적용해서 1대당 총 120달러를 적용해 주십시오.

☐ **17**12월 31일 이후 주문하겠습니다. 1대당 160달러와 1대당 배송비 35달러를 청구해 주십시오.

- - - - - - - - - -

어휘 | concentrate 집중시키다, 모으다 by contrast 대조적으로, 그에 반해서 evenly 고르게, 균등하게 comfortable temperature 쾌적 온도 consumption 소비 sturdy 견고한 lightweight 경량의 effortless 수월하게, 힘들이지 않고 patented 특허를 받은 humidity 습도 retail price 소매가 full refund 전액 환불

15 난방 시스템의 장점으로 언급되지 않은 것은?

(A) 공기를 건조하게 만들지 않는다.
(B) 효율적인 에너지 사용을 촉진한다.
(C) 유사 제품들보다 저렴하다.
(D) 쉽게 옮길 수 있다.

해설 | Not/True
안내 책자의 두 번째 단락 마지막 문장에서 '공기를 건조하게 하는 대부분의 실내 난방기와 달리 써모제스트 특허 시스템은 정상 습도를 유지할 수 있도록 돕는다(Unlike most space heaters, which dry out the air, our patented system helps maintain normal humidity)'고 했으므로 (A)가 언급되었고, 첫 단락 마지막 문장에서 '사용 중인 방만 난방하므로 에너지 소비량을 줄여준다(the Thermozest system reduces your energy consumption)'고 했으므로 (B)가 언급되었다.

두 번째 단락 첫 문장에서 '써모제스트에는 회전 바퀴 및 견고하지만 경량의 핸들 세트가 함께 들어 있어 자리 이동이 수월하다(making transferring it between locations effortless)'고 했으므로 (D)가 언급되었다. 하지만 유사 제품들보다 저렴하다는 이야기는 없으므로 (C)가 정답이다.

어휘 | efficient 효율적인

패러프레이징
지문의 helps maintain normal humidity
→ 보기의 avoids making the air drier
지문의 reduces your energy consumption
→ 보기의 promotes efficient energy use
지문의 making transferring it between locations effortless → 보기의 be moved easily

16 고객들이 배송비를 내지 않는 방법은?

(A) 기한 이전에 주문한다.
(B) 2대 이상 구매한다.
(C) 1년짜리 서비스 계약을 맺는다.
(D) 웹사이트에 코드를 입력한다.

해설 | 세부 사항
shipping을 키워드로 잡고 shipping이 언급되는 부분에서 답을 찾아야 한다. 세 번째 단락 첫 문장에서 '12월 31일까지 우편 또는 온라인으로 접수된 주문 건은 25퍼센트 할인에 무료 배송까지 받으실 수 있다(Orders received by mail or online by December 31 will receive a 25% discount PLUS free shipping)'고 했으므로 (A)가 정답이다.

어휘 | contract 계약

패러프레이징
지문의 by December 31 → 보기의 before a deadline

17 난방기의 정상 소매가는?

(A) 25달러
(B) 35달러
(C) 120달러
(D) 160달러

해설 | 세부 사항
retail price를 키워드로 잡고 retail price가 언급되는 부분에서 답을 찾아야 한다. 세 번째 단락 두 번째 문장에서 '해당 일자 12월 31일 이후에는 정상 소매가와 1대당 35달러의 배송비가 청구될 예정(After that date, customers will be billed the normal retail price plus $35 shipping per unit)'이라고 하였고, 안내 책자 마지막 부분에서 '12월 31일 이후 주문하는 경우 1대당 160달러와 1대당 배송비 35달러를 청구한다'고 했으므로 정상 소매가는 160달러임을 알 수 있다. 따라서 (D)가 정답이다.

[18-20] 광고

> ## 무딘 칼날 때문에 힘드십니까? 스킬포인트가 도와드리겠습니다!
>
> 스킬포인트는 토론토 도시권의 식당, 식료품점, 상업용 주방에서 칼을 최상의 상태로 유지할 수 있게 도와드립니다. **18얼마나 무디고 손상됐는지에 관계없이 모든 종류의 칼을 갈아드립니다. 또한** 푸드 프로세서, 슬라이서, 강판, 가위 등의 날도 작업해 드립니다.
>
> **아래의 선택사항 중에서 고르세요:**
>
> • **19(A)물건을 저희에게 가져다주세요.** 매주 금요일 오전 8시부터 정오까지 웨스트 파크 가 4512번지에서 영업합니다. 날을 가는 동안 기다려 주세요. 보통 15분이면 됩니다.
>
> • **19(B)다운타운 파머스 마켓을 방문하세요. 주말마다 오전 9시에서 오후 1시 사이에 저희 야외 부스에 칼날을 맡기셔도 됩니다.** 쇼핑을 마치고 찾아가세요!
>
> • 저희가 방문합니다. **19(C)계시는 곳으로 숙련된 전문가를 보내 현장에서 칼날을 갈아드립니다.** 월요일부터 목요일까지 오전, 오후, 저녁 시간대가 있습니다. **20저희 웹사이트 www.torontosp.com을 방문하셔서 편리한 시간을 신청하세요.**
>
> 어휘 | commercial 상업적인 no matter how 아무리 ~ 해도 grater 강판 experienced 경험이 풍부한, 숙련된 dispatch 보내다, 파견하다 premises 구내, 건물 on-site 현장에서 sign up for ~에[을] 신청하다

18 스킬포인트가 제공하는 서비스는?

(A) 중고 장비 구입
(B) 주방 도구 연마
(C) 식품 품질 및 준비 평가
(D) 요식업 종사자 교육

해설 | 세부 사항
광고의 첫 단락 두 번째 문장에서 '얼마나 무디고 손상됐는지에 관계없이 모든 종류의 칼을 갈아드린다(We sharpen all types of knives)'고 한 후, '푸드 프로세서, 슬라이서, 강판, 가위 등의 날도 작업해 드린다(We also work on blades for food processors, slicers, graters, and scissors)'고 했으므로 (B)가 정답이다.

어휘 | rate 평가하다

패러프레이징
지문의 knives, food processors, slicers, graters, and scissors → 보기의 kitchen tools

19 스킬포인트의 서비스를 이용하는 방법으로 언급되지 않은 것은?

(A) 매장 방문하기
(B) 야외 시장 방문하기
(C) 직원 방문 받기
(D) 요식업계 대회 참석하기

해설 | Not / True
첫 번째 선택사항에서 '물건을 영업점에 가져다 달라(Bring your items to us)'고 했으므로 (A)는 언급되었고, 두 번째 선택사항에서 '다운타운 파머스 마켓을 방문하라(Visit the Downtown Farmers Market)'고 한 후 '주말마다 오전 9시에서 오후 1시 사이에 저희 야외 부스에 칼날을 맡겨도 된다(you can drop off your blades at our open-air booth ~)'고 했으므로 (B)가 언급되었다. 세 번째 선택사항에서 '계시는 곳으로 숙련된 전문가를 보내 현장에서 칼날을 갈아드린다(An experienced professional will be dispatched to your premises to sharpen all your blades on-site)'고 했으므로 (C)가 언급되었다. 요식업계 대회 참석에 관한 이야기는 없으므로 (D)가 정답이다.

어휘 | storefront 점포, 상점 representative 대표, 대리인

패러프레이징
지문의 Bring your items to us
→ 보기의 Visiting a storefront location
지문의 open-air → 보기의 outdoor
지문의 An experienced professional
→ 보기의 a representative

20 광고에 따르면, 고객이 회사 웹사이트를 통해 할 수 있는 것은?

(A) 가격 견적서 요청하기
(B) 예약 잡기
(C) 서비스 관련 의견 남기기
(D) 보도 자료 읽기

해설 | 세부 사항
Web site를 키워드로 잡고 Web site가 언급되는 부분에서 답을 찾아야 한다. 마지막 단락 마지막 문장에서 '저희 웹사이트 www.torontosp.com을 방문하셔서 편리한 시간을 신청하라(Visit our Web site ~ to sign up for a convenient time)'고 했으므로 예약을 잡으라는 것을 알 수 있다. 따라서 (B)가 정답이다.

어휘 | price estimate 가격 견적서 press release 보도 자료

패러프레이징
지문의 sign up for a convenient time
→ 보기의 Make an appointment

[21-24] 안내문

> ### 코빌 음악 축제
>
> 모든 종류의 훌륭한 음악을 즐기며 시간을 기부하고 싶으십니까? 그렇다면 제15회 연례 코빌 음악 축제에서 자원봉사를 해 보세요! **21**올해 축제는 9월 24일부터 30일까지 코빌 카운티 축제 마당에서 개최되며 지역에서 인기 있는 비레오스 팝 밴드, 재즈 마블스, 치앙 현악 4중주단을 비롯해 50여 개 이상의 재능 있는 그룹의 음악이 포함됩니다.
>
> **자원봉사자는 이런 업무를 해야 합니다:**
> - **23(D)**9월 1일부터 모든 전단을 디자인 및 게시하고 보도 자료를 보내는 등 홍보 관련 업무를 도와야 합니다.
> - 9월 22일부터 28일까지 음악가들을 맞이하고 배정된 숙소 위치 파악을 할 수 있도록 도와야 합니다. **22**타 지역 음악가들 모두 지역 내 가정에서 맞을 예정입니다.
> - **23(A)**매표소를 운영하고 **23(C)**축제 중에는 방문객들에게 주차장을 안내하며 전반적인 정보를 제공해야 합니다.
>
> 감사의 의미로 **24**각 자원봉사자는 코빌 음악 축제의 한정판 티셔츠와 무료 입장권 4장을 받으시게 됩니다.
>
> 자원봉사 의향이 있으시다면 8월 17일까지 마타 세드락에게 msedlak@corvillemusicfest.org로 연락 주십시오.
>
> ---
> 어휘 | donate 기부하다 fairground 축제 마당 publicity 홍보 flyer 전단 press release 언론 발표, 보도 자료 assignment 배정 host 주인으로서 ~을 접대하다 appreciation 감사 complimentary 무료의

21 축제에 대해 명시된 것은?

(A) 9월 1일에 개최될 예정이다.
(B) 다양한 음악 유형이 포함된다.
(C) 전문 음악가에 의해 개최된다.
(D) 우천 시 일정이 변경될 수 있다.

해설 | Not / True
안내문의 첫 단락 세 번째 문장에서 '올해 축제는 9월 24일부터 30일까지 개최된다(This year's festival runs from September 24 to 30)'고 했으므로 (A)는 오답이다. 첫 단락 마지막 문장에서 '올해 축제는 지역에서 인기 있는 비레오스 팝 밴드, 재즈 마블스, 치앙 현악 4중주단을 비롯해 50여 개 이상의 재능 있는 그룹의 음악이 포함된다(features music from more than 50 talented groups, including local favorites Vireos Pop Band, Jazz Marvels, and Chiang String Quartet)'고 했으므로 (B)가 정답이다.

어휘 | a variety of 다양한

패러프레이징
지문의 local favorites Vireos Pop Band, Jazz Marvels, and Chiang String Quartet
→ 보기의 a variety of music types

22 일부 연주자에 대해 암시된 것은?

(A) 중고 악기를 기부할 것이다.
(B) 축제 포스터를 제공할 것이다.
(C) 코빌 내 가정에 머무를 것이다.
(D) 축제에서 주요 상을 받을 것이다.

해설 | 추론
자원봉사자가 해야 할 두 번째 업무에서 '타 지역 음악가들 모두 지역 내 가정에서 맞을 예정(All out-of-town musicians will be hosted by area families)'이라고 했으므로 일부 연주자들은 코빌 내 가정에 머물 것이라는 것을 짐작할 수 있다. 따라서 (C)가 정답이다.

어휘 | instrument 악기

패러프레이징
지문의 musicians → 질문의 performers

23 자원봉사자가 하지 않을 업무는?

(A) 축제 공연 표 판매하기
(B) 음악가들을 축제 마당으로 이동시키기
(C) 방문객들에게 주차 장소 안내하기
(D) 홍보 자료 배포하기

해설 | Not/True
자원봉사자가 해야 할 업무 항목에서 답을 찾아야 한다. 세 번째 업무에서 '매표소를 운영하고 축제 중에는 방문객들에게 주차장을 안내해야 한다(operate the ticket booth, direct guests to the parking areas during the festival)'고 했으므로 (A)와 (C)가 언급되었다. 첫 업무에서 '9월 1일부터 모든 전단을 디자인 및 게시하고 보도 자료를 보내는 등 홍보 관련 업무를 도와야 한다(help with publicity—designing and posting all flyers and sending press releases—starting September 1)'고 했으므로 (D)가 언급되었다. 하지만 음악가들을 축제 마당으로 이동시키기에 대한 이야기는 없으므로 (B)가 정답이다.

어휘 | distribute 배포하다, 나눠주다

패러프레이징
지문의 operate the ticket booth
→ 보기의 Selling tickets
지문의 direct guests to the parking areas
→ 보기의 Showing visitors where to park
지문의 sending press releases
→ 보기의 Distributing publicity materials

24 자원봉사자들이 무료로 받을 것은?

(A) 의류 한 벌
(B) 무대 뒤 공간 출입증
(C) 축제 녹화 동영상
(D) 축제 기간 중 간식 및 식사

해설 | 세부 사항
receive를 키워드로 잡고 receive가 언급되는 부분에서 답을 찾아야 한다. 세 번째 단락에서 '각 자원봉사자는 코빌 음악 축제의 한정판 티셔츠와 무료 입장권 4장을 받게 된다(each volunteer will receive a limited edition Corville Music Festival T-shirt and four complimentary tickets)'고 했으므로 (A)가 정답이다.

어휘 | article 물품, 물건

패러프레이징
지문의 T-shirt → 보기의 An article of clothing

UNIT 04 기사

기출 예제 본책 p.092

웰컴백이 나왔습니다

[1]페어밀 웰컴 협회(FWA)는 새로운 주민들을 위한 멋진 선물을 결정했습니다. 페어밀 관련 정보가 가득 담긴 재활용 가능한 장바구니 가방입니다. 천으로 된 이 가방은 앞면에 '페어밀 기념'이라고 인쇄되고 지역사회 최신 소식, 쿠폰, 협회 회원들이 집에서 구운 간식 등으로 채워질 예정입니다. [2]본 프로젝트 자금을 지원하고자 하는 지역 업체는 비용을 지불하고 가방 뒷면에 로고를 인쇄할 수 있습니다. [3]페어밀 주민 여러분은 이 가방을 각 가정에 직접 가져다주면서 새 이웃을 환영해 주십시오. 신청하시려면 온라인에서 최근 업데이트한 저희 지역사회 웹사이트 fairmillwa.org를 방문하세요.

어휘 | resident 주민, 거주자 **treat** 간식 **fund** 자금을 대다

기출 ETS TEST 본책 p.094

1 (A)	**2** (B)	**3** (C)	**4** (D)	**5** (B)
6 (D)	**7** (B)	**8** (D)	**9** (C)	**10** (C)
11 (D)	**12** (D)	**13** (D)	**14** (C)	**15** (A)
16 (C)	**17** (B)	**18** (B)	**19** (A)	**20** (D)
21 (D)	**22** (A)	**23** (D)	**24** (A)	**25** (B)
26 (C)	**27** (D)	**28** (C)		

[1-3] 기사

트래딘 카운티, 파크 프로젝트 행사 개최

[1]트래딘 카운티에서는 트래딘 캐니언랜드를 야생동물 보호 시설 및 교육 시설로 개조하는 일이 포함된 대규모 계획인

파크 프로젝트에서 일할 직원 채용 행사를 개최한다.

마케팅과 교육뿐 아니라 건설, 유지 보수, 조경 등에서 75개가 넘는 일자리가 있다. 행사는 3월 31일 토요일 카운티 대경기장에서 열릴 예정이다.

파크 프로젝트 고용 기회에 관한 정보를 얻거나 지원서를 다운로드하려면 www.tradeencounty.gov를 방문하면 된다. **²3월 31일 이전 온라인으로 등록한 사람들은 면접 일정을 미리 잡을 수 있다.** 현장 접수 지원자들도 행사 당일에 참여 가능하다. 모든 면접은 오전 10시부터 오후 4시 사이에 이루어진다.

³파크 프로젝트는 야생동물 서식지 보호 증진을 목적으로 최근 통과된 법안에 대응하여 카운티 공무원들이 시작한 것이다.

어휘 | large-scale 대규모의 initiative 계획 convert 전환하다, 개조하다 refuge 피난처, 보호 시설, 쉼터 landscaping 조경 application 지원, 신청서 in advance 미리 walk-in 예약이 안 된 candidate 지원자, 후보자 in response to ~에 대응하여 habitat 서식지

1 행사에 참여하는 이유는 무엇이겠는가?

(A) 일자리를 구하려고
(B) 새 법안에 대해 논의하려고
(C) 야생동물 보호에 대해 배우려고
(D) 공원 개장을 기념하려고

해설 | 추론
기사의 첫 단락 첫 문장에서 '트래딘 카운티에서는 트래딘 캐니언랜드를 야생동물 보호 시설 및 교육 시설로 개조하는 일이 포함된 대규모 계획인 파크 프로젝트에서 일할 직원 채용 행사를 개최한다(Tradeen County is holding an event to recruit workers for the Park Project)'고 했으므로 (A)가 정답이다.

어휘 | attend 참석하다

2 행사 이전에 신청한 사람들이 할 수 있을 것은?

(A) 등록비 할인 결제
(B) 면담 시간 예약
(C) 특별 견학 참여
(D) 행사에 일찍 입장

해설 | 세부 사항
두 번째 단락 두 번째 문장에서 '3월 31일 이전 온라인으로 등록한 사람들은 면접 일정을 미리 잡을 수 있다(Those who register online prior to March 31 will be able to schedule an interview in advance)'고 했으므로 (B)가 정답이다.

어휘 | sign up 신청하다 reserve 예약하다

패러프레이징
지문의 register → 질문의 sign up
지문의 schedule an interview
→ 보기의 Reserve a meeting time

3 기사에 언급된 법안이 지지하는 것은?

(A) 도시 개발
(B) 컴퓨터 교육
(C) 자연 환경 보호
(D) 트래딘 카운티에 대학교 개교

해설 | 세부 사항
law를 키워드로 잡고 law가 언급되는 부분에서 답을 찾아야 한다. 마지막 단락에서 '파크 프로젝트는 야생동물 서식지 보호 증진을 목적으로 최근 통과된 법안에 대응하여 카운티 공무원들이 시작한 것(The Park Project was initiated by county officials in response to a recently passed law aimed at increasing habitat protection for wildlife)'이라고 했으므로 (C)가 정답이다.

어휘 | preserve 보존하다, 보호하다 environment 환경

패러프레이징
지문의 habitat protection for wildlife
→ 보기의 Preserving the natural environment

[4-6] 기사

'디스커버 포트 스노우덴' 앱 이용 가능

9월 22일 – 포트 스노우덴 기업 협회(PSBC)는 대부분의 태블릿과 휴대전화에서 새로운 앱 '디스커버 포트 스노우덴'을 무료로 다운받을 수 있게 됐다고 오늘 발표했다.

앱의 가장 인기 있는 기능 중 하나는 지역 명소에 대한 맞춤형 길 안내를 제공하는 대화형 지도이다. 또한 지역 식당 명부, 숙소 전체 목록과 음악회, 극장, 기타 행사에 대한 월별 안내도 포함되어 있다. **⁴대중교통 노선 및 시간표, 공사 구역, 교통편 지연 관련 최신 정보로 다니기가 훨씬 수월해진다.**

앱을 개발한 프로그래머 젠스 헤닝센은 "종이 지도와 안내 책자는 변경사항이 있을 때마다 종종 지난 정보가 됩니다. **⁵이 앱을 사용해 버튼을 클릭하기만 하면 주요 정보를 추가 또는 변경할 수 있어요.**"라고 설명한다.

정보를 최신으로 유지해주는 기능이 PSBC가 프로젝트를 추진하기로 결정한 주요 이유이다. '**⁶디스커버 포트 스노우덴' 개발 비용은 PSBC 회원들에게 모금한 연회비로 충당됐다.**

어휘 | at no charge 무료로 interactive 대화식의, 상호적인 customized 개개인의 요구에 맞춘 attraction 명소 comprehensive 포괄적인, 종합적인 up-to-date 최신의 public transit 대중교통 dated 구식의 annual dues 연회비

4 앱에 대해 명시된 것은?

(A) 명소 할인을 제공한다.
(B) 호텔 예약 기능이 있다.
(C) 식당 메뉴를 보여줄 수 있다.
(D) 교통편 관련 정보를 제공한다.

해설 | Not / True
기사의 두 번째 단락 마지막 문장에서 '대중교통 노선 및 시간표, 공사 구역, 교통편 지연 관련 최신 정보로 다니기가 훨씬 수월해진다(Getting around is made easier with up-to-date information about public transit routes and schedules, construction zones, and traffic delays)'고 했으므로 (D)가 정답이다.

어휘 | reservation 예약

패러프레이징
지문의 public transit routes → 보기의 transportation

5 기사에 따르면, PSBC는 왜 앱을 개발하도록 했는가?

(A) 관광업을 진흥하기 위해서
(B) 업데이트가 쉬워져서
(C) 비용을 아낄 수 있어서
(D) 일자리가 창출될 수 있어서

해설 | 세부 사항
developed를 키워드로 잡고 developed가 언급되는 부분에서 답을 찾아야 한다. 세 번째 단락에서 '앱을 개발한 프로그래머 젠스 헤닝센(Jens Henningsen, the programmer who developed the application)은 이 앱을 사용해 버튼을 클릭하기만 하면 주요 정보를 추가 또는 변경할 수 있다(important information can be added or changed with the click of a button)'고 했으므로 (B)가 정답이다.

어휘 | promote 촉진하다, 홍보하다

패러프레이징
지문의 important information can be added or changed with the click of a button
→ 보기의 easy to update

6 PSBC는 앱을 위한 자금을 어디서 구했는가?

(A) 판매 수입에서
(B) 지역사회 기부를 통해서
(C) 추가 세금을 통해서
(D) 회비에서

해설 | 세부 사항
마지막 단락 마지막 문장에서 '디스커버 포트 스노우덴' 개발 비용은 PSBC 회원들에게 모금한 연회비로 충당됐다(The cost of developing *Discover Port Snowden* was coved by the annual dues collected from PSBC members)'고 했으므로 (D)가 정답이다.

어휘 | sales revenue 매출 수입 **donation** 기부

패러프레이징
지문의 annual dues collected from PSBC members
→ 보기의 membership fees

[7-9] 보도 자료

> 베이우드 역사 학회(BHS)는 100년 이상 전에 설계되고 지어진 것과 똑같이 타워 밀을 재건하는 계획을 어제 발표했다. 그 풍차는 1년 반 전 화재로 소실됐다. 지난 50년간 가동하지는 않았지만 지어진 이래 베이우드 지역의 중심이었다. 이렇듯 사랑받는 랜드마크가 된 것은 위치 때문이다. 도시 변두리의 목가적인 환경에 위치한 타워 밀은 무수히 많은 졸업식, 결혼식, 기념 행사의 배경이 되었다. 작은 시골 마을에서의 삶에 관한 TV 다큐멘터리 세 편에도 등장한 바 있다.
>
> **8**풍차의 원래 설계를 재현하는 프로젝트는 마인즈아이 매터스 주식회사에게 돌아갔다. 건설 도급업체와의 협상이 진행 중이다. **7**시의회는 프로젝트에 10만 달러를 책정한 한편, 지역 업체들은 7만 5천 달러 넘게 기부하였다. BHS는 회계 담당자 자닌 추이가 이끌 모금 프로젝트들을 통해 추가 5만 달러를 모을 계획이다. 6월 6일, **9(B)**BHS 회장 가번 로크는 프로젝트에 대해 논의하고 **9(D)**원래 풍차에 관한 BHS 기록 보관소의 역사적 정보를 제공할 예정이다. 또한 **9(A)**추이 씨는 7월 27일 토요일로 잠정 계획된 기금 마련 만찬 계획의 개요를 설명할 것이다. 6월 6일 행사는 월트햄로 151번지에 있는 BHS 사무실에서 오후 7시에 개최된다.
>
> **어휘 | mill** 풍차 **reconstruct** 재건하다 **mainstay** 중심, 주축, 중추 **be situated in** ~에 위치하다 **idyllic** 목가적인 **backdrop** 배경, 환경 **untold** 말로 다 할 수 없는, 막대한 **negotiation** 협상 **ongoing** 진행 중인 **in excess of** ~을 초과하여 **amass** 모으다, 축적하다 **fund-raising** 모금 **treasurer** 회계 담당자 **archive** 기록 보관소 **benefit dinner** 기금 마련 만찬 **tentatively** 잠정적으로

7 타워 밀에 대해 암시된 것은?

(A) 설계가 다수의 시골 마을 풍차와 유사하다.
(B) 다양한 원천에서 재건 자금을 조달할 것이다.
(C) 거의 50년 전 재건된 적이 있다.
(D) 베이우드 중심부에 있다.

해설 | 추론
기사의 두 번째 단락 세 번째 문장에서 '시의회는 프로젝트에 10만 달러를 책정한 한편, 지역 업체들은 7만 5천 달러 넘게 기부하였다(The Town Council has allocated $100,000 toward the project while local businesses have given donations in excess of $75,000)'고 했으며 'BHS는 회계 담당자 자닌 추이가 이끌 모금 프로젝트들을 통해 추가 5만 달러를 모을 계획(The BHS intends to amass an additional $50,000 through a series of fund-raising projects)'이라고 했으므로 타워 밀은

시의회, 지역 업체, 모금 프로젝트와 같은 다양한 원천에서 재건 자금을 조달할 것이라는 것을 짐작할 수 있다. 따라서 (B)가 정답이다.

8 마인즈아이 매터스 주식회사는 어떤 종류의 업체이겠는가?

(A) 건설   (B) 촬영
(C) 조경   (D) 건축

해설 | 추론
Mindseye Matters, Inc.를 키워드로 잡고 Mindseye Matters, Inc.가 언급되는 부분에서 답을 찾아야 한다. 두 번째 단락 첫 문장에서 '풍차의 원래 설계를 재현하는 프로젝트는 마인즈아이 매터스 주식회사에게 돌아갔다(The project to re-create the original design of the mill was awarded to Mindseye Matters, Inc.)'고 했으므로 마인즈아이 매터스 주식회사는 건축 회사임을 짐작할 수 있다. 따라서 (D)가 정답이다.

9 베이우드 역사 학회에 대해 명시되지 않은 것은?

(A) 7월에 모금 행사를 개최할 계획이다.
(B) 로크 씨가 이끌고 있다.
(C) 대중에게 프로젝트 최신 소식을 정기적으로 제공할 계획이다.
(D) 타워 밀의 역사적 변천 과정에 관한 정보를 가지고 있다.

해설 | Not / True
두 번째 단락 후반부에서 '추이 씨는 7월 27일 토요일로 잠정 계획된 기금 마련 만찬 계획의 개요를 설명할 것 (Ms. Tsui will outline plans for a benefit dinner ~)' 이라고 했으므로 (A)가 언급되었고, 'BHS 회장 가번 로크(BHS President Garvan Locke)'라는 말이 나오므로 (B)도 언급되었다. '원래 풍차에 관한 BHS 기록 보관소의 역사적 정보를 제공할 예정(BHS President Garvan Locke will ~ provide historical information from the BHS archives about the original mill)'이라고 했으므로 (D)도 언급되었지만, 대중에게 프로젝트 최신 소식을 정기적으로 제공할 계획에 대한 이야기는 없으므로 (C)가 정답이다.

패러프레이징
지문의 a benefit dinner → 보기의 a fund-raising event
지문의 President → 보기의 headed
지문의 historical information from the BHS archives about the original mill → 보기의 information about the historical development of the Tower Mill

[10-12] 신문 기사

시내 더 이상의 무료 주차는 없어

5월 21일

알리시아 그랜저

10모리스타운 중심부 혼잡을 제한하려는 노력의 일환으로 시의회에서 주차 규정 변경을 계획하고 있다. "거리는 종종 저녁 시간에 가장 붐빕니다." **11**모리스타운 시의회 대변인 지나 톰슨이 말한다. "주민과 비거주민 모두 식당, 극장, 콘서트 장소 등에 가기 위해 도심 지역을 방문하기 때문입니다. 사람들은 주차장을 피하는 경향이 있어요. 요금을 청구하니까요. 그들이 무료 도로 주차 공간을 찾아 돌아다니느라 이로 인해 혼잡도가 증가됩니다."

11현재 도로 주차 요금은 오전 6시부터 오후 5시까지만 요구되며, 야간에는 주차 요금이 부과되지 않는다. "이것이 바뀌어야 해요." 톰슨 씨가 말한다. "24시간 요금을 내는 다른 도시들의 선례를 따르고자 합니다."

제안된 변경사항이 실시되면 최근 몇 개월간 두 번째 변화가 된다. **12**3월에 새로운 주차 요금 징수기가 설치되었는데, 이는 동전과 신용카드 둘 다 받을 뿐 아니라, 모리스타운 특별 주차 카드도 이용 가능하다. 4월에 나온 이 카드는 시에서 구매 가능하다.

어휘 | in an effort to ~하기 위한 노력으로 congestion 혼잡 regulation 규정, 규제 spokesperson 대변인 currently 현재 go into effect 발효되다, 실시되다 install 설치하다

10 모리스타운에 대해 암시된 것은?

(A) 도로 보수가 필요하다.
(B) 새 도로 건설을 위한 기금을 마련해야 한다.
(C) 교통 문제가 있다.
(D) 주민들은 시 주차장에 무료로 주차할 수 있다.

해설 | 추론
기사의 첫 단락 첫 문장에서 '모리스타운 중심부 혼잡을 제한하려는 노력의 일환으로(In an effort to limit congestion in the center of Morristown) 시의회에서 주차 규정 변경을 계획하고 있다'고 했으므로 모리스타운에 교통 문제가 있다는 것을 짐작할 수 있다. 따라서 (C)가 정답이다.

어휘 | in need of ~을 필요로 하는 raise funds 기금을 마련하다

패러프레이징
지문의 congestion → 보기의 a traffic problem

11 시의회가 고려하고 있는 것은?

(A) 기존 주차 공간 확장
(B) 새 주차 공간 조성
(C) 시간당 주차 요금 인상
(D) 저녁 시간대 주차 요금 도입

해설 | 세부 사항
두 번째 단락에서 '현재 도로 주차 요금은 오전 6시부터 오후 5시까지만 요구되며, 야간에는 주차 요금이 부과되지 않는데(no parking fee is charged at night) 이것이

바뀌어야 한다면서, 24시간 요금을 내는 다른 도시들의 선례를 따를 것(payment is required 24 hours a day)이라는 톰슨 씨의 인터뷰 내용이 언급되었다. 첫 단락 두 번째 문장에서 '지나 톰슨이 모리스타운 시의회 대변인(Gina Thompson, spokesperson for the Morristown City Council)'이라고 했으므로 시의회는 야간 주차 요금 도입을 고려한다고 할 수 있다. 따라서 (D)가 정답이다.

어휘 | enlarge 확장하다, 확대하다 existing 기존의 hourly rate 시간당 요금 introduce 도입하다

12 모리스타운에 최근 어떤 일이 있었는가?

(A) 일부 도심 주차장이 폐쇄됐다.
(B) 시의회가 주차를 위한 추가 부지를 매입했다.
(C) 주차 요금 징수기가 수리됐다.
(D) 새로운 주차 요금 결제 방식이 수립됐다.

해설 | 세부 사항
마지막 단락 두 번째 문장에서 '3월에 새로운 주차 요금 징수기가 설치되었는데, 이는 동전과 신용카드 둘 다 받을 뿐 아니라, 모리스타운 특별 주차 카드도 이용 가능하다(In March, new parking meters were installed that accept both coins and credit cards, as well as special Morristown parking cards)'고 했으며, 기사 작성일이 5월 21일이므로 최근에 있었던 일이라는 것을 알 수 있다. 따라서 (D)가 정답이다.

어휘 | establish 수립하다, 설립하다

패러프레이징
지문의 coins and credit cards, ~ parking cards
→ 보기의 payment options

[13-16] 기사

메트로-에더블스 사, 새 방향 발표

5월 7일 – 메트로-에더블스 사는 수프 앤 샐러드 센트럴이라고 부르는 패스트푸드 체인을 개발할 계획이라고 발표했다. 새 체인은 메트로-에더블스의 홍콩 본부에서 관리할 예정이며 이 다국적 기업은 최종적으로 200개의 수프 앤 샐러드 센트럴 지점을 아시아 및 유럽 전역에 소개하고자 한다.

13"편의 식품 부문은 지난 10년간 전 세계적인 성장을 보였습니다." 비즈니스트렌드 닷컴의 업계 분석가 루이스 머키가 말한다. "메트로-에더블스는 이런 동향을 현명하게 활용하고 있습니다."

14메트로-에더블스가 작년 한 해 동안 시행한 설문 조사에서 소비자들은 외식할 때 더 건강식을 사먹는 것으로 나타났다. 15(C)메트로-에더블스 최고 경영자 네하 라미세티는 보통 업계에서 튀긴 음식에 중점을 덜 두고 신선한 재료와 영양가에 더 많이 집중한다는 점을 언급했다.

15(B)"저희 역시 이런 식으로 접근하며, 점심과 저녁 식사는 평균 7.50달러에, 아침 식사와 간식은 더 저렴하게 제공할 것입니다." 라미세티 씨가 말했다. "15(D)뿐만 아니라 더 빠른 생활 방식을 가진 도시 거주자들의 구미에 대부분 맞출 것입니다. 그러므로 저희 메뉴가 제공하는 편의성을 그들이 환영하리라고 생각합니다."

16메트로-에더블스 사는 최근 만든 자회사 수프 앤 샐러드 센트럴이 영업 2년째에 이윤을 내기 시작할 것이라고 낙관하고 있다. 업체는 현재 기업을 창립하며 빌린 장기 부채 일부를 아직 갖고 있다.

어휘 | multinational 다국적의 eventually 결국, 마침내 take advantage of ~을 이용하다 reveal 밝히다, 드러내다 wholesome food 건강식 in general 보통, 일반적으로 place emphasis on ~에 중점을 두다, 강조하다 nutritional value 영양가 cater to ~의 구미에 맞추다, ~을 충족시키다 appreciate 환영하다, 고마워하다 optimistic 낙관적인 subsidiary 자회사 turn profits 이윤을 남기다 debt 빚 enterprise 기업, 회사

13 머키 씨는 누구이겠는가?

(A) 메트로-에더블스 사의 법률 고문
(B) 홍콩 은행원
(C) 영양 전문가
(D) 식품업계 연구원

해설 | 추론
Mr. Merkey를 키워드로 잡고 Mr. Merkey가 언급되는 부분에서 답을 찾아야 한다. 기사의 두 번째 단락에서 '편의 식품 부문은 지난 10년간 전 세계적인 성장을 보였다(The convenience food sector has shown worldwide growth over the last decade)'고 비즈니스트렌드 닷컴의 업계 분석가 루이스 머키가 말했으므로 Mr. Merkey는 식품업계 분석가임을 짐작할 수 있다. 따라서 (D)가 정답이다.

어휘 | expert 전문가

패러프레이징
지문의 industry analyst → 보기의 industry researcher

14 메트로-에더블스 사에 대해 보도된 것은?

(A) 신임 지도자를 채용했다.
(B) 업계의 느린 성장에 영향을 받았다.
(C) 사람들의 식사 선호를 조사했다.
(D) 본사 이전을 계획하고 있다.

해설 | 세부 사항
세 번째 단락 첫 문장에서 '메트로-에더블스가 작년 한 해 동안 시행한 설문 조사에서 소비자들은 외식할 때 더 건강식을 사먹는 것으로 나타났다(A survey conducted by Metro-Edibles over the last year revealed that consumers are choosing to purchase more

wholesome foods when eating out)'고 했으므로 (C)가
정답이다.

어휘 | affect 영향을 주다 investigate 조사하다, 연구하다
preference 선호

패러프레이징
지문의 choosing to purchase more wholesome foods
when eating out → 보기의 dining preferences

15 수프 앤 샐러드 센트럴의 식사에 대해 라미세티 씨가
명시하지 않은 것은?

(A) 비슷한 식당의 식사보다 저렴할 것이다.
(B) 하루 종일 이용 가능하다.
(C) 건강에 좋은 재료를 넣을 것이다.
(D) 빠르게 제공할 것이다.

해설 | Not/True
세 번째 단락 두 번째 문장에서 라미세티 씨가 업계에서
신선한 재료와 영양가에 더 많이 집중한다는 점을
언급했다는 내용에 이어 제시된 '저희 역시 이런 식으로
접근하며, 점심 식사와 저녁 식사는 평균 7.50달러에,
아침 식사와 간식은 더 저렴하게 제공할 것(We are
offering this approach too, at an average price
of US $7.50 for a lunch or dinner, with cheaper
options for breakfast and snacks)'이라고 한 말에서
(B)와 (C)가 언급되었다. 이어서 '더 빠른 생활 방식을
가진 도시 거주자들의 구미에 대부분 맞출 것(we will
cater mostly to urban residents with faster-
paced lifestyles)'이라고 했으므로 (D)도 언급되었다.
하지만 비슷한 식당의 식사보다 저렴할 것이라는 이야기는
없으므로 (A)가 정답이다.

어휘 | available 이용 가능한

패러프레이징
지문의 a lunch or dinner, ~ for breakfast and snacks
→ 보기의 throughout the day
지문의 fresh ingredients
→ 보기의 healthful ingredients
지문의 faster-paced → 보기의 quickly

16 수프 앤 샐러드 센트럴에 대해 암시된 것은?

(A) 실적이 좋지 않은 메트로-에더블스 기업을 대체한다.
(B) 메뉴 조리법을 고객에게 제공할 것이다.
(C) 즉시 이윤을 낼 것으로 기대하지 않는다.
(D) 주로 작은 도시에 지점을 낼 것이다.

해설 | 추론
마지막 단락 첫 문장에서 '메트로-에더블스 사는 최근 만든
자회사 수프 앤 샐러드 센트럴이 영업 2년째에 이윤을 내기
시작할 것이라고 낙관하고 있다(Metro-Edible Corp. is
optimistic that Soup and Salad Central, its newest
subsidiary, will start to turn profits by its second

year of operations)'고 했으므로 (C)가 정답이다.

어휘 | replace 대신하다, 대체하다 profitable 이득이 되는,
수익성이 있는

패러프레이징
지문의 turn profits → 보기의 be profitable

[17-20] 기사

DA, 남아메리카로 사업 방향 전환

1월 23일 – **17도이치 오토콘체른 AG(DA)는 브라질
쿠리티바에 자동차 공장을 설립할 계획을 이번 주 초에
발표했다.** 건축 설계는 최종 승인이 아직 남아있지만, 독일
자동차 제조업체의 첫 남아메리카 공장 건설이 오는 3월
시작될 예정이다.

가격이 적당하고 연비가 좋은 DA 차량은 라이프치히 조립
라인에서 처음 출시되자마자 유럽 소비자들에게 인기를
끌었다. 회사의 최고 경영자인 한스 디에트리히 카우프만은
보도 자료에서 "남아메리카 전역의 소비자들이 우리 제품과
서비스를 이용할 수 있도록 해서 그들 역시 가격 경쟁력이
있는 고품질 자동차를 탈 수 있게 만들고 싶다"고 밝혔다.

시장 분석가들은 이 소식이 놀랍지 않다고 지적한다.
**17,18DA는 거의 3년 전, 세계에서 입지를 넓힐 포괄적
전략을 발표했다.** 이에 관계없이 분석가들은 DA의
최고 경영자가 언급한 건설 기간에 대해 회의적이었다.
**18,19바흐마이어 오토파브리크에서 25년간 근무하다 2년 전
DA의 최고 경영자 자리를 수락한 카우프만은 "DA는 항상
생산 역량을 확대하고자 했으며 쿠리티바 공장이 1년 후면
가동할 것으로 확신한다."고 말했다.**

시장 분석가 멜리나 나시멘토는 지난 4년간 회사 수익이
꾸준히 증가했다는 사실에 주목한다. **20이러한 재정적 성공은
유럽 소비자들이 DA의 제품과 고객 서비스에 깊은 인상을
받았다는 사실에 기인한다고 보았다.** 나시멘토는 남아메리카
소비자들도 같은 생각으로 이 회사의 재정을 더욱 강화시킬
것으로 크게 기대하고 있다.

어휘 | pending ~을 기다리는 동안 approval 승인
architectural 건축학의, 건축술의 affordable (가격이)
적당한, 감당할 수 있는 fuel-efficient 연비가 좋은 assembly
조립 press release 보도 자료 competitively priced 가격
경쟁력을 갖춘 comprehensive 포괄적인 strategy 전략
presence 존재, 참석 regardless 상관하지 않고 skeptical
회의적인 operational 가동 준비가 갖춰진 attribute
A to B A를 B의 덕분으로 여기다 sentiment 정서, 감정
strengthening 강화, 보강

17 기사에 따르면, DA는 왜 쿠리티바에 공장을 건설할
계획인가?

(A) 바흐마이어 오토파브리크와의 합병을 용이하게 하려고
(B) 세계적으로 입지를 강화하려고
(C) 새 디자인에 기반한 차량을 생산하려고
(D) 라이프치히 공장을 대체하려고

해설 | 세부 사항
기사의 첫 단락 첫 문장에서 '도이치 오토콘체른 AG (DA)는
브라질 쿠리티바에 자동차 공장을 설립할 계획(it plans to
build an automobile plant in Curitiba, Brazil)을 이번
주 초에 발표했다'고 했으며, 세 번째 단락 두 번째 문장에서
'DA는 거의 3년 전, 세계에서 입지를 넓힐 포괄적 전략을
발표했다(DA had released a comprehensive strategy
to broaden its presence around the world nearly
three years ago)'고 했으므로 DA의 쿠리티바 공장 건설은
세계 입지 전략 때문이라는 것을 알 수 있다. 따라서 (B)가
정답이다.

어휘 | facilitate 가능하게 하다, 용이하게 하다 **merger** 합병

패러프레이징
지문의 broaden its presence around the world
→ 보기의 strengthen its presence internationally

18 기사에서 DA에 관해 암시하는 것은?

(A) 차량 가격을 인상했다.
(B) 얼마 전부터 새 공장을 열 계획을 하고 있었다.
(C) 유럽에 자동차 공장을 여러 곳 갖고 있다.
(D) 남아메리카에서 심한 경쟁에 직면하고 있다.

해설 | 추론
세 번째 단락 두 번째 문장에서 'DA는 거의 3년 전,
세계에서 입지를 넓힐 포괄적 전략을 발표했다(DA had
released a comprehensive strategy to broaden
its presence around the world nearly three years
ago)'고 했으며, 세 번째 단락 마지막 문장 카우프만의
인터뷰에서 '쿠리티바 공장이 1년 후면 가동할 것으로
확신한다(we are confident that our Curitiba plant
will be operational in a year's time)'고 했으므로 얼마
전부터 새 공장을 개소할 계획을 하고 있었다는 것을 짐작할
수 있다. 따라서 (B)가 정답이다.

어휘 | competition 경쟁

패러프레이징
지문의 our Curitiba plant will be operational
→ 보기의 open a new plant

19 카우프만 씨에 따르면, 새 공장은 언제 문을 열 것인가?

(A) 1년 후   (B) 2년 후
(C) 3년 후   (D) 4년 후

해설 | 세부 사항
세 번째 단락 마지막 문장 카우프만의 인터뷰에서 '쿠리티바
공장이 1년 후면 가동할 것으로 확신한다(we are
confident that our Curitiba plant will be operational
in a year's time)'고 했으므로 정답은 (A)이다.

패러프레이징
지문의 be operational → 질문의 open
지문의 in a year's time → 보기의 In one year

20 나시멘토 씨는 왜 DA가 남아메리카에서 성공을 거둘
것이라고 믿는가?

(A) 유럽 이외 지역에서 좋은 평판을 얻었으므로
(B) 대규모 광고 캠페인을 시작할 것이므로
(C) 고객들이 공장에서 직접 차를 구매할 수 있을 것이므로
(D) 고객들이 업체가 제공하는 사항을 마음에 들어 할
    것이므로

해설 | 세부 사항
Ms. Nascimento를 키워드로 잡고 Ms. Nascimento가
언급되는 부분에서 답을 찾아야 한다. 마지막 단락 두
번째 문장에서 '멜리나 나시멘토는 재정적 성공이 유럽
소비자들이 DA의 제품과 고객 서비스에 깊은 인상을
받았다는 사실에 기인한다(She attributes this financial
success to the fact that European consumers are
impressed with DA's products and its customer
service)고 했고, 이어서 '남아메리카 소비자들도 같은
생각으로 회사의 재정을 더욱 강화시킬 것으로 크게
기대하고 있다(Nascimento fully expects that South
Americans will share this sentiment, resulting in a
further strengthening of the company's finances)'고
했으므로 (D)가 정답이다.

어휘 | reputation 명성, 평판 **extensive** 대규모의, 광범위한

패러프레이징
지문의 are impressed with DA's products and its
customer service
→ 보기의 like what the company has to offer

[21-24] 보도 자료

더블린 (8월 30일) – 이번 달 초, 더블린 클론타프 대학교의
최근 졸업생 2인이 그들의 첫 상업적 벤처 사업의 문을
열었다. **²¹아달 맥피와 조 힐리는 운동과 빨래를 한 군데서
할 수 있는 아일랜드 최초의 시설, 스핀 사이클을 창립했다.**
대학교 근처 번화가의 킨코라 로에 위치한 이 업체는 시간이
많이 소요되는 빨래에 건강이라는 발상의 전환을 제공한다.
"어느 날 캠퍼스에서 벗어나 걷고 있는데 창문에 매매라는
표지판이 붙은 붐비는 빨래방을 봤어요. 주인이 가족과 시간을
더 보내기 위해 은퇴하느라 매장을 매각하고 싶어한다는
것을 알게 됐죠. 조와 저는 그 자리가 우리의 첫 벤처 사업을
하기에 이상적이라고 생각했습니다." 맥피 씨가 설명했다.

맥피 씨와 힐리 씨는 빨래방에 정기적으로 가는 것이 수고스럽다는 것을 개인적으로 경험해 알고 있었다. 이들은 돋보이고 싶다면 서비스에 창의적인 변화를 주어야 한다는 것을 깨달았다. **24(B)그들은 사업 계획서를 쓰고 24(C)상업 대출을 받은 후** 빨래방 옆 빈 매장을 매입할 수 있었다. **24(D)공동 벽면에 이 공간을 빨래방으로 연결하는 통로를 내고 청소와 페인트칠을 했다.** 이후 12대의 자전거 운동 기구를 설치했다. 스핀 사이클이 고객을 위해 **23준비됐다.**

젊은 기업가들의 직감이 성공을 거둔 듯하다. 맥피 씨와 힐리 씨에 따르면 사업은 이미 이윤을 내고 있다. 지역 내 많은 주민들은 기숙사나 소형 아파트에 거주하는데 그곳에는 종종 세탁기나 건조기를 넣을 공간이 없다. **22스핀 사이클에서 고객들은 90분 이내에 빨래를 세탁 및 건조하고 갤 수 있도록 프론트데스크에 맡기거나** 셀프 서비스 기계를 이용한다. 어느 쪽이든 활기찬 운동을 마치고 깨끗한 옷을 찾아갈 수 있다.

어휘 | graduate 졸업생 commercial 상업적인 launderette 빨래방 establishment 기관, 시설 bustling 붐비는, 북적북적하는 diversion 전환 chore 하기 싫은 일, 허드렛일 stand out 돋보이다 install 설치하다 stationary bicycle 운동용 자전거 entrepreneur 기업가 instinct 본능, 직감 pay off 성공하다 accommodate ~을 위한 충분한 공간을 제공하다 fold 개다 energizing 활기찬, 활기를 북돋는 workout 운동

21 기사를 쓴 목적은?

(A) 매장 관리 방법을 설명하려고
(B) 개업식 행사를 알리려고
(C) 두 명의 동료가 가진 생각을 비교하려고
(D) 색다른 사업 개념을 서술하려고

해설 | **주제/목적**
기사의 첫 단락 두 번째 문장에서 '아달 맥피와 조 힐리는 운동과 빨래를 한 군데서 할 수 있는 아일랜드 최초의 시설, 스핀 사이클을 창립했다(Ardal McFee and Joe Healy have created Spin Cycle, a one-stop exercise and launderette destination, Ireland's first such establishment)'고 하므로 (D)가 정답이다.

어휘 | colleague 동료

패러프레이징
지문의 first such establishment
→ 보기의 unusual business

22 스핀 사이클에 대해 암시된 것은?

(A) 더블린에 사는 가족이 운영한다.
(B) 대학교 캠퍼스 내에 위치해 있다.
(C) 고객은 세탁해 달라고 빨래를 맡길 수 있다.
(D) 세탁기를 최근 교체했다.

해설 | **추론**
마지막 단락 세 번째 문장에서 '스핀 사이클에서 고객들은 90분 이내에 빨래를 세탁 및 건조하고 갤 수 있도록 프론트데스크에 맡길 수 있다(At Spin Cycle, customers can leave their laundry at the front desk to be washed, dried, and folded within 90 minutes)'고 했으므로 (C)가 정답이다.

어휘 | replace 대신하다, 대체하다

패러프레이징
지문의 leave their laundry at the front desk
→ 보기의 drop off their laundry

23 두 번째 단락 13행에 쓰인 "set"과 의미상 가장 가까운 것은?

(A) 확실한
(B) 단호한
(C) 뚜렷한
(D) 준비된

해설 | **동의어**
'be set for'는 문맥상 '~을 위해 준비되다'의 의미로 쓰였으므로 정답은 (D) prepared이다.

24 맥피 씨와 힐리 씨가 스핀 사이클을 열기 전 하지 않은 것은?

(A) 고객 설문 조사 실시
(B) 사업 계획서 작성
(C) 자금 마련
(D) 공간 개조

해설 | **Not/True**
두 번째 단락 세 번째 문장에서 '사업 계획서를 쓰고 상업 대출을 받은 후(After writing a business plan and securing a commercial loan) 빨래방 옆 빈 매장을 매입할 수 있었다'고 했으므로 (B)와 (C)가 언급되었다. 이어서 '공동 벽면에 이 공간을 빨래방으로 연결하는 통로를 내고 청소와 페인트칠을 했다(They cut a doorway in the common wall, connecting the area to the launderette, and cleaned and painted the area)'고 했으므로 (D)가 언급되었다. 하지만 고객 설문 조사 실시에 대한 이야기는 없으므로 (A)가 정답이다.

어휘 | conduct 하다 obtain 얻다, 구하다

패러프레이징
지문의 writing a business plan
→ 보기의 Develop a business plan
지문의 securing a commercial loan
→ 보기의 Obtain funding
지문의 cut a doorway, ~ painted the area
→ 보기의 Renovate a space

[25-28] 기사

> ### 나이로비 데일리 저널
> #### 4월 2일
>
> **25**현재 케냐에서는 두 슈퍼마켓 체인이 1위가 되기 위해 경쟁하고 있다. AT 마트와 두간즈 두 소매 업체는 소비자들 사이에서 기필코 1위가 될 것이라고 발표했다.
>
> 영국에 본사를 둔 AT 마트는 3월에 나이로비 내의 첫 매장을 열 계획이라고 발표했다. AT 마트는 세계적으로 가장 큰 슈퍼마켓 체인 중 하나이다. 반면 두간즈는 아프리카 외 지역에서는 잘 알려져 있지 않지만 남아공에서 가장 압도적인 우위를 차지하고 있는 슈퍼마켓 체인으로 이 지역에서 확실한 존재감을 확립했다. 현재 케냐에는 단골 고객층을 확보하고 있는 두간즈 매장이 8개 있다.
>
> 슈퍼마켓을 열기에 좋은 자리의 임대료는 보통 지나치게 비싸다. **28**미국에 본사를 둔 웬트워스와 같은 몇몇 슈퍼마켓 체인점은 손님이 그다지 많지 않은데 지나치게 비싼 임대료라고 생각하는 금액을 지불하고 싶지는 않았다. 그 결과 **26**웬트워스는 케냐에서 불과 2년 만에 매장 세 곳을 모두 폐점했다.
>
> 그런데 두간즈에는 이점이 있다. **27(A)두간즈는 자체적으로 부동산 사업부인 D 프라퍼티즈 주식회사를 설립했다.** 이 회사는 4개의 쇼핑 단지를 건설하여 각 단지마다 두간즈를 주된 세입자로 두었다. 게다가 두간즈는 제품을 현지 문화에 맞추는 데 특별히 신경을 썼다. 또한 **27(C)두간즈의 유명한 매장 내 제과점, 정육점 및 농산물 코너에 서비스를 제공하기 위해 27(B)효과적인 공급 및 배송 시스템을 개발하였다.** AT 마트가 훨씬 더 널리 알려져 있을지는 모르지만 인기 있는 두간즈와 경쟁하기 위해서는 좀 더 혁신적이어야 할 것이다.
>
> - 수잔 코터 기자

어휘 | compete 경쟁하다 retailer 소매업체 announce 발표하다 be determined to ~하기로 다짐하다 consumer 소비자 base ~에 본사를 두다 launch 출시하다, 개시하다 well-known 잘 알려진 dominant 우세한 establish 설립하다, 확립하다 presence 존재 loyal customer base 단골 고객층 be willing to 기꺼이 ~하다 exorbitant 과도한, 지나친 leasing fee 임대료 significant 상당한 as a result 그 결과 advantage 이점, 장점 real estate 부동산 tenant 세입자 tailor 맞추다 inventory 물품 목록, 재고 effective 효과적인 on-site 현장의 butcher 정육점 produce 농산물 recognition 인정, 알아봄 innovative 혁신적인

25 기사는 주로 무엇에 관한 것인가?

(A) 효과적인 사업 전략
(B) 업계 내 경쟁
(C) 케냐에서 싼 물건을 찾을 수 있는 곳
(D) 새로운 쇼핑몰의 성장

해설 | 주제 / 목적
기사의 첫 단락 첫 문장에서 '현재 케냐에서는 두 슈퍼마켓 체인이 1위가 되기 위해 경쟁하고 있다(Two supermarket chains are currently competing ~)'고 했고, 그 아래 단락들에서 AT 마트와 두간즈 두 소매 업체를 소개하고 있으므로 (B)가 정답이다.

어휘 | strategy 전략 bargain 싸게 사는 물건 growth 성장

26 웬트워스에 대해 암시된 것은?

(A) 단골 고객층이 있다.
(B) 지점은 주로 남아공에 있었다.
(C) 케냐에서의 사업은 상대적으로 수명이 짧았다.
(D) 가족 소유 기업이다.

해설 | 추론
세 번째 단락에 Wentworth's에 대한 이야기가 나온다. 세 번째 단락 마지막 문장에서 '웬트워스는 케냐에서 불과 2년 만에 매장 세 곳을 모두 폐점했다(Wentworth's closed all three of its stores after only two years in Kenya)'고 했으므로 케냐에서의 사업은 상대적으로 수명이 짧았다는 것을 짐작할 수 있다. 따라서 (C)가 정답이다.

어휘 | relatively 상대적으로 short-lived 수명이 짧은 enterprise 기업

패러프레이징
지문의 after only two years → relatively short-lived

27 두간즈의 성과로 언급되지 않은 것은?

(A) 부동산 사업부 설립
(B) 효율적인 배송 시스템 구축
(C) 매장 내 제과점 설치
(D) 세계적인 명성 구축

해설 | Not / True
Duggan's의 성과가 언급된 부분에서 찾아야 한다. 마지막 단락 두 번째 문장에서 '두간즈는 자체적으로 부동산 사업부인 D 프라퍼티즈 주식회사를 설립했다(The company created its own real estate division, D Properties Ltd.)'고 했으므로 (A)가 언급되었다. 다섯 번째 문장에서 '두간즈의 유명한 매장 내 제과점, 정육점 및 농산물 코너에 서비스를 제공하기 위해 효과적인 공급 및 배송 시스템을 개발하였다(It also has developed an effective supply-and-delivery system to service its famous on-site bakeries ~)'고 했으므로 (B)와 (C)가 언급되었다. 하지만 세계적인 명성 구축에 대한 이야기는 없으므로 (D)가 정답이다.

어휘 | efficient 효율적인 reputation 명성, 평판

패러프레이징
지문의 advantage → 질문의 accomplishment
지문의 created → 보기의 Establishing
지문의 developed an effective supply-and-delivery system
→ 보기의 Creating an efficient delivery system

28 [1], [2], [3], [4]로 표시된 곳 중에서 다음 문장이 들어가기에 가장 적합한 곳은?

"슈퍼마켓을 열기에 좋은 자리의 임대료는 보통 지나치게 비싸다."

(A) [1]   (B) [2]   (C) [3]   (D) [4]

해설 | 문장 삽입
제시된 문장에서 지나치게 비싼 임대료에 대해 언급하고 있으므로 임대료를 언급한 내용의 앞이나 뒤에 위치해야 한다. [3] 뒤에서 '미국에 본사를 둔 웬트워즈와 같은 몇몇 슈퍼마켓 체인점은 지나치게 비싼 임대료라고 생각하는 금액을 지불하고 싶지는 않았다(Some supermarket chains, such as Wentworth's, which is based in the United States, ~ exorbitant leasing fees)는 내용이 왔으므로 제시된 문장이 [3]에 들어가면 자연스럽게 연결된다. 따라서 (C)가 정답이다.

어휘 | desirable 바람직한 extremely 극도로

UNIT 05 웹페이지/양식

기출 예제

본책 p.102

노스 리버 호텔
¹당일 세탁/건조/개기 서비스

- 오전 8시 30분 전에 접수처에 맡기세요.
- 오후 6시까지 준비됩니다.
- 비용: 가방당 10달러

가방 속 품목	수량
셔츠 또는 블라우스	4
바지 또는 치마	3
원피스	
스웨터 또는 조끼	
반바지	1
양말(쌍)	2

²이름 및 객실번호: 리디아 리, 603
수령인: 다넬 리드
날짜: 1월 19일
총 비용: 10달러

어휘 | fold 접다 drop off 맡기다 reception 접수처 cost 비용 per ~마다 quantity 수량 vest 조끼 shorts 반바지

---

1 (B)	**2** (A)	**3** (A)	**4** (B)	**5** (D)	**6** (A)
7 (C)	**8** (B)	**9** (C)	**10** (A)	**11** (B)	**12** (C)
13 (A)	**14** (D)	**15** (A)	**16** (B)	**17** (C)	**18** (C)
19 (A)	**20** (A)	**21** (D)	**22** (C)	**23** (A)	**24** (D)

[1-2] 초대장

산 버나디노 콘도미니엄
펠드스톤 가
7월 7일 금요일 개장

¹BC 주 스프링턴 시, V8B 2KO 소재의
노스 리버 부동산에서 즉시 구입 가능한
멋진 부동산 매물들을 만나 보시라고
여러분을 초대합니다!

오후 4시부터 오후 8시까지 투어가 계속되며
음료와 간식이 제공됩니다.

²J. D. 폰지에게 (604) 555-0139로 연락하셔서
부동산 세부 사항과 대출 정보를 확인하세요.

어휘 | real estate 부동산 cordially 다정하게, 몹시 property 부동산, 건물 immediate 즉각적인 mortgage (담보) 대출, 융자

1 행사가 열리는 이유는?

(A) 지역사회에 공사 계획을 알리려고
(B) 지역 내 새 집을 소개하려고
(C) 본사 수리 개조를 기념하려고
(D) 회사 취업 면접 일정을 잡으려고

해설 | 주제/목적
초대장의 첫 문장에서 '노스 리버 부동산에서 즉시 구입 가능한 멋진 부동산 매물들을 볼 수 있도록 초대한다(North River Real Estate ~ cordially invites you to view our SPECTACULAR properties available for immediate purchase)'고 했으므로 (B)가 정답이다.

어휘 | renovate 개조하다 employment 고용, 직장

패러프레이징
지문의 properties available for immediate purchase
→ 보기의 new housing

2 J. D. 폰지의 직업은 무엇이겠는가?

(A) 매매 중개인
(B) 인테리어 디자이너
(C) 출장 요리 서비스 관리자
(D) 시티 투어 담당자

해설 | 추론
J. D. Ponge를 키워드로 잡고 J. D. Ponge가 언급되는 부분에서 답을 찾아야 한다. 마지막 문장에서 'J. D. 폰지에게 연락하여 부동산 세부 사항과 대출 정보를 확인하라(Contact J. D. Ponge ~ for property details and mortgage information)'고 하였으므로 J. D. 폰지는 부동산 중개인임을 짐작할 수 있다. 따라서 (A)가 정답이다.

어휘 | profession 직업

[3-5] 웹페이지

http://www.callex.com

홈	제품	지원	**특별 할인**	내 계정

칼렉스 전자제품 보상 판매 프로그램

오래된 칼렉스 노트북 컴퓨터나 기타 전자 기기를 처리하고 싶으십니까? 수리가 안 되거나 품질 보장 기한이 지났나요? 걱정 마십시오! 저희에게 보내주시고 할인된 가격으로 칼렉스의 새로운 기기를 구입하세요. 절차는 간단하여 3단계로 처리할 수 있습니다.

1단계: 제품 페이지에서 칼렉스 제품 종류를 선택하세요. ³저희 온라인 계산기가 여러분의 보상 판매 기기의 가치를 평가합니다.

2단계: 여러분의 기기를 온라인에 제공된 주소로 30일 이내에 보내주세요. 기기를 보내시고 나면 안에 있는 데이터를 다시는 찾지 못할 수도 있습니다. ⁴배송하기 전에 기기에서 모든 개인 정보를 삭제하실 것을 적극 추천합니다.

3단계: ⁵기기가 수령되면 최종 평가 금액의 칼렉스 상품권이 귀하에게 발송됩니다. 상품권은 어떤 종류의 제품이든 칼렉스 전 매장 또는 온라인 구매시 사용하실 수 있습니다.

어휘 | trade-in 보상 판매 get rid of 없애다, 처리하다 assess 평가하다 retrieve 되찾아 오다, 회수하다 delete 삭제하다 prior to ~에 앞서

3 온라인 계산기는 무엇을 추산하는가?

(A) 제품이 얼마의 값어치가 있는지
(B) 제품을 배송하는 데 비용이 얼마나 드는지
(C) 제품을 수리하는 데 얼마나 오래 걸리는지
(D) 제품이 얼마나 빨리 배송될 수 있는지

해설 | 세부 사항
online calculator를 키워드로 잡고 online calculator가 언급되는 부분에서 답을 찾아야 한다. Step 1에서 '온라인 계산기가 보상 판매 기기의 가치를 평가한다(our online calculator will assess the value of your trade-in device)'고 했으므로 (A)가 정답이다.

어휘 | estimate 추산하다, 추정하다

패러프레이징
지문의 the value of your trade-in device → 보기의 How much an item is worth

4 고객에게 무엇을 하라고 조언하는가?

(A) 가격 비교
(B) 데이터 삭제
(C) 추가 품질 보증서 구매
(D) 제품 배송 현황 확인

해설 | 세부 사항
Step 2 마지막 문장에서 '배송하기 전에 기기에서 모든 개인 정보를 삭제할 것을 적극 추천한다(It is strongly recommended that you delete all personal information from your device prior to shipping)'고 했으므로 (B)가 정답이다.

어휘 | compare 비교하다 status 상황

패러프레이징
지문의 recommended → 질문의 advised
지문의 delete all personal information → 보기의 Erase data

5 고객들은 무엇을 받을 것인가?

(A) 무료 수리 서비스
(B) 개인 맞춤 기술 서비스
(C) 향후 할인 행사 알림
(D) 향후 구매에 사용할 금액 포인트

해설 | 세부 사항
Step 3에서 '기기가 수령되면 최종 평가 금액의 칼렉스 상품권(a Callex gift card)이 발송되며, 상품권은 어떤 종류의 제품이든 칼렉스 전 매장 또는 온라인 구매 시 사용하실 수 있다(The card can be used at any Callex store or for online purchase in any product category)'고 했으므로 (D)가 정답이다.

어휘 | customized 개개인의 요구에 맞춘 credit (가게) 포인트

패러프레이징
지문의 a Callex gift card → 보기의 Credit

[6-7] 양식

잇츠 포토 랩
104 퍼스트 가
세인트 자카리, QC GOM 2C0

고객명: 셀리나 김플

특별 주문:

동봉한 사진을 스캔해서 아카이브 품질 용지에 사진당 2매씩 출력해 주세요. 해당 사진들을 디지털 형식으로 꼭 저장해 주시고, 주문 건과 함께 두 장의 CD를 넣어 주세요. **6오래된 사진이니 취급하실 때 특별히 신경 써 주시기 바랍니다.**

출력 크기: 4x6   (5x7)

후가공: (유광)   무광

수령 일자: 5월 24일 오후 3시 이후 아무 때나

총 금액: 60달러

· 프로모션 할인 10%(최초 고객만 해당)가 적용됩니까?
                           (네)   아니요

 총 금액: -6달러

· 선결제 25% (30달러 이상 모든 주문 건에 해당): -13.50달러

7수령 시 잔액: 40.50달러

- -
어휘 | enclose 동봉하다 matte 무광 applicable 해당되는, 적용되는 up front 선불 remainder 나머지

---

6 김플 씨가 제공한 사진에 대해 암시된 것은?

(A) 손상되기 쉽다.
(B) 색상이 밝다.
(C) 역사적 건물들이 나온다.
(D) 디지털 카메라로 찍었다.

해설 | 추론
특별 주문(Special Instructions)의 마지막 문장에서 '오래된 사진이니 취급하실 때 특별히 신경 써 주시기 바란다(These are old photographs, so please take great care when handling them)'고 했으므로 사진이 손상되기 쉽다는 것을 짐작할 수 있다. 따라서 (A)가 정답이다.

어휘 | fragile 취약한, 손상되기 쉬운 **brightly** 환히

패러프레이징
지문의 old → 보기의 fragile

7 김플 씨는 5월 24일에 얼마를 내야 하는가?

(A) 6.00달러
(B) 13.50달러
(C) 40.50달러
(D) 60.00달러

해설 | 세부 사항
양식의 마지막 부분에서 '수령 시 잔액(Remainder Due at Pickup)이 40.50달러'라고 했으므로 (C)가 정답이다.

어휘 | owe 빚지다

패러프레이징
지문의 Remainder due → 질문의 owe

[8-10] 영수증

┌───┐
요크 직물 & 실
79 웰치 로, 요크, UK Y031 3LP
¹⁰70년이 넘는 미세모, 실, 직물 조달 업체

고객: 세바스천 그레이엄
주문: 78-3L2 (6월 8일 주문)
청구서 발송 주소: 25 카나리 로, 리딩 RG31 2RE
8배송 주소: 그렌다 그레이엄, 13 리드 가, 완티지 OX12 2T

수량	제품	단가	제품 가격
1.5kg	**셰틀랜드 양모**	14파운드/kg	21.00파운드
	원산지: 올드 그로브 양 목장, 러윅		
2.5kg	**레스터 양모**	16파운드/kg	40.00파운드
	원산지: 아놀드 농장, 아네스비		
	⁹선물 포장	**무료**	
	소계		61.00파운드
	운송		7.00파운드
	총 주문금액		68.00파운드
	신용카드 결제 금액		68.00파운드
	미지급액		0.00파운드

본 서류는 청구용 영수증입니다. 배송품에 들어 있는 선물용 영수증에는 금액이 명시되지 않습니다.
└───┘

- -
어휘 | purveyor 조달 업자 fine 미세한, 가느다란 balance due 미지불액 gift receipt 가격이 표시되지 않는 선물용 영수증

---

8 소포는 어디로 발송되겠는가?

(A) 요크   (B) 완티지
(C) 러윅   (D) 리딩

해설 | 추론
영수증 상단의 배송 주소(Shipping address)가 Wantage OX12 2T로 되어 있으므로 (B)가 정답이다.

9 상품에 대해 암시된 것은?

(A) 현금으로 지불했다.
(B) 양 목장에서 구매했다.
(C) 선물로 구매했다.
(D) 트럭으로 운송됐다.

해설 | 추론
선물 포장(Gift wrapping)이 무료(Free)라고 했으므로 선물로 구매했다는 것을 짐작할 수 있다. 따라서 (C)가 정답이다.

어휘 | in cash 현금으로

10 요크 직물 & 실에 대해 명시된 것은?

(A) 수십 년간 영업했다.
(B) 온라인 소매업체이다.
(C) 대량 주문 건은 무료로 배송된다.
(D) 두 번째 지점을 열 계획이다.

해설 | Not / True

영수증 맨 위 칸에서 '요크 직물 & 실은 70년이 넘는 미세모, 실, 직물 조달 업체(Purveyors of fine wool, yarns, and textiles for over 70 years)'라고 했으므로 (A)가 정답이다.

어휘 | decade 10년 **retailer** 소매업체

패러프레이징
지문의 for over 70 years → 보기의 for decades

[11-14] 웹페이지

```
http://www.citywidesportsemporium.com.nz/about
```

시티와이드 스포츠 엠포리움

소개	홈	매장 위치	제품	서비스

시티와이드 스포츠 엠포리움 소개

[11,14]사업 및 테니스 동료인 그레이스 클레이와 아멜리아 로스는 10년 전 보웬 가 164번지에 첫 시티와이드 스포츠 엠포리움(CSE)을 [12]설립했습니다. [13]그들은 당시 대부분의 스포츠용품 소매업체들은 예를 들면 암벽 등반이나 카약 장비 같은 모험 스포츠 상품에 집중하고 있었으며 그런 스포츠에 그다지 관심이 없는 웰링턴 주민들은 혜택을 받지 못하고 있다는 것을 깨달았습니다. 보웬 가 매장을 열고 2년 후 CSE는 램턴 키 23번지에 매장을 열었습니다. 이후 웰링턴 이외의 지역으로 확장하는 데 성공했습니다. [13]이제는 전국에서 테니스, 사이클, 육상 애호가 전용 최고의 매장이 되었습니다.

올해 CSE는 올림픽 출전 육상 선수 숀 와그너가 디자인한 의류 제품 시티와이드 스포츠 어타이어를 당당히 선보였습니다. 이 제품은 모든 매장과 본 웹사이트에서 구매하실 수 있습니다. 편안하고 다채로운 남녀 의상 및 신발을 보시려면 **제품**을 클릭하세요.

[14]아울러 본점에서만 단독으로 이용하실 수 있는 특별 서비스가 있습니다. 해당 서비스에는 자전거 및 러닝머신 수리, 테니스 라켓 줄 교체 등이 포함됩니다. **서비스**를 클릭하셔서 수리 일정을 잡거나 문의사항을 남겨주세요.

어휘 | concentrate on ~에 집중하다 **underserved** 서비스나 혜택이 부족한 **expand** 확대시키다, 확장되다 **exclusively** 독점적으로, 배타적으로 **enthusiast** 애호가 **debut** 신상품으로 소개하다, 데뷔하다 **attire** 의복, 복장 **reconditioning** 수리 **restringing** 줄 교체 **inquiry** 문의

11 CSE 소유주에 대해 명시된 것은?

(A) 스포츠웨어를 디자인한다.
(B) 함께 테니스를 친다.
(C) 사이클 프로 선수이다.
(D) CSE 체인점을 매각할 의향이 있다.

해설 | Not / True

첫 번째 단락 첫 문장에서 '사업 및 테니스 동료(Business and tennis partners)인 그레이스 클레이와 아멜리아 로스가 첫 시티와이드 스포츠 엠포리움(CSE)을 설립했다'고 했으므로 (B)가 정답이다.

패러프레이징
지문의 tennis partners → 보기의 play tennis together

12 첫 번째 단락 1행에 쓰인 "established"와 의미상 가장 가까운 것은?

(A) 보여주었다
(B) 도전했다
(C) 소개했다
(D) 제공했다

해설 | 동의어

established는 '설립했다'는 의미로 쓰였기에 '소개했다, 도입했다'를 뜻하는 (C) introduced가 정답이다.

13 CSE에 대해 암시된 것은?

(A) 모험 스포츠 장비를 판매하지 않는다.
(B) 웰링턴 이외 지역에 매장을 가지고 있지 않다.
(C) 제품을 더 이상 온라인으로 판매하지 않는다.
(D) 램턴 키에서 더 이상 매장을 운영하지 않는다.

해설 | 추론

첫 단락 두 번째 문장에서 'CSE는 설립 당시 대부분의 스포츠용품 소매업체들이 모험 스포츠 상품에 집중하고 있으며 그런 스포츠에 관심이 없는 웰링턴 주민들은 혜택을 받지 못하고 있다는 것을 깨달았다(They realized that most sporting goods retailers at the time were concentrating on adventure sports merchandise ~ and Wellington residents with less extreme interests were underserved)'고 했고, 첫 단락 마지막 문장에서 '이제는 전국에서 테니스, 사이클, 육상 애호가 전용 최고의 매장이 되었다(CSE is the top destination exclusively for tennis, cycling, and running enthusiasts across the country)'고 했으므로 CSE는 모험 스포츠 상품을 판매하지 않는다고 짐작할 수 있다. 따라서 (A)가 정답이다.

어휘 | no longer 더 이상 ~ 않는

패러프레이징
지문의 adventure sports merchandise
→ 보기의 adventure sports gear

14 CSE 고객이 보웬 가 매장에서만 이용할 수 있는 것은?

(A) 운동화
(B) 운동 수업
(C) 운동복
(D) 장비 수리

해설 | 세부 사항

마지막 단락에서 '본점에서만 단독으로 이용하실 수 있는 특별 서비스가 있다면서(special services are available exclusively at our original location), 해당 서비스에는 자전거 및 러닝머신 수리, 테니스 라켓 줄 교체 등이 포함된다(These services include bicycle and treadmill reconditioning, tennis racquet restringing ~)'고 했다. 첫 단락 첫 문장에서 '그레이스 클레이와 아멜리아 로스가 10년 전 보웬 가 164번지에 첫 시티와이드 스포츠 엠포리움을 설립했다(established the first Citywide Sports Emporium (CSE) at 164 Bowen Street a decade ago)'고 했으므로 보웬 가 매장이 본점인 것을 알 수 있고 그곳에서만 장비 수리가 가능하다고 했으므로 (D)가 정답이다.

어휘 | athletic 육상의

패러프레이징
지문의 bicycle and treadmill reconditioning, tennis racquet restringing → 보기의 Equipment repair

[15-17] 설문지

프랭크 자동차 정비소
센트럴 가 112번지

고객용 설문지

고객님의 의견은 저희에게 중요합니다. 저희는 이 조사에서 수집된 정보를 바탕으로 저희의 서비스를 개선할 것입니다. 고객님께서 자동차 정비업체를 선택하실 때 다음의 요소들이 각각 얼마나 중요한지 표시해 주십시오. 1-6의 숫자에 동그라미로 표시해 주세요.

	중요하지 않음				아주 중요함	
가격	1	2	3	4	⑤	6
¹⁵편리한 위치	1	②	3	4	5	6
숙련된 정비사	1	2	3	4	5	⑥
친절한 사무실 직원	1	2	3	④	5	6

저희 직원들이:
¹⁶고객님의 자동차에 필요한 작업에 대해 명확하게 설명했습니까?   아니요 X   네 ___
¹⁶⁽ᴰ⁾고객님에게 예의 바르고 공손하게 처신했습니까?
                                                   아니요 ___   네 X
¹⁶⁽ᶜ⁾작업 소요 시간을 정확하게 예상했습니까?
                                                   아니요 ___   네 X
¹⁶⁽ᴬ⁾고객님의 자동차를 수리하기 전에 비용에 대해 말했습니까?   아니요 ___   네 X

의견:
전 제 자동차에 뭐가 고장 났는지를 잘 알 수 없었는데 정비사들은 쉽고 빠르게 수리할 수 있었습니다. ¹⁷가격 역시 적당했습니다. 하지만 다음에는 ¹⁶수리 작업에 대해 좀 더 자세히 알려 주시면 도움이 될 것 같습니다.

어휘 | auto repair 자동차 정비[수리] factor 요인, 요소 automotive 자동차의 convenient 편리한 mechanic 수리공, 정비사 courteous 공손한, 친절한 vehicle 탈것, 차량 accurately 정확히, 틀림없이 estimate 어림하다, 견적서를 작성하다 reasonable 적당한; (가격이) 비싸지 않은

15 고객이 자동차 정비 서비스를 선택할 때 중요시하지 않는 것은?

(A) 정비소의 위치
(B) 직원들이 보여준 배려
(C) 정비사의 경력
(D) 정비 서비스의 가격

해설 | 세부 사항
고객은 평가 요소들 중에서 정비소의 위치(Convenient Location)를 가장 중요하지 않은 것(2점)으로 꼽았으며, 정비사의 경력(Experienced Mechanics)을 가장 중요한 것(6점)으로 평가했다. 따라서 (A)가 정답이다.

16 고객은 서비스의 어떤 면에 만족하지 못했는가?

(A) 필요한 부품의 가격
(B) 정비 작업에 대한 정보의 양
(C) 정비에 소요되는 시간
(D) 직원들의 공손함

해설 | Not / True
서비스 부분에 대한 상세한 내용은 Yes / No 질문 섹션에서 찾아볼 수 있다. (A), (C), (D)에 해당되는 항목들은 'Yes'에 표시되어 있지만, 자동차에 필요한 작업에 대해 명확하게 설명했는가(Clearly explain the work your vehicle needed) 항목에는 'No'에 표시되어 있고, Comments 항목에서 '다음에는 수리 작업에 대해 좀 더 자세히 알려 주면 좋을 것 같다(But it would be helpful next time if I could get more information about the repair)'고 했으므로 (B)가 정답이다.

어휘 | aspect 측면, 양상 part 부품, 부속품

17 고객에 대해 암시된 것은?

(A) 한 번 이상 정비소를 이용했다.
(B) 다시는 프랭크 정비소와 거래하지 않을 것이다.
(C) 수리비에 대해 만족했다.
(D) 자동차에 어떤 문제가 있었는지 알았다.

해설 | 추론
Comments의 두 번째 문장에서 가격이 적당했다(The price was reasonable)고 했으므로 고객은 자동차 수리 비용에 만족했음을 알 수 있다. 따라서 (C)가 정답이다.

어휘 | do business with ~와 거래를 하다

http://www.asterbooks.com/invoice_58579

애스터 북스

주문 번호: 58579
18주문 일자: 2월 8일
예상 배송 일자: 2월 12일

19배송 주소:　　　　**18청구지 발송 주소:**
카디자 알 풀란 씨　　**에이프릴 드류 씨**
93 카버 가, Apt. 16　　231 롬바드 가
뉴욕, NY 10007　　　　체리뷰, NJ 08172

19제목	**저자**	**가격**
<관리 전략>	레오나드 포레스트	32.95달러
<관리자의 성공 단계>	엘리너 츠	42.49달러

소계: 75.44달러
세금: 5.28달러
20배송 및 취급: 무료
신용카드 총 청구 금액: 80.72달러

18선물용 주문인 경우 카드 포함 여부 (추가 요금 없음)
　　　　　　　　　　　X 네 ＿＿＿ 아니요

19카드 메시지: 새 직장 입사를 축하해요! 이 책들이 새로운
직책에 도움이 되길 바랍니다. 벌써 보고 싶네요.

드류 & 이케다 법률 서비스 직원

어휘 | estimated 추측의 strategy 전략 managerial
경영의, 관리의 at no extra charge 추가 요금 없이, 무료로

18 드류 씨가 2월 8일에 한 일은?

(A) 소포 찾기
(B) 배송 취소
(C) 선물 구매
(D) 책 반납

해설 | 세부 사항
청구지 발송 주소(Bill to: Ms. April Drew) 정보에서 드류
씨가 구매자임을 알 수 있다. 주문 일자(Order Date)가 2월
8일로 되어 있고, 하단에서 선물용 주문인 경우 카드 포함
여부(Include card if your order is a gift)를 묻는 질문에
네(Yes)라고 답변하였으므로 드류 씨가 2월 8일에 선물을
구매했음을 알 수 있다. 따라서 (C)가 정답이다.

19 알 풀란 씨에 대해 암시된 것은?

(A) 최근 관리자로 채용됐다.
(B) 대학 과정에 등록했다.
(C) 드류 씨의 관리자이다.
(D) 책을 썼다.

해설 | 추론
배송 주소 정보(Ship to: Ms. Kadija Al-Fulan)에서
알 풀란 씨가 수령자임을 알 수 있다. 하단의 카드
메시지(Message for card)에서 '새 직장 입사를
축하한다(Congratulations on your new job)'고 한
후, '이 책들이 새로운 직책에 도움이 되길 바란다(We
hope these books will be helpful in your new
position)'고 했다. 구입한 도서 제목(Title)이 <관리
전략>(Management Strategies)과 <관리자의 성공
단계>(Steps to Managerial Success)이므로 관리자를
대상으로 한 도서임을 알 수 있다. 따라서 도서 수령자인 알
풀란 씨는 최근 관리자로 채용됐다고 짐작할 수 있으므로
(A)가 정답이다.

어휘 | enroll in ~에 등록하다

패러프레이징
지문의 your new job → 보기의 was recently hired

20 애스터 북스에 대해 명시된 것은?

(A) 추가 요금 없이 주문 물품을 배송했다.
(B) 잡지를 출판한다.
(C) 상품권을 판매한다.
(D) 주문을 받고 하루 지나서 주문 물품을 배송했다.

해설 | Not / True
배송 및 취급(Shipping and Handling)이 무료(Free)라고
했으므로 애스터 북스는 추가 요금 없이 주문 물품을
배송했다는 것을 알 수 있다.

어휘 | publish 출판하다

패러프레이징
지문의 Free → 보기의 at no additional charge

[21-24] 웹페이지

http://www.eypf.org.uk/

엘리스 영 시 축제

아카이브	EYPF 소개	입장권	홈

엘리스 영 시 축제는 영국 최대 시 축제 중 하나로 유명한
동시대 시인들과 수백 명의 다른 참가자들이 전 세계에서
찾고 있습니다. **21(B)상단의 '아카이브' 탭을 클릭하셔서 참여
시인들의 간단한 약력**과 **21(A)지난 축제의 낭송 동영상**을
확인하세요.

올해 축제는 7월 6일과 7일에 페이즐리에 있는 로즈힐
가든에서 개최됩니다. 입장권은 성인 15파운드, 12세 이하
아동 10파운드입니다. **21(C)예매 입장권은 5월 20일부터**
www.eypf.org.uk/tickets (상단 '입장권' 탭)에서
온라인으로 구매하실 수 있습니다.

발표작 제출

축제에서의 정식 발표를 위해 누구나 자신의 작품을 제출할 수 있습니다. **22제출물에는 100~400행 길이의 작품 견본이 반드시 있어야 합니다.** 작품 견본은 장편 시 한 편 또는 여러 편의 단편 시로 구성하시면 됩니다. 출판작과 미출판작 모두 제출 가능합니다. 지원자의 작품 낭송 동영상은 도움이 되지만 필수사항은 아닙니다.

제출물은 늦어도 3월 25일까지 수신되어야 합니다. 본인의 제출 상황에 관한 문의는 삼가 주십시오. **23모든 지원자는 우편으로 접수 확인서를 수신하게 되며** 선발된 지원자에게는 4월 25일까지 연락을 드릴 예정입니다. 제출품이 많은 관계로 선발 과정 마무리 단계에서 발표 초청을 받는 지원자에게만 연락드릴 수 있습니다.

다음 주소로 심사할 작품을 보내주세요.
엘리스 영 시 축제, 캐리 우드 앞
사서함 29001, 던디 DD1 4BG

축제 기간 동안 수차례의 공개 낭송회도 열립니다. **24청중 앞에서 시 낭송을 하고 싶으신 분은 이 낭송회에 와 주십시오. 이 경우 사전에 지원하지 않으셔도 됩니다.**

어휘 | renowned 유명한, 저명한 contemporary 동시대의 attendee 참석자 biography 전기 advance sale 예매 submission 제출 eligible (자격을 갖춘) ~할 수 있는 consist of ~로 구성되다 any number of 많은 no later than 늦어도 ~까지는 refrain from ~을 삼가다 status 상황 acknowledgement 접수 통지 due to ~ 때문에 application 지원, 신청

21 축제 웹사이트에서 할 수 있는 것으로 명시되지 않은 것은?

(A) 지난 공연 녹화분 보기
(B) 유명 시인들의 삶에 관해 읽기
(C) 축제 입장권 구매하기
(D) 시 강좌 참석 등록하기

해설 | Not / True
웹페이지의 첫 단락 마지막 문장에서 '상단의 '아카이브' 탭을 클릭하셔서 참여 시인들의 간단한 약력(short biographies of the featured poets)과 지난 축제의 낭송 동영상을 확인하라(see videos of readings at past festivals)'는 부분에서 (A)와 (B)가 언급되었다. 두 번째 단락 마지막 문장에서 '예매 입장권은 5월 20일부터 온라인으로 구매하실 수 있다(Advance sale tickets will be available for purchase online ~)'고 했으므로 (C)가 언급되었다. 하지만 시 강좌 참석 등록에 대한 이야기는 없으므로 (D)가 정답이다.

어휘 | register 등록하다

패러프레이징
지문의 videos of readings at past festivals
→ 보기의 recordings of past performances

지문의 biographies of the featured poets
→ 보기의 lives of famous poets
지문의 purchase → 보기의 buy

22 지원자의 시 제출 요건은?

(A) 미출판작이어야 한다.
(B) 동영상으로 녹화해야 한다.
(C) 명시된 길이여야 한다.
(D) 특정 형식으로 써야 한다.

해설 | 세부 사항
발표작 제출(Presentation Submissions)의 첫 단락에서 '제출물에는 100~400행 길이의 작품 견본이 반드시 있어야 한다(Submissions must include a work sample containing between 100 and 400 lines)'고 했으므로 (C)가 정답이다.

어휘 | requirement 필요조건, 요건 specified 명시된

패러프레이징
지문의 between 100 and 400 lines
→ 보기의 a specified length

23 축제에 작품을 제출한 모든 사람이 받게 될 것은?

(A) 작품 접수 확인 서신
(B) 검수자들의 최종 결정을 명시한 서신
(C) 작품평 목록
(D) 축제 독점 행사 출입증

해설 | 세부 사항
발표작 제출(Presentation Submissions)의 두 번째 단락에서 '모든 지원자는 우편으로 접수 확인서를 수신하게 된다(All applicants will receive a letter of acknowledgement by post)'고 했으므로 (A)가 정답이다.

어휘 | receipt 수령 exclusive 독점적인

패러프레이징
지문의 a letter of acknowledgement
→ 보기의 A letter confirming receipt

24 공개 낭송회에 대해 암시된 것은?

(A) 일반 대중들이 무료로 참석할 수 있다.
(B) 축제 공식 개막 이전에 개최된다.
(C) 여기에서 낭송하는 시인들은 청중의 피드백을 받는다.
(D) 지원이 거절된 시인들은 여기에서 낭송할 수 있다.

해설 | 추론
open reading sessions가 언급되는 마지막 단락에서 '청중 앞에서 시 낭송을 하고 싶으신 분은 이 낭송회에 올 수 있으며 이 경우 사전에 지원하지 않아도 된다(All those wishing to perform their poetry ~ are welcome at these sessions, which do not require advance application)'고 했으므로 지원을 하지 않거나 거절된

시인들이 낭송할 수 있다는 것을 짐작할 수 있다. 따라서 (D)가 정답이다.

어휘 | reject 거부하다

UNIT 06 문자 메시지/온라인 채팅

기출 예제   본책 p.112

성미 정 (오전 9시 24분)
토니, 부카르 씨가 모두의 7월 판매 실적을 요청하고 있어요. 지난주가 마감이었어요. 언제 당신의 것을 보내줄 수 있나요?

토니 발레리오 (오전 9시 30분)
죄송해요. 제가 아파서 결근했거든요. 지금 작업 중입니다.

성미 정 (오전 9시 35분)
아, 몰랐네요. 회복하셔서 다행입니다. **¹목표는 달성하신 것 같나요?**

토니 발레리오 (오전 9시 40분)
모르겠어요. 정오까지 보내 드리겠습니다.

성미 정 (오전 9시 45분)
감사합니다. 전반적으로 **²지난달만큼 차를 많이 팔지 못했는데,** 영업사원 중 다수가 휴가였기 때문인 듯합니다.

어휘 | figure 수치 due ~하기로 되어 있는 be out sick 아파서 결근하다 aware 아는 tell 알다 overall 전반적으로 previous 이전의 possibly 아마 on vacation 휴가 중인

기출 ETS TEST

본책 p.114

1 (C)	**2** (B)	**3** (A)	**4** (D)	**5** (A)	**6** (B)
7 (C)	**8** (C)	**9** (C)	**10** (D)	**11** (B)	**12** (D)
13 (A)	**14** (B)	**15** (D)	**16** (D)	**17** (C)	**18** (C)
19 (A)	**20** (A)	**21** (B)	**22** (A)	**23** (B)	**24** (D)

[1-2] 문자 메시지

이즈라 혼 [오전 11시] 아이야, **¹저와 양 씨와 오늘 정오에 점심을 같이 하시겠어요?** 우리는 회사 구내식당으로 걸어서 갈 예정입니다.

아이야 타나카 [오전 11시 3분] 전 지금 다른 고객의 사무실에 있어요. **¹하지만 오늘 오후 회의에서 뵙겠습니다.**

이즈라 혼 [오전 11시 4분] 회의가 있나요? 언제인가요?

아이야 타나카 [오전 11시 7분] 오후 2시에 있어요. **²코스모 애슬레틱스의 새로운 수영복 라인을 홍보하기 위한 전략을 논의할 것입니다.**

이즈라 혼 [오전 11시 9분] 상기시켜 주셔서 감사해요. 제가 준비해야 할 것이 있나요?

아이야 타나카 [오전 11시 12분] 포커스 그룹의 결과지를 여섯 부 인쇄해 주세요. 제 책상 위에 있는 폴더 안에 있어요. 감사합니다.

어휘 | promote 홍보하다 swimwear 수영복 reminder 상기시키는 것 focus group 포커스 그룹(시장 조사나 여론 조사를 위해 각 계층을 대표하도록 뽑은 소수의 사람들로 이뤄진 그룹)

1 오전 11시 3분에 타나카 씨가 "전 지금 다른 고객의 사무실에 있어요"라고 쓴 의도는 무엇이겠는가?

(A) 책상 위에 두고 온 문서가 필요하다.
(B) 계약을 도와줄 수 없다.
(C) 초대를 수락할 수 없다.
(D) 잘못된 건물 주소로 갔다.

해설 | 의도 파악
11시에 혼 씨가 '오늘 정오에 점심을 같이 할 것(would you like to join Mr. Yang and me for lunch today at noon?)'을 제안하면서 '회사 구내식당으로 걸어서 갈 예정(We are going to walk over to the company cafeteria)'이라고 하자 타나카 씨가 '지금 다른 고객의 사무실에 있는데(I'm at another client's office) 오늘 오후 회의에서 만나자(But I will see you at the meeting this afternoon)'고 했다. 이는 타나카 씨가 혼 씨의 점심 초대를 수락할 수 없음을 의미한다. 따라서 (C)가 정답이다.

어휘 | document 서류, 문서 assist 돕다, 보조하다 contract 계약(서)

2 오후 회의에 대해 명시된 것은?

(A) 더 큰 회의실로 옮길 것이다.
(B) 새로운 제품 라인을 마케팅하는 방법에 초점을 맞출 것이다.
(C) 원래 예정된 것보다 일찍 시작할 것이다.
(D) 양 씨의 프레젠테이션이 포함될 것이다.

해설 | Not / True
11시 7분에 '코스모 애슬레틱스의 새로운 수영복 라인을 홍보하기 위한 전략을 논의할 것(We will be discussing strategies to promote a new line of swimwear for Cosmo Athletics)'이라고 했으므로 (B)가 정답이다.

어휘 | focus on ~에 초점을 맞추다, 집중하다 market 시장에 내놓다 originally 원래

패러프레이징
지문의 be discussing → 보기의 focus on
지문의 strategies promote a new line of swimwear
→ 보기의 how to market a new product line

[3-4] 온라인 채팅

> **라이브 채팅**
>
> **로저 발란드 (오후 12시 21분)**
> 안녕하세요. 코플린 미술용품의 24시간 고객 지원
> 채팅창입니다. 제 이름은 로저입니다. 무엇을 도와드릴까요?
>
> **샤이나 오브스 (오후 12시 22분)**
> ³저는 온라인으로 주문한 제품 4가지를 기다리고 있는데
> 현재 주문이 취소되었다고 확인됩니다. 코플린에서 자주
> 주문을 하는데 전에는 전혀 문제가 없었습니다. ⁴제 계정을
> 확인해 주시겠습니까?
>
> **로저 발란드 (오후 12시 24분)**
> 지금 확인 중입니다. ⁴저희 측에 등록하신 신용카드가
> 만료되어 결제를 처리할 수 없다고 나오네요. 고객 계정에
> 로그인하시면 결제 정보를 업데이트하실 수 있습니다. 그런
> 다음 주문 번호를 클릭하시면 시스템에서 다시 주문을 하실
> 수 있을 겁니다.
>
> **샤이나 오브스 (오후 12시 26분)**
> 지금 바로 해 보겠습니다. 도와주셔서 감사합니다!
>
> ---
> 어휘 | supply 용품　support 지원　cancel 취소하다　bring
> up (컴퓨터 화면에) 띄우다　state 진술하다　expire 만료되다
> process 처리하다　payment 결제　place an order 주문하다

3　오브스 씨가 고객 지원 센터에 연락한 이유는?

(A) 주문품이 도착하지 않았다.
(B) 제품이 파손되었다.
(C) 소포가 실수로 발송되었다.
(D) 제품이 품절되었다.

해설 | 주제/목적
12시 22분에 오브스 씨가 '온라인으로 주문한 제품 4가지를
기다리고 있는데 현재 주문이 취소되었다고 확인된다
(I have been waiting ~ the order was canceled)'고
했으므로 주문품이 배송되지 않고 취소되어 확인하려고
연락했음을 알 수 있다. 따라서 정답은 (A)이다.

어휘 | damaged 파손된　package 소포　out of stock
품절된

4　오후 12시 24분에 발란드 씨가 "지금 확인 중입니다"라고 쓴
의도는 무엇이겠는가?

(A) 상사에게 그 문제에 대해 언급하고 있다.
(B) 오브스 씨가 새 비밀번호를 만드는 것을 돕고 있다.

(C) 일부 품목에 할인을 적용하고 있다.
(D) 오브스 씨의 계정 내역을 보고 있다.

해설 | 의도 파악
12시 22분에 오브스 씨가 '자신의 계정을 확인해 줄 수
있는지(Can you check my account?)' 묻자 12시
24분에 발란드 씨가 '지금 확인 중(I'm bringing it up
now)'이라고 대답하며 '저희 측에 등록하신 신용카드가
만료되어 결제를 처리할 수 없다고 나온다(It states here
~ not process the payment)'고 계정 확인 내용에 대해
설명하고 있는 것으로 보아 오브스 씨의 계정의 세부 내역을
보고 있다는 의도로 한 말임을 알 수 있다. 따라서 (D)가
정답이다.

[5-6] 문자 메시지

> **멜리타 윌슨 (오전 7시 43분)**
> ⁵안타깝게도 어젯밤 제 차가 고장 나서 오늘 출근을 할 수가
> 없어요.
>
> **홍 장 (오전 7시 44분)**
> 유감이네요, 멜리타. 중요한 일정이 있나요?
>
> **멜리타 윌슨 (오전 7시 45분)**
> 네, ⁵오늘 애들레이드 부츠 제조업체의 징 치웬과 내년도
> 마케팅 전략 논의를 위한 약속이 있어요. 오전 10시
> 30분으로 예정되어 있어요.
>
> **홍 장 (오전 7시 46분)**
> 중요한 고객이네요. 우리가 3년 동안 컨설팅을 해 온
> 곳이네요. 회의를 대신 맡아 줄 다른 사람이 있나요, 아니면
> 일정을 다시 잡아야 할까요?
>
> **멜리타 윌슨 (오전 7시 48분)**
> 다시 잡지 말기로 해요. 약속을 잡기가 쉽지 않았어요. ⁶제
> 비서인 벤자민 케니가 이 고객을 위한 제 일에 긴밀히 관여해
> 왔어요. 그러니 그가 저를 대신할 수 있을 겁니다.
>
> **홍 장 (오전 7시 50분)**
> 좋은 생각이네요. 지금 벤자민에게 알리겠습니다.
>
> ---
> 어휘 | unfortunately 안타깝게도　appointment 약속
> manufacturer 제조업체　strategy 전략　cover 대신하다
> arrange 주선하다　assistant 보조원　closely 밀접하게
> involve 관련시키다　fill in 대신하다　notify 알리다

5　윌슨 씨에 대해 암시된 것은?

(A) 회의에 참석할 수 없다.
(B) 치웬 씨의 상사이다.
(C) 새로운 사업주이다.
(D) 긴급한 프로젝트가 없다.

해설 | 추론
7시 43분에 윌슨 씨가 '안타깝게도 어젯밤 차가 고장 나서

오늘 출근을 할 수가 없다(Unfortunately, my car ~ into the office today)'고 했고, 또한 7시 45분에 '오늘 애들레이드 부츠 제조업체의 징 치웬과 내년도 마케팅 전략 논의를 위한 약속이 있다(I have an appointment ~ for next year)'고 했으므로 윌슨 씨는 징 치웬과의 회의에 참석할 수 없음을 짐작할 수 있다. 따라서 정답은 (A)이다.

어휘 | urgent 긴급한

6 오전 7시 50분에 장 씨가 "좋은 생각이네요"라고 쓴 의도는 무엇이겠는가?

(A) 윌슨 씨가 제안한 마케팅 아이디어가 마음에 든다.
(B) 케니 씨가 적절한 대체자가 될 것이라고 생각한다.
(C) 케니 씨가 승진해야 한다는 데에 동의한다.
(D) 약속 일정을 재조정해야 한다고 생각한다.

해설 | 의도 파악
7시 48분에 윌슨 씨가 '비서인 벤자민 케니가 이 고객을 위한 제 일에 긴밀히 관여해 왔으니 그가 저를 대신할 수 있을 것(My assistant, Benjamin Kenney ~ he could fill in for me)'이라고 한 데 대해 7시 50분에 장 씨가 '좋은 생각이다(Sounds good)'라고 했으므로, 케니 씨가 윌슨 씨를 대신할 수 있을 거라는 윌슨 씨의 생각에 동의하려는 의도로 한 말임을 알 수 있다. 따라서 정답은 (B)이다.

패러프레이징
지문의 fill in for ~ → 보기의 replacement

[7-10] 온라인 채팅

제인 코바 [오전 8시 48분] 안녕하세요, 스탠. 공식 발표예요! 우리 소프트웨어 신제품인 DT-3 '인벤토리 매니저'가 다음 달에 출시할 준비가 되었어요.

스탠 밀턴 [오전 8시 50분] 일정대로네요! 곧 이 제품을 어떻게 시연할지 우리 영업사원들을 교육해야겠네요.

제인 코바 [오전 8시 52분] 아! **7가장 경험이 풍부한 사내 강사인 래리 황 씨가 다음 주에 실습을 겸한 설명회를 당신 팀에 해줄 거예요.**

스탠 밀턴 [오전 8시 53분] 하지만 그는 본사에서 일하잖아요. 거기에서 교육받아요?

제인 코바 [오전 8시 54분] 아니요, 그가 회사 셔틀버스를 타고 여기로 올 거예요. 우린 프로그램 일정만 준비하면 돼요. 다음 주 화요일이나 수요일이 팀 일정에 괜찮은가요?

스탠 밀턴 [오전 8시 55분] 지금 단체 이메일을 보내서 사람들이 어느 요일을 선호하는지 알아볼게요.

제인 코바 [오전 8시 57분] 좋아요. 저한테 계속 알려주시고 나중에 더 이야기해요.

마이크 베드퍼드 [오전 9시 46분] 안녕하세요, 좀 늦게 접속해서 미안해요. '교육'이라는 제목의 이메일을 받았어요. **8오늘 워크숍이 있나요? 저는 참석할 수…**

스탠 밀턴 [오전 9시 48분] 아, 아니요. 그 이메일은 DT-3에 대한 실습교육 건이에요.

마이크 베드퍼드 [오전 9시 49분] 아, 좋습니다. **9언제 교육받나요? 교육은 얼마나 오래 할까요?**

스탠 밀턴 [오전 9시 50분] 아직 준비 중이에요.

제인 코바 [오전 9시 52분] 네, 필요한 게 있으시면 뭐든지 제가 준비해드릴게요. **10그리고 이건 영업팀에서 DT-3의 상세 제품 설명을 보실 수 있는 암호(링크)예요.** 명심하세요. 이 암호는 지금은 기밀입니다.

스탠 밀턴 [오전 9시 53분] 알겠어요. 고맙습니다.

어휘 | official 공식적인 release 출시 demonstrate 시연하다 in-house 내부의 hands-on 직접 해보는 headquarters 본사, 본부 put together 준비하다 keep someone posted ~에게 계속 알려주다 work on ~에 대해 작업하다 set up 준비하다 description 설명, 소개 confidential 기밀의

7 래리 황 씨는 누구인가?

(A) 창고 관리자
(B) 소프트웨어 디자이너
(C) 교육 강사
(D) 회장

해설 | 세부 사항
8시 52분에 제인 코바 씨가 '가장 경험이 풍부한 사내 강사인 래리 황 씨가 다음 주에 실습을 겸한 설명회를 당신 팀에 해줄 것(Larry Huang, our most experienced in-house trainer, will give your team a hands-on presentation next week)'이라고 했으므로 정답은 (C)이다.

패러프레이징
지문의 trainer → 보기의 training instructor

8 베드퍼드 씨가 대화에 합류한 이유는 무엇이겠는가?

(A) 영업 회의에 대한 세부 내용을 알려주기 위해
(B) 행사 준비에 대해 다른 사람들에게 감사를 표하기 위해
(C) 행사에 참석할 수 있음을 확인해 주기 위해
(D) 이메일 프로그램에 대한 문제를 상의하기 위해

해설 | 추론
9시 46분에 마이크 베드퍼드 씨가 '오늘 워크숍이 있나요? 저는 참석할 수…(Do we have a workshop today? I can attend…)' 라고 했으므로 정답은 (C)이다.

패러프레이징
지문의 attend → 보기의 be present at

9 오전 9시 50분에 밀턴 씨가 "아직 준비 중이에요"라고 쓴 의도는 무엇인가?

(A) 한 팀원이 결석할 것이다.
(B) 제품 출시가 지연될 것이다.
(C) 일정이 확정되지 않았다.
(D) 입금되지 않았다.

해설 | 의도 파악

9시 49분에 마이크 베드퍼드 씨가 '언제 교육받아요? 교육은 얼마나 오래 할까요?(When will we train? And how long is the training?)'라고 물었을 때 '아직 준비 중이에요(We're still working on it)'라고 대답했다. 이것은 아직 일정이 확정되지 않았다는 의미이므로 정답은 (C)이다.

10 코바 씨가 영업팀에게 제공한 것은?

(A) 교육 매뉴얼
(B) 고객 명단
(C) 계약서
(D) 암호

해설 | 세부 사항

오전 9시 52분에 코바 씨가 '그리고 이건 영업팀에서 DT-3의 상세 제품 설명을 보실 수 있는 암호(And, for the whole sales team, here is the password to view the DT-3's full product description)'라고 했으므로 정답은 (D)이다.

[11-12] 문자 메시지

마리나 뮐러 15시 6분
¹¹오전 투어 그룹의 한 관광객이 모르고 당신의 버스에 선글라스를 두고 내리셨다고 하시네요. 왼쪽 뒤편에 앉았었다고 하시고요. 아직 있는지 확인해 주실래요?

빈센트 듀몬트 15시 7분
그럼요. 지금 당장은 도보 관광 중이니까, 버스로 돌아가는 대로 바로 확인해 볼게요.

마리나 뮐러 15시 7분
고맙습니다. 그렇게 전달할게요.

빈센트 듀몬트 15시 43분
돌아왔는데요. 사각형 렌즈에 빨간 테인가요?

마리나 뮐러 15시 45분
네. 그거 맞아요. 가능하면 오늘 밤에 사무실로 가지러 오고 싶으시대요. 당신 투어는 5시에 끝나지만, 우리는 6시에 닫죠. 한 시간 내에 올 수 있겠어요? ¹²**꽤 멀리 나갔고 차가 많이 막히겠지만요.**

빈센트 듀몬트 15시 46분
보통 그렇게 심하지는 않아요. 늦을 것 같으면 알려 드릴게요.

어휘 | accidentally 우연히 frames 안경테 square 사각 collect ~을 가지러[데리러] 가다

---

11 뮐러 씨가 언급한 문제는?

(A) 등산로가 폐쇄되어 있다.
(B) 한 방문객이 물건을 잃어버렸다.
(C) 버스가 고장 났다.
(D) 투어가 취소되었다.

해설 | 세부 사항

15시 6분에 뮐러 씨가 보낸 메시지에서 '한 관광객이 실수로 선글라스를 놓고 내렸다(A tourist from your morning tour group ~ left her sunglasses on your bus)'는 말이 나오므로, 정답은 (B)이다.

어휘 | hiking trail 등산로 misplace 물건을 잃어버리다 break down 고장 나다

12 15시 46분에 듀몬트 씨가 "보통 그렇게 심하지는 않아요."라고 말할 때 암시하는 것은?

(A) 사람들은 도보 관광을 한 시간 후에 끝낼 수 있다.
(B) 교통체증은 금요일에 가장 심하다.
(C) 대부분의 사람이 투어에 만족하는 것 같다.
(D) 6시까지 사무실로 돌아갈 수 있다.

해설 | 의도 파악

15시 45분에 뮐러 씨가 '꽤 멀리 나갔고 차가 많이 막히겠지만요(I know you're a bit far away and there might be a lot of traffic)'라고 했는데 이에 대해 듀몬트 씨는 '보통 그렇게 심하지는 않다(It's usually not that bad)'고 했다. 즉, 교통 체증이 그렇게 심하지 않아서 6시까지 사무실로 돌아갈 수 있다는 의미이므로 정답은 (D)이다.

[13-16] 온라인 채팅

줄리 펄로우 (오전 10시 5분)
안녕하세요, 조 그리고 오티스. ¹⁵제가 오후 1시에 사토 씨를 기차역으로 모시러 가겠다고 했는데 지금 몸이 좀 안 좋아요. 두 분 중 한 분이 해 주실 수 있을까요?

오티스 호크스워스 (오전 10시 6분)
¹³도와드리고 싶지만, 저는 오후 1시 30분부터 회의에 참석해야 해요.

줄리 펄로우 (오전 10시 9분)
¹⁴사토 씨도 같은 회의에 참석하나요? 그렇다면 어차피 그 없이 회의를 시작할 수 없겠네요.

오티스 호크스워스 (오전 10시 10분)
¹⁴그렇지 않을걸요. 사토 씨는 면접에 참석하러 여기 오는 겁니다.

조 버그도프 (오전 10시 11분)
¹⁵제가 모시러 갈게요. 점심 먹고 사무실로 돌아갈 건데 가는 길에 모시러 갈 수 있습니다.

줄리 펄로우 (오전 10시 12분)
아, 그러네요, 오티스. **14**이번 주에 영업사원 자리를 충원할 계획인 걸 깜빡했어요.

줄리 펄로우 (오전 10시 13분)
완벽해요, 조. 큰 도움이 될 것 같아요.

조 버그도프 (오전 10시 14분)
16사토 씨를 어떻게 알아보죠? 뵌 적이 없어요.

줄리 펄로우 (오전 10시 15분)
16그의 직원 프로필을 보내드릴게요. 사진이 담겨 있어요.

조 버그도프 (오전 10시 16분)
감사합니다!

어휘 | attend 참석하다 on one's way 도중에 recognize 알아보다

---

13 호크스워스 씨가 펄로우 씨를 도울 수 없는 이유는?

(A) 회의에 참석할 예정이다.
(B) 기차역에 있을 예정이다.
(C) 사토 씨를 만난 적이 없다.
(D) 몸이 좋지 않다.

해설 | 세부 사항
10시 6분에 호크스워스 씨가 '도와드리고 싶지만 오후 1시 30분부터 회의에 참석해야 한다(I would offer to help, but I need to be in a meeting starting at 1:30 P.M.)'고 했으므로 (A)가 정답이다.

14 사토 씨가 오는 이유는?

(A) 호크스워스 씨와의 회의에 참석하려고
(B) 영업직 지원자 면접에 참석하려고
(C) 승진을 요청하려고
(D) 펄로우 씨와 점심을 먹으려고

해설 | 세부 사항
10시 9분에 펄로우 씨가 '사토 씨도 같은 회의에 참석하는지(Is Mr. Sato going to the same meeting?)' 묻자 10시 10분에 호크스워스 씨가 '그렇지 않을 것 같다(I don't think so)'며 '그는 면접에 참석하러 여기 오는 것(He's coming to town to attend all the interviews)'이라고 말했다. 또한 10시 12분에 펄로우 씨가 '이번 주에 영업사원 자리를 충원할 계획인 걸 깜빡했다 (I had forgotten ~ fill the salesperson position this week)'고 한 것으로 보아 사토 씨는 영업직 면접에 참석하러 오는 것이므로 정답은 (B)이다.

어휘 | participate in ~에 참여하다 candidate 후보자 promotion 승진

15 오전 10시 13분에 펄로우 씨가 "완벽해요, 조"라고 쓴 의도는 무엇이겠는가?

(A) 버그도프 씨가 사무실로 점심을 가져올 거라서 기쁘다.
(B) 버그도프 씨가 적임자라고 믿는다.
(C) 그날 늦게 버그도프 씨를 만나기를 기대하고 있다.
(D) 역으로 사토 씨를 마중 가겠다는 버그도프 씨의 계획에 찬성한다.

해설 | 의도 파악
10시 5분에 펄로우 씨가 '오후 1시에 사토 씨를 기차역으로 모시러 가겠다고 했는데 몸이 좋지 않다(I offered to pick up Mr. Sato ~ I'm feeling a little sick)'며 '두 분 중 한 분이 해 주실 수 있느냐(Could either of you do it?)'고 도움을 요청했고, 10시 11분에 버그도프 씨가 '내가 모시러 가겠다(I can pick him up)'며 '점심 먹고 사무실로 돌아갈 건데 가는 길에 모시러 갈 수 있다(I will be coming back ~ on my way)'고 한 말에 대해 10시 13분에 펄로우 씨가 '완벽해요, 조(Perfect, Zoe)'라고 호응했다. 따라서 버그도프 씨가 사토 씨를 역으로 모시러 간다는 제안에 찬성하려는 의도로 한 말이므로 (D)가 정답이다.

어휘 | look forward to ~을 기대하다 approve of ~을 찬성하다

16 펄로우 씨가 버그도프 씨에게 사토 씨의 사진을 보내려고 하는 이유는?

(A) 버그도프 씨가 사토 씨의 지원서에 사진을 붙일 수 있도록
(B) 버그도프 씨가 사토 씨의 직원 파일을 수정할 수 있도록
(C) 버그도프 씨가 경비실에 사진을 보낼 수 있도록
(D) 버그도프 씨가 사토 씨를 알아볼 수 있도록

해설 | 세부 사항
10시 14분에 버그도프 씨가 '사토 씨를 어떻게 알아볼지(How will I recognize him?)'를 물으며 '만난 적이 없다(We've never met)'고 하자 10시 15분에 펄로우 씨가 '그의 직원 프로필을 보내주겠다(I'll send you his employee profile)'고 했고 '사진이 담겨 있다(It includes a photo)'고 했다. 따라서 펄로우 씨는 버그도프 씨가 사토 씨를 알아볼 수 있도록 사진이 담긴 직원 프로필을 보낸다는 것을 알 수 있으므로 (D)가 정답이다.

어휘 | add 추가하다 application 지원서 security 보안

[17-20] 문자 메시지

마커스 파본 (오후 12시 40분) 안녕하세요 라라, **17**오늘 오전 영업회의에서 적은 메모를 저에게 이메일로 보내주실 수 있나요?

라라 뉴 (오후 12시 41분) **18**내일 보내드려도 될까요? 먼저 정리를 좀 하고 싶어서요.

마커스 파본 (오후 12시 42분) 그러실 필요 없어요. **18**분명 이해할 수 있을 거예요.

¹⁹라라 뉴 (오후 12시 43분) 알았어요. 지금 구내 식당에서 마무리하고 있어요. 책상에 가자마자 보낼게요.

마커스 파본 (오후 12시 44분) 좋습니다. 언제쯤 될까요?

라라 뉴 (오후 12시 45분) 15분쯤 후에요. 왜 그렇게 서두르세요?

마커스 파본 (오후 12시 46분) ¹⁷분기 보고서를 위한 자료를 검토해야 하거든요. 기한이 오늘 오후까지예요.

라라 뉴 (오후 12시 47분) 아, 그래요! 다음 주 월요일이나 되는 줄 알았어요.

마커스 파본 (오후 12시 48분) 그랬는데 타일러 켈소 씨가 기한을 앞당겼어요.

라라 뉴 (오후 12시 49분) 알았어요, 곧 메모를 보낼게요. ²⁰보고서를 제출하시기 전에 제가 교정을 봐 드리길 원하시면 알려주세요.

마커스 파본 (오후 12시 50분) 고맙습니다! 그렇게 할게요.

어휘 | figure out 이해하다 quarterly 분기의 due ~하기로 되어 있는 proofread 교정을 보다

---

17 파본 씨가 뉴 씨의 메모를 요청하는 이유는?

(A) 자신이 쓴 메모를 잃어버렸다.
(B) 영업 자료 일부가 마음에 들지 않았다.
(C) 쓰고 있는 보고서 때문에 필요하다.
(D) 누가 회의에 참석했는지 알고 싶어한다.

해설 | 세부 사항
12시 40분에 파본 씨는 뉴 씨에게 '오늘 오전 영업회의에서 적은 메모를 이메일로 보내줄 수 있는지(can you e-mail me your notes ~)'를 요청한 후, 12시 46분에 '분기 보고서를 위한 자료를 검토해야 한다(I need to review some of the data for my quarterly report)'고 했으므로 (C)가 정답이다.

패러프레이징
지문의 can you e-mail me your notes
→ 질문의 request Mr. Niu's notes

18 오후 12시 42분에 파본 씨가 '그러실 필요 없어요'라고 쓴 의도는 무엇이겠는가?

(A) 메모의 필요성에 대해 마음을 바꿨다.
(B) 메모를 직접 찾으러 갈 수 없다.
(C) 정리가 안 된 메모로 작업하겠다.
(D) 다음 주 월요일까지 메모를 기다리고 싶다.

해설 | 의도 파악
12시 41분에 뉴 씨가 '내일 보내드려도 되는지(Do you mind if I send them tomorrow)' 묻고 나서 '먼저 정리를 좀 하고 싶다(I'd like to organize them first)'고 하자, 파본 씨가 '그러실 필요 없어요'(No need)'라고 한 후 '분명

이해할 수 있을 거라고(I'm sure I can figure them out)' 했다. 이는 정리가 안 된 메모가 괜찮다는 의도이므로 (C)가 정답이다.

어휘 | in person 직접

19 뉴 씨는 문자 메시지를 보내는 동안 무엇을 하고 있겠는가?

(A) 점심 식사
(B) 회의 참석
(C) 자료 수집
(D) 독서

해설 | 추론
12시 43분에 뉴 씨가 '지금 구내 식당에서 마무리하고 있다(I'm finishing up at the cafeteria now)'고 했으므로 점심 식사 중이라는 것을 짐작할 수 있다. 따라서 (A)가 정답이다.

어휘 | text (휴대전화로) 문자를 보내다

20 뉴 씨는 무엇을 하겠다고 제안하는가?

(A) 보고서 오류 검토
(B) 보고서 기한 변경
(C) 켈소 씨에게 연락
(D) 파본 씨를 위한 서신 전달

해설 | 세부 사항
12시 49분에 뉴 씨가 '보고서를 제출하시기 전에 교정을 봐 드리길 원하시면 알려달라(Let me know if you'd like me to proofread the report ~)'고 했으므로 (A)가 정답이다.

패러프레이징
지문의 proofread the report
→ 보기의 Check a report for errors

[21-24] 온라인 채팅

롤란다 타피아 (오후 4시 46분) 안녕하세요, 엔버. ²¹오늘 오후에 홍보 부서 3층 수도관이 터졌다는 소식을 들으셨는지 모르겠네요.

엔버 아타이 (오후 4시 47분) 전 듣지 못했어요. 해결이 되었나요?

롤란다 타피아 (오후 4시 48분) 유지보수 팀에서 2~3일이 소요될 것이라고 합니다. ²³여기 바닥에 물이 흥건하게 차서 홍보 부서의 저희 6명은 금요일까지 원래 책상에 앉을 수가 없어요. 비어 있는 장소를 찾으려고 합니다. ²¹,²²,²³회계 부서에 빈 책상이 몇 개 있죠?

엔버 아타이 (오후 4시 49분) ²³책상 3개가 있는 방이 하나 더 있어요. 당신의 직원 모두를 환영해요. 또한, 우리 층에 있는 회의실을 3명이 사용할 수 있는지 ²²우리 부서 관리자인 가르셀에게 확인할게요. 그녀를 이 대화에 초대하겠습니다.

22가르셀 베누아 (오후 4시 51분) 롤란다와 엔버, 안녕하세요. 앞으로 3일 동안의 회의실 일정을 살펴보았는데, 거기에서는 내일 아침에만 회의가 한 번 있어요.

엔버 아타이 (오후 4시 53분) ²⁴내 사무실에서 대신 회의를 해도 돼요. 여기에서 이야기를 마무리하면 회의 초대를 변경하겠습니다.

롤란다 타피아 (오후 4시 54분) 완벽하네요. 가르셀, 우리 부서 직원들이 어디에 앉을지 결정하는 것을 당신에게 맡길 수 있을까요? 전 그들이 쓸 임시 노트북 설치에 대해 IT 부서에 연락을 할게요.

엔버 아타이 (오후 4시 55분) 더 필요한 것이 있으면 알려주세요.

가르셀 베누아 (오후 4시 56분) 물론이죠.

롤란다 타피아 (오후 4시 57분) 두 분 모두 정말 감사합니다!

어휘 | fix 수리하다 maintenance 유지 accounting 회계 administrator 관리자 temporary 임시의

21 타피아 씨가 아타이 씨에게 글을 쓴 이유는?

(A) 직원에 대한 정보를 얻기 위해
(B) 문제에 대한 도움을 요청하기 위해
(C) 작업이 완료되었음을 알리기 위해
(D) 회의에 대해 알리기 위해

해설 | 주제/목적
4시 46분에 타피아 씨가 '오늘 오후에 홍보 부서 3층 수도관이 터졌다는 소식을 들으셨는지 모르겠다(I don't know if you've heard that this afternoon, a water pipe broke on the third floor in the advertising department)'고 한 후, 4시 48분에 '회계 부서에 빈 책상이 몇 개 있는지(You have a few empty desks in the accounting department, right?)'를 묻고 있으므로 (B)가 정답이다.

22 베누아 씨에 대해 암시된 것은?

(A) 회계 부서에서 일한다.
(B) IT 부서를 관리한다.
(C) 유지 보수 팀의 일원이다.
(D) 아타이 씨의 고객이다.

해설 | 추론
4시 48분에 타피아 씨가 '회계 부서에 빈 책상이 몇 개 있는지(You have a few empty desks in the accounting department, right?)'를 묻는 질문에 4시 49분에 아타이 씨가 '우리 부서 관리자인 가르셀(my department administrator, Garcelle)'에게 확인을 하겠다고 했으므로 베누아 씨는 회계 부서에서 일한다는 것을 짐작할 수 있다. 따라서 (A)가 정답이다.

23 오후 4시 49분에 아타이 씨가 "당신의 직원 모두를 환영해요"라고 쓴 의도는 무엇이겠는가?

(A) 신입 직원이 자신의 부서에 합류한 것을 기뻐한다.
(B) 홍보 부서 직원들이 자신의 부서 공간을 사용할 수 있다.
(C) 직원들이 견학에 참여하기를 원한다.
(D) 일부 동료들이 그가 프로젝트를 완료하는 데 도움을 줄 수 있다.

해설 | 의도 파악
4시 48분에 타피아 씨가 '바닥에 물이 흥건하게 차서 홍보 부서의 6명은 금요일까지 원래 책상에 앉을 수 없다(The floor is covered ~ six of us from advertising can't be at our regular desks until Friday)'고 한 후, '회계 부서에 빈 책상이 몇 개 있는지(You have a few empty desks in the accounting department, right?)'를 묻자 4시 49분에 회계 부서의 아타이 씨가 '책상 3개가 있는 방이 하나 더 있다(We do have an extra room with three desks in it)'고 답했는데 이는 회계 부서 공간을 사용할 수 있다는 의미이다. 따라서 (B)가 정답이다.

어휘 | hire 신입 사원 personnel 직원들 colleague 동료

패러프레이징
지문의 extra room → 보기의 space

24 아타이 씨는 다음에 무엇을 하겠는가?

(A) 사무실이 청소되도록 주선한다.
(B) 명단을 요청한다.
(C) IT 부서에 새 노트북들을 요청한다.
(D) 회의 장소 변경을 알린다.

해설 | 추론
4시 53분에 아타이 씨가 '내 사무실에서 대신 회의를 열 수 있다(I can hold the meeting in my office instead)'고 한 후, '이야기를 마무리하면 회의 초대를 변경하겠다(I'll make the change to the meeting invitation when we're done here.)'고 했으므로 회의 장소에 대한 변경 정보를 알리려고 한다는 것을 짐작할 수 있다. 따라서 (D)가 정답이다.

어휘 | arrange 주선하다 request 요청하다

패러프레이징
지문의 the meeting in my office
→ 보기의 a meeting location

UNIT 07   이중 지문

기출 예제   이메일 + 전단   본책 p. 122

팀 여러분께,

다음 주에 열릴 점심시간 워크숍 전단을 첨부했습니다. 이는 최근 우리 회사 최고 경영자가 시작한 기업 활동의 일부입니다. **첫 번째 워크숍 시간은 주간 팀 회의와 일정이 겹치지만,** 나머지 두 개 중 하나에는 참석하실 수 있을 겁니다. 여러분의 시간을 할애할 가치가 있을 것입니다.

감사합니다.
아마릴리아 산타나
품질보증팀 책임자

어휘 | attach 첨부하다 flyer 전단 corporate 회사의 initiative 사업 계획 recently 최근에 launch 시작하다 session (특정 활동) 시간 conflict (일정이) 겹치다 worth ~의 가치가 있는 quality 품질 assurance 보증

9월 점심 & 학습 워크숍

이번 달 워크숍은 직원들이 예산 편성, 투자, 장기 재무 계획 수립의 미묘한 차이를 이해하는 데 도움이 될 것입니다. 단 60분 만에, 여러분은 동료들과 점심을 즐기며 금융 감각을 향상시킬 수 있습니다!

강사: 바이 셴은 DBH 인터내셔널의 투자 컨설턴트입니다.

다가오는 워크숍 일정 (모두 오후 12시 30분에 시작):
9월 5일 월요일
9월 6일 화요일
9월 8일 목요일

워크숍에 등록하려면 인사부의 네이트 스테파니 (내선번호 8571)에게 연락하십시오.

어휘 | nuance 미묘한 차이, 뉘앙스 budgeting 예산 편성 investment 투자 long-term 장기적인 financial 재무의 acumen 감각 instructor 강사 register 등록하다

기출 ETS PRACTICE   본책 p. 123

Q (D)

이메일 + 이메일

발신: 리처드 백스터
수신: 제시카 샤이어
전송일: 11월 12일 화요일, 오전 10시 12분
제목: 영업 컨퍼런스

제시카 씨께,

다음 달 디트로이트에서 열리는 연례 마케팅 컨퍼런스에 저 대신 참석하기로 해주셔서 감사합니다. 그 주에 몇몇 한국 고객들이 방문하기로 되어 있는데, 제가 이곳 뉴욕 사무소에서 그들을 만나야 합니다. 작년에 시카고에서 열린 그 회의에 참석했을 때, 저는 그 경험이 매우 보람이 있음을 알게 되었고, 유용한 만남도 많이 가졌습니다. 우리 여행 부서에 연락하여 당신의 항공편과 호텔 예약을 준비하도록 요청하였습니다. 항공편은 12월 1일 일요일 오후 1시에 필라델피아를 출발하여 오후 4시 45분에 디트로이트에 도착할 것입니다. 항공편, 호텔, 렌터카 비용은 EBR 인더스트리즈가 미리 지불할 것입니다. 식비 지원을 위한 수당이 나오지만, 돌아와서 환급을 받아야 합니다. 그러므로 반드시 모든 영수증을 간직했다가 돌아온 후 경리부에 그것을 제출해 주십시오.

컨퍼런스 세미나 일정은 다음과 같습니다. **월요일에는 오전 9시부터 11시 30분까지 전시 마케팅**, 오후 1시 30분부터 4시 30분까지 브랜드 마케팅이 있습니다. 화요일에는 오전 9시부터 11시 30분까지 인터넷 마케팅, 오후 1시 30분부터 4시 30분까지 표적 마케팅이 있습니다.

즐거운 여행 되세요!
리처드

어휘 | take one's place ~를 대신하다 annual 연례의 client 고객 rewarding 보람 있는 make contacts 접촉하다 flight 항공편 make arrangements 준비하다 car rental 자동차 대여 in advance 사전에, 미리 allowance 수당 cover (비용을) 보상하다 reimburse 환급하다 submit 제출하다 accounts payable department 경리부

발신: 제시카 샤이어
수신: 리처드 백스터
전송일: 12월 4일 수요일, 오후 2시 11분
제목: 회신: 영업 컨퍼런스

리처드 씨께,

저는 어젯밤 늦게 마케팅 컨퍼런스에서 돌아왔습니다. **유감스럽게도, 월요일 오전 세미나는 참석률 저조로 취소되었지만, 다른 세미나들은 일정대로 진행되었습니다.** 제가 아주 상세히 메모를 해 놓았고, 이번 주 말까지는 당신에게 완성된 서면 보고서를 제출할 수 있을 겁니다. 이곳에서 있었던 당신의 회의가 순조롭게 진행되었기를 바랍니다. EBR의 영업부를 대표하여 이번 컨퍼런스에 참석할 기회를 주셔서 감사합니다.

제시카

어휘 | due to ~ 때문에 attendance 출석, 참석 take place (행사가) 개최되다, 열리다 as scheduled 일정대로 take notes 기록하다 detailed 상세한 represent 대표하다 sales department 영업부

Q 컨퍼런스에서 어떤 세미나가 취소되었는가?

(A) 브랜드 마케팅

(B) 인터넷 마케팅

(C) 표적 마케팅

(D) 전시 마케팅

해설 | 연계

두 번째 이메일의 두 번째 문장에서 제시카 샤이어는 '월요일 오전 세미나가 참석률 저조로 취소되었다(the Monday morning seminar was canceled due to poor attendance)'고 밝혔다. 그리고 첫 번째 이메일 두 번째 단락에 제시된 회의 일정 중 '월요일에는 오전 9시부터 11시 30분까지 전시 마케팅(On Monday from 9:00 to 11:30 A.M. is Exhibit Marketing)'이라고 했으므로 취소된 세미나가 전시 마케팅임을 알 수 있다. 따라서 (D)가 정답이다.

기출 ETS TEST

본책 p. 124

1 (B)	2 (D)	3 (B)	4 (B)	5 (A)
6 (C)	7 (B)	8 (D)	9 (B)	10 (C)
11 (D)	12 (A)	13 (D)	14 (C)	15 (B)
16 (B)	17 (C)	18 (D)	19 (B)	20 (C)
21 (C)	22 (A)	23 (B)	24 (C)	25 (D)

[1-5] 안내 책자 + 이메일

노르버그 커뮤니티 센터
장소 임대

¹새로 단장한 노르버그 커뮤니티 센터 (NCC)는 비즈니스 회의 및 사교 행사를 위한 장소를 임대합니다. 다음 세부 정보를 참조하십시오.

객실	시간당 비용	수용인원(좌석/입석)
A회의실	$75	20/44
B회의실	$100	60/126
식당	$120	40/84
이벤트 홀	$150	80/170

- ³학교 및 자선 단체는 할인된 가격으로 이용할 수 있습니다.
- ²객실에는 테이블, 의자, 마이크 및 프로젝터가 있습니다.
- ⁵예약 날짜로부터 최소 30일 이상 전에 예약을 취소하는 경우 25달러의 취소 수수료가 발생합니다. 예약 날짜로부터 30일간의 여유를 두지 않고 취소하는 경우 50달러의 수수료가 발생합니다. reservations@norburgcommunitycenter.org로 취소 요청서를 제출하십시오.

어휘 | refurbish 새로 꾸미다 charitable organization 자선단체 incur 초래하다 in advance of ~에 앞서

발신: mari.reed@joycecochranefoundation.org

수신: reservations@norburgcommunitycenter.org

⁵날짜: 6월 25일

제목: 취소 통지

NCC 관계자께,

⁴예상치 못한 비용 발생으로 인해 조이스 코크런 재단(JCF)은 계획대로 NCC에서 연례 자원봉사 감사 만찬을 주최할 수 없습니다. ⁴,⁵이에 11월 14일 예약을 취소합니다. 불편을 끼쳐 드려 유감스럽게 생각합니다.

³우리 자선단체는 지난 8년 동안 NCC에서 이 행사를 개최했으며 지속적으로 우수한 서비스를 받았습니다. NCC는 아름다운 세레니티 호수를 내려다보고 있기 때문에 우리의 축하 모임은 항상 차원이 다른 운치를 만끽해왔습니다. 내년에 귀하의 시설에서 이 행사를 개최할 수 있기를 기대합니다.

감사합니다.

마리 리드

JCF 회장

어휘 | volunteer 자원봉사자 appreciation 감사 regret 유감스럽게 생각하다 charity 자선 단체 consistently 일관되게 overlook (건물 등이) 내려다보다 festive 기념일의, 축하하는 elegance 기품 facility 시설

1 안내 책자에서 NCC에 대해 암시하는 것은?

(A) 프로젝터에 대해서는 추가 요금을 부과한다.

(B) 최근에 개조되었다.

(C) 경영진이 바뀌었다.

(D) 출장 연회 서비스를 제공한다.

해설 | 추론

안내 책자의 첫 번째 단락 첫 문장에서 '새로 단장한 노르버그 커뮤니티 센터 (NCC)(The newly refurbished Norburg Community Center (NCC))'라고 했으므로 NCC는 최근에 개조되었다는 것을 짐작할 수 있다. 따라서 (B)가 정답이다.

어휘 | charge 청구하다 renovate 개조하다 catering service 출장 연회 서비스

패러프레이징

지문의 newly refurbished → 보기의 recently renovated

2 NCC에서 장소를 빌리는 비용에 포함되는 것은?

(A) 사전 이벤트 준비   (B) 청소 서비스

(C) 미니 뷔페 이용   (D) 시청각 장비

해설 | 세부 사항

안내 책자의 중간 부분에서 '객실에는 테이블, 의자, 마이크 및 프로젝터가 있다(Rooms come with tables, chairs, microphones, and projectors)'고 했으므로 (D)가

정답이다.

어휘 | setup 준비, 설정 food station 미니 뷔페
audiovisual equipment 시청각 장비

패러프레이징
지문의 microphones, projectors
→ 보기의 Audiovisual equipment

3 JCF에 대해 암시된 것은?

(A) NCC로부터 매년 자금을 받는다.
(B) NCC로부터 할인을 받을 자격이 있었다.
(C) 설립된 지 8년이 안 되었다.
(D) 현재 자원봉사자를 모집하고 있다.

해설 | 연계
키워드 JCF를 찾아 보도록 한다. 이메일의 첫 문장에서
JCF가 조이스 코크런 재단임을 알 수 있는데, 이메일 두
번째 단락에서 '우리 자선단체(Our charity)'라고 표현한
것을 볼 수 있다. 첫 번째 지문인 안내 책자의 표 아래 첫
문장을 보면 '학교 및 자선 단체는 할인된 가격으로 이용할
수 있다(Discounted rates are available for schools
and charitable organizations)'고 했다. 따라서 JCF는
자선단체로서 NCC로부터 할인 받을 자격이 있다는 것을
짐작할 수 있으므로 정답은 (B)이다.

어휘 | fund 기금 annually 매년 be eligible for ~할 자격이
있다 recruit 모집하다

패러프레이징
지문의 Discounted rates are available → 보기의 It was
eligible for a discount

4 이메일에 따르면, JCF가 예약을 취소해야 하는 이유는?

(A) 더 큰 공간이 필요하다.
(B) 예상치 못한 비용이 발생했다.
(C) 자원봉사자들이 특별한 메뉴를 요청했다.
(D) 회원들이 다른 장소를 선호한다.

해설 | 세부 사항
이메일의 첫 단락 첫 문장에서 '예상치 못한 비용 발생으로
인해(Due to unexpected expenses) NCC에서 연례
자원봉사 감사 만찬을 주최할 수 없다'고 하면서 이에 11월
14일 예약을 취소한다고 했으므로 (B)가 정답이다.

어휘 | unforeseen 예측하지 못한

패러프레이징
지문의 unexpected expenses → 보기의 unforeseen
costs

5 JCF는 취소 수수료로 얼마를 지불해야 하는가?

(A) 25달러
(B) 50달러
(C) 75달러
(D) 100달러

해설 | 연계
cancellation fee를 키워드로 잡고 cancellation fee가
언급되는 부분에서 답을 찾아야 한다. 이메일의 첫 단락
두 번째 문장에서 '11월 14일 예약을 취소한다(We are
canceling the reservation made for November
14)'고 했는데 이메일의 작성 일자는 6월 25일(June
25)이므로 예약 날짜로부터 30일 전에 예약을 취소함을
알 수 있다. 안내 책자에서 '예약 날짜로부터 최소 30일
이상 전에 예약을 취소하는 경우 25달러의 취소 수수료가
발생한다(A $25 cancellation fee will be incurred
if the reservation is canceled at least 30 days in
advance of the reserved date)'고 했으므로 JCF는
취소 수수료로 25달러를 지불해야 함을 알 수 있다. 따라서
(A)가 정답이다.

[6-10] 웹사이트 안내문 + 이메일

주간해양청 (IMA)

홈	소개	서비스	뉴스	채용 기회

인턴십 프로그램

IMA는 연중 내내 인턴을 모집합니다. 현재 IMA의 회계,
홍보, 해양공학 등의 부서에서 인턴을 찾고 있습니다. 인턴십
지원 자격을 위해 지원자는 다음을 필요로 합니다.

- **[10]대학교 마지막 학년 재학 중**
- 신청서 작성
- 이력서 제출
- 대학 강사 1인에게 받은 추천서 제출

인턴은 진행 중인 프로젝트에 IMA 전문가들과 함께 기여하게
됩니다. **[6]인턴은 예정된 기한을 맞추고 부서 동료들과 잘
협력해야 하며 독립적으로 일할 수 있어야 합니다.**

신청서는 www.ima.ti/applications에서 다운받을 수
있습니다. 탄카이 아일랜드 술론 로 11번지 TI442Z로
IMA의 경력 개발 관리자 라메시 나약 씨에게 모든 자료를
보내주십시오. 주의사항: **[7]내부 위원회에서 모든 신청서를
꼼꼼히 검토하므로** 선발 과정은 최대 2개월까지 소요될
수 있습니다. 신청서는 수신일자로부터 1년 동안 IMA
데이터베이스에 보관됩니다.

어휘 | interstate 주간의 accounting 회계 qualify
for ~의 자격을 얻다 applicant 지원자 submit 제출하다
contribute to ~에 기여하다 meet a deadline 기한에
맞추다 collaborate 협력하다 independently 독립적으로,
자주적으로 retain 보유하다, 유지하다

수신: 프로젝트 관리자
발신: 에이미 페리노
날짜: 7월 15일
제목: 다음 회의
첨부: 빌라로보스 입사 의향서

안녕하세요 여러분,

8,10 9월 1일부터 알리시아 빌라로보스가 인턴으로 들어올 예정입니다. 알리시아는 스페인어를 매우 9 **자유자재로 구사하며**, 우리 부서의 다른 업무를 수행하면서 아울러 번역 서비스를 제공할 것입니다. 알리시아가 인턴십 지원서와 함께 제출한 의향서 첨부 파일을 읽어 보세요. **8 8월 1일 회의 중 알리시아가 우리와 함께 일할 4개월간 어떻게 하면 그녀의 역량을 최대한 활용할 수 있을지 논의할 수 있도록 준비해 주십시오.** 회의 직후 알리시아에게 어떤 프로젝트를 맡게 되는지 알리려고 합니다.

감사합니다.

에이미 페리노
홍보부서장

- -

어휘 | have a command of ~을 자유자재로 구사하다
in addition to ~ 이외에, ~에 더하여 letter of interest 의향서
utilize 활용하다

6 안내문에 따르면, 인턴은 무엇을 할 수 있어야 하는가?

(A) 회계 소프트웨어 사용
(B) 스페인어로 보고서 작성
(C) 팀의 일원으로 업무 처리
(D) 전일 근무 일정 준수

해설 | 세부 사항
웹페이지 안내문의 두 번째 단락 마지막 문장에서 '인턴은 부서 동료들과 잘 협력해야 하며 독립적으로 일할 수 있어야 한다(Interns are expected to ~ successfully collaborate with department colleagues, and work independently)'고 했으므로 인턴은 팀의 일원으로 업무 처리를 할 수 있어야 한다는 것을 알 수 있다.

어휘 | maintain 유지하다, 지키다

7 인턴십 신청서에 대해 암시된 것은?

(A) 최대 2개월까지 데이터베이스에 저장된다.
(B) IMA 직원으로 구성된 위원회가 읽어본다.
(C) IMA 웹사이트에서 제출해야 한다.
(D) 지원자의 작업 견본과 함께 내야 한다.

해설 | 추론
applications를 키워드로 잡고 applications가 언급되는 부분에서 답을 찾아야 한다. 웹사이트 안내문 마지막 단락의 Note에서 '내부 위원회에서 모든 신청서를 꼼꼼히 검토한다(all applications are carefully reviewed by an internal committee)'고 했으므로 IMA 직원들로 구성된 위원회에서 검토한다는 것을 알 수 있다. 따라서 (B)가 정답이다.

어휘 | accompany 동반하다

패러프레이징
지문의 reviewed → 보기의 read

지문의 an internal committee
→ 보기의 a panel of IMA employees

8 이메일을 쓴 목적은?

(A) 나약 씨에게 프로젝트 제안서를 제출하라고 관리자들에게 요청하려고
(B) 페리노 씨의 근무시간 변경을 알리려고
(C) 관리자 회의가 연기되었음을 알리려고
(D) 임시직 직원에게 업무를 할당하는 데 도움을 요청하려고

해설 | 주제 / 목적
이메일의 첫 단락 첫 문장에서 '9월 1일부터 알리시아 빌라로보스가 인턴으로 들어올 예정(Starting 1 September, Alicia Villalobos will be joining us as an intern)'이라고 한 후, 네 번째 문장에서 '8월 1일 회의 중 알리시아가 우리와 함께 일할 4개월간 어떻게 하면 그녀의 역량을 최대한 활용할 수 있는지 논의할 수 있도록 준비해달라(Be ready, ~ to discuss how we can best utilize Alicia's skills during the four months she will be with us)'고 했으므로 (D)가 정답이다.

어휘 | postpone 연기하다, 미루다 temporary 임시의, 일시적인

패러프레이징
지문의 during the four months she will be with us
→ 보기의 temporary

9 이메일의 첫 번째 단락 2행에 쓰인 "command"와 의미상 가장 가까운 것은?

(A) 존경   (B) 숙달
(C) 설명   (D) 감사

해설 | 동의어
'알리시아는 스페인어를 매우 자유자재로 구사한다(Alicia, who has a strong command of the Spanish language)'고 했으므로 문맥상 '능력'이라는 뜻으로 쓰였다. 따라서 정답은 (B) mastery이다.

10 빌라로보스 씨에 대해 암시된 것은?

(A) IMA와 1년 근무 계약을 맺었다.
(B) 지원 자료들을 다시 제출하라는 요청을 받았다.
(C) 현재 대학생이다.
(D) 엔지니어 자리를 찾고 있다.

해설 | 연계
이메일의 첫 문장에서 '알리시아 빌라로보스가 인턴으로 들어올 예정(Alicia Villalobos will be joining us as an intern)'이라고 했는데, 웹페이지 안내문에서 '인턴십 지원자는 대학교 마지막 학년 재학 중(be in their final year of university study)'이어야 한다는 필수요건이 있으므로 빌라로보스 씨가 현재 대학생이라고 짐작할 수 있다. 따라서 (C)가 정답이다.

어휘 | contract 계약하다

[11-15] 기사 + 양식

T.E. 하스의 아카이브 전시

댈러스 (5월 2일) – 11,13와이가 23번지에 위치한 인문학 연구도서관 드레이턴 센터에서 연구를 위해 소설가 T.E. 하스의 아카이브를 이용할 수 있게 됐다. 140개가 넘는 상자를 채운 아카이브는 도서관 몬머스실에 소장되어 있다. 11이 대량 문서에는 그의 주요 작품 전부와 12(B)초기 저서들의 자필 원본까지 포함되어 있는데 이는 하스의 생애와 이력을 밝혀준다. 아카이브에는 등장인물 관련 메모, 줄거리 아이디어, 그의 작품에 기반을 둔 영화 여러 편의 홍보 자료 등도 포함된다.

"12(C)T.E. 하스는 우리나라에서 가장 존경받는 작가 중한 분입니다." 13드레이턴 센터 직원인 에블린 브라우넬이 말했다. "그의 소설 25편과 12(D)단편소설집 세 권은 수십 년간 문학도들의 보물이었습니다. 드레이턴 센터는 하스의 자료들을 연구자들이 이용할 수 있도록 하여 동시대 문학도들을 위한 멋진 기회를 마련한 것이죠."

14드레이턴 센터는 원고, 희귀 서적, 시각 자료, 기타 문서들을 연구 목적에 한해서 이용할 수 있게 해 준다. 15신규 회원은 안내데스크에서 드레이턴 센터의 규정을 읽고 서명해야 한다. 또한 2층을 찾아 시설 이용 및 자료 취급에 관한 짧은 동영상을 시청해야 한다. 드레이턴 센터는 월요일부터 금요일, 오전 9시부터 오후 5시까지 운영된다.

어휘 | archive 아카이브, 기록 보관소 humanities 인문학 house 소장하다, 보관하다 publicity 홍보 respected 존경받는, 훌륭한 volume 낱권 treasure 보물 literary 문학의 contemporary 동시대의 manuscript 원고 patron 고객, 후원자 regulation 규정

드레이턴 센터
회원 규정 동의서

드레이턴 센터에 오신 것을 환영합니다. 연구에 도움이 되는 환경을 제공하고 소장품을 보존하며 그것들을 계속 이용할 수 있도록 하기 위해 고객은 도서관 자료 이용에 관한 규정을 준수해야 합니다. 15첨부된 문서를 전부 읽으신 후 드레이턴 센터 규정에 동의하시면 페이지 하단에 서명해 주십시오. 본 서식을 유효한 신분증과 함께 안내데스크에 제출하시고 1년 회원 카드를 받으십시오. 드레이턴 센터는 자료를 센터 밖으로 반출하는 것을 허용하지 않습니다. 고객이 도서관에서 퇴장할 때 모든 가방을 검사합니다.

저는 드레이턴 센터 자료 이용 약관을 숙지하였으며 이에 동의합니다.

날짜: 4월 22일

이름: 제레미 크웰러

15서명: 제레미 크웰러

어휘 | conducive to ~에 도움이 되는 preserve 보존하다 ongoing 진행 중인 concerning ~에 관한 in its entirety 전부, 온전히 그대로 acceptance 수락, 동의 valid 유효한 be subject to ~의 대상이다, ~을 해야 하다 terms and conditions 조건, 약관

---

11 기사에 따르면, 방문자들이 드레이턴 센터에서 할 수 있는 것은?

(A) 자료 보관법 배우기
(B) 글쓰기 워크숍 참석
(C) 인기 저자의 강연 청취
(D) 소장 도서 열람

해설 | 세부 사항
기사의 첫 단락 첫 문장에서 '인문학 연구도서관 드레이턴 센터에서 연구를 위해 소설가 T.E. 하스의 아카이브를 이용할 수 있게 됐다(The archives of fiction writer T.E. Hass are now available for research at the Drayton Center, a humanities research library ~)'고 한 후, 세 번째 문장에서 '이 대량 문서에는 그의 주요 작품 전부가 포함되어 있다(The bulk of the documents, which include all of his major writings ~)'고 했으므로 방문자들은 소장 도서를 열람할 수 있다. 따라서 (D)가 정답이다.

어휘 | lecture 강연, 강의 a collection of ~의 모음

12 T.E. 하스에 대해 언급되지 않은 것은?

(A) 5월에 최신작을 발표할 예정이다.
(B) 일부 작품의 자필본을 만들었다.
(C) 많은 사람들의 존경을 받는다.
(D) 단편소설집을 여러 권 썼다.

해설 | Not / True
기사의 첫 단락 세 번째 문장에서 '이 대량 문서에는 그의 주요 작품 전부와 초기 저서들의 자필 원본(even some original handwritten copies of his earlier books)까지 포함되어 있다'고 했으므로 (B)를, 기사의 두 번째 단락의 첫 문장에서 'T.E. 하스는 우리나라에서 가장 존경받는 작가 중 한 분(T.E. Hass is one of the country's most respected writers)'이라고 했으므로 (C)를, 이어서 '그의 소설 25편과 단편소설집 세 권(His twenty-five novels and three volumes of short stories)은 수십 년간 문학도들의 보물이었다'고 했으므로 (D)를 언급하였다. 하지만 5월에 최신작을 발표할 예정이라는 이야기는 없으므로 (A)가 정답이다.

어휘 | admire 존경하다

13 브라우넬 씨는 누구인가?

(A) 저자
(B) 연구원
(C) 영화제작자
(D) 도서관 직원

해설 | 세부 사항
Ms. Brownell을 키워드로 잡고 Ms. Brownell이 언급되는
부분에서 답을 찾아야 한다. 기사의 두 번째 단락에서
'드레이턴 센터 직원인 에블린 브라우넬(Drayton Center
staff member Evelyn Brownell)'이라고 했으며, 첫
단락 첫 문장에서 '인문학 연구도서관 드레이턴 센터(the
Drayton Center, a humanities research library)'라고
했으므로 브라우넬 씨는 도서관 직원임을 알 수 있다.
따라서 (D)가 정답이다.

14 드레이턴 센터에 대해 명시된 것은?

(A) 정책을 업데이트하고 있다.
(B) 새 자료를 찾고 있다.
(C) 연구원들만 이용 가능하다.
(D) 보관 공간을 확장하고 있다.

해설 | Not/True
기사의 세 번째 단락 첫 문장에서 '드레이턴 센터는 원고,
희귀 서적, 시각 자료, 기타 문서들을 연구 목적에 한해서
이용할 수 있게 해 준다(for research purposes only)'고
했으므로 (C)가 정답이다.

어휘 | expand 확대하다, 확장하다

15 크웰러 씨는 무엇을 하라고 요청받았는가?

(A) 회비 납부
(B) 안내 동영상 시청
(C) 작품 견본 제공
(D) 대출한 자료 연장

해설 | 연계
Mr. Kweller를 키워드로 잡고 Mr. Kweller가 언급되는

부분을 우선 찾아야 한다. 양식의 하단에 Mr. Kweller가
서명을 하였으며, 양식의 세 번째 문장에서 '드레이턴 센터
규정에 동의하시면 페이지 하단에 서명해 달라(Please ~
confirm your acceptance of the Drayton Center's
regulations by signing at the bottom of the page)'고
했으므로 Mr. Kweller가 드레이턴 센터 신규 회원 가입을
했음을 알 수 있다. 기사의 마지막 단락 두 번째와 세 번째
문장에서 '신규 회원은 안내데스크에서 드레이턴 센터의
규정을 읽고 서명해야 하며 2층을 찾아 시설 이용 및 자료
취급에 관한 짧은 동영상을 시청해야 한다(They must also
visit the second floor, where they will view a short
video presentation ~)'고 했으므로 크웰러 씨가 안내
동영상을 시청해야 한다는 것을 알 수 있다. 따라서 (B)가
정답이다.

어휘 | renew 갱신하다, 연장하다

[16-20] 공지 + 웹페이지

앤티가 바부다 상하수도청
공지

앤티가 바부다 상하수도청(WASAAB)은 3월 4일,
세인트 존스 시의 하수도 개선 프로젝트 제3단계(SIP)를
시작합니다. 프로젝트의 목적은 도시 내에서 더욱 효과적인
하수 처리를 가능하게 하는 것입니다.

16,17(B)향후 몇 개월 동안 도심 상업지구 내 기존 하수관이
새 하수관으로 교체될 예정입니다. **16**본 작업으로 인해
많은 도로를 폐쇄해야 합니다. 우회 표지판을 게시하여
영향을 받는 지역 운전자들을 안내할 것입니다. 2월
25일에는 구체적인 도로 폐쇄를 상세히 담은 일정표가 모든
지역 신문에 게재됩니다. 해당 일정표는 3단계 기간 내내
상하수도청 웹사이트 www.wasaab.gov.ag/sipp3에서도
보실 수 있습니다.

183단계는 5월 31일에 완료될 예정이지만 저희
상하수도청은 명시된 기한 전에 단계를 완료할 수 있도록
최선을 다하겠습니다. 단, 예상치 못한 상황이 발생할 경우
해당 기한이 미뤄져야 할 수도 있습니다.

세인트 존스 모든 주민들에게 도움이 될 이 필수 개선
작업을 완료하는 데 있어 안내해주시고 양해해주셔서
감사드립니다. 문의사항 또는 우려사항이 있으실 경우
홍보관 레녹스 코드링턴 씨에게 555-0139로 전화하시거나
lcodrington@wasaab.gov.ag로 이메일을 보내주십시오.

어휘 | sewerage 하수도, 하수 시설 phase 단계 allow for
~을 고려하다, ~이 가능하게 하다 effective 효과적인

---

http://www.abputrans.com.ag

소개	노선	**알림**	연락처

압푸트랜스
앤티가 바부다 대중교통 서비스
버스 정류장 이전

[18]압푸트랜스에서 2월에 발표한 버스 정류장 임시 이전의
마지막 건이 6월 10일부터 시행될 예정입니다. 본 이전은
세인트 존스 하수도 개선 프로젝트(SIP) 제3단계로 시행
중인 작업의 결과입니다. [17(A)]영향을 받는 버스 정류장들은
플리머스 가와 샌달우드 길 사이 블룸필드 로를 따라서
위치해 있습니다. [17(D),19]6월 10일부로 해당 지역 내 18번,
24번, 27번 노선 버스에 탑승하고자 하시는 승객은 칼라바시
가와 쉐이디 파인스 길 사이 프레데릭 로에서 탑승하셔야
합니다. 임시 버스 정류장은 압푸트랜스 로고가 있는 밝은
노란색 표지판으로 표시할 예정입니다. [20]본 조치는 6월
말까지 시행될 예정이나 www.abputrans.com.ag에서 최신
업데이트를 확인해 주시기 바랍니다.

어휘 | alert 경보 advisory 경보, 주의보 public transit
대중교통 relocation 이전 take effect 시행되다, 효력을
발생하다 temporary 임시의, 일시적인 be in effect 시행되다

---

16 공지가 발행된 이유는?

(A) 도시 하수 관리에 관한 문의에 대처하려고
(B) 대중에게 앞으로 있을 도로 폐쇄에 대해 알리려고
(C) 대중에게 프로젝트 승인에 대해 알리려고
(D) 지역사회 프로젝트에 대한 논평을 받으려고

해설 | **주제/목적**
공지의 두 번째 단락의 첫 문장에서 '향후 몇 개월 동안
도심 상업지구 내 기존 하수관이 새 하수관으로 교체될
예정(Over the next several months, existing sewer
pipes will be replaced by new ones in the city's
central business district)'이라고 한 후, '본 작업으로
인해 많은 도로를 폐쇄해야 한다(This work will require
that a number of streets be closed to the public)'고
했으므로 (B)가 정답이다.

어휘 | upcoming 다가오는, 곧 있을 approval 승인
패러프레이징
지문의 Over the next several months
→ 보기의 upcoming
지문의 a number of streets be closed
→ 보기의 road closures

---

17 블룸필드 로에 대해 명시되지 않은 것은?

(A) 부분적으로 대중이 통행할 수 없을 것이다.
(B) 도시 상업 지구에 위치해 있다.
(C) 최근 버스 노선으로 도입되었다.
(D) 여러 버스 노선이 지나간다.

해설 | **연계**
Bloomfield Road를 키워드로 잡고 Bloomfield
Road가 언급되는 부분에서 답을 찾아야 한다. 웹페이지의
세 번째 문장에서 '작업의 영향을 받는 버스 정류장들은
블룸필드 로를 따라서 위치해 있다(The stops that will
be affected are located along Bloomfield Road
~)'고 했으므로 (A)를, 공지의 두 번째 단락의 첫 문장에서
'향후 몇 개월 동안 도심 상업지구 내 기존 하수관이 새
하수관으로 교체될 예정(existing sewer pipes will be
replaced by new ones in the city's central business
district)'이라고 했으므로 (B)를, 웹페이지의 네 번째
문장에서 '6월 10일부로 해당 지역(블룸필드 로) 내 18번,
24번, 27번 노선 버스에 탑승하고자 하시는 승객(riders
who wish to board bus lines 18, 24, and 27)'에서
(D)가 언급되었다. 하지만 최근 버스 노선으로 도입되었다는
이야기는 없으므로 (C)가 정답이다.

어휘 | partially 부분적으로 inaccessible 접근할 수 없는
recently 최근
패러프레이징
지문의 in the city's central business district
→ 보기의 in the city's business section
지문의 bus lines 18, 24, and 27
→ 보기의 multiple bus lines

---

18 하수도 개선 프로젝트 제3단계에 대해 암시된 것은?

(A) 신규 도로 건설이 포함됐다.
(B) 대중의 비판을 받았다.
(C) 널리 홍보되지 못했다.
(D) 원래 예정대로 완료되지 못했다.

해설 | **연계**
공지의 세 번째 단락 첫 문장에서 '3단계가 5월 31일에
완료될 예정(Phase 3 is scheduled to be completed
by 31 May)'이라는 내용이 있는데 웹페이지의 첫 문장에서
'압푸트랜스에서 2월에 발표한 버스 정류장 임시 이전의
마지막 건이 6월 10일부터 시행될 예정(The last in the
series of temporary bus stop relocations ~ will take
effect beginning 10 June)'이며 '본 이전은 세인트 존스
하수도 개선 프로젝트(SIP) 제3단계로 시행 중인 작업의
결과'라고 했으므로 제3단계는 원래 예정대로 완료되지
못했다는 것을 알 수 있다. 따라서 (D)가 정답이다.

어휘 | involve 수반하다, 포함하다 criticize 비판하다
publicize 홍보하다

19 임시 버스 정류장이 위치할 곳은?

(A) 칼라바시 가
(B) 프레데릭 로
(C) 플리머스 가
(D) 샌달우드 길

해설 | 세부 사항
웹페이지의 네 번째 문장에서 '6월 10일부로 해당 지역 내 18번, 24번, 27번 노선 버스에 탑승하고자 하시는 승객은 프레데릭 로에서 탑승하셔야 한다(riders who wish to board bus lines 18, 24, and 27 in the area affected should now do so along Frederic Road ~)'고 했으므로 (B)가 정답이다.

20 7월에 무슨 일이 있을 것인가?

(A) 압푸트랜스가 웹사이트를 다시 디자인한다.
(B) 압푸트랜스가 새 로고를 도입한다.
(C) 일부 버스가 정규 노선으로 복귀한다.
(D) 임시 버스 정류장 일부가 설치된다.

해설 | 추론
웹페이지의 마지막 문장에서 '버스정류장 이전 조치는 6월 말까지 시행될 예정(this measure is scheduled to be in effect through the end of June)'이라고 했으므로 7월에는 정규 노선으로 복구될 것이라고 짐작할 수 있다. 따라서 (C)가 정답이다.

어휘 | install 설치하다

[21-25] 설명서 + 후기

²¹릴커 ECD-2 무선 드릴

릴커의 ECD-2 무선 드릴은 항상 힘이 넘치는 제품입니다. 이제 이 가격대에서 가장 다목적으로 자리매김하게 해 줄 새롭게 향상된 기능을 자랑합니다. ²¹ECD-2의 새롭게 변경된 디자인으로 가장 힘든 작업부터 가장 섬세한 작업에 이르기까지, 어떤 집 수리 작업이든 자신 있게 해결할 수 있습니다. 독점적인 기능을 살펴보시기 바랍니다.

²⁴균형 잡힌 손잡이: ECD-2의 새로운 인체 공학적 손잡이 디자인은 미끄럼 방지 표면을 갖췄으며 손에 꼭 맞는 모양으로 만들어져 피로를 최소화합니다.

세 가지 속도 설정: 이전의 빠름, 느림 설정에 더해 정밀 작업을 위한 매우 느림 설정이 추가됐습니다. 세 가지 속도 모두 앞방향과 역방향으로 작업 가능해 수월한 드릴 작업을 위한 최상의 속도와 방향을 맞추기가 쉽습니다.

팬 냉각 모터: ²²릴커가 특허를 받은 팬 냉각 시스템은 드릴이 과열되는 것을 막아주고 모터 마모를 줄여주어 드릴 수명을 크게 연장시켜 줍니다.

충전 가능한 배터리: 급속 충전 7.2볼트 배터리는 완전히

충전하는 데 두 시간이면 됩니다. ECD-2를 이용하면 프로젝트로 더 빨리 돌아갈 수 있습니다!

어휘 | boast 자랑하다 **feature** 기능 **versatile** 다목적의, 다용도의 **price range** 가격대 **tackle** 씨름하다 **delicate** 섬세한 **exclusive** 독점적인 **ergonomic** 인체 공학의 **fatigue** 피로 **precision** 정확, 정밀 **reverse** 반대, 역 **patented** 특허 받은, 독특한 **extend** 늘리다, 연장하다 **rechargeable** 충전 가능한, 재충전되는

고객 후기

온라인 사용자 네이든 펠톨라; 디트로이트, MI
9월 9일 오전 10시 21분
고객 평점: ★★★★☆ (5점 만점 중 4점)

²³저의 릴커 ECD 드릴이 몇 년 쓰니 마침내 작동을 멈췄습니다. 2주 전 신제품에 대해 알고 바로 구입했죠. 가격은 매우 적당했고 솔직히 더 나은 드릴은 써 보지 못했네요. 다양한 목공 프로젝트를 여러 건 완료하는 동안 어떤 종류의 나무든 잘 뚫을 수 있어 좋았습니다. ²⁴새 드릴의 손잡이는 저에게 훨씬 더 편안하게 맞아서, 손과 손목이 원래 ²⁵모델을 사용했을 때처럼 피로하지 않습니다. 약간 더 넓은 보관함도 마음에 들었어요. 한 가지 불만사항이 있다면 팬을 넣어 재설계한 모터가 이전 드릴의 모터보다 가끔 더 시끄럽고 진동이 심합니다. 하지만 전체적으로 ECD-2는 이미 좋은 제품이 더욱 개선되었군요.

어휘 | rating 등급, 평점 **function** 작동하다, 기능하다 **reasonable** 합당한, 적정한 **carpentry** 목공일, 목공품 **roomy** 널찍한 **vibrate** 진동하다 **previous** 이전의 **overall** 전반적으로 **improvement** 개선, 향상

21 설명서는 어디에서 볼 수 있겠는가?

(A) 지역 업체 명부
(B) 목공 수업 교육 교재
(C) 집 수리 물품 웹사이트
(D) 건설업체 안내 책자

해설 | 추론
설명서의 제목에서 '릴커 ECD-2 무선 드릴(Rilker ECD-2 Cordless Drill)' 제품이 언급되었고, 설명서의 첫 단락 세 번째 문장에서 'ECD-2의 새롭게 변경된 디자인으로 어떤 집 수리 작업이든 자신 있게 해결할 수 있다(With the updated design of the ECD-2, you will feel confident tackling any home-improvement job ~)'고 ECD-2 드릴을 집 수리 물품으로 언급하였다. 따라서 설명서의 출처를 집 수리 물품 웹사이트로 추측할 수 있으므로 (C)가 정답이다.

어휘 | directory 명부, 안내 책자 **carpentry** 목수일

22 ECD-2 드릴에 대해 암시된 것은?

(A) 독특한 냉각 시스템을 갖췄다.
(B) 건설업계 종사자들을 위해 특별 설계됐다.
(C) 전통적인 스타일의 손잡이가 있다.
(D) 가격이 변동되지 않았다.

해설 | **추론**

설명서의 세 번째 독점적인 기능에서 '릴커가 특허를 받은 팬 냉각 시스템(Rilker's patented fan-cooled system)'이라고 했으므로 독특한 냉각 시스템을 갖췄다는 것을 짐작할 수 있다. 따라서 (A)가 정답이다.

어휘 | professional 전문직 종사자 traditional 전통적인

패러프레이징
지문의 patented → 보기의 unique

23 펠톨라 씨에 대해 명시된 것은?

(A) 릴커 직원이었다.
(B) 과거에 릴커 제품을 갖고 있었다.
(C) 반품하고 환불을 받았다.
(D) 최근 집을 지었다.

해설 | **Not / True**

후기의 첫 문장에서 펠톨라 씨가 '릴커 ECD 드릴이 몇 년 쓰니(after years of use) 마침내 작동을 멈췄으며, 2주 전 신제품에 대해 알고 바로 구입했다(When I learned about the updated product two weeks ago, I purchased it right away)'고 했으므로 과거에 릴커 제품을 갖고 있었다는 것을 알 수 있다. 따라서 (B)가 정답이다.

어휘 | associate (직장) 동료 refund 환불

24 펠톨라 씨가 설명서에 열거된 신규 기능 중 특히 인정하는 것은?

(A) 급속 충전 배터리
(B) 향상된 보관함
(C) 미끄럼 방지 손잡이
(D) 환불 보장

해설 | **연계**

후기의 다섯 번째 문장에서 '새 드릴의 손잡이는 훨씬 더 편안하게 맞아서, 손과 손목이 피로하지 않다(The handle on this new drill fits me much more comfortably, and my hand and wrist never get tired ~)'고 했으며, 설명서의 첫 번째 독점적인 기능 설명에서 'ECD-2의 새로운 인체 공학적 손잡이 디자인은 피로를 최소화한다(The ECD-2's new ergonomic grip design features a nonslip surface ~ minimizing fatigue)'고 했으므로 (C)가 정답이다.

어휘 | guarantee 보장

25 후기의 첫 번째 단락 7행에 쓰인 "model"과 의미상 가장 가까운 것은?

(A) 패턴
(B) 목적
(C) 예시
(D) 버전

해설 | **동의어**

original model은 '원래 모델'이라는 의미로 쓰였기에 '버전'을 뜻하는 (D) version이 정답이다.

UNIT 08 삼중 지문

기출 예제 구인 광고 + 이메일 + 달력 본책 p. 134

<온라인 데일리> 웹 편집자

인기 전자 출판물인 <온라인 데일리>에서 웹 편집자를 구하고 있습니다. 이 직책은 주로 기사가 문법과 문체 표준을 준수하는지 확인하기 위해 검토하는 일을 담당합니다. **¹최소 4년의 편집 경력이 기대됩니다.**

어휘 | electronic 전자의 publication 출판(물) seek 구하다 primarily 주로 ensure 반드시 ~이게 하다 adhere to ~을 충실히 지키다 editorial 편집의

안녕하세요 최 씨,

¹<온라인 데일리>의 웹 편집자 자리에 관심을 보여주셔서 감사합니다. 면접 절차를 시작할 수 있도록 귀하를 초대하고 싶습니다. **²채용 지원자는 당사 웹사이트 www.theonlinedaily.com에서 편집 능력 평가를 다운로드 및 완료하여 6월 27일 수요일까지 저희에게 보내주십시오.**

감사합니다.
첼시 트랙스

어휘 | process 과정 prospective 장래의 hire 신입사원 complete 완료하다 assessment 평가

이름: 애나 최		월: 6월
24	일요일	이력서 세 통 발송
25	월요일	편집 능력 평가 시작
²26	**화요일**	**편집 능력 평가 제출**
27	수요일	휴가 여행 계획 작성
28	목요일	10:00: 자동차 정비 예약
29	금요일	트랙스 씨에게 연락

어휘 | car mechanic 자동차 정비공 appointment 약속

이메일 + 광고 + 목록

에레라 씨께,

귀하를 만나 뵙고 저희 임대 아파트 목록 일부를 보여 드릴 기회가 있어서 참 좋았습니다. 일을 추진하는 동안 몇 가지 중요한 사항을 말씀드리려고 이메일을 보냅니다.

저는 귀하가 매물을 찾는 것을 도울 선임 임대 중개인으로 리사 레프케 씨(lisa@altafinders.com)를 배정했습니다. 언제든지 궁금한 사항이 있으시면 555-0143번으로 그녀에게 연락 주십시오. 제가 드렸던 썬마드 빌딩에 대한 광고 전단을 보셨기를 바랍니다. 이 건물은 현재 몇 개의 매물이 나와 있습니다. **¹이 건물의 부동산 관리회사와 맺은 계약 덕분에 저희 중개소는 해당 건물의 아파트 임대에 대한 독점적인 권한을 보유하고 있습니다.** 저희는 언제든지 구경하실 수 있도록 준비해 드릴 수 있습니다.

귀하의 기본 요구 조건을 레프케 씨에게 전달하면서, **²귀하의 최대 임대료 예산이 월 1,700달러이고, 사이델 공원이 보이는 것 중에 가능한 한 가장 큰 세대를 선호하신다는** 내용도 언급했습니다.

다시 한 번 귀하의 일을 맡을 수 있기를 기대합니다.

테드 먼슨
소유주 / 경영자, 알타 파인더스 사

어휘 | rental 임대 assign 배정하다 flyer 전단 vacant 비어 있는 agreement 동의, 협정 property management company 부동산 관리회사 exclusive 독점적인 authorization 권한, 허가 lease 임대하다 viewing 구경 requirement 요구조건 budget 예산

썬마드 빌딩에서 살아보세요

☞ 시내 중심가의 바로 북쪽, 역사적인 극장 지구에 위치한 썬마드 빌딩은 다양하고 훌륭한 거주 조건을 제공합니다. 주민들은 이 건물에서 적당한 금액의 어떤 세대를 선택하더라도 도시 전체의 파노라마 전경을 볼 수 있습니다. 편의 시설은 다음과 같습니다:

- 모든 세대에 신형 냉장고 및 전기 오븐
- 아파트 전용 구내 체력단련실- 모든 입주자에게 무료
- 넉넉한 발코니와 대형 복도 벽장

☞ **¹썬마드 빌딩은 바치 부동산 관리회사에서 관리합니다.** www.bacciproperty.com을 방문하세요.

어휘 | historical 역사적인 panoramic 파노라마의 affordable 가격이 알맞은 amenities 편의 시설 tenant 입주자 spacious 넉넉한 closet 수납장, 벽장

디나 에레라 씨를 위해 선별한 썬마드 빌딩 매물 목록

#1170 동향의 침실 하나짜리 세대 (시내 조망),
　　1,675달러/월　　　　　　　크기: 677제곱피트

#1432 남향의 대형 원룸 세대 (강변 조망),
　　1,575달러/월　　　　　　　크기: 524제곱피트

#1214 서향의 침실 하나짜리 세대 (사이델 공원 조망),
　　1,775달러/월　　　　　　　크기: 636제곱피트

²#1502 서향의 침실 하나짜리 세대 (사이델 공원 조망),
　　1,690달러/월　　　　　　크기: 611제곱피트

어휘 | vacancy 빈 방 generate 만들어 내다 face ~을 향하다 studio 원룸 아파트

---

1 바치 부동산 관리회사에 대한 사실로 가장 적절한 것은?

(A) 먼슨 씨의 회사를 통해 공간을 임대한다.
(B) 상업용 건물과 주거용 건물을 모두 관리한다.
(C) 리사 레프케 씨가 창립했다.
(D) 다른 회사와 합병을 계획 중이다.

해설 | 연계
이메일 두 번째 단락에서 '이 건물의 부동산 관리회사와 맺은 계약 덕분에 저희 중개소는 해당 건물의 아파트 임대에 대한 독점적인 권한을 보유하고 있다(Thanks to an agreement with the building's property management company, my agency has exclusive authorization to lease their apartments)'고 했다. 그리고 두 번째 지문에서 '썬마드 빌딩은 바치 부동산 관리회사에서 관리한다(The Sunmard Building is managed by Bacci Property Ltd.)'고 했다. 이를 통해 바치 부동산 관리회사는 이메일 발신자인 먼슨 씨의 회사를 통해 임대가 된다는 사실을 알 수 있다. 따라서 (A)가 정답이다.

패러프레이징
지문의 lease their apartments → 보기의 rent spaces

2 에레라 씨의 요구사항에 가장 잘 맞는 매물은 무엇이겠는가?

(A) #1170　　　　　　　(B) #1214
(C) #1432　　　　　　　(D) #1502

해설 | 연계
첫 번째 지문인 이메일 세 번째 단락에서 '귀하의 최대 임대료 예산이 월 1,700달러이고, 사이델 공원이 보이는 것 중에 가능한 한 가장 큰 아파트를 선호하신다(your maximum rental budget is $1,700 a month and that you prefer the largest unit available with a view

of Sidell Park)'고 했다. 그리고 세 번째 지문에서 #1502 아파트가 '사이델 공원 조망, 1,690달러/월(view of Sidell Park), $1,690/month)'이라고 명시되어 있으므로 정답은 (D)이다.

기출 ETS TEST 본책 p.136

1 (C)	**2** (B)	**3** (B)	**4** (A)	**5** (D)
6 (D)	**7** (B)	**8** (A)	**9** (D)	**10** (A)
11 (D)	**12** (A)	**13** (C)	**14** (B)	**15** (D)
16 (A)	**17** (A)	**18** (C)	**19** (B)	**20** (A)
21 (B)	**22** (D)	**23** (B)	**24** (A)	**25** (C)

[1-5] 안내 책자 + 카드 + 일정표

쥬얼 피트니스 클럽

1쥬얼 피트니스 클럽 - 신규 회원 특가

❖ 기본 카드 – 월 20달러
❖ 골드 카드 – 월 30달러

1쥬얼 피트니스 클럽에서 여러분은 건강과 운동을 통한 다이어트를 위해 원하는 모든 것을 찾을 수 있습니다. 저희는 모든 지점에서 모든 종류의 운동 기구, 모든 수준에 맞춘 피트니스 수업, 대형 사이즈의 실내 수영장을 제공합니다.

가족이 소유하고 운영하는 업체인 쥬얼 피트니스 클럽은 최고의 트레이너들을 직원으로 두고 있으며 맞춤형 피트니스 프로그램, 각종 그룹 수업 프로그램을 갖추고 있다는 자부심을 갖고 있습니다. **4우리 강사들은 채용되기 전에 피트니스 업계에서 최소 5년의 경력을 갖고 있어야 합니다.**

기본 카드 회원은 모든 운동 기기 및 장비, 그룹 운동 수업을 이용할 수 있습니다. 매일 아침 저희 접수처에서 오전 11시까지 다양한 무료 음료를 이용할 수 있습니다.

골드 카드 회원은 개인 트레이닝 시간 할인 혜택을 추가로 받을 수 있습니다. **3골드 카드 회원은 또한 일주일에 7일 오전 9시부터 오후 9시까지 실내 수영장을 이용할 수 있습니다.**

쥬얼 피트니스 클럽의 회원이 되시려면 몬트리올 올드 시티, 듀건 대로 821번지에 있는 저희 본점을 방문해 주세요. **2회원이 되려면 18세 이상이어야 합니다.**

어휘 | regimen 식이 요법 location 지점 complete 완전한 an array of 다양한 workout 운동 equipment 장비 operate 운영하다 proud 자랑스러운 top-notch 최고의 physical 신체의 customized 맞춤의 instructor 강사 industry 산업 full 완전한 access 접근, 이용 reception 접수처 a selection of 다양한 complimentary 무료의

beverage 음료 additional 추가의 advantage 이점 session (특정 활동) 시간

쥬얼 피트니스 클럽

이름: 조안 스탠포드
쥬얼 피트니스 클럽 회원: 20256
3회원권 유형: 골드, 연간
시작일: 9월 15일

어휘 | effective 시행되는

4쥬얼 피트니스 클럽
듀건 대로 지점
10월 1일 월요일 수업 시간표

주의사항: 수업 참가 최대 인원은 15명입니다.

10월 1일 월요일	수업	강사
오전 7시 30분	5입문 에어로빅	유후아 D.
오전 9시	웨이트리프팅	애니 P.
오후 5시	유산소 댄스 운동	앙투안 G.
오후 6시 30분	5에어로빅 2단계	4사라 J.
오후 7시	의자 요가와 부드러운 스트레칭	마크 T.

어휘 | reminder 상기시켜 주는 메모 cap 한도를 정하다 participant 참가자

1 쥬얼 피트니스 클럽에 대해 암시된 것은?
(A) 새로운 수업을 시간표에 도입하고 있다.
(B) 국영 기업이다.
(C) 고객 수를 늘리기를 원한다.
(D) 지점을 늘리고 있다.

해설 | 추론
안내 책자에서 쥬얼 피트니스 클럽의 신규 회원 특가(Jewel Fitness Club - New Member Special)를 내세우며 첫 문장에서 '쥬얼 피트니스 클럽에서 여러분은 건강과 운동을 통한 다이어트를 위해 원하는 모든 것을 찾을 수 있다(You will find everything ~ Jewel Fitness Club)'고 홍보하고 있다. 따라서 쥬얼 피트니스 클럽은 특가 행사를 통해 신규 회원을 모집하기를 원한다는 것을 알 수 있으므로 (C)가 정답이다.

어휘 | introduce 도입하다 national 국가의 corporation 기업 increase 늘리다 clientele 고객 expand 확장하다 branch 지점

2 안내 책자에 따르면, 회원에게 요구되는 것은?
(A) 일주일에 적어도 두 개의 수업을 들어야 한다.
(B) 최소 18세여야 한다.
(C) 일회성 등록비를 지불해야 한다.
(D) 의사의 승인을 받아야 운동할 수 있다.

안내 책자의 마지막 문장에서 '회원이 되려면 18세 이상이어야 한다(Members must be 18 or older to join)'고 했으므로 (B)가 정답이다.

어휘 | attend 참석하다 at least 최소한 registration 등록 fee 수수료 approval 승인

패러프레이징

지문의 18 or older → 보기의 at least eighteen years

3 스탠포드 씨는 어떤 회원권 혜택을 받을 수 있는가?

(A) 무료 주차 지정 구역

(B) 수영장 매일 이용

(C) 야외 운동 구역 이용

(D) 손님용 무료 이용권

해설 | 연계

Stanford라는 이름이 나오는 부분부터 찾아야 한다. 두 번째 지문인 카드를 보면 스탠포드 씨의 회원권 유형(Membership Type)이 골드(Gold)라고 나온 것을 볼 수 있다. 안내 책자의 네 번째 단락 두 번째 문장에서 '골드 카드 회원은 일주일에 7일 오전 9시부터 오후 9시까지 실내 수영장을 이용할 수 있다(They also have access to our indoor pool ~ seven days a week)'고 했으므로 정답은 (B)이다.

어휘 | designated 지정된 open-air 야외의

4 사라 J.라는 이름의 강사에 대한 설명으로 사실인 것은?

(A) 5년 이상의 전문적인 경력을 가지고 있다.

(B) 초급반을 지도하고 있다.

(C) 하나 이상의 지점에서 수업을 진행한다.

(D) 최근에 고용되었다.

해설 | 연계

Sarah J라는 이름부터 찾아보도록 한다. 마지막 지문인 시간표에 보면 에어로빅 2단계를 가르치는 강사임을 알 수 있다. 안내 책자의 두 번째 단락 두 번째 문장에서 '우리 강사들은 채용되기 전에 피트니스 업계에서 최소 5년의 경력을 갖고 있어야 한다(Our instructors must have at least five years of fitness industry experience before they are hired)'고 했으므로 정답은 (A)이다. 에어로빅 2단계를 가르치고 있으므로 (B)는 오답, 듀건 대로 지점의 시간표만 나와 있으므로 (C)는 알 수 없고, 최근 고용되었는지에 대한 언급도 나와 있지 않으므로 (D)도 답이 될 수 없다.

패러프레이징

지문의 industry experience → 보기의 professional experience

5 시간표에 명시된 것은?

(A) 모든 수업은 추가 비용이 든다.

(B) 일부 수업이 취소되었다.

(C) 각 수업은 하루에 두 번 제공된다.

(D) 수업 중 하나는 두 가지 난이도로 제공된다.

해설 | Not / True

시간표에 따르면 에어로빅 수업에는 입문 에어로빅(Aerobics for Beginners)과 에어로빅 2단계(Aerobics Level 2) 두 가지 수준의 수업이 있으므로 (D)가 정답이다.

어휘 | cancel 취소하다 difficulty 난이도

[6-10] 회람 + 이메일 + 카드

수신: 전 직원

발신: 인사부

날짜: 9월 10일

[7]제목: 정책 업데이트

프리 앤 클리어 회계법인 직원 안내서

[7]선물 금지 정책

직원들과 접촉하는 모든 개인 및 조직에 대한 공정하고 공평한 대우를 보장하기 위해, 모든 프리 앤 클리어 회계 직원들은 다음의 선물 금지 정책을 준수해야 합니다.

직원들은 현재 또는 잠재적 판매업체, 공급업체 또는 고객이 제공하는 어떠한 종류의 선물도, 그 가치에 관계없이, 언제든지, 직장 내에서든 외부에서든 받아서는 안 됩니다.

선물의 예로는 펜, 모자, 티셔츠, 열쇠고리 같은 작은 물건뿐 아니라 더 가치 있는 물건들도 포함됩니다. 이 선물 금지 정책은 음식이나 음료에도 적용됩니다. 단, **[6]직원들은 업무 회의 중 고객의 식사 비용 지불을 위해 법인 카드를 사용할 수는 있습니다.** 문의사항이 있으면 인사부로 직접 문의해 주시기 바랍니다.

어휘 | policy 정책 accounting 회계 handbook 안내서 ensure 보장하다 fair 공평한 impartial 공정한 treatment 대우 organization 조직 abide by 준수하다 value 가치 current 현재의 potential 잠재적인 vendor 판매업체 supplier 공급업체 accept 받다 premises 부지 apply 적용되다 beverage 음료 direct 보내다

수신: 인사부

발신: 노튼 탄

날짜: 9월 12일

제목: 선물 정책

인사부 관계자께,

[8]저는 프리 앤 클리어의 호치민 사무실에서 일하는 직원입니다. [8,10]어제 동료 두 명과 저는 이곳에서 우리 회사의 가장 큰 고객사인 팜 수입업체와의 회의에 참석했습니다. [7,10]회의가 끝날 때 고객사의 최고 재무책임자가 그들의 제품이 가득 담긴 커다란 선물 바구니를 저희에게 주었습니다. 저희는 이틀 전에 온

인사부의 회람을 읽지 못하고 사무실로 바구니를 가져왔습니다. 어떻게 해야 할까요? 선물을 돌려줌으로 인해 팜 수입업체 직원들이 불쾌해 하는 일이 없도록 조심하고 싶습니다.

어떻게 처리해야 할지 알려주십시오.

노튼 탄

어휘 | associate 동료 coworker 동료 importer 수입업체 offend 불쾌하게 하다 proceed 진행하다

9월 15일

탄 씨께,

저는 귀사에 대해 들어본 적이 없어서 ^{9,10}**귀하의 선물 바구니가 도착했을 때 무척 놀랐습니다.** 그리고 나서 귀하께서 동봉하신 귀하의 고충을 설명하는 쪽지를 보았습니다. ¹⁰**선물을 받지 못하신다니 안타깝지만 저희 입주자들이 근사한 프랑스와 이탈리아 음식을 아주 맛있게 드실 거라고 장담드릴 수 있습니다.**

⁹**귀하의 배려에 감사드립니다.**

한나 딥
고령자를 위한 골든 로투스 홈 책임자

어휘 | enclosed 동봉된 explain 설명하다 predicament 곤경 assure 장담하다 fancy 근사한 thoughtfulness 배려

---

6 회람에서 프리 앤 클리어 회계 직원들에 대해 명시한 것은?

(A) 새로운 판매업체와 공급업체를 찾고 있다.
(B) 복장 규정을 따라야 한다.
(C) 고객들에게 종종 펜과 열쇠고리를 제공한다.
(D) 고객들에게 식사 대접을 할 수 있다.

해설 | **Not / True**
회람의 세 번째 단락 세 번째 문장에서 '직원들은 업무 회의 중 고객의 식사 비용 지불을 위해 법인 카드를 사용할 수 있다(employees may use a company credit card to pay for a client's meal during a business meeting)'고 했으므로 (D)가 정답이다.

패러프레이징
지문의 use a company credit card to pay for a client's meal → 보기의 take clients out to eat

7 탄 씨에 대해 암시된 것은?

(A) 최근에 호치민 시로 이사했다.
(B) 정책 변경에 대해 알지 못했다.
(C) 회사의 최고 재무책임자이다.
(D) 전 직원에게 회람을 보냈다.

해설 | **연계**
Thanh이라는 이름을 먼저 찾아보도록 한다. 두 번째 지문인 이메일의 발신자가 탄 씨임을 알 수 있다. 이메일의

세 번째 문장에서 탄 씨가 '회의가 끝날 때 고객사의 최고 재무책임자가 그들의 제품이 가득 담긴 커다란 선물 바구니를 저희에게 주었다(At the end of the meeting ~ with their products)'고 했고 '이틀 전에 온 인사부의 회람을 읽지 못하고 사무실로 바구니를 가져왔다(We had not read ~ back to the office)'고 했다. 첫 번째 지문인 회람의 제목이 '정책 업데이트(Subject: Policy update)'이며 선물 금지 정책(No-Gift Policy)이라는 새로 바뀐 정책에 대해 설명하는 내용이므로 탄 씨는 회람을 읽지 않아 선물 금지에 관한 정책 변경 내용을 몰랐다는 것을 알 수 있다. 따라서 정답은 (B)이다.

어휘 | recently 최근에 be unaware of ~에 대해 모르다

8 팜 수입업체에 대해 암시된 것은?

(A) 호치민 시에 사무실이 있다.
(B) 프리 앤 클리어 회계법인의 새로운 고객이다.
(C) 다른 나라에 지사가 있다.
(D) 이 도시에서 가장 큰 수입업체이다.

해설 | **추론**
이메일의 첫 문장에서 탄 씨가 '프리 앤 클리어의 호치민 사무실에서 일하는 직원(I am an associate ~ Free-and-Clear)'이라고 소개했고 '어제 동료 두 명과 이곳에서 우리 회사의 가장 큰 고객인 팜 수입업체와의 회의에 참석했다(Yesterday, my two coworkers ~ largest client here, Pham Importers)'고 했다. 따라서 팜 수입업체는 탄 씨가 근무 중인 호치민에 있는 회사임을 알 수 있으므로 정답은 (A)이다.

9 카드의 목적은?

(A) 서비스 요청   (B) 음식 주문
(C) 사업 광고   (D) 감사 표시

해설 | **주제 / 목적**
카드의 첫 문장에서 '귀하의 선물 바구니가 도착했을 때 무척 놀랐다(I was very surprised when your gift basket arrived)'고 했고, 마지막 문장에서 '귀하의 배려에 감사드린다(Thank you for your thoughtfulness)'고 했으므로 선물 바구니를 보내준 데 대해 감사를 표하려고 카드를 보냈음을 알 수 있다. 따라서 (D)가 정답이다.

어휘 | advertise 광고하다 express 표현하다 gratitude 감사

패러프레이징
지문의 Thank you → 보기의 gratitude

10 팜 수입업체는 무엇을 판매할 것 같은가?

(A) 해외 식품   (B) 인사 카드
(C) 사무용품   (D) 티셔츠

해설 | **연계**
이메일에 나온 내용을 요약해보면, 탄 씨가 팜 수입업체와의 회의에 참석했다가 회람을 읽지 못한 관계로 선물 바구니를

받아왔다고 했다. 그런데 카드의 첫 문장에서 탄 씨에게 '귀하의 선물 바구니가 도착했을 때 무척 놀랐다(I was very surprised when your gift basket arrived)'면서, 첫 단락의 마지막 문장에서 '선물을 받지 못하신다니 안타깝지만 우리 입주자들이 근사한 프랑스와 이탈리아 음식을 아주 맛있게 드실 거라고 장담드릴 수 있다(I am sorry ~ food items very much)'고 했다. 따라서 팜 수입업체의 제품으로 채워진 선물 바구니에 프랑스와 이탈리아 음식이 담겨 있었음을 알 수 있으므로 (A)가 정답이다.

패러프레이징
지문의 French and Italian food items
→ 보기의 International foods

[11-15] 쿠폰 + 영수증 + 피드백 양식

알타드라이브
10% 할인

다음 서비스에 한해 인시니타스 지점에서 5월 1일부터 31일까지 유효합니다:

1 - 오일 교환
2 - 브레이크 수리
3 - 타이어 정렬
4 - 배터리 교체

예약으로만 가능합니다. www.altadrive.com/mayoffer에서 서비스 일정을 잡으세요. **¹¹재방문 고객에게는 15% 추가 할인 혜택이 제공됩니다.**

¹⁵월요일부터 금요일까지는 오전 7시부터 오후 6시, 토요일에는 오전 7시부터 오후 5시까지 영업합니다.

어휘 | valid 유효한 location 지점 repair 수리 alignment 정렬 replacement 교체 appointment 약속 in addition to ~에 더하여 benefit 혜택

알타드라이브
323 메인 가, 인시니타스, CA 92024
(760) 555-0145

¹¹이름: 케빈 키벨슨   **자동차 제조사: 네투카르**
주소: 137 세이지브러쉬 로   **모델: 스피디**
　　　샌페드로, CA 92007   **색상: 은색**

5월 25일
- 오일 교환　　　　　35달러
- 브레이크 수리　　　400달러
소계　　　　　　　　435달러
10% 할인　　　　　　-43.50달러　(쿠폰)
¹¹¹¹5% 할인　　　　-65.25달러　(감사합니다!)
　　　　　　　　　　326.25달러
타이어 땜질　　　　25달러
총계　　　　　　　351.25달러

정비사 참고 사항: 고객께서 타이어 공기압 경고등이 켜진다고 알려 오심. **¹²조석석 앞 타이어에 금속 조각이 박혀 타이어에서 공기가 새는 것을 발견함.** 금속 조각을 제거하고 타이어를 때운 뒤 타이어 공기압 경고등을 재설정 함.

¹³6월에 예약을 잡으시고 전면유리 와이퍼 교체 및 에어컨 서비스 할인을 받으세요!

어휘 | subtotal 소계 patch 때우다 technician 기술자 pressure 압력 passenger 승객 lodge 박다 leak 새다 remove 제거하다 windshield 전면유리

알타드라이브
고객 만족도 조사

최근 알타드라이브를 방문해 주셔서 감사합니다. 저희는 고객들로부터 의견을 듣고 싶습니다! 다음 사항에 대한 서비스를 평가해 주세요. 1은 '형편 없음,' 5는 '훌륭함'을 의미합니다.

	1	2	3	4	5
팀 지식					X
팀 친절					X
서비스 속도					X
서비스 가치					X

추가 의견이 있으시나요?
전반적으로 훌륭한 정비에 감사드립니다! 쿠폰으로 정비를 받을 만한 가치가 있었습니다. 국경일 하루 전에 정비를 받으러 가서 **¹⁵직원이 충분하지 않았는데도 당일 서비스를 제공해 주셔서 그날 오후 6시 30분에 정비를 마쳤습니다.** 오일 교환과 브레이크 수리만 약속을 잡았지만 타이어 공기압 등에 불이 들어와서 그 문제도 해결해 주셨습니다. **¹⁴대기실은 아주 편안하고 조명이 좋았으며 무료 다과도 감사했습니다.** 하지만 가장 좋았던 것은 높은 테이블로, 노트북을 놓고 쉽게 일을 할 수 있었습니다. 무엇보다도 다음 날 아침에 휴가를 떠날 수 있게 되어 좋았습니다.

케빈 키벨슨

어휘 | satisfaction 만족 survey (설문) 조사 recent 최근의 rate 평가하다 knowledge 지식 courtesy 친절 value 가치 overall 전체적으로 worth 가치가 있는 national holiday 국경일 fully 완전히 staffed 직원이 있는 manage to ~해내다 take care of ~을 돌보다 issue 문제 comfortable 편안한 appreciate 감사하다 complimentary 무료의 refreshment 다과 feature 특징

---

11 키벨슨 씨에 대해 암시된 것은?
　(A) 수리 서비스에 현금을 지불했다.
　(B) 전면유리의 와이퍼를 교체했다.
　(C) 알타드라이브와 같은 지역에 산다.
　(D) 이전에 알타드라이브를 방문했다.

해설 | 연계

Kivelson이라는 이름부터 찾아보도록 한다. 영수증의 이름 란에 케빈 키벨슨(Kevin Kivelson)이라고 나와 있고 15% 할인(15% discount -$65.25)이 추가로 적용되어 있음을 볼 수 있는데, 첫 번째 지문인 쿠폰의 하단에 '재방문 고객에게는 15% 추가 할인 혜택이 제공된다(Discount is in addition ~ returning customers)'고 했다. 따라서 키벨슨 씨가 알타드라이브를 재방문한 고객임을 알 수 있으므로 (D)가 정답이다.

어휘 | previously 이전에

12 영수증에 따르면, 정비사는 어떤 문제를 발견했는가?

(A) 타이어에 금속 조각이 박혀 있었다.
(B) 타이어 땜질 결함이 공기가 새는 원인이었다.
(C) 타이어 공기압 등이 고장 났다.
(D) 타이어 여러 개를 교체해야 했다.

해설 | 세부 사항

영수증의 정비사 참고사항 두 번째 문장에서 '조수석 앞 타이어에 금속 조각이 박혀 타이어에서 공기가 새는 것을 발견했다(We found the customer's ~ tire to leak air)'고 했으므로 (A)가 정답이다.

어휘 | result 결과 faulty 결함이 있는 replace 교체하다

패러프레이징

지문의 the tire had a piece of metal lodged in it → 보기의 A piece of metal was stuck in a tire

13 알타드라이브가 에어컨 서비스에 대해 암시한 것은?

(A) 정비사가 키벨슨 씨에게 추천했다.
(B) 일 년에 한 번씩 일정을 잡아야 한다.
(C) 6월에 할인이 적용된다.
(D) 스피디 모델에 정기적으로 필요하다.

해설 | 추론

영수증의 마지막 문장에서 '6월에 예약을 잡으시고 전면유리 와이퍼 교체 및 에어컨 서비스 할인을 받으시라(Schedule an appointment for June ~ air-conditioning service!)'고 했으므로 6월에 에어컨 서비스를 할인해주는 행사가 있음을 알 수 있다. 따라서 (C)가 정답이다.

어휘 | recommend 추천하다 regularly 정기적으로

14 키벨슨 씨가 대기실에서 가장 마음에 들었던 특징은?

(A) 음료   (B) 테이블
(C) 조명   (D) 의자

해설 | 세부 사항

피드백 양식의 마지막 단락 다섯 번째 문장에서 키벨슨 씨가 '대기실은 아주 편안하고 조명이 좋았으며 무료 다과도 감사했다(Your waiting room is ~ complimentary refreshments)'면서 가장 좋았던 것은 높은 테이블로 노트북을 놓고 쉽게 일을 할 수 있었다(However, my favorite ~ get work done)고 했으므로 (B)가 정답이다.

15 키벨슨 씨의 자동차 수리에 대해 암시된 것은?

(A) 그가 예상했던 것보다 더 비쌌다.
(B) 이른 아침 시간에 예약되었다.
(C) 국경일에 행해졌다.
(D) 영업 시간 이후에 완료되었다.

해설 | 연계

키벨슨 씨가 작성한 피드백 양식을 보면, 마지막 단락 세 번째 문장에서 '직원이 충분하지 않았는데도 당일 서비스를 제공해 주셔서 그날 오후 6시 30분에 정비를 마쳤다(you weren't fully staffed, ~ finished at 6:30 p.m.)'고 했다. 그런데 쿠폰의 마지막 문장을 보면 알타드라이브는 '월요일부터 금요일까지는 오전 7시부터 오후 6시, 토요일에는 오전 7시부터 오후 5시까지 영업한다(Open Monday to Friday, ~ 5:00 p.m.)'고 했다. 따라서 카벨슨 씨의 차량 정비는 영업 시간이 종료된 이후에 완료되었음을 알 수 있으므로 정답은 (D)이다.

어휘 | anticipate 예상하다 complete 완료하다

[16-20] 이메일 + 일정표 + 이메일

발신: 앤소니 밋포드 <a.mitford@rhyta.com.au>
수신: 후안 유 추 <tsou81@bgg.com.sg>
날짜: 5월 4일
제목: 교육 과정
첨부: 📎 일정표

추 씨께,

175월 10일 화요일 본사의 라이타 센터 빌딩에서 귀하를 모시고 직원들을 위한 교육 과정을 진행할 예정입니다. 첨부된 일정표를 보시고 모든 세부 사항이 맞는지 확인해 주세요.

귀하께서 이끌 교육은 3층 회의실에서 진행될 예정으로, 와이파이 연결, 오디오 장비, 영상 디스플레이 시스템이 완비되어 있습니다. **16**귀하의 교육 과정에 직원들의 관심이 매우 높았습니다. 모든 과정은 이미 예약이 꽉 찼습니다. **19**오전 교육에는 직원 15명이, 오후 교육에는 각각 20명씩 등록했습니다.

20교육을 위해 도착하시면 오전 8시 30분에 접수 데스크에서 카이 고메즈 씨를 만나실 겁니다. 그가 회의실로 안내해 드릴 것입니다. 화요일 오전에 호텔로 모시러 갈 사람을 보내야 하는지도 알려 주세요.

앤소니 밋포드
모범 경영 팀

어휘 | training session 교육 (과정) attached 첨부된 confirm 확인하다 details 세부 사항 fully 완전히 equipped 장비를 갖춘 equipment 장비 a great deal of 많은 book 예약하다 sign up 등록하다 best practice 모범 경영

CHAPTER 2

UNIT 08

교육 과정 – 5월 10일 화요일
후안 유 추 (BGG 솔루션)

오전 9시 – 10시	아침식사
¹⁹오전 10시 – 정오	¹⁸,¹⁹"제품을 팔지 않고도 사게 만드는 법: 소셜 미디어 활용을 위한 10가지 전략"
정오 – 오후 1시	점심식사
오후 1시 – 3시	¹⁸"최고의 홍보: 1분 안에 제품을 설명하는 방법"
오후 3시 – 3시 30분	휴식
오후 3시 30분 – 5시 30분	¹⁸"고객의 기대치 관리: 제품의 한계에 대해 설명하는 방법"
오후 5시 30분 – 6시	종료

어휘 | pitch (판매나 설득을 위해 하는) 홍보, 권유 expectation 기대 limitation 한계 wrap up 마무리하다

발신: 후안 유 추 <tsou81@bgg.com.sg>
수신: 앤소니 밋포드 <a.mitford@rhyta.com.au>
날짜: 5월 5일
답장: 교육 과정

밋포드 씨께,

알려주셔서 감사합니다. 일정표는 좋아 보이고 요청하신 대로 저는 오전 8시 30분에 도착할 예정입니다. 첫 교육을 시작하기 전에 제가 장비에 익숙해질 수 있도록 여분의 시간이 있으면 좋겠습니다. 제가 렌트한 차로 직접 그곳까지 운전해서 갈 계획이라 데리러 오시지 않아도 됩니다. 그런데 ²⁰그날 아침 건물에서 저를 만나기로 한 직원이 저를 위해 유인물 출력을 도와줄 수 있을까요?

후안 유 추

어휘 | familiarize A with B A를 B에 익숙하게 하다 rental 임대물 assist 돕다 handout 유인물

16 밋포드 씨가 다가오는 교육 과정에 대해 언급한 것은?

(A) 추가 참석자를 위한 자리가 더 이상 없다.
(B) 참석자들은 몇 가지 자료를 챙겨 와야 한다.
(C) 몇몇 직원들은 여러 과정에 등록했다.
(D) 각 참석자들에게 컴퓨터가 제공될 것이다.

해설 | Not/True
첫 이메일의 두 번째 단락 두 번째 문장에서 '귀하의 교육 과정에 직원들의 관심이 매우 높았다(There has been a great deal of employee interest in your sessions)'며 '모든 과정은 이미 예약이 꽉 찼다(all of them are already fully booked)'고 했으므로 (A)가 정답이다.

어휘 | space 공간 additional 추가의 attendee 참석자

participant 참가자 material 자료 register 등록하다 multiple 다수의 workstation 단말기

패러프레이징
지문의 fully booked → 보기의 no more space for additional attendees

17 추 씨에 대해 명시된 것은?

(A) 밋포드 씨의 직장에서 직원들을 훈련시킬 것이다.
(B) 전에 라이타 센터 빌딩을 방문한 적이 있다.
(C) 밋포드 씨와 워크숍을 함께 이끌 것이다.
(D) 기술 지원 제공을 위해 채용되었다.

해설 | Not/True
첫 이메일의 첫 문장에서 밋포드 씨가 추 씨에게 '5월 10일 화요일 본사의 라이타 센터 빌딩에서 귀하를 모시고 직원들을 위한 교육 과정을 진행할 예정(We will be hosting you ~ our staff on Tuesday, 10 May)'이라고 했으므로 (A)가 정답이다.

어휘 | workplace 직장 previously 이전에 colead 함께 이끌다 support 지원

18 교육 동안 다뤄질 주요 주제는?

(A) 법률 문제
(B) 안전 시스템
(C) 영업 기법
(D) 관리 관행

해설 | 추론
일정표에 나온 교육 과정이 "제품을 팔지 않고도 사게 만드는 법: 소셜 미디어 활용을 위한 10가지 전략", "최고의 홍보: 1분 안에 제품을 설명하는 방법", "고객의 기대치 관리: 제품의 한계에 대해 설명하는 방법"인 것으로 미루어 보아 교육 과정의 주요 주제는 판매, 즉 영업 기법임을 알 수 있다. 따라서 정답은 (C)이다.

19 소셜 미디어에 관한 교육에 얼마나 많은 인원이 참석할 예정인가?

(A) 10
(B) 15
(C) 20
(D) 25

해설 | 연계
첫 이메일의 두 번째 단락 마지막 문장에서 '오전 교육에는 직원 15명이, 오후 교육 각각에는 20명씩 등록했다(There are 15 employees signed up for the morning session and 20 for each of the afternoon sessions)'고 했고, 일정표에 따르면 소셜 미디어 관련 교육은 "소셜 미디어 활용을 위한 10가지 전략"("Ten Strategies for Using Social Media")으로 오전 10시부터 정오까지(10:00-Noon) 오전 시간대에 열리므로 15명이 참석할 것임을 알 수 있다. 따라서 정답은 (B)이다.

20 고메즈 씨는 무엇을 할 것 같은가?

(A) 문서를 복사한다.
(B) 차량을 마련한다.
(C) 계획보다 일찍 도착한다.
(D) 교육 시작 시간을 바꾼다.

해설 | 연계
첫 이메일의 세 번째 단락 첫 문장에서 추 씨에게 '교육을
위해 도착하면 오전 8시 30분에 접수 데스크에서 카이
고메즈 씨를 만날 것(Kai Gomez will meet ~ arrive for
your sessions)'이라고 했고, 두 번째 이메일의 마지막
문장에서 추 씨가 '그날 아침 건물에서 만나기로 한 직원이
유인물 출력을 도와줄 수 있는지(could the employee
who is planning to meet me ~ printing out some
handouts for me?)'를 묻고 있다. 따라서 고메즈 씨는
교육날 아침에 추 씨를 도와 문서 인쇄를 하게 될 것이라고
짐작할 수 있으므로 (A)가 정답이다.

어휘 | arrange 마련하다 transportation 차량

패러프레이징
지문의 printing out some handouts
→ 보기의 Create copies of documents

[21-25] 일정표 + 이메일 + 기사

바토스키 매뉴팩처링
생산 시험 가동 일정
제품: 구아디아나 사무용 의자

날짜	활동
7월 8일 일요일	• 데이비드 마테야 씨 빌고라이 도착
217월 9일 월요일	• 기계 제작 준비 작업 설정 • **21**지정된 사양으로 장비 교정 및 조정
237월 10일 화요일	• 부품 생산 및 조립
7월 11일 수요일	• 내구성 테스트 (무게, 저항력 및 재료 품질)
7월 12일 목요일	• 데이비드 마테야 씨 브라티슬라바로 출발

어휘 | manufacturing 제조업 trial-run 시운전
preproduction 제작 준비 단계의, 생산 개시 이전의 setup
설치, 설정 calibrate 눈금을 매기다, 측정하다 adjust
조정하다 designated 지정된 specifications 사양,
명세서 assembly 조립하다 part 부품 durability 내구성
resistance 저항(력) depart for ~을 향해 떠나다

발신: dmateja@nostilde.sk
수신: thammond@nostilde.it
제목: 구아디아나 시험 가동
24날짜: 7월 13일

하몬드 씨께,

바토스키 매뉴팩처링의 구아디아나 시험 가동에 대한
업데이트입니다. 다행히도 공장이 우리의 설계 사양에 따라
의자를 제조할 여건이 되고 **22**예상 생산 비용도 사업 파트너
관계를 맺을 만한 수치를 보여줍니다.

23월요일에 장비 교정을 감독했고, 그 다음 날 시험 가동
중에 금속 부품을 칠하는 데 사용된 페인트가 우리 사양에
맞지 않는다는 것을 발견했습니다. 제가 문제를 지적한
후에 정확한 페인트로 바로 다시 칠해졌습니다. 그 외에
다른 문제는 없었습니다. 수요일에 의자를 테스트했고 모두
통과했습니다.

24오늘 마틴 하브래넥과 전화상으로 생산 일정을 논의했고
우리의 유통 정책에 따라 출시 날짜에 맞추어 모든 소매점에
의자가 준비되어 있어야 한다고 설명했습니다. **24**하브래넥은
바토스키 매뉴팩처링이 마감 기한을 맞추기 위해 상당한
투자를 할 준비가 되어 있다고 나에게 장담했습니다.

데이비드 마테야

어휘 | be capable of ~ 할 수 있다 per 각 ~에 대하여, ~당
estimated 예상되는, 추정되는 viable 실행 가능한
supervise 감독하다 calibration 측정, 눈금 매기기 coat
칠하다 distribution 유통, 분배 retail 소매 assure
확신시키다 make an investment 투자하다 significant
상당한

폴란드 회사, 노스틸드와 계약 체결

7월 22일 – 폴란드의 빌고라이에 소재한 바토스키
매뉴팩처링은 세계적인 가구 브랜드 노스틸드와 사무용 의자
생산 계약을 체결했다.

노스틸드는 약 20만 개의 의자를 유럽 연합 내 모든 자사
매장에서 배송할 계획이다. 이는 바토스키가 지금까지 받은
가장 큰 주문이다. **24**수요를 충족하기 위해 바토스키는 추가
장비에 투자하여 공장의 생산 능력을 높이기로 약속했다.

"우리는 몇 년째 대규모 장비 구매를 염두에 두고
있었습니다. 공간도 있고 인력 동원도 가능합니다. **25**새로운
장비가 갖추어지면 숙련된 인력을 대거 투입해 즉시 작업할
수 있습니다"라고 마틴 하브래넥 바토스키 매뉴팩처링
사장이 설명했다.

어휘 | Polish 폴란드의 secure a contract 계약을 체결하다
pledge 약속하다, 맹세하다 additional 추가의 capacity
능력, 용량 contemplate 생각하다, 고려하다 large-scale
대규모의 labour[labor] pool 노동 인력 skilled 숙련된
applicant 지원자, 신청자

21 일정에 따르면, 7월 9일에 무슨 일이 있었는가?

(A) 사양이 인쇄되었다.
(B) 기계가 조정되었다.
(C) 직원들이 교육을 받았다.
(D) 품질이 테스트되었다.

해설 | 세부 사항
July 9를 키워드로 잡고 July 9가 언급되는 부분에서 답을 찾아야 한다. 일정에 보면 7월 9일 월요일에 '지정된 사양으로 장비 교정 및 조정(Calibrating and adjusting equipment ~)'이 있다고 했으므로 (B)가 정답이다.

어휘 | personnel 인력 **train** 교육시키다, 훈련하다

패러프레이징
지문의 equipment → 보기의 Machines

22 마테야 씨가 생산 비용에 대해 암시하는 것은?

(A) 하브래넥 씨에 의해 확인될 것이다.
(B) 협상하기 어려웠다.
(C) 수정되었다.
(D) 받아들일 만하다.

해설 | 추론
production costs를 키워드로 잡고 production costs가 언급되는 부분에서 답을 찾아야 한다. 이메일의 첫 단락 마지막 문장에서 '예상 생산 비용도 사업 파트너 관계를 맺을 만한 수치를 보여준다(the estimated production costs suggest that this would be a viable partnership)'고 했으므로 생산 비용은 받아들일 만하다는 것을 짐작할 수 있다. 따라서 (D)가 정답이다.

어휘 | negotiate 협상하다 **revise** 수정하다 **acceptable** 받아들일 만한

23 마테야 씨는 사양을 맞추기 위해 언제 변경을 요청했겠는가?

(A) 7월 8일
(B) 7월 10일
(C) 7월 11일
(D) 7월 12일

해설 | 연계
이메일의 두 번째 단락 첫 문장에서 '월요일에 장비 교정을 감독했고, 그 다음 날 시험 가동 중에 금속 부품을 칠하는 데 사용된 페인트가 우리 사양에 맞지 않는다는 것을 발견하고 나서(On Monday, I supervised the calibration of the equipment, and the next day ~ I noticed that the paint that was used to coat the metal elements did not meet our specifications)' 문제를 지적한 후에 정확한 페인트로 바로 다시 칠해졌다고 했으므로 화요일에 사양을 맞추기 위해 변경을 요청했다는 것을 알 수 있다. 일정표에서 화요일은 7월 10일이므로 (B)가 정답이다.

24 7월 13일에 마테야 씨가 약속 받은 것은?

(A) 바토스키 매뉴팩쳐링이 생산 장비를 추가 구입할 것
(B) 몇몇 고객에게 긴급 배송이 가능할 것
(C) 노스틸드 의자 생산이 당장 시작될 것
(D) 대부분의 재료가 폴란드에서 공급될 것

해설 | 연계
우선 질문에 등장한 날짜 July 13을 찾아보도록 한다. 이메일의 날짜가 7월 13일인 것을 확인하고 읽어보면, 이메일의 세 번째 단락 첫 문장에서 마테야 씨가 '오늘 마틴 하브래넥과 전화상으로 생산 일정을 논의했다(Today, I discussed our production schedule by telephone with Martin Havranec)'고 한 말이 나온다. 마지막 문장에서는 '하브래넥은 바토스키 매뉴팩쳐링이 마감 기한을 맞추기 위해 상당한 투자를 할 준비가 되어 있다(Bartowsky Manufacturing was prepared to make a significant investment)고 장담했다'고 했다. 기사의 두 번째 단락 마지막 문장에서 '수요를 충족하기 위해 바토스키는 추가 장비에 투자하여 공장의 생산 능력을 높이기로 약속했다(the company pledged to invest in additional equipment to increase the factory's production capacity)'고 했으므로 마테야 씨가 약속 받은 것은 바토스키 매뉴팩쳐링의 생산 장비 추가 구매라는 것을 짐작할 수 있다. 따라서 (A)가 정답이다.

어휘 | expedited delivery 긴급 배송 **source** 공급 받다

패러프레이징
지문의 pledged → 질문의 be promised
지문의 additional equipment to increase the factory's production capacity
→ 보기의 additional production equipment

25 하브래넥 씨가 바토스키 매뉴팩쳐링에 대해 암시하는 것은?

(A) 이전에 노스틸드를 위해 제품을 생산했다.
(B) 노스틸드를 위해 독점적으로 의자를 디자인했다.
(C) 자격을 갖춘 근로자를 쉽게 찾을 것이다.
(D) 공장의 한 구역을 수리할 것이다.

해설 | 추론
기사의 마지막 단락 마지막 문장에서 마틴 하브래넥 바토스키 매뉴팩쳐링 사장이 '새로운 장비가 갖추어지면 숙련된 인력을 대거 투입해 즉시 작업할 수 있다(we will be able to put many skilled applicants to work immediately)'고 설명했으므로 자격을 갖춘 근로자를 쉽게 찾을 것이라는 것을 의미한다. 따라서 (C)가 정답이다.

어휘 | exclusively 독점적으로 **qualified** 자격을 갖춘 **section** 부분, 구역

패러프레이징
지문의 be able to put many skilled applicants to work immediately → 보기의 easily find qualified workers

ETS 실전 모의고사 01 본책 p.149

147 (B)	**148** (D)	**149** (D)	**150** (B)	**151** (A)
152 (D)	**153** (B)	**154** (A)	**155** (C)	**156** (C)
157 (D)	**158** (B)	**159** (A)	**160** (D)	**161** (D)
162 (A)	**163** (D)	**164** (C)	**165** (D)	**166** (B)
167 (B)	**168** (B)	**169** (C)	**170** (D)	**171** (A)
172 (B)	**173** (A)	**174** (D)	**175** (B)	**176** (C)
177 (D)	**178** (A)	**179** (D)	**180** (C)	**181** (D)
182 (B)	**183** (C)	**184** (A)	**185** (D)	**186** (C)
187 (D)	**188** (B)	**189** (B)	**190** (A)	**191** (B)
192 (A)	**193** (C)	**194** (D)	**195** (C)	**196** (B)
197 (A)	**198** (A)	**199** (D)	**200** (B)	

[147-148] 광고

다음 단계: 성공!
메리웨더 컨벤션 홀
6월 8일 오전 9시~오후 4시
인사부 담당자들과 만나세요!

주요 사항
- 무료 입장
- **147**300곳 이상의 기업 일자리
- **147**예약제로 운영되는 이력서 작성 지원 (소정의 수수료 적용)
- **147**취업 알선 서비스 이용
- 오늘날 치열한 경쟁 환경에서 직업을 구하고 유지하는 일에 대한 강연 및 토론

148많은 다양한 직종의 종사자들이 참석할 예정입니다: 사무직, 회계, 보안, 판매 및 홍보, 운송 및 하역 등.

어휘 | representative 대리인, 대표 admission 입장 résumé 이력서 appointment 약속 fee 수수료 apply 적용되다 placement 취업 알선 lecture 강의 discussion 토론 competitive 경쟁이 있는 environment 환경 profession (특정 직종) 종사자 represent 대표하다 shipping 운송

147 어떤 행사가 홍보되고 있는가?

(A) 작문 워크숍
(B) 채용 박람회
(C) 컴퓨터 네트워킹 세미나
(D) 인적 자원 관리 강좌

해설 | 주제/목적
행사의 주요 사항이 300곳 이상의 기업 일자리(Open positions with over 300 companies), 예약제로 운영되는 이력서 작성 지원(Résumé-writing help by appointment), 취업 알선 서비스 이용(Professional placement services available) 등으로 구성된 것으로 보아 홍보되고 있는 행사는 채용 박람회임을 알 수 있다. 따라서 (B)가 정답이다.

148 행사에 대해 명시된 것은?

(A) 이틀에 걸쳐 열릴 것이다.
(B) 사무실 건물에서 열릴 것이다.
(C) 모든 활동 및 서비스가 무료이다.
(D) 여러 회사에서 담당자들이 참석할 예정이다.

해설 | Not/True
광고의 하단에 많은 다양한 직종의 종사자들이 참석할 예정(Many different professions will be represented)이라며 사무직, 회계, 보안, 판매 및 홍보, 운송 및 하역 등(office work ~ and more)의 업종을 열거하고 있는 것으로 보아 (D)가 정답이다.

어휘 | take place 열리다 activity 활동 free of charge 무료로

패러프레이징
지문의 professions → 보기의 representatives

[149-150] 문자 메시지

세레나 키타무라 (오후 7시 15분)
안녕하세요, 알렉스. 오늘 사이클로퀘스트에서 우리 동료들은 어땠나요?

알렉스 샐리나스 (오후 7시 16분)
리지로드 팀이 잘 했어요. **149**미카와 조나스는 내리막 경주에서 공동 2위를 했고, 딜런은 크로스컨트리 경기에서 3위로 들어왔어요. 몇 가지 사소한 문제는 있었지만요.

세레나 키타무라 (오후 7시 16분)
정말요? 무슨 일이었는데요?

알렉스 샐리나스 (오후 7시 17분)
미카의 브레이크에 문제가 있어서 우리가 그 다음 경주 전에 고쳤어요. 그 외에도 딜런은 오르막 구간에서 다리 근육이 결렸고요. 그래도 내일이면 괜찮아질 것 같아요.

세레나 키타무라 (오후 7시 18분)
그건 그렇고, **149**이번 주 스틸 프레임 자전거의 온라인 판매가 눈에 띄게 상승했어요. 사실 오늘만 30개 이상

팔렸답니다. **149, 150**리지로드 이글에서 올해
사이클퀘스트의 후원사가 되기로 결정해서 정말
다행이에요.

알렉스 샐리나스 (오후 7시 19분)
맞아요. 정말 잘 풀렸어요, 그렇죠?

어휘 | colleague 동료 **tie for** 공동으로 ~이 되다 **race** 경주
minor 사소한 **pull a muscle** 근육이 결리다 **incidentally**
그건 그렇고 **significant** 중요한 **bump** 격상 **work out** (일이)
잘 풀리다

149 사이클퀘스트는 무엇인가?

(A) 기업 교육 프로그램
(B) 운동 일정
(C) 관광 여행
(D) 자전거 경기

해설 | 세부 사항
7시 16분에 알렉스가 미카와 조나스는 내리막 경주에서
공동 2위를 했고 딜런은 크로스컨트리 경기에서 3위로
들어왔다(Mika and Jonas tied for ~ in cross-
country)고 했으므로 사이클퀘스트가 경주 대회임을 알
수 있다. 또한 7시 18분에 세레나가 이번 주 스틸 프레임
자전거의 온라인 판매가 눈에 띄게 상승했다(this week
we've seen ~ our steel-frame bicycles)며 리지로드
이글에서 올해 사이클퀘스트의 후원사가 되기로
결정해서 정말 다행(I'm glad ~ sponsor of this year's
Cycloquest)이라고 했으므로 리지로드 이글은 자전거
회사이고 사이클퀘스트는 자전거 관련 행사임을 알 수
있다. 이를 종합해 보면 사이클퀘스트는 자전거 경주
대회이므로 정답은 (D)이다.

패러프레이징
지문의 race → 보기의 competition

150 오후 7시 19분에 샐리나스 씨가 "맞아요. 정말 잘 풀렸어요,
그렇죠?"라고 쓴 의도는 무엇이겠는가?

(A) 행사가 재미있었다.
(B) 후원이 성공적이었다.
(C) 그룹의 몸 상태가 좋다.
(D) 판매팀이 열심히 노력 중이다.

해설 | 의도 파악
7시 18분에 세레나가 리지로드 이글에서 올해
사이클퀘스트의 후원사가 되기로 결정해서 정말 다행(I'm
glad ~ sponsor of this year's Cycloquest)이라고
하자, 7시 19분에 샐리나스 씨가 맞다(Yes)고 맞장구치며
정말 잘 풀렸다(it really worked out well, didn't it?)고
덧붙였다. 샐리나스 씨가 후원을 한 일이 잘되었다는
세레나의 말에 동의하려는 의도로 한 말이므로 정답은
(B)이다.

어휘 | sponsorship 후원 **physical** 신체의

[151-152] 편지

2월 14일

커스 가리베이 씨
케임브리지 가 155번지
팁퍼러리 E34 A039

회신: 사례 번호 1253

가리베이 씨께,

귀하의 계좌에 승인되지 않은 요금이 부과된 건은 진심으로
유감입니다.

151, 152귀하의 사례와 같은 불만 사항은 보통 당사의 소비자
보호 부서에서 처리하므로 해당 건을 디나 레가스피 씨에게
넘겼습니다. 영업일 기준 2일 이내에 그녀로부터 전화를 받게
되실 겁니다.

151또한, 추가적인 문제를 예방하기 위해 귀하의 계좌를
해지했습니다. 영업일 기준 5~7일 이내에 새로운 신용
카드와 함께 새 계좌 번호를 받게 되실 겁니다.

귀하의 문제에 대해 언제든지 저희에게 연락하셔야 할 경우,
이 편지의 상단에 있는 사례 번호를 이용하십시오.

다바오 은행과 지속적으로 거래해 주셔서 감사합니다.

아르만도 에체베리아
계좌 처리 부서, 다바오 은행

어휘 | sincerely 진심으로 **regret** 유감이다 **incident** 사건
involve 관련시키다 **unapproved** 승인되지 않은 **charge**
요금 **complaint** 불만 **ordinarily** 보통 때는 **address**
처리하다 **prevent** 예방하다 **further** 추가의

151 고객은 왜 이 편지를 받았는가?

(A) 문제에 대해 해결 방법을 보고하려고
(B) 보안 기능 추가를 권장하려고
(C) 정책 변경을 명시하려고
(D) 가능한 한 빠른 은행 방문을 요청하려고

해설 | 주제 / 목적
두 번째 단락의 첫 문장에서 귀하의 사례와 같은 불만
사항은 보통 당사의 소비자 보호 부서에서 처리하므로 해당
건을 디나 레가스피 씨에게 넘겼다(As complaints like
yours ~ Ms. Dina Legaspi)고 했고, 세 번째 단락의
첫 문장에서 또한 추가적인 문제를 예방하기 위해 귀하의
계좌를 해지했다(Moreover, to prevent ~ closed
your account)며 고객에게 발생한 문제가 처리되고 있는
방식에 대해 설명하고 있으므로 (A)가 정답이다.

어휘 | resolution 해결 **recommend** 권장하다 **add**
추가하다 **security** 보안 **feature** 기능 **indicate** 나타나다
policy 정책

패러프레이징
지문의 the incident → 보기의 a problem

152 레가스피 씨에 대해 암시된 것은?

(A) 가리베이 씨의 계좌를 해지했다.
(B) 가리베이 씨에게 사례 번호를 배정해 주었다.
(C) 신규 신용 카드 발급을 담당하고 있다.
(D) 소비자 보호 부서에서 일한다.

해설 | 추론
두 번째 단락의 첫 문장에서 귀하의 사례와 같은 불만
사항은 보통 당사의 소비자 보호 부서에서 처리하므로 해당
건을 디나 레가스피 씨에게 넘겼다(As complaints like
yours ~ Ms. Dina Legaspi)고 한 것으로 보아 레가스피
씨는 소비자 보호 부서에서 근무하고 있다는 것을 짐작할
수 있다. 따라서 정답은 (D)이다.

어휘 | assign 배정하다 in charge of ~을 담당하는 issue
발급하다

[153-154] 웹페이지

슬레서 신발 반품 정책

153구입하신 상품은 구매일로부터 60일 이내에 반품이
가능합니다. **153(D)**사용하지 않은 물품만 환불 및 교환하실
수 있습니다. 다시 말씀드리지만 저희는 사용되었거나
더럽혀진 신발에 대해서는 환불 또는 교환을 해드릴 수
없습니다.

154온라인 구매: 주문 처리 센터로 온라인 구매품을
우편 발송해 주십시오. **153(A)**4달러의 처리 수수료가
환불 총액에서 공제됩니다. **153(C)**환불금은 원래 구매에
사용하셨던 동일 계정에 마일리지 포인트 형태로
지급됩니다. 환불 처리에는 영업일 기준 5일의 시간이
소요됩니다.

154매장 내 구매: 고객님이 계신 지역의 슬레서 신발
소매점에서 신발을 구입하신 경우 상품을 반품하거나
교환하기 위해서는 동일한 매장으로 방문해 주셔야 합니다.

어휘 | policy 방침 eligible ~을 할 수 있는 refund 환불
exchange 교환 soil 더럽히다 processing 처리 fee 요금
deduct 공제하다 form 형태 credit 마일리지 account
계정 original 원래의 process 처리하다 retail store 소매점
merchandise 상품

153 반품 방침에 언급되지 않은 것은?

(A) 처리 수수료가 부과될 수 있다.
(B) 제품은 구매일로부터 5일 이내에 반품되어야 한다.
(C) 마일리지 포인트가 청구 계정으로 지급될 것이다.
(D) 제품은 사용하지 않은 상태여야 한다.

해설 | Not / True
첫 문장에서 구입한 상품은 구매일로부터 60일 이내에
반품이 가능하다(Purchases may be returned within
60 days of the purchase date)고 했으므로 (B)가
정답이다. 사용하지 않은 물품만 환불 및 교환할 수
있다(Only items that are in unused condition are
eligible for refund or exchange)에서 (D), 4달러의
처리 수수료가 환불 총액에서 공제된다(A $4 processing
fee will be deducted from all refund amounts)에서
(A), 환불금은 구매 시 사용한 동일 계정에 마일리지 포인트
형태로 지급된다(Your refund will come ~ you used
for the original purchase)에서 (C)를 찾을 수 있다.

어휘 | charge 청구하다 issue 지급하다

154 슬레서 신발에 대해 명시된 것은?

(A) 온라인과 매장에서 모두 신발을 판매한다.
(B) 웹페이지를 업데이트할 계획이다.
(C) 주문품에 대해 익일 배송 옵션을 제공한다.
(D) 여러 나라에서 제품을 판매한다.

해설 | Not / True
신발 반품 방침을 온라인 구매(Online purchases) 시와
매장 내 구매(In-store purchases) 시로 따로 나누어
안내한 것으로 보아 슬레서 신발은 온라인과 매장에서
모두 신발을 판매하고 있음을 알 수 있다. 따라서 (A)가
정답이다.

[155-157] 보도 자료

긴급 보도

미디어 연락처: 레일라 베커
<lbecker@birdwingmedia.co.za>

프리토리아(**155**10월 22일)—남아프리카 공화국에서 가장
큰 엔터테인먼트 회사 중 하나이자 큰 인기를 끈 영화
<나이트 로켓>과 <비치 오브 노 리턴>의 제작사인 버드윙
멀티미디어는 수요일에 놀라운 발표를 했다. 제네사
치카온다 사장 대행은 **155**회사 설립자 프레드릭 보슬루가
사장직에서 즉시 사임한다고 보고했다. 보슬루 씨는 3월
업계 컨퍼런스에서 연내 은퇴를 암시했지만 발표 시점은
예상되지 못했다. 치카온다 씨에 의하면 보슬루 씨는 다른
길을 모색하고 싶어 한다. 그녀는 **156**버드윙 멀티미디어가
다음 달 케이프타운에 있는 새 본사로 이전할 준비로 한창일
때 보슬루 씨가 발표를 했다고 말했다. "이번 변화와 함께,
157회사는 리더십 변화에도 대비할 준비가 되었습니다."
치카온다 씨는 새 사장을 찾을 때까지 버드윙 멀티미디어
경영을 계속할 것이다.

어휘 | acting 대행 step down 퇴진하다 industry 산업,
업계 retire 은퇴하다 unexpected 예상 밖의 explore
탐구하다 avenue (나아갈) 길, 방안 headquarters 본사, 본부

155 보도 자료의 주제는?

  (A) 새 영화   (B) 승진
  (C) 은퇴   (D) 회의

해설 | **주제 / 목적**
첫 문장에서 엔터테인먼트 회사의 놀라운 발표가 있었음을 전하며 두 번째 문장에서 회사 설립자 프레드릭 보슬루가 사장직에서 즉시 사임한다고 보고했다(reported ~ stepping down immediately from his position as president)고 했으므로 정답은 (C)이다.

어휘 | retirement 퇴직, 은퇴

156 보도 자료에 따르면, 버드윙 멀티미디어는 11월에 무엇을 하는가?

  (A) 리더십 회의를 주최한다.
  (B) 다른 지역으로 확장한다.
  (C) 본사를 이전한다.
  (D) 합병을 준비한다.

해설 | **세부 사항**
보도 자료의 보도일이 10월 22일이고, 다섯 번째 문장에서 버드윙 멀티미디어가 다음 달 케이프타운에 있는 새 본사로 이전할 준비로 한창이다(Birdwing Multimedia is preparing to move into its new headquarters in Cape Town next month)라고 했으므로 정답은 (C)이다.

어휘 | host 주최하다 relocate 이전하다 merger 합병

157 [1], [2], [3], [4]로 표시된 곳 중에서 다음 문장이 들어가기에 가장 적합한 위치는?

"치카온다 씨는 새 사장을 찾을 때까지 버드윙 멀티미디어 경영을 계속할 것이다."

  (A) [1]   (B) [2]   (C) [3]   (D) [4]

해설 | **문장 삽입**
'새 사장을 찾을 때까지 경영을 계속한다'는 주어진 문장의 내용으로 보아 경영자가 곧 바뀜(the company is also ready for a change in leadership)을 알 수 있는 마지막 문장 뒤에 들어가는 것이 가장 적절하다. [1], [2]번 위치는 지문에서 Ms. Chikaonda가 소개되기 전이므로 오답이고, [3]번 위치는 앞뒤 문장이 보슬루 씨의 은퇴 발표 시점과 그의 계획이 이어지고 있으므로 치카온다 씨에 대한 소식을 전하는 제시문은 들어가기에 적합하지 않다. 따라서 정답은 (D)이다.

[158-160] 이메일

> 수신: 전 직원
> 발신: 가브리엘 페트레스쿠
> 날짜: 5월 3일, 월요일
> 제목: 중요한 정보

직원 여러분께:

158우리 고객 응대 부서에 당장 필요했던 접수 담당자 자리를 채워 줄 사람을 찾았다는 소식을 알리게 되어 기쁩니다. 오늘부터 시나 웅 씨가 우리 직원으로 합류합니다. 웅 씨는 상근 접수 담당자를 공식적으로 구인159**하는 동안** 임시직으로 주 3일 근무할 예정입니다.

웅 씨는 의료 및 제약 업계에서 접수원으로서 폭넓은 경험을 가지고 있습니다. 따라서 많은 전화 통화에 응답하고 예약을 기록하고 큰 사무실에서 매일 방문객을 맞이하는 일에 익숙합니다.

웅 씨는 월요일, 화요일, 수요일에는 오전 9시부터 오후 5시까지 정규 근무 시간 동안 접수처에서 근무할 예정입니다. **160상근 접수 담당자를 채용할 때까지 목요일에는 랄프 닐슨이, 그 다음 날에는 제인 심이 근무를 대신할 것입니다.**

오늘 저희 접수처에 들러 웅 씨를 직접 환영해 주시기 바랍니다.

가브리엘 페트레스쿠
인사 담당자

어휘 | announce 발표하다 fill 충족시키다 immediate 즉각적인 temporary 임시의 basis 기준 conduct (특정 활동을) 하다 formal 공식적인 permanent 영구적인 extensive 폭넓은 pharmaceutical 제약의 consequently 그 결과 accustomed 익숙한 appointment 예약 on duty 근무 중 regular 정기적인 fill in ~을 대신하다

158 이메일의 목적은?

  (A) 고객 응대 부서 직책 홍보
  (B) 신입 사원 소개
  (C) 관리자 직무 논의
  (D) 새로운 업무 시간 발표

해설 | **주제 / 목적**
첫 문장에서 우리 고객응대 부서에 당장 필요했던 접수 담당자 자리를 채워 줄 사람을 찾았다는 소식을 알리게 되어 기쁘다(I am happy to announce ~ in our front office)며 오늘부터 시나 웅 씨가 우리 직원으로 합류한다(Beginning today, Sina Ung will be joining our staff)고 신입 접수 담당자인 웅 씨를 소개하고 있으므로 정답은 (B)이다.

어휘 | advertise 광고하다 duty 직무

159 첫 번째 단락 3행의 "conduct"와 의미가 가장 가까운 단어는?

  (A) 수행하다
  (B) 수송하다
  (C) 처신하다
  (D) 묘사하다

해설 | 동의어

의미상 공식적인 구인 활동을 '한다'는 뜻으로 쓰인 것이므로 정답은 (A) perform이다.

160 금요일에는 누가 접수처에서 일하는가?

(A) 페트레스쿠 씨
(B) 웅 씨
(C) 닐슨 씨
(D) 심 씨

해설 | 세부 사항

세 번째 단락의 두 번째 문장에서 상근 접수 담당자를 채용할 때까지 목요일에는 랄프 닐슨이 근무를 대신하고(Until we hire ~ fill in on Thursdays), 그 다음 날에는 제인 심이 근무를 대신할 것(Jane Sim will fill in on the following day)이라고 했으므로 금요일에는 심 씨가 접수처에서 근무할 예정임을 알 수 있다. 따라서 (D)가 정답이다.

[161-163] 공지

토마토 통조림 자발적 리콜 공지

9월 25일

식품 생산 회사인 자이스만 프로듀스 주식회사는 28온스 용량의 썬 토마토 통조림 일부를 예방 차원에서 리콜하고 있습니다. 통조림 통의 구조적 결함과 관련하여 시행하는 자발적 리콜입니다. 문제는 제조 단계에서의 결함으로 거슬러 올라갑니다. 현재 대상이 되는 모든 통조림은 식료품점 선반에서 치워졌습니다.

161제품이 리콜의 대상이 되는지 알아보기 위해 소비자가 직접 자이스만 프로듀스의 28온스 용량의 썬 토마토 통조림 통 바닥에 찍힌 코드를 확인할 것을 권장합니다. **162**제품 코드 803471 및 803472가 리콜 대상에 포함됩니다. 이 코드 중 하나가 포함된 통조림이 있는 경우 **162**최초 구매처에 반품하여 환불을 요청하십시오. 리콜에 대한 추가 정보는 당사 웹사이트 www.zeissmannproduce.com/recall 을 통해, 혹은 314-555-0183으로 전화하여 확인할 수 있습니다.

이로 인해 유발될 수 있는 불편에 사과드립니다. **163**우리 자이스만 프로듀스사는 과일, 야채 및 수프 통조림의 품질에 자부심을 가지고 있습니다. 다시는 이런 일이 발생하지 않도록 조치를 취하고 있으니 안심하십시오.

161항상 우리 제품을 찾아 주시는 여러분께 감사드립니다.

마틸다 림, CEO
자이스만 프로듀스 주식회사

어휘 | recall 리콜(하다) out of an abundance of caution 예방 차원에서 dice 깍둑썰기를 하다 voluntary 자발적인 relate to ~와 관련되다 defect 결함 structure 구조, 구조물 be traced to 거슬러 올라가다 remove 치우다

---

purchase 구입 quality 질, 우수함 assure 장담하다, 확언하다 take a step 조치를 취하다

161 공지는 누구를 위한 것인가?

(A) 식료품점 점원
(B) 식료품점 주인
(C) 자이스만 프로듀스 주식회사 직원
(D) 자이스만 프로듀스 주식회사 고객

해설 | 세부 사항

통조림 제품의 리콜 소식을 알리며, 두 번째 문단 첫 문장에서 소비자가 직접 통조림 통 바닥에 찍힌 코드를 확인할 것(We recommend that consumers check ~)을 권했고, 마지막 문장에서 고객에게 감사하는 인사로 공지를 마무리(Thank you for your loyalty)하고 있으므로 정답은 (D)이다.

어휘 | grocery 식료품 clerk 점원, 직원

162 림 씨가 추천하는 한 가지 행동은?

(A) 환불을 위해 반품하기
(B) 온라인 양식 작성하기
(C) 다른 제품으로 교환하기
(D) 고객 서비스 담당자에게 연락하기

해설 | 세부 사항

두 번째 문단 두 번째 문장에서 리콜 대상이 되는 상품 코드를 알려주며, 이어서 최초 구매처에 반품하여 환불을 요청하라(please return it to the original place of purchase for a refund)고 했으므로 정답은 (A)이다.

어휘 | contact 연락하다 customer service representative 고객 서비스 담당자(직원)

163 자이스만 프로듀스 주식회사에 대해 언급된 것은?

(A) 신규 웹사이트가 있다.
(B) 국제적인 기업이다.
(C) 제품이 유기농이다.
(D) 통조림 수프를 판매한다.

해설 | Not/True

세 번째 문단 두 번째 문장에서 자이스만 프로듀스사는 과일, 야채 및 수프 통조림의 품질에 자부심을 가지고 있다(We here at Zeissmann Produce, Inc., ~ canned fruits, vegetables, and soups)라고 했으므로 정답은 (D)이다.

어휘 | international 국제적인 organic 유기농의

[164-167] 이메일

수신: 레일라 앨리자데
발신: 사라 크랜머
날짜: 2월 2일
제목: 요청 사항

앨리자데 씨,

164요청하신 대로 5월까지 출장 준비를 해 놓았습니다. 항공편 스케줄은 다음과 같습니다.

3월	**167보스턴 출발**	쿠알라룸푸르 도착
	3월 1일 오전 11시 20분, 셀랑고르 항공 23G편	3월 2일 오후 9시 45분
	166쿠알라룸푸르 출발	**167보스턴 도착**
	1663월 14일 오후 2시 20분, 셀랑고르 항공 54A편	**166**3월 14일 오후 5시 25분
4월	**167보스턴 출발**	베이징 도착
	4월 10일 오전 11시 55분, 레고 항공 3471편	4월 11일 오후 1시 45분
	베이징 출발	**167보스턴 도착**
	4월 22일 오후 3시 45분, 레고 항공 4498편	4월 22일 오후 5시 30분
5월	**165, 167보스턴 출발**	필라델피아 도착
	5월 3일 오전 6시 40분, 로렐 항공 117편	5월 3일 오전 8시 10분
	필라델피아 출발	**165, 167보스턴 도착**
	5월 3일 오후 8시 55분, 로렐 항공 109편	**5월 3일 오후 10시 15분**

상기 항공편은 어느 것이든 여행사를 통해 2월 15일까지는 위약금 없이 변경 가능합니다. **1663월 14일에 돌아오는 항공편을 정오 전에 출발하는 항공편으로 예약해 달라고 요청하셨는데요.** 안타깝게도 가능한 항공편이 하나도 없습니다. 그날 예약 가능한 가장 빠른 항공편은 오후 2시 20분에 출발합니다.

마지막으로, 각각의 출장 날짜가 다가오면, 공항까지의 지상 교통편을 예약하겠습니다.

이 일정표가 괜찮으신지 알려 주세요.

사라 크랜머

어휘 | business travel arrangement 출장 준비 per ~에 따라서 as follows 다음과 같이 travel agency 여행사 penalty 벌금, 위약금 regarding ~에 관하여 ground transportation 지상 교통편 itinerary 여행 일정표 suit ~의 마음에 들다

164 크랜머 씨가 앨리자데 씨에게 이메일을 쓴 이유는?

(A) 회의 준비를 위해 여러 날짜를 제안하기 위하여
(B) 직원 휴가 일정에 관한 최신 정보를 제공하기 위하여
(C) 곧 있을 출장 준비에 관해 알리기 위하여
(D) 항공사 방침 변경에 관해 상기시키기 위하여

해설 | 주제 / 목적
첫 번째 단락 첫 문장에서 요청하신 대로 5월까지 출장 준비를 해 놓았다(I have made your business travel

arrangements ~ per your request)라고 했고, 항공편 스케줄은 다음과 같다(Your flight schedule is as follows)며, 항공편 예약 상황을 보고하고 있으므로 정답은 (C)이다.

165 일정표에 따르면 앨리자데 씨가 당일 출장을 가는 때는?

(A) 2월   (B) 3월
(C) 4월   (D) 5월

해설 | 세부 사항
표에서 5월 3일 출장은 오전 6시 40분에 출발(Depart Boston May 3, 6:40 A.M.)하여 필라델피아에 갔다가 당일 오후 10시 15분에 보스턴에 도착(Arrive Boston May 3, 10:15 P.M.)하는 것으로 나오므로 정답은 (D)이다.

166 앨리자데 씨는 어느 도시에서 정오 전에 출발하기를 원하는가?

(A) 보스턴   (B) 쿠알라룸푸르
(C) 베이징   (D) 필라델피아

해설 | 세부 사항
두 번째 단락 두 번째 문장에서 3월 14일에 돌아오는 항공편을 정오 전에 출발하는 항공편으로 예약해 달라고 요청하셨다(Regarding your return flight on March 14, you had requested ~ leaves before noon)고 했는데, 표에서 3월 14일 돌아오는 항공편은 쿠알라룸푸르에서 출발하는 것으로 나와 있다. 따라서 정답은 (B)이다.

167 앨리자데 씨에 대해 암시된 것은?

(A) 여행사에서 근무한다.
(B) 회사가 보스턴 지역에 있다.
(C) 레고 항공의 우대 고객이다.
(D) 비서가 그녀를 공항까지 태워다 준다.

해설 | 추론
표의 항공편이 전부 보스턴을 출발해 다시 보스턴으로 돌아오는 일정(Depart Boston, Arrive Boston)이므로 이를 통해 앨리자데 씨가 근무하는 회사가 보스턴 지역에 있음을 짐작할 수 있다. 따라서 정답은 (B)이다.

[168-171] 온라인 채팅

루시 플레츠 (오전 8시 54분)
안녕하세요, 여러분. **168, 169금요일 경영진 회의 시간과 장소에 대해 알고 계신 게 있을까요?**

콜린 마에다 (오전 8시 56분)
169평소처럼 6번 회의실에서 10시에 합니다.

루시 플레츠 (오전 8시 57분)
회계부의 로버트가 그 방은 그 시간에 고객과의 회의로 예약이 되었다던데요.

콜린 마에다 (오전 9시)

안 돼요! 그 방에 있는 프로젝터를 사용해야 하는 슬라이드 프레젠테이션이 있어요. 지금 6호실이 중복 예약된 게 올해에만 두 번째예요. 답답하네요!

루시 플레츠 (오전 9시 01분)

여기는 회의 장소 구하기가 하늘의 별 따기예요! ¹⁷⁰**생각나는 유일한 다른 장소는 구내식당뿐이네요.**

콜린 마에다 (오전 9시 02분)

거기는 시끄러울 수 있어요. 프로젝터를 둘 수도 없고요. 회사 도서관은 어떨까요?

루시 플레츠 (오전 9시 03분)

여름에는 금요일에 문을 닫아요.

빈센트 골딩(오전 9시 04분)

직원 휴게실은요? ¹⁷¹**제가 시청각 부서에 휴대용 프로젝터와 스크린을 요청할 수 있어요.**

콜린 마에다 (오전 9시 05분)

자리가 좀 비좁을 것 같아요.

루시 플레츠 (오전 9시 06분)

그건 해결할 수 있어요.

어휘 | as usual 평소처럼 accounting 회계 book 예약하다 double-booked 이중으로 예약된 frustrating 답답한 space 공간 at a premium 구하기 힘든 spot 장소 noisy 시끄러운 capability 능력 corporate 기업의 portable 휴대용의

168 플레츠 씨는 왜 온라인 채팅을 시작했는가?

(A) 대체 회의 시간을 요청하기 위해
(B) 회의 장소를 문의하기 위해
(C) 일부 장비가 수리되었음을 보고하기 위해
(D) 시청각 부서에 도움을 요청하기 위해

해설 | 주제/목적
8시 54분에 플레츠 씨가 금요일 경영진 회의 시간과 장소에 대해 알고 있는 것이 있는지(Do you know anything about ~ management meeting?)에 대한 질문으로 온라인 채팅을 시작했다. 따라서 정답은 (B)이다.

어휘 | alternate 대안의 inquire 문의하다 equipment 장비 repair 수리하다 assistance 도움

169 경영진 회의는 주로 어디서 열리는가?

(A) 도서관
(B) 구내식당
(C) 6번 회의실
(D) 직원 휴게실

해설 | 세부 사항
8시 54분에 플레츠 씨가 금요일 경영진 회의 시간과

장소에 대해 알고 있는 것이 있는지(Do you know anything about ~ management meeting?) 묻자 8시 56분에 마에다 씨가 평소처럼 6번 회의실에서 10시에 한다(It's at ten ~ Room 6, as usual)고 했으므로 (C)가 정답이다.

170 오전 9시 2분에 마에다 씨가 "거기는 시끄러울 수 있어요"라고 쓴 의도는 무엇이겠는가?

(A) 6번 회의실 근처에 혼잡한 복도가 있다.
(B) 경영진이 평소 조용하지 않다.
(C) 프로젝터 모터가 매우 시끄럽다.
(D) 구내식당에서는 잘 들리지 않는다.

해설 | 의도 파악
9시 1분에 플레츠 씨가 생각나는 유일한 다른 장소는 구내식당뿐(The only other spot I can think of is the cafeteria)이라며 대체 장소를 제안하자 9시 2분에 마에다 씨가 거기는 시끄러울 수 있다(That can get noisy)고 했으므로, 구내식당은 시끄러워서 잘 들리지 않는다며 플레츠 씨의 제안에 동의하지 않는다는 의도로 한 말임을 알 수 있다. 따라서 정답은 (D)이다.

어휘 | hallway 복도 loud 시끄러운

171 골딩 씨는 무엇을 하겠다고 제안하는가?

(A) 장비 대여 주선
(B) 휴게실에 몇 자리 추가
(C) 회의 의제 수정
(D) 도서관 예비용 키 입수

해설 | 세부 사항
9시 4분에 골딩 씨가 자신이 시청각 부서에 휴대용 프로젝터와 스크린을 요청할 수 있다(I can request ~ audiovisual department)고 했으므로 (A)가 정답이다.

어휘 | arrange 주선하다 agenda 의제 spare 예비용의

패러프레이징
지문의 a portable projector and screen
→ 보기의 some equipment

[172-175] 회람

날짜: 1월 7일
수신: 모든 신입 사원
발신: 인사부
제목: 워크숍

¹⁷²**인사 워크숍 시리즈와 관련해 모든 신입 사원에게 알립니다.** 참석은 의무 사항이라는 것을 기억하세요. ¹⁷⁵**워크숍은 1월 14일, 16일, 18일에 3층 대회의실에서 열릴 예정입니다.** C 회의실을 가리키는 표지판을 찾으세요. ¹⁷³**편하게 만나서 인사할 수 있는 아침식사가 아침 8시 30분에 제공되며** 워크숍은 오전 9시부터 오후 1시까지

진행되고 오전 10시 45분과 11시 15분 사이에 커피 및 간단한 다과를 위한 휴식 시간도 있습니다. **174워크숍 주제에 대한 구체적인 정보는 조만간 각자에게 발송될 것입니다.** 오후 1시부터 시작되는 점심시간은 신입 사원들이 배정된 멘토들과 만날 수 있는 기회가 될 것입니다.

다음 주에 여러분 모두와 만나기를 기대합니다.

프란시스 레지스, 인사부 담당자

어휘 | hire 신입 사원 human resources 인사부 reminder 상기시켜 주는 메모 attendance 참석 mandatory 의무적인 informal 편안한 session (특정 활동) 시간 refreshments 다과 specific 구체적인 shortly 곧 assigned 배정된

---

172 회람의 목적은?

(A) 직원들에게 근무 시간 기록표를 일찍 제출하도록 요청하는 것
(B) 신입 사원들에게 필수 교육에 대해 상기시키는 것
(C) 멘토들에게 일부 워크숍 수강을 추천하는 것
(D) 인사부 직원에게 새로운 방침에 대해 알리는 것

해설 | 주제 / 목적
첫 문장에서 인사 워크숍 시리즈와 관련해 모든 신입 사원에게 알린다(This is a reminder ~ HR workshop series)며 참석은 의무 사항이라는 것을 기억하라(Please remember that attendance is mandatory)고 했으므로 정답은 (B)이다.

어휘 | time sheet 근무 시간 기록표 policy 방침

패러프레이징
지문의 mandatory → 보기의 required

173 워크숍 시리즈에 대해 암시된 것은?

(A) 친목을 도모할 시간이 있을 것이다.
(B) 저녁 식사는 선택 사항이다.
(C) 점심 식사 후에 수업이 시작된다.
(D) 초청 연사들이 발표를 할 것이다.

해설 | 추론
첫 단락의 네 번째 문장에서 편하게 만나서 인사할 수 있는 아침 식사가 아침 8시 30분에 제공된다(An informal meet-and-greet breakfast will be served at 8:30 A.M.)고 했으므로 (A)가 정답이다.

어휘 | socialize (사람들과) 어울리다 instruction 교육

패러프레이징
지문의 meet-and-greet → 보기의 socialize

174 레기스 씨에 따르면, 이 회람을 받는 사람들은 곧 무엇을 받을 예정인가?

(A) 아침 및 점심 식사 메뉴
(B) 멘토링 시간을 위한 의제
(C) 자세한 주행 경로 안내
(D) 워크숍 주제에 대한 세부 사항

해설 | 세부 사항
첫 단락의 다섯 번째 문장에서 워크숍 주제에 대한 구체적인 정보는 조만간 각자에게 발송될 것(Specific information about workshop topics will be sent to each of you shortly)이라고 했으므로 (D)가 정답이다.

어휘 | agenda 의제 detailed 자세한 direction 방향 detail 세부 사항

패러프레이징
지문의 Specific information → 보기의 details

175 [1], [2], [3], [4]로 표시된 곳 중에서 다음 문장이 들어가기에 가장 적합한 위치는?

"C 회의실을 가리키는 표지판을 찾으세요."

(A) [1]　　　(B) [2]　　　(C) [3]　　　(D) [4]

해설 | 문장 삽입
제시된 문장은 'C 회의실을 가리키는 표지판을 찾으라'며 장소를 찾기 위한 정보를 주고 있다. 따라서 워크숍은 3층 대회의실에서 열릴 예정(Workshop will be held ~ in the large conference room on the third floor)이라며 행사 장소를 알려 주는 문장 뒤에 들어가는 것이 글의 흐름상 자연스러우므로 (B)가 정답이다.

[176-180] 안내 책자 + 이메일

만돌린 서비스

고객을 감동시킬 수 있는 깨끗하고 매력적인 작업 공간을 유지할 수 있도록 도와드립니다!

우리 전문가들은 어떠한 사무실 작업도 처리할 수 있습니다. **176(A)우리는 나무와 타일 바닥에서 흙먼지와 모래를 제거하는 일을 전문으로 합니다.** 우리는 또한 진공청소기로 청소하고, **176(B), (D)쓰레기통을 비우고, 책상과 의자에서 먼지를 털어내고 광택을 내고, 물품을 채워 넣는 일도 합니다.** 심지어 전구도 교체해 드립니다!

177우리는 고객님의 요구를 수용하기 위해 다양한 서비스 플랜을 제공합니다.

177아침: 인원이 보통이거나 월요일부터 금요일 정규 업무 시간 동안 고객이 자주 방문하지 않는 사무실용. 업무 시간 이후 직원이 상주하는 사무실에 권장됨.

177,179야간: 인원이 많고 정기적으로 고객이 방문하는 사무실용. 걸레질한 뒤 마를 시간을 감안해 타일 바닥(카펫이나 대형 깔개가 없는 바닥)이 있는 사무실에 권장됨.

177토요일: 인원이 적거나 고객 방문이 거의 없는 사무실용. 서비스는 토요일 오전 또는 오후 시간대에 예약 가능.

견적 일정을 잡으시려면 help@mandolinservices.ca로 이메일을 보내시거나 (250) 555-0141로 전화 주세요. 만돌린 서비스 팀은 여러분을 도울 준비가 되어 있습니다!

어휘 | maintain 유지하다 inviting 매력적인 workspace 작업 공간 impress 깊은 인상을 주다 professional 전문가 handle 다루다 specialise in ~을 전문으로 하다 dirt 흙, 먼지 grit 모래 vacuum 진공청소기로 청소하다 empty 비우다 garbage bin 쓰레기통 dust 먼지를 털다 polish 닦다 restock 다시 채우다 supplies 물품 replace 교체하다 light bulb 전구 a variety of 다양한 accommodate 수용하다 traffic 방문량 infrequently 드물게 recommend 추천하다 regular 정기적인 rug 깔개 mop 대걸레로 닦다 estimate 견적

발신: 나탈리 메디나 <nmedina@medinaadvisors.ca>
수신: 고객 서비스 <help@mandolinservices.ca>
날짜: 2월 6일 월요일
제목: 서비스 견적

안녕하세요,

178, 179저는 캠루프에 있는 제 사무실에서 서비스를 위한 견적 일정을 잡고 싶습니다. 178현재 서비스 제공 업체와 계약이 3월 31일에 끝나는데, 더 좋은 가격을 찾으려고 알아보는 중입니다. 저는 귀사의 일일 서비스 플랜 중 하나에 관심이 있습니다. **179귀사의 안내 책자에 나온 정보에 따르면, 야간 서비스가 제 사무실에 적합할 것 같습니다.** 저는 다음 주 오전 아무 때나 시간이 가능하지만 목요일이나 금요일이 가장 **180적당합니다.**

답장 기다리겠습니다.

나탈리 메디나, 업주
메디나 어드바이저

어휘 | contract 계약 current 현재의 provider 제공자 rate 요금 brochure 안내 책자 appropriate 적절한 available 시간이 되는 suit 맞다

176 만돌린 서비스 팀의 손질을 받는 것으로 언급되지 않은 것은?

(A) 바닥 (B) 가구
(C) 창문 (D) 휴지통

해설 | Not / True
안내 책자의 두 번째 단락 두 번째 문장에서 우리는 나무와 타일 바닥에서 흙먼지와 모래를 제거하는 일을 전문으로 한다(We specialise in ~ wood and tile floors)고 했으므로 (A), 또한 쓰레기통을 비우고 책상과 의자에서 먼지를 털어내고 광택을 낸다(empty garbage bins, dust and polish desks and chairs)고 했으므로 (B)와 (D)는 업체의 서비스를 받는 대상임을 알 수 있다. 창문에 대한 언급은 없으므로 (C)가 정답이다.

어휘 | attention 처리, 손질

패러프레이징
지문의 garbage → 보기의 Trash
지문의 desks and chairs → 보기의 Furniture

177 만돌린 서비스에 대해 명시된 것은?

(A) 산업상을 받았다.
(B) 유연한 일정을 제공한다.
(C) 가족이 운영하는 사업체이다.
(D) 일주일에 7일 서비스를 제공한다.

해설 | Not / True
안내 책자의 세 번째 단락에서 우리는 고객님의 요구를 수용하기 위해 다양한 서비스 플랜을 제공한다(We offer a variety of service plans to accommodate your needs)고 했고, 아침(Mornings), 야간(Nighttimes), 토요일(Saturdays)로 다양한 서비스 시간대를 제공하고 있으므로 (B)가 정답이다.

어휘 | industry 산업 award 상 flexible 유연한 family-operated 가족이 운영하는

178 왜 메디나 씨는 이메일을 썼는가?

(A) 서비스 비용을 줄이고 싶어 한다.
(B) 현재 서비스 품질에 만족하지 못한다.
(C) 서비스 제공업체가 폐업한다는 것을 알게 되었다.
(D) 신도시에 사무실을 개업할 계획이다.

해설 | 주제 / 목적
이메일의 첫 문장에서 메디나 씨가 캠루프에 있는 제 사무실에서 서비스를 위한 견적 일정을 잡고 싶다(I would like to ~ office in Kamloops)고 했고, 현재 서비스 제공 업체와 계약이 3월 31일에 끝나는데 더 좋은 가격을 찾으려고 알아보는 중(The contract I have ~ a better rate)이라고 했으므로 서비스 비용이 더 저렴한 업체를 알아보려고 이메일을 썼음을 알 수 있다. 따라서 (A)가 정답이다.

어휘 | reduce 줄이다 expense 비용 out of business 폐업한

179 캠루프 사무실에 대해 암시된 것은?

(A) 카펫이 있다.
(B) 방이 여러 개 있다.
(C) 개조될 예정이다.
(D) 고객들이 정기적으로 방문한다.

해설 | 연계
이메일의 첫 문장에서 메디나 씨가 캠루프에 있는 제 사무실에서 서비스를 위한 견적 일정을 잡고 싶다(I would like to ~ office in Kamloops)고 했고, 네 번째 문장에서 귀사의 안내 책자에 나온 정보에 따르면 야간 서비스가 제 사무실에 적합할 것 같다(Based on the information

~ appropriate for my office)고 했다. 안내 책자의 야간(Nighttimes) 서비스 설명에 인원이 많고 정기적으로 고객이 방문하는 사무실용(For offices with heavy traffic and with regular client visits)이라고 나와 있으므로 메디나 씨의 캠루프 사무실은 많은 고객들이 정기적으로 방문하고 있음을 알 수 있다. 따라서 정답은 (D)이다.

180 이메일에서 첫 번째 단락 5행의 "suit"와 의미가 가장 가까운 단어는?

(A) 옷을 입다 (B) 바꾸다
(C) 맞다 (D) 묘사하다

해설 | 동의어
의미상 다음 주 오전 아무 때나 가능하지만 목요일이나 금요일이 가장 '적당하다'는 뜻으로 쓰인 것이므로 정답은 (C) fit이다.

[181-185] 기사 + 이메일

> 더반 (8월 4일)—181홈 앤 패션 센터(HFC)는 예전에 노던 몰로 알려졌던 새로 단장한 쇼핑 플라자로 완전히 새로운 상점들이 들어서 있다. 181,182현재는 8개의 실내 인테리어와 의류 부티크, 카페 그리고 8개 스크린 영화관을 뽐내고 있다. 182이 상점들은 모두 온라인 쇼핑객들에게는 유명하지만 오프라인 지점이 있었던 적은 없다.
>
> 182요하네스버그에 본사를 둔 쿠퍼스 가정용품은 HFC에 입점한 8개 상점 중 하나이다. "온라인 스토어에서 정말 많은 주문을 받고 있어 여기 HFC에 오프라인 매장을 열기로 한 선택은 당연한 것이었습니다."라고 데니스 블레이 쿠퍼스 가정용품 마케팅 부사장은 말했다.
>
> 184HFC 매장은 월요일부터 토요일에는 오전 9시 30분부터 오후 8시 30분까지, 일요일에는 오후 12시 30분부터 오후 5시까지 문을 연다. 영화관은 일주일에 7일 오전 10시부터 오후 11시까지 문을 연다.
>
> ---
> **어휘 |** formerly 이전에 feature ~을 특징으로 하다 completely 완전히 boast 뽐내다 physical 실물의 location 지점 houseware 가정용품 based in ~에 본사를 둔 fill (주문 등을) 이행하다 brick-and-mortar store 오프라인 매장 obvious 명백한 vice president 부사장

> 수신: 사무엘 디디자 <sdidiza@tiptop.co.za>
> 발신: 리아 아야르 <layyar@coopershousewares.co.za>
> 날짜: 8월 27일
> 제목: 쿠퍼스 가정용품에 오신 것을 환영합니다.
> 첨부: 🖇 서류 작업
>
> 디디자 씨께:
>
> 쿠퍼스 가정용품 판매팀에 오신 것을 환영합니다. 이곳에서 즐겁게 일하기를 바랍니다.

당신은 판매 사원으로서 매장 내 고객을 돕게 될 것입니다. 184, 1859월 1일 수요일, 매장이 문을 열 때 출근을 보고하시기 바랍니다. 오리엔테이션은 오전 10시에 시작해 오후 12시 30분까지 계속될 예정입니다. 185점심시간을 짧게 가진 후 나머지 팀들과 만나고 수석 판매 사원인 카울라 씨의 근무 시간이 끝날 때까지 그녀를 수행하게 될 것입니다. 그런 다음 남은 한 주 동안 당신의 업무 일정을 받게 될 것입니다.

183당신의 채용과 관련된 모든 서류를 첨부해 드리니 확인하세요. 모든 문서를 인쇄해 작성한 후 근무 첫날 가져오시기 바랍니다.

당신이 우리 팀이 되는 것을 기대하고 있습니다.

리아 아야르
매장 관리자

어휘 | sales associate 판매 사원 assist 돕다 in-store 매장 내의 last 지속되다 rest 나머지 shadow 수행하다 shift 교대 근무 (시간) attached 첨부된 pertinent 관련 있는

181 기사의 목적은?

(A) 쇼핑 몰에서 이용 가능한 매장 목록 나열
(B) 더반의 다양한 쇼핑 구역 강조
(C) 쿠퍼스 가정용품의 판매 제품에 대한 설명
(D) 쇼핑 플라자의 새 단장 발표

해설 | 주제/목적
기사의 첫 문장에서 홈 앤 패션 센터(HFC)는 예전에 노던 몰로 알려졌던 새로 단장한 쇼핑 플라자로 완전히 새로운 상점들이 들어서 있다(Home and Fashion Centre ~ completely new stores)고 했고, 현재는 8개의 실내 인테리어와 의류 부티크, 카페 그리고 8개 스크린 영화관을 뽐내고 있다(It boasts eight ~ eight-screen cinema)며 새롭게 바뀐 쇼핑 플라자에 대해 소개하고 있으므로 (D)가 정답이다.

어휘 | list 나열하다 highlight 강조하다 describe 묘사하다 announce 발표하다

182 쿠퍼스 가정용품에 대해 암시된 것은?

(A) 더반에 본사가 있다.
(B) 최근에 첫 번째 오프라인 매장을 열었다.
(C) 토요일과 일요일에는 문을 닫는다.
(D) 카페 옆에 있다.

해설 | 추론
기사의 첫 단락 두 번째 문장에서 HFC가 8개의 실내 인테리어와 의류 부티크, 카페 그리고 8개 스크린 영화관을 뽐내고 있다(It boasts eight ~ eight-screen cinema)고 했고 이 상점들은 모두 온라인 쇼핑객들에게는 유명하지만 오프라인 지점이 있었던 적은 없다(The stores are all well known ~ a physical location)고 했으며, 두

번째 단락 첫 문장에서 요하네스버그에 본사를 둔 쿠퍼스 가정용품은 HFC에 입점한 8개 상점 중 하나(Cooper's Housewares ~ found a home at HFC)라고 했다. 따라서 쿠퍼스 가정용품은 HFC에 첫 오프라인 매장을 열었음을 알 수 있으므로 (B)가 정답이다.

183 아야르 씨는 디디자 씨에게 무엇을 보냈는가?

(A) 지역의 지도
(B) 판매 보고서
(C) 채용 서류
(D) 고객 설문지

해설 | 세부 사항
이메일의 세 번째 단락 첫 문장에서 아야르 씨가 디디자 씨에게 당신의 채용과 관련된 모든 서류를 첨부했으니 확인하라(Attached please find all the paperwork pertinent to your hiring)고 했으므로 정답은 (C)이다.

패러프레이징
지문의 the paperwork pertinent to your hiring
→ 보기의 Employment forms

184 디디자 씨는 언제 매장에 도착해야 하는가?

(A) 오전 9시 30분
(B) 오전 10시
(C) 오후 12시 30분
(D) 오후 5시

해설 | 연계
이메일의 두 번째 단락 두 번째 문장에서 디디자 씨에게 9월 1일 수요일, 매장이 문을 열 때 출근을 보고하라(Please report for work ~ when the store opens)고 했는데, 기사의 세 번째 단락 첫 문장에서 HFC 매장은 월요일부터 토요일에는 오전 9시 30분부터 오후 8시 30분까지 문을 연다(The stores at HFC ~ Monday through Saturday)고 했다. 따라서 디디자 씨는 수요일 매장 개점 시간에 출근해야 하고 기사에 따르면 평일 매장 개점 시간은 오전 9시 30분이므로 정답은 (A)이다.

185 디디자 씨는 수요일 오후에 무엇을 할 것인가?

(A) 일부 서류 읽기
(B) 수업 참석
(C) 쿠퍼스 가정용품에서 쇼핑
(D) 카울라 씨와 만남

해설 | 세부 사항
이메일의 두 번째 단락 두 번째 문장에서 디디자 씨에게 9월 1일 수요일에 출근하라(Please report for work on Wednesday)고 했고, 같은 단락 네 번째 문장에서 점심시간을 짧게 가진 후 나머지 팀원들과 만나고 수석 판매 사원인 카울라 씨의 근무 시간이 끝날 때까지 그녀를 수행하게 될 것(After a short lunch break, ~ shadow our senior sales associate, Ms. Khawula, until the

end of her shift)이라고 했다. 따라서 디디자 씨가 첫 출근일인 수요일 오후에 카울라 씨를 만나게 될 것임을 알 수 있으므로 정답은 (D)이다.

[186-190] 이메일 + 명함 + 온라인 후기

수신: 개빈 타가트 <gtaggart@northdalebank.com>
발신: 올모 가족 치과 <appt@olmofamilydental.com>
날짜: 3월 2일
제목: 예약 알림 메시지

타가트 씨께,

1873월 10일 오전 9시에 올모 가족 치과에 예약이 있다는 것을 알려 드리는 메시지입니다. 예약을 확정하기 위해 이 이메일에 답장해 주시기 바랍니다.

사진이 있는 신분증과 결제 수단을 예약 방문 시 지참해 주세요. **186**이번이 저희 병원에서 첫 진료이기 때문에 몇 가지 양식 작성을 위해 예약 시간 15분 전에 도착해 주시기 바랍니다. 그 후, **189**폴 엘윈 선생님이 부러진 치아를 손봐주실 것입니다.

정성껏 모시겠습니다.

토드 데쉔느
올모 가족 치과 접수 담당

- - - - - - - - - - - - - - - - - - - -
어휘 | appointment 약속 reminder 상기시켜주는 편지 confirm 확정하다 form 양식 payment 지불 fill out 작성하다 repair 보수하다

올모 가족 치과
4428 산 아마로 가 NE
앨버커키, 뉴멕시코 87109
info@olmofamilydental.com

187진료 시간: 월요일부터 금요일까지 오전 10시~오후 6시
토요일 오전 8시~오후 1시

olmofamilydental.com에서 우리 치과와 직원에 대해 알아보세요.

188예약 또는 문의 사항에 관해서는 (505) 555-0114로 전화하세요. 온라인 결제를 하시려면 olmofamilydental. com/pay를 방문하세요.

http://www.olmofamilydental.com/reviews

189어제 올모 가족 치과에서 치과 치료를 받았는데 마리나 나르바에즈 선생님의 진료에 아주 만족했습니다. 산타페에서 앨버커키로 이사 온 지 하루 만인 이번 주 초에 부서진 이를 고쳐 주셨습니다. 나르바에즈 선생님은 훌륭한 치과 의사일 뿐 아니라 흥미로운 이력의 소유자입니다.

그녀는 앨버커키에서 자랐지만 미시간주 디트로이트에 있는 대학과 치의대를 다녔습니다. 그녀는 지난해 올모 가족 치과에 채용되었을 때 앨버커키로 돌아왔습니다. 나르바에즈 선생님의 말씀에 따르면, 올모 가족 치과는 불과 5년 전에 개원했지만 이미 이 도시 최고의 치과 병원 중 하나라고 합니다. 그리고 **190저의 새 직장에서 바로 길 위쪽에 위치해 편리합니다.**

나르바에즈 선생님을 적극 추천합니다. 치과 치료가 더 필요하게 되면 꼭 올모 가족 치과로 다시 가려고 합니다.

– 3월 11일, 개빈 타가트

어휘 | fix 고치다 dentist 치과 의사 background 이력 practice (의사·변호사 등의) 사무실 conveniently 편리하게 recommend 추천하다 certainly 확실히

186 이메일에서 타가트 씨는 무엇을 요청받는가?

(A) 양식을 작성해 가져올 것
(B) 데쉔느 씨에게 전화할 것
(C) 일찍 도착할 것
(D) 신용 카드를 사용할 것

해설 | 세부 사항
이메일의 두 번째 단락 두 번째 문장에서 타가트 씨에게 이번이 저희 병원에서 첫 진료이기 때문에 몇 가지 양식 작성을 위해 예약 시간 15분 전에 도착해 주시기 바란다(As this will be ~ arrive fifteen minutes before your appointment time to fill out some forms)고 했으므로 (C)가 정답이다.

187 타가트 씨의 진료 예약은 언제인가?

(A) 월요일
(B) 화요일
(C) 금요일
(D) 토요일

해설 | 연계
이메일의 첫 문장에서 타가트 씨에게 3월 10일 오전 9시에 올모 가족 치과에 예약이 있다는 것을 알려 드리는 메시지(This is a reminder ~ at 9:00 A.M.)라고 했고, 명함에는 진료 시간(Office hours)이 월요일부터 금요일까지 오전 10시~오후 6시(10:00 A.M. to 6:00 P.M., Monday to Friday), 토요일 오전 8시~오후 1시(8:00 A.M. to 1:00 P.M. on Saturday)라고 나와 있다. 평일에는 오전 9시에 진료를 하지 않으므로 타가트 씨의 진료 예약은 토요일임을 알 수 있다. 따라서 (D)가 정답이다.

188 명함에 따르면, 환자는 어떻게 올모 가족 치과에 진료 예약을 잡아야 하는가?

(A) 온라인 양식을 작성하여
(B) 이메일을 발송하여

(C) 사무실로 전화하여
(D) 문자 메시지를 발송하여

해설 | 세부 사항
명함의 하단에 예약 또는 문의 사항에 관해서는 (505) 555-0114로 전화하라(For appointments or questions, call (505) 555-0114)고 나와 있으므로 (C)가 정답이다.

189 나르바에즈 선생님에 대해 암시된 것은?

(A) 어린이를 위한 치과 치료를 전문으로 한다.
(B) 원래 타가트 씨의 진료에 예약되어 있지 않았다.
(C) 올모 가족 치과에서 5년 동안 치과 의사로 일했다.
(D) 원래 앨버커키 출신이 아니다.

해설 | 연계
이메일의 두 번째 단락 마지막 문장에서 타가트 씨에게 폴 엘윈 선생님이 부러진 치아를 손봐주실 것(Dr. Paul Elwin will repair your broken tooth)이라고 했는데, 타가트 씨가 작성한 온라인 후기의 첫 문장에서 어제 올모 가족 치과에서 치과 치료를 받았는데 마리나 나르바에즈 선생님의 진료에 아주 만족했다(I received dental care ~ service provided by Dr. Marina Narvaez)고 했으므로 타가트 씨의 진료 예약 의사가 엘윈에서 나르바에즈로 바뀌었음을 알 수 있다. 따라서 (B)가 정답이다.

어휘 | specialize in ~을 전문으로 하다 originally 원래

190 온라인 후기에서 타가트 씨에 대해 암시된 것은?

(A) 최근에 새 일을 시작했다.
(B) 나르바에즈 선생님에게 몇 년 동안 진료를 받았다.
(C) 추가 진료 예약을 잡았다.
(D) 디트로이트에 거주했다.

해설 | 추론
온라인 후기의 첫 단락 마지막 문장에서 타가트 씨가 치과가 저의 새 직장에서 바로 길 위쪽에 위치해 편리하다(it is conveniently located just up the street from my new workplace)고 했으므로 (A)가 정답이다.

패러프레이징
지문의 my new workplace → 보기의 a new job

[191-195] 광고 + 이메일 + 일정

오벌 오차드 렌탈에 오신 것을 환영합니다!

저희는 나이로비 웨스트랜드 중심부에 위치한 두 채의 주거용 건물을 운영하고 있습니다. 전 세대는 안락한 현관, 서재, 설비를 갖춘 주방, 넉넉한 창고, 세탁실, 그리고 지붕이 있는 주차장이 있습니다. 주간 청소 서비스, 전기, 인터넷 서비스, 위성 텔레비전 모두 각 아파트의 임대료에 포함됩니다.

194저희 란타나 가 빌딩은 침실 3개짜리 아파트로 로투스 비즈니스 단지와 버스 정류장에서 걸어서 단 2분 거리에 있습니다. 랍타 가 빌딩은 침실 4개짜리 아파트로 일본 대사관 가깝게 쾌적하게 자리 잡고 있습니다. **191**추가적으로 각각의 랍타 가 아파트에는 그릴, 식탁, 라운지 가구, 해먹이 구비된 개인 전용 야외 정원이 있어 웨스트랜드라는 대도시의 분주함을 벗어난 완벽한 휴식처가 되어 줍니다.

192아름다운 저희 아파트를 보시려면 www.ovalorchardrentals.co.ke를 방문하셔서 오픈 하우스 행사 중 하나에 등록하시면, 경험 많은 저희 직원이 둘러보실 수 있도록 안내하고 궁금하신 점이 있으면 답변해 드릴 것입니다.

- -

어휘 | operate 운영하다 residential 주거의 centrally 중심부에 flat 아파트 feature 특징으로 하다 entrance hall 현관 로비 well-appointed 잘 설비된 ample 충분한 storage 보관 space 공간 laundry 세탁 covered 지붕이 덮인 satellite 위성 rent 임대(료) pleasantly 쾌적하게 situated 위치한 embassy 대사관 additionally 게다가 private 전용의 equipped ~장비를 갖춘 dining 식사 hammock 해먹 retreat 조용한 곳, 휴식처 cosmopolitan 도회적인, 세계적인 rush 분주함

수신: 프레드릭 매킨크 <f.makkink@quincemail.com>
발신: 하미다 청아 <hamida@ovalorchardrentals.co.ke>
제목: 회신: 침실 3개짜리 아파트
날짜: 3월 16일
첨부: 📎 오픈 하우스 정보

매킨크 씨께:

제 이름은 하미다 청아이고, 오벌 오차드 렌탈의 직원입니다. **193**저희 매력적인 주거 공간 중 하나를 임대하는 것에 관심을 보여 주셔서 감사드리며 최근 나이로비로 이사하셨다는 소식을 듣게 되어 기쁩니다. **193**고객님의 이메일에서 침실 3개짜리 아파트에 대해 문의하셨는데요. **194, 195**란타나 가에 월 15만 케냐 실링에 침실 3개짜리 아파트가 딱 한 채 남아 있습니다. 고객님의 새 직장에서 2분밖에 안 걸리는 곳이라 마음에 드실 것 같습니다.

195아파트를 직접 보시고 싶으시면 다음 주 오픈 하우스에 참석해 주세요. 이 이메일에 첨부된 일정을 확인해 주세요. 제가 거기서 아파트를 보여 드리겠습니다.

하미다 청아, 렌탈 직원

- -

어휘 | agent 대리인 express 표현하다 interest 관심 delighted 아주 즐거운 recently 최근에 unit (아파트 같은 공동 주택 내의) 한 가구 appreciate 감사하다 workplace 직장 in person 직접 attend 참석하다 attach 첨부하다

오벌 오차드 오픈 하우스 공개 시간, 3월 20-23일		
	요일 및 시간	장소
월요일	오전 8시 30분~오전 11시	랍타 가 빌딩 5호
화요일	일정 없음	일정 없음
195수요일	오전 10시~오후 12시	**195**란타나 가 빌딩 2호
목요일	오전 8시 30분~오전 11시	랍타 가 빌딩 8호

191 광고에 따르면, 랍타 가 빌딩에 있는 아파트의 추가적인 특징은?

(A) 주간 청소 서비스
(B) 개인 전용 정원
(C) 실내 주차 구역
(D) 세탁실

해설 | 세부 사항
광고의 두 번째 단락 세 번째 문장에서 추가적으로 각각의 랍타 가 아파트에는 그릴, 식탁, 라운지 가구, 해먹이 구비된 개인 전용 야외 정원이 있어 웨스트랜드라는 대도시의 분주함을 벗어난 완벽한 휴식처가 되어 준다(Additionally, each Rhapta Road flat ~ cosmopolitan rush of Westlands)고 했으므로 정답은 (B)이다.

192 관심 있는 사람들은 오픈 하우스에 참석하기 전에 무엇을 하라고 지시받는가?

(A) 온라인 등록
(B) 중개료 지불
(C) 중개인과 전화 통화
(D) 고용주로부터 서류 제출

해설 | 세부 사항
광고의 세 번째 단락 첫 문장에서 아름다운 저희 아파트를 보려면 www.ovalorchardrentals.co.ke를 방문하여 오픈 하우스 행사 중 하나에 등록하라(To view our beautiful flats, visit ~ register for one of our open house events)고 했으므로 정답은 (A)이다.

어휘 | register 등록 fee 수수료 employer 고용주

193 이메일의 목적은?

(A) 환불 요청
(B) 일정 변경 공지
(C) 문의 응답
(D) 교통 정보 제공

해설 | 주제 / 목적
이메일의 첫 단락 두 번째 문장에서 저희 매력적인 주거 공간 중 하나를 임대하는 것에 관심을 보여 주셔서 감사드린다(Thank you for ~ lovely living spaces)고 했고, 세 번째 문장에서 고객님의 이메일에서 침실 3개짜리 아파트에 대해 문의하셨다(In your e-mail, you asked

about our three-bedroom flats)고 했다. 따라서 이 이메일은 수신인인 매킨크 씨가 전에 보낸 문의 이메일에 답변을 하기 위한 것임을 알 수 있으므로 (C)가 정답이다.

어휘 | announce 알리다 respond 응답하다 inquiry 문의 transportation 교통편

194 청아 씨의 이메일에서 매킨크 씨에 대해 암시하는 것은?

(A) 일본 대사관에 약속이 있다.
(B) 규칙적으로 버스를 타고 출근한다.
(C) 몇 년 전에 랍타 가 인근에 살았다.
(D) 로투스 비즈니스 단지에서 일한다.

해설 | 연계
이메일의 첫 단락 네 번째 문장에서 매킨크 씨에게 란타나 가에 월 15만 케냐 실링에 침실 3개짜리 아파트가 딱 한 채 남아 있다(We have just one ~ 150,000 per month)며 고객님의 새 직장에서 2분밖에 안 걸리는 곳이라 마음에 드실 것 같다(I think you would appreciate ~ your new workplace)고 했는데, 광고의 두 번째 단락 첫 문장에서 란타나 가 빌딩이 침실 3개짜리 아파트로 로투스 비즈니스 단지와 버스 정류장에서 걸어서 단 2분 거리에 있다(Our Lantana Road building ~ a bus stop)고 했다. 따라서 매킨크 씨의 새 직장은 란타나 가 빌딩에서 2분 거리에 위치한 로투스 비즈니스 단지에 있다는 것을 알 수 있으므로 정답은 (D)이다.

어휘 | appointment 약속 regularly 규칙적으로

195 매킨크 씨는 언제 오픈 하우스에 참석할 것 같은가?

(A) 월요일
(B) 화요일
(C) 수요일
(D) 목요일

해설 | 연계
이메일의 첫 단락 네 번째 문장에서 매킨크 씨에게 란타나 가에 월 15만 케냐 실링에 침실 3개짜리 아파트가 딱 한 채 남아 있다(We have just one ~ 150,000 per month)고 했고 두 번째 단락 첫 문장에서 아파트를 직접 보고 싶으면 다음 주 오픈 하우스에 참석하라(If you wish to see ~ open house next week)고 했다. 시간표에 따르면 매킨크 씨가 보고 싶어 할 란타나 가 아파트의 오픈 하우스는 수요일에 예정되어 있으므로 (C)가 정답이다.

[196-200] 광고+이메일+고객 의견

http://www.tighesautopainting.ca/home_page

| 홈페이지 | 서비스 | 고객 의견 | 연락처 |

티게의 오토 페인팅
우수한 가격에 최고급 작업

저희는 승용차, 승합차, 보트, 항공기 등 매우 다양한 차량을 위한 도장, 세차, 왁싱 작업을 제공합니다. 저희의 꼼꼼한 세차 서비스는 타의 추종을 불허합니다. 차를 안팎으로 새것처럼 보이게 할 수 있습니다.

196이제 이동식 서비스도 제공합니다. 정기적으로 당신의 사무실이나 작업 현장을 방문하여 차량에 서비스를 제공합니다. 여기에는 세차, 왁싱, 벗겨진 페인트 자국을 손보는 작업이 포함됩니다. 저희 트럭이 전동 세척기, 수건, 진공청소기 등 필요한 모든 장비를 가지고 갑니다. **197상거래에 대한 자세한 정보를 원하시거나 계약 옵션을 검토하시려면 앨리슨 맥카시에게 amccarthy@tighesautopainting.ca 또는 416-555-0146, 내선 번호 4번으로 연락 주십시오.**

199특별 판촉 행사: 12월 4일까지 주간 또는 월간 서비스 계약을 체결하시고 15% 할인 혜택을 받으세요!

어휘 | premium 고급의 excellent 우수한 a wide variety of 매우 다양한 vehicle 차량 detailing 정밀 세차 mobile 이동식의 site 현장 fleet (버스·택시 등의) 무리 regular 정기적인 paint chip 벗겨진 페인트 자국 carry 운반하다 necessary 필요한 equipment 장비 vacuum 진공 청소기 commercial 상업의 account 신용 거래 review 검토하다 contract 계약 ext. 내선 번호 promotion 판촉

수신: 프레스턴 워드 <pwarde@polluxelectrical.ca>
발신: 아쇼크 디어 <adheer@polluxelectrical.ca>
제목: 업데이트
199날짜: 11월 22일
첨부: 🖇 나보아_아프레_정보

워드 씨께,

198, 199우리가 논의했던 대로 새로운 승합차 몇 대를 구입하고 티게의 오토 페인팅에 가입했습니다. 그들이 차량에 우리 로고를 칠해 줄 겁니다. 또한 기존에 가지고 있던 승합차에도 페인트 칠을 해줄 수 있습니다. **199그 후에는 매주 목요일마다 와서 우리 주차장에 있는 승합차를 세차하고 왁스 작업을 할 겁니다.** 6개월 뒤에는 계약을 재평가하고 그들과 거래를 계속할지 알아볼 수 있습니다.

또한 **200우리가 고용할 전기 기사인 맥스 나보아와 클로드 아프레에 대한 정보를 첨부합니다.** 둘 다 운전 면허증이 있고 우리 승합차와 같은 승합차를 운전한 적이 있습니다.

아쇼크 디어, 운영 총괄

어휘 | discuss 논의하다 purchase 구입하다 own 소유하다 lot 지역 reevaluate 재평가하다 continue 계속하다 attach 첨부하다 regarding ~에 관해 electrician 전기 기사 driver's license 운전 면허증

http://www.polluxelectrical.ca/customer_commetns

| 홈페이지 | 서비스 | **고객 의견** | 연락처 |

폴룩스 일렉트리칼을 이용하면 실망하지 않을 겁니다. 저는 최근에 서점을 샀는데 전기 시스템을 업데이트해야 했습니다. 전화로 상의한 뒤, 예약을 했습니다. 그 다음 날 시스템은 수리되었습니다. **200전기 기사인 맥스 나보아는 매우 예의 바르고 능률적이었습니다.** 그는 그의 승합차에 필요한 모든 도구를 구비하고 있었습니다. 작업은 몇 시간밖에 걸리지 않았습니다. 가격도 합리적이었습니다.

– **200사라 아덴**, 12월 20일

어휘 | disappoint 실망시키다 recently 최근에 electrical 전기의 discussion 논의 appointment 약속 book 예약하다 fix 고치다 polite 예의 바른 efficient 효율적인 reasonable 합리적인

196 광고에 따르면, 티게의 오토 페인팅의 새로운 점은?

(A) 업체명
(B) 서비스 유형
(C) 페인트 상표
(D) 가전제품 세트

해설 | 세부 사항
광고의 두 번째 단락 첫 문장에서 이제 이동식 서비스도 제공한다(We now offer mobile service)고 했으므로 티게의 오토 페인팅에서 최근에 새로운 유형의 서비스를 추가했다는 것을 알 수 있다. 따라서 (B)가 정답이다.

197 맥카시 씨는 누구일 것 같은가?

(A) 상업 거래처 관리자
(B) 정밀 세차 서비스 일정 관리자
(C) 장비 및 자재 주문 담당자
(D) 웹페이지를 업데이트하는 마케팅 전문가

해설 | 추론
광고의 두 번째 단락 마지막 문장에서 상거래에 대한 자세한 정보를 원하거나 계약 옵션을 검토하려면 앨리슨 맥카시에게 amccarthy@tighesautopainting.ca 또는 416-555-0146, 내선 번호 4번으로 연락하라(For more information ~ 416-555-0146, Ext. 4)고 했으므로 맥카시 씨는 상거래 계약을 관리하고 있음을 짐작할 수 있다. 따라서 (A)가 정답이다.

어휘 | material 자재 specialist 전문가

198 이메일에서 디어 씨와 워드 씨에 대해 명시된 것은?

(A) 이전에 차량 서비스에 대해 이야기한 적이 있다.
(B) 일자리 공석을 위한 면접을 준비해야 한다.
(C) 오래된 승합차를 교체할 계획이다.
(D) 둘 다 청소 서비스 업체에서 근무한다.

해설 | Not / True
이메일의 첫 문장에서 디어 씨가 워드 씨에게 우리가 논의했던 대로 새로운 승합차 몇 대를 구입하고 티게의 오토 페인팅에 가입했다(As we discussed ~ Tighe's Auto Painting)고 했으므로 디어 씨와 워드 씨는 전에 차량 구입 및 서비스에 관해 이야기한 적이 있다는 것을 알 수 있다. 따라서 정답은 (A)이다.

199 디어 씨가 이메일에서 언급한 계약에 대해 사실일 것 같은 것은?

(A) 기간이 2년짜리였다.
(B) 목요일에 갱신될 예정이다.
(C) 새로운 승합차의 구매를 성사시켰다.
(D) 주간 서비스 할인이 포함되어 있다.

해설 | 연계
광고의 마지막 문장에서 특별 판촉 행사를 홍보하며 12월 4일까지 주간 또는 월간 서비스 계약을 체결하고 15% 할인 혜택을 받으라(Special promotion sign ~ receive 15% off!)고 했는데, 이메일의 작성 날짜가 11월 22일(Date 22 November)이고 첫 문장에서 논의했던 대로 티게의 오토 페인팅에 가입했다(As we discussed ~ Tighe's Auto Painting)고 했다. 이어서 네 번째 문장에서 그 후에는 매주 목요일마다 와서 우리 주차장에 있는 승합차를 세차하고 왁스 작업을 할 것(After that, they'll come ~ that are in our lot)이라고 했다. 따라서 디어 씨는 판촉 행사 기간 동안 티게의 오토 페인팅에서 주간 서비스를 체결해 15% 할인을 받았음을 알 수 있다. 따라서 정답은 (D)이다.

어휘 | period 기간 finalize 마무리 짓다

200 아덴 씨가 받은 서비스에 대해 암시된 것은?

(A) 불만족스러웠다.
(B) 새로운 직원이 관여되었다.
(C) 끝내는 데 오래 걸렸다.
(D) 일정을 변경해야 했다.

해설 | 연계
고객 의견의 다섯 번째 문장에서 아덴 씨는 전기 기사인 맥스 나보아가 매우 예의 바르고 능률적이었다(The electrician, Max Naboa, was so polite and efficient)고 평가했는데, 이메일의 두 번째 단락 첫 문장에서 디어 씨가 우리가 고용할 전기 기사인 맥스 나보아와 클로드 아프레에 대한 정보를 첨부한다(I'm attaching the information ~ Max Naboa and Claude Affre)고 했다. 따라서 아덴 씨는 새로 고용된 직원으로부터 서비스를 받았음을 알 수 있으므로 (B)가 정답이다.

어휘 | unsatisfactory 불만족스러운 involve 관련시키다 complete 완료하다

CHAPTER 3

실전 모의고사 01

109

147 (B)	**148** (C)	**149** (B)	**150** (D)	**151** (A)
152 (B)	**153** (B)	**154** (C)	**155** (A)	**156** (C)
157 (A)	**158** (C)	**159** (A)	**160** (B)	**161** (C)
162 (B)	**163** (D)	**164** (B)	**165** (C)	**166** (A)
167 (B)	**168** (A)	**169** (D)	**170** (B)	**171** (A)
172 (C)	**173** (B)	**174** (C)	**175** (B)	**176** (C)
177 (A)	**178** (B)	**179** (D)	**180** (D)	**181** (A)
182 (D)	**183** (C)	**184** (B)	**185** (A)	**186** (C)
187 (B)	**188** (A)	**189** (D)	**190** (B)	**191** (C)
192 (B)	**193** (C)	**194** (D)	**195** (B)	**196** (D)
197 (C)	**198** (C)	**199** (B)	**200** (D)	

[147-148] 웹페이지

http://www.kitchencarts.com

천연 원목 조리대가 있는 흰색 주방 카트

➤ 고정 높이 86cm, 폭 57cm, 길이 98cm

➤ 2개의 탈착식 철제 바구니가 달린 조정 불가능한 선반 포함

➤ **147**간편한 이동성을 제공하는 바퀴(잠금 장치 포함)가 특징

148할인 코드 KSPROMO로 25% 할인 받으세요. 6월 8일부터 6월 10일까지 모든 가구가 할인됩니다. 배송비가 부과됩니다.

어휘 | natural 천연의 countertop 조리대 fixed 고정된 height 높이 width 폭 length 길이 nonadjustable 조정할 수 없는 shelf 선반 removable 제거할 수 있는 wire 철사 feature 특징으로 하다 caster (가구 밑에 달린) 바퀴 mobility 이동성 charge 요금 apply 적용되다

147 주방 카트의 어떤 특징이 언급되는가?

(A) 탈착 가능한 선반이 있다.
(B) 이동이 가능하다.
(C) 다양한 색상으로 나온다.
(D) 도구로 쉽게 조절할 수 있다.

해설 | Not / True
네 번째 문장에서 간편한 이동성을 제공하는 바퀴(잠금 장치 포함)가 특징(Features caster wheels (with locks) to provide easy mobility)이라고 했으므로 (B)가 정답이다.

어휘 | a variety of 다양한 adjust 조절하다 tool 도구

패러프레이징
지문의 mobility → 보기의 can be moved around

148 할인 행사에 대해 명시된 것은?

(A) 열흘 동안 지속된다.
(B) 단종된 상품에 대한 것이다.
(C) 특별 코드가 필요하다.
(D) 무료 배송을 포함한다.

해설 | Not / True
다섯 번째 문장에서 할인 코드 KSPROMO로 25% 할인 받으라(Get 25 percent off with promo code KSPROMO)며 6월 8일부터 6월 10일까지 모든 가구가 할인된다(All furniture on sale from June 8 to June 10)고 한 것으로 보아 코드가 있으면 모든 가구에 할인을 받을 수 있음을 알 수 있다. 따라서 (C)가 정답이다.

어휘 | last 지속하다 discontinued 단종된 require ~이 필요하다

[149-150] 회람

회람

수신: 모든 카페 직원
150발신: 이베트 파트리지, 총지배인
날짜: 4월 12일
제목: 주간 예약

다음 지시 사항은 모든 웨이터, 카운터 직원 및 관리자에게 적용됩니다. **149**조식이나 점심 식사 예약 요청은 고객에게 확인증을 발급하기 전에 저에게 승인을 받아야 합니다. 또한, 예약 요청이 들어오면 고객의 이름과 성, 전화번호, 예약을 요청한 날짜와 시간을 반드시 적어 두기 바랍니다. 그런 다음, 고객에게 24시간 내에 회신 전화가 갈 것임을 알리세요. **150**브래들리 씨와 저는 조식과 점심 식사 예약이 점차 인기를 얻고 있어 무척 기쁩니다. 정원 초과 예약과 같은 실수를 피하는 것이 더욱 중요한 이유는 우리 측의 잘못으로 인해 고객을 잃기를 원하지 않기 때문입니다.

어휘 | reservation 예약 directive 지시 apply to ~에 적용되다 authorize 인가하다 confirmation 확인(서) inform 알리다 return call 회신 전화 thrilled 아주 신이 난 imperative 중요한 overbooking 초과 예약 shortcoming 결점

149 회람에 따르면, 조식과 점심 식사 예약은 누가 확정할 수 있는가?

(A) 웨이터
(B) 파트리지 씨
(C) 관리자
(D) 브래들리 씨

해설 | 세부 사항
두 번째 문장에서 조식이나 점심 식사 예약 요청은 고객에게 확인증을 발급하기 전에 저에게 승인을 받아야 한다(Please be advised that ~ confirmation is

issued to a customer)고 했고, 이 회람의 작성자 즉, 발신인은 이베트 파트리지 총지배인이므로 정답은 (B)이다.

150 파트리지 씨와 브래들리 씨에 대해 명시된 것은?

(A) 카운터 직원이었다.
(B) 전 직원을 대상으로 교육을 실시할 예정이다.
(C) 조식 및 점심 식사 서비스 시간을 연장할 예정이다.
(D) 카페에 예약 요청이 늘고 있어 기분이 좋다.

해설 | Not / True
다섯 번째 문장에서 브래들리 씨와 저는 조식과 점심 식사 예약이 점차 인기를 얻고 있어 무척 기쁘다(Mr. Bradley and I are thrilled that breakfast and lunch reservations are becoming more popular)고 했고 '저'는 회람의 작성자인 파트리지 씨이므로 브래들리 씨와 파트리지 씨는 카페 예약이 늘고 있어 즐거워하고 있다는 것을 알 수 있다. 따라서 정답은 (D)이다.

[151-152] 구인 광고

노스포트 미술관의 서아프리카 미술 큐레이터

서아프리카 미술 큐레이터는 주로 나이지리아와 아이보리 코스트에서 습득한 미술품을 보존, 정리, 분류, 전시 및 추천합니다. **151**큐레이터는 전략적 기획에 참여하고 다른 미술관 직원들과 협력하여 우리 기관의 교육, 연구 및 공공 서비스 행사를 개발합니다. **152(C)**프랑스어, 이보어, 디울라어를 읽는 능력은 필수적입니다. 서아프리카에서 사용되는 하우사어, 아랍어, 또는 기타 언어에 대한 독해 지식이 우대됩니다. 소장품을 대중에게 소개하기 위한 기본으로서 **152(D)**서아프리카 역사와 문화, 미술 간의 상호 관계에 대한 폭넓은 지식이 요구됩니다. **152(A)**서아프리카 문화에 중점을 둔 미술사 또는 인류학의 석사 또는 박사 학위가 요구됩니다. 지원하시려면 www.northfortmuseum. org / openpositions를 방문하십시오.

어휘 | preserve 보존하다 organize 정리하다 categorize 분류하다 recommendation 추천 acquisition 습득 primarily 주로 participate in ~에 참여하다 strategic 전략적인 collaborate 협력하다 personnel 직원 further 발전시키다 institution 기관 instructional 교육용의 research 연구 essential 필수적인 knowledge 지식 desirable 우대하는 extensive 폭넓은 interrelationship 상호 관계 basis 기초, 기반 present 제시하다 advanced degree 석·박사 학위 anthropology 인류학 apply 지원하다

151 큐레이터의 책무 중 하나는?

(A) 미술관 직원과 상담
(B) 방문객을 위한 견학 진행

(C) 미술품 판매
(D) 예술가 홍보

해설 | 세부 사항
두 번째 문장에서 큐레이터는 전략적 기획에 참여하고 다른 미술관 직원들과 협력하여 우리 기관의 교육, 연구 및 공공 서비스 행사를 개발한다(The curator participates in ~ and public service events)고 했으므로 (A)가 정답이다.

어휘 | consult 상담하다 lead 이끌다 promote 홍보하다
패러프레이징
지문의 collaborates with other museum personnel → 보기의 Consulting with museum staff

152 이 직책의 요건으로 언급되지 않은 것은?

(A) 관련 학문 분야의 전문화
(B) 해외 출장 의향
(C) 일부 언어에 대한 숙련도
(D) 서아프리카 문화에 대한 전문 지식

해설 | Not / True
세 번째 문장에서 프랑스어, 이보어, 디울라어를 읽는 능력이 필수(The ability to read ~ is essential)라고 했으므로 (C), 다섯 번째 문장에서 서아프리카 역사와 문화, 미술 간의 상호 관계에 대한 폭넓은 지식이 요구된다(Extensive knowledge is ~ collection to the public)고 했으므로 (D), 여섯 번째 문장에서 서아프리카 문화에 중점을 둔 미술사 또는 인류학의 석사 또는 박사 학위가 요구된다(An advanced degree ~ is required)고 했으므로 (A)가 직책의 요건으로 언급되었으며, 해외 출장에 관한 내용은 없으므로 (B)가 정답이다.

어휘 | specialization 전문화 relevant 관련된 academic 학문의 field 분야 willingness 의향 abroad 해외로 skillfulness 숙련도 expertise 전문 지식

[153-154] 온라인 채팅

제임스 레이스 (오전 8시 07분)
로라, **153**제가 에어컨 수리를 요청했어요. 어떤 분이 제 사무실에 오시기는 했는데, 문제가 해결되지 않았어요.

로라 쉬에 (오전 8시 08분)
죄송합니다. 문제가 뭐죠?

제임스 레이스 (오전 8시 11분)
제 에어컨 냉방이 충분히 시원하지 않아요. 적정 온도로 맞춰도 사무실이 여전히 너무 더워요.

로라 쉬에 (오전 8시 13분)
불편하시겠어요. 제가 재방문 통지를 보내 기사가 오늘 당신의 사무실을 우선적으로 처리하도록 할게요.

제임스 레이스 (오전 8시 14분)

좋아요. 그런데 ¹⁵⁴돈을 두 번 내고 싶지는 않아요. 서비스는 무료인가요?

로라 쉬에 (오전 8시 16분)

물론이죠. 기사가 첫 방문 때 문제를 해결하지 못할 경우 재방문은 무료입니다.

어휘 | repair 수리 fix 고치다 issue 문제 properly 제대로 comfortable 편안한 temperature 온도 frustrating 불만스러운 recall 소환 technician 기술자 prioritize 우선시하다 complimentary 무료의

---

153 레이스 씨는 왜 쉬에 씨에게 연락하는가?

(A) 사무실 대여를 원한다.
(B) 유지 보수 문제가 있다.
(C) 에어컨 구입을 원한다.
(D) 계좌에 잔액이 남아 있다.

해설 | 주제/목적

8시 7분에 레이스 씨가 에어컨 수리를 요청했다(I requested a repair for my air conditioner)고 했고, 어떤 분이 제 사무실에 오시기는 했는데 문제가 해결되지 않았다(Someone came by my office, but the problem has not been fixed)고 한 것으로 보아 에어컨 수리에 문제가 있음을 알리려고 연락했다는 것을 알 수 있다. 따라서 정답은 (B)이다.

어휘 | rent 빌리다 maintenance (기계 등을 점검·보수하는) 유지 balance 잔액

패러프레이징

지문의 repair → 보기의 maintenance

154 오전 8시 16분에 쉬에 씨가 "물론이죠"라고 쓴 의도는 무엇이겠는가?

(A) 기술자가 수리를 했다.
(B) 레이스 씨의 사무실에 들를 예정이다.
(C) 서비스 요금이 부과되지 않을 것이다.
(D) 아직 돈을 내지 않았다.

해설 | 의도 파악

8시 14분에 레이스 씨가 돈을 두 번 내고 싶지 않다(I don't want to pay twice)며 서비스가 무료인지(Is this a free service?)를 묻자 8시 16분에 쉬에 씨가 물론이죠(Absolutely)라고 답한 것이므로 쉬에 씨는 서비스가 무료임을 확인해 주려는 의도로 한 말임을 알 수 있다. 따라서 (C)가 정답이다.

어휘 | stop by 들르다 charge 부과하다

패러프레이징

지문의 a free service → 보기의 A service fee will not be charged.

[155-157] 표

타마기 전자 악기
JZ-9M 키보드의 문제 해결 팁

¹⁵⁵스탠드형 JZ-9M 타마기 키보드를 구입해 주셔서 감사합니다. 악기에 문제가 발생할 경우 이 표를 이용해 문제를 해결하십시오. 일부 문제는 키보드를 공장 초기 설정으로 복원하여 해결할 수도 있습니다(사용 설명서 16페이지 참조). ¹⁵⁶문제가 지속되면 타마기 서비스 센터로 연락 주십시오.

문제	의심되는 원인	해결책
소리가 나지 않는다.	악기가 꺼져 있거나 전원에 연결되어 있지 않다.	ON/OFF 스위치를 "ON"으로 켜주세요.
¹⁵⁷기기가 갑자기 꺼진다.	자동 끄기가 활성화되어 있다.	¹⁵⁷자동 끄기 스위치를 길게 눌러 이 기능을 꺼주세요.
낮은 음 소리가 약하거나 들리지 않는다.	메인 슬라이더 버튼과 옥타브 슬라이더 버튼이 모두 활성화되어 있다.	옥타브 슬라이더 버튼을 내려 오디오 출력을 조정해 주세요.

어휘 | instrument 악기 resolve 해결하다 restore 복원하다 instruction manual 사용 설명서 persist 지속되다 unexpectedly 갑자기 note 음 inaudible 들리지 않는 suspected 의심되는 cause 원인 enable 가능하게 하다 octave 옥타브 engaged 사용 중인 deactivate 비활성화시키다 feature 특징 adjust 조정하다 output 출력

---

155 이 정보의 대상은 누구인가?

(A) JZ-9M 키보드 소유자
(B) 타마기 사의 직원
(C) 서비스 센터 전화 담당자
(D) 제품 조립 라인 작업자

해설 | 세부 사항

첫 문장에서 스탠드형 JZ-9M 타마기 키보드를 구입해 주셔서 감사하다(Thank you for purchasing the JZ-9M Tamagi keyboard with stand)고 한 것으로 보아 JZ-9M 타마기 키보드의 소유자를 대상으로 한 글임을 알 수 있다. 따라서 (A)가 정답이다.

어휘 | representative 대리인 assembly-line 조립 라인

156 타마기 서비스 센터에 전화해야 하는 이유로 언급된 것은?

(A) 키보드를 공장 초기 설정으로 복원하려고
(B) 키보드 스탠드를 교체하려고
(C) 반복되는 문제에 대한 도움을 받으려고
(D) 구매에 대한 환불을 받으려고

해설 | 세부 사항

첫 단락 마지막 문장에서 문제가 지속되면 타마기 서비스 센터로 연락하라(If problems persist, contact a Tamagi Service Center)고 했으므로 정답은 (C)이다.

어휘 | recurring 되풀이하여 발생하는 obtain 얻다 refund 환불

<u>패러프레이징</u>
지문의 problems persist → 보기의 a recurring problem

157 사용자가 스위치를 길게 눌러야 하는 이유는?

(A) 악기가 갑자기 꺼지기 때문에
(B) 소리가 크게 재생되지 않기 때문에
(C) 옥타브 슬라이더 스위치가 활성화되어 있기 때문에
(D) 전기 케이블이 분리되지 않기 때문에

해설 | 세부 사항

표 두 번째 칸에 기기가 갑자기 꺼지는(Instrument turns off unexpectedly) 경우 해결책(Solution)으로 자동 끄기 스위치를 길게 눌러 이 기능을 끄라(Press and hold the auto-off switch to deactivate this feature)고 했으므로 (A)가 정답이다.

어휘 | detach 분리되다

[158-160] 이메일

수신: bella.mcintyre@cumulusmail.net
발신: customersupport@synchette.com
날짜: 6월 23일
제목: 최신 버전

매킨타이어 씨께,

귀사의 사업에 싱셰트 백업 및 복구 소프트웨어를 선택해 주셔서 감사합니다.

158, 159당사의 기록에 따르면 귀사는 현재 소프트웨어 8.0 버전을 사용하고 있습니다. 8월 1일부터 저희는 그 버전을 더 이상 지원하지 않습니다. 158귀사의 소프트웨어를 즉시 업데이트하실 것을 권장 드립니다. 160지금부터 8월 1일까지 현재 업계 표준인 10.5 버전을 정가에서 15달러 할인된 가격에 구매하실 수 있습니다.

싱셰트 10.5 버전의 강력한 기능에 대해 자세한 내용을 확인하시려면 당사의 웹사이트 www.synchette.com을 방문하십시오.

싱셰트 고객 지원 부서

- -
어휘 | recovery 복구 indicate 나타내다 currently 현재 no longer 더 이상 ~않다 support 지원하다 immediately 즉시 current 현재의 industry 업계 feature 기능

158 싱셰트 고객 지원 부서에서 왜 이메일을 보냈는가?

(A) 고객에게 가격 인상에 대해 알리려고
(B) 기술 문제에 대한 도움을 제공하려고
(C) 고객에게 즉각적인 조치를 취하도록 알리려고
(D) 프로그램의 기능에 대해 의견을 요청하려고

해설 | 주제 / 목적

두 번째 단락의 첫 문장에서 당사의 기록에 따르면 귀사는 현재 소프트웨어 8.0 버전을 사용하고 있다(Our records indicate ~ of the software)고 했고 8월 1일부터는 그 버전을 더 이상 지원하지 않는다(As of August 1 ~ support that version)며 귀사의 소프트웨어를 즉시 업데이트할 것을 권한다(We advise you to update your software immediately)고 했다. 따라서 정답은 (C)이다.

어휘 | notify 알리다 increase 인상 immediate 즉각적인 take action 조치를 취하다

159 이메일에 따르면, 싱셰트는 8월 1일에 무엇을 할 예정인가?

(A) 소프트웨어 8.0 버전에 대한 지원을 중단한다.
(B) 최신 버전의 소프트웨어를 출시한다.
(C) 소프트웨어를 온라인으로 시연한다.
(D) 매킨타이어 씨에게 새 소프트웨어에 대한 청구서를 발송한다.

해설 | 세부 사항

두 번째 단락의 첫 문장에서 당사의 기록에 따르면 귀사는 현재 소프트웨어 8.0 버전을 사용하고 있다(Our records indicate ~ of the software)고 했고 8월 1일부터는 그 버전을 더 이상 지원하지 않는다(As of August 1 ~ support that version)고 했다. 따라서 정답은 (A)이다.

어휘 | release 출시하다 latest 최신의 demonstration 시연 invoice 청구서

<u>패러프레이징</u>
지문의 will no longer support
→ 보기의 Stop supporting

160 싱셰트 고객 지원 부서는 무엇을 권하는가?

(A) 이메일로 답장하기
(B) 낮은 가격 혜택 이용하기
(C) 모든 시스템 파일 백업하기
(D) 담당자에게 연락하기

해설 | 세부 사항

두 번째 단락의 마지막 문장에서 지금부터 8월 1일까지 현재 업계 표준인 10.5 버전을 정가에서 15달러 할인된 가격에 구매할 수 있다(Between now and August 1 ~ $15.00 off the list price)고 했으므로 (B)가 정답이다.

어휘 | respond 답장하다 take advantage of ~을 이용하다 representative 직원

¹⁶¹5년마다 하트풀 시 의회가 고용한 기술자들이 보도에 파손된 부분이 있는지 점검합니다. 지난주에 보도 점검이 완료되었습니다.

¹⁶¹, ¹⁶²보수 예정인 보도는 빨간 동그라미로 표시되어 있습니다. ¹⁶²하트풀 웹사이트인 www.townofhart pool.gov의 지도에도 나와 있습니다. 집이나 사업장이 표시된 보도와 인접해 있는 경우 보수 작업 시기를 알리는 통지문을 받게 됩니다. 통지문에는 보수 작업으로 어떤 영향을 받게 될지에 대한 문의 사항이 있을 경우에 대비해 연락처가 포함될 예정입니다. 만약 귀하의 진입로가 표시된 보도와 닿아 있다면, 이틀간의 보수 작업 기간 동안 도로에 주차해야 할 것입니다.

¹⁶³시 의회는 아직 보수 공사 건으로 건설업체들로부터 입찰을 받고 있습니다. 한 곳이 선정되면 주민 모두 안내를 받게 될 것입니다. 이 프로젝트는 5월 초에 시작해 날씨가 허락한다면 5주가 걸릴 것으로 예상됩니다.

어휘 | council 의회 inspect 점검하다 sidewalk 보도 damaged 파손된 slate 계획하다 repair 수리하다; 보수 adjacent 인접한 notify 알리다 take place 일어나다 affect 영향을 미치다 driveway (도로에서 집·차고까지의) 진입로 connect 연결되다 period 기간 bid 입찰 permit 허락하다

161 공지의 목적은?

(A) 진입로 점검 예약
(B) 계약자에게 입찰 제출 요청
(C) 주민에게 공사 작업 공지
(D) 일부 보도의 파손 경위 설명

해설 | 주제/목적
첫 단락에서 5년마다 하트풀 시 의회가 고용한 기술자들이 보도에 파손된 부분이 있는지 점검한다(Every five years ~ damaged areas)며 지난주에 보도 점검이 완료되었다(A sidewalk inspection was completed last week)고 했고, 두 번째 단락 첫 문장에서 보수 예정인 보도는 빨간 동그라미로 표시되어 있다(Sidewalks that are ~ with red circles)고 했다. 따라서 공지문은 하트풀 마을 주민에게 보도 점검 결과에 따른 보수 공사 작업에 대해 안내하기 위한 것이므로 (C)가 정답이다.

162 공지에 따르면, 보수 위치를 파악할 수 있는 한 가지 방법은?

(A) 시 의회로 전화한다.
(B) 시의 웹사이트를 방문한다.
(C) 지역 신문을 읽는다.
(D) 건물에 게시된 표지판을 찾아본다.

해설 | 세부 사항
두 번째 단락의 첫 문장에서 보수 예정인 보도는 빨간 동그라미로 표시되어 있다(Sidewalks that are

slated ~ with red circles)고 했고, 하트풀 웹사이트인 www.townofhartpool.gov의 지도에도 나와 있다(They are also shown ~ www.townofhartpool.gov)고 했으므로 정답은 (B)이다.

163 [1], [2], [3], [4]로 표시된 곳 중에서 다음 문장이 들어가기에 가장 적합한 위치는?

"한 곳이 선정되면 주민 모두 안내를 받게 될 것입니다."

(A) [1]　　　(B) [2]　　　(C) [3]　　　(D) [4]

해설 | 문장 삽입
제시된 문장의 when one has been selected가 문제 해결의 단서이다. '한 곳이 선정되면'이라는 내용으로 보아 여러 곳을 두고 무엇인가를 선택하는 과정에 있음을 알 수 있으므로, 주어진 문장 앞에는 복수 명사와 함께 선택 및 선정과 관련된 내용이 와야 한다. 따라서 보수 공사 건으로 여러 건설업체(construction companies)로부터 입찰을 받고 있다는 문장 뒤인 (D)가 정답이다.

트렌턴 (4월 4일)—¹⁶⁴라벤더 스킨 케어 회사의 최고 경영자 도널드 맥그래스는 회사의 본사를 뉴저지주 해밀턴에서 아이다호주 보이시로 옮길 의사를 밝혔다. 이러한 변화는 내년 초에 이루어질 예정이다. ¹⁶⁶이 계획에 대한 ¹⁶⁵추진 요인은 비용 절감의 필요성에 있는 것으로 보인다. 맥그래스 씨는 부동산세가 더 낮은 지역으로 이전하여 이를 달성하기를 희망한다고 언급했다.

¹⁶⁷지난 10월 마케팅 부사장에서 승진한 이후 맥그래스 씨는 회사에 여러 변화를 주었다. 이러한 변화 중 일부에는 최고 재무 책임자 교체와 실적이 저조한 몇몇 상품 중단이 포함된다.

어휘 | announce 발표하다 intention 의사 corporate 기업의 base 본부, 본사 operation 사업 shift 변화 take place 발생하다 driving 추진하는 factor 요인 appear 나타나다 reduce 줄이다 cost 비용 accomplish 달성하다 tax 세금 property 부동산 tend 경향이 있다 promotion 승진 replace 교체하다 chief financial officer 최고 재무 책임자 discontinue 중단하다 underperforming 실적이 저조한

164 기사는 주로 무엇에 관한 것인가?

(A) 회사 임원의 임명
(B) 본사 이전
(C) 지역 회사의 최근 수익 보고서
(D) 기업의 인력 확충

해설 | 주제/목적
첫 문장에서 라벤더 스킨 케어 회사의 최고 경영자 도널드 맥그래스는 회사의 본사를 뉴저지주 해밀턴에서

아이다호주 보이시로 옮길 의사를 밝혔다(Lavender Skin Care Company CEO ~ New Jersey, to Boise, Idaho)며 관련 내용을 이어가고 있으므로 기사의 주제는 기업의 본사 이전이다. 따라서 정답은 (B)이다.

어휘 | executive 임원 appointment 임명 headquarters 본사 latest 최근의 earnings 수익 workforce 인력 expansion 확대

패러프레이징
지문의 move its corporate base of operations
→ 보기의 A company headquarters relocation

165 첫 번째 단락 7행의 "driving"과 의미가 가장 가까운 단어는?

(A) 통근   (B) 운영상의
(C) 동기부여가 되는   (D) 집착하는

해설 | 동의어
의미상 계획을 '추진하게 된' 요인이라는 뜻으로 쓰인 것이므로 정답은 (C) motivating이다.

166 맥그래스 씨는 어떤 비용을 줄이기를 희망하는가?

(A) 세금   (B) 공과금
(C) 급여   (D) 교육

해설 | 세부 사항
첫 단락의 세 번째 문장에서 이 계획에 대한 추진 요인은 비용 절감의 필요성에 있는 것으로 보인다(The driving factor ~ reduce costs)고 했고, 맥그래스 씨는 부동산세가 더 낮은 지역으로 이전하여 이를 달성하기를 희망한다고 언급했다(Mr. McGrath noted that ~ taxes on property tend to be lower)고 했다. 따라서 맥그래스 씨는 부동산세 절감을 통해 비용을 줄이기를 바라는 것이므로 정답은 (A)이다.

167 맥그래스 씨의 이전 직책은?

(A) 최고 재무 책임자   (B) 부사장
(C) 재무 고문   (D) 시장

해설 | 세부 사항
두 번째 단락의 첫 문장에서 지난 10월 마케팅 부사장에서 승진한 이후 맥그래스 씨는 회사에 여러 변화를 주었다(Since his promotion from vice president ~ changes to the company)고 했으므로 정답은 (B)이다.

[168-171] 안내

지역 공동체를 위한 게시판 공간

168무어링타운 도서관은 지역 사회 주민분들을 도서관 정문 외부에 위치한 새로운 게시판에 있는 무료 광고란을 사용하실 수 있도록 안내드리게 되어 기쁩니다. 게시판의 공간은 한 번에 4주까지 쓰실 수 있습니다.

169(C)광고물은 도서관 안내 데스크에서 미리 승인을 받아야 하며, 다음의 요건을 충족해야 합니다. 모든 내용은 공공 게시용으로 적합해야 합니다. **169(A)광고물은 가로 8.5인치 x 세로 11인치, 또는 가로 5.5인치 x 세로 8.5인치 크기의 표준 용지에 쓰거나 인쇄되어야 합니다. 169(B), 171희망 게시일의 시작과 끝 날짜를 맨 앞 오른쪽 아래에 적어야 합니다.** 광고물을 붙이는 사람의 이름과 전화번호가 뒷면에 잘 보이도록 적혀 있어야 합니다. **171이 요건들에 맞지 않는 광고물은 고려되지 않고 폐기될 것입니다.**

지금 무어링타운 도서관 안내 데스크에서 접수 중입니다. **170방문 시 게시하고자 하는 형태, 즉 실제 광고물을 갖고 오세요.** 업무일 기준 1일 내에 광고물이 게시판에 게재되었음을 확인해 드리는 전화를 받으실 것입니다.

무어링타운 도서관
www.mooringtownlib.co.au

어휘 | noticeboard 게시판 available 사용 가능한 community group 지역 공동체 approve 승인하다 requirement 요건 content 내용 display 게시, 전시 dimension 크기, 치수 discard 폐기하다 submission 제출 format 포맷, 형식 business day 영업일, 업무일

168 무어링타운 도서관 게시판의 광고 공간에 대해 명시된 것은?

(A) 무료로 사용이 가능하다.
(B) 사용 기간 제한이 없다.
(C) 모든 분야의 사업체에 개방돼 있다.
(D) 주로 스포츠 행사를 위한 용도이다.

해설 | Not / True
첫 단락 첫 문장에서 무어링타운 도서관은 지역 사회 주민분들을 도서관 정문 외부에 위치한 새로운 게시판에 있는 무료 광고란을 사용할 수 있도록 안내하게 되어 기쁘다(Mooringtown Library is pleased to invite ~ on its new notice board)고 했으므로 정답은 (A)이다.

169 게시판에 게재될 광고물의 요건으로 언급되지 않은 것은?

(A) 규정된 크기이어야 한다.
(B) 게시 날짜가 표시되어야 한다.
(C) 사전에 검토되어야 한다.
(D) 사서의 서명을 받아야 한다.

해설 | Not / True
두 번째 단락에서 광고물은 도서관 안내 데스크에서 미리 승인을 받아야 한다(Notices must be approved in advance ~)고 했으므로 (C)를, 가로 8.5인치 x 세로 11인치, 또는 가로 5.5인치 x 세로 8.5인치 크기의 표준 용지에 쓰거나 인쇄되어야 한다(The notice must be written ~ 5.5 in x 8.5 in)에서 (A)를, 희망 게시일의 시작과 끝 날짜를 맨 앞 오른쪽 아래에 적어야 한다(The desired start and end date ~ bottom right corner)에서 (B)를 알 수 있으므로 정답은 (D)이다.

170 광고물을 제출하러 도서관에 올 때 가져와야 할 것은?

(A) 계획한 내용의 개요
(B) 광고물 완성본
(C) 작성된 제출 양식
(D) 기관에서 받은 편지

해설 | 세부 사항
세 번째 단락 두 번째 문장에서 방문 시 게시하고자 하는 형태, 즉 실제 광고물을 갖고 오라(Please have the actual notice, ~ when you arrive)고 했으므로 정답은 (B)이다.

171 [1], [2], [3], [4]로 표시된 곳 중에서 다음 문장이 들어가기에 가장 적절한 위치는?

"광고물을 붙이는 사람의 이름과 전화번호가 뒷면에 잘 보이도록 적혀 있어야 합니다."

(A) [1]   (B) [2]   (C) [3]   (D) [4]

해설 | 문장 삽입
제시된 문장은 광고물의 요건에 해당되므로 요건을 나열한 문장과, 이러한 요건이 충족되지 않을 시 폐기된다(Any notices that do not meet these requirements ~ will be discarded)는 문장 사이에 들어가는 것이 가장 적합하다. 따라서 정답은 (A)이다.

[172-175] 문자 메시지

웨이린 잉 (오전 9시 7분)
안녕하세요, 샨토야. **172토론토에서 출발하는 비행기가 연착되는 바람에 제 매출 보고서 발표 시간에 맞춰 보스턴으로 복귀하지 못할 것 같아요.**

샨토야 블랙웰 (오전 9시 8분)
비행 편 소식을 듣게 되어 유감이네요.

웨이린 잉 (오전 9시 9분)
늘 있는 일인걸요. **174바삼 사이드가 저랑 그 보고서를 작성했기 때문에 그가 발표를 넘겨받을 수 있을 거예요.** 다만, 연락이 닿지를 않네요.

샨토야 블랙웰 (오전 9시 10분)
아마 **173, 174그가 갑자기 쿠웨이트로 떠나게 돼서** 그럴 거예요.

웨이린 잉 (오전 9시 12분)
173그가 집에 갔다고요? 왜요?

샨토야 블랙웰 (오전 9시 13분)
죄송하지만 저도 자세한 내용은 몰라요. **174당신의 발표 말인데요.** 시카고 지사에 있는 케이코 하야시에게 연락해 보시길 제안해요.

웨이린 잉 (오전 9시 13분)
좋아요, 해 볼게요.

샨토야 블랙웰 (오전 9시 40분)
케이코가 뭐라고 하던가요?

웨이린 잉 (오전 9시 41분)
네, **174그녀가 도와준다고 했어요. 그래서 문제가 해결됐어요.**

샨토야 블랙웰 (오전 9시 43분)
잘됐네요. **172토론토에서 열린 무역 박람회는 어땠어요?**

웨이린 잉 (오전 9시 44분)
대단했어요. **175많은 소매업자들이 우리 아동복에 관심을 보였어요.**

샨토야 블랙웰 (오전 9시 45분)
놀랍지는 않네요. **175제가 어디에 가든 우리 옷을 입은 아이들이 보이니까요.**

어휘 | flight 항공편 delay 지연시키다 present 발표하다 take over 인계받다 reach 연락이 닿다 probably 아마 suddenly 갑자기 detail 세부 사항 solve 해결하다 retailer 소매업자 express 표하다 apparel 의류

172 잉 씨에 대해 암시된 것은?

(A) 최근에 영업부에 합류했다.
(B) 시카고에서 하야시 씨와 처음 만났다.
(C) 출장에서 돌아오는 길이다.
(D) 정기적으로 무역 박람회에 참석한다.

해설 | 추론
9시 7분에 잉 씨가 토론토에서 출발하는 비행기가 연착되는 바람에 매출 보고서 발표 시간에 맞춰 보스턴으로 복귀하지 못할 것 같다(My flight out of Toronto ~ my sales report)고 했고, 9시 43분에 블랙웰가 잉 씨에게 토론토에서 열린 무역 박람회는 어땠는지(So how was that trade show in Toronto?)를 묻는 것으로 보아 잉 씨는 토론토에 출장을 갔다가 돌아오는 길임을 알 수 있다. 따라서 정답은 (C)이다.

173 사이드 씨에 대해 암시된 것은?

(A) 보스턴에 산다.
(B) 쿠웨이트 출신이다.
(C) 블랙웰 씨의 상관이다.
(D) 가족을 자주 방문한다.

해설 | 추론
9시 10분에 블랙웰 씨가 그(Bassam Saeed)가 갑자기 쿠웨이트로 떠나게 됐다(he suddenly had to leave for Kuwait)고 하자 9시 12분에 잉 씨가 그가 집에 갔다고요?(He went home?)라며 되묻고 있다. 따라서 사이드 씨의 집이 쿠웨이트에 있음을 알 수 있으므로 (B)가 정답이다.

174 오전 9시 41분에 잉 씨가 "그래서 문제가 해결됐어요"라고 쓴 의도는?

(A) 우편으로 새로운 티켓을 받을 것이다.
(B) 보고서가 경영진에게 이메일로 전송되었다.
(C) 동료가 그의 업무를 인계받을 것이다.
(D) 비행기 출발이 발표되었다.

해설 | 의도 파악
9시 9분에 잉 씨가 바삼 사이드가 저랑 그 보고서를 작성했기 때문에 그가 발표를 넘겨받을 수 있을 것(Bassam Saeed and I ~ presentation from me)인데 연락이 닿지를 않는다(Only, I haven't been able to reach him)고 하자, 블랙웰 씨가 9시 10분에 그가 쿠웨이트로 떠나야 했다(he suddenly had to leave for Kuwait)고 알려 주며 9시 13분에 발표 건에 대해 시카고 지사에 있는 케이코 하야시에게 연락해 볼 것을 제안한다(about your presentation ~ our Chicago office)고 했다. 그리고 잠시 후 9시 41분에 잉 씨가 그녀가 도와준다고 했다(She said she would help)며 그래서 문제가 해결되었다(so the problem is solved)고 했으므로 케이코 하야시가 잉 씨의 발표를 대신해 주기로 동의해서 더 이상 문제될 것이 없다는 의도로 한 말임을 알 수 있다. 따라서 정답은 (C)이다.

어휘 | coworker 동료 assignment 업무 departure 출발 announce 발표하다

175 메시지 작성자들은 어느 업종에 근무하겠는가?

(A) 여행
(B) 의류
(C) 엔터테인먼트
(D) 통신

해설 | 추론
9시 44분에 잉 씨가 많은 소매업자들이 우리 아동복에 관심을 보였다(Lots of retailers have expressed interest in our kids' wear)고 했고, 9시 45분에 블랙웰 씨가 제가 어디에 가든 우리 옷을 입은 아이들이 보인다(I see children wearing our apparel everywhere I go)고 한 것으로 보아 메시지 작성자들은 아동복 업체에서 근무하고 있음을 알 수 있다. 따라서 정답은 (B)이다.

패러프레이징
지문의 kids' wear, apparel → 보기의 clothing

[176-180] 영수증 + 양식

타우너 서점
영수증

176고객 정보: 토마스 카브랄, 씨뷰 로 8번지, 카디프 CF4
176저희 온라인 서점에서 쇼핑해 주셔서 감사합니다!
주문번호 9207411번에 대한 영수증입니다.

제품 설명	수량	가격
177에리카 에스테스의 <안토니오 가르시아 전기> (최종 판매)	1	15.00파운드
사무엘 엡슨의 <세상에서 가장 유명한 요리사의 실화>	1	18.50파운드
아그네스 밀롯의 <파리에서의 성장: 회고록>	1	9.95파운드
헨리 살의 **179<사진의 역사>**	1	**21.25파운드**
총		64.70파운드

177참고: 최종 판매 품목은 환불 또는 교환이 불가능합니다.

주문 상태: 완료
배송 횟수: 1

어휘 | description 설명 quantity 수량 biography 전기 memoir 회고록 eligible ~을 할 수 있는 refund 환불 exchange 교환 status 상황 complete 완료된 shipment 배송

타우너 서점
상품 반품 정책 및 절차

이 양식의 모든 항목을 작성하시고 인쇄본을 반품하고자 하는 제품과 함께 동봉해 주십시오. 반품은 주문일로부터 90일 이내에 수령되어야 합니다. 반품 요청이 처리될 때까지 1-2주의 시간을 기다려 주십시오. **180선호하시는 연락 방법을 통해 통지해 드립니다.**

주문 번호: 9207411
고객 성함/주소: 토마스 카브랄, 씨뷰 로 8번지, 카디프 CF4
이메일: tcabral@knet.co.uk
전화번호: 029 5550 0161

180선호하시는 연락 방법은?
우편 □ 이메일 □ 전화 □ 문자 메시지 ☑

제품 설명	반품 사유	거래 유형
179<사진의 역사>	**178표지가 찢어짐**	**179환불 ☑ 교환 □**

어휘 | merchandise 상품 policy 정책 procedure 절차 complete 작성하다 section 부문 form 양식 enclose 동봉하다 process 처리하다 notify 통지하다 via ~을 통하여 prefer 선호하다 method 방법 credit 신용 거래

176 카브랄 씨가 구매한 책에 대해 암시된 것은?

(A) 같은 저자에 의해 집필되었다.
(B) 카디프에서 선적되었다.
(C) 온라인으로 주문되었다.
(D) 양장본이다.

해설 | 추론
영수증의 고객 정보(Customer Information)에 고객 이름이 토마스 카브랄(Thomas Cabral)이고, 저희

온라인 서점에서 쇼핑해 주셔서 감사하다(Thank you for shopping at our online bookshop!)고 나와 있는 것으로 보아 카브랄 씨는 온라인으로 책을 구매했음을 알 수 있다. 따라서 (C)가 정답이다.

어휘 | author 저자 ship 선적하다 hardcover 양장본

177 <안토니오 가르시아 전기>에 대해 명시된 것은?

(A) 교환할 수 없다.
(B) 손님들에게 인기가 많다.
(C) 절판되었다.
(D) 우편으로 따로 발송되었다.

해설 | Not / True
영수증의 표에 에리카 에스테스의 <안토니오 가르시아 전기>(The Biography of Antonio Garcia by Erica Estes)는 최종 판매(final sale)라고 나와 있고, 표 아래 참고(Note)에 따르면 최종 판매 품목은 환불 또는 교환이 불가능하다(Final sale items are not eligible for refunds or exchanges)고 했으므로 (A)가 정답이다.

어휘 | mail 우편으로 보내다 separately 따로

패러프레이징
지문의 not eligible for ~ exchanges
→ 보기의 cannot be exchanged

178 카브랄 씨는 왜 양식을 작성했는가?

(A) 주문하지 않은 물건을 받았다.
(B) 파손된 물건을 받았다.
(C) 주문할 때 실수를 했다.
(D) 자신의 연락처를 수정하기를 원했다.

해설 | 주제 / 목적
양식 하단의 반품 사유(Reason for Return)에 표지가 찢어졌다(Front cover is torn)고 했으므로 카브랄 씨는 손상된 제품이 배송되어 반품하기 위해 양식을 작성했음을 알 수 있다. 따라서 정답은 (B)이다.

어휘 | damaged 파손된 mistake 실수

패러프레이징
지문의 torn → 보기의 damaged

179 카브랄 씨는 얼마를 환불받을 것인가?

(A) 9.95 파운드   (B) 15.00 파운드
(C) 18.50 파운드   (D) 21.25 파운드

해설 | 연계
양식 하단에 따르면 카브랄 씨가 사진의 역사(The History of Photography) 제품의 환불(Refund)을 신청했고, 영수증의 표에 <사진의 역사>(The History of Photography)가 21.25파운드(£21.25)라고 명시되어 있으므로 카브랄 씨가 환불받을 금액은 21.25파운드임을 알 수 있다. 따라서 (D)가 정답이다

180 서점은 어떤 방식으로 카브랄 씨에게 반품 상태에 대해 알리겠는가?

(A) 이메일로   (B) 전화로
(C) 문자 메시지로   (D) 우편으로

해설 | 세부 사항
양식의 첫 단락 마지막 문장에서 선호하시는 연락 방법을 통해 통지해 드린다(You will be notified via your preferred method of contact)고 했고, 양식의 하단에 선호하는 연락 방법(How do you prefer to be contacted?)을 묻는 항목에서 카브랄 씨는 문자 메시지에 표시하였으므로 (C)가 정답이다.

[181-185] 이메일 + 이메일

발신: rsutriono@caston.com
수신: reservations@rideselect.com
제목: 렌트 문의
날짜: 7월 16일, 월요일, 오후 4시 34분

예약 담당자께,

귀사의 웹사이트를 통해 예약을 할 수 없어 이 이메일을 보냅니다. 차량을 선택하도록 되어 있는 웹페이지가 계속 열리지 않습니다.

181우리 가족과 저는 다음 주 목요일에 비행기를 타고 오거스타로 가서 일주일간 휴가를 보낼 예정으로, 방문 기간 동안 차를 한 대 렌트하고 싶습니다. **182**다섯 사람이 편하게 앉을 수 있고, 큰 가방 세 개를 넣을 트렁크 공간이 있으면서 가격이 주당 250달러를 넘지 않는 차를 찾고 있습니다.

2년 전 귀사의 서비스를 이용했을 때, 귀사에서 자전거 거치대와 같은 다양한 부대용품을 제공한다는 것을 알게 되었습니다. 아직도 이런 것들을 제공하고 계시나요? 마지막으로, 제가 혜택을 받을 수 있는 다른 서비스가 있을까요?

도와주셔서 감사합니다.

라흐마트 수트리오노

어휘 | inquiry 문의 reservation 예약 be supposed to ~하기로 되어 있다 select 선택하다 vehicle 차량 consistently 지속적으로 duration 기간 notice 알아차리다 various 다양한 accessories 부대용품 rack 거치대 benefit 득을 보다

발신: yan_fung@rideselect.com
수신: rsutriono@caston.com
답신: 렌트 문의
날짜: 7월 16일, 월요일, 오후 5시 19분

수트리오노 씨께,

저희 웹사이트의 오류로 인해 불편을 끼쳐 드려 죄송합니다. 향후 3시간 이내에 제대로 운영될 테니 저녁 8시 이후에 다시 시도해 주시기 바랍니다.

렌트 차량에 관해서는, **182고객님께서 말씀하신 모든 기준에 부합하므로 라인랜더 QT를 제안합니다.** 언급하신 부대용품은 추가 요금을 내시면 이용하실 수 있습니다. 또한, **183저희 환대 프로그램에 참여하는 호텔 중 한 곳에 투숙을 예약하시면 호텔 숙박비에서 10%를 할인 받으실 수 있다는 점도 알아 두세요.**

185참고로, 855-555-0167로 전화하시면 예약을 184잡을 수 있습니다. 또한 이러한 용도로 최근에 출시된 저희 앱을 사용하셔도 됩니다.

고객님의 문의에 만족스러운 답변이 되었기를 바랍니다.

얀 펑, 예약 담당자
라이드셀렉트

어휘 | inconvenience 불편 malfunctioning 고장
operational 가동할 준비가 갖춰진 as for ~에 관해 말하자면
criteria 기준 specify 명시하다 reference 언급하다
additional 추가의 fee 수수료 stay 숙박 participate in
~에 참여하다 hospitality 환대 bill 청구서 reservation 예약
launch 출시하다 purpose 용도

181 첫 이메일에서 수트리오노 씨에 대해 명시하는 것은?

(A) 오거스타에 산다.
(B) 라이드셀렉트를 처음 이용한다.
(C) 7일 동안 렌터카가 필요하다.
(D) 최근에 자전거를 샀다.

해설 | Not / True
첫 이메일의 두 번째 단락 첫 문장에서 우리 가족과 저는 다음 주 목요일에 비행기를 타고 오거스타로 가서 일주일간 휴가를 보낼 예정으로 방문 기간 동안 차를 한 대 렌트하고 싶다(My family and I will be flying ~ rent a car for the duration of our visit)고 했으므로 정답은 (C)이다.

패러프레이징
지문의 one-week → 보기의 seven days

182 라인랜더 QT에 대해 사실인 것은?

(A) 임대료가 주당 250달러 이상이다.
(B) 트렁크 공간이 확장 가능하다.
(C) 라이드셀렉트에서 가장 인기 있는 렌터카이다.
(D) 다섯 명이 탈 공간이 있다.

해설 | 연계
두 번째 이메일의 두 번째 단락 첫 문장에서 고객님께서 말씀하신 모든 기준에 부합하므로 라인랜더 QT를 제안한다(I suggest the Rhinelander QT ~ criteria you have specified)고 했는데, 해당 조건은 첫 이메일의 두 번째 단락 두 번째 문장에서 다섯 사람이 편하게 앉을 수

있고 큰 가방 세 개를 넣을 트렁크 공간이 있으면서 가격이 주당 250달러를 넘지 않는 차를 찾고 있다(I am looking for a vehicle ~ $250 per week)에 해당하므로 라인랜더 QT는 다섯 사람이 탈 수 있어야 한다는 요건을 충족시킴을 알 수 있다. 따라서 (D)가 정답이다.

어휘 | expand 확장하다 room 공간

패러프레이징
지문의 seat five → 보기의 has room for five people

183 펑 씨는 수트리오노 씨에게 무엇을 제안하는가?

(A) 자전거 거치대 무료 이용
(B) 무료 가방
(C) 호텔 숙박 시 할인된 가격
(D) 렌터카 요금 할인

해설 | 세부 사항
두 번째 이메일의 두 번째 단락 세 번째 문장에서 펑 씨가 저희 환대 프로그램에 참여하는 호텔 중 한 곳에 투숙을 예약하시면 호텔 숙박비에서 10%를 할인 받으실 수 있다는 점도 알아 두라(note that if you book a stay ~ 10 percent discount on your hotel bill)고 했으므로 (C)가 정답이다.

어휘 | usage 이용 complimentary 무료의

패러프레이징
지문의 a 10 percent discount on your hotel bill → 보기의 a reduced price on a hotel stay

184 두 번째 이메일에서 세 번째 단락 1행의 "placed"와 의미가 가장 가까운 단어는?

(A) 확인하다
(B) 미리 정하다
(C) 추정하다
(D) 권고하다

해설 | 동의어
의미상 855-555-0167로 전화하면 예약을 잡을 수 있다는 뜻으로 쓰였고 여기서 '잡다'는 '계획하여 정하다'의 의미이므로 정답은 (B) arranged이다.

185 두 번째 이메일에서 라이드셀렉트에 대해 암시하는 것은?

(A) 새로운 예약 방법을 추가했다.
(B) 웹사이트의 정기적인 유지 관리 일정을 잡았다.
(C) 최근에 지점을 몇 군데 더 열었다.
(D) 경쟁사들보다 더 나은 임대료를 제시한다.

해설 | 추론
두 번째 이메일의 세 번째 단락 첫 문장에서 855-555-0167로 전화하면 예약을 할 수 있다(reservation may be placed over the phone by calling 855-555-0167)고 했고 또한 이러한 용도로 최근에 출시된 앱을 사용해도 된다(You can also use

our recently launched app for this purpose)고 했으므로 새로 나온 앱을 통해서도 예약이 가능해졌음을 알 수 있다. 따라서 정답은 (A)이다.

어휘 | add 추가하다 location 지점 rate 요금 competitor 경쟁사

[186-190] 웹페이지 + 이메일 + 고객 후기

http://www.sportsol.com/products/detergent

스포츠올
세제

잘 지워지지 않는 얼룩을 위한 딥 클렌징 농축액

✓ 효소 분해 방식으로 풀과 흙 때문에 생긴 가장 없애기 힘든 얼룩을 녹입니다.

✓ **186합성 및 천연 섬유에 모두 안전하게 사용할 수 있습니다.**

✓ 시트러스 계열의 성분으로 자연 분해되며 환경적으로 안전합니다.

다음과 같은 편리한 크기로 제공됩니다.

제품 번호	설명	양	세탁 횟수
A20	견본 크기	4온스 봉투	10
A30	싱글 팩	1병	20
A40	트윈 팩	2병	40
189A50	슈퍼 팩	**1894병**	80

어휘 | detergent 세제 concentrate 농축물 stain 얼룩 enzyme 효소 formula 공식[방식] dissolve 녹이다 stubborn 없애기 힘든 grass 풀 soil 흙 synthetic 합성의 citrus 감귤류 과일 ingredient 재료[성분] biodegradable 생분해성의 environmentally 환경적으로 convenient 편리한 ounce 온스(무게 단위, 28.35그램)

수신: 리즈 잉그램
발신: 딜런 캠벨
날짜: 10월 6일
제목: 답신: 요청하신 정보

안녕하세요, 잉그램 씨

187요청하신 대로, 스포츠올 세제에 대한 최신 마케팅 자료를 보내 드립니다.

187작년 3월에 온라인 판매를 시작한 이후로 이 제품의 판매가 꾸준히 증가하고 있습니다. 사실, 이번 분기 말에는 판매가 지난 분기 대비 12% 증가할 것으로 예상하고 있습니다. 이러한 성장세와 전적으로 일관되게, 이 제품은 별 5개 중 평균 4.5개를 받으며 고객 평가가 상당히 긍정적이었습니다.

하지만 한 가지 문제가 있습니다. **190가장 최근에 병을 다시**

디자인한 뒤, 비록 아주 적은 양이지만 제품에서 액체가 샌다는 보고를 받고 있습니다. 이 문제는 포장 디자인 팀으로 전달되었고, 현재 적절한 해결책을 마련하기 위해 조사 중입니다.

딜런 캠벨, 책임자
마케팅 팀

어휘 | per one's request ~의 요청대로 current 현재의 steadily 꾸준히 quarter 분기, 4분의 1 wholly 전적으로 in line with ~와 일치하는 positive 긍정적인 score 득점을 올리다 average 평균의 rating 등급 leak out (액체가) 새다 attention 관심 investigate 조사하다 come up with 마련하다 proper 적절한

http://www.sportsol.com/products/detergent/review

스포츠올
세제

스포츠올 세제 점수 ★ ★ ★ ★ ★

환상적인 제품을 만들어 주셔서 감사합니다! **188저는 10살에서 14살짜리 남자애가 셋 있는데** 운동 훈련과 경기가 끝난 후 유니폼과 작업복 바지를 세탁하는데 거의 매일 이 세제를 사용합니다. 이 제품은 얼룩 제거와 하얀색을 최상으로 유지하는 데 최고의 제품입니다. **189우리 집은 매달 자동으로 4병 묶음 패키지를 받고 있습니다.** 또한 **190최근 병뚜껑 위에 비닐 수축 포장지를 추가해 주셔서 감사합니다.** 이제 제품이 새지 않고 온전한 상태로 옵니다.

– 애나 D.

어휘 | lad 남자아이 nearly 거의 dungaree 작업복 바지 remove 제거하다 household 가정 automatically 자동으로 plastic shrink-wrap 비닐 수축 포장 bottle cap 병뚜껑 in good shape 상태가 좋은 spillage 흘림

186 스포츠올 세제에 대해 명시된 것은?

(A) 병으로만 판매된다.
(B) 반드시 서늘한 곳에 보관해야 한다.
(C) 여러 종류의 원단을 안전하게 세탁한다.
(D) 슈퍼마켓에서 쉽게 구할 수 있다.

해설 | Not / True
웹페이지의 세 번째 문장에서 스포츠올 세제가 합성 및 천연 섬유에 모두 안전하게 사용할 수 있다(Safe for use with both synthetic and natural fabrics)고 했으므로 (C)가 정답이다.

187 캠벨 씨가 이메일을 보낸 이유는?

(A) 신제품에 대한 광고 아이디어를 제안하기 위해
(B) 제품의 판매 상황을 설명하기 위해

(C) 패키지 디자인에 대한 도움을 요청하기 위해

(D) 독특한 제품을 개발한 직원을 축하하기 위해

해설 | 주제/목적

이메일의 첫 문장에서 요청에 따라 스포츠올 세제에 대한 최신 마케팅 자료를 보낸다(Per your request ~ Sportsol detergent)고 했고, 작년 3월에 온라인 판매를 시작한 이후로 이 제품의 판매가 꾸준히 증가하고 있다(Sales of the product have been growing ~ last March)는 내용을 시작으로 제품의 판매 및 예측에 대해 설명하고 있으므로 캠벨 씨는 데이터와 함께 세제의 판매 현황 보고를 위해 이메일을 쓴 것임을 알 수 있다. 따라서 (B)가 정답이다.

어휘 | status 상황 assistance 도움 congratulate 축하하다

---

188 고객 후기에 따르면, 애나 D.에 대해 사실인 것은?

(A) 아이가 몇 명 있다.

(B) 유니폼을 입고 출근한다.

(C) 카펫에 묻은 얼룩을 제거할 계획이다.

(D) 스포츠올 세제를 처음 사용했다.

해설 | Not/True

고객 후기의 두 번째 문장에서 작성자인 애나가 10살에서 14살짜리 남자애가 셋 있다(I have three lads, ages 10 to 14)고 했으므로 (A)가 정답이다.

패러프레이징

지문의 lads → 보기의 children

---

189 애나 D.가 주로 구매하는 제품의 번호는?

(A) A20

(B) A30

(C) A40

(D) A50

해설 | 연계

고객 후기의 네 번째 문장에서 애나가 우리 집은 매달 자동으로 4병 묶음 패키지를 받고 있다(Our household receives the four-bottle package automatically each month)고 했고 웹페이지의 표에 따르면 4병씩 판매되는 제품은 A50이므로 정답은 (D)이다.

---

190 스포츠올의 직원은 일부 고객에게 영향을 미친 결함에 어떻게 대응했는가?

(A) 제품의 제조 방식을 변경했다.

(B) 병뚜껑을 단단히 고정시키는 재료를 추가했다.

(C) 제품 포장의 크기를 키웠다.

(D) 운송 회사를 변경했다.

해설 | 연계

이메일의 세 번째 단락 두 번째 문장에서 가장 최근에

병을 다시 디자인한 뒤 적은 양이지만 제품에서 액체가 샌다는 보고를 받고 있다(Following the most recent redesign ~ in very small amounts)며 이 문제는 포장 디자인 팀으로 전달되었고, 적절한 해결책 마련을 위해 조사 중(This issue has been brought ~ come up with a proper solution)이라고 했고, 고객 후기의 다섯 번째 문장에서 최근 병뚜껑 위에 비닐 수축 포장지를 추가해 주셔서 감사하다(thanks for recently adding ~ bottle caps)며 이제 제품이 새지 않고 온전한 상태로 온다(Now the product arrives in good shape with no spillage)고 했다. 따라서 스포츠올의 포장 디자인 팀이 제품이 새는 문제를 포장재를 추가함으로써 해결했다는 것을 알 수 있으므로 정답은 (B)이다.

어휘 | secure (단단히) 고정시키다 shipping 운송

[191-195] 이메일+표+이메일

발신: 조앤 나기 <jnagy@sjs.com>

수신: 데니 스미스 <dsmith@doodlemail.com>

날짜: 11월 18일

제목: 정보

첨부: ⬚ 양식

스미스 씨께,

저는 시거 존스 소프트웨어(SJS) 채용팀의 조앤 나기입니다. **191, 192당사에 귀하에게 적합할 만한 새로운 사업 개발직이 최근 창출되었습니다.** 이 직책은 당사의 소프트웨어 도구를 주요 기관에 소개하는 영업 전략을 수립하는 일을 수반합니다. 또한 이 업무는 시장의 요구를 충족시킬 수 있도록 제품 개발에 대한 의견을 줄 수 있어야 합니다.

191이 기회에 대해 더 논의할 수 있도록 가능한 한 빨리 다음 주에 만날 수 있는 시간을 알려 주시기 바랍니다. 모든 입사 후보자들이 사전에 작성해야 하는 몇 가지 양식을 첨부했습니다. **193귀하의 현재 이력서를 당사의 직원 규정 준수 담당자에게 보내는 것을 우선시해 주십시오.** 이메일 주소는 첨부된 양식 하단에 있습니다.

감사합니다.

조앤 나기

어휘 | form 양식 recruiting 인력 채용 development 개발 role 직무 suit 맞다 involve 수반하다 strategy 전략 introduce 소개하다 tool 도구 major 주요한 institution 기관 input 조언 meet 충족시키다 convenience 편리 availability 가능한 시간 discuss 논의하다 opportunity 기회 further 더 attach 첨부하다 prospective 장래의 in advance 미리 prioritize 우선시하다 résumé 이력서 compliance (규정) 준수 representative 대리인 bottom 하단

시거 존스 소프트웨어: 인사부
파일 체크리스트: 데니 스미스

양식	완료일	전달받은 직원
1. 이력 조회 허가	11월 23일	휴 설리반
1952. 고용 추천서 목록	보류	루이스 엘즈베리
1933. 이력서	11월 20일	크리스틴 피터스
4. 작성 완료된 SJS 지원서	11월 23일	수미 정

어휘 | forward 전달하다 permission 허가 reference 추천서 pending 미결인 application 지원서

발신: 데니 스미스 <dsmith@doodlemail.com>
수신: 조앤 나기 <jnagy@sjs.com>
날짜: 11월 27일
제목: 사업 개발 직책

나기 씨께,

저의 지원서와 관련하여 글을 씁니다. **194**제가 한 가지 양식을 더 제출해야 하는데 이전 관리자인 마유미 타다 씨가 현재 해외 출장 중임을 방금 알게 되었습니다. **195**타다 씨와 연락이 닿는 대로 다음 주에 마지막 추천서를 제출해도 될까요?

데니 스미스

어휘 | with regard to ~에 관해 discover 발견하다 currently 현재 abroad 해외에 reach 연락하다

---

191 첫 번째 이메일의 목적은?

(A) 소프트웨어 프로그램에 대한 피드백 요청
(B) 구직자에 대한 의견 요청
(C) 만날 시간 조율
(D) 승진 발표

해설 | 주제/목적
첫 이메일의 첫 단락 두 번째 문장에서 당사에 귀하에게 적합할 만한 새로운 사업 개발직이 최근 창출되었다(We have just created ~ may suit you well)고 했고, 두 번째 단락 첫 문장에서 이 기회에 대해 더 논의할 수 있도록 가능한 한 빨리 다음 주에 만날 수 있는 시간을 알려 주기 바란다(At your earliest ~ discuss this opportunity further)고 했으므로 면접 일정을 정하려고 이메일을 보냈음을 알 수 있다. 따라서 정답은 (C)이다.

어휘 | opinion 의견 applicant 지원자 arrange (미리) 정하다 announce 발표하다 promotion 승진

192 사업 개발 직책에 대해 암시된 것은?

(A) 다음 주에 시작한다.
(B) 최근에 만들어졌다.

(C) 나기 씨의 이전 직책이었다.
(D) 온라인으로 광고될 예정이다.

해설 | 추론
첫 이메일의 첫 단락 두 번째 문장에서 당사에 귀하에게 적합할 만한 새로운 사업 개발직이 최근 창출되었다(We have just created ~ may suit you well)고 했으므로 (B)가 정답이다.

패러프레이징
지문의 just created → 보기의 created recently

193 직원 규정 준수 담당자는 누구일 것 같은가?

(A) 설리반 씨
(B) 엘즈베리 씨
(C) 피터스 씨
(D) 정 씨

해설 | 연계
첫 이메일의 두 번째 단락 세 번째 문장에서 스미스 씨에게 현재 이력서를 당사의 직원 규정 준수 담당자에게 보내는 것을 우선시해 달라(Please prioritize sending ~ compliance representative)고 했고, 표에 따르면 스미스 씨의 이력서(3. Résumé)를 전달받은 직원은 크리스틴 피터스(Kristen Peters)이므로 피터스 씨가 직원 규정 준수 담당자임을 알 수 있다. 따라서 정답은 (C)이다.

194 두 번째 이메일에서 타다 씨에 대해 암시하는 것은?

(A) 추천서를 제공하기를 꺼린다.
(B) 몇 가지 양식을 처리할 것이다.
(C) SJS의 관리자이다.
(D) 스미스와 함께 일했다.

해설 | 추론
두 번째 이메일의 두 번째 문장에서 스미스 씨가 한 가지 양식을 더 제출해야 하는데 이전 관리자인 마유미 타다 씨가 현재 해외 출장 중임을 방금 알게 되었다(I have one more ~ currently abroad on business)고 했다. 스미스 씨가 타다 씨를 이전 관리자라고 했으므로 정답은 (D)이다.

어휘 | unwilling 꺼리는 process 처리하다

195 스미스 씨는 나기 씨에게 보낸 이메일에서 어떤 양식을 언급하는가?

(A) 양식 1
(B) 양식 2
(C) 양식 3
(D) 양식 4

해설 | 연계
두 번째 이메일의 마지막 문장에서 타다 씨와 연락이 닿는 대로 다음 주에 마지막 추천서를 제출해도 되는지(Would it be possible ~ once I am able to reach Ms. Tada?)를 물으며 추천서를 언급했는데, 표에 따르면 보류(Pending)라고 나와 있는 스미스 씨의 고용 추천서 목록(List of employment references)은 2번 양식이다. 따라서 (B)가 정답이다.

http://www.doringtonow.com/services

도링턴 사무실 작업 - 서비스

고객님의 예산과 일정에 맞춰, 우리 디자인 전문가들이 작은 변화 혹은 대규모 보수 작업을 활용해 사무실 공간을 재구성할 수 있도록 도와드립니다.

베이직 – 196기존 사무실 배치를 개선하기 위해 미술품 및 장식품을 선택하고 설치할 수 있도록 지원합니다.

플러스 – 베이직 서비스를 기반으로 198색상 상담을 제공하고 벽을 페인트칠하고 보완이 되는 미술품 및 장식품을 추가합니다.

컴플릿 – 198디자인 서비스를 한 단계 추가해 사무실 가구(적합할 경우, 칸막이 포함)를 선택할 수 있도록 지원하고, 벽면 처리 및 미술품을 어울리게 맞춥니다.

맥시멈 – 공간을 전체적으로 개선하기 위해 198카펫 또는 카펫 타일, 가구, 벽면 및 장식품을 업그레이드하는 과정까지 안내합니다.

지금 바로 design@doringtonow.com으로 연락하시고 바로 시작하세요!

어휘 | depending on ~에 따라 budget 예산 timeline 일정표 reimagine 재구성하다 renovation 보수 select 선택하다 install 설치하다 enhance 개선하다 existing 기존의 layout 배치 complementary 상호 보완적인 layer 층[단계] cubicle 사무실 칸막이 appropriate 적합한 coordinate 꾸미다 treatment 처리 process 과정

수신: 마이클 노 <michael.noe@finleynoeassociates.com>
발신: 제인 핑크 <janef@doringtonow.com>
날짜: 5월 6일
제목: 업데이트

노 씨께,

지난주에 다시 만나 뵙게 되어 즐거웠습니다. 197직원들이 받을 업무 방해를 최소화하기 위해 처음 논의했던 보수 작업의 범위를 축소하기를 원하시는 것으로 알고 있습니다. 197, 198귀사의 사무실 카펫 상태가 양호하기 때문에, 바닥재 변경은 더 이상 저희 디자인에 포함되지 않습니다.

제시된 기한 내에 프로젝트를 완료하려면 몇 가지 결정을 빨리 내려야 합니다. 198가구 배치에 대한 스케치와 가구용 커버 원단 샘플, 페인트 색상, 액자 인쇄물을 보여 드리기 위해 만나 뵙고 싶습니다. 199현재로서는 제가 5월 13일 월요일 오전 10시부터 정오까지, 5월 14일 화요일 오후 2시부터 오후 4시까지는 확실히 시간이 됩니다. 하지만

이 시간대에 만나는 것이 힘들 경우 제 일정은 어느 정도 유동적이므로 알려 주시기 바랍니다.

제인 핑크
실내 디자인 전문가
도링턴 사무실 작업

어휘 | pleasure 기쁨 in the interest of ~을 위하여 minimize 최소화하다 disruption 방해 decrease 줄이다 scope 범위 initially 처음에 involve 포함하다 flooring 바닥재 proposed 제안된 timeframe 일정, 기간 present 제시하다 arrangement 배치, 배열 upholstery (소파 등의) 커버 fabric 천 framed 틀에 끼운 availability 시간이 됨 somewhat 다소 flexible 유연한

회의록. 제인 핑크 작성. 도링턴 사무실 작업
1995월 14일, 오후 4시~오후 6시
프로젝트: 마이클 노, 핀리 앤 노 어소시에이츠

프로젝트의 시작일은 6월 17일로 확정되었다. 모든 작업은 시작일로부터 4주 이내에 완료되어야 한다.

페인트 선택 완료:
• 시사이드 탠 – 접수 구역 및 복도용
• 웜 스톤 – 사무실용
• 퓨어 세이지 – 휴게실용

기타 예비 선택 사항:
• 200캐주얼 크래프트 퍼니처의 아르투로 그랑 시리즈. 해당 가구 구매는 대량 주문 가격 적용 대상이라 대폭 할인 가능.

어휘 | meeting notes 회의록 complete 완료하다 selection 선택된 것들 finalize 마무리 짓다 preliminary 예비의 bulk (큰) 규모[양] eligible 자격이 되는 significant 상당한 apply 적용하다

---

196 웹페이지에서 도링턴 사무실 작업에 대해 명시하는 것은?

(A) 역사적인 건물을 복원한다.
(B) 독창적인 예술 작품을 만든다.
(C) 가구를 제작한다.
(D) 설치 서비스를 제공한다.

해설 | Not / True
웹페이지의 베이직 서비스 항목에서 기존 사무실 배치를 개선하기 위해 미술품 및 장식품을 선택하고 설치할 수 있도록 지원한다(We assist you in selecting and installing ~ office layout)고 했으므로 (D)가 정답이다.

어휘 | restore 복원하다 historic 역사적인 manufacture 제조하다 installation 설치

패러프레이징
지문의 assist you in installing ~
→ 보기의 provides installation services

197 이메일의 목적은?

(A) 상세 견적 요청
(B) 미술품 선택 절차 완료
(C) 프로젝트 변경 사항 확인
(D) 핑크 씨의 디자인 이력 설명

해설 | 주제 / 목적
이메일의 첫 단락 두 번째 문장에서 직원들이 받을 업무 방해를 최소화하기 위해 처음 논의했던 보수 작업의 범위를 축소하기를 원하시는 것으로 알고 있다(I understand that ~ we initially discussed)며 귀사의 사무실 카펫 상태가 양호하기 때문에 바닥재 변경은 더 이상 저희 디자인에 포함되지 않는다(Since your office carpeting ~ changes to the flooring)고 프로젝트의 변경 내용을 확인하고 있으므로 (C)가 정답이다.

어휘 | detailed 상세한 estimate 견적(서) acknowledge 알고 있음을 알리다 describe 설명하다

198 도링턴 사무실 작업은 노 씨에게 어떤 서비스를 제공할 것 같은가?

(A) 베이직　　　　　　(B) 플러스
(C) 컴플릿　　　　　　(D) 맥시멈

해설 | 연계
이메일의 첫 단락 세 번째 문장에서 귀사의 사무실 카펫 상태가 양호하기 때문에 바닥재 변경은 더 이상 저희 디자인에 포함되지 않는다(Since your office carpeting ~ changes to the flooring)고 했고, 두 번째 단락 두 번째 문장에서 가구 배치에 대한 스케치와 가구용 커버 원단 샘플, 페인트 색상, 액자 인쇄물을 보여 드리기 위해 만나 뵙고 싶다(I would like to meet ~ and framed prints)고 했다. 웹페이지에서 플러스는 색상 상담(color consultation), 컴플릿은 플러스 서비스에 사무실 가구 선택, 벽면 처리 및 미술품 맞추기(Adding another layer ~ and artwork), 맥시멈은 카펫 또는 카펫 타일 작업이 추가(upgrading carpet or carpet tiles)된다고 했다. 이메일에서 카펫 작업은 제외된다고 했고 가구, 장식품, 페인트 색상 서비스를 제공하는 것으로 보아 노 씨는 컴플릿 서비스를 받는다는 것을 알 수 있으므로 정답은 (C)이다.

199 노 씨에 대해 암시된 것은?

(A) 새로운 프로젝트 시작일을 요청했다.
(B) 대체 회의 시간을 제안했다.
(C) 사무실 칸막이를 설치할 공간이 충분하지 않다.
(D) 5월 14일 회의에서 액자 장식을 결정했다.

해설 | 연계
이메일의 두 번째 단락 세 번째 문장에서 핑크 씨가 노 씨에게 현재로서는 제가 5월 13일 월요일 오전 10시부터 정오까지, 5월 14일 화요일 오후 2시부터 오후 4시까지는 확실히 시간이 된다(As of now, I know ~ 2:00 P.M.

to 4:00 P.M.)고 했고, 하지만 이 시간대에 만나는 것이 힘들 경우 제 일정은 어느 정도 유동적(However, my schedule is ~ do not work for you)이니 알려 달라(Let me know)고 했는데, 회의록의 일시가 5월 14일 오후 4시~오후 6시(May 14, 4:00-6:00 P.M.)로 나와 있는 것으로 보아, 노 씨가 핑크 씨가 앞서 언급한 시간이 아닌 다른 시간을 제안했다고 짐작할 수 있다. 따라서 정답은 (B)이다.

어휘 | alternative 대안이 되는

200 회의록에 따르면, 선택된 제품 중 비용이 절감되는 것은?

(A) 시사이드 탠　　　　(B) 웜 스톤
(C) 퓨어 세이지　　　　(D) 아르투로 그랑

해설 | 세부 사항
회의록의 기타 예비 선택 사항에서 캐주얼 크래프트 퍼니처의 아르투로 그랑 시리즈("Arturo Grand" Series by Casual Craft Furniture)에 대해서 해당 가구 구매는 대량 주문 가격 적용 대상이라 대폭 할인이 가능하다(This furniture purchase ~ discount will be applied)고 했으므로 아르투로 그랑의 구입 비용이 줄어들 것임을 알 수 있다. 따라서 (D)가 정답이다.

ETS	실전 모의고사 03			본책 p. 193
147 (B)	**148** (C)	**149** (C)	**150** (D)	**151** (D)
152 (C)	**153** (B)	**154** (C)	**155** (B)	**156** (D)
157 (A)	**158** (B)	**159** (C)	**160** (C)	**161** (A)
162 (C)	**163** (B)	**164** (B)	**165** (D)	**166** (A)
167 (D)	**168** (D)	**169** (A)	**170** (A)	**171** (C)
172 (C)	**173** (C)	**174** (B)	**175** (D)	**176** (A)
177 (C)	**178** (C)	**179** (B)	**180** (B)	**181** (D)
182 (B)	**183** (B)	**184** (C)	**185** (A)	**186** (A)
187 (D)	**188** (B)	**189** (B)	**190** (D)	**191** (D)
192 (B)	**193** (B)	**194** (B)	**195** (A)	**196** (D)
197 (C)	**198** (A)	**199** (C)	**200** (B)	

[147-148] 쿠폰

브라질 커피 원두 회사
2파운드 이상 주문 시 10% 할인

- 147,148브라질 바이아 지역에서 재배되는 신선한 커피 원두가 파운드당 단 15달러!
- 50달러 이상 주문 시 미국 내 무료 배송

쿠폰 코드: LIKE-008; 유효 기간은 9월 30일까지
온라인으로 커피를 주문하시려면 당사 웹사이트를
방문해 주세요.
www.braziliancoffeebean.com

147 회사에 대해 명시된 것은?

(A) 새로운 경영진이 관리하고 있다.
(B) 브라질의 한 지역에서 재배된 커피 원두를 판매한다.
(C) 브라질에 여러 지점을 열었다.
(D) 커피 제품을 소매점으로 배송한다.

해설 | Not / True
쿠폰의 첫 항목에서 브라질 바이아 지역에서 재배되는 신선한 커피 원두가 파운드당 15달러(Just $15 per pound ~ in Brazil's Bahia region!)라고 했으므로 정답은 (B)이다.

어휘 | management 경영진 location 지점 ship 배송하다 retail store 소매점

148 고객은 무엇을 15달러에 살 수 있는가?

(A) 두 가지 커피 품종으로 구성된 샘플 꾸러미
(B) 다음 주문 시 10% 할인권
(C) 커피 1파운드
(D) 커피 머그잔

해설 | 세부 사항
쿠폰의 첫 항목에서 브라질 바이아 지역에서 재배되는 신선한 커피 원두가 파운드당 15달러(Just $15 per pound ~ in Brazil's Bahia region!)라고 했다. 따라서 15달러에 커피 원두 1파운드를 살 수 있으므로 (C)가 정답이다.

어휘 | pack 꾸러미 variety 품종

패러프레이징
지문의 per pound → 보기의 a single pound

[149-150] 보도 자료

> **149고고학적 유물의 기록 추적을 용이하게 하는 새로운 데이터베이스**
>
> **149섹터시스사는** 고고학적 유적지에서 발견된 유물을 광범위한 데이터베이스로 구축하기 위해 세계 각국의 **박물관 및 고고학협회와 곧 협력할 예정임을 발표하게 되어 기쁩니다.** 에릭 요하네센 섹터시스 CEO는 "고대 세계의 유물에 대한 정보는 대부분 상세히 기록돼 있지 않고 손쉽게 이용할 수도 없습니다. **149,150우리는 박물관 및 관련 분야 전문가들이 유물에 대한 온전한 해설을 찾아볼 수 있도록 전자 데이터베이스를 구축할 계획입니다.**"라고 말합니다. 데이터베이스는 30만 점의 유물에 대한 정보를 시작으로 지속적으로 갱신해 나갈 것입니다.

어휘 | facilitate 용이하게 하다 tracking 추적 archaeological finds 고고학적 유물 team up with ~와 협력하다 society 사회, 협회 extensive 광범위한

artifact 유물, 공예품 discover 발견하다 archaeological sites 고고학적 유적지 treasure 보물 ancient 고대의 document (상세한 내용을) 기록하다; 문서 readily 손쉽게 available 이용 가능한 description 묘사, 해설 initially 초기에 object 물건, 유물 continually 지속적으로

149 섹터시스는 어떤 제품을 내놓을 것인가?

(A) 고고학적 발굴에 필요한 용품
(B) 박물관용 도난 방지 경보 장치
(C) 유물에 대한 정보를 담은 소프트웨어
(D) 가짜 유물 감지 장치

해설 | 세부 사항
고고학적 유물의 기록 추적을 용이하게 하는 데이터베이스(New Database to Facilitate Tracking of Archaeological Finds)라는 제목과 함께 섹터시스가 구축하는 데이터베이스에 대한 발표가 이어지고 있으므로 정답은 (C)이다.

어휘 | dig 발굴; (구멍을) 파다 antitheft alarm system 도난 방지 경보 장치 detect 감지하다 fake 가짜의

패러프레이징
지문의 archaeological finds → 보기의 artifacts
지문의 contain → 보기의 holds

150 보도 자료에 따르면, 제품은 누가 사용할 것인가?

(A) 골동품을 사고 파는 상인
(B) 박물관 경비원
(C) 고고학 관련 서적을 출판하는 회사
(D) 박물관 직원 및 고고학자

해설 | 세부 사항
세 번째 문장에서 우리는 박물관 및 관련 분야 전문가들이 유물에 대한 온전한 해설을 찾아볼 수 있도록 전자 데이터베이스를 구축할 계획이다(We plan on organizing ~ museums and professionals working in the field)라고 했으므로 정답은 (D)이다.

어휘 | old object 골동품 security guard 경비원 archaeologist 고고학자

패러프레이징
지문의 professionals working in the field
→ 보기의 archaeologists

[151-152] 이메일

수신: 에리카 여 <ericayeo@zmail.com>
발신: 리차드 박 <r.park@maquarium.org>
제목: 맥코넬 수족관
날짜: 1월 10일

여 씨께,

맥코넬 수족관의 소중한 회원이 되어주셔서 감사합니다.

회원권이 1월 30일에 만료될 예정이니 참고 바랍니다. 연회비 단 35달러로 회원권을 갱신하시면 놀라운 혜택을 계속 즐기실 수 있습니다. **151(B), (C)**혜택에는 저희 수중 극장의 해양 및 수상 생물에 관한 영화 무료 입장, 축제 모임을 위한 연회실 예약 시 15% 할인, <월간 아쿠아티카> 전자 잡지 및 기타 다양한 전자 데이터베이스 이용권 등이 있습니다.

151(A)추가로 회원들은 저희의 최신 전시회인 <아마존 유역의 수상 생물>을 포함한 특별 행사를 독점 관람하실 수 있습니다. 이 전시회의 회원 전용 시사회는 2월 22일 토요일에 열릴 예정입니다. **152**이 기회를 놓치지 않으시려면 오늘 555-0122로 전화하셔서 회원권을 갱신하세요. 또는 www.maquarium.org/membership으로 웹사이트를 방문하세요.

지속적으로 애용해 주셔서 감사합니다.

리차드 박
맥코넬 수족관 회원권 관리자

어휘 | aquarium 수족관 valued 소중한 expire 만료되다 renew 갱신하다 annual 연례의 fee 요금 continue 계속하다 amazing 놀라운 benefit 혜택 advantage 이익 admission 입장 marine 해양의 aquatic 수생의 reserve 예약하다 banquet room 연회실 festive 축제의 gathering 모임 access 이용(권) various 다양한 electronic 전자의 additionally 게다가 exclusive 독점적인 latest 최신의 exhibit 전시 basin 유역 preview 시사회 miss 놓치다 opportunity 기회 patronage 애용

151 회원 혜택이 아닌 것은?

(A) 특별 행사 참석
(B) 바다 생물에 관한 영화 관람
(C) 전자 자료 이용
(D) 선물 가게 제품 할인

해설 | Not / True
첫 단락의 네 번째 문장에서 혜택에는 수중 극장의 해양 및 수상 생물에 관한 영화 무료 입장, 연회실 예약 시 15% 할인, <월간 아쿠아티카> 전자 잡지 및 기타 다양한 전자 데이터베이스 이용권 등이 있다(Among the advantages ~ various other electronic databases)고 했으므로 (B)와 (C)는 사실이고, 두 번째 단락의 첫 문장에서 추가로 회원들은 최신 전시회인 <아마존 유역의 수상 생물>을 포함한 특별 행사를 독점 관람할 수 있다(Additionally, members have exclusive access ~ *Amazon Basin*)고 했으므로 (A)도 사실이다. 선물 가게 제품 할인에 대한 내용은 언급되지 않았으므로 정답은 (D)이다.

어휘 | attend 참석하다 material 자료

패러프레이징
지문의 electronic databases
→ 보기의 electronic materials

152 여 씨는 무엇을 하라고 요청받는가?

(A) 연회실 예약   (B) 잡지 기사 작성
(C) 맥코넬 수족관 연락   (D) 회의 참석

해설 | 세부 사항
두 번째 단락의 세 번째 문장에서 이 기회를 놓치지 않으려면 오늘 555-0122로 전화해 회원권을 갱신하라(So as not to miss ~ call us today at 555-0122 to renew your membership)고 했으므로 정답은 (C)이다.

패러프레이징
지문의 call → 보기의 Contact

[153-154] 문자 메시지

> **개럿 제퍼슨 (오전 11시 15분)**
> 안녕하세요, 디브야. **153**오늘 제가 칼라와 몇 시에 만나기로 했는지 다시 알려 주실 수 있나요?
>
> **디브야 아가왈 (오전 11시 19분)**
> 물론이죠! 확인해 볼게요.
>
> **개럿 제퍼슨 (오전 11시 21분)**
> 고마워요. **153**제 일정표가 핸드폰에 동기화가 안 되는데, 왜 그런지 모르겠네요.
>
> **디브야 아가왈 (오전 11시 23분)**
> **154**당신과 칼라는 오늘 회의가 두 건이 있는 것 같아요. 하나는 지역 신문 편집장과 하는 거고, 다른 하나는 5개년 계획에 대해 둘이서만 하는 거네요.
>
> **개럿 제퍼슨 (오전 11시 24분)**
> 아! **154**브루노 산타모스와의 회의를 깜빡했네요. 오후 3시 30분 맞죠?
>
> **디브야 아가왈 (오전 11시 25분)**
> 네, 그리고 5개년 계획 관련 회의는 그 직후인 오후 4시 30분이고요.
>
> **개럿 제퍼슨 (오전 11시 26분)**
> 알겠어요. 몇 시간 뒤에 봅시다.
>
> **디브야 아가왈 (오전 11시 27분)**
> 이따 뵐게요.
>
> ----
> **어휘 |** remind 상기시키다 synch 동기화하다 chief editor 편집장

153 오전 11시 19분에 아가왈 씨가 "확인해 볼게요"라고 쓴 의도는 무엇이겠는가?

(A) 회의가 끝났는지 확인할 것이다.
(B) 제퍼슨 씨의 일정표를 확인할 것이다.
(C) 의뢰인이 도착했는지 확인할 것이다.
(D) 회의 일정을 조정하려고 노력할 것이다.

해설 | 의도 파악

11시 15분에 제퍼슨 씨가 자신이 오늘 칼라와 몇 시에 만나기로 했는지 다시 알려 줄 수 있냐(Can you remind me what time I am meeting with Carla today?)고 묻자 아가왈 씨가 11시 19분에 확인해 보겠다(Let me check)고 대답했고 11시 21분에 제퍼슨 씨가 일정표가 핸드폰에 동기화가 안 되는데 왜 그런지 모르겠다(My schedule is not ~ not sure why)고 했다. 제퍼슨 씨가 핸드폰으로 자신의 일정표를 확인할 수 없자 아가왈 씨에게 미팅 일정을 봐 달라고 요청한 것이므로, 제퍼슨 씨의 일정표를 대신 확인해 주겠다는 의도로 대답한 것임을 알 수 있다. 따라서 정답은 (B)이다.

어휘 | conclude 끝나다 reschedule 일정을 변경하다

154 산타모스 씨에 대해 암시된 것은?

(A) 오후 4시 30분 회의에 참석할 것이다.
(B) 제퍼슨 씨와 같은 사무실을 쓴다.
(C) 지역 신문사에서 일한다.
(D) 업무 일정이 매우 바쁘다.

해설 | 추론

11시 23분에 아가왈 씨가 당신과 칼라는 오늘 회의가 두 건이 있는 것 같다(It looks like you and Carla have two meetings today)며 하나는 지역 신문 편집장과 하는 거고 다른 하나는 5개년 계획에 대해 둘이서만 하는 것(One is with the chief editor ~ two about the 5-year plan)이라고 하자 11시 24분에 제퍼슨 씨가 브루노 산타모스와의 회의를 깜빡했다(I forgot about our meeting with Bruno Santamos)고 했다. 따라서 브루노 산타모스가 지역 신문 편집장임을 알 수 있으므로 정답은 (C)이다.

[155-157] 공지

제3회 허그 더 쇼어 5K에 오늘 신청하세요!

6월 20일 토요일 오전 10시

허그 더 쇼어는 5킬로미터 도보 경주입니다. **155코스는** 샌디 마일 공원의 분수대에서 시작하고 끝납니다. 등록비는 25달러입니다. 모든 수익금은 퓨어 오션 프로미스에 기부될 예정입니다. **156참가 주자들은 티셔츠를 받게 되며, 공원에서 도보로 5분 거리에 있는 현지 인기 레스토랑인 캡틴 케이트즈 그릴에서 행사가 끝난 후 기념하는 자리에 초대됩니다.**

157퓨어 오션 프로미스는 지역 해변을 안전하고 청정하게 유지하기 위해 노력하는 비영리 단체입니다. 지역 주민을 대상으로 환경 교육을 제공하고, 매월 해변 청소 활동을 진행하며, 해양 친화적 제품을 홍보하고 있습니다. 주최측은 경주 행사 키트에 무료 재사용 물병을 포함시킬 예정입니다.

어휘 | sign up 등록하다 annual 매년의 footrace 도보 경주 fountain 분수 registration fee 등록비 proceeds 수익금 donate 기부하다 nonprofit 비영리의 organization 단체 strive to ~하려고 애쓰다 pollution-free 무공해의 environmental 환경의 education 교육 resident 주민 host 주최하다 endorse 홍보하다 ocean-friendly 해양 친화적인 organizer 조직자 complimentary 무료의 reusable 재사용 가능한 packet (선물) 꾸러미

155 첫 번째 단락 1행의 "course"와 의미가 가장 가까운 단어는?

(A) 수업   (B) 경로
(C) 식사   (D) 해결책

해설 | 동의어

앞 문장에서 허그 더 쇼어는 5킬로미터의 도보 경주(Hug the Shore is a five-kilometer footrace)라고 한 것으로 보아 문맥상 course는 경주의 '경로'라는 뜻으로 쓰인 것이므로 정답은 (B) route이다.

156 캡틴 케이트즈 그릴에 대해 암시된 것은?

(A) 상품을 증정한다.
(B) 샌디 마일 공원에 있다.
(C) 건강한 음식을 제공한다.
(D) 인기가 좋다.

해설 | 추론

첫 단락 다섯 번째 문장에서 참가 주자들은 티셔츠를 받게 되며 공원에서 도보로 5분 거리에 있는 현지 인기 레스토랑인 캡틴 케이트즈 그릴에서 행사가 끝난 후 기념하는 자리에 초대된다(Runners will receive a T-shirt ~ walk away from the park)고 했으므로 (D)가 정답이다.

패러프레이징
지문의 popular → 보기의 well liked

157 공지에 따르면, 퓨어 오션 프로미스가 지역 사회에 도움을 주는 방식은?

(A) 교육 기회를 제공한다.
(B) 재활용 서비스를 제공한다.
(C) 매년 여름마다 수영 경기를 주최한다.
(D) 여름에 수영장을 이용할 수 있게 한다.

해설 | 세부 사항

두 번째 단락 첫 문장에서 퓨어 오션 프로미스는 지역 해변을 안전하고 청정하게 유지하기 위해 노력하는 비영리 단체(Pure Ocean Promise is a nonprofit ~ safe and pollution-free)라고 소개하면서 지역 주민을 대상으로 환경 교육을 제공한다(It provides environmental education to area residents)고 했으므로 (A)가 정답이다.

어휘 | opportunity 기회 available 이용 가능한

패러프레이징
지문의 provides ~ education
→ 보기의 offering educational opportunities

[158-160] 이메일

수신: lynn.popal@camisat.net
발신: ckinsella@ubi.com
제목: 문의
날짜: 5월 26일

포팔 씨께,

유니온 이발 협회의 4주 마스터 이발 프로그램에 대해 문의
주셔서 감사합니다. 다음 기간 7월 1일~7월 26일, 9월
9일~10월 4일, 11월 4일~11월 29일 중 하나에 등록하실 수
있습니다.

158원하시는 강좌 수강 기간을 결정하신 뒤 입학 담당자인
파리드 하즈라티 씨에게 555-0144번 또는 fhazrati@
ubi.com으로 연락하시면 귀하를 등록하고 수업료 첫
50달러를 수납할 것입니다.

159, 160이발 도구를 포함한 모든 수업 자료의 구입은
직접 하셔야 합니다. 160필요한 자료의 전체 목록은 강의
웹사이트에서 확인하실 수 있습니다. 저희 물품 매장은 평일
정오부터 오후 5시까지 운영됩니다. 159수업 첫날에는 강의
교재를 지참해 주시기 바랍니다.

귀하를 만나 뵙기를 기대하며 저희 프로그램이 유익하다고
느끼시리라 믿습니다.

카렌 킨셀라
유니온 이발 협회 보조 프로그램 책임자

어휘 | inquiry 문의 barbering 이발 institute 기관[협회]
sign up for ~에 등록하다 period 기간 admission 입학
coordinator 조정자 enroll 등록하다 accept 받아들이다
tuition fee 수업료 material 자료 tool 도구 available 이용
가능한 rewarding 보람 있는, 유익한

158 포팔 씨가 하즈라티 씨에게 연락하라고 권고받은 이유는?

(A) 만날 약속을 정하기 위해
(B) 교육 프로그램에 등록하기 위해
(C) 연락처를 수정하기 위해
(D) 강의 자료 목록을 구하기 위해

해설 | 세부 사항
두 번째 단락 첫 문장에서 원하는 강좌 수강 기간을 결정한
뒤 입학 담당자인 파리드 하즈라티 씨에게 555-0144번
또는 fhazrati@ubi.com으로 연락하면 귀하를 등록하고
수업료 첫 50달러를 수납할 것(Once you decide ~
enroll you and accept the first $50 of your tuition

fee)이라고 했으므로 (B)가 정답이다.

어휘 | educational 교육의 obtain 얻다

패러프레이징
지문의 enroll → 보기의 sign up

159 이메일에서 학생들에 대해 암시하는 것은?

(A) 세 개의 별도 과정을 이수해야 한다.
(B) 강좌가 시작되기 전에 수업료 전액을 내야 한다.
(C) 교실에서 사용할 교과서를 구입해야 한다.
(D) 저녁에 모이는 수업을 선택할 수 있다.

해설 | 추론
세 번째 단락 마지막 문장에서 수업 첫날에 강의 교재를
지참하라(Please bring the course textbook with
you on the first day of class)고 했는데, 같은 단락 첫
문장에서 모든 수업 자료의 구입은 직접 해야 한다(Please
note that you are responsible for buying all course
materials)고 했다. 따라서 학생들은 강의 교재를 직접
구입해서 가져와야 함을 알 수 있으므로 (C)가 정답이다.

어휘 | separate 별도의

160 [1], [2], [3], [4]로 표시된 곳 중에서 다음 문장이
들어가기에 가장 적합한 위치는?

"저희 물품 매장은 평일 정오부터 오후 5시까지
운영됩니다."

(A) [1]   (B) [2]   (C) [3]   (D) [4]

해설 | 문장 삽입
제시된 문장은 '물품 매장은 평일 정오부터 오후 5시까지
운영된다'며 물품을 판매하는 매장의 영업시간을 안내하고
있다. 따라서 수업 자료 구입은 직접 해야 하고(Please
note that you are responsible for buying all course
materials) 필요한 자료의 전체 목록을 강의 웹사이트에서
확인할 수 있다(The complete list of necessary
materials is available on the course Web site)며
물품을 직접 사야 한다는 사실과 함께 사야할 물품에 대한
확인 방법을 알려 주는 문장 뒤에 들어가면 글의 흐름상
자연스러우므로 (C)가 정답이다.

[161-163] 웹페이지

https://www.jhpc.com.jm

소개	연락처	향후 프로젝트	이전 프로젝트	**소식**

161자메이카 역사 보존 컨소시엄(JHPC)의 공동 창립자인
다리우스 로키어가 회장직에서 물러난다. 로키어 씨는 4월
7일 회의에서 소식을 전했다. "제가 몹시 사랑하는 일을
그만두는 것은 쉽지 않습니다. 그러나 JHPC를 잘 맡기고
저는 떠납니다. 저의 정원에서 그리고 또 아내와 손주들과

함께 즐거운 시간을 보낼 계획입니다."라고 그는 말했다. **¹⁶²그는 이 협회의 두 번째 회장으로, 기디언 모리슨이 8년 전 은퇴한 후 현 직위로 승진했다. ¹⁶³로키어 씨의 마지막 공식 역할은 JHPC의 연례 회의를 주재하는 것이다. 올해는 6월 3일부터 5일까지 킹스턴 팜 스위프트 호텔에서 열릴 예정이다.** 티아 알우드가 7월 1일부터 회장 대행으로서 업무를 시작한다. 알우드 씨는 수년간 이 단체에서 활동해 왔다.

어휘 | cofounder 공동 창립자 historical 역사적 preservation 보존 consortium 컨소시엄, 협력단 step down 퇴진하다 role 직무 announcement 발표 grandchildren 손주 organisation 단체 promote 승진하다 retire 은퇴하다 official 공식적인 function 기능 preside 주재하다 annual 연례의 serve 일하다 acting 대행

161 웹페이지의 목적은?

(A) 은퇴 발표
(B) 일정 변경 제안
(C) 제휴 체결 환영
(D) 프로젝트 보고

해설 | 주제 / 목적
첫 문장에서 자메이카 역사 보존 컨소시엄(JHPC)의 공동 창립자인 다리우스 로키어가 회장직에서 물러난다(Darius Lockyer, cofounder ~ his role as president)고 소식을 전하고 있으므로 (A)가 정답이다.

어휘 | announce 발표하다 retirement 은퇴 propose 제안하다 partnership 동업

패러프레이징
지문의 stepping down → 보기의 retirement

162 모리슨 씨에 대해 암시된 것은?

(A) 호텔 체인의 사장이다.
(B) 4월 7일 회의에 참석했다.
(C) 로키어 씨와 동시에 JHPC에서 일했다.
(D) 알우드 씨와 7월 행사를 계획 중이다.

해설 | 추론
여섯 번째 문장에서 그는 이 협회의 두 번째 회장으로, 기디언 모리슨이 8년 전 은퇴한 후 현 직위로 승진했다(He is the second president ~ eight years ago)라고 했으므로 은퇴하기 전 모리슨 씨와 로키어 씨는 JHPC에서 같이 근무했음을 알 수 있다. 따라서 정답은 (C)이다.

163 웹페이지에 따르면, 6월에 무슨 일이 있을 예정인가?

(A) 알우드 씨가 JHPC를 떠난다.
(B) 회의가 열릴 예정이다.
(C) 새 직책이 생긴다.
(D) 로키어 씨가 가족과 함께 여행을 떠난다.

해설 | 세부 사항
일곱 번째 문장에서 로키어 씨의 마지막 공식 역할은 JHPC의 연례 회의를 주재하는 것(Mr. Lockyer's last

official ~ annual conference)이며 올해는 6월 3일부터 5일까지 킹스턴 팜 스위프트 호텔에서 열릴 예정(This year it will ~ 3 to 5 June)이라고 했으므로 정답은 (B)이다.

[164-167] 일정

엑셀란차 관광으로 여행을 예약해 주셔서 감사합니다. 다음은 귀하의 단체 여행 일정표입니다.

관광 일자	계획된 일정	숙박	날짜
1	카프리 도착. 호텔 체크인.	벨리시마 카프리	7월 7일
2	아말피 해안을 따라 항해하고, **¹⁶⁴그림 같이 아름다운 동굴인 그로타 아주라를 탐험. ¹⁶⁷선택 가능한 아침 여행:** 아우구스투스 정원 관광 및 멋진 현지 레스토랑에서 식사.	위와 동일	**¹⁶⁴7월 8일**
3	배로 만을 횡단하고 관광버스로 나폴리를 지나 이동. 유명 요리사와 만나 그의 레스토랑에서 식사를 한 후 나폴리 인 체크인. 늦은 오후와 저녁 때 지역을 직접 둘러볼 수 있는 자유 시간이 제공됨.	나폴리 인	7월 9일
4	베니스로 이동하여 크라운 호텔 체크인. 도보로 도시를 관광하고, 입으로 불어 만드는 유리 제품 공장과 상점 방문.	크라운 호텔	7월 10일
5	베니스에서 마음껏 오전 시간을 보냄. 버스는 크라운 호텔에서 오후 1시 30분에 출발해서 **¹⁶⁵저녁에 피렌체에 도착. 카사 피렐로 체크인. ¹⁶⁷선택 가능한 아침 여행:** 흥을 돋우는 사공이 모는 곤돌라, 즉 노로 젓는 좁은 배를 타고 베니스 운하를 여행함.	카사 피렐로	7월 11일
6	가이드가 안내하는 피렌체 관광을 하며 가장 유명한 관광 명소들을 방문. **¹⁶⁶카사 피렐로** **¹⁶⁶호텔 레스토랑에서 송별연으로 하루를 마감함.**	**¹⁶⁶카사 피렐로**	7월 12일
7	셔틀 버스가 오전 10시 30분에 호텔에서 출발하여, 주요 기차 터미널과 공항에 정차함.		7월 13일

유의 사항: **¹⁶⁶이 여행은 위의 여행 일정표에 열거된 7일간의 교통편, 호텔, 식사를 포함합니다.** 하지만 본인이 참가 여부를 결정하는 선택 가능한 여행은 추가 비용이 발생합니다. 자세한 내용은 관광 안내 책자를 참조하세요.

CHAPTER 3

실전 모의고사 03

어휘 | accommodation 숙박 시설　check in(to) (호텔 등에서) 체크인하다　picturesque 그림 같은, 매우 아름다운　optional 선택적인　excursion (단체로 하는) 짧은 여행, 유람　dine 식사를 하다　charming 매력적인, 멋진　gulf 만　inn 여관, (작은) 호텔　glass-blowing 유리 불기(녹인 유리 덩어리를 대롱 끝에 붙여서 입으로 불어 제품을 만드는 방법)　canal 운하, 수로　gondola 곤돌라　rowboat 노로 젓는 배　gondolier 곤돌라 사공　tourist attraction 관광 명소　farewell dinner 송별연　transportation 수송, 교통 수단　itinerary 여행 일정(표)　incur (비용을) 발생시키다　detail 세부 사항, 상세한 내용

164 7월 8일에는 무엇이 계획되어 있는가?

(A) 도시 관광
(B) 동굴 방문
(C) 정원에서 제공되는 식사
(D) 가이드가 인솔하는 버스 여행

해설 | 세부 사항
7월 8일 일정에서 그림 같이 아름다운 동굴인 그로타 아주라를 탐험한다(explore the Grotta Azzurra, a picturesque cave)고 했으므로 정답은 (B)이다.

165 5일차에 여행객들은 어디에서 묵을 것인가?

(A) 카프리
(B) 나폴리
(C) 베니스
(D) 피렌체

해설 | 세부 사항
일정표의 Day 5에서 저녁에 피렌체에 도착하여 카사 피렐로에 체크인한다(arrive in Florence in the evening ~ at the Casa Pirello)고 되어 있으므로 정답은 (D)이다.

166 여행 비용에 포함되어 있는 것은?

(A) 카사 피렐로에서의 식사
(B) 요리 강습
(C) 유리 공장의 기념품
(D) 운하에서 배로 여행하기

해설 | 세부 사항
일정표 하단의 유의 사항을 보면 이번 여행은 여행 일정표에 열거된 7일간의 교통수단, 호텔, 식사를 포함한다(The tour includes transportation for the seven days, hotels, and the meals listed in the above itinerary)고 명시되어 있는데 카사 피렐로에서의 식사는 7월 12일 여행 일정에 포함된 사항이므로 정답은 (A)이다.

어휘 | souvenir (관광지의) 기념품, 선물

167 선택 가능한 여행에 대해 명시된 것은?

(A) 나폴리에서 참가할 수 있다.
(B) 사전 예약을 해야 한다.
(C) 박물관 관광이 포함되어 있다.
(D) 아침에 이루어진다.

해설 | Not / True
일정표에서 7월 8일과 7월 11일에 선택 가능한 오전 여행(Optional morning excursion)이 있으므로 정답은 (D)이다.

[168-171] 문자 메시지

더크 넬슨 [오후 2시 33분] 안녕하세요, 제프리 그리고 리사. 방금 린넨 공급업체에서 연락을 받았어요. **168토요일까지 우리가 요청했던 색상으로 식탁보를 배달할 수 없을 것 같아요.**

제프리 림 [오후 2시 34분] 그렇지만 **168개관 행사는 이번 주 금요일 저녁인데요. 169저는 주문이 확정된 것으로 생각했어요. 169,170월요일에 확인서를 받지 않았나요?**

리사 콥 [오후 2시 35분] **169,170**네, 그랬어요. 제가 바로 여기 갖고 있어요. **170**어두운 녹색의 대형 식탁보 24개를 배송받기로 되어 있었어요.

더크 넬슨 [오후 2시 36분] 공급업체의 창고에 혼선이 있었던 것 같습니다. 다른 색상을 받아주면 할인해 준다고 하네요.

제프리 림 [오후 2시 37분] 다른 색상은 어떤 게 있나요?

리사 콥 [오후 2시 38분] 지금 그쪽 웹사이트를 보는 중이에요. 저라면 은은한 금색을 고르겠어요.

제프리 림 [오후 2시 39분] 그러면 되겠네요. 모든 테이블 중앙에 대비되는 꽃 장식을 배치하면 되거든요.

더크 넬슨 [오후 2시 40분] 좋은 생각이에요. **171린넨 공급업체에 전화해서 은은한 금색으로 바꿀 테니 이번 주 목요일까지 반드시 배송해 달라고 전달할게요.**

어휘 | supplier 공급업체　tablecloth 식탁보　confirm 확정하다　confirmation 확인(서)　dozen 12개짜리 한 묶음　apparently 보아 하니　mix-up 혼선　warehouse 창고　accept 받아들이다　available 입수 가능한　arrange 준비하다　contrasting 대비되는　floral 꽃으로 만든　centerpiece 중앙부 장식

168 메시지 작성자들은 무슨 일을 하는 것 같은가?

(A) 창고 관리　　　　(B) 린넨 제조
(C) 경관 설계　　　　(D) 행사 기획

해설 | 추론

2시 33분에 넬슨 씨가 공급업체에서 토요일까지 우리가 요청했던 색상으로 식탁보를 배달할 수 없을 것 같다(They will not be able ~ we requested until Saturday)고 하자 2시 34분에 림 씨가 그렇지만 개관 행사는 이번 주 금요일 저녁(the grand opening event is this Friday evening)이라고 한 것으로 보아 메시지 작성자들은 행사를 위해 식탁보가 필요한 것이고, 행사를 준비하는 일을 하는 사람들임을 알 수 있다. 따라서 정답은 (D)이다.

169 언제 주문이 확정되었는가?

(A) 월요일   (B) 목요일
(C) 금요일   (D) 토요일

해설 | 세부 사항

2시 34분에 림 씨가 주문이 확정된 것으로 생각했다(I thought we had confirmed the order)며 월요일에 확인서를 받지 않았는지(Didn't we receive a confirmation on Monday?)를 묻자, 2시 35분에 콥 씨가 그랬다(Yes, we did)고 답했으므로 정답은 (A)이다.

170 오후 2시 35분에 콥 씨가 "제가 바로 여기 갖고 있어요"라고 쓴 의도는 무엇이겠는가?

(A) 공급업체에서 온 메시지를 보고 있다.
(B) 온라인으로 연한 금색 샘플을 보고 있다.
(C) 책상 위에서 중앙 꽃 장식에 대한 청구서를 발견했다.
(D) 식탁보를 배송받았다.

해설 | 의도 파악

2시 34분에 림 씨가 월요일에 확인서를 받지 않았는지(Didn't we receive a confirmation on Monday?) 묻자 2시 35분에 콥 씨가 그랬다(Yes, we did)고 답했고 바로 여기 갖고 있다(I have it right here)며 어두운 녹색의 대형 식탁보 24개를 배송받기로 되어 있었다(We were expecting ~ in dark green)고 내용을 확인해 주고 있는 것으로 보아 공급업체로부터 받은 확인서를 보고 있다는 의도로 한 말임을 알 수 있다. 따라서 정답은 (A)이다.

어휘 | view 보다 invoice 청구서 shipment 수송품

171 넬슨 씨는 다음에 무엇을 할 것 같은가?

(A) 식당에 연락
(B) 회사 웹사이트 방문
(C) 이전 주문 업데이트
(D) 사업 관계 취소

해설 | 추론

2시 40분에 넬슨 씨가 린넨 공급업체에 전화해서 은은한 금색으로 바꿀 테니 이번 주 목요일까지 반드시 배송해 달라고 전달하겠다(I'll call the linen supplier ~ should be delivered this Thursday)고 했으므로 정답은 (C)이다.

어휘 | previous 이전의 cancel 취소하다 relationship 관계

[172-175] 추천 글

저는 건축 회사의 마케팅 이사입니다. **172우리 웹사이트에 쓸 동료들의 얼굴 사진과 사무실 공간의 파노라마 사진을 찍어줄 사람을 찾고 있었고**, 경험이 풍부하면서도 가격이 적당한 사진작가를 찾느라 애를 먹고 있었습니다. 한 친구가 사진 사업을 하는 카테리나 맥밀란을 추천해 주었습니다. 저는 그녀에게 연락했고, 그녀는 견적서, 가능한 시간대, 작품 샘플과 함께 신속하게 답장을 했습니다. 그녀의 요금은 합리적이고, **175우리가 이용했던 사무실 사진 촬영 패키지와 같은 174(A)대규모 작업을 위한 여러 할인 패키지를 제공합니다.** 그 패키지는 우리의 요구 사항에 안성맞춤이었습니다. 촬영 당일 맥밀란 씨는 우리 회의실 중 한 곳에 임시 인물 사진 스튜디오를 마련했습니다. **173, 174(D)그녀는 추가 요금을 받고 사진 보정 서비스를 제공하지만, 우리는 큰 규모의 그래픽 아트 부서가 내부에 있어서 그 서비스를 거절했습니다.** 모두 맥밀란 씨의 작업에 만족했고 **174(C)그녀는 제가 함께 작업한 사진작가 중 최고입니다.**

– 에릭 앵글러, 6월 3일

어휘 | architecture 건축 firm 회사 headshot 얼굴 사진 colleague 동료 space 공간 struggle 애쓰다 experienced 경험 많은 affordable 가격이 알맞은 own 소유하다 respond 응답하다 quote 견적(서) availability 이용 가능성 rate 가격 reasonable 합리적인 set up 설치하다 temporary 임시의 portrait 인물 사진 fee 요금 decline 거절하다 sizable 꽤 큰 on-site 현장에

172 추천 글에 따르면, 앵글러 씨는 왜 사진을 찍기를 원했는가?

(A) 판매할 제품을 제작하려고
(B) 사무실 건물을 장식하려고
(C) 웹사이트에 시각 자료를 추가하려고
(D) 건축가의 요청을 충족시키려고

해설 | 세부 사항

두 번째 문장에서 앵글러 씨가 우리 웹사이트에 쓸 동료들의 얼굴 사진과 사무실 공간의 파노라마 사진을 찍어줄 사람을 찾고 있었다(I was looking for someone ~ for our Web site)고 했으므로 정답은 (C)이다.

어휘 | decorate 장식하다 content 내용물 satisfy 만족시키다 architect 건축가

173 앵글러 씨의 회사에 대해 사실인 것은?

(A) 사내 대형 인물 사진 스튜디오가 있다.
(B) 여러 건물에서 운영된다.
(C) 그래픽 아티스트 팀을 고용하고 있다.
(D) 맥밀란 씨가 찾기 어려웠다.

일곱 번째 문장에서 맥밀란 씨는 추가 요금을 받고 사진 보정 서비스를 제공하지만 우리는 큰 규모의 그래픽 아트 부서가 내부에 있어서 그 서비스를 거절했다(She offers a photo-retouching ~ graphic arts department on-site)고 했으므로 앵글러 씨의 회사에는 그래픽 아트 부서가 있음을 알 수 있다. 따라서 (C)가 정답이다.

어휘 | operate 운영하다 employ 고용하다

패러프레이징
지문의 have a sizable graphic arts department
→ 보기의 employs a team of graphic artists

174 맥밀란 씨에 대해 명시되지 않은 것은?

(A) 대형 작업 할인을 제공한다.
(B) 풍경을 촬영한다.
(C) 함께 일하기 편하다.
(D) 요청하면 사진을 보정해 준다.

해설 | Not / True
다섯 번째 문장에서 대규모 작업을 위한 여러 할인 패키지를 제공한다(she offers several discount packages for large jobs)고 했으므로 (A), 일곱 번째 문장에서 추가 요금을 받고 사진 보정 서비스를 제공한다(she offers a photo-retouching service for an extra fee)고 했으므로 (D), 마지막 문장에서 그녀는 함께 작업한 사진작가 중 최고(she is the best photographer I've ever worked with)라고 했으므로 (C)는 모두 언급되었고, 풍경을 촬영한다는 내용은 없으므로 (B)가 정답이다.

어휘 | volume discount 대량 주문 할인 landscape 풍경 retouch 수정하다 upon request 요청에 따라

패러프레이징
지문의 discount packages for large jobs
→ 보기의 volume discounts

175 [1], [2], [3], [4]로 표시된 곳 중에서 다음 문장이 들어가기에 가장 적합한 위치는?

"그 패키지는 우리의 요구 사항에 안성맞춤이었습니다."

(A) [1] (B) [2] (C) [3] (D) [4]

해설 | 문장 삽입
제시된 문장의 The package가 문제 해결의 단서이다. '그 패키지'라고 언급한 것으로 보아, 주어진 문장 앞에서도 패키지에 대한 내용이 와야 한다. 따라서 맥밀란 씨의 대규모 작업 할인 패키지(discount packages for large jobs)에 대해 소개하며 우리가 이용했던 패키지도 여기에 포함된다(including the ~ package, which we used)는 문장 뒤인 (B)가 정답이다.

[176-180] 회람 + 이메일

아포 플레이버 회사
회람

발신: 에이미 지라드
수신: 아포 플레이버사 전 직원
날짜: 7월 6일
제목: 사무실 이전

176다음 주에 우리는 새 사무실로 이전할 예정입니다. 풍부한 자연광뿐 아니라 이 사무실보다 더 널찍한 공간에 만족하게 될 것이라고 생각합니다. 우리와 계약한 이사업체는 하루에 한 부서씩 옮길 예정입니다. 아래 일정대로 여러분 부서의 이사 날짜를 기억해 두세요.

날짜	부서	연락 담당
7월 11일	IT	칼리 모턴
7월 12일	180연구 개발	180앨런 듀벡
7월 13일	178회계	178브라이언 스미스
7월 14일	마케팅	네이트 하비슨
7월 15일	인사	에이미 지라드

이사 날짜에 책상, 서류 캐비닛, 책장에서 모든 물건을 치워 주세요. **177상자에 물건을 넣은 다음 각 상자에 이름, 부서 및 메모(예를 들어 상자에 깨지기 쉬운 물건이 있는 경우)를 적은 표를 붙여 주세요. 178, 180문의 사항이나 우려 사항이 있는 경우 여러분의 부서에 해당하는 연락 담당자에게 연락하세요.**

어휘 | transition 이동하다 spacious 널찍한 layout 배치 abundance 풍부 natural 자연의 relocation 이전 contractor 계약자 remove 치우다 label 표를 붙이다 contain ~이 들어 있다 breakable 깨지기 쉬운 object 물건 reach 연락하다 concern 우려

발신: 제일라 윌리엄스
수신: 앨런 듀벡
날짜: 7월 7일
제목: 이사일

180듀벡 씨께,

179다음 주에 리스본에서 열리는 PEN 식품 과학 컨퍼런스에서 발표를 하기로 되어 있어 저희 부서 이사 예정일에 제가 사무실에 없을 것 같습니다. 저는 목요일에 사무실로 돌아올 예정입니다.

대신 그 주 마지막 날에 제 짐을 옮기는 것이 가능할까요? 어떻게 진행해야 할지 알려 주세요.

감사합니다.

제일라 윌리엄스

176 새로운 사무실 건물에 대해 암시된 것은?

(A) 창문이 많다.
(B) 바닥 면적이 협소하다.
(C) 가구가 이미 갖추어져 있다.
(D) 다른 지역에 위치해 있다.

해설 | 추론
회람의 첫 문장에서 다음 주에 우리는 새 사무실로 이전할 예정(Next week, we will transition to our new offices)이라고 했고 풍부한 자연광뿐 아니라 이 사무실보다 더 널찍한 공간에 만족하게 될 것이라고 생각한다(We think you will ~ abundance of natural light)고 했다. 자연광이 풍부하다고 한 것으로 보아 볕이 들 수 있는 창문이 많다고 짐작할 수 있으므로 (A)가 정답이다.

어휘 | limited 한정된 space 공간 furnished 가구가 비치된

177 지라드 씨는 직원들에게 무엇을 하라고 지시하는가?

(A) 책상 위에 상자를 쌓을 것
(B) 파손되기 쉬운 물품은 개인적으로 옮길 것
(C) 상자에 식별 정보를 붙일 것
(D) 양식을 제출하여 특정 이사 날짜를 요청할 것

해설 | 세부 사항
회람의 두 번째 단락 두 번째 문장에서 상자에 물건을 넣은 다음 각 상자에 이름, 부서 및 메모(예를 들어 상자에 깨지기 쉬운 물건이 있는 경우)를 적은 표를 붙여 주라(Pack your things ~ boxes contain breakable objects)고 했으므로 (C)가 정답이다.

어휘 | stack 쌓다 fragile 깨지기 쉬운 identifying 식별 specific 특정한 submit 제출하다 form 양식

패러프레이징
지문의 label each box with your name, department
→ 보기의 Add identifying information to boxes

178 회계부서 직원들은 질문이 있을 때 누구에게 연락해야 하는가?

(A) 모턴 씨   (B) 듀벡 씨
(C) 스미스 씨   (D) 지라드 씨

해설 | 세부 사항
회람의 두 번째 단락 마지막 문장에서 문의 사항이나 우려 사항이 있는 경우 여러분의 부서에 해당하는 연락 담당자에게 연락하라(Reach out to the contact ~ any questions or concerns)고 했고, 회람의 표에 따르면 회계부서(Accounting)의 연락 담당자는 브라이언 스미스(Brian Smith)이므로 정답은 (C)이다.

179 이메일의 목적은?

(A) 휴가 신청
(B) 겹치는 일정 설명
(C) 컨퍼런스 참석 요청
(D) 특별 프로젝트 관련 보고

해설 | 주제 / 목적
이메일의 첫 문장에서 다음 주에 리스본에서 열리는 PEN 식품 과학 컨퍼런스에서 발표를 하기로 되어 있어 저희 부서 이사 예정일에 제가 사무실에 없을 것 같다(I will be presenting ~ department's scheduled move)고 했으므로 (B)가 정답이다.

어휘 | time off 휴가 explain 설명하다 scheduling conflict 일정 겹침

180 윌리엄스 씨는 어느 부서에서 일하는 것 같은가?

(A) IT
(B) 연구 개발
(C) 마케팅
(D) 인사

해설 | 연계
회람의 두 번째 단락 마지막 문장에서 문의 사항이나 우려 사항이 있는 경우 여러분의 부서에 해당하는 연락 담당자에게 연락하라(Reach out to the contact ~ any questions or concerns)고 했는데, 윌리엄스 씨가 듀벡 씨(Mr. Dubeck)에게 이사와 관련된 문의를 했고 회람의 표에 따르면 앨런 듀벡(Alan Dubeck)은 연구 개발(Research and Development)의 연락 담당자이므로 윌리엄스 씨는 연구 개발 부서에서 일하고 있음을 알 수 있다. 따라서 정답은 (B)이다.

[181-185] 양식 + 이메일

182HIH – 호손 인터내셔널 호텔
182직원 객실 복지 서비스 – 예약 양식

프로그램에 참여 자격이 있는 직원은 이 양식을 이용해 온라인으로 예약을 해야 합니다. 호텔이나 콜센터로 직접 연락하지 마세요.

181이름: 아차라 분프라산   직원 ID: 7931-4782-0201
181근무하는 호텔 지점: 룸피니   이메일: aboonprasan@
                                   hihbangkok.com
181국가, 도시: 태국, 방콕   전화번호: 02-5861252
오늘 날짜: 4월 15일

방문 국가, 도시: 대한민국, 서울
요청 날짜: 8월 22-27일
숙박일수: 5
호텔 지점: 이태원동
183대안 지점 1: 인사동
대안 지점 2: 홍대

181(C), 184특별 요청: 서울 여행은 이번이 처음이라 전망이 좋은 위층 객실로 요청하고 싶습니다.

182조식 그리고 이용 가능한 곳일 경우 체육관 및 수영장 이용이 예약에 포함됩니다. 제출 후 48시간 이내에 예약 정보가 포함된 이메일을 받게 되실 겁니다. 질문이나 우려 사항이 있는 경우 해외 지원팀에 연락하세요.

어휘 | benefit 혜택 form 양식 eligible ~에 자격이 있는 book 예약하다 reservation 예약 directly 직접 location 지점 alternative 대안의 upper floor 위층 available 이용 가능한 access 이용 submission 제출 support 지원 concern 우려

수신: 아차라 분프라산 <aboonprasan@hihbangkok.com>
발신: 사라 로웰 <slowell@hihcorporate.com>
날짜: 4월 16일
제목: 귀하의 예약

분프라산 씨께,

귀하의 직원 객실 요청을 접수했습니다. 안타깝게도, **183이태원동 지점은 예약이 다 찼지만 귀하의 제1 대안 지점에 객실을 예약할 수 있었습니다.** 귀하의 확인 번호는 908X-W752입니다. **184시내 조망이 딸린 위층 객실은 체크인 시 이용 가능 여부가 결정됩니다.** 체크아웃 시 직원 **185요금**이 부과될 것입니다. 즐거운 서울 여행 되시기 바랍니다.

사라 로웰

어휘 | unfortunately 안타깝게도 fully 완전히 reserve 예약하다 confirmation 확인 be subject to ~의 대상이다 availability 이용 가능성 charge 부과하다 rate 요금

181 분프라산 씨에 대해 명시된 것은?

(A) 한국으로 전근 갈 예정이다.
(B) 콜센터에서 일했었다.
(C) 서울로 자주 여행을 간다.
(D) 태국에서 온다.

해설 | Not / True
양식에 아차라 분프라산 씨(Name Achara Boonprasan)가 근무하는 호텔 지점은 룸피니(Location of the hotel you work for Lumphini), 국가, 도시는 태국, 방콕(City, country Bangkok, Thailand)이라고 나와 있으므로 정답은 (D)이다. 특별 요청에 서울 여행은 이번이 처음(This will be my first trip to Seoul)이라고 나와 있으므로 (C)는 오답, 전근이나 콜센터 근무 경력에 관한 언급은 없으므로 (A)와 (B)는 답이 될 수 없다.

어휘 | transfer 전근 가다

182 HIH 직원 객실 복지 제도에 대해 명시된 것은?

(A) 모든 직원이 이용할 수 있다.
(B) 호텔에 직접 전화해서 예약할 수 있다.
(C) 객실 예약에는 조식이 포함되어 있다.
(D) 모든 참여 호텔에 체육관과 수영장이 있다.

해설 | Not / True
양식의 상단에 HIH 직원 객실 복지 서비스를 위한 예약 양식(Employee Room Benefit Services - Booking Form)이라고 나와 있고, 하단에 조식 그리고 이용 가능한 곳일 경우 체육관 및 수영장 이용이 예약에 포함된다(Breakfast and, ~ included in your reservation)고 했다. 따라서 HIH 직원 객실 복지 프로그램을 통한 객실 예약에는 조식이 포함되어 있으므로 (C)가 정답이다.

어휘 | participate 참여하다

183 분프라산 씨는 여행 중 어디서 묵을 것 같은가?

(A) 룸피니
(B) 이태원동
(C) 인사동
(D) 홍대

해설 | 연계
이메일의 두 번째 문장에서 분프라산 씨에게 이태원동 지점은 예약이 다 찼지만 귀하의 제1 대안 지점에 객실을 예약할 수 있었다(the Itaewon-dong location ~ at your first alternative location)고 했는데, 양식에 따르면 분프라산 씨가 신청한 대안 지점 1은 인사동 지점(Alternative choice 1: Insa-dong)이다. 따라서 분프라산 씨는 인사동 지점에서 숙박하게 될 것임을 알 수 있으므로 (C)가 정답이다.

184 로웰 씨에 대해 암시된 것은?

(A) HIH의 시간제 직원이다.
(B) 분프라산 씨의 문의를 HIH의 해외 지원 부서로 보냈다.
(C) 분프라산 씨의 특별 요청을 들어줄 수 없다.
(D) 방콕에 방문한 적이 있다.

해설 | 연계
양식의 특별 요청란(Special requests)에 분프라산 씨가 서울 여행은 이번이 처음이라 전망이 좋은 위층 객실로 요청하고 싶다(This will be ~ I would like to request a room on an upper floor with a view)고 했는데, 이메일의 네 번째 문장에서 로웰 씨가 시내 조망이 딸린 위층 객실은 체크인 시 이용 가능 여부가 결정된다(The upper floor rooms ~ upon check-in)고 했으므로 (C)가 정답이다.

어휘 | refer 보내다 be unable to ~할 수 없다 honor 요구에 따르다

185 이메일에서 첫 번째 단락 4행의 "rate"와 의미가 가장 가까운 단어는?

(A) 가격　　　　　(B) 등급
(C) 양　　　　　　(D) 평가

해설 | 동의어
의미상 체크아웃 시 직원 '요금'이 부과될 것이라는 뜻으로 쓰인 것이므로 정답은 (A) price이다.

[186-190] 제품 정보 + 이메일 + 이메일

프리츠 앤 로건 퍼니처: 콘템포 컬렉션
www.fritzlogan.com / contempocollecion

품목 코드	설명	가격
CC01	4인용 쿠션 소파	680달러
188CC02	**188**2인용 쿠션 소파	560달러
CC03	안락의자 및 어울리는 오토만	430달러
CC04	**186, 190**커피 탁자	**190**200달러
CC05	**186**작은 탁자	140달러

제품 세부 정보:

• 소파, 안락의자, 오토만은 검정 또는 갈색 가죽, 연회색 극세사 직물로 구매 가능합니다.
• 가죽 가구는 진공청소기로 청소하거나 젖은 천으로 닦아야 합니다.
• **186(D)**극세사 직물은 비누와 물로 얼룩을 닦아낼 수 있습니다.
• 모든 가구는 사전 조립된 상태로 배송됩니다.

문의 사항이 있거나 특별 할인에 대해 알고 싶으시면 sales@fritzlogan.com으로 연락 주십시오.

어휘 | armchair 안락의자　matching 어울리는　ottoman 오토만(안에 물건을 보관하고 윗부분을 의자로 쓰는 가구)　end table (소파 곁에 놓는) 작은 테이블　leather 가죽　microfiber 극세사　fabric 천　vacuum 진공청소기로 청소하다　wipe 닦다　damp 축축한　cloth 천　spot 얼룩　preassembled 조립된

수신: sales@fritzlogan.com
발신: ecooper@selodydecor.com
날짜: 9월 13일
제목: 콘템포 컬렉션

안녕하세요,

187저는 셀로디 데코에서 일하고 있습니다. 대형 회사 사무실의 접수처 구역에 있는 공용 공간을 디자인하고 있습니다. 콘템포 컬렉션의 품목들은 제 고객의 많은 요구 사항들을 충족합니다. **188**저는 특히 2인용 쿠션 소파에 관심이 있습니다. 만약 이 소파를 6개 구입한다면 제 주문이 대량 주문 가격을 적용받을 수 있을까요?

빠른 답변 주시면 감사하겠습니다.

엘리스 쿠퍼

어휘 | public 공공의　space 공간　reception 접수처　corporate 회사의　requirement 요건　especially 특히　qualify for ~에 자격이 되다　bulk pricing 대량 주문 가격

수신: ecooper@selodydecor.com
발신: jevans@fritzlogan.com
날짜: 9월 14일
제목: 회신: 콘템포 컬렉션

쿠퍼 씨께,

문의 주셔서 감사합니다. **189**한 품목을 5개 이상 구매하시면 20% 할인을 받으실 수 있습니다. 대량 가구 구매에는 100달러의 정액 배송료가 적용됩니다.

190고객님이 관심을 갖고 있는 컬렉션에 대한 판촉 행사를 진행 중입니다. 9월 30일까지 주문하시면 동일 가구 세트에서 무료 커피 탁자를 받으실 수 있습니다. 구입하실 준비가 되면 알려 주세요. 기쁜 마음으로 도와드리겠습니다.

제임스 에반스

어휘 | inquiry 문의　flat (가격·요금이) 균일한　shipping 배송　apply 적용하다　promotion 판촉 (활동)　interest ~의 관심을 끌다　complimentary 무료의　assist 돕다

186 제품 정보에 명시된 것은?

(A) 한 종류 이상의 탁자를 구입할 수 있다.
(B) 고객이 직접 제품을 운반할 수 있다.
(C) 미리 조립된 제품은 추가 요금이 부과된다.
(D) 직물을 씌운 제품은 전문적으로 세척되어야 한다.

해설 | Not / True
제품 정보의 표에 따르면 탁자는 커피 탁자와 작은 탁자 두 종류가 있으므로 정답은 (A)이다. 제품 세부 정보의 네 번째 항목에서 모든 가구는 사전 조립된 상태로 배송된다(All furniture is delivered preassembled)고만 했고 고객이 직접 운반할 수 있는지 여부와 추가 요금에 대한 언급이 없으므로 (B)와 (C)는 답이 될 수 없다. 또한 세 번째 항목에서 극세사 직물은 비누와 물로 얼룩을 닦아낼 수 있다(Microfiber fabric can be ~ soap and water)고 했으므로 (D)도 오답이다.

어휘 | kind 종류　transport 운반하다　be subject to ~의 대상이다　professionally 전문적으로

187 쿠퍼 씨는 누구일 것 같은가?

(A) 가구 판매원
(B) 사무실 접수원
(C) 실내 장식가
(D) 기업 관리자

해설 | 추론

첫 번째 이메일의 첫 문장에서 작성자인 쿠퍼 씨가 저는 셀로디 데코에서 일하고 있다(I work for Selody Décor)고 했고, 대형 회사 사무실의 접수처 구역에 있는 공용 공간을 디자인하고 있다(I am designing the public ~ large corporate office)고 자신을 소개하고 있으므로 (C)가 정답이다.

188 쿠퍼 씨는 어떤 품목에 가장 관심 있는가?

(A) CC01   (B) CC02
(C) CC03   (D) CC04

해설 | 연계

첫 번째 이메일의 네 번째 문장에서 쿠퍼 씨가 저는 특히 2인용 쿠션 소파에 관심이 있다(I am especially interested in the two-seat cushion sofa)고 했고, 제품 정보의 표에 따르면 2인용 쿠션 소파는 CC02이므로 (B)가 정답이다.

189 두 번째 이메일에서 대량 주문 가격에 대해 언급된 것은?

(A) 총 주문액이 100달러 이상인 고객이 이용할 수 있다.
(B) 콘템포 컬렉션의 제품을 구입하는 사람에게 적용된다.
(C) 할인된 배송비를 받을 수 있다.
(D) 한정된 기간 동안 제공되고 있다.

해설 | Not / True

두 번째 이메일 두 번째 문장에서 한 품목을 5개 이상 구매하면 20% 할인을 받을 수 있다(Purchases of five or more ~ 20 percent discount)고 했고 대량 가구 구매에는 100달러의 정액 배송료가 적용된다(A flat $100 shipping fee is applied to bulk furniture purchases)며 대량 주문에 대한 할인 혜택을 설명하고 있다. 따라서 (C)가 정답이다. 100달러는 배송료 할인에 대한 내용이므로 (A)는 오답, 한 품목을 5개 이상 구매하는 사람에게 적용되는 것이므로 (B)도 오답, 9월 30일까지 주문 시 무료 커피 탁자를 받을 수 있다고 했으므로 한정된 기간 동안 제공되는 것은 대량 주문 가격에 관한 것이 아니므로 (D)도 오답이다.

어휘 | total 총 ~이 되다 reduced 할인된 limited 한정된

190 프리츠 앤 로건 퍼니처 판촉 행사에서 제공되는 사은품의 정가는 얼마인가?

(A) 140달러   (B) 200달러
(C) 430달러   (D) 560달러

해설 | 연계

두 번째 이메일의 두 번째 단락 첫 문장에서 고객님이 관심을 갖고 있는 컬렉션에 대한 판촉 행사를 진행 중(We are running a promotion ~ interests you)이라며, 9월 30일까지 주문하면 동일 가구 세트에서 무료 커피 탁자를 받을 수 있다(If you place an order ~ same furniture grouping)고 했다. 제품 정보의 표에 따르면 커피 탁자는

200달러이므로 (B)가 정답이다.

[191-195] 이메일 + 기사 + 이메일

수신: 사이먼 애딩턴 <saddington@happenings.co.uk>
발신: 라비 티파니스 <rtipanis@happenings.co.in>
제목: 정보
날짜: 3월 22일
첨부: 📎 eng.report.doc

애딩턴 씨께,

192하이데라바드의 새 캠퍼스에 대한 진행 상황을 알려 드리고자 합니다. **191**각 건물에 대한 엔지니어링 점검은 잘 되었고, 191, **192**6월 중순 개관 일정에 맞춰 진행되고 있습니다. **191**참고하실 수 있도록 보고서를 첨부했습니다. 궁금하신 점이 있으시면 알려 주십시오.

라비 티파니스

어휘 | progress 진행 inspection 점검 on schedule 예정대로 attach 첨부하다 for your reference 참고할 수 있도록

---

www.globalbusinesswire.com

192, 193런던에 본사를 둔 전자 상거래 회사인 해프닝스 코퍼레이션이 8월 4일 마침내 하이데라바드에 새 캠퍼스를 열었다. 뭄바이에 분류 센터가 있기는 하지만 이곳은 영국을 벗어난 첫 번째 주요 캠퍼스이다.

194사이먼 애딩턴 해외 시설 관리 수석 부사장은 개관식을 위해 에든버러에서 비행기를 타고 왔다. 애딩턴 씨는 8월 31일 은퇴를 앞두고 있으므로 이 행사는 그의 마지막 공식 임무가 될 것이다.

다른 손님들로는 해프닝스 코퍼레이션 인도 지사의 부사장인 비닛 바핫 씨와 다양한 정부 관료들이 있었다. 새 캠퍼스는 수천 명의 직원을 고용할 예정이다. 회사는 여전히 소프트웨어 엔지니어부터 유지 관리 직원에 이르기까지 다양한 직책을 고용 중에 있다. 일자리에 대한 정보는 www.happenings.co.in/jobs에서 확인할 수 있다.

어휘 | e-commerce 전자 상거래 headquartered in ~에 본사를 둔 major 주요한 sorting 분류 vice president 부사장 facility 시설 mark 나타내다, 기념하다 official 공식적인 duty 임무 retire 은퇴하다 include 포함하다 various 다양한 government official 공직자 employ 고용하다 a variety of 다양한 maintenance 유지 보수 job opening 일자리

수신: 마리솔 말리나 <mmalina@happenings.com.mx>
발신: 니콜라스 셀리 <ncely@happenings.co.uk>
제목: 정보

날짜: 9월 20일
첨부: 📎 Cely_1.doc

마리솔 씨께:

과달라하라 창고에 대한 보고서에 감사드립니다. 보고서는 상당히 유익했습니다. 그곳의 일상 업무를 상당히 잘 이해할 수 있었습니다. 12월 2일 멕시코 시티행 항공편을 예약했습니다. 12월 3일에 비행기를 타고 과달라하라로 가서 12월 4일에 현장 방문을 할 예정입니다. 그곳에서 런던으로 돌아올 계획입니다. **195저의 일정표를 첨부했습니다.** 만나 뵙기를 기대합니다.

194니콜라스 셀리
해외 시설 관리 수석 부사장
해프닝스 코퍼레이션

- -
어휘 | warehouse 창고 informative 유익한 day-to-day 매일 행해지는 operation 작업 book 예약하다 flight 항공편 on-site 현장의 itinerary 일정표

191 첫 번째 이메일에서 엔지니어링 보고서에 대해 암시하는 것은?

(A) 4월 말에 제출되었다.
(B) 미완성이다.
(C) 티파니스 씨에 의해 거절당했다.
(D) 어떠한 큰 문제도 드러나 있지 않다.

해설 | **추론**
첫 이메일의 두 번째 문장에서 각 건물에 대한 엔지니어링 점검은 잘 되었고 6월 중순 개관 일정에 맞춰 진행되고 있다(The engineering inspections ~ mid-June opening)며 참고하실 수 있도록 보고서를 첨부했다(I've attached the reports for your reference)고 했으므로 (D)가 정답이다.

어휘 | submit 제출하다 incomplete 미완성의 reject 거절하다 indicate 나타내다

192 하이데라바드 캠퍼스에 대해 어떤 결론을 내릴 수 있는가?

(A) 직원 채용이 완료되었다.
(B) 예상보다 늦게 문을 열었다.
(C) 원래 계획했던 것만큼 크지 않다.
(D) 주요 캠퍼스로 간주되지 않는다.

해설 | **연계**
첫 이메일의 첫 문장에서 하이데라바드의 새 캠퍼스에 대한 진행 상황을 알려 드린다(I just wanted to ~ campus in Hyderabad)며 6월 중순 개관 일정에 맞춰 진행되고 있다(we're on schedule for a mid-June opening)고 했고, 기사의 첫 문장에서 런던에 본사를 둔 전자 상거래 회사인 해프닝스 코퍼레이션이 8월 4일 마침내 하이데라바드에 새 캠퍼스를 열었다(Happenings

Corporation ~ in Hyderabad on 4 August)고 했다. 따라서 하이데라바드 캠퍼스는 원래 일정보다 늦게 문을 열었음을 알 수 있으므로 (B)가 정답이다.

어휘 | staff 직원을 제공하다 originally 원래 consider 고려하다

193 기사에 따르면, 해프닝스 코퍼레이션의 본사는 어디에 있는가?

(A) 뭄바이
(B) 하이데라바드
(C) 에든버러
(D) 런던

해설 | **세부 사항**
기사의 첫 문장에서 런던에 본사를 둔 전자 상거래 회사인 해프닝스 코퍼레이션(Happenings Corporation, the e-commerce company headquartered in London)이라고 했으므로 정답은 (D)이다.

194 셀리 씨에 관해 사실일 것 같은 것은?

(A) 과달라하라에 거주한다.
(B) 말리나 씨의 친구이다.
(C) 애딩턴 씨의 후임자이다.
(D) 하이데라바드 캠퍼스 개관식에 참석했다.

해설 | **연계**
두 번째 이메일에 셀리 씨의 직함이 해외 시설 관리 수석 부사장(Senior Vice President of Global Facilities)이라고 나와 있는데, 기사의 두 번째 단락에서 사이먼 애딩턴 해외 시설 관리 수석 부사장은 개관식을 위해 에든버러에서 비행기를 타고 왔다(Simon Addington ~ opening from Edinburgh)며 애딩턴 씨는 8월 31일 은퇴를 앞두고 있으므로 이 행사는 그의 마지막 공식 임무가 될 것(The event marked ~ retiring on 31 August)이라고 했다. 따라서 애딩턴 씨가 8월에 은퇴한 뒤 니콜라스 셀리가 후임으로 온 것을 알 수 있으므로 (C)가 정답이다.

어휘 | replace 대신하다

195 셀리 씨는 이메일과 함께 무엇을 보냈는가?

(A) 여행 일정표
(B) 멕시코 사진 몇 장
(C) 창고 보고서
(D) 관광 정보

해설 | **세부 사항**
두 번째 이메일의 일곱 번째 문장에서 셀리 씨가 저의 일정표를 첨부했다(I've attached my itinerary)고 했으므로 (A)가 정답이다.

패러프레이징
지문의 itinerary → 보기의 travel schedule

[196-200] 웹페이지 + 이메일 + 이메일

---

www.highlandsrestaurant.co.nz/privatediningrooms

196새로 단장한 하이랜즈 레스토랑은 메인 식당 구역 바로 옆에 전용실 두 개를 추가했습니다. **198**각각의 전용실에는 25명까지 앉을 수 있습니다. 이 전용실 두 개는 50명까지 앉을 수 있는 큰 식당 공간으로 개방되고 합쳐질 수 있습니다. 이 새로운 구역은 회의나 파티와 같은 점심 또는 저녁 행사에 완벽합니다.

전용실에는 연설 및 발표를 위한 장비 설치가 가능합니다. 귀하의 요구 사항에 따라 인터넷 사용, 디지털 프로젝터, 스크린, 디지털 화이트보드, 마이크를 제공할 수 있습니다.

식사에는 네 가지 옵션이 제공됩니다:

- **옵션 A:** 샐러드와 메인 요리가 포함된 2코스 점심 메뉴
- **옵션 B:** 샐러드, 메인 요리, 디저트가 포함된 3코스 점심 메뉴
- **199옵션 C:** 샐러드, 메인 요리, 디저트가 포함된 3코스 저녁 메뉴
- **옵션 D:** 전채 요리, 샐러드, 메인 요리, 디저트가 포함된 4코스 저녁 메뉴

비공개 행사 일정을 잡으시려면 skone@highlandsrestaurant.co.nz으로 사라 코네에게 연락하세요.

- - - - - - - - - -

어휘 | renovated 개조된 private (개인 등) 전용의 dining 식사 seat 앉히다 combine 결합하다 section 구획 equip 장비를 갖추다 speech 연설 requirement 요건

수신: 토마스 웰던 <twheldon@wrightrealty.co.nz>
발신: 사라 코네 <skone@highlandsrestaurant.co.nz>
날짜: 10월 12일
제목: 예약

웰던 씨께:

197, 19811월 1일 저녁 6시 30분에 이곳 하이랜즈 레스토랑에서 열리는 라이트 부동산의 비공개 만찬 행사에 관해 확인을 드리고자 합니다. 현재 예약하신 인원은 46명입니다. 전채 요리는 전원, 닭고기는 18, 쇠고기는 22, 채식 요리는 6인 분량을 요청하셨습니다. 디저트는 전원 분량으로 초콜릿 케이크를 고르셨습니다.

처음 말씀 나눴을 때 어떤 장비가 행사에 필요할지 잘 모르겠다고 하셨습니다. 혹시 결정이 났을까요? 그렇다면 저희가 제대로 장비를 갖춰 놓을 수 있도록 알려 주시기 바랍니다.

예약 내용이 변경될 경우 연락 주십시오.

비공개 행사 담당자 사라 코네
하이랜즈 레스토랑

어휘 | reservation 예약 regarding ~에 관하여 current 현재의 vegetarian 채식주의자 select 선택하다 uncertain 잘 모르는 determine 결정하다 ensure 보장하다 properly 제대로 detail 세부 사항

수신: 사라 코네 <skone@highlandsrestaurant.co.nz>
발신: 토마스 웰던 <twheldon@wrightrealty.co.nz>
날짜: 10월 14일
제목: 회신: 예약

코네 씨께:

이메일을 보내 주셔서 감사합니다. 11월 1일 우리 회사의 시상식 만찬에 약간의 변화가 생겼습니다. **198현재 48명이 참석 예정이며**, 기존 주문에 닭고기 메인 요리 2인분이 추가로 필요합니다. **199저녁 만찬에 전채 요리는 포함시키지 않기로 결정했습니다.** 시상식은 저녁 7시에 시작할 계획이며 그 시간에 식사 서비스를 시작해 주셨으면 합니다. **200발표를 위해 디지털 프로젝터, 스크린, 마이크가 필요할 것 같습니다.**

도와주셔서 감사합니다.

토마스 웰던
부동산 중개 보조
198라이트 부동산

- - - - - - - - - -

어휘 | award 시상 additional 추가의 include 포함하다 ceremony 기념행사

---

196 웹페이지에서 하이랜즈 레스토랑에 대해 명시하는 것은?

(A) 보수 공사를 위해 문을 닫을 예정이다.
(B) 채식 전문점이다.
(C) 새로 생긴 식당이다.
(D) 확장되었다.

해설 | Not / True
웹페이지의 첫 문장에서 새로 단장한 하이랜즈 레스토랑은 메인 식당 구역 바로 옆에 전용실 두 개를 추가했다(The newly renovated Highlands Restaurant ~ our main dining area)고 했으므로 (D)가 정답이다. 새로 단장했다고 했으므로 (A)와 (C)는 오답, 채식을 전문으로 한다는 언급은 없으므로 (B)는 답이 될 수 없다.

패러프레이징
지문의 added two ~ rooms → 보기의 expanded

197 첫 번째 이메일의 목적은?

(A) 회의 일정 잡기
(B) 식사 장소 선택
(C) 행사의 세부 사항 확인
(D) 호텔 객실 예약

해설 | 주제/목적

첫 이메일의 첫 문장에서 11월 1일 저녁 6시 30분에 이곳 하이랜즈 레스토랑에서 열리는 라이트 부동산의 비공개 만찬 행사에 관해 확인을 드리고자 한다(I wanted to check ~ November at 6:30 p.m.)고 했으므로 (C)가 정답이다.

198 라이트 부동산의 비공개 행사에 대해 암시된 것은?

(A) 결합된 공간에서 열릴 것이다.
(B) 전원이 채식을 먹을 것이다.
(C) 전 사무실이 참석할 예정이다.
(D) 연례 행사이다.

해설 | 연계

첫 번째 이메일의 첫 번째 문장에서 해당 메일이 라이트 부동산의 비공개 만찬 행사에 관해 확인하는 메일임을 알 수 있고, 그에 대한 회신인 두 번째 이메일에서 라이트 부동산에서는 현재 48명이 참석 예정(We now have 48 people attending)이라는 것을 알 수 있다. 웹페이지의 첫 단락 두 번째 문장에서 25명까지 앉을 수 있는 전용실(Each private ~ up to 25 people)이 소개되며 두 전용실을 합쳐서 50명까지 앉을 수 있다(These two private rooms ~ seat up to 50)고 했으므로 48명이 참석하는 라이트 부동산의 비공개 행사는 두 개의 전용실이 합쳐진 공간에서 열릴 것임을 알 수 있다. 따라서 정답은 (A)이다.

어휘 | entire 전체의 annual 연례의

199 시상식 만찬에는 어떤 식사 옵션이 제공될 것 같은가?

(A) 옵션 A
(B) 옵션 B
(C) 옵션 C
(D) 옵션 D

해설 | 연계

두 번째 이메일의 네 번째 문장에서 저녁 만찬에 전채 요리는 포함시키지 않기로 결정했다(We have decided that we do not want to include starters with our dinner)고 했는데, 웹페이지에 나온 메뉴 중 옵션 C와 D가 저녁 메뉴이고 그중 전채 요리를 포함하지 않는 것은 옵션 C이므로 정답은 (C)이다.

200 웰던 씨는 어떤 장비를 요청하는가?

(A) 음악 재생기
(B) 디지털 프로젝터
(C) 컴퓨터
(D) 비디오 카메라

해설 | 세부 사항

두 번째 이메일의 첫 단락 마지막 문장에서 발표를 위해 디지털 프로젝터, 스크린, 마이크가 필요할 것 같다(We will need a digital projector ~ for our presentation)고 했으므로 정답은 (B)이다.

147 (C)	**148** (A)	**149** (B)	**150** (D)	**151** (D)
152 (B)	**153** (D)	**154** (B)	**155** (C)	**156** (B)
157 (C)	**158** (D)	**159** (B)	**160** (B)	**161** (A)
162 (D)	**163** (B)	**164** (C)	**165** (C)	**166** (B)
167 (D)	**168** (B)	**169** (C)	**170** (B)	**171** (A)
172 (C)	**173** (A)	**174** (C)	**175** (A)	**176** (B)
177 (A)	**178** (D)	**179** (C)	**180** (C)	**181** (C)
182 (A)	**183** (B)	**184** (A)	**185** (B)	**186** (B)
187 (B)	**188** (D)	**189** (C)	**190** (D)	**191** (D)
192 (A)	**193** (B)	**194** (A)	**195** (C)	**196** (B)
197 (D)	**198** (C)	**199** (A)	**200** (D)	

[147-148] 초대장

[147] 바인 스트리트 종합 병원의 신임 최고 경영자인 다프네 마티아스를 만나 환영하는 자리에 여러분을 정중히 초대합니다.

10월 27일 오후 4시~오후 5시 30분
2층 주 회의실

뉴 호프 병원에서 병원 관리자로 오래 근무했던 다프네 마티아스는 의료 센터에서 일한 경력이 25년을 넘습니다.

[148] 마티아스 씨에게 바인 스트리트 종합 병원에 대한 그녀의 비전에 대해 물어볼 기회를 가질 수 있을 것입니다. 간단한 다과가 제공될 예정입니다.

관심 있는 손님들은 바인 스트리트 종합 병원의 새로 단장한 병동을 둘러볼 수 있습니다.

어휘 | cordially 진심으로 greet 환영하다 chief executive officer 최고 경영자 administrator 관리자 opportunity 기회 refreshments 다과 renovated 개조된

147 마티아스 씨에 대해 암시된 것은?

(A) 뉴 호프 병원에서 일한다.
(B) 곧 은퇴할 계획이다.
(C) 최근에 새로운 일을 시작했다.
(D) 10월 27일 회의에 참석할 예정이다.

해설 | 추론

초대장의 첫 문장에서 바인 스트리트 종합 병원의 신임 최고 경영자인 다프네 마티아스를 만나 환영하는 자리에 여러분을 정중히 초대한다(You are cordially invited ~ Vine Street General Hospital)고 했으므로, 마티아스 씨는 최근에 바인 스트리트 종합 병원의 임직원이 되었음을 알 수 있다. 따라서 정답은 (C)이다.

어휘 | retire 은퇴하다 recently 최근에

148 손님들은 무엇을 할 수 있는가?

(A) 질문
(B) 예약
(C) 간식 구입
(D) 공사 도면 보기

해설 | 세부 사항
두 번째 단락 첫 문장에서 마티아스 씨에게 바인 스트리트 종합 병원에 대한 그녀의 비전에 대해 물어볼 기회를 가질 수 있을 것(You will have the opportunity to ask ~ General Hospital)이라고 했으므로 정답은 (A)이다.

어휘 | appointment 약속 purchase 구입하다 renovation 보수

[149-150] 온라인 후기

---

http://www.lakehouselodge.co.ke/reviews

고객이 남기는 말…

친구와 나는 케냐로 여행을 떠나 레이크 하우스 숙소에 며칠 동안 머물렀다. **149**전에 케냐에 가 본 적은 없었는데 정말 마음이 따뜻해지는 곳이었다. **150(A)**우리는 얼룩말과 원숭이를 포함한 그 지역의 멋진 동물들을 보기 위해 반나절짜리 사파리에 두 번 참여했다. 우리 객실의 창문에서 우리는 숙소 부지 주변을 자유롭게 거니는 기린들을 볼 수 있었다. 몇몇 기린들은 잘 길들여져 있어 우리가 직접 간식을 먹일 수도 있었다. **150(B), (C)**야생 동물들의 사진을 찍으며 아침을 보낸 뒤 오후에는 사랑스러운 정원에서 다른 방문객들과 함께 차를 즐겼다. 숙소 직원들과 사파리 가이드들은 친절하고 세심했다. 이번 휴가는 특별했으며 우리는 다시 방문하기를 바란다.

– 월터 브레이어, 2월 2일

어휘 | lodge 숙소 welcoming (방문객에게) 따뜻한 safari 사파리 peek 엿봄 region 지역 including ~을 포함하여 wander 거닐다 property 건물 구내 tame 길들여진 hand-feed 손으로 먹이를 주다 treat 간식 wildlife 야생 동물 attentive 세심한 vacation 휴가

---

149 후기에서 브레이어 씨가 명시하는 것은?

(A) 케냐 여행이 매우 비쌌다.
(B) 처음으로 케냐를 방문했다.
(C) 휴가가 며칠 단축되어야 했다.
(D) 사업 회의로 케냐에 돌아갈 예정이다.

해설 | Not / True
두 번째 문장에서 전에 케냐에 가 본 적은 없었다(We had never been to Kenya before)고 했으므로 (B)가 정답이다.

어휘 | shorten 단축하다

패러프레이징
지문의 had never been to Kenya before
→ 보기의 visiting Kenya for the first time

150 브레이어 씨가 언급한 활동이 아닌 것은?

(A) 현지 야생 동물 관찰
(B) 숙소 투숙객들과의 휴식
(C) 사진 촬영
(D) 야외 캠핑

해설 | Not / True
세 번째 문장에서 얼룩말과 원숭이를 포함한 그 지역의 멋진 동물들을 보기 위해 반나절짜리 사파리에 두 번 참여했다(We joined a couple of half-day safaris ~ including zebras and monkeys)고 했으므로 (A)는 사실, 여섯 번째 문장에서 야생 동물들의 사진을 찍으며 아침을 보낸 뒤 오후에는 사랑스러운 정원에서 다른 방문객들과 함께 차를 즐겼다(After spending the mornings taking photos ~ visitors in the lovely garden)고 했으므로 (B)와 (C)도 사실이다. 야외 캠핑에 대한 언급은 없으므로 (D)가 정답이다.

패러프레이징
지문의 get a peek at ~ the animals in the region
→ 보기의 Observing local wildlife
지문의 enjoyed ~ tea with ~ lodge visitors
→ 보기의 Relaxing with lodge guests

[151-152] 문자 메시지

자말 나이트 [오후 1시 9분]
안녕하세요, 민. **151**오후 1시 45분 회의가 B 회의실로 바뀌어서 알려 드리려고요. 사무실 문이 닫혀 있어서 안에 계시는지, 이메일을 보셨는지 알 수 없었어요.

민 지아 [오후 1시 13분]
알려 주셔서 감사합니다. 점심을 먹으려고 일찍 건물을 나왔어요. 메시지는 못 봤어요. **152**회의 전에 잠깐 우리 발표에 대해 논의할 시간이 있을까요?

자말 나이트 [오후 1시 14분]
152물론이죠. 지금 인쇄 자료도 제가 다 가지고 있어요.

민 지아 [오후 1시 16분]
152좋아요. 저는 지금 사무실에 있어요.

자말 나이트 [오후 1시 17분]
네. 이야기하고 나서 회의실로 같이 걸어가면 되겠네요.

어휘 | inform 알리다 material 자료

151 나이트 씨는 지아 씨에게 왜 연락했는가?

(A) 사무실 문을 닫을 것을 상기시켜 주려고
(B) 업무상 점심 회식에 초대하려고

(C) 회의실 예약을 부탁하려고

(D) 새로운 회의 장소를 알려 주려고

해설 | 주제/목적

1시 9분에 나이트 씨가 오후 1시 45분 회의가 B 회의실로 바뀌어서 알려 드리려 한다(I wanted to inform you ~ moved to Conference Room B)며 연락한 이유를 언급하고 있으므로 (D)가 정답이다.

152 오후 1시 16분에 지아 씨가 "저는 지금 사무실에 있어요"라고 쓴 의도는 무엇이겠는가?

(A) 나이트 씨가 실수를 했다고 생각한다.

(B) 나이트 씨와 지금 만날 수 있다.

(C) 프로젝트 때문에 매우 바쁘다.

(D) 이메일 메시지를 읽고 있다.

해설 | 의도 파악

1시 13분에 지아 씨가 회의 전에 잠깐 우리 발표에 대해 논의할 시간이 있을지(Do you have a few minutes to discuss our presentation before the meeting?) 묻자 나이트 씨가 1시 14분에 물론(Sure)이라고 답했고, 1시 16분에 지아 씨가 좋다(Great)며 지금 사무실에 있다(I'm in my office)고 했다. 따라서 지아 씨가 자신의 사무실에서 만나 발표에 대해 이야기하자는 의도로 한 말이므로 정답은 (B)이다.

[153-155] 이메일

수신: 베이뷰 아파트 전 주민

발신: 다니엘 로메로, 건물 관리인

날짜: 9월 1일

제목: 9월 15일부터 16일까지 전기 유지 보수 작업

153주민 여러분께 알립니다:

1539월 15일 월요일에 A 빌딩, 9월 16일 화요일에 B 빌딩에서 정전이 있을 예정입니다. 각 날짜 오전 9시 이후에 전력이 차단될 예정이며 오후 5시까지는 복구될 것으로 예상됩니다. 이러한 정전 계획은 올베이 전기 회사와 함께 편성되었습니다. 이 기간 동안 우리의 노후한 기계 시스템이 업그레이드되고 필수 정비가 이루어질 것입니다.

155귀하의 건물이 해당되는 날에 다음 예방 조치를 따르십시오. 비상 발전기로 로비와 계단 통로에 전기가 공급될 것입니다. 엘리베이터보다는 계단을 이용하십시오. **154**텔레비전과 컴퓨터와 같은 전자 장치의 플러그를 뽑으십시오. 냉장고와 냉동고의 온도를 유지하기 위해 문을 열고 닫는 것을 최소화하십시오.

문의는 저에게 d.romero@bayviewapt.com으로 연락 주십시오. 양해해 주셔서 감사합니다.

어휘 | resident 주민 property 건물 electrical 전기의 maintenance (점검·보수하는) 유지 interruption 중단 restore 복구하다 planned 계획된 coordinate 편성하다

period 기간 aging 노후한 mechanical 기계와 관련된 essential 필수적인 perform 수행하다 precaution 예방 조치 affect 영향을 미치다 emergency 비상 generator 발전기 stairwell 계단 통로 unplug 플러그를 뽑다 electronic equipment 전자 장치 maintain 유지하다 refrigerator 냉장고 freezer 냉동고 temperature 온도 minimize 최소화하다 reach out 연락하다 appreciate 감사하다 patience 인내

153 이메일의 목적은?

(A) 서로 다른 계약자 간의 작업을 조율하는 것

(B) 전기 회사의 변화를 발표하는 것

(C) 제안된 청구 인상에 대해 설명하는 것

(D) 서비스 중단 계획을 알리는 것

해설 | 주제/목적

첫 문장에서 주민 여러분께 알립니다(Attention, residents)라며 9월 15일 월요일에 A 빌딩, 9월 16일 화요일에 B 빌딩에서 정전이 있을 예정(Interruptions to electric power ~ September 16)이라고 전기 공급 중단 계획에 대해 공지하고 있으므로 정답은 (D)이다.

어휘 | contractor 계약자 announce 발표하다 explain 설명하다 proposed 제안된 billing 청구 increase 인상 disruption 중단

패러프레이징

지문의 Interruptions → 보기의 disruption

154 주민들은 무엇을 하라고 지시받는가?

(A) 발전기를 구입할 것

(B) 전자 제품 플러그를 뽑을 것

(C) 창문을 닫아 둘 것

(D) 로메로 씨와 만날 것

해설 | 세부 사항

두 번째 단락 중반부에 텔레비전과 컴퓨터와 같은 전자 장치의 플러그를 뽑으라(Unplug electronic equipment such as televisions and computers)고 지침을 내리고 있으므로 (B)가 정답이다.

155 [1], [2], [3], [4]로 표시된 곳 중에서 다음 문장이 들어가기에 가장 적합한 위치는?

"엘리베이터보다는 계단을 이용하십시오."

(A) [1]   (B) [2]   (C) [3]   (D) [4]

해설 | 문장 삽입

제시된 문장은 '엘리베이터보다는 계단을 이용하라'는 안전 지침이므로 귀하의 건물이 해당되는 날 다음 예방 조치를 따르라(Please take the following precautions on the day your building will be affected)고 지침을 내리며 비상 발전기로 로비와 계단 통로에 전기가 공급될 것(An emergency generator will provide electric service to lobbies and stairwells)이라고 계단과 관련된 내용을

언급한 문장 뒤에 들어가야 글의 흐름상 자연스럽다.
따라서 정답은 (C)이다.

[156-158] 안내문

카르도나 타운 스위트에 오신 것을 환영합니다!

156저희 숙소는 투숙객 여러분께 가정의 편안함과 사무실의 편리함을 제공하기 위해 설계되었습니다. 저희의 많은 편의 시설이 마음에 드시리라 확신합니다.

157, 158(C)무료 조식은 매일 아침 아이비룸에서 오전 7시부터 10시까지 제공되며, 그곳에서 커피, 차, 간식은 하루 종일 즐기실 수 있습니다. 매우 합리적인 가격의 저녁 뷔페는 화요일과 목요일 저녁에 날씨 상황에 따라 테라스나 주회의실에서 제공됩니다. 세탁 시설은 주차 구역의 동쪽에 위치한 시설 관리 건물에 있습니다. **158(A)**동전 세탁기와 건조기는 종일 이용 가능합니다.

저희 셀프 서비스 비즈니스 센터에는 필수 사무용품이 구비되어 있으며, **158(B)**무료 인터넷 접속과 컴퓨터 및 프린터 이용 서비스를 제공해 드리고 있습니다. **158(D)**미리 알려 주시면 안내 데스크 직원이 고객님을 위해 회의실을 예약해 드립니다.

저희 숙소에 머무시는 동안 생산적이고 즐거우시기를 바랍니다.

어휘 | accommodation 숙소 comfort 편안함 convenience 편리 amenities 편의 시설 complimentary 무료의 serve 제공하다 reasonably 합리적으로 patio 테라스 laundry 세탁 facility 시설 housekeeping 시설 관리 coin-operated washer 동전 세탁기 dryer 건조기 available 이용 가능한 stock 갖추다 essential 필수의 office supplies 사무용품 reserve 예약하다 advance 사전의 notice 통지 productive 생산적인

156 카르도나 타운 스위트는 주로 어떤 투숙객을 끌겠는가?

(A) 자녀가 있는 가족
(B) 출장 여행자
(C) 대학생
(D) 현지 방문 관광객

해설 | 추론
첫 문장에서 우리 숙소는 투숙객 여러분께 가정의 편안함과 사무실의 편리함을 제공하기 위해 설계되었습니다(Our accommodations ~ conveniences of an office)고 했으므로 주로 업무상 출장 중 숙소가 필요한 사람들을 위한 호텔임을 알 수 있다. 따라서 (B)가 정답이다.

157 투숙객은 낮에 어디에서 가벼운 간식을 구할 수 있는가?

(A) 안내 데스크   (B) 테라스
(C) 아이비룸   (D) 회의실

해설 | 세부 사항
두 번째 단락 첫 문장에서 무료 조식은 매일 아침 아이비룸에서 오전 7시부터 10시까지 제공되며 그곳에서 커피, 차, 간식은 하루 종일 즐기실 수 있다(A complimentary breakfast is served ~ snacks can be enjoyed there throughout the day)고 했으므로 정답은 (C)이다.

158 정보에 따르면, 투숙객이 직접 할 수 있는 일이 아닌 것은?

(A) 옷 세탁   (B) 문서 출력
(C) 식품 입수   (D) 회의실 예약

해설 | Not/True
세 번째 단락 마지막 문장에서 미리 알려 주시면 안내 데스크 직원이 고객님을 위해 회의실을 예약해 드린다(Front desk staff can reserve ~ with advance notice)고 안내하고 있으므로 정답은 (D)이다. 커피, 차, 간식은 하루 종일 즐길 수 있다고 했으므로 (C), 동전 세탁기와 건조기는 종일 이용 가능하다고 했으므로 (A), 무료 인터넷 접속과 컴퓨터 및 프린터를 이용할 수 있다고 했으므로 (B)는 모두 투숙객이 직접 할 수 있는 일이다.

[159-161] 편지

아보 항공 신용 카드
앤더슨 가 178번지
브리즈번 퀸즐랜드 4001

존 라오 씨
뱅크시아 코트 90
도츠우드 퀸즐랜드 4820

라오 씨께,

159새로운 아보 항공 신용 카드 소지자는 여행 포인트 5만점을 빠르게 적립할 수 있다는 것을 알고 계셨나요? 가입하는 것만으로 여행 포인트 2만점을 적립하실 수 있습니다. 그런 다음 아보 항공 신용 카드 사용 후 첫 3개월 이내에 천 달러를 쓰시면 3만 포인트가 추가로 적립됩니다. 75곳의 국내 및 해외 목적지로 비행하실 때에도 포인트가 적립됩니다. **160**또한 우리 항공편을 이용하실 때 아보 항공 신용 카드로 조기 탑승에 대한 자격이 부여됩니다. 뿐만 아니라 당사의 소중한 제휴 업체에서 할인을 받으실 수도 있습니다. 연회비 단 99달러로 이 모든 **161**혜택을 누리세요. 추가 정보를 원하시면, www.avoairlines.com/cc를 방문하세요.

데비 어바노, 회원 서비스
아보 항공 신용 카드

어휘 | sign up 등록하다 additional 추가의 national 국내의 destination 목적지 entitle 자격을 주다 boarding 탑승 eligible ~을 할 수 있는 valued 소중한 access 접근, 이용 benefit 혜택 annual fee 연회비

159 라오 씨는 아보 항공 신용 카드 개설 시 몇 점의 여행 포인트를 자동으로 받을 수 있는가?

(A) 10,000   (B) 20,000
(C) 30,000   (D) 50,000

해설 | 세부 사항
첫 문장에서 새로운 아보 항공 신용 카드 소지자는 여행 포인트 5만점을 빠르게 적립할 수 있다는 것을 알고 있는지(Did you know ~ Avo Airlines credit card holder?) 물으며 가입하는 것만으로 여행 포인트 2만점을 적립할 수 있다(Just for signing up, you will earn 20,000 travel points)고 했으므로 (B)가 정답이다.

160 아보 항공 신용 카드 소지자에 대해 언급된 것은?

(A) 항공권을 99달러 할인해 준다.
(B) 회사 항공편에서 우선 탑승 서비스를 누린다.
(C) 첫해에는 연회비를 내지 않는다.
(D) 포인트를 사용하여 비즈니스석으로 업그레이드할 수 있다.

해설 | Not / True
다섯 번째 문장에서 우리 항공편 이용 시 아보 항공 신용 카드로 조기 탑승에 대한 자격이 부여된다(Your Avo Airlines credit card ~ when flying with us)고 했으므로 (B)가 정답이다. 연회비 단 99달러로 이 모든 혜택을 누릴 수 있다고 했으므로 (A)는 오답이고 (C)와 (D)에 관련해서는 언급된 내용이 없으므로 답이 될 수 없다.

어휘 | priority 우선 seat 좌석

패러프레이징
지문의 early boarding → 보기의 priority boarding

161 첫 번째 단락 7행의 "benefits"와 의미가 가장 가까운 단어는?

(A) 이익   (B) 요청
(C) 지불   (D) 행사

해설 | 동의어
의미상 연회비 단 99달러로 이 모든 '혜택'을 누리라는 뜻으로 쓰인 것이므로 정답은 (A) advantages이다.

[162-164] 공지

일자리를 구하시나요?

¹⁶²배링턴 공공 도서관의 효과적인 구직 활동에 관한 시리즈 강연에 오세요!

¹⁶²⁽ᶜ⁾3월 4, 11, 18, 25일 수요일
¹⁶²⁽ᴮ⁾오후 6:30 – 오후 9:00

세션 1: 구직 기회 알아보기
세션 2: 이력서 작성하기

세션 3: 자기소개서 쓰기
세션 4: 효과적으로 면접 보기

전문 편집자 캐서린 트라우트맨과 함께 원하는 일자리를 얻는 업계의 비결을 배우세요. ¹⁶³특출한 이력서와 자기소개서를 작성하여 지원서를 눈에 띄게 만드는 방법을 가르쳐 드립니다.

행사는 무료이지만 각 세션은 선착순 응답자 40명으로 제한됩니다. ¹⁶⁴회답하시려면 eliebowitz@bpl.org 에이탄 리보위츠에게 이메일을 보내세요. 시리즈 전체 또는 개별 세션을 신청하실 수 있습니다.

어휘 | effective 효과적인 identify 알아보다 cover letter 자기소개서 trick 비결 application 지원(서) outstanding 특출한 respondent 응답자 RSVP 회답하다 registration 신청

162 시리즈에 대해 명시된 것은?

(A) 여러 곳에서 진행될 예정이다.
(B) 오전에 진행될 예정이다.
(C) 매달 제공될 예정이다.
(D) 도서관에서 열릴 예정이다.

해설 | Not / True
첫 문장에서 배링턴 공공 도서관의 효과적인 구직 활동에 관한 시리즈 강연에 오라(Come to Barrington Public Library's series ~ job search!)고 했으므로 정답은 (D)이다. 3월 소식만 있고(Wednesdays, March 4, 11, 18, 25), 오후 시간대로 편성되어 있으므로(6:30 P.M.–9:00 P.M.) (B), (C)는 오답이다.

163 시리즈에 참여하는 것에 대한 혜택으로 언급된 것은?

(A) 여러 업계 전문가의 일대일 도움
(B) 자기소개서 작성 요령
(C) 다른 참가자와 면접 연습
(D) 인맥을 쌓을 기회

해설 | Not / True
두 번째 문단 두 번째 문장에서 특출한 이력서와 자기소개서를 작성하여 지원서를 눈에 띄게 만드는 방법을 가르쳐 준다(She will teach you how to ~ outstanding résumé and cover letter)고 했으므로 정답은 (B)이다.

164 참가자가 세션에 등록하기 위해 해야 하는 것은?

(A) 트라우트맨 씨에게 대금 보내기
(B) 온라인 양식 작성하기
(C) 리보위츠 씨에게 연락하기
(D) 이력서 사본 제출하기

해설 | 세부 사항
마지막 문단 두 번째 문장에서 회답하려면 에이탄 리보위츠에게 이메일을 보내라(To RSVP, e-mail

Eitan Liebowitz at eliebowitz@bpl.org)고 했고, 이어서 시리즈 전체 또는 개별 세션을 신청할 수 있다(Registration is available ~ an individual session)고 했으므로 정답은 (C)이다.

[165-167] 이메일

발신: 마크 쿠니야
수신: 전 직원
제목: 섀넌 화이트
날짜: 5월 9일

전 직원 여러분:

165섀넌 화이트가 5월 12일에 중부 지역의 시카고 담당 영업 이사로 커리 조명 회사에 합류하게 됨을 발표하게 되어 기쁩니다. 우리 팀에 합류하기 전에 섀넌은 에너지 대사 법인(EAC)에서 다양한 역할로 근무했습니다. 섀넌은 대학을 나오자마자 EAC에서 영업 사원으로 경력을 시작하여 마침내 에반스턴 지점의 매장 관리자가 되었습니다. 마지막으로 섀넌은 지난 5년간 EAC의 영업 지점장으로 근무했습니다.

166섀넌은 동부 캘리포니아 대학교에서 경영학 학사 학위와 MBA 학위를 받았습니다. 재학 중 그녀는 싱가포르에서 지속 가능한 성장에 대해 연구를 수행했습니다. 여가 시간에는 현지 자선 단체에 자원해 어린이들에게 미술을 가르치고 있습니다. 또한 **167장거리 달리기를 즐기고 올해 말까지 첫 마라톤을 완주하기를 희망하고 있습니다.**

저와 함께 섀넌이 커리 조명 기구 팀에 오는 것을 환영해 주세요!

마크 쿠니야
영업 부사장
커리 조명 회사

어휘 | pleasure 기쁨 announce 발표하다 light fixture 조명 기구 region 지역 serve 근무하다 a variety of 다양한 ambassador 대사 corporation 회사 sales associate 영업 사원 eventually 결국 location 지점 regional 지역의 bachelor 학사 degree 학위 conduct 수행[실행]하다 sustainable 지속 가능한 spare 여분의, 여가의 volunteer 자원봉사하다 charity 자선 단체 distance running 장거리 경주

165 이메일의 목적은?

(A) 채용 공고
(B) 대학 프로그램 홍보
(C) 신규 직원 소개
(D) 이전 발표

해설 | 주제 / 목적
첫 문장에서 섀넌 화이트가 5월 12일에 중부 지역의 시카고 담당 영업 이사로 커리 조명 회사에 합류하게 됨을

발표하게 되어 기쁘다(It is my pleasure to announce ~ Sales Director for the central region)고 했으므로 새로운 직원을 소개하기 위한 글임을 알 수 있다. 따라서 정답은 (C)이다.

어휘 | advertise 광고하다 job opening 일자리 promote 홍보하다 introduce 소개하다 relocation 이전

166 화이트 씨에 대해 사실인 것은?

(A) EAC를 공동 창립했다.
(B) 두 개의 학위를 가지고 있다.
(C) 대학 수업을 가르쳐 왔다.
(D) 커리 조명 회사에서 여러 직책을 맡아 왔다.

해설 | Not / True
두 번째 단락 첫 문장에서 섀넌은 동부 캘리포니아 대학교에서 경영학 학사 학위와 MBA 학위를 받았다(Shannon has a bachelor's degree in business and an MBA degree from East California University)고 했으므로 (B)가 정답이다.

어휘 | co-found 공동 창립하다 academic 학업의 position 직책

167 화이트 씨는 연말까지 무엇을 할 계획인가?

(A) 지역 자선 단체 설립
(B) 싱가포르에서 구직
(C) 연구 프로젝트 완료
(D) 스포츠 행사 참가

해설 | 세부 사항
두 번째 단락 마지막 문장에서 섀넌이 장거리 달리기를 즐기고 올해 말까지 첫 마라톤을 완주하기를 희망하고 있다(She also enjoys distance running ~ complete her first marathon by the end of this year)고 했으므로 (D)가 정답이다.

어휘 | establish 설립하다 compete (시합 등에) 참가하다
패러프레이징
지문의 marathon → 보기의 a sports event

[168-171] 기사

6월 5일, 웨이브리지—**168, 171요리사인 로베르토 비앙키 씨와 안토니오 콘티 씨는 지난 10년간 런던 사람들을 위해 이탈리아 요리를 만들어 왔다.** 이제 그들은 도시 외곽에 그들의 첫 번째 식당을 개업했다. **171웨이브리지 플로어쌤 가에 있는 작은 식당인 포모도로는 5월 17일 개업하여 대단한 평가를 받았다.** **168지역 투자자인 케네스 멀그루 씨의 재정적 지원을 받은 그 식당은** 현대적인 실내 장식을 갖춘 아름다운 2층 벽돌 건물에 자리잡고 있다. 오전 11시에서 오후 10시까지 영업하는 포모도로는 이탈리아와 영국의 전통 음식을 혼합한 메뉴를 제공한다. 비앙키 씨는 "안토니오와 저는 영국 요리와 런던 문화에 크게 영향을 받았어요. 그런

부분을 저희 식당에서 제공하는 음식에 담고 싶어요."라고 말한다.

성공한 이 두 사람은 런던 웨스트엔드에 세 개의 식당을 소유하고 있다. **169이탈리아 카프리 근처에서 자란 비앙키 씨**는 아버지의 요리가 그에게 영감을 주었다고 말한다. "아버지께서 매일 밤 옛날식 가족 요리법으로 정성 들여 저녁 식사를 준비하셨어요." 이탈리아 요리를 정식으로 2년간 연구하고 수많은 워크숍에 참석한 후 **169비앙키 씨는 어린 시절 이웃인 안토니오 콘티 씨와 함께** 런던에 와서 벨라 리스토란테를 개업했다. 두 친구는 그 이후 식당 주인으로 성공했다.

콘티 씨는 "저희는 도시에 살고 있지 않는 사람들도 저희 음식을 즐길 수 있도록 만들려고 합니다. **170주변 도시로 쉽게 왕래할 수 있는 지역 기차역이 있어서 웨이브리지가 적합한 장소였어요.**"라고 설명한다.

포모도로는 예약을 받지만 일찌감치 예약해야 한다.

어휘 | cuisine 요리(법) bistro 작은 식당 review 평가 financial 재정적인 backing 지원 investor 투자자 contemporary 현대적인 fuse 융합시키다 incorporate A into B A를 B에 포함시키다 serve (음식을) 제공하다 cite A as B A를 B의 예로 들다 inspiration 영감, 기발한 생각 numerous 수많은 childhood 어린 시절 restaurateur 식당 주인 accessible 접근[이용] 가능한 logical 합당한, 이치에 맞는 surrounding 주변의

---

168 멀그류 씨는 비앙키 씨와 콘티 씨에게 무엇을 제공했겠는가?

(A) 부동산 목록
(B) 사업 자금
(C) 장식 서비스
(D) 메뉴 아이디어

해설 | 추론
첫 번째 단락 중반부에 지역 투자자인 케네스 멀그류 씨의 재정적 지원을 받은 그 식당(With the financial backing of Kenneth Mulgrew, a local investor, the restaurant ~)이라고 했고, 그 식당은 비앙키 씨와 콘티 씨의 식당을 가리키므로 정답은 (B)이다.

패러프레이징
지문의 the financial backing → 보기의 Funding

169 콘티 씨에 대해 암시된 것은?

(A) 웨이브리지에 거주한다.
(B) 비앙키 씨와 요리 학교에 다녔다.
(C) 이탈리아에서 자랐다.
(D) 영국 요리에 대한 수업을 들었다.

해설 | 추론
두 번째 단락 두 번째 문장에서 이탈리아 카프리 근처에서 자란 비앙키 씨(Mr. Bianchi, who grew up near Capri,

Italy)라고 했고, 이어서 네 번째 문장에서 비앙키 씨는 어린 시절 이웃인 안토니오 콘티 씨와 함께(Mr. Bianchi, together with his childhood neighbor Antonio Conti)라는 내용이 언급된다. 이를 통해 비앙키 씨와 마찬가지로 안토니오 콘티 씨도 이탈리아에서 자랐다는 것을 알 수 있으므로 정답은 (C)이다.

170 식당 부지로 웨이브리지가 선정된 이유는?

(A) 그곳에서 영업을 하는 것이 저렴하다.
(B) 다른 지역에서 그곳으로 가기 쉽다.
(C) 인구 밀도가 매우 높은 지역이다.
(D) 경치가 빼어난 해변 지역이다.

해설 | 세부 사항
세 번째 단락 마지막 문장에서 주변 도시로 쉽게 왕래할 수 있는 지역 기차역이 있어서 웨이브리지가 적합한 장소였다(Weybridge was a logical location because the local rail station makes it easy to get to and from surrounding towns)고 했으므로 정답은 (B)이다.

패러프레이징
지문의 surrounding towns → 보기의 other towns

171 [1], [2], [3], [4]로 표시된 곳 중에서 다음 문장이 들어가기에 가장 적절한 위치는?

"이제 그들은 도시 외곽에 그들의 첫 번째 식당을 개업했다."

(A) [1]   (B) [2]   (C) [3]   (D) [4]

해설 | 문장 삽입
주어진 문장의 '이제(Now)', '그들은(they)'을 통해, 현재까지 그들이 무엇을 했는지 소개되는 내용이 제시문 앞에 놓여야 한다는 것을 알 수 있다. [1] 앞에서 '그들'이라고 지칭할 수 있는 두 사람(Roberto Bianchi and Antonio Conti)이 소개되었고, 지난 10년간 런던 사람들을 위해 이탈리아 요리를 만들어 왔다(have been preparing Italian cuisine for Londoners for the past ten years)며 현재까지 해 온 일을 언급하고 있으므로 제시문이 [1]에 들어갈 수 있는 조건이 충족된다. 또한 지금까지는 런던 사람들을 위해서 요리했지만 런던이 아닌 도시 외곽에서 개업한 것은 처음이라는 연결도 자연스럽다. [1] 뒤에는 그 첫 번째 식당 이름(Pomodoro)이 등장하면서 해당 식당에 대한 소개가 이어지므로 앞뒤로 모두 자연스럽다. 따라서 정답은 (A)이다.

[172-175] 온라인 채팅

레티시아 클라크 (오후 1시 15분)
안녕하세요, 애나. **172퐁테 북스 판매 페이지에 무슨 문제가 있는지 아세요?**

애나 와이저 (오후 1시 17분)
죄송해요, 문제가 있는 줄 몰랐어요. 확인해 보겠습니다.

레티시아 클라크 (오후 1시 18분) **173**25분 전 즈음부터
고객 지원 센터에서 관련 전화를 받기 시작했어요. 지금은
점점 더 빈번해지고 있고요.

애나 와이저 (오후 1시 19분) 지금 보고 있어요. **172**고객이
"지금 구매" 버튼을 클릭하면 장바구니에 담긴 책이
사라지네요.

레티시아 클라크 (오후 1시 20분) 맞아요.

애나 와이저 (오후 1시 21분) 안녕하세요, 조셉. 퐁테 북스
온라인 주문서에 문제가 있는 것 같아요. **174, 175**제가
상황을 해결하는 동안 "유지 보수 관계로 페이지 중단"이라는
메시지를 게시해 주시겠어요?

조셉 일로모 (오후 1시 22분) 그럴게요. **175**얼마나 걸릴 것
같나요?

애나 와이저 (오후 1시 23분) **175**한 40분가량이요.

조셉 일로모 (오후 1시 24분) 좋아요.

레티시아 클라크 (오후 1시 25분) 고마워요, 애나.

애나 와이저 (오후 1시 26분) 당연한 걸요. 최대한 빨리 다시
순조롭게 운영되도록 조치하고 끝나면 두 분께 알릴게요.

어휘 | help line 고객 지원 센터 frequent 빈번한 disappear
사라지다 post 게시하다 maintenance 유지 보수 sort out
해결하다 smoothly 순조롭게 notify 알리다

172 채팅 토론에서 확인된 문제는?

(A) 콜센터에 일손이 부족하다.
(B) 인기 있는 책이 품절되었다.
(C) 온라인 쇼핑 포털사이트에서 주문을 처리할 수 없다.
(D) 기술 지원팀이 연결 문제를 해결할 수 없다.

해설 | 세부 사항
1시 15분에 클라크 씨가 애나에게 퐁테 북스 판매 페이지에
무슨 문제가 있는지 아는지(Do you know what ~ sales
page?) 물었고 1시 19분에 애나가 고객이 "지금 구매"
버튼을 클릭하면 장바구니에 담긴 책이 사라진다(When
a customer clicks ~ shopping cart disappear)고
했다. 따라서 웹페이지의 주문 절차에 문제가 생겼음이
확인되었으므로 정답은 (C)이다.

어휘 | understaffed 일손이 부족한 process 처리하다
crew 작업반 fix 고치다 connectivity 연결

173 클라크 씨는 누구로부터 전화를 받고 있는가?

(A) 도서 저자   (B) 사무실 직원
(C) 고객   (D) 판매 사원

해설 | 세부 사항
1시 18분에 클라크 씨가 25분 전 즈음부터 고객 지원
센터에서 관련 전화를 받기 시작했다(I started getting

calls ~ 25 minutes ago)고 했으므로 정답은 (C)이다.

174 일로모 씨는 무엇을 하라고 요청받는가?

(A) 판매 거래 완료
(B) 지사 연락
(C) 임시 메시지 게시
(D) 유지 보수 작업 연기

해설 | 세부 사항
1시 21분에 애나가 일로모 씨에게 자신이 상황을 해결하는
동안 "유지 보수 관계로 페이지 중단"이라는 메시지를
게시해 줄 수 있는지(Can you post a "Page down
for maintenance" message while I get everything
sorted out?)를 묻고 있으므로 (C)가 정답이다.

어휘 | branch 지사 temporary 임시의 postpone
연기하다 task 작업

패러프레이징
지문의 post → 보기의 Display

175 오후 1시 24분에 일로모 씨가 "좋아요"라고 쓴 의도는
무엇이겠는가?

(A) 제안된 계획을 받아들인다.
(B) 동료들과 곧 만날 예정이다.
(C) 마케팅 아이디어가 성공할 것이라고 생각한다.
(D) 와이저 씨가 회의록을 계속 작성하는 것에 기뻐한다.

해설 | 의도 파악
1시 21분에 애나가 일로모 씨에게 자신이 상황을 해결하는
동안 "유지 보수 관계로 페이지 중단"이라는 메시지를
게시해 줄 것(Can you post ~ everything sorted
out?)을 요청하자 1시 22분에 일로모 씨가 얼마나 걸릴
것 같냐(How long do you think you'll need?)고
물었고 1시 23분에 애나가 40분가량(Maybe about
40 minutes)이라고 대답하자 1시 24분에 일로모 씨가
좋다(Sounds good)고 대답했다. 따라서 메시지를
게시해달라는 애나의 제안을 수락하려는 의도로 한
말이므로 (A)가 정답이다.

어휘 | accept 받아들이다 proposed 제안된 colleague
동료 shortly 곧 meeting notes 회의록

[176-180] 이메일 + 이메일

수신: 칼 피커링 <kpickering@drakedistribution.org>
발신: no-reply@drakedistribution.org
날짜: 2월 3일
제목: 귀하의 비밀번호

드레이크 유통 직원께,

176귀하의 회사 비밀번호가 2월 8일에 만료되도록 설정되어
있습니다. 급여 포털, 직원 메시지 게시판, 드레이크 런즈

직업 개발 허브, **180회계 부서의 수치 기록 데이터베이스를** 포함한 모든 네트워크 서비스에 대한 이용이 영향을 받습니다.

이러한 네트워크 서비스를 중단 없이 이용하려면, 먼저 기존의 비밀번호를 사용해 직원 홈페이지에 로그인하십시오. 홈페이지의 오른쪽 상단 모서리에 있는 "설정" 탭을 누른 다음 "비밀번호 업데이트"를 선택하십시오. 새 비밀번호는 최소한 10자 이상이고, 대문자, 숫자 및 특수 문자를 하나 이상 포함해야 합니다. 새 비밀번호는 이전에 사용하던 것과 같아서는 안 됩니다. **177회사 비밀번호는 90일마다 변경해야 함을 알아 두세요.**

도움이 필요하시면 네트워크 관리자에게 helpdesk@drakedistribution.org로 연락하십시오.

어휘 | distribution 유통 corporate 기업의 expire 만료되다 access 접근 affect 영향을 미치다 payroll 급여 professional 전문적인 development 개발 accounting 회계 avoid 피하다 interrupt 중단하다 current 현재의 select 선택하다 character 문자 contain 포함하다 capital letter 대문자 previously 이전에 revise 변경하다 administrator 관리자

수신: helpdesk@drakedistribution.org
발신: 칼 피커링 <kpickering@drakedistribution.org>
날짜: 2월 5일
제목: 비밀번호 재설정

업무 지원 직원께,

귀하의 부서로부터 도움이 필요합니다. **179제가 사용하고자 하는 새 비밀번호는 귀하의 이메일에 명시된 사양에 178부합하며 전에 사용한 적도 없습니다. 하지만 반복된 시도에도 불구하고 저의 로그인 정보를 성공적으로 업데이트하지 못하고 있습니다.** 회사 시스템에 계속 접속할 수 있도록 도와주시겠습니까? **180금요일에 발표를 해야 해서 회계 데이터베이스에서 매출 통계가 필요합니다.** 오늘 근무 종료 전에 이 문제를 해결할 수 있도록 도와주시기 바랍니다.

칼 피커링

어휘 | reset 재설정 specification 명세 (사항) outline 개요를 서술하다 repeat 반복하다 attempt 시도 continue 계속하다 statistics 통계 resolve 해결하다

---

176 첫 번째 이메일의 목적은?

(A) 새로운 회사 정책 발표
(B) 직원에게 만료일 통지
(C) 새로운 직업 개발 과정 소개
(D) 계정이 삭제된 이유 설명

해설 | 주제 / 목적
첫 이메일의 첫 문장에서 직원에게 귀하의 회사 비밀번호가

2월 8일에 만료되도록 설정되어 있다(Your corporate password is set to expire on 8 February)고 알리고 있으므로 (B)가 정답이다.

어휘 | announce 발표하다 policy 정책 notify 통지하다 introduce 소개하다 explain 설명하다 delete 삭제하다

패러프레이징
지문의 expire on ~ → 보기의 a deadline

177 첫 번째 이메일에 명시된 것은?

(A) 로그인 정보를 주기적으로 변경해야 한다.
(B) 직원 홈페이지가 최근에 새롭게 구성되었다.
(C) 일부 데이터베이스는 유지 관리를 위해 오프라인 상태이다.
(D) 각 직원은 업무 지원 부서에 연락해야 한다.

해설 | Not / True
첫 이메일의 두 번째 단락 마지막 문장에서 회사 비밀번호는 90일마다 변경해야 함을 알아 두라(Please note that corporate passwords must be revised every 90 days)고 했으므로 (A)가 정답이다.

어휘 | periodically 주기적으로 recently 최근에 maintenance 유지 관리

패러프레이징
지문의 revised every 90 days → 보기의 changed periodically

178 두 번째 이메일에서, 첫 번째 단락 1행의 "meets"와 의미가 가장 가까운 단어는?

(A) 마주치다　　　　　　(B) 위치를 찾다
(C) 나타나다　　　　　　(D) 만족시키다

해설 | 동의어
의미상 새 비밀번호가 명시된 사양에 '부합한다'는 뜻으로 쓰인 것이므로 정답은 (D) satisfies이다.

179 피커링 씨에게 무슨 문제가 있는가?

(A) 업무 지원 부서에 건 전화에 회신을 받지 못했다.
(B) 직원 홈페이지 접속이 중단되었다.
(C) 비밀번호를 재설정할 수 없다.
(D) 웹페이지 링크가 없어졌다.

해설 | 세부 사항
두 번째 이메일의 두 번째 문장에서 제가 사용하고자 하는 새 비밀번호는 귀하의 이메일에 명시된 사양에 부합하며 전에 사용한 적도 없다(The new password ~ not been used before)고 했고 하지만 반복된 시도에도 불구하고 저의 로그인 정보를 성공적으로 업데이트하지 못하고 있다(Despite repeated attempts ~ login information successfully)고 했다. 따라서 피커링 씨는 비밀번호 변경에 어려움을 겪고 있는 것이므로 (C)가 정답이다.

어휘 | suspend 중단하다 lose 잃어버리다

<u>패러프레이징</u>
지문의 update → 보기의 reset

180 피커링 씨는 발표에 필요한 정보를 어디서 찾을 수 있을 것 같은가?

(A) 급여 포털
(B) 드레이크 런즈
(C) 수치 기록 데이터베이스
(D) 직원 메시지 게시판

해설 | 연계
두 번째 이메일의 다섯 번째 문장에서 피커링 씨가 금요일에 발표를 해야 해서 회계 데이터베이스에서 매출 통계가 필요하다(I must give a presentation on Friday and need the sales statistics from the accounting database for it)고 했는데, 첫 이메일의 두 번째 문장 마지막 부분(the accounting department's Figuretrack database)을 통해 회계 부서의 데이터베이스가 수치 기록 데이터베이스임을 알 수 있다. 따라서 정답은 (C)이다.

[181-185] 임대 계약서 + 이메일

임대 계약서

이 계약은 <u>11월 20일</u> 알렉스 에드워즈 (임대인)와 <u>조슈아 애들러와 메이지 애들러</u> (세입자) 사이에 이루어진 것으로 다음과 같은 조건으로 <u>오크 플레이스 42번지</u>에 위치한 주택을 임대한다.

항목 1: 거주
181세입자는 1월 1일부터 12월 31일까지 건물에 거주할 수 있다. 184해당 건물에서의 거주는 조슈아 애들러와 메이지 애들러 그리고 그들의 자녀들로 제한된다. 세입자의 손님은 1회 방문 시 연속 10일까지 건물에 머무를 수 있다.

항목 2: 지불
세입자는 매달 1,500달러를 지불하기로 동의한다. **185월세는 매월 1일 또는 그 전에 내야 한다.**

항목 3: 보증금
182세입자는 한 달치 월세에 상응하는 보증금을 지불한다. 이는 거주 기간 동안 발생할 수 있는 모든 훼손에 대해 보상하기 위한 것이다. 세입자가 입주 당시와 같은 상태로 퇴거할 경우, 보증금 전액은 반환된다. 임대인은 또한 미납된 월세를 충당하는 데 보증금을 사용할 수 있다.

항목 4: 공과금
세입자는 전기 요금, 가스 요금, 인터넷 요금을 공급업체에 직접 납부해야 한다. **183주간 쓰레기 수거 및 수도와 관련된 비용에 대해서는 임대인이 부담한다.**

임대인: <u>알렉스 에드워즈</u>
세입자: <u>조슈아 애들러, 메이지 애들러</u>
날짜: <u>11월 20일</u>

어휘 | agreement 계약(서) landlord 주인 renter 세입자 dwelling 주택 terms and conditions (계약 등의) 조건 occupancy (건물 등의) 사용 occupy (건물 등을) 사용[거주]하다 premises 부지 property 건물 consecutive 연이은 due (돈을) 지불해야 하는 security deposit 임대 보증금 intend 의도하다 cover (비용 등을) 보상하다 damage 훼손 occur 발생하다 entire 전체의 utilities 공과금 directly 직접 supplier 공급업자 associated with ~와 관련된 trash 쓰레기

발신: 메이지 애들러
수신: 알렉스 에드워즈
날짜: 6월 20일
제목: 임대 계약

에드워즈 씨께,

부탁이 하나 있습니다. **184저희 어머니께서 저희와 함께 2주 동안 지내셔도 될까요?** 어머니께서 8월 초에 집을 공사하실 계획인데 그 기간 동안 다른 거주하실 곳이 없습니다.

그리고 **185다음 달 월세를 수표로 방금 발송해 드렸으니 7월 1일 전에 받으실 수 있을 겁니다.** 지시하신 대로 새 주소로 보냈으니 참고하십시오.

배려해 주셔서 감사합니다.

메이지 애들러

어휘 | construction 공사 housing 주택 option 선택 사항 period 기간 check 수표 direct 지시하다

181 임대 계약서에 대해 명시된 것은?

(A) 1인 임차인을 위한 것이다.
(B) 오크 플레이스 42번지에서 서명되었다.
(C) 계약 기간은 1년이다.
(D) 갱신이 가능하다.

해설 | Not / True
임대 계약서 항목 1의 첫 문장에서 세입자는 1월 1일부터 12월 31일까지 건물에 거주할 수 있다(The renters may occupy the premises from January 1 through December 31)고 했으므로 임대 계약 기간이 1년임을 알 수 있다. 따라서 (C)가 정답이다.

<u>패러프레이징</u>
지문의 from January 1 through December 31 → 보기의 for one year

182 임대 보증금에 대해 언급된 것은?

(A) 한 달 치 월세와 같은 금액이다.

(B) 수표로 지불해야 한다.
(C) 첫 달 치 월세를 포함한다.
(D) 미납 공과금에 적용될 수 있다.

해설 | Not / True
임대 계약서 항목 3의 첫 문장에서 세입자는 한 달치 월세에 상응하는 보증금을 지불한다(The renters will pay a security deposit equal to one month's rent)고 했으므로 정답은 (A)이다.

패러프레이징
지문의 equal to one month's rent
→ 보기의 the same amount as a month's rent

183 임대인은 어떤 서비스에 대해 지불하는가?

(A) 전기   (B) 가스
(C) 인터넷   (D) 수도

해설 | 세부 사항
임대 계약서 항목 4의 두 번째 문장에서 주간 쓰레기 수거 및 수도와 관련된 비용에 대해서는 임대인이 부담한다(The landlord will be responsible ~ trash pickup and water)고 했으므로 정답은 (D)이다.

184 애들러 씨는 임대 계약서의 어떤 부분에 대해 예외를 요청했는가?

(A) 항목 1   (B) 항목 2
(C) 항목 3   (D) 항목 4

해설 | 연계
임대 계약서 항목 1의 두 번째 문장에서 해당 건물에서의 거주는 조슈아 애들러와 메이지 애들러 그리고 그들의 자녀들로 제한된다(Occupancy of this property ~ and their children)며 세입자의 손님은 1회 방문 시 연속 10일까지 건물에 머무를 수 있다(Guests of the renters ~ ten consecutive days per visit)고 했는데, 이메일의 첫 단락 두 번째 문장에서 애들러 씨가 어머니가 2주 동안 함께 지내도 되는지(Would it be possible ~ with us for two weeks?)를 묻고 있다. 어머니 즉, 손님이 14일간 머무는 것은 항목 1에 반하는 사항이므로 정답은 (A)이다.

185 애들러 씨가 월세 수표에 대해 암시하는 것은?

(A) 잘못된 주소로 보내졌다.
(B) 제때에 도착할 것이다.
(C) 새 계좌로부터 발급된 것이다.
(D) 배달 중에 분실되었을 수 있다.

해설 | 연계
임대 계약서 항목 2의 두 번째 문장에서 월세는 매월 1일 또는 그 전에 내야 한다(The rent is due on or before the first of every month)고 했고, 이메일의 두 번째 단락 첫 문장에서 다음 달 월세를 수표로 방금 발송해 드렸으니

7월 1일 전에 받을 수 있을 것(I have just mailed the check ~ before July 1st)이라고 했다. 따라서 월세 수표가 계약서에 명시된 때에 맞춰 도착할 것임을 암시한 것이므로 (B)가 정답이다.

[186-190] 이메일+일정+공지

수신: faisal-ali@znetmail.com
발신: a.skartsi@tourism.lavidas.gov
날짜: 7월 24일
제목: 회신: 최종 정보

알리 씨께,

1867월 30일에 있을 라비다스의 관광 재부흥 컨퍼런스를 위한 환영 만찬과 관련해 이메일을 주셔서 감사합니다. **187**채식 식사를 제공받으실 손님 명단에 귀하의 성함을 추가했습니다.

188컨퍼런스는 아이리스 호텔에서 열릴 예정입니다. 대중교통을 이용하시면, 포트 제임스 정류장에서 3번 버스나 5번 버스를 타시면 됩니다. 아이리스 호텔은 종점 바로 건너편 편리한 위치에 있습니다. 이 지역의 다른 두 호텔 모두 아이리스 호텔 입구에서 보여서 귀하께서 어느 호텔에 묵으시든 쉽게 찾아가실 수 있을 것입니다.

더 궁금하신 점이나 고민이 있으시면 알려 주세요.

알리샤 스카치

어휘 | reviving 되살아나는 vegetarian 채식주의자 public transportation 대중교통 depot 정류장 conveniently 편리하게 visible 보이는 entrance 입구 reach 도달하다

라비다스 섬 버스 시간표
5월부터 8월까지 월요일-일요일

#	노선	출발 시간	
		포트 제임스발	포트 제임스행
1	포트 제임스-멜라-암프라	오후 12시 30분, 오후 7시 30분	오전 8시, 오전 11시 30분
2	포트 제임스-카니시	오후 6시 45분	오전 8시 15분
1883	**포트 제임스-플라타-엘로디아**	오후 4시 30분	오전 7시 45분
1894	**포트 제임스-사미롤라**	오전 8시 15분, 오후 6시 30분	오전 7시, 오후 6시
1885	**포트 제임스-멜라-엘로디아**	오후 12시 45분, 오후 6시 45분	오전 9시 30분, 오전 11시 45분
6	포트 제임스-공항	오전 9시 30분, 정오, 오후 3시 15분	오전 10시 30분, 오후 1시, 오후 5시

186 알리 씨는 어떤 목적으로 라비다스 섬에 가는가?

(A) 현지 요리에 관한 수업을 하려고
(B) 섬의 관광 산업에 대해 배우려고
(C) 교통 세미나에 참석하려고
(D) 호텔을 시찰하려고

해설 | 세부 사항
이메일의 첫 문장에서 알리 씨에게 7월 30일에 있을 라비다스의 관광 재부흥 컨퍼런스를 위한 환영 만찬과 관련해 이메일을 주셔서 감사하다(Thank you for your e-mail ~ Tourism in Lavidas conference)고 한 것으로 보아 알리 씨는 라비다스의 관광 산업을 주제로 하는 컨퍼런스에 참석하고자 함을 알 수 있다. 따라서 (B)가 정답이다.

어휘 | cuisine 요리 inspection 시찰

187 스카치 씨는 알리 씨에 대해 어떤 정보를 알고 있는 것 같은가?

(A) 섬에 도착하는 시간
(B) 식단 요구 사항
(C) 체류하는 호텔
(D) 거주 국가

해설 | 추론
이메일의 첫 단락 두 번째 문장에서 스카치 씨가 알리 씨에게 채식 식사를 제공받으실 손님 명단에 귀하의 성함을 추가했다(I've added your name to the list of guests who will receive a vegetarian meal)고 한 것으로 보아 스카치 씨는 알리 씨의 채식 선호 성향을 이미 알고 있음을 알 수 있다. 따라서 (B)가 정답이다.

패러프레이징
지문의 meal → 보기의 dietary

188 아이리스 호텔은 어느 지역에 있는가?

(A) 포트 제임스
(B) 멜라

(C) 사미롤라
(D) 엘로디아

해설 | 연계
이메일의 두 번째 단락 첫 문장에서 컨퍼런스는 아이리스 호텔에서 열릴 예정(The conference will be held at the Iris Hotel)이며 대중교통을 이용하려면 포트 제임스 정류장에서 3번 버스나 5번 버스를 타면 된다(If you use public transportation ~ Port James depot)고 했다. 버스 시간표에 따르면 포트 제임스 정류장에서 출발하는 3번과 5번 버스의 공통적인 목적지는 엘로디아이므로 아이리스 호텔은 엘로디아에 위치하고 있음을 알 수 있다. 따라서 (D)가 정답이다.

189 7월 30일에 취소된 버스 노선은?

(A) 노선 1
(B) 노선 2
(C) 노선 4
(D) 노선 6

해설 | 연계
공지의 첫 문장에서 오늘 (7월 30일) 사미롤라로 가는 버스는 운행하지 않는다는 것을 알려 드리게 되어 유감(We are sorry to inform ~ no buses running to Samirola)이라고 했고, 버스 시간표에 따르면 운행이 취소된 사미롤라 행 버스는 노선 4번이므로 정답은 (C)이다.

190 공지에서 섬의 레스토랑에 대해 명시하는 것은?

(A) 버스표를 판매한다.
(B) 버스 정류장 가까이에 있다.
(C) 관광 성수기에는 연장 영업을 한다.
(D) 관광객들에게 기념품을 판매한다.

해설 | Not / True
공지의 두 번째 단락 두 번째 문장에서 승차권은 포트 제임스의 라비다스 버스 본사 또는 공항에서 구입하실 수 있다(Tickets are available ~ or in the airport)고 했고 섬 전역에 있는 레스토랑 및 상점에서도 판매되고 있다(They are also for sale in restaurants and shops across the island)고 했으므로 섬의 레스토랑에서 버스표를 판다는 것을 알 수 있다. 따라서 (A)가 정답이다.

어휘 | extend 연장하다 souvenir 기념품

[191-195] 웹페이지 + 회람 + 이메일

---
http://www.jlc.com

제이 리더십 컨설팅

홈	워크숍	코치 시간표	연락처

오늘날 비즈니스 환경에서, 제이 리더십 컨설팅은 귀사가

강력한 지도자와 효과적인 팀을 키울 수 있도록 지원합니다. **191우리는 소규모 그룹 워크숍 및 장기 개별 맞춤형 코칭 서비스를 제공하며, 모두 귀사의 작업 현장에서 편리하게 누리실 수 있습니다.** 두 코치 모두 15년 이상의 경력을 갖고 있으며 이 지역에서 가장 성공적인 조직들과 함께 일했습니다. 저명한 작가인 류칭 왕 박사는 직원들의 동기 부여를 보장하는 팀워크 개발 워크숍을 진행합니다. **195이본 제퍼슨은 리더십 기술과 성장 전략 개발을 위해 전문가들과 개별적으로 협력합니다.** www.jcl.com/coach_availability에서 온라인으로 코치들의 시간표를 확인하세요.

어휘 | environment 환경 effective 효과적인 personalized 개인 맞춤형의 conveniently 편리하게 region 지역 organization 조직 distinguished 저명한 facilitate 원활히 진행시키다 guarantee 보장하다 motivate 동기를 부여하다 professional 전문가 individual 개별적인 basis 기반 strategy 전략 availability 이용 가능성

회람

수신: SRT 부서 전문 직원
발신: 켄달 하킨, 본부장
날짜: 10월 12일
제목: 워크숍

날란 엔터프라이즈는 류칭 왕 박사님이 다음 주 이틀 동안 우리와 다시 함께하는 것을 기쁘게 생각합니다. **194왕 박사님이 워크숍을 진행하실 예정으로 여러분 중 많은 인원이 참석하기를 바랍니다.** 이 워크숍들에 대한 피드백은 항상 아주 좋았기 때문에 저는 여러분이 가능하면 참석할 것을 강력히 추천합니다.

강한 팀 만들기	10월 18일, 오전 9시 30분~오전 11시 30분	B 라운지, 3층
194아이디어 실행하기	10월 19일, 오전 10시~오전 11시 30분	웨스턴 룸

좌석이 한정되어 있으니, 날란의 온라인 이벤트 포털을 이용해 가능한 한 빨리 등록하세요. **192평소와 같이 워크숍에 참석하는 동안 업무상 책임이 완수될 있도록 사전에 담당 관리자와 확인하시기 바랍니다.**

어휘 | division 부서 positive 긍정적인 recommend 추천하다 seating 좌석 register 등록하다 beforehand 사전에

수신: info@jlc.com
발신: 알렉스 윌리
날짜: 10월 22일
제목: 다음 단계

안녕하세요.

194며칠 전, 저는 날란 엔터프라이즈에서 열린 왕 박사님의 워크숍 중 하나에 참석했습니다. 전날 워크숍에 대한 동료들의 긍정적인 평가를 듣고 등록했습니다. 저는 운이 좋게도 이 매우 고무적인 상호 소통형 워크숍에서 마지막 남은 자리를 차지하게 되었습니다. 우리가 했던 그룹 활동은 매우 유익했습니다.

193, 195왕 박사님이 도중에 제이 리더십 컨설팅이 1대 1 코칭도 제공하고 있다고 언급하셨는데요. 제 상관인 하킨 씨와 그 코칭의 이용 가능성에 대해 이야기했는데, 하킨 씨가 제 생각을 지지해 주셨습니다. 옵션에 대해 좀 더 알려 주시겠습니까?

감사합니다.

알렉스 윌리

어휘 | participate in ~에 참여하다 sign up 등록하다 colleague 동료 previous 이전의 inspiring 고무적인 interactive 상호 작용을 하는 beneficial 유익한 possibility 가능성 support 지지하다

---

191 제이 리더십 컨설팅 워크숍은 보통 어디에서 진행되는가?

(A) 호텔 연회장
(B) 인터넷
(C) 본사
(D) 고객 사무실

해설 | 세부 사항
웹페이지의 두 번째 문장에서 우리(제이 리더십 컨설팅)는 소규모 그룹 워크숍 및 장기 개별 맞춤형 코칭 서비스를 제공하며 모두 귀사의 작업 현장에서 편리하게 누릴 수 있다(We offer small-group workshops ~ conveniently delivered at your work site)고 했으므로 (D)가 정답이다.

패러프레이징
지문의 work site → 보기의 offices

192 회람은 워크숍 참석자들에게 무엇을 하라고 지시하는가?

(A) 상관과 상의할 것
(B) 새로운 사업 아이디어를 개발할 것
(C) 다른 사람에게 워크숍을 추천할 것
(D) 워크숍에 대해 피드백을 제공할 것

해설 | 세부 사항

회람의 두 번째 단락 마지막 문장에서 평소와 같이 워크숍에 참석하는 동안 업무상 책임이 완수될 수 있도록 사전에 담당 관리자와 확인하기 바란다(As usual, check with your manager ~ attending the workshop)고 지시했으므로 정답은 (A)이다.

어휘 | consult 상의하다 supervisor 관리자

패러프레이징
지문의 check with your manager
→ 보기의 Consult their supervisors

193 월리 씨는 왜 이메일을 보냈는가?

(A) 추천서를 제공하려고
(B) 프로그램에 대해 문의하려고
(C) 약속을 연기하려고
(D) 워크숍에 대해 불평하려고

해설 | 주제 / 목적

이메일의 두 번째 단락 첫 문장에서 왕 박사님이 제이 리더십 컨설팅이 1대 1 코칭도 제공하고 있다고 언급했다(At one point, Dr. Wang ~ one-on-one coaching)고 했고, 상관인 하킨 씨와 그 코칭의 이용 가능성에 대해 이야기했는데 하킨 씨가 제 생각을 지지해 주었다(I spoke with my boss ~ supported the idea)며 옵션에 대해 좀 더 알려 줄 수 있는지(Can you tell me more about the options?)를 묻고 있다. 따라서 월리 씨는 제이 리더십 컨설팅의 1대 1 코칭에 대해 문의하려고 이메일을 작성한 것이므로 (B)가 정답이다.

어휘 | reference 추천서 inquire 문의하다 postpone 연기하다

194 〈아이디어 실행하기〉 워크숍에 대해 사실일 것 같은 것은?

(A) 정원으로 진행되었다.
(B) 나중으로 연기되었다.
(C) 오후 늦게 열렸다.
(D) 참석자들로부터 형편없는 피드백을 받았다.

해설 | 연계

회람의 첫 단락 두 번째 문장에서 왕 박사님이 워크숍을 진행한다(Dr. Wang will be leading workshops)고 했고 아래에 있는 표에 따르면 이틀째 되는 날 〈아이디어 실행하기〉 워크숍을 진행했음을 알 수 있다. 이메일의 첫 문장에서 월리 씨는 며칠 전 날란 엔터프라이즈에서 열린 왕 박사님의 워크숍 중 하나에 참석했다(A couple of days ago ~ Narlan Enterprises)며 전날 워크숍에 대한 동료들의 긍정적인 평가를 듣고 등록했고(I signed up ~ previous day's workshop) 운 좋게도 이 워크숍에서 마지막 남은 자리를 차지하게 되었다(I was lucky ~ interactive workshop)고 했다. 이를 종합해 보면 월리 씨는 둘째 날에 왕 박사님의 워크숍 즉, 〈아이디어 실행하기〉에 참석했고 마지막 자리를 차지하게 되었다고 했으므로 워크숍 인원이 꽉 찼음을 알 수 있다. 따라서

정답은 (A)이다.

195 월리 씨의 이메일을 받은 사람은 어떤 대응을 할 것 같은가?

(A) 월리 씨에게 환불해 준다.
(B) 등록 양식을 작성한다.
(C) 제퍼슨 씨의 서비스를 제안한다.
(D) 팀워크 개발 기회에 대해 정보를 제공한다.

해설 | 연계

이메일의 두 번째 단락 첫 문장에서 왕 박사님이 제이 리더십 컨설팅이 1대 1 코칭도 제공하고 있다고 언급했다(At one point, Dr. Wang ~ one-on-one coaching)며 옵션에 대해 좀 더 알려 줄 수 있는지(Can you tell me more about the options?)를 묻고 있다. 1대 1 코칭 옵션에 대해서는 웹페이지의 다섯 번째 문장에서 이본 제퍼슨은 리더십 기술과 성장 전략 개발을 위해 전문가들과 개별적으로 협력한다(Yvonne Jefferson works ~ skills and strategies for growth)는 정보가 있으므로 이메일 수신인은 이본 제퍼슨의 개인 코칭을 제안할 것임을 짐작할 수 있다. 따라서 (C)가 정답이다.

어휘 | registration 등록 form 양식 opportunity 기회

[196-200] 보도 자료 + 이메일 + 초대장

긴급 보도
10월 13일

연락처: 루비 레이몬드,
rraymond@sunnyplazahotel.com.jm

(킹스턴)—**196**킹스턴의 세인트 루시아 가에 위치한 **198**서니 플라자 호텔은 10월 28일에 레스토랑 선샤인 그릴을 재개점한다고 오늘 발표했다. **196, 198**이 레스토랑은 대대적인 보수 공사를 거쳐 30명 이상의 손님을 위해 예약될 수 있는 연회장을 추가하였다. 마크 실바는 모든 레스토랑 운영을 감독하는 총괄 요리사로 남고, 레이카 엘리슨이 연회 및 음식 공급 부문을 위한 수석 요리사 역할을 맡게 된다.

서니 플라자 매니저인 데릭 코르도바는 "우리는 이번 변화에 대해 기대가 큽니다. 서니 플라자는 하룻밤 투숙객들을 위해 항상 최고의 경험을 선사해 왔습니다. 이제는 비즈니스 및 사교 행사를 위한 환경도 제공할 수 있게 되었습니다."라고 말했다. **197**서니 플라자 호텔은 70개의 객실, 피트니스 구역, 비즈니스 센터 및 회의 공간을 제공하고 있다.

어휘 | immediate 즉각적인 release 보도 announce 발표하다 extensive 광범위한 remodeling 개보수 addition 추가 banquet 연회 space 공간 reserve 예약하다 remain 남아 있다 executive chef 총괄 요리사 oversee 감독하다 operation 운영 assume 맡다 role 역할 catering 음식 공급 top-notch 최고의 overnight 하룻밤 동안의 setting 환경[장소] social 사회적인

수신: 데릭 코르도바
발신: 레이카 엘리슨
날짜: 10월 20일
제목: 예약 요청

안녕하세요, 데릭.

¹⁹⁸킹스턴 과학 협회(KSA)의 연례 만찬 행사를 이곳 서니 플라자 호텔에 있는 우리 연회장에서 개최해 달라는 요청을 전달해 주셔서 감사합니다. 괜찮으시다면 **²⁰⁰KSA 행사일을 11월 25일로 확정하기 전에 10월 31일까지 기다리고 싶습니다.** 주방은 현재 전 직원으로 운영되지만 서비스 직원에는 여전히 약간의 공백이 있습니다. KSA처럼 대규모 단체 손님을 응대하려면 최소 12명의 서버가 필요합니다. 행사일까지 직원들이 충분히 교육을 받을 거라고 확신할 수 있도록 일정을 약속하기 전에 직원부터 충원하고 싶습니다. 이로 인한 약간의 지연이 문제가 되는지 알려 주세요.

감사합니다.

레이카

어휘 | forward 전달하다 request 요청 association 협회 annual 연례의 acceptable 받아들일 수 있는 confirm 확정하다 fully 완전히 staffed 직원이 있는 gap 공백 handle 처리하다 fill 채우다 commit 약속하다 confident 자신 있는 delay 지연

KSA

¹⁹⁹킹스턴 과학 협회(KSA)는 레오넬 아빌라를 웅거 기술 및 혁신상의 첫 수상자로 지명하게 된 것을 자랑스럽게 생각합니다. 협회의 연례 만찬에서 이 성과를 축하하는 자리에 함께해 주시기 바랍니다.

²⁰⁰12월 29일 금요일 오후 6시 30분
노던 뷰 컨퍼런스 센터, 오팔 룸
킹스턴 시모어 가 130번지

킹스턴 비즈니스 경영인 에드워드 웅거의 아낌없는 후원으로 가능해진 이 상을 본드라 스티븐스 KSA 회장이 시상할 예정입니다.

12월 20일까지 jblissett@ksa.com.jm으로 행사 진행자인 재닌 블리셋에게 회신해 주십시오.

어휘 | recognise 인정하다 recipient 수령인 innovation 혁신 award 상 celebrate 축하하다 achievement 성과 president 회장 present 제시하다 generous 후한 sponsorship 후원 respond 응답하다 coordinator 진행자

---

196 보도 자료에서 무엇을 발표하는가?

(A) 새로운 호텔 건설
(B) 보수 공사의 완료

(C) 총괄 요리사 채용
(D) 레스토랑 메뉴 업데이트

해설 | **주제/목적**
보도 자료의 첫 문장에서 킹스턴의 세인트 루시아 가에 위치한 서니 플라자 호텔은 10월 28일에 레스토랑 선샤인 그릴을 재개점한다고 오늘 발표했다(The Sunny Plaza Hotel ~ Sunshine Grill, on 28 October)며 이 레스토랑은 대대적인 보수 공사를 거쳐 30명 이상의 투숙객을 위해 예약될 수 있는 연회장을 추가하였다(The restaurant has gone ~ 30 or more guests)고 했다. 호텔 레스토랑의 보수 공사 완료 및 재개점을 발표하고 있으므로 (B)가 정답이다.

어휘 | construction 건설 completion 완료
패러프레이징
지문의 remodeling → 보기의 a renovation project

197 보도 자료에 따르면, 서니 플라자 호텔은 무엇을 제공하는가?

(A) 대규모 그룹에 대한 할인
(B) 드라이클리닝 서비스
(C) 수영장
(D) 운동 기구

해설 | **세부 사항**
보도 자료의 마지막 문장에서 서니 플라자 호텔은 70개의 객실, 피트니스 구역, 비즈니스 센터 및 회의 공간을 제공하고 있다(The Sunny Plaza Hotel offers 70 guest rooms, ~ a meeting space)고 했으므로 정답은 (D)이다.

패러프레이징
지문의 a fitness area → 보기의 Exercise equipment

198 엘리슨 씨가 받은 예약 요청에 대해 암시된 것은?

(A) 바로 확정될 것이다.
(B) 12개의 객실에 대한 것이다.
(C) 최소 30명 이상의 손님이 있는 행사이다.
(D) 레이몬드 씨가 처리할 것이다.

해설 | **연계**
이메일의 첫 문장에서 엘리슨 씨가 킹스턴 과학 협회(KSA)의 연례 만찬 행사를 이곳 서니 플라자 호텔에 있는 우리 연회장에서 개최해 달라는 요청을 전달해 주셔서 감사하다(Thank you for forwarding ~ Sunny Plaza Hotel)고 했다. 서니 플라자 호텔에 대해서는 보도 자료의 첫 번째 문장에서 소개하며 이 레스토랑은 대대적인 보수 공사를 거쳐 30명 이상의 손님을 위해 예약될 수 있는 연회장을 추가하였다(The restaurant has gone ~ 30 or more guests)고 했으므로 엘리슨 씨는 30명 이상을 위해 예약될 수 있는 연회장에서 행사를 열겠다는 요청을 받은 것이 된다. 따라서 (C)가 정답이다.

실전 모의고사 04

패러프레이징
지문의 30 or more guests → 보기의 at least 30 guests

199 초대장에 따르면, 누가 상을 받을 예정인가?

(A) 아빌라 씨　　　　　(B) 스티븐스 씨
(C) 블리셋 씨　　　　　(D) 웅거 씨

해설 | 세부 사항
초대장의 첫 문장에서 킹스턴 과학 협회(KSA)는 레오넬 아빌라를 웅거 기술 및 혁신상의 첫 수상자로 지명하게 된 것을 자랑스럽게 생각한다(The Kingston Science Association ~ Innovation Award)고 했으므로 (A)가 정답이다.

200 KSA 행사에 대해 암시된 것은?

(A) 처음으로 열린다.
(B) 오후 6시 30분에 끝날 예정이다.
(C) 서니 플라자 호텔에서 열린다.
(D) 다른 날짜로 옮겨졌다.

해설 | 연계
이메일의 두 번째 문장에서 KSA 행사일을 11월 25일로 확정하기 전에 10월 31일까지 기다리고 싶다(I would like to wait ~ KSA event date of 25 November)고 했는데, 초대장의 두 번째 단락에 적힌 행사 일자는 12월 29일 금요일(Friday, 29 December)인 것으로 보아 KSA의 행사일이 바뀐 것을 알 수 있다. 따라서 정답은 (D)이다.

ETS 실전 모의고사 05　　　　본책 p. 237

147 (C)	**148** (D)	**149** (C)	**150** (D)	**151** (D)
152 (C)	**153** (C)	**154** (B)	**155** (B)	**156** (C)
157 (A)	**158** (C)	**159** (B)	**160** (D)	**161** (B)
162 (A)	**163** (D)	**164** (C)	**165** (D)	**166** (B)
167 (A)	**168** (B)	**169** (C)	**170** (B)	**171** (C)
172 (A)	**173** (B)	**174** (C)	**175** (C)	**176** (C)
177 (D)	**178** (B)	**179** (A)	**180** (A)	**181** (C)
182 (B)	**183** (A)	**184** (C)	**185** (A)	**186** (B)
187 (C)	**188** (A)	**189** (B)	**190** (D)	**191** (A)
192 (C)	**193** (A)	**194** (D)	**195** (B)	**196** (B)
197 (D)	**198** (D)	**199** (A)	**200** (C)	

[147-148] 전단

> **홀랜드빌 공공 도서관**
> **연례 도서 판매**
> **10월 12일 금요일부터 10월 16일 화요일까지**
>
> • 모든 장르의 중고 책을 헐값에 구입하세요!

• 도서 기부는 9월 15일부터 10월 7일까지 받습니다. 기부하시려면 조심스럽게 사용한 책들을 안내 데스크로 가져오세요.
• 판매는 도서관 카페 바깥쪽 B실에서 진행됩니다.
• **147모든 수익금은 어린이 소장 도서를 업데이트하는 데 쓰일 예정입니다.**
• **1485달러의 정액 요금에는 입장료와 멋진 각인 책갈피가 포함됩니다.**

어휘 | annual 연례의　purchase 구입하다　genre 장르　bargain 값싼　donation 기부　accept 받아 주다　donate 기부하다　gently 부드럽게　proceeds 수익금　collection 소장품　flat fee 정액 요금　admission 입장　engraved 새겨진　bookmark 책갈피

147 홀랜드빌 공공 도서관에 대해 명시된 것은?

(A) 첫 번째 도서 판매를 주최한다.
(B) 일년 내내 도서 판매 기부를 받는다.
(C) 어린이 도서 부문이 개선될 것이다.
(D) 도서 판매에서 일할 자원봉사자를 찾고 있다.

해설 | Not / True
네 번째 항목에서 모든 수익금은 어린이 소장 도서를 업데이트하는 데 쓰일 예정(All proceeds will go ~ children's collection)이라고 했으므로 어린이 도서 부문이 개선될 것임을 알 수 있다. 따라서 (C)가 정답이다.

어휘 | host 주최하다　section 부문　volunteer 자원봉사자

패러프레이징
지문의 updating → 보기의 improved

148 입장료에는 무엇이 포함되는가?

(A) 책
(B) 카페 상품권
(C) 회원 할인
(D) 책갈피

해설 | 세부 사항
마지막 항목에서 5달러의 정액 요금에는 입장료와 멋진 각인 책갈피가 포함된다(A flat fee of ~ engraved bookmark)고 했으므로 (D)가 정답이다.

[149-150] 문자 메시지

> **샤디아 알로타이비 (오전 10시 15분)**
> 로시오, **149지난주 채용 박람회에서 저와 이야기해 주셔서 다시 한 번 감사드려요.** 이력서 작성에 대한 팁이 도움이 되었습니다. 만나서 제 이력서를 검토해 주시기로 한 것이 아직 가능한가요?
>
> **로시오 수자 (오전 10시 16분)**
> 물론이에요. 시내에 있는 제 사무실에 들를 수 있나요? 오후 4시 이후 아무 때나 좋아요.

샤디아 알로타이비 (오전 10시 18분)

죄송하지만 오늘은 안 되겠어요. 제 차가 종일 자동차 정비소에 있을 예정이에요.

로시오 수자 (오전 10시 19분)

¹⁵⁰저는 지역 남동부에 살고 있어요. 당신이랑 가깝지 않나요? 퇴근 후에 근처 어딘가에서 만날 수 있을 거예요.

샤디아 알로타이비 (오전 10시 20분)

그게 더 수월하겠네요. 레몬 트리 카페 아세요? 그럼, 오늘 저녁 6시 30분 어떨까요?

로시오 수자 (오전 10시 22분)

방금 제 일정을 확인했는데, 네, 거기 어딘지 알아요. 그때 봐요!

어휘 | career fair 채용 박람회 résumé 이력서 review 검토하다 stop by 들르다 auto shop 자동차 정비소 in the vicinity 근처에서

---

149 알로타이비 씨는 왜 수자 씨에게 연락하고 있는가?

(A) 후속 취업 면접을 잡기 위해
(B) 자동차 정비소 서비스에 대해 보고하기 위해
(C) 전문적인 지도를 요청하기 위해
(D) 약속을 놓친 것에 대해 사과하기 위해

해설 | 주제 / 목적
10시 15분에 알로타이비 씨가 지난주 채용 박람회에서 저와 이야기해 주셔서 다시 한 번 감사드린다(thanks again for ~ last week)고 했고 이력서 작성에 대한 팁이 도움이 되었다(Your tips on résumé writing helped)며 만나서 제 이력서를 검토해 주시기로 한 것이 아직 가능한지(Are you still able to meet to review mine?) 묻고 있으므로 정답은 (C)이다.

어휘 | arrange 주선하다 follow-up 후속의 professional 전문적인 guidance 지도 apologize 사과하다 miss 놓치다 appointment 약속

150 오전 10시 20분에 알로타이비 씨가 "그게 더 수월하겠네요"라고 쓴 의도는 무엇이겠는가?

(A) 그녀의 동네에는 카페가 많다.
(B) 수자 씨의 사무실 건물이 익숙하다.
(C) 시내로 가는 버스 노선이 많다.
(D) 제안된 만남이 편하다.

해설 | 의도 파악
10시 19분에 수자 씨가 저는 지역 남동부에 살고 있다(I live in the southeast part of town)고 했고 당신이랑 가깝지 않냐(Isn't that close to you?)고 물으며 퇴근 후에 근처 어딘가에서 만날 수 있을 것(We could meet somewhere in the vicinity after work hours)이라고 하자 10시 20분에 알로타이비 씨가 그게 더

수월하겠다(That might be easier)고 했다. 따라서 퇴근 후 남동부 지역에서 만나자는 수자 씨의 제안이 편할 것 같다고 호응하며 한 말이므로 (D)가 정답이다.

어휘 | neighborhood 동네 familiar 익숙한 suggested 제안된 convenient 편리한

[151-152] 제품 설명

애더슨 산업
보안 경보 시스템

애더슨 산업 경보는 보안상 조기 감지가 중대한 건물 구역을 위해 설계되었습니다. ¹⁵¹일반적으로 실험실, 산업용 건물 및 기록 보관소에 설치되며 해당 시스템이 설치되는 특정 환경에 맞게 조정이 가능합니다. ¹⁵¹최신 카메라 기술 외에도, 적외선 온도 센서와 상시 감시 옵션이 있습니다.

시스템은 최첨단 무선 및 자동화 기술을 이용해 움직임이나 온도 변화를 감지하면 수 초 이내에 중앙 감시소로 알림을 보냅니다. ¹⁵²월 단위 또는 연 단위로 모니터링 계약이 가능합니다.

어휘 | security 보안 alarm 경보 detection 감지 critical 중요한 typically 일반적으로 install 설치하다 laboratory 실험실 industrial 산업용의 archive 기록 보관소 adjust 조정하다 specific 특정한 infrared 적외선의 temperature 온도 24-7 (하루 24시간, 7일간이라는 뜻으로) 항상 monitoring 감시 state-of-the-art 최첨단의 automation 자동화 notification 알림 detect 감지하다 annual 매년의

151 제품에 대해 언급된 것은?

(A) 주거 건물용이다.
(B) 문자 메시지 알림을 보낸다.
(C) 야외에서 사용하기에 적합하다.
(D) 열 변화를 감지하는 센서가 있다.

해설 | Not / True
첫 단락의 마지막 문장에서 최신 카메라 기술 외에도 적외선 온도 센서와 상시 감시 옵션이 있다(In addition to the newest ~ 24-7 monitoring)고 했으므로 정답은 (D)이다. 일반적으로 실험실, 산업용 건물 및 기록 보관소에 설치된다고 했으므로 (A)와 (C)는 오답이고, 문자 메시지에 대한 언급은 없으므로 (B)도 답이 될 수 없다.

어휘 | intend 의도하다 residential 주거의 suitable 적합한 outdoor 야외의

패러프레이징
지문의 temperature → 보기의 heat

152 고객에게 이용 가능한 옵션은?

(A) 카메라 업그레이드
(B) 추가 전화선
(C) 연간 모니터링 계약
(D) 무료 설치

해설 | 세부 사항
두 번째 단락의 마지막 문장에서 월 단위 또는 연 단위로 모니터링 계약이 가능하다(Contracts for monitoring on a monthly or annual basis are available)고 했으므로 (C)가 정답이다.

패러프레이징
지문의 annual → 보기의 Yearly

[153-154] 안내

http://www.cosdhr.gov

스틸즈빌 시
인사부
개정된 입사 지원 절차 공지

¹⁵³6월 1일부터, 스틸즈빌 시 인사부(DHR)는 오로지 인터넷으로 제출된 입사 지원서만 받을 예정입니다. 서면으로 작성된 지원서는 거부됩니다.

절차를 시작하려면 www.cosdhr.gov/sign-up으로 방문하여 개인 프로필을 생성하세요. 그 다음 제출 버튼을 누르고 사용자 이름과 비밀번호를 설정하십시오. 로그온 인증을 통해 귀하의 관심사와 능력에 부합하는 직책을 고용 데이터베이스에서 검색할 수 있습니다. 적합한 직책을 찾고 나면 이름을 클릭하고 지원서를 작성한 뒤 이력서와 자기소개서를 업로드하십시오. ¹⁵⁴자기소개서에 지원서 상단에 있는 직책의 참조 번호를 기입해 주십시오. 주의: 이 두 문서가 없는 지원서는 검토되지 않습니다.

웹사이트에 문제가 있을 경우, 555-0125번으로 24시간 기술 지원 센터에 전화하시거나 techsupport@cosdhr.gov로 이메일을 보내 주십시오.

어휘 | notice 공지 revised 개정된 application 지원 process 절차 effective 시행되는 accept 받다 employment 고용 electronically 인터넷으로 decline 거절하다 credential 인증(서) enable 가능하게 하다 appropriate 적합한 reference number 참조 번호 support 지원

---

153 안내에서 DHR에 대해 명시하는 것은?

(A) 더 이상 이력서를 제출할 필요가 없다.
(B) 고용 데이터베이스를 매주 갱신한다.
(C) 종이 서류로 제출된 입사 지원서를 거부할 것이다.
(D) 고용 문의에 24시간 이내에 응답한다.

해설 | Not / True
첫 문장에서 6월 1일부터 스틸즈빌 시 인사부(DHR)는 오로지 인터넷으로 제출된 입사 지원서만 받을 예정(Effective June 1, the Department of Human Resources ~ submitted electronically)이라며 서면으로 작성된 지원서는 거부된다(Paper-based applications will be declined)라고 했으므로 (C)가 정답이다.

어휘 | submission 제출 inquiry 문의

패러프레이징
지문의 Paper-based applications will be declined. → 보기의 will refuse job applications submitted on paper

---

154 구직자들은 무엇을 하라고 요청받는가?

(A) 정기적으로 사용자 이름을 변경할 것
(B) 자기소개서에 참조 번호를 표기할 것
(C) 지원서에 경력 목표를 기재할 것
(D) 각 지원서마다 추천서 두 장을 제출할 것

해설 | 세부 사항
두 번째 단락 후반부에 자기소개서에 지원서 상단에 있는 직책의 참조 번호를 기입하라(Please include the position's reference number ~ in your cover letter)고 했으므로 (B)가 정답이다.

어휘 | regularly 정기적으로

[155-157] 뉴스 기사

인도 뭄바이 6월 3일—지난 5년 동안 뭄바이의 유력 항공사였던 ¹⁵⁵스타 에어웨이즈가 보유하고 있는 모든 항공기를 유럽산 스카이스트림 제트기로 교체할 계획이라고 밝혔다. 스타 에어웨이즈는 일차적으로 제트기 90대를 구매하고, ¹⁵⁶기체 변경을 완료하기까지 10년이 걸릴 것으로 예상하고 있다. ¹⁵⁷(C), (D)새로운 항공기들은 낙후된 항공기들을 교체하는 동시에 이 항공사가 국제 항로를 확장할 수 있도록 할 것이다. 스타 에어웨이즈와 스카이스트림은 목요일에 브뤼셀 에어쇼에서 항공기 주문에 신형 AWB850 항공기 17대가 포함되어 있음을 공동 발표했다. ¹⁵⁷(B)이로써 스타 에어웨이즈는 AWB850 기종을 이용하는 첫 번째 인도 항공사가 될 것이며, 이는 이 강력한 제트기가 처음 생산된 이래로 스타 에어웨이즈가 품어 왔던 목표이다.

어휘 | dominant 지배적인, 가장 유력한 airline 항공사 replace 교환하다 aircraft 항공기 fleet (한 회사 소속의) 항공기, 선박 jet 제트기 initial 초기의 purchase 구매 changeover 전환, 변경 decade 10년 complete 완료하다 expand 확장하다 replacement 대체, 교환 aging 노화하는, 고물이 되어 가는 joint announcement 공동 발표 carrier 항공 회사 aim 목표

155 이 기사의 목적은?

(A) 공항의 최근 보수 공사에 대해 설명하는 것
(B) 새로운 사업 계약을 발표하는 것
(C) 투자자들에게 최신 프로젝트 계획을 알리는 것
(D) 두 항공사 간의 합병을 발표하는 것

해설 | 주제 / 목적
첫 번째 문장에서 스타 에어웨이즈가 보유하고 있는 모든 항공기를 유럽산 스카이스트림 제트기로 교체할 계획이라고 밝혔다(Star Airways ~ European-produced Skystream jets)고 했으므로 정답은 (B)이다.

패러프레이징
지문의 has reported it is planning to replace
→ 보기의 announce a new business agreement

156 변경에는 시간이 얼마나 걸릴 것으로 예상되는가?

(A) 3년
(B) 5년
(C) 10년
(D) 17년

해설 | 세부 사항
두 번째 문장에서 기체 변경을 완료하기까지 10년이 걸릴 것으로 예상하고 있다(Star Airways expects the changeover to take a decade to complete)고 했으므로 정답은 (C)이다.

157 스타 에어웨이즈의 목표로 보고되지 않은 것은?

(A) 국제 본부를 이전하는 것
(B) 새로운 항공기를 이용하는 첫 번째 회사들 중 하나가 되는 것
(C) 보유하고 있는 오래된 항공기들을 교체하는 것
(D) 취항지의 수를 늘리는 것

해설 | Not / True
세 번째 문장에서 새로운 항공기들은 낙후된 항공기들을 교체하는 동시에 이 항공사가 국제 항로를 확장할 수 있도록 할 것(The new planes will enable the airline ~ aging fleet of jet planes)이라고 했으므로 (C), (D), 마지막 문장에서 이로써 스타 에어웨이즈는 AWB850 기종을 이용하는 첫 번째 인도 항공사가 될 것(This will make Star Airways the first ~ to fly the AWB850)이라고 했으므로 (B)를 알 수 있다. 따라서 정답은 (A)이다.

패러프레이징
지문의 enable the airline to expand its international routes → 보기의 increase its number of flight destinations

발신: omtproject@avhmuseum.org
수신: khandzlik@mediomail.com
날짜: 9월 23일
제목: OMT 프로젝트

한트즐릭 씨께,

158온라인 박물관 번역 프로젝트에 100달러를 기부해 주셔서 감사합니다. **160**귀하와 같은 커뮤니티 회원들의 후원은 박물관 포털 사이트를 스페인어와 프랑스어로 번역하는 데 필요한 자금 조달에 도움이 되고 있으며, 이 프로젝트는 현재 거의 완성 단계에 있습니다. 이러한 기부금의 중요성은 아무리 **159**강조해도 지나치지 않습니다. 기부금 없이는 우리는 번역가들에게 그들의 서비스에 대한 대가를 지불할 수 없을 것입니다.

앨버커키 밸리 역사 박물관

어휘 | express 표하다 appreciation 감사 contribution 기부금 translation 번역 support 지원 finance 자금을 대다 near 다가오다 stress 강조하다 translator 번역가

158 이메일이 한트즐릭 씨에게 발송된 이유는?

(A) 서비스 제공을 요청하기 위해
(B) 최근 방문에 대해 문의하기 위해
(C) 그녀의 기부에 감사하기 위해
(D) 박물관 입장권을 제공하기 위해

해설 | 주제 / 목적
첫 문장에서 한트즐릭 씨에게 온라인 박물관 번역 프로젝트에 100달러를 기부해 주셔서 감사하다(We would like to express ~ Museum Translation Project)고 했으므로 (C)가 정답이다.

어휘 | inquire 묻다 recent 최근의 donation 기부

패러프레이징
지문의 express our appreciation for your contribution
→ 보기의 thank her for a donation

159 첫 번째 단락 4행의 "stressed"와 의미가 가장 가까운 단어는?

(A) 기진맥진한
(B) 강조된
(C) 강요된
(D) 걱정스러운

해설 | 동의어
의미상 기부금의 중요성은 아무리 '강조해도' 지나치지 않는다는 뜻으로 쓰인 것이므로 정답은 (B) emphasized이다.

160 현재 박물관은 어떤 프로젝트에 관여하고 있는가?

(A) 커뮤니티 행사 조직
(B) 오래된 건물 보수
(C) 새로운 전시품 구입
(D) 웹사이트의 새로운 언어 버전 생성

해설 | 세부 사항
두 번째 문장에서 귀하와 같은 커뮤니티 회원들의 후원은 박물관 포털 사이트를 스페인어와 프랑스어로 번역하는 데 필요한 자금 조달에 도움이 되고 있으며 이 프로젝트는 현재 거의 완성 단계에 있다(Support from community members ~ a project that is now nearing completion)고 했으므로 (D)가 정답이다.

패러프레이징
지문의 translation of our Museum Web portal
→ 보기의 Creating new language versions of its Web site

[161-163] 정보

직원 포상 프로그램

시 직원으로부터 특별히 주목할 만한 수준의 서비스를 받은 경험이 있으십니까? **161직원 감사 프로그램은 시민에게 뛰어난 서비스를 제공하는 브리즈번 시 공무원의 공로를 인정하기 위해 고안되었습니다.** 추천은 일반 시민뿐 아니라 동료 직원들도 할 수 있습니다. 추천서를 제출하는 사람은 브리즈번 거주자가 아니어도 됩니다. 추천인은 그 직원의 모범적인 성과 및 전문성을 보여주는 논평이나 증빙 서류를 제출해야 합니다. **162제출물은 각 분기별 시 집행 위원회 회의 때 고려되어 후보자가 선정됩니다.** **163수상자는 그 후 즉시 발표되며 시청에서 간단한 기념식을 하는 동안 상패를 받게 됩니다.** 수상자는 지역 언론 보도에도 기재됩니다.

- -

어휘 | recognition (공로 등에 대한) 인정 **noteworthy** 주목할 만한 **appreciation** 감사 **recognise** 인정하다 **government** 정부 **excel** 뛰어나다 **nomination** 지명, 추천 **fellow** 동료 **resident** 주민 **nominator** 추천인 **commentary** 논평 **evidence** 증거 **exemplary** 모범적인 **performance** 성과 **submission** 제출물 **quarterly** 분기별의 **executive committee** 집행 위원회 **candidate** 후보자 **recipient** 수령인 **announce** 발표하다 **afterwards** 그 후 **plaque** 상패 **brief** 간단한 **ceremony** 기념식

---

161 프로그램의 목적은?

(A) 다년간 근무한 직원에게 감사를 표하는 것
(B) 일을 잘한 직원에게 상을 주는 것
(C) 은퇴한 직원을 기억하는 것
(D) 새 업무에 직원을 추천하는 것

해설 | 세부 사항
두 번째 문장에서 직원 감사 프로그램은 시민에게 뛰어난 서비스를 제공하는 브리즈번 시 공무원의 공로를 인정하기 위해 고안되었다(The Staff Appreciation Programme is designed to recognise ~ excel in service to the public)고 했으므로 정답은 (B)이다.

어휘 | acknowledge 감사를 표하다 **reward** 보상하다 **retire** 은퇴하다 **assignment** 업무

162 선발 절차는 누가 담당하는가?

(A) 위원회 구성원
(B) 직원 관리자들
(C) 브리즈번 기업 경영진
(D) 브리즈번 시장

해설 | 세부 사항
여섯 번째 문장에서 제출물은 각 분기별 시 집행 위원회 회의 때 고려되어 후보자가 선정된다(Submissions are considered ~ candidate is selected)고 했으므로 시 집행 위원회의 구성원들이 선발 작업을 하고 있음을 알 수 있다. 따라서 정답은 (A)이다.

163 [1], [2], [3], [4]로 표시된 곳 중에서 다음 문장이 들어가기에 가장 적합한 위치는?

"수상자는 지역 언론 보도에도 기재됩니다."

(A) [1]   (B) [2]   (C) [3]   (D) [4]

해설 | 문장 삽입
제시된 문장의 The honoree is also featured가 문제 해결의 단서이다. 수상자에게 일어나는 일에 대해 언급하며 also를 사용했으므로 주어진 문장 앞에서도 수상자와 관련된 사항에 대해 안내하는 내용이 와야 한다. 따라서 수상자 발표 일정과 기념식(The recipient is announced ~ a brief ceremony at the city hall)에 대한 내용 뒤인 (D)가 정답이다.

어휘 | honoree 수상자 **feature** 특별히 포함하다

[164-167] 문자 메시지

지나 권 (오후 1시 9분)
안녕하세요, 짐. **165제가 루드밀라의 사무실에 제 USB 드라이브를 두고 온 것 같아요.** 스내커란디아 이사회를 위한 프레젠테이션이 거기에 있거든요. 찾아서 좀 가져다주실 수 있을까요?

짐 스미스 (오후 1시 10분)
165그럼요. 벌써 그쪽 장소에 계신 건가요?

지나 권 (오후 1시 12분)
아뇨, 콘치타 커피 하우스에 있어요. 마지막으로 한 번 더 프레젠테이션의 핵심 요소들을 살펴보려고 했는데 저한테 USB가 없다는 것을 깨달았어요.

짐 스미스 (오후 1시 13분)

걱정 마세요. 우리는 잘 해낼 거예요. 어쨌든, **¹⁶⁴지난 두 달 동안 매일 그 디지털 광고 캠페인을 기획해 왔잖아요.** 지금 루드밀라의 사무실로 가는 중이에요.

지나 권 (오후 1시 17분)

그래서 **¹⁶⁶USB를 찾았나요?**

짐 스미스 (오후 1시 18분)

이를 어쩌죠, 지나. **¹⁶⁶루드밀라가 퇴근해서 사무실 문을 잠근 것 같아요.** 경비실에 전화해서 그녀의 사무실 문을 열어 달라고 할게요.

지나 권 (오후 1시 19분)

그러실 필요 없어요. **¹⁶⁷공유 드라이브의 "신규 프로젝트" 폴더에서 "Snackadcamp"라는 이름으로 문서를 찾으시면 돼요. USB 드라이브에 복사만 해 주세요.**

짐 스미스 (오후 1시 22분)

좋아요. 비밀번호로 보호되어 있나요?

지나 권 (오후 1시 23분)

아니요, 그렇지 않아요.

짐 스미스 (오후 1시 25분)

그럼 바로 해 볼게요. 또 다른 건 없나요?

지나 권 (오후 1시 26분)

없어요. 감사합니다. **¹⁶⁵거기서 봬요.**

어휘 | board of directors 이사회 go over 검토하다 element 요소 notice 알다 after all 어쨌든 advertising 광고 leave for the day 퇴근하다 security 경비

164 글쓴이들은 어떤 업계에 종사하고 있는가?

(A) 컴퓨터 기술 (B) 건물 보안
(C) 광고 (D) 식품 서비스

해설 | 세부 사항

1시 13분에 스미스 씨가 우리는 지난 두 달 동안 매일 그 디지털 광고 캠페인을 기획해 왔다(we have been designing that digital advertising campaign every day for the last two months)고 했으므로 글쓴이들은 광고를 기획하는 일을 한다는 것을 알 수 있다. 따라서 (C)가 정답이다.

165 스미스 씨에 대해 암시된 것은?

(A) 스내커란디아 임원을 상대로 한 프레젠테이션이 호평을 받았다.
(B) 권 씨와 정기적으로 프레젠테이션을 한다.
(C) 그의 사무실은 루드밀라의 사무실 옆에 있다.
(D) 곧 회의에 참석할 것이다.

어휘 | official 임원 well received 호평을 받는

해설 | 추론

1시 9분에 권 씨가 루드밀라의 사무실에 제 USB 드라이브를 두고 온 것 같다(I think I left my USB drive in Ludmilla's office)고 했고 스내커란디아 이사회를 위한 프레젠테이션이 거기에 있다(Our presentation ~ is on it)며 찾아서 좀 가져다줄 수 있는지(Can you get it and bring it with you?) 묻자 1시 10분에 스미스 씨가 그러겠다(Sure)며 벌써 그쪽 장소에 있는지(Are you at their location already?)를 물었고, 1시 26분에 권 씨가 스미스 씨에게 거기서 보자(See you there)고 했다. 따라서 스미스 씨는 곧 스내커란디아 이사회 회의 장소로 향할 것임을 알 수 있으므로 (D)가 정답이다.

166 오후 1시 18분에 스미스 씨가 "이를 어쩌죠, 지나"라고 쓴 의도는?

(A) 권 씨가 발표를 다시 해야 해서 기분이 언짢다.
(B) 권 씨의 USB 드라이브를 구하지 못해 미안해하고 있다.
(C) 권 씨가 아직 스내커란디아 사무실에 있지 않아 속상하다.
(D) 권 씨가 그 프로젝트를 작업하는 데 두 달이 걸린 것을 유감스럽게 생각한다.

해설 | 의도 파악

1시 17분에 권 씨가 USB를 찾았는지(Did you get it?) 묻자 1시 18분에 스미스 씨가 이를 어쩌죠(Sorry)라며 루드밀라가 퇴근해서 사무실 문을 잠근 것 같다(It seems Ludmilla has left for the day and has locked her office)고 했으므로 사무실 문이 잠겨 USB를 찾지 못해 미안함과 안타까움을 표현하려는 의도로 한 말임을 알 수 있다. 따라서 (B)가 정답이다.

어휘 | apologetic 미안해하는 regret 유감스럽게 생각하다

167 다음에 무슨 일이 일어날 것 같은가?

(A) 파일이 복사된다.
(B) 비밀번호가 변경된다.
(C) 일부 폴더가 생성된다.
(D) 일부 소프트웨어가 설치된다.

해설 | 추론

1시 19분에 권 씨가 공유 드라이브의 "신규 프로젝트" 폴더에서 "Snackadcamp"라는 이름으로 문서를 찾으면 된다(You'll find the document ~ under the name "Snackadcamp")며 스미스 씨에게 USB 드라이브에 복사만 해 달라(Just copy it on a USB drive)고 부탁하고 있으므로 (A)가 정답이다.

[168-171] 편지

WYB 테크놀로지스사
웨스트 45번가 456번지
뉴호프, 텍사스 75009

1월 5일
사이먼 콴
사서함 352
맥킨니, 텍사스 75071

169콴 씨께:

168, 169이 편지는 귀하가 소프트웨어 교육 컨설턴트로서 WYB 테크놀로지스사에 제공하는 서비스에 관한 상호간의 합의 사항을 확인하기 위한 것입니다.

귀하가 맡은 일은 2월 15일 시작하여 6월 15일에 종료됩니다. 여기에는 **170(C),(D)**당사의 세 지사 각각에서 교육을 진행하고, **170(A)**모든 정기 월례 회의에 참석하는 것이 포함됩니다.

우리가 논의한 대로, 귀하가 제공하는 서비스에 대해 총 1,400달러의 보수를 받게 됩니다.
금액은 다음과 같이 분할 지급됩니다.

3월 15일: 350달러   4월 15일: 350달러
5월 15일: 350달러   6월 15일: 350달러

이 일은 시간제 임시 업무이므로 귀하는 휴일 및 휴가 수당을 받을 수 없으며, 근무 시간 외에 업무 준비를 위해 들인 시간에 대해서도 보수가 지급되지 않습니다.

168,171이러한 사전 타협의 수락을 확인하기 위해 서명을 하신 후 이 편지를 인사부로 반송해 주시기 바랍니다.

저는 당사가 필요로 하는 소프트웨어 교육에 도움을 주시고자 귀하가 저희와 함께 해 주신 것에 기쁘고, 귀하의 WYB 입사를 환영하는 바입니다. 저희는 하루빨리 귀하와 함께 일하고 싶습니다.

제가 도와드릴 일이 있다면, 839-555-0392번으로 제게 연락주십시오.

크리스틴 드제네로
인사부장
피고용인 서명: <u>사이먼 콴</u> 날짜: <u>1월 11일</u>
        사이먼 콴

어휘 | confirm 확인하다, 확정하다 **agreement** 합의, 계약 **assignment** 과제, 임무 **conduct** 실시하다, 처리하다 **training session** 교육 (과정), 연수회 **regional office** 지사, 지점 **compensate** 보상하다, (보수를) 지불하다 **payment** 지불금, 납부액 **disseminate** 퍼뜨리다, 보급시키다 **as follows** 다음과 같이 **temporary** 일시적인, 임시의 **vacation pay** 휴가 수당 **outside of** ~ 이외에 **working hour** 근무 시간 **appointment** 약속, 사전 타협 **human resources** 인사부 **be of assistance to** ~에게 도움이 되다

168 편지의 목적은?

(A) 구인 광고를 하는 것
(B) 고용 제의를 확인하는 것
(C) 신입 사원 교육에 대해 상의하는 것
(D) 급여 인상을 발표하는 것

해설 | 주제 / 목적
편지의 첫 문단에서 이 편지는 귀하가 소프트웨어 교육 컨설턴트로서 WYB 테크놀로지스사에 제공하는 서비스에 관한 상호간의 합의 사항을 확인하기 위한 것(This letter is to confirm ~ for WYB Technologies, Inc.)이라고 했고 다섯 번째 문단에서 이러한 사전 타협의 수락을 확인하기 위해 서명을 하신 후 이 편지를 인사부로 반송해 주시기 바란다(To confirm your acceptance of this appointment, please ~ human resources)고 했으므로 정답은 (B)이다.

패러프레이징
지문의 confirm our agreement for your services → 보기의 confirm an offer of employment

169 편지의 수신인은 누구인가?

(A) 인사부장   (B) 판매원
(C) 컨설턴트   (D) 회사 사장

해설 | 세부 사항
수신인은 콴 씨이며(Dear Mr. Kwan), 첫 문장에서 귀하가 소프트웨어 교육 컨설턴트로서 WYB 테크놀로지스사에 제공하는 서비스(your services as a software-training consultant for WYB Technologies, Inc.)라고 언급하므로 정답은 (C)이다.

170 직무의 필수 사항으로 열거되지 않은 것은?

(A) 회의 참석하기
(B) 주간 업무 계획 제출하기
(C) WYB의 여러 지사 방문하기
(D) 교육 실시하기

해설 | Not / True
두 번째 문단의 당사의 세 지사 각각에서 교육을 진행하고(conducting training sessions at each of our three regional offices)에서 (C)와 (D), 모든 정기 월례 회의에 참석하는 것이 포함된다(attending all regular monthly meetings)에서 (A)를 알 수 있다. 따라서 정답은 (B)이다.

171 편지에 언급된 것은?

(A) 매달 15일에 회의가 있다.
(B) 직원들은 입사 3달 후에 휴일 및 휴가 수당을 받을 것이다.
(C) 편지는 수신인이 서명을 해야 한다.
(D) 취업 지원자들은 전화 면접을 볼 것이다.

해설 | Not / True

다섯 번째 문단에서 서명을 하신 후 이 편지를 인사부로 반송해 주시기 바란다(please sign and return this letter to the office of human resources)고 했으므로 정답은 (C)이다.

[172-175] 이메일

수신: humuranaka@myemail.com
발신: tours@mammothcanyonpark.org
날짜: 1월 2일
제목: 투어 확인
첨부: 오시는 길 지도

무라나카 씨께,

매머드 캐년 파크에서 히든 패스웨이 투어를 예약해 주셔서 감사합니다. 이 이메일은 입장권으로 쓰일 수 없다는 점을 유의하시기 바랍니다. 173방문자 센터에서 직접 티켓을 수령해야 하며 이때 사진이 부착된 신분증을 제시해야 합니다. 오시는 길 지도가 첨부되어 있습니다.

또한 겨울철에는 일부 도로가 폐쇄될 수 있음을 참고 부탁드립니다. 출발 전에 172방문자 센터 (208) 555-0136으로 전화하여 도로 폐쇄 및 우회로에 대해 문의하십시오.

175아래 주문 세부 정보를 검토하여 모든 정보가 정확한지 확인해 주십시오. mammothcanyonpark.org/tours를 방문하여 예약을 변경하실 수 있습니다. 히든 패스웨이 투어는 약 3시간 동안 진행되므로 따뜻한 옷과 적당한 부츠를 착용하고 174하이킹을 위한 충분한 물과 간식을 준비하는 것이 좋습니다.

확인 코드: HPT010201	투어 날짜 및 시간: 1월 10일, 오전 10시
구입일: 1월 2일	수량: 5
지불 유형: 신용 카드	총계: 50달러

이 구매를 연간 회원권에 적용하는 방법을 알아보려면 공원 관리인에게 문의하십시오!

모험을 위해 매머드 캐년 파크를 고려해 주셔서 감사합니다. 우리는 고객님을 맞이하는 것을 기대하고 있으며 즐거운 방문이 되시기를 희망하고 있습니다.

어휘 | serve ~의 역할을 하다 admission 입장 produce 보여 주다 detour 우회로 ranger 공원 관리원

172 이메일에 따르면, 고객은 왜 방문자 센터에 전화하겠는가?

(A) 도로 상황을 확인하기 위해
(B) 영업시간을 묻기 위해
(C) 매머드 캐년 파크로 가는 방법을 묻기 위해
(D) 투어 가이드에게 늦게 도착하는 것을 알리기 위해

해설 | 세부 사항

두 번째 단락 두 번째 문장에서 방문자 센터 (208) 555-0136으로 전화하여 도로 폐쇄 및 우회로에 대해 문의하라(be sure to call our Visitor Center ~ to ask about road closures and detours)고 했으므로 정답은 (A)이다.

173 무라나카 씨가 티켓을 수령할 때 제공해야 하는 것은?

(A) 파크 멤버십 카드
(B) 사진이 부착된 신분증
(C) 확인 이메일
(D) 신용 카드 번호

해설 | 세부 사항

첫 번째 단락 세 번째 문장에서 방문자 센터에서 직접 티켓을 수령해야 하며 이때 사진이 부착된 신분증을 제시해야 한다(You must pick up your tickets in person ~ must produce photo identification at that time)고 했으므로 정답은 (B)이다.

174 무라나카 씨는 여행에 무엇을 가지고 오라는 조언을 받는가?

(A) 등산 스틱 (B) 손전등
(C) 간식 (D) 우비

해설 | 세부 사항

세 번째 단락 표 이전에 하이킹을 위한 충분한 물과 간식을 준비하는 것이 좋다(we advise that ~ bring enough water and a snack for the hike)고 했으므로 정답은 (C)이다.

175 [1], [2], [3], [4]로 표시된 곳 중에서 다음 문장이 들어가기에 가장 적합한 위치는?

"mammothcanyonpark.org/tours를 방문하여 예약을 변경하실 수 있습니다."

(A) [1] (B) [2] (C) [3] (D) [4]

해설 | 문장 삽입

예약 변경에 관한 내용은 예약 정보를 확인시켜 주고 난 다음에 오는 것이 흐름상 맞으므로 모든 정보가 정확한지 확인해 달라(Please review the details of your order ~ all the information is correct)는 내용 다음인 [3]에 오는 것이 적절하다. 따라서 정답은 (C)이다.

[176-180] 이메일 + 열차 시간표

수신: 줄리안 리드 <juliannereid@farlanduniversity.ac.uk>
발신: 에바 맥클린 <emaclean@sandington.gov.uk>
날짜: 7월 26일
제목: 8월 행사

리드 씨께,

176지역 사회 구성원들에게 다시 문을 열고 우리 도서관 복원

및 보수 사업의 결과를 소개하는 8월 25일 기념식에서 연설하기로 동의해 주셔서 아주 기쁩니다. **177**당신의 발표에서 제공하는 역사적 관점은 건물 재설계를 맡은 건축가가 해 줄 강연의 기술적 요소를 보완해 줄 것입니다. **178**모든 것이 준비될 수 있도록 당신의 기술적 요구 사항에 대해 알려 주십시오. 아침 9시 30분에 손님들이 도착하기 시작할 예정이며 가벼운 아침 식사가 제공될 것입니다. **179**그날의 첫 번째 연사이시므로 9시까지 도착해 주시기 바랍니다. 도서관은 샌딩턴 기차역에서 조금만 걸어오시면 됩니다.

177샌딩턴 마을과 도서관의 역사를 우리 이용객들과 공유하는 일에 기꺼이 응해 주셔서 감사합니다. 우리 소장 도서와 시설에 대해 수개월 동안 이용이 제한되었던지라 이용객들은 이 공동체 공간으로 돌아오기를 간절히 고대하고 있습니다.

에바 맥클린

어휘 | delighted 즐거운 celebration 기념 행사 community 지역 사회 introduce 소개하다 restoration 복원 renovation 보수 historical 역사의 perspective 관점 complement 보완하다 element 요소 talk 강연 architect 건축가 responsible 책임이 있는 serve 제공하다 appreciate 감사하다 willingness 기꺼이 하는 마음 patron 이용객 limited 제한된 access 이용 collection 소장품 facility 시설 eagerly 열렬히 anticipate 고대하다 space 공간

여객 철도 시스템 – 파랜드 라인

열차 번호	역 및 도착 시간				
	파랜드 대학교	볼드윈	램지 센터	노르몬트	샌딩턴
17922	08:10	08:22	08:31	08:36	**179**08:45
34	08:55	09:07	09:16	09:21	09:30
75	09:30	09:42	09:51	09:56	10:05
96	10:05	10:17	10:26	10:31	10:40

알림: **180**현재 볼드윈역의 매표기가 고장 난 상태임을 알려 드립니다. 볼드윈역에서 탑승하는 승객들은 열차 내에서 승차권을 구입하셔야 합니다.

어휘 | notice 알림 out of order 고장 난 passenger 승객 board 탑승하다

---

176 8월 25일에는 어떤 행사가 열리는가?

(A) 책 사인회
(B) 역사 사진 전시회
(C) 건물의 재개관
(D) 시상

해설 | 세부 사항
이메일의 첫 문장에서 지역 사회 구성원들에게 다시 문을 열고 우리 도서관 복원 및 보수 사업의 결과를 소개하는 8월 25일 기념식에서 연설하기로 동의해 주셔서 아주 기쁘다(I am delighted ~ renovation project)고 한 것으로 보아 도서관 재개관 기념식이 열리는 것을 알 수 있다. 따라서 (C)가 정답이다.

어휘 | exhibit 전시회 historical 역사의 presentation 수여 award 상

177 리드 씨는 누구일 것 같은가?

(A) 사서
(B) 건축가
(C) 뉴스 기자
(D) 역사학자

해설 | 추론
이메일의 첫 단락 두 번째 문장에서 리드 씨에게 당신의 발표에서 제공하는 역사적 관점은 건물 재설계를 맡은 건축가가 해 줄 강연의 기술적 요소를 보완해 줄 것(The historical perspective provided by your ~building's redesign)이라고 했고, 두 번째 단락 첫 문장에서 샌딩턴 마을과 도서관의 역사를 우리 이용객들과 공유하는 일에 기꺼이 응해 주셔서 감사하다(We appreciate your ~ history of the town of Sandington and its library)고 한 것으로 보아 (D)가 정답이다.

178 맥클린 씨는 리드 씨에게 어떤 정보를 요청하는가?

(A) 여행 세부 정보
(B) 기술 요구 사항
(C) 식단 선호도
(D) 강연료

해설 | 세부 사항
이메일의 첫 단락 세 번째 문장에서 맥클린 씨가 리드 씨에게 모든 것이 준비될 수 있도록 당신의 기술적 요구 사항에 대해 알려 달라(Please let us know ~ ready for you)고 했으므로 (B)가 정답이다.

어휘 | detail 세부 사항 requirement 요건 dietary 식사의 preference 선호 fee 수수료

패러프레이징
지문의 needs → 보기의 requirements

179 리드 씨는 제시간에 도착하기 위해 어떤 기차를 타야 할 것 같은가?

(A) 22번
(B) 34번
(C) 75번
(D) 96번

해설 | 연계
이메일의 첫 단락 다섯 번째 문장에서 리드 씨에게 그날의 첫 번째 연사이므로 9시까지 도착해 주기 바란다(You are the first speaker ~ arrive by 9:00)며 도서관은 샌딩턴 기차역에서 조금만 걸어오면 된다(The library is just

~ Sandington train station)고 했고, 열차 시간표에 따르면 샌딩턴 역에 9시 전에 도착하는 기차는 8시 45분에 도착하는 22번 기차이므로 (A)가 정답이다.

180 현재 어느 역에서 표를 구매할 수 없는가?

(A) 볼드윈
(B) 램지 센터
(C) 노르몬트
(D) 샌딩턴

해설 | 세부 사항
열차 시간표의 알림에 현재 볼드윈역의 매표기가 고장 난 상태임을 알린다(Please be advised ~ out of order at this time)며 볼드윈역에서 탑승하는 승객들은 열차 내에서 승차권을 구입해야 한다(Passengers who board ~ purchase their tickets on the train)고 했으므로 정답은 (A)이다.

[181-185] 서평 + 이메일

마르티나 한센의 <로마: 단조의 수수께끼>
마이클 슈라 작성

¹⁸¹마르티나 한센의 베스트셀러 소설인 <로마: 단조의 수수께끼>는 한센이 지역 잡지에서 읽은 실화에서 영감을 받았다. ¹⁸³이 소설은 이탈리아 혈통으로 덴마크에서 태어나고 자란 젊은 여성인 에바 롬바르도의 이야기를 담고 있다. 에바의 가족은 연락을 거부하는 유명한 작곡가인 에바의 할머니와 소원해진다. 신문 기사에서 예기치 못한 소식을 접하자 에바는 할머니를 만나러 로마로 향하지만 상황은 그녀가 상상했던 것보다 훨씬 더 복잡하다는 것을 깨닫는다. 비록 결말은 다소 어둡고 암울하지만 많은 독자들이 이 이야기를 감동적이라고 느낄 것이고, 주인공들이 솜씨 있게 ¹⁸²그려져 있다.

어휘 | minor key 단조 **novel** 소설 **inspired** 영감을 받은 **descent** 혈통 **estrange** 멀어지게 하다 **composer** 작곡가 **refuse** 거절하다 **unexpected** 예상치 못한 **confront** 맞서다 **situation** 상황 **complicated** 복잡한 **bleak** 암울한 **moving** 감동적인 **skillfully** 솜씨 있게

수신: 마르티나 한센 <mhansen@inkwell.com>
발신: 피터 커 <keo.p@sturbridge.edu>
날짜: 2월 15일
회신: 초대

한센 씨께,

^{183, 184, 185}3월 6일 목요일에 스터브리지 대학교를 방문해 저의 창작 작문 수업에서 학생들에게 강연해 주시기로 동의해 주셔서 감사합니다. 이들은 모두 소설 기법에 대해 어느 정도 지식을 갖고 있는 상급 학생들입니다. 학생들은 당신이 소재를 구성하고 인물을 발전시키는 방법에 대해

많은 질문을 갖고 있습니다. ¹⁸³모두들 당신이 작곡가를 실존 인물을 바탕으로 한 것인지 알고 싶어합니다!

¹⁸⁵12번 버스를 타고 캠퍼스로 오신다고 알고 있습니다. 버스는 도서관 바로 앞에서 정차합니다. 2시에 거기서 뵙고 카유가 홀까지 함께 걸어서 가겠습니다.

피터 커

어휘 | agree 동의하다 **advanced** 상급의 **knowledge** 지식 **fictional** 소설의 **technique** 기법 **organize** 체계화하다 **material** 자료 **directly** 바로

181 한센 씨의 소설에 대해 명시된 것은?

(A) 덴마크에서 집필되었다.
(B) 많이 팔리지 않았다.
(C) 실제 사건을 기반으로 한다.
(D) 결말이 즐겁다.

해설 | Not / True
서평의 첫 문장에서 마르티나 한센의 베스트셀러 소설인 <로마: 단조의 수수께끼>는 한센이 지역 잡지에서 읽은 실화에서 영감을 받았다(*Rome: Mystery in a Minor Key* ~ true story Hansen read in a local magazine)고 했으므로 (C)가 정답이다.

패러프레이징
지문의 true story → 보기의 real events

182 서평에서 첫 번째 단락 8행의 "drawn"과 의미가 가장 가까운 단어는?

(A) 당겨진   (B) 묘사되는
(C) 이해되는   (D) 수행되는

해설 | 동의어
의미상 소설 속에서 주인공들이 솜씨 있게 '그려져' 있다는 뜻으로 쓰인 것이므로 정답은 (B) described이다.

183 창작 작문 수업을 듣는 학생들에 대해 암시된 것은?

(A) <로마: 단조의 수수께끼>를 읽었다.
(B) 초보 작가들이다.
(C) 로마로 여행을 갈 계획이다.
(D) 야간 수업에 등록되어 있다.

해설 | 연계
이메일의 첫 문장에서 커 씨가 한센 씨에게 저의 창작 작문 수업에서 학생들에게 강연해 주시기로 동의해 주셔서 감사하다(Thank you for ~ creative writing class)고 했고 첫 단락 마지막 문장에서 모두들 당신이 작곡가를 실존 인물을 바탕으로 한 것인지 알고 싶어 한다(Everybody wants to ~ on a real person!)고 했다. 여기서 학생들이 궁금해하는 작곡가는 한센의 소설에 등장하는 인물로, 서평에서 소개되는 소설 <로마: 단조의 수수께끼> 속의 등장 인물이므로(The novel tells the

story of ~ a famous composer who refuses to have any contact with them) 커 씨의 창작 작문 수업을 듣는 학생들이 이 소설을 읽었음을 짐작할 수 있다. 따라서 정답은 (A)이다.

어휘 | enroll in ~에 등록하다

184 커 씨는 누구일 것 같은가?

(A) 서평가　　　　　(B) 버스 기사
(C) 대학 교수　　　(D) 도서관 보조원

해설 | 추론
이메일의 첫 문장에서 커 씨가 3월 6일 목요일에 스터브리지 대학교를 방문해 저의 창작 작문 수업에서 학생들에게 강연해 주시기로 동의해 주셔서 감사하다(Thank you for agreeing ~ my creative writing class)고 한 것으로 보아 커 씨는 대학에서 작문을 가르치고 있음을 알 수 있으므로 (C)가 정답이다.

185 이메일에서 한센 씨에 대해 암시하는 것은?

(A) 3월 6일에 대중교통을 탈 것이다.
(B) 스터브리지 대학을 졸업했다.
(C) 카유가 홀에서 일한다.
(D) 초대에 응하지 않았다.

해설 | 추론
이메일의 첫 문장에서 한센 씨에게 3월 6일 목요일에 스터브리지 대학교를 방문해 저의 창작 작문 수업에서 학생들에게 강연해 주시기로 동의해 주셔서 감사하다(Thank you for agreeing ~ my creative writing class)고 했고, 두 번째 단락 첫 문장에서 12번 버스를 타고 캠퍼스로 오신다고 알고 있다(I understand that ~ on the number twelve bus)고 했다. 따라서 한센 씨는 3월 6일에 버스를 타고 스터브리지 대학교에 올 것임을 짐작할 수 있으므로 (A)가 정답이다.

어휘 | public transportation 대중교통 graduate 졸업하다 accept 수락하다

패러프레이징
지문의 bus → 보기의 public transportation

[186-190] 메모+표+이메일

킴벌리 수목원

우리의 20에이커 규모 부지는 많은 지역에서 온 나무들을 위한 보호 구역입니다. 쾌적한 현지 날씨와 온실 기술로 우리는 세계 각국에서 온 비침입종 수목을 돌볼 수 있습니다.

우리는 현재 프로그램 진행을 도와줄 자원봉사자 5명을 모집하고 있습니다. 자원봉사자는 우리가 돌보는 나무에 대해 더 많이 배우고 방문객들에게 가이드 투어를 제공할 기회를 갖게 될 것입니다. 일부 자원봉사자들은 또한 수목원에서 나무 돌보는 일을 도울 예정입니다. **186지원자는 식물학과**

교육에 관심이 있는 고등학생 또는 대학생이어야 하며, 대중과 효과적으로 소통할 수 있어야 합니다. 이전 경력은 필요하지 않으며 지원자는 일주일에 6시간 이상을 할애할 수 있어야 합니다. **188자세한 내용 및 지원서 제출은 jhou@kimberlyarboretum.org로 관리 보조원인 진 허우 씨에게 연락 주시기 바랍니다.**

어휘 | arboretum 수목원 property 부지 sanctuary 보호 구역 region 지역 pleasant 쾌적한 greenhouse 온실 noninvasive 비침입성의 opportunity 기회 tend 돌보다 applicant 지원자 interest 관심 botany 식물학 education 교육 effectively 효과적으로 previous 이전의 be willing to 기꺼이 ~하다 commit 전념하다 submit 제출하다 administrative 관리상의 assistant 보조원

킴벌리 수목원 주간 봉사 일지

187이름: 스테파니 크로스　　　　주간 총 시간: **8시간**

	시작	종료	시작	종료	총 시간
월요일	–	–	–	–	–
화요일	오전 10시	오전 11시	–	–	1
187수요일	**오전 9시**	**오전 11시**	**오후 2시**	**오후 4시**	**4**
190목요일	오전 10시	오후 12시	오후 6시	오후 7시	3
금요일	–	–	–	–	–

188수신: 진 허우

발신: 스테파니 크로스
제목: 질문
날짜: 3월 9일

허우 씨께,

지난 한 달 동안 이곳에서 일하는 것, 특히 대학교에서 공부했던 나무들 주변에서 보고 일하는 것이 정말 즐거웠습니다.

189최근 아프리카 나무 구역의 에드워드 님스와 이야기했는데, 그쪽 나무들을 돌보는 데 도움이 필요하다고 들었습니다. 그가 탄자니아의 야생 보호 구역에서 일하는 동안 습득한 나무에 관한 지식과 현재 그 지식을 수목원 관리에 어떻게 적용하고 있는지 듣는 것도 재미있었습니다.

저는 화요일, 수요일, 목요일 아침에 가이드 투어를 진행하고 있습니다. **190남미 수목 전시회에 자원봉사자가 두 명 더 늘었으니 제가 남미 구역에서 근무하는 날 저녁에 님스 씨를 도와도 되는지 궁금합니다.** 이 변경 사항에 승인해 주실 수 있는지 알려 주세요.

스테파니 크로스

186 자원봉사자 지원자에게 요구되는 것은?

(A) 대학 학위

(B) 좋은 소통 능력

(C) 운전면허

(D) 나무에 대한 상당한 지식

해설 | 세부 사항

메모의 두 번째 단락 네 번째 문장에서 지원자는 식물학과 교육에 관심이 있는 고등학생 또는 대학생이어야 하며 대중과 효과적으로 소통할 수 있어야 한다(Applicants must be ~ communicate effectively with the public)고 했으므로 (B)가 정답이다.

어휘 | degree 학위 license 면허 significant 상당한

187 크로스 씨는 수요일에 보통 몇 시간 동안 일하는가?

(A) 1시간   (B) 3시간

(C) 4시간   (D) 8시간

해설 | 세부 사항

표에서 스테파니 크로스(Name Stephanie Cross)는 수요일(Wednesday)에 총 4시간(Total Hours - 4)을 일한다고 나와 있으므로 (C)가 정답이다.

188 크로스 씨는 누구에게 이메일을 보냈는가?

(A) 관리 보조

(B) 수목원 자원봉사자

(C) 대학 교수

(D) 급여 관리자

해설 | 연계

메모의 마지막 문장에서 자세한 내용 및 지원서 제출은 jhou@kimberlyarboretum.org로 관리 보조원인 진 허우 씨에게 연락하기 바란다(For more information ~ at jhou@kimberlyarboretum.org)고 했고, 크로스 씨가 보낸 이메일의 수신자는 진 허우(To Jin Hou)이므로 (A)가 정답이다.

189 이메일에 따르면, 님스 씨는 무엇을 책임지고 있는가?

(A) 모집 공고문 작성

(B) 전문 수목 관리 제공

(C) 아프리카 해외여행 인솔

(D) 무료 강좌를 위한 강의 계획 작성

해설 | 세부 사항

이메일의 두 번째 단락 첫 문장에서 최근 아프리카 나무 구역의 에드워드 님스와 이야기했는데 그쪽 나무들을 돌보는 데 도움이 필요하다고 들었다(I recently

spoke with ~ the care of the trees there)고 했고, 그가 습득한 지식을 수목원 관리에 어떻게 적용하는지 들었다(hear about the knowledge ~ to care of the arboretum)고 했으므로 님스 씨는 현재 아프리카 나무의 관리를 책임지고 있다는 것을 알 수 있다. 따라서 (B)가 정답이다.

어휘 | recruitment 모집 notice 공고문 specialized 전문적인 lead 이끌다 overseas 해외의

190 크로스 씨는 언제 님스 씨와 일하고 싶어 하는가?

(A) 월요일   (B) 화요일

(C) 수요일   (D) 목요일

해설 | 연계

이메일의 세 번째 단락 두 번째 문장에서 크로스 씨는 남미 수목 전시회에 자원봉사자가 두 명 더 늘었으니 제가 남미 구역에서 근무하는 날 저녁에 님스 씨를 도와도 되는지 궁금하다(Now that the South ~ working in the South American section)고 했고, 표에 따르면 크로스 씨는 목요일 오후 6시~7시(Thursday Time in 6 P.M., Time out 7:00 P.M.)에만 유일하게 저녁 시간대에 근무하고 있으므로 크로스 씨가 님스 씨의 일을 돕고 싶다고 한 날은 목요일임을 알 수 있다. 따라서 정답은 (D)이다.

[191-195] 제품 설명서 + 후기 + 이메일

193쿨 컴팩트 시스템 3은 창문에 장착되는 소형 에어컨으로 최대 14제곱미터 크기의 작은 방을 빠르게 냉방할 수 있도록 설계되었습니다. 당사의 최첨단 기술이 불필요한 소음 없이 시원함을 유지시켜 줍니다. **191**물세척이 가능한 필터망으로 먼지를 가두어 공기를 깨끗하게 해 주며 저전력 시동으로 에너지를 절약합니다.

http://www.coolcompact.com/reviews

데이비드 톰킨스가 작성한 후기, 7월 8일

192,193저는 작년에 쿨 컴팩트 웹사이트에서 직접 시스템 3을 저희 집 각 침실마다 한 대씩 4대 구입했습니다. 지난 여름 내내 저의 침실을 금세 시원하게 해 주었지만 제가 예상했던 것보다는 시끄러웠습니다. 거슬리는 윙윙거리는 소리가 났습니다. 겨울에는 에어컨을 벽장에 보관했다가 지난주에 꺼냈는데, 4대 중 3대가 작동하지 않았습니다.

194고객 서비스 센터에 전화를 걸었지만 공휴일이라 통화가 불가능했습니다. 다음날 드디어 담당자와 통화할 수 있게 되었을 때 보증 기간이 1년이고 전날 만료되었다는 말을 들었습니다. 공휴일이었다는 상황을 설명한 뒤에도

담당자는 기기 교체를 거부했습니다. 저는 이 회사에 몹시 실망했습니다.

수신: 데이비드 톰킨스 <dthompkins@rmail.com>
발신: 라나 그레이 <lgray@coolcompact.com>
제목: 쿨 컴팩트 시스템 3
날짜: 7월 10일

톰킨스 씨께,

방금 웹사이트에 게시하신 후기를 읽었으며, 쿨 컴팩트 시스템 3과 고객 서비스와 관련된 고객님의 경험에 대해 사과드리고 싶습니다. 최근 저희의 기술이 향상되어 신제품은 작년에 고객님께서 구매하셨던 것보다 훨씬 조용해졌습니다. **194저희는 고객들이 편안하고 마음의 평온을 누리시기를 원하기 때문에 당사의 모든 에어컨은 2년 동안 품질이 보증됩니다.**

쿨 컴팩트에 대한 고객님의 신뢰를 회복하고자 이 문제를 즉시 처리할 수 있기를 원합니다. **195불량 에어컨 3대뿐 아니라 작동이 되는 1대까지 모두 교체해 드리겠습니다.** 고객님 댁으로 제품 배송을 준비할 수 있도록 저에게 전화 주시기 바랍니다.

라나 그레이
고객 서비스 관리자
(609) 555-0143

191 제품 설명서에서 쿨 컴팩트 시스템 3에 대해 명시하는 것은?

(A) 물세척이 가능한 필터가 있다.
(B) 어떤 방이든 한 시간 안에 시원해진다.
(C) 한 방향으로만 공기를 보낼 수 있다.
(D) 배터리로 작동된다.

해설 | Not/True
제품 설명서의 마지막 문장에서 물세척이 가능한 필터망으로 먼지를 가두어 공기를 깨끗하게 해 주며 저전력 시동으로 에너지를 절약한다(Its washable mesh filter ~ start-up conserves energy)고 쿨 컴팩트 시스템 3의 특징을 설명하고 있으므로 물세척 가능 필터가 탑재되어 있음을 알 수 있다. 따라서 (A)가 정답이다.

어휘 | feature 특징으로 삼다 blow (바람이) 불다

direction 방향 operate (기계를) 가동하다

192 후기에서 톰킨스 씨가 자신이 구입한 제품에 대해 명시하는 것은?

(A) 구입품 중 일부를 이미 반품했다.
(B) 할인을 받았다.
(C) 웹사이트에서 주문했다.
(D) 친구를 위해 구입했다.

해설 | Not/True
후기의 첫 문장에서 톰킨스 씨가 작년에 쿨 컴팩트 웹사이트에서 직접 시스템 3을 각 침실마다 한 대씩 4대 구입했다(I purchased four System 3 units last year directly from the Cool Compact Web site, one for each bedroom in my house)고 했으므로 (C)가 정답이다.

패러프레이징
지문의 purchased → 보기의 ordered

193 톰킨스 씨 집의 침실에 대해 암시된 것은?

(A) 14제곱미터보다 크지 않다.
(B) 시끄러운 거리를 향해 있다.
(C) 여름에 자연 냉방만으로도 시원하다.
(D) 커다란 창문이 있다.

해설 | 연계
후기의 첫 문장에서 톰킨스 씨가 작년에 쿨 컴팩트 웹사이트에서 직접 시스템 3을 각 침실마다 한 대씩 4대 구입했다(I purchased four System 3 units ~ for each bedroom in my house)고 했다. 제품 설명서의 첫 문장에서 쿨 컴팩트 시스템 3은 창문에 장착되는 소형 에어컨으로 최대 14제곱미터 크기의 작은 방을 빠르게 냉방할 수 있도록 설계되었다(The Cool Compact System 3 ~ 14 square meters in size)고 했으므로 톰킨스 씨의 침실은 14제곱미터 크기를 넘지 않는다는 것을 알 수 있다. 따라서 정답은 (A)이다.

어휘 | face ~을 향하다 naturally 자연적으로

패러프레이징
지문의 up to 14 square meters
→ 보기의 no bigger than 14 square meters

194 톰킨스 씨는 고객 서비스 상담 중에 어떤 잘못된 정보를 받았는가?

(A) 고객 서비스가 휴일에도 가능했다는 점
(B) 에어컨이 벽장에 안전하게 보관될 수 있다는 점
(C) 그레이 씨가 모든 고객 후기에 대응한다는 점
(D) 에어컨의 보증 기간이 만료되었다는 점

해설 | 연계

후기의 두 번째 단락 첫 문장에서 고객 서비스 센터에 전화를 걸었지만 공휴일이라 통화가 불가능했고(I called customer service ~ national holiday) 다음날 담당자와 통화할 수 있게 되었을 때 보증 기간이 1년이고 전날 만료되었다는 말을 들었다(When I was finally ~ expired the day before)고 했는데, 이메일의 첫 단락 마지막 문장에서 고객 서비스 관리자가 저희는 고객들이 편안하고 마음의 평온을 누리시기를 원하기 때문에 당사의 모든 에어컨은 2년 동안 품질이 보증된다(Because we want our customers ~ two-year warranty)고 했으므로 톰킨스 씨는 보증 기간에 대해 잘못된 정보를 들었음을 알 수 있다. 따라서 (D)가 정답이다.

195 그레이 씨는 톰킨스 씨에게 무엇을 제안하는가?

(A) 전액 환불
(B) 새로운 에어컨 4대
(C) 상품권 몇 장
(D) 보증기간 연장

해설 | 세부 사항

이메일의 두 번째 단락 두 번째 문장에서 그레이 씨가 톰킨스 씨에게 불량 에어컨 3대뿐 아니라 작동이 되는 1대까지 모두 교체해 드리겠다(We will replace ~ the functional one)고 했으므로 (B)가 정답이다.

[196-200] 블로그 게시글 + 기사 + 이메일

---

https://www.karisblog.com.au

9월 5일

196<콜링 마리나>는 해니 어워즈를 염두에 둔 바로 그 시점에 맞추어 10월 10일에 개봉될 예정입니다. **198**이 영화는 6월에 개봉될 예정이었지만 일련의 차질을 겪게 되었습니다. 첫째, 야쿱 비텍이 마커스 블레인을 대체해서 감독으로 들어왔습니다. 그러던 중 프랑스에 위치한 촬영장에 뜻밖의 비가 내렸습니다. **197**배우 중에 떠오르는 스타 엘리스 모로의 모든 의상이 물에 젖어 사용할 수 없게 되었습니다. **의상 팀 직원들은 그 문제를 해결하기 위해 할 일이 많았습니다!** 그러나 내가 본 영화 장면들은 멋있어 보였고, 앞으로 꼭 볼 영화로 찍어 놓았습니다!

다음 게시물에서는 최근 중국에서 촬영 중인 액션 영화에 대해 이야기해 보겠습니다.

제 사이트를 방문해 주셔서 감사합니다!

– 카리

어휘 | release 개봉하다 be supposed to ~하기로 되어 있다 suffer 겪다 setback 차질 replace 대체하다 costume 의상 wardrobe 의상 post (posting) 인터넷 토론 방에 올리는 글 film 촬영하다

애들레이드 주변

10월 12일

198킴버 시네마는 8개월간의 보수 공사 끝에 오늘 다시 문을 연다. 재개관을 기념하기 위해 극장은 스릴러물인 <콜링 마리나>를 포함해 3편의 새로운 영화를 상영할 예정이다. 오늘과 내일 입장료는 반값이다.

관리자인 에나 피리피는 극장을 다시 열게 되어 기쁘며 하츠랜드 가 쇼핑센터의 다른 사업체들도 기뻐하고 있다는 것을 알고 있다고 말했다. 주차장의 공사 차량과 도로 우회로로 인해 쇼핑센터에 진입하기가 어려웠다. **199**로사즈 카페의 소유주인 엔조 로리타는 공사가 진행되는 동안 장사가 부진했다고 말했다. 사실 그는 주방을 수리하고 새로운 피자 오븐을 설치하기 위해 그의 이탈리아 레스토랑을 임시로 닫기에 좋은 시기라고 판단했다. **199, 200**그와 공동 소유주인 요하나 스테이스는 재오픈을 했으므로 사업이 호황을 누릴 것으로 기대하고 있으며 추가 직원을 고용하고 있다.

어휘 | renovation 보수 admission 입장료 delighted 매우 기뻐하는 detour 우회로 vehicle 차량 temporarily 임시로 install 설치하다 now that ~이기 때문에

수신: 웬디 조 <wcho@starmail.com.au>
발신: 요하나 스테이스 <jstace@zinmail.com.au>
200날짜: 10월 20일
제목: 새로운 시작

안녕하세요, 웬디.

만나서 반가웠어요. 우리 직원으로 합류하게 되어 기쁩니다.

200로리타 씨가 10월 30일을 당신이 일을 시작하는 날로 계획해 놓았다는 것을 알고 있지만 당신과 그가 가장 최근에 이야기한 날 이후로 예약이 증가하게 되었어요.

토요일 저녁에 모든 테이블의 예약이 다 찼어요. **200**이번 주에 일을 시작하는 것이 가능할까요? 최대한 빨리 알려주세요.

요하나

어휘 | reservation 예약 book 예약하다

---

196 블로그 게시물의 목적은?

(A) 영화제 수상자 발표하기
(B) 영화에 대한 소식 제공하기
(C) 기상 정보에 대해 보고하기
(D) 인기 있는 영화 제작 장소 논평하기

해설 | 주제 / 목적

첫 번째 문장에서 영화 제목을 언급하며 <콜링 마리나>는 해니 어워즈를 염두에 둔 바로 그 시점에 맞추어 10월

10일에 개봉될 예정(*Calling Marina* is expected to be released on 10 October, just in time for consideration for the Hanny Awards)이라고 했고, 이어서 이 영화는 6월에 개봉될 예정이었지만 일련의 차질을 겪게 되었다(The movie was supposed to be out in June but suffered a series of setbacks)며 해당 영화에 대한 세부 소식을 전하고 있으므로 정답은 (B)이다.

어휘 | award 상 recipient 수령인 review 논평[비평]하다

197 블로그 게시물에서 모로 씨에 대해 암시하는 것은?

(A) 프랑스에서 태어났다.
(B) 유명한 영화 감독이다.
(C) 그녀의 비행기가 날씨로 인해 연착되었다.
(D) 영화에서 입을 의상이 교체되어야 했다.

해설 | **추론**
다섯 번째 문장에서 배우 중에 떠오르는 스타 앨리스 모로의 모든 의상이 물에 젖어 사용할 수 없게 되었다(One of the actors, rising star ~ her costumes were water damaged and unusable)고 했고, 이어서 의상 팀 직원들은 그 문제를 해결하기 위해 할 일이 많았다(The wardrobe staff had quite a job to do to fix that problem!)라고 했으므로 젖은 의상이 교체되어야 했음을 짐작할 수 있다. 따라서 정답은 (D)이다.

어휘 | director 감독 flight 비행 편 wardrobe 옷, 의상 팀 replace 대체하다

198 기사가 킴버 시네마에 대해 명시하는 것은?

(A) 8개월 후에 다시 문을 열 것이다.
(B) 주차장이 공사 중이다.
(C) 매주 반값 티켓을 제공할 것이다.
(D) 제작이 지연되어야 했던 영화를 상영할 것이다.

해설 | **연계**
기사 첫 문장에서 킴버 시네마는 8개월간의 보수 공사 끝에 오늘 다시 문을 연다(The Kimber Cinema reopens today after an eight-month renovation)고 했고 재개관을 기념하기 위해 극장은 스릴러물인 <콜링 마리나>를 포함해 3편의 새로운 영화를 상영할 예정(To celebrate the reopening, ~ including the thriller *Calling Marina*)이라고 했는데, 블로그 게시글 두 번째 문장에서 해당 영화는 6월에 개봉될 예정이었지만 일련의 차질을 겪게 되었다(The movie was supposed to be out in June but suffered a series of setbacks)고 했으므로 지연되었던 영화, 즉 <콜링 마리나>가 킴버 시네마에서 상영됨을 할 수 있다. 따라서 정답은 (D)이다.

어휘 | under construction 공사중인 production 제작

199 기사에서 로리타 씨가 자신의 사업에 대해 언급하는 것은?

(A) 잠시 문을 닫았었다.
(B) 더 적은 피자 종류를 제공한다.
(C) 새 위치로 인해 혜택을 누렸다.
(D) 메뉴들의 가격을 인상했다.

해설 | **Not / True**
기사 두 번째 단락 세 번째 문장에서 엔조 로리타 씨의 사업체인 로사즈 카페(Rosa's Café)가 언급되며, 임시로 닫는 것을 결정했고(decided it was a good time to temporarily close ~) 재오픈을 했다(now that they have reopened)고 했으므로 정답은 (A)이다.

어휘 | brief 짧은 benefit 득을 보다 raise 올리다

200 스테이스 씨가 조 씨에게 하도록 요청하는 것은?

(A) 특별 행사장 예약하기
(B) 토요일 직원 교육에 참석하기
(C) 예상보다 빨리 로사즈 카페에서 근무 시작하기
(D) 매니저에게 자신을 소개하기

해설 | **연계**
기사 마지막 문장에서 요하나 스테이스는 엔조 로리타 씨의 로사즈 카페 동업자(co-owner)임을 알 수 있고, 현재 추가 직원을 고용하고 있다(are hiring additional staff)고 했다. 이메일에서는 스테이스 씨가 계획된 날짜(30 October)가 아닌 이번 주에 일을 시작하는 것이 가능한지(Could you possibly start this week?) 묻고 있는데, 이메일을 쓴 날짜가 10월 20일(Date 20 October)이므로 정답은 (C)이다.

어휘 | reserve 예약하다 attend 참석하다